W9-DBV-772

CONTENTS

Solo
Leveling

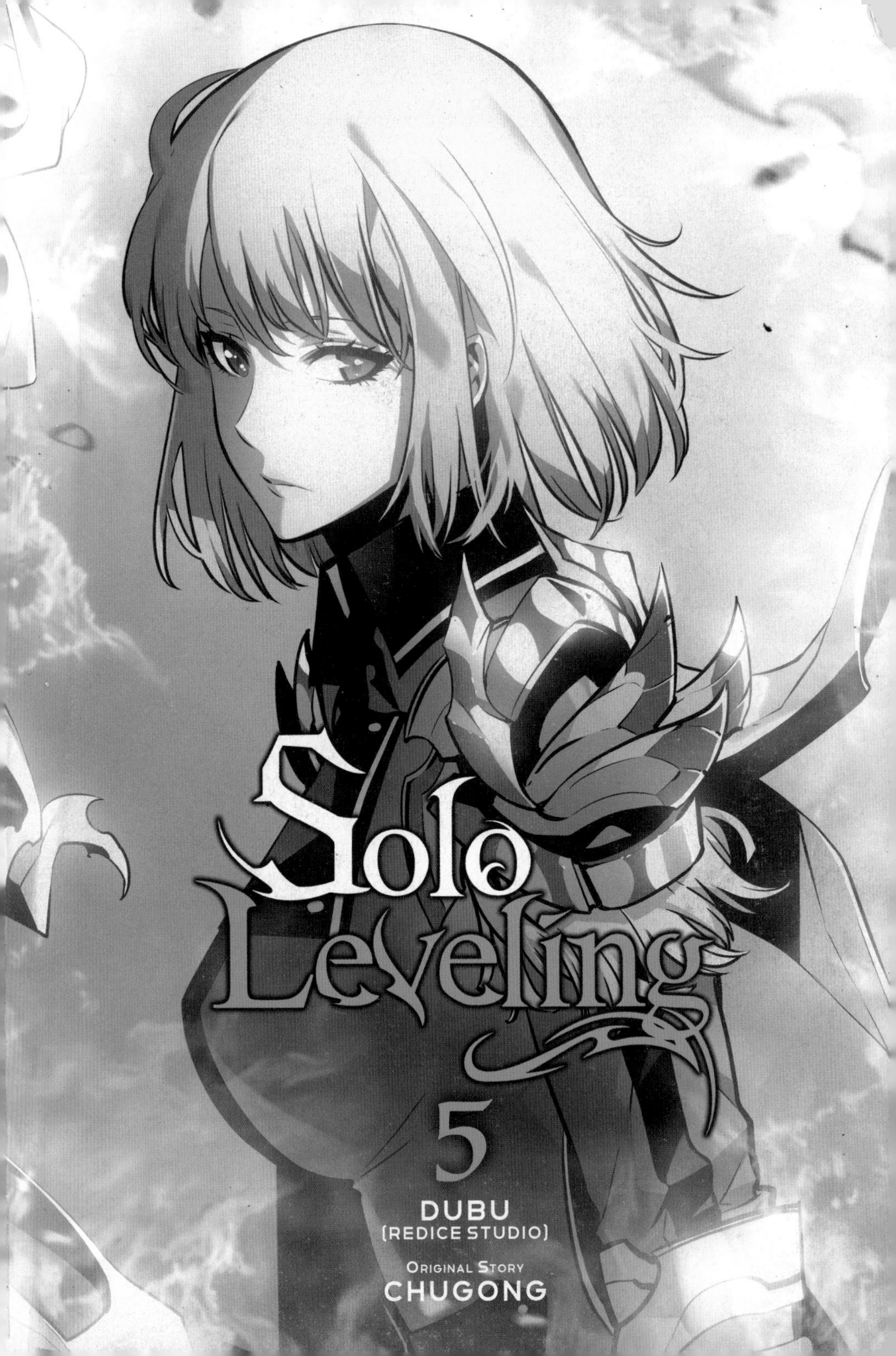
Solo Leveling
5
DUBU
(REDICE STUDIO)
Original Story
CHUGONG

CHARACTERS

Jinwoo Sung

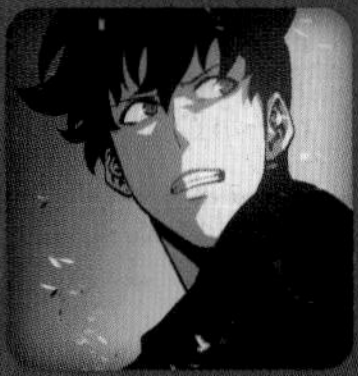

S-rank Hunter

Haein Cha

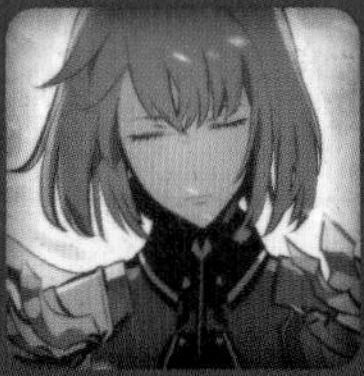

S-rank Hunter, Hunters Guild

Kihoon Son

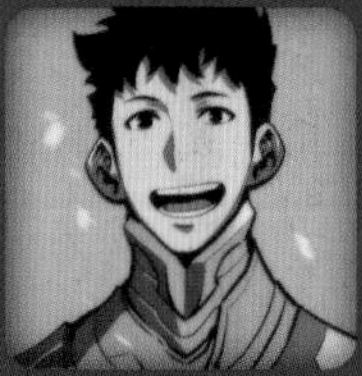

A-rank Hunter, Hunters Guild

Gunhee Go

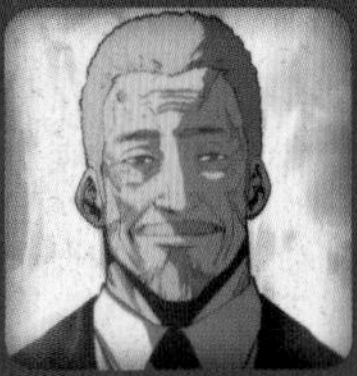

S-rank Hunter, Hunter's Association of Korea

Jinchul Woo

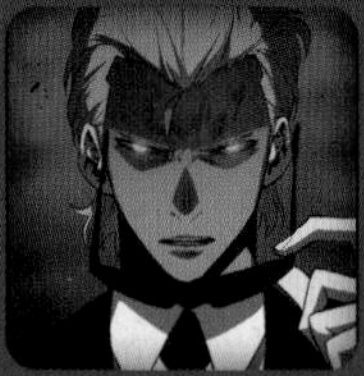

A-rank Hunter, Hunter's Association of Korea

Jinho Yoo

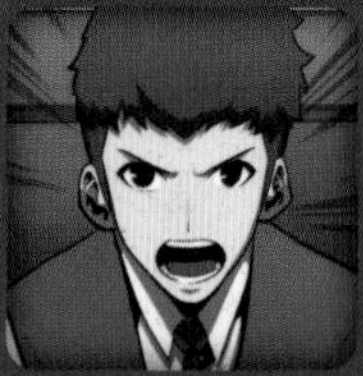

D-rank Hunter

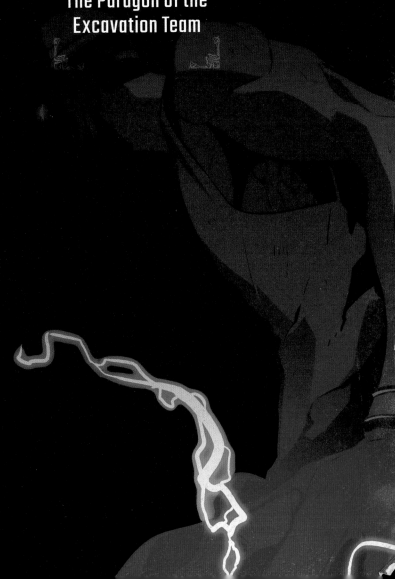

CHAPTER 11

The Paragon of the Excavation Team

Solo Leveling

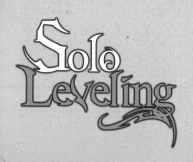

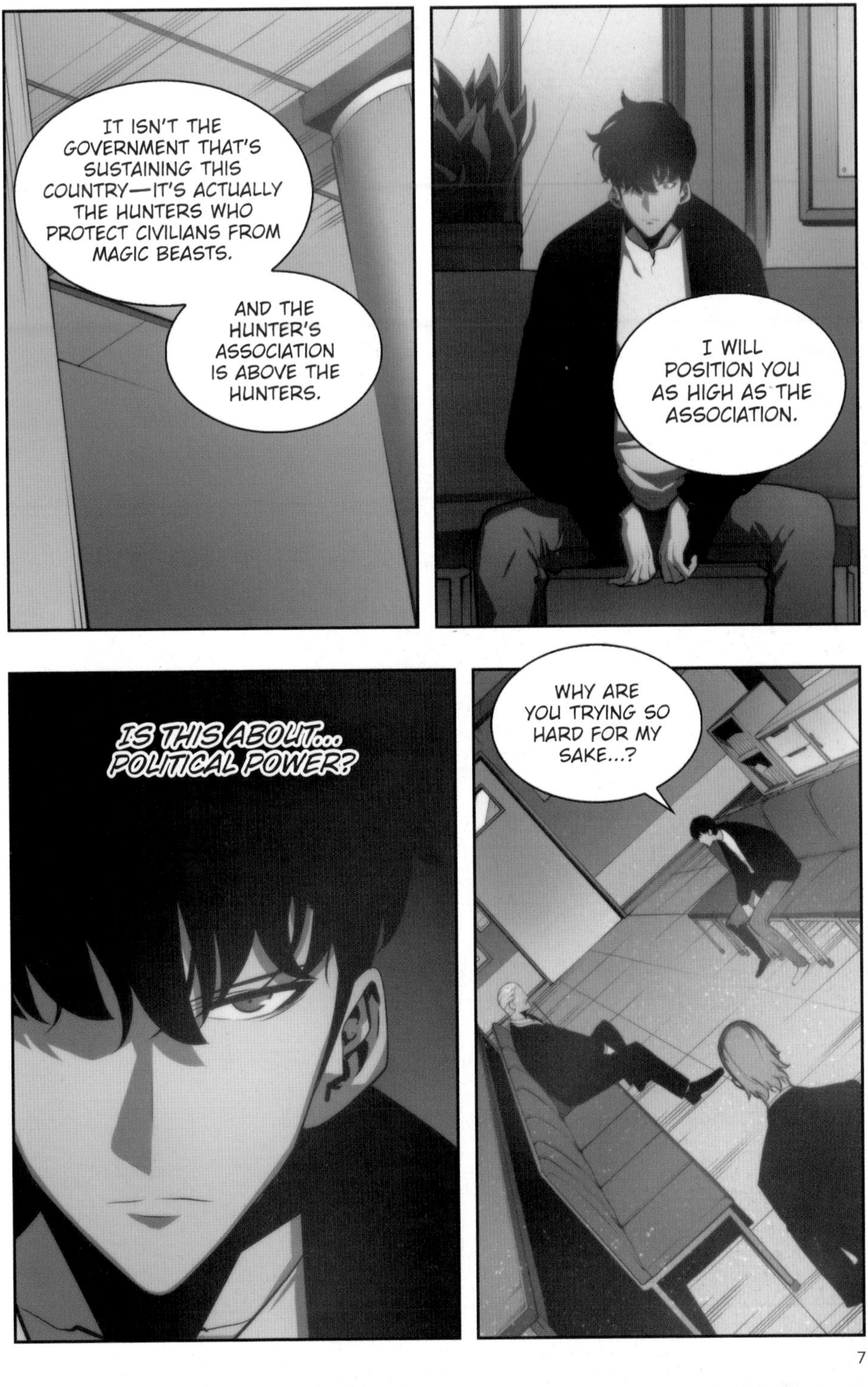
IT ISN'T THE GOVERNMENT THAT'S SUSTAINING THIS COUNTRY—IT'S ACTUALLY THE HUNTERS WHO PROTECT CIVILIANS FROM MAGIC BEASTS.
AND THE HUNTER'S ASSOCIATION IS ABOVE THE HUNTERS.
I WILL POSITION YOU AS HIGH AS THE ASSOCIATION.
IS THIS ABOUT... POLITICAL POWER?
WHY ARE YOU TRYING SO HARD FOR MY SAKE...?

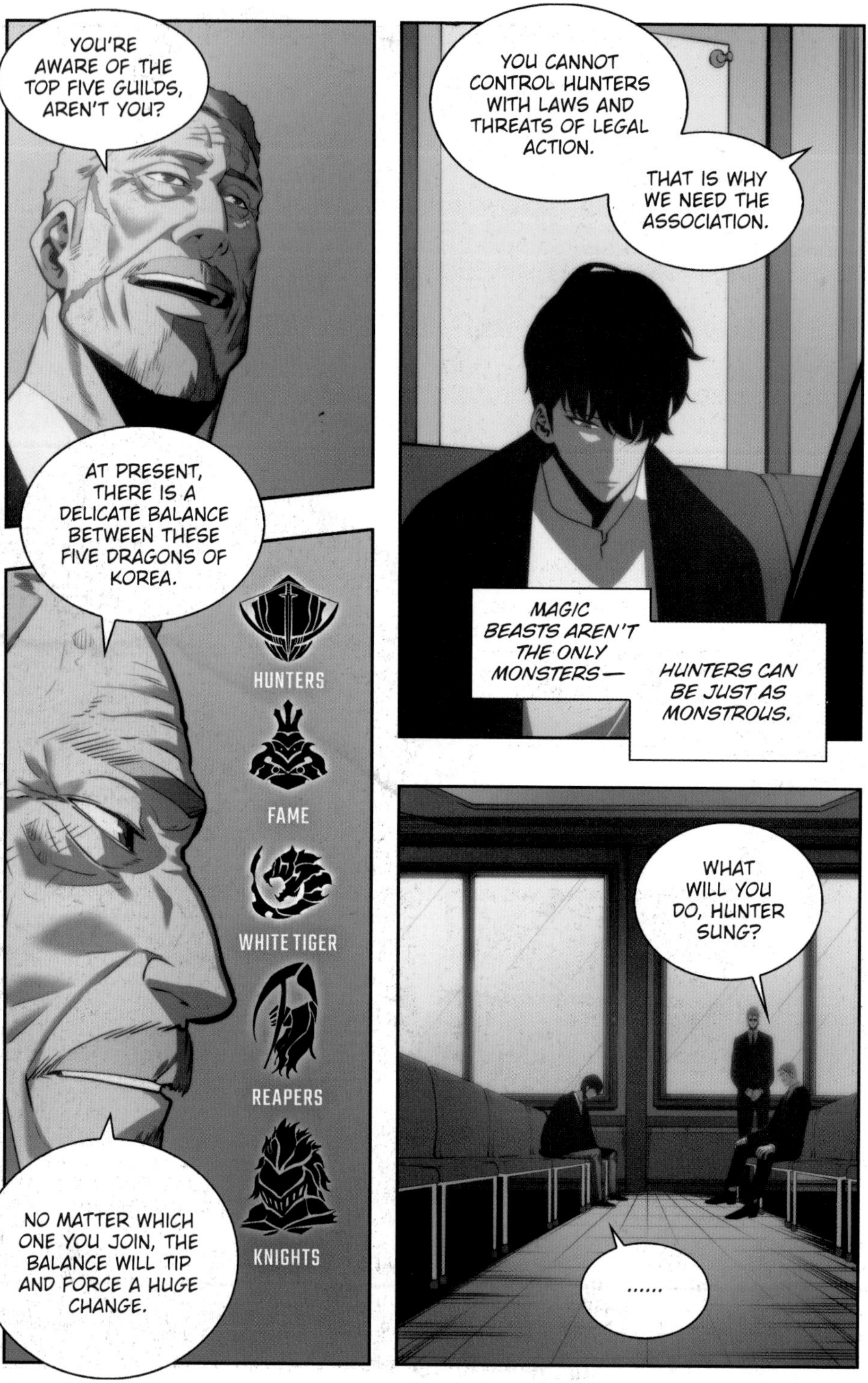
YOU'RE AWARE OF THE TOP FIVE GUILDS, AREN'T YOU?
AT PRESENT, THERE IS A DELICATE BALANCE BETWEEN THESE FIVE DRAGONS OF KOREA.
HUNTERS
FAME
WHITE TIGER
REAPERS
KNIGHTS
NO MATTER WHICH ONE YOU JOIN, THE BALANCE WILL TIP AND FORCE A HUGE CHANGE.
YOU CANNOT CONTROL HUNTERS WITH LAWS AND THREATS OF LEGAL ACTION.
THAT IS WHY WE NEED THE ASSOCIATION.
MAGIC BEASTS AREN'T THE ONLY MONSTERS—
HUNTERS CAN BE JUST AS MONSTROUS.
WHAT WILL YOU DO, HUNTER SUNG?
......

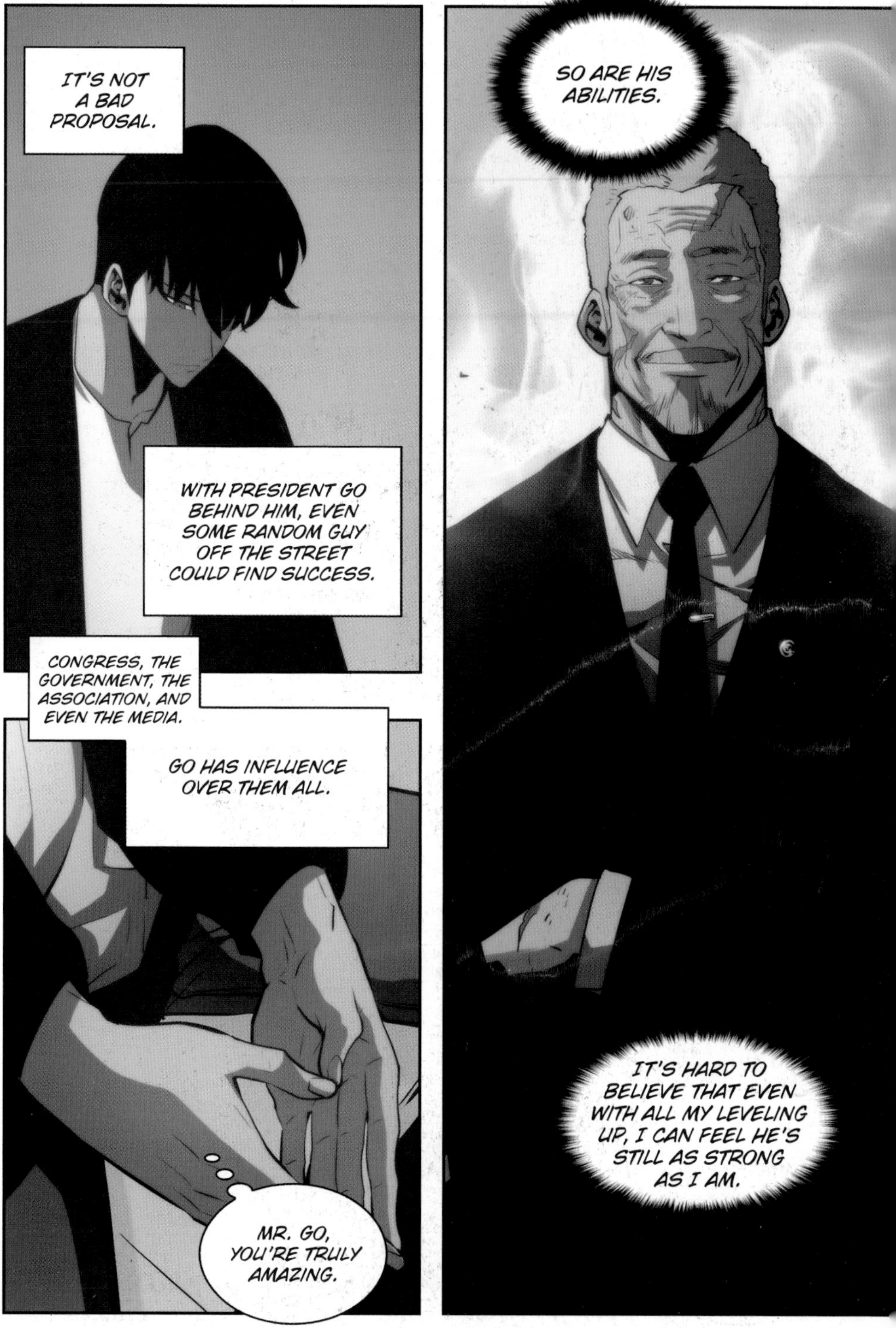
IT'S NOT A BAD PROPOSAL.
WITH PRESIDENT GO BEHIND HIM, EVEN SOME RANDOM GUY OFF THE STREET COULD FIND SUCCESS.
CONGRESS, THE GOVERNMENT, THE ASSOCIATION, AND EVEN THE MEDIA.
GO HAS INFLUENCE OVER THEM ALL.
MR. GO, YOU'RE TRULY AMAZING.
SO ARE HIS ABILITIES.
IT'S HARD TO BELIEVE THAT EVEN WITH ALL MY LEVELING UP, I CAN FEEL HE'S STILL AS STRONG AS I AM.

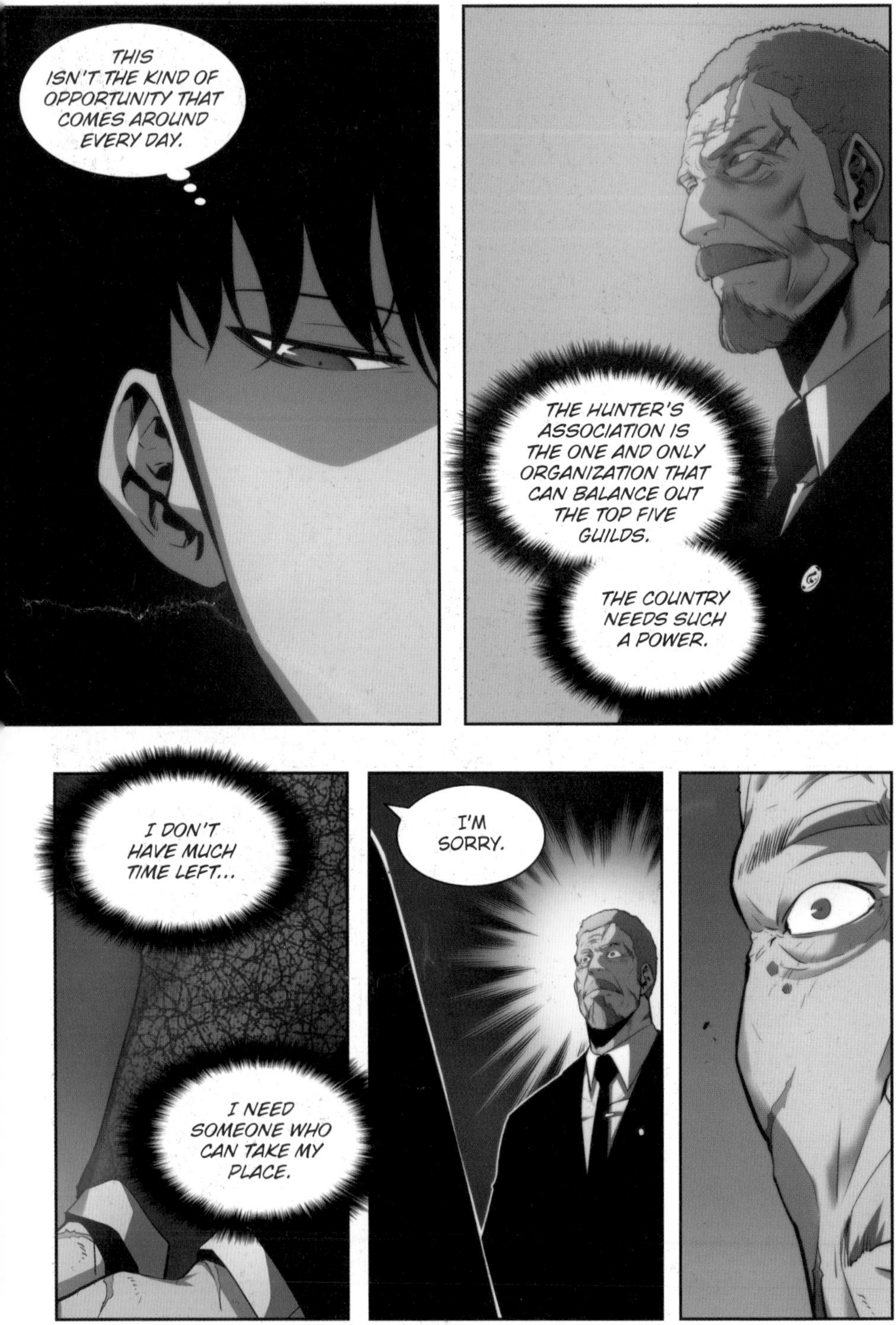
THIS ISN'T THE KIND OF OPPORTUNITY THAT COMES AROUND EVERY DAY.
THE HUNTER'S ASSOCIATION IS THE ONE AND ONLY ORGANIZATION THAT CAN BALANCE OUT THE TOP FIVE GUILDS.
THE COUNTRY NEEDS SUCH A POWER.
I DON'T HAVE MUCH TIME LEFT...
I NEED SOMEONE WHO CAN TAKE MY PLACE.
I'M SORRY.

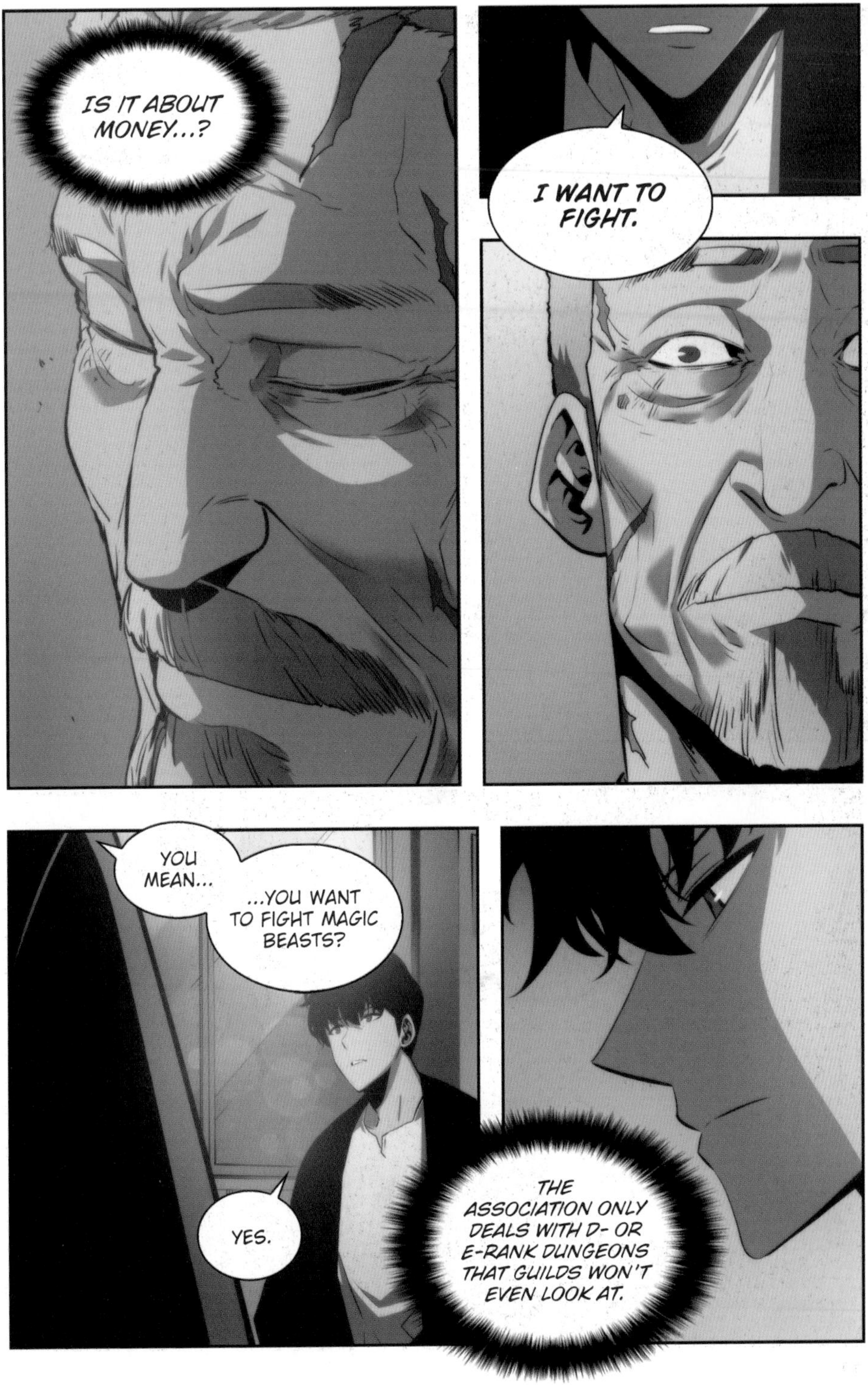
IS IT ABOUT MONEY...?
I WANT TO FIGHT.
YOU MEAN...
...YOU WANT TO FIGHT MAGIC BEASTS?
YES.
THE ASSOCIATION ONLY DEALS WITH D- OR E-RANK DUNGEONS THAT GUILDS WON'T EVEN LOOK AT.

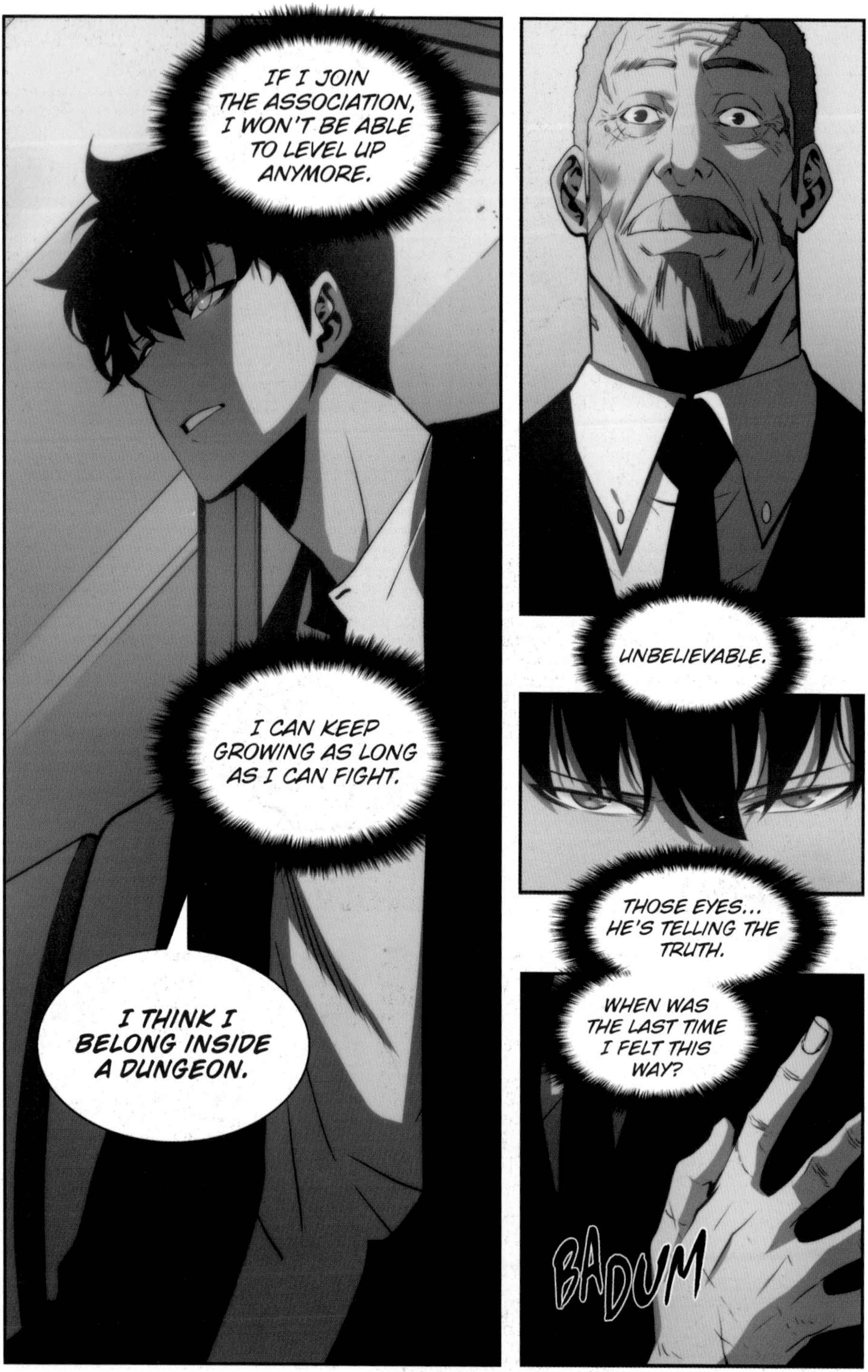
IF I JOIN THE ASSOCIATION, I WON'T BE ABLE TO LEVEL UP ANYMORE.
I CAN KEEP GROWING AS LONG AS I CAN FIGHT.
I THINK I BELONG INSIDE A DUNGEON.
UNBELIEVABLE.
THOSE EYES... HE'S TELLING THE TRUTH.
WHEN WAS THE LAST TIME I FELT THIS WAY?
BADUM

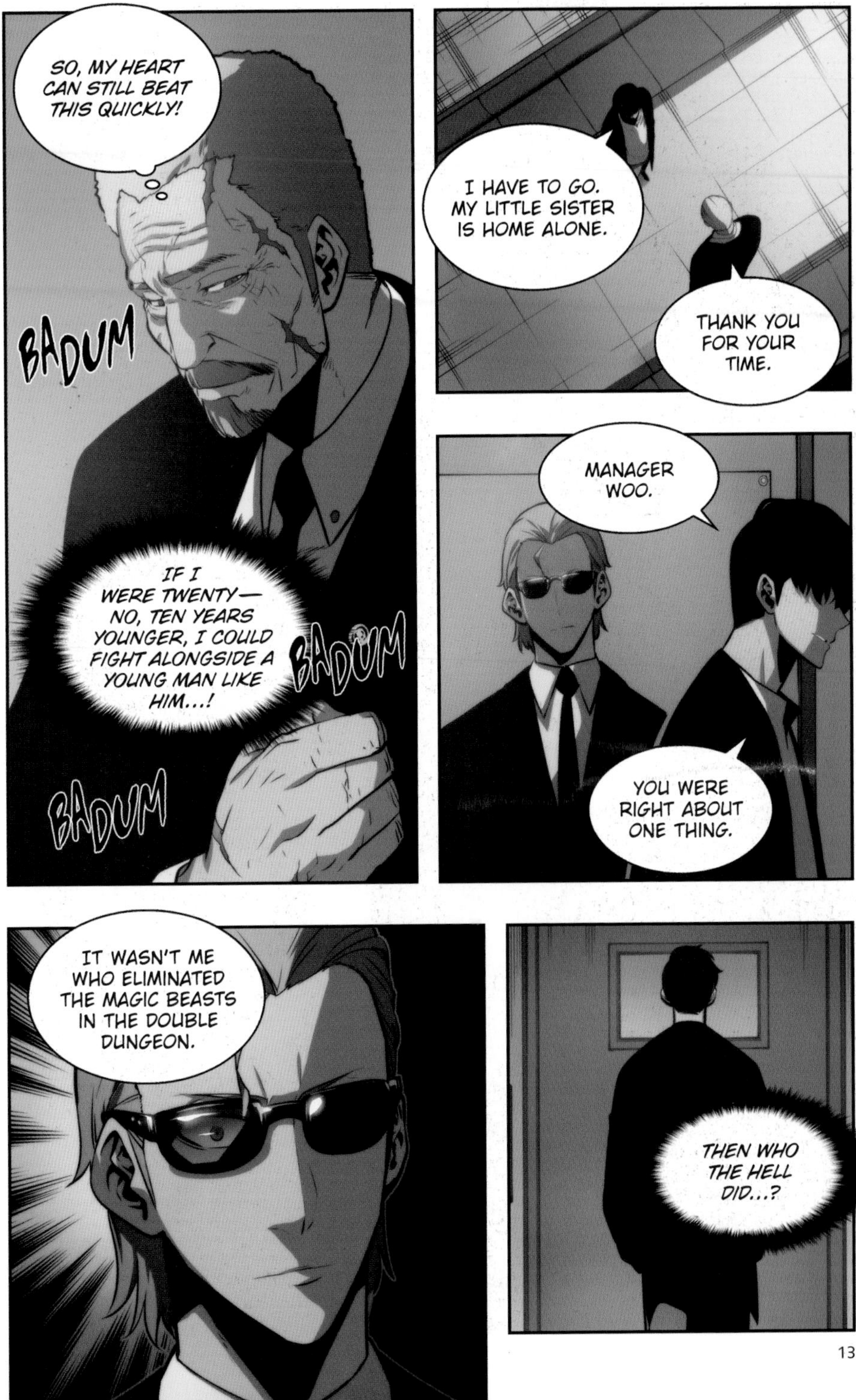

SO, MY HEART CAN STILL BEAT THIS QUICKLY!
BADUM
IF I WERE TWENTY— NO, TEN YEARS YOUNGER, I COULD FIGHT ALONGSIDE A YOUNG MAN LIKE HIM...!
BADUM
BADUM
I HAVE TO GO. MY LITTLE SISTER IS HOME ALONE.
THANK YOU FOR YOUR TIME.
MANAGER WOO.
YOU WERE RIGHT ABOUT ONE THING.
IT WASN'T ME WHO ELIMINATED THE MAGIC BEASTS IN THE DOUBLE DUNGEON.
THEN WHO THE HELL DID...?

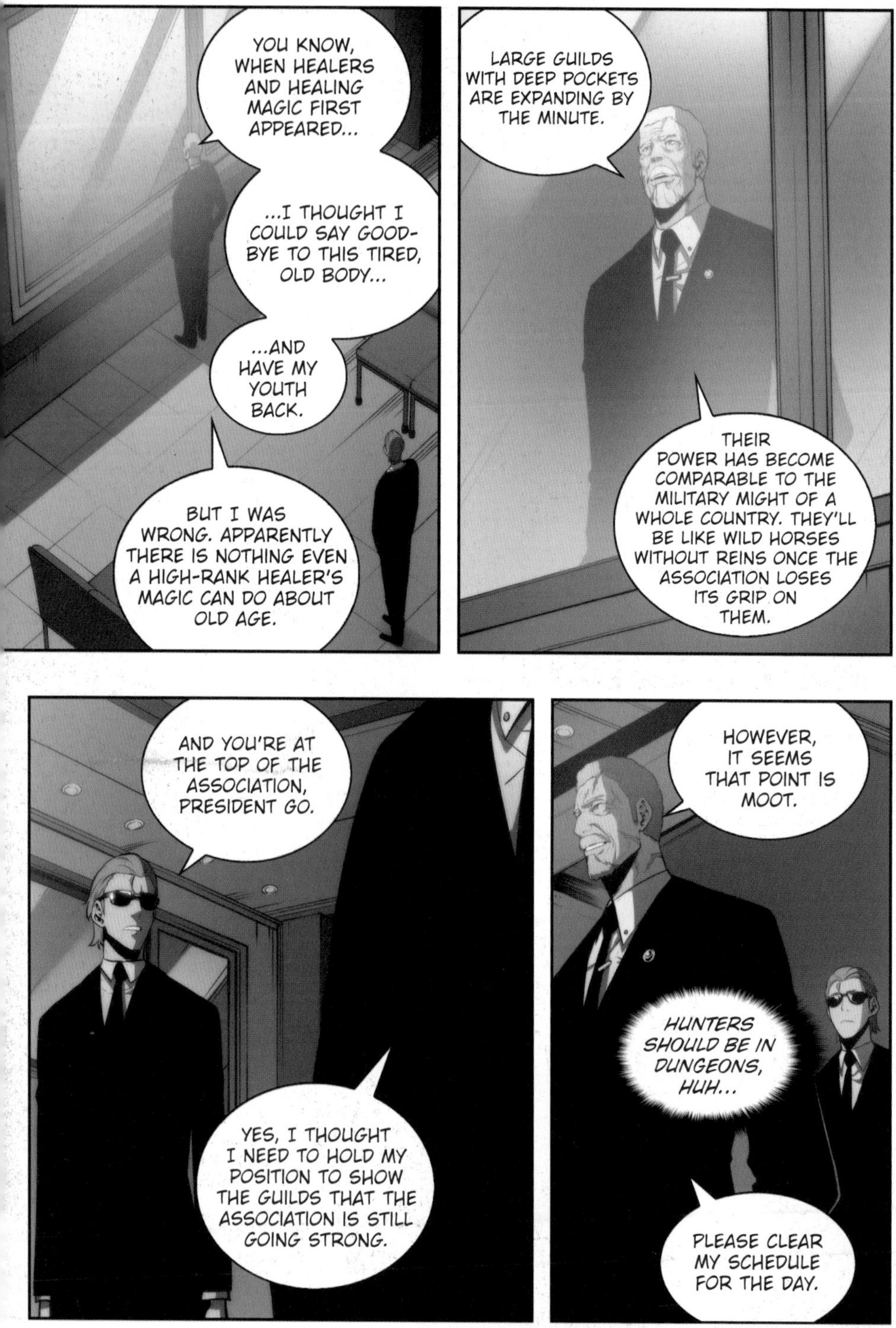
YOU KNOW, WHEN HEALERS AND HEALING MAGIC FIRST APPEARED...
...I THOUGHT I COULD SAY GOOD-BYE TO THIS TIRED, OLD BODY...
...AND HAVE MY YOUTH BACK.
BUT I WAS WRONG. APPARENTLY THERE IS NOTHING EVEN A HIGH-RANK HEALER'S MAGIC CAN DO ABOUT OLD AGE.
LARGE GUILDS WITH DEEP POCKETS ARE EXPANDING BY THE MINUTE.
THEIR POWER HAS BECOME COMPARABLE TO THE MILITARY MIGHT OF A WHOLE COUNTRY. THEY'LL BE LIKE WILD HORSES WITHOUT REINS ONCE THE ASSOCIATION LOSES ITS GRIP ON THEM.
AND YOU'RE AT THE TOP OF THE ASSOCIATION, PRESIDENT GO.
YES, I THOUGHT I NEED TO HOLD MY POSITION TO SHOW THE GUILDS THAT THE ASSOCIATION IS STILL GOING STRONG.
HOWEVER, IT SEEMS THAT POINT IS MOOT.
HUNTERS SHOULD BE IN DUNGEONS, HUH...
PLEASE CLEAR MY SCHEDULE FOR THE DAY.

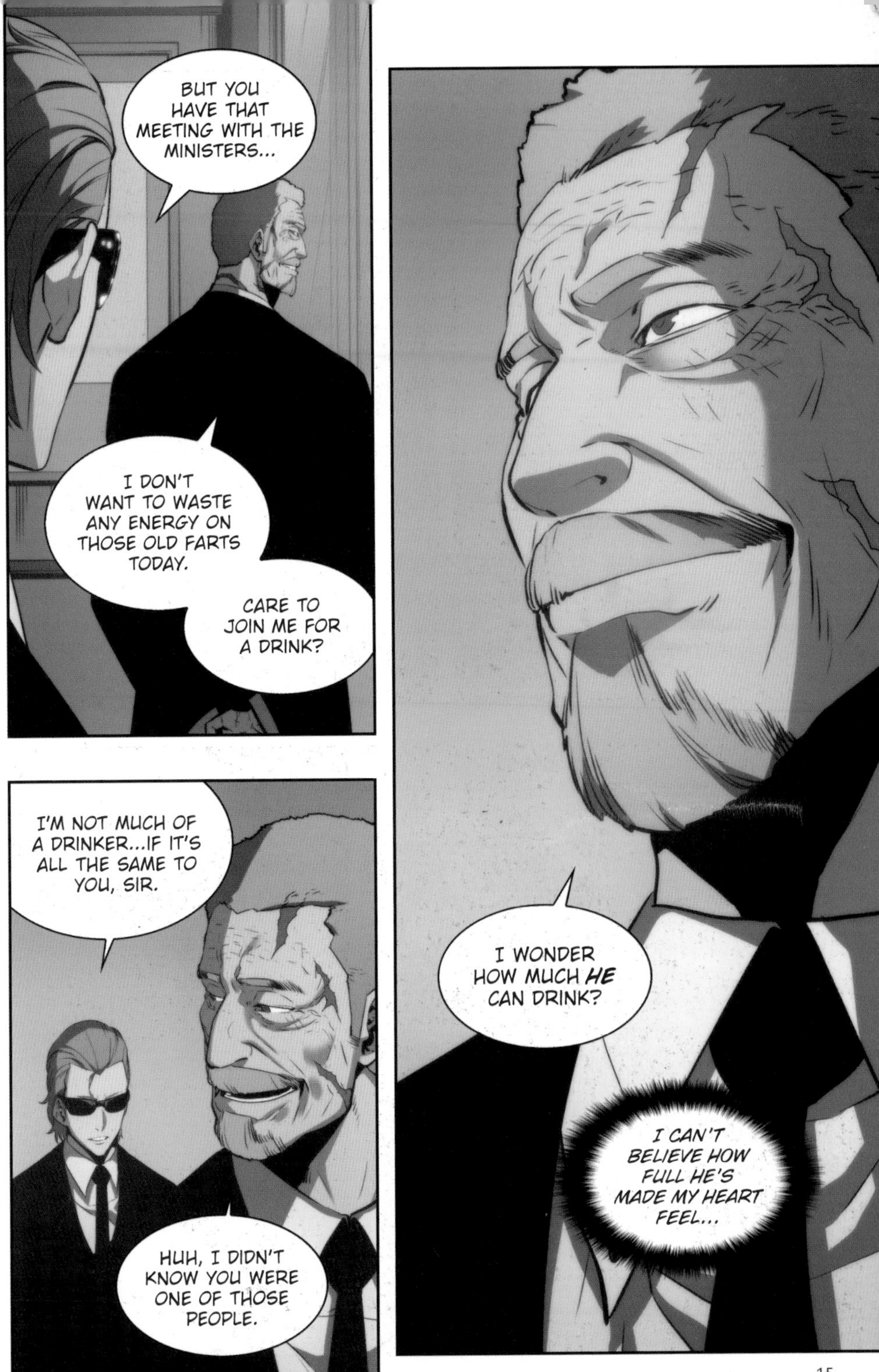
BUT YOU HAVE THAT MEETING WITH THE MINISTERS...
I DON'T WANT TO WASTE ANY ENERGY ON THOSE OLD FARTS TODAY.
CARE TO JOIN ME FOR A DRINK?
I'M NOT MUCH OF A DRINKER...IF IT'S ALL THE SAME TO YOU, SIR.
HUH, I DIDN'T KNOW YOU WERE ONE OF THOSE PEOPLE.
I WONDER HOW MUCH *HE* CAN DRINK?
I CAN'T BELIEVE HOW FULL HE'S MADE MY HEART FEEL...

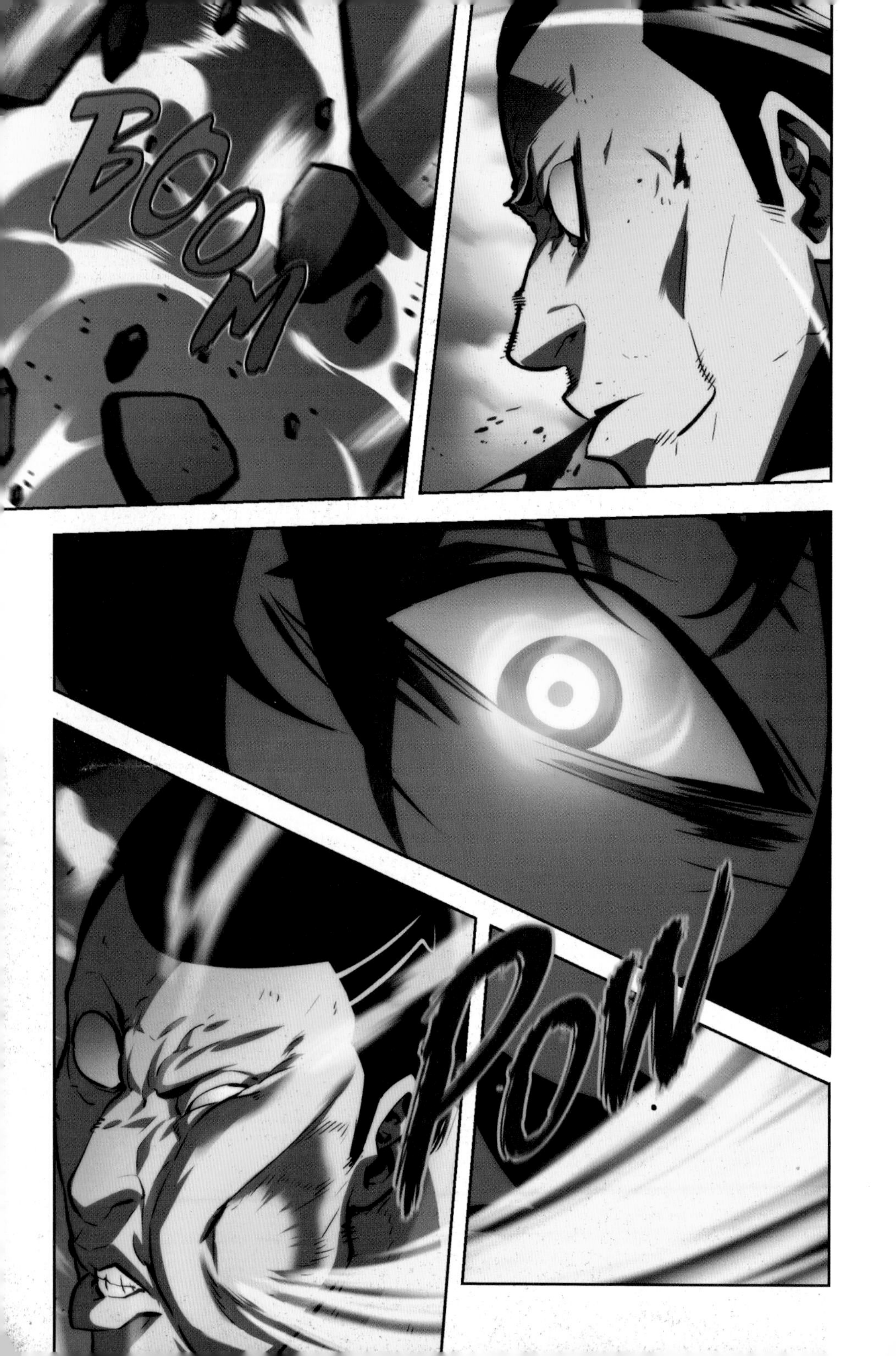
BOOM
POW

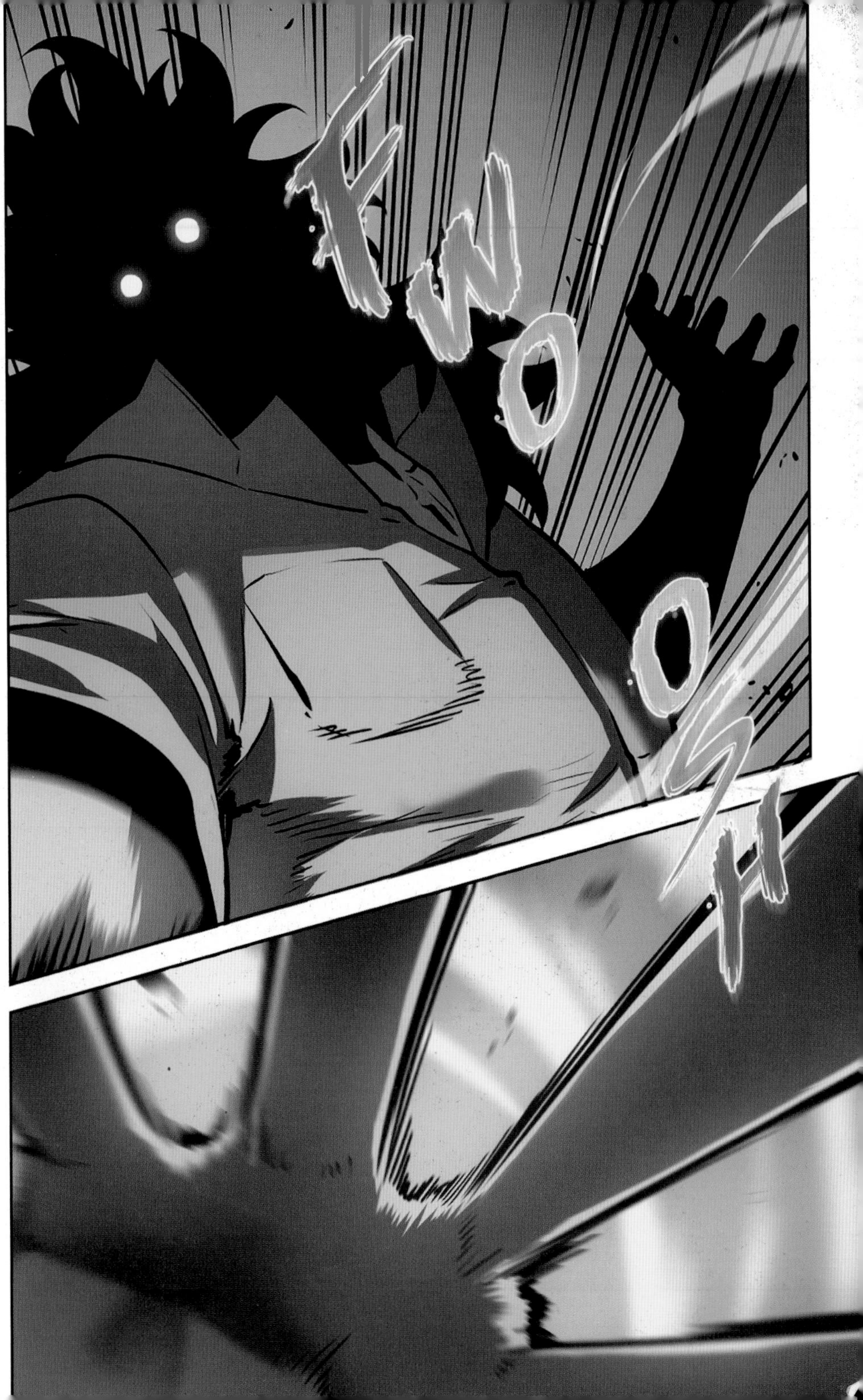
FWOOSH

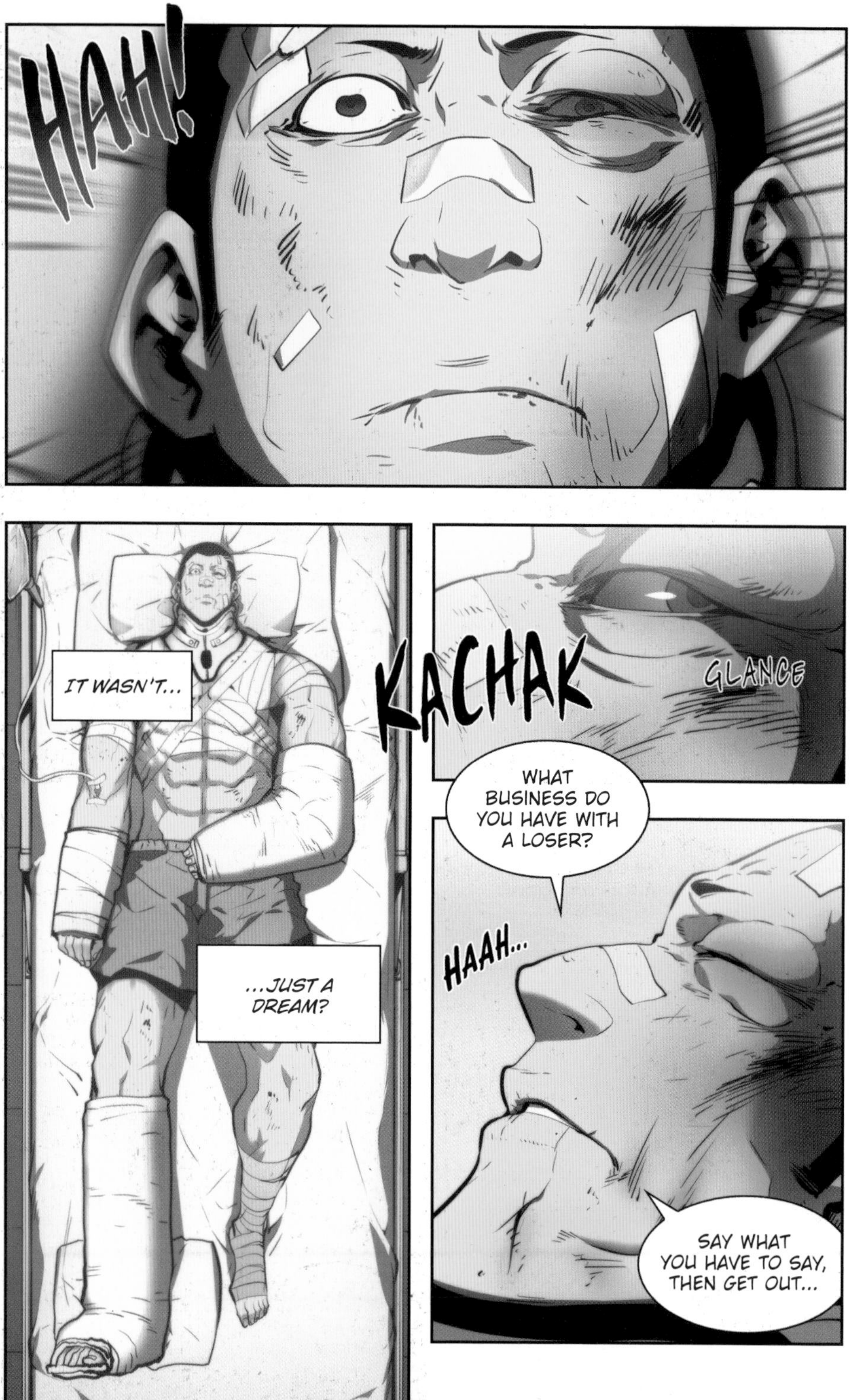
HAH!
IT WASN'T...
...JUST A DREAM?
KACHAK
GLANCE
WHAT BUSINESS DO YOU HAVE WITH A LOSER?
HAAH...
SAY WHAT YOU HAVE TO SAY, THEN GET OUT...

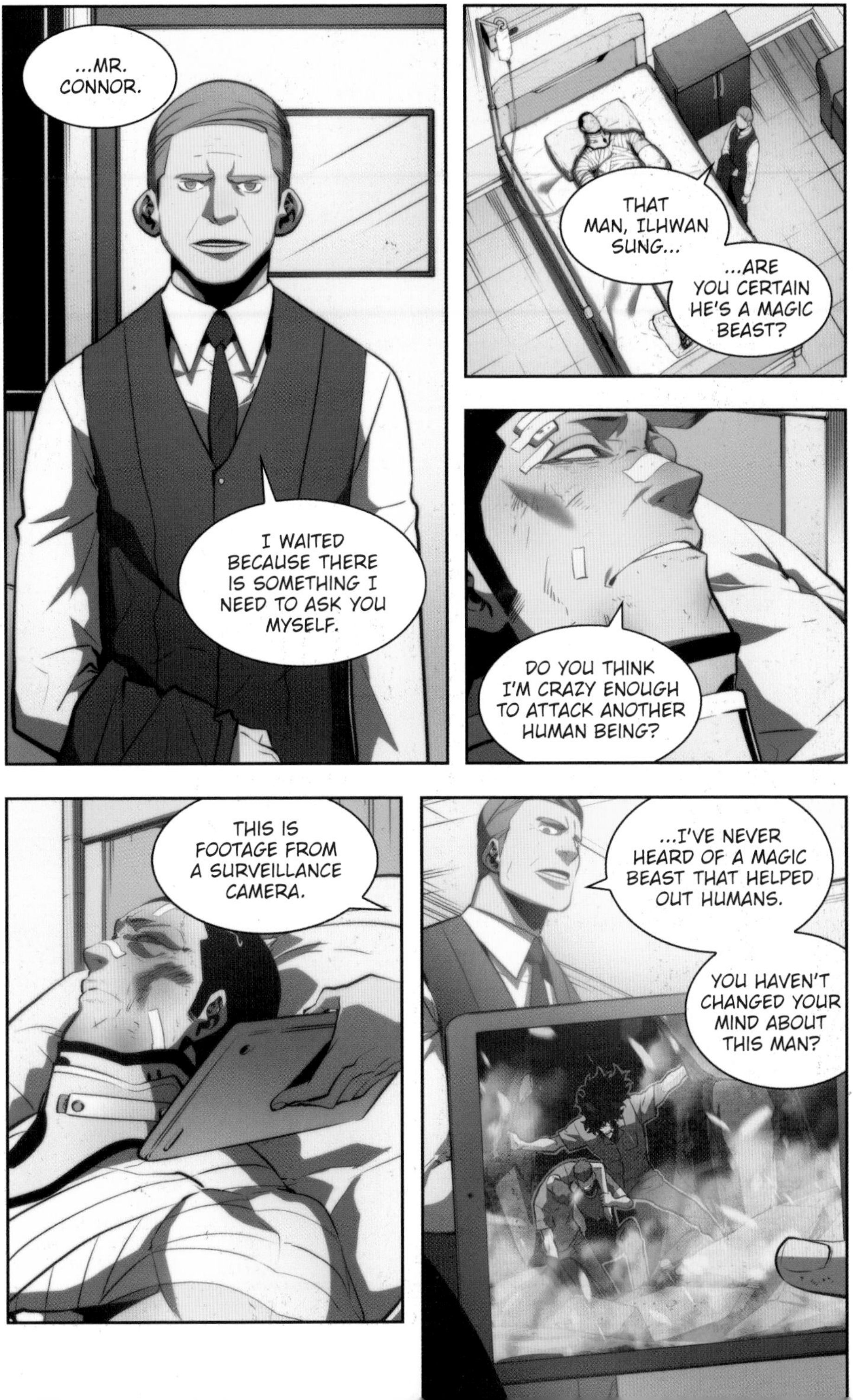
...MR. CONNOR.
I WAITED BECAUSE THERE IS SOMETHING I NEED TO ASK YOU MYSELF.
THAT MAN, ILHWAN SUNG...
...ARE YOU CERTAIN HE'S A MAGIC BEAST?
DO YOU THINK I'M CRAZY ENOUGH TO ATTACK ANOTHER HUMAN BEING?
THIS IS FOOTAGE FROM A SURVEILLANCE CAMERA.
...I'VE NEVER HEARD OF A MAGIC BEAST THAT HELPED OUT HUMANS.
YOU HAVEN'T CHANGED YOUR MIND ABOUT THIS MAN?

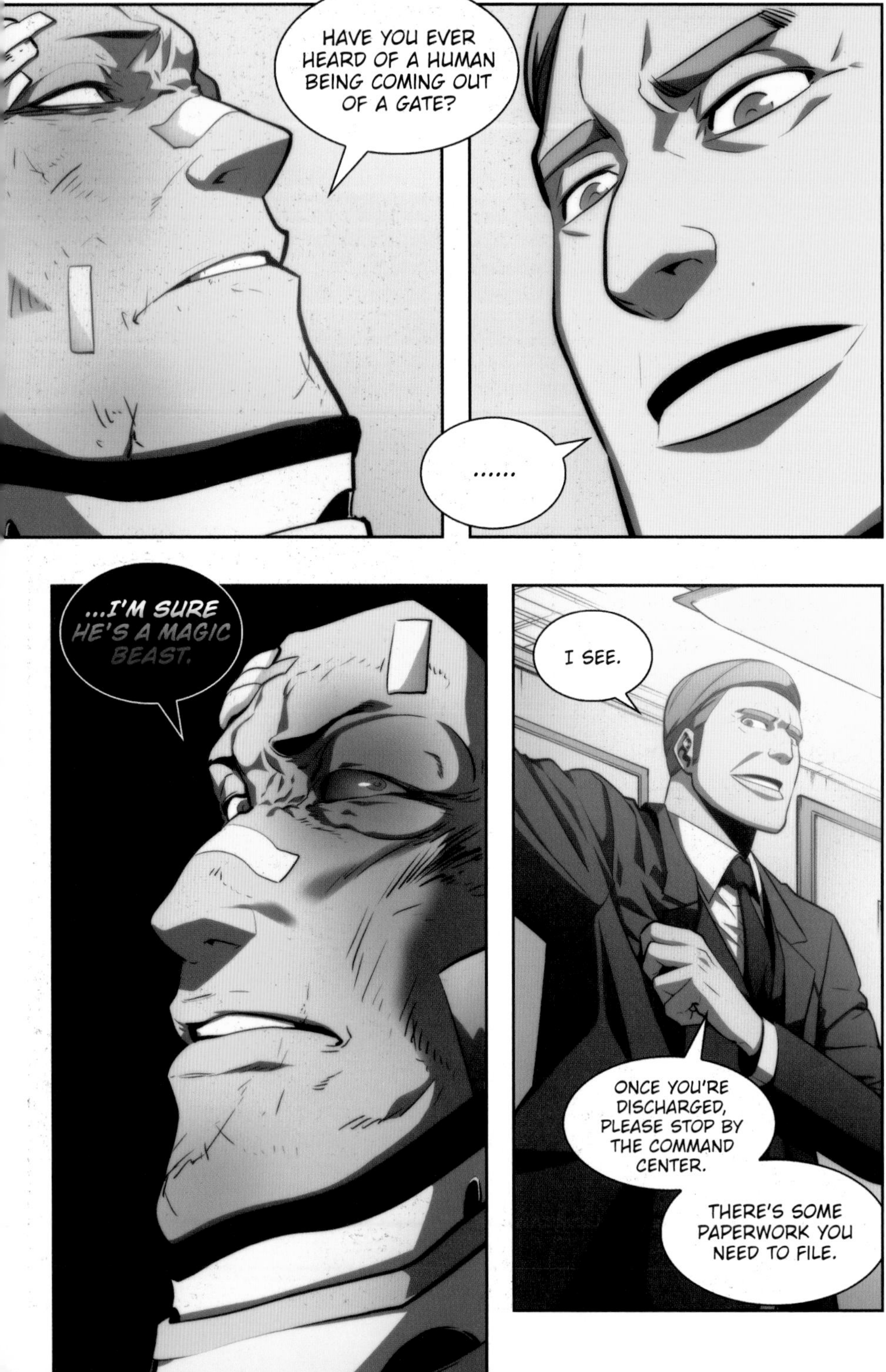
HAVE YOU EVER HEARD OF A HUMAN BEING COMING OUT OF A GATE?
......
...I'M SURE HE'S A MAGIC BEAST.
I SEE.
ONCE YOU'RE DISCHARGED, PLEASE STOP BY THE COMMAND CENTER.
THERE'S SOME PAPERWORK YOU NEED TO FILE.

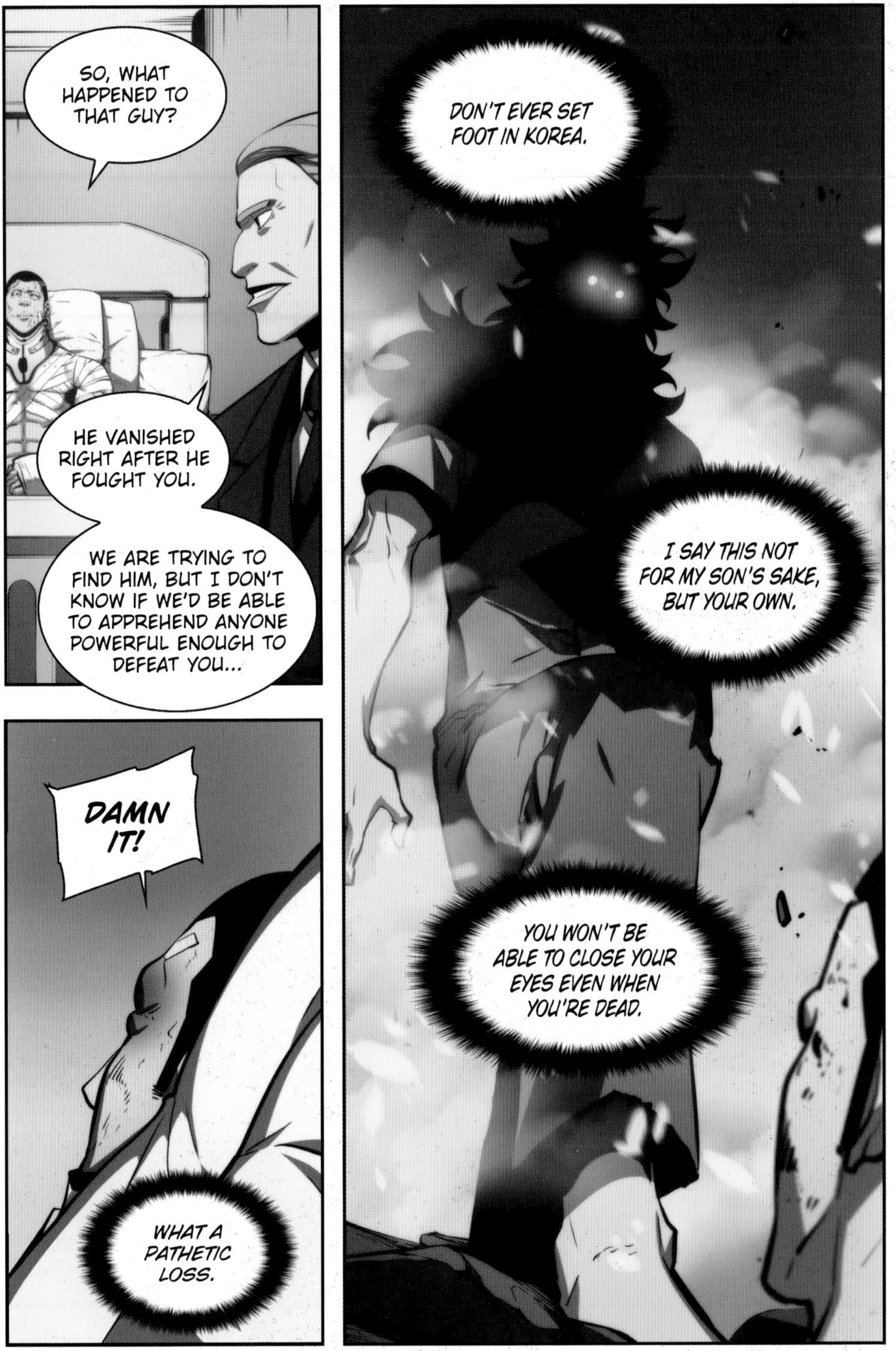
SO, WHAT HAPPENED TO THAT GUY?
HE VANISHED RIGHT AFTER HE FOUGHT YOU.
WE ARE TRYING TO FIND HIM, BUT I DON'T KNOW IF WE'D BE ABLE TO APPREHEND ANYONE POWERFUL ENOUGH TO DEFEAT YOU...
DAMN IT!
WHAT A PATHETIC LOSS.
DON'T EVER SET FOOT IN KOREA.
I SAY THIS NOT FOR MY SON'S SAKE, BUT YOUR OWN.
YOU WON'T BE ABLE TO CLOSE YOUR EYES EVEN WHEN YOU'RE DEAD.

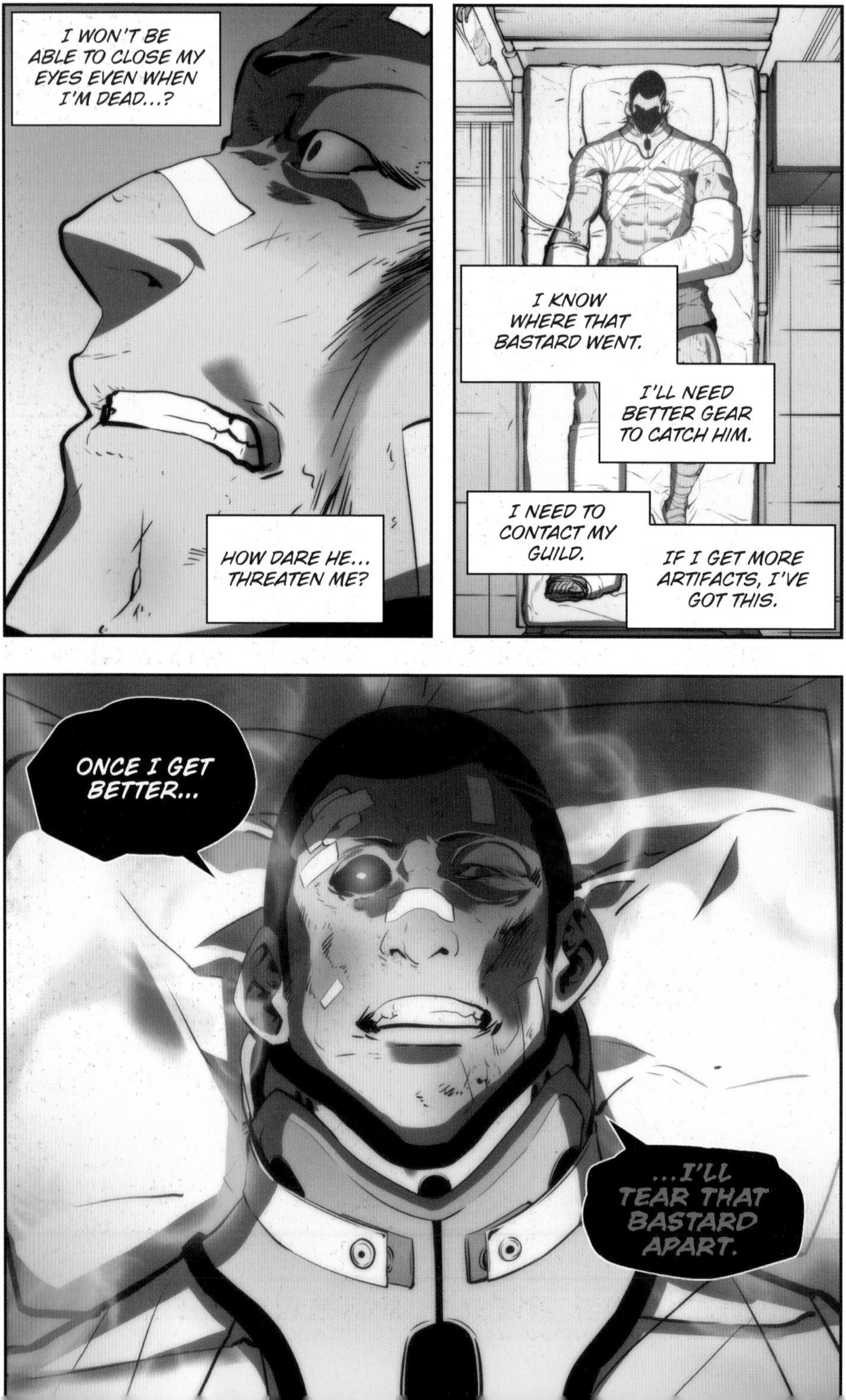
I WON'T BE ABLE TO CLOSE MY EYES EVEN WHEN I'M DEAD...?
HOW DARE HE... THREATEN ME?
I KNOW WHERE THAT BASTARD WENT.
I'LL NEED BETTER GEAR TO CATCH HIM.
I NEED TO CONTACT MY GUILD.
IF I GET MORE ARTIFACTS, I'VE GOT THIS.
ONCE I GET BETTER...
...I'LL TEAR THAT BASTARD APART.

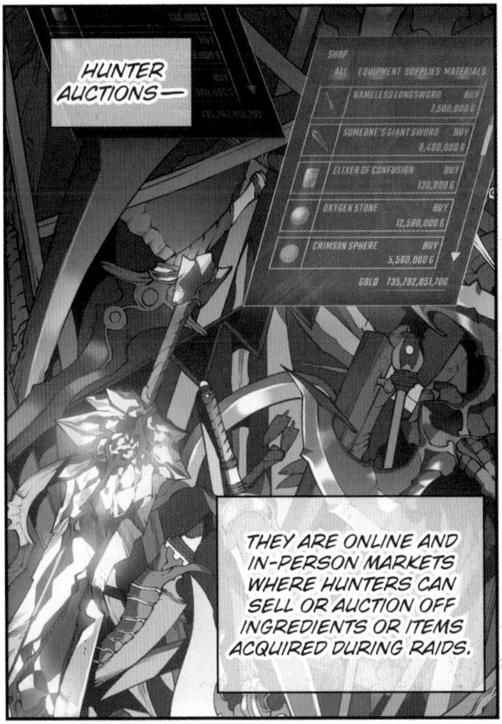
HUNTER AUCTIONS—
SHOP
ALL EQUIPMENT SUPPLIES MATERIALS
NAMELESS LONGSWORD BUY 7,500,000 G
SOMEONE'S GIANT SWORD BUY 8,400,000 G
ELIXER OF CONFUSION BUY 130,000 G
OXYGEN STONE BUY 12,560,000 G
CRIMSON SPHERE BUY 5,560,000 G
GOLD 735,792,051,700
THEY ARE ONLINE AND IN-PERSON MARKETS WHERE HUNTERS CAN SELL OR AUCTION OFF INGREDIENTS OR ITEMS ACQUIRED DURING RAIDS.

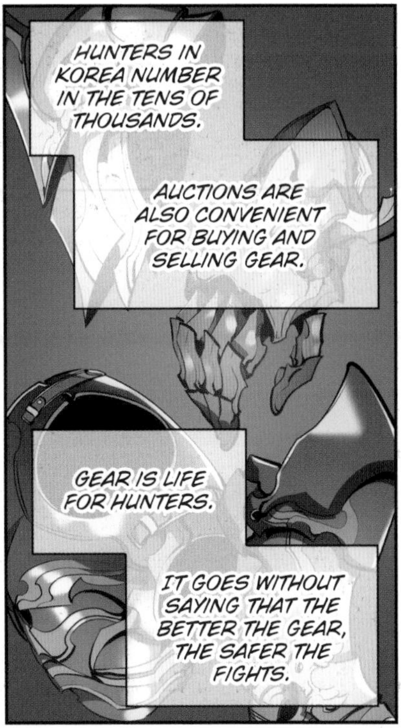
HUNTERS IN KOREA NUMBER IN THE TENS OF THOUSANDS.
AUCTIONS ARE ALSO CONVENIENT FOR BUYING AND SELLING GEAR.
GEAR IS LIFE FOR HUNTERS.
IT GOES WITHOUT SAYING THAT THE BETTER THE GEAR, THE SAFER THE FIGHTS.

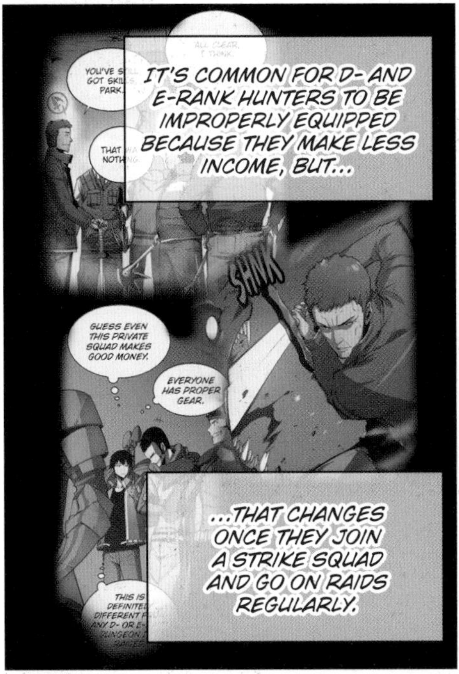
IT'S COMMON FOR D- AND E-RANK HUNTERS TO BE IMPROPERLY EQUIPPED BECAUSE THEY MAKE LESS INCOME, BUT...
SHNK
GUESS EVEN THIS PRIVATE SQUAD MAKES GOOD MONEY.
EVERYONE HAS PROPER GEAR.
...THAT CHANGES ONCE THEY JOIN A STRIKE SQUAD AND GO ON RAIDS REGULARLY.

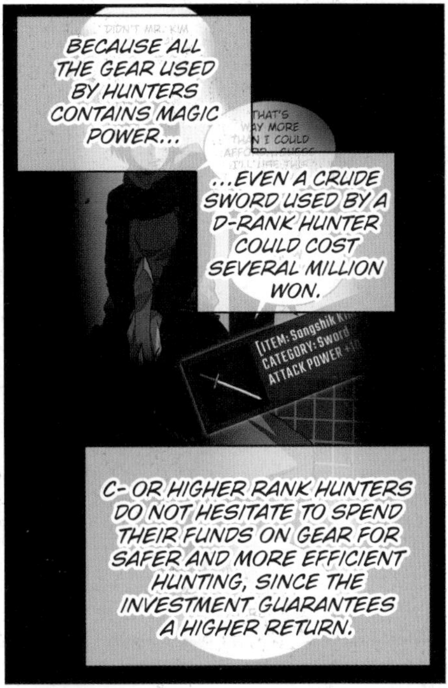
BECAUSE ALL THE GEAR USED BY HUNTERS CONTAINS MAGIC POWER...
...EVEN A CRUDE SWORD USED BY A D-RANK HUNTER COULD COST SEVERAL MILLION WON.
C- OR HIGHER RANK HUNTERS DO NOT HESITATE TO SPEND THEIR FUNDS ON GEAR FOR SAFER AND MORE EFFICIENT HUNTING, SINCE THE INVESTMENT GUARANTEES A HIGHER RETURN.

While exchange rates fluctuate daily, an easy conversion estimate is about 1,000 KRW to 1 USD.

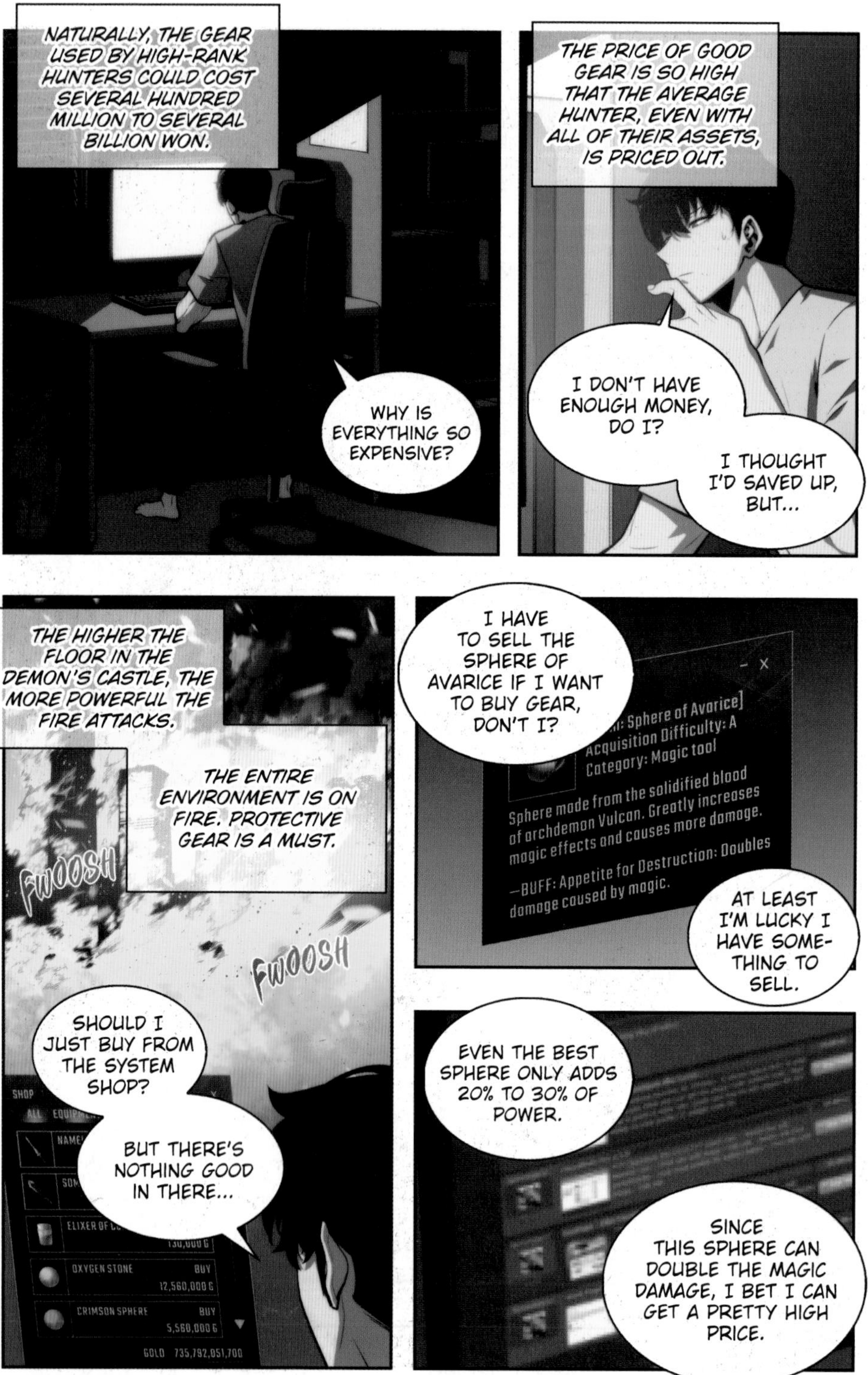
NATURALLY, THE GEAR USED BY HIGH-RANK HUNTERS COULD COST SEVERAL HUNDRED MILLION TO SEVERAL BILLION WON.
WHY IS EVERYTHING SO EXPENSIVE?
THE PRICE OF GOOD GEAR IS SO HIGH THAT THE AVERAGE HUNTER, EVEN WITH ALL OF THEIR ASSETS, IS PRICED OUT.
I DON'T HAVE ENOUGH MONEY, DO I?
I THOUGHT I'D SAVED UP, BUT...
THE HIGHER THE FLOOR IN THE DEMON'S CASTLE, THE MORE POWERFUL THE FIRE ATTACKS.
THE ENTIRE ENVIRONMENT IS ON FIRE. PROTECTIVE GEAR IS A MUST.
FWOOSH
FWOOSH
SHOULD I JUST BUY FROM THE SYSTEM SHOP?
BUT THERE'S NOTHING GOOD IN THERE...
SHOP
ALL
130,000 G
OXYGEN STONE
BUY
12,560,000 G
CRIMSON SPHERE
BUY
5,560,000 G
GOLD 735,792,051,700
I HAVE TO SELL THE SPHERE OF AVARICE IF I WANT TO BUY GEAR, DON'T I?
Sphere of Avarice]
Acquisition Difficulty: A
Category: Magic tool
Sphere made from the solidified blood of archdemon Vulcan. Greatly increases magic effects and causes more damage.
—BUFF: Appetite for Destruction: Doubles damage caused by magic.
AT LEAST I'M LUCKY I HAVE SOME-THING TO SELL.
EVEN THE BEST SPHERE ONLY ADDS 20% TO 30% OF POWER.
SINCE THIS SPHERE CAN DOUBLE THE MAGIC DAMAGE, I BET I CAN GET A PRETTY HIGH PRICE.

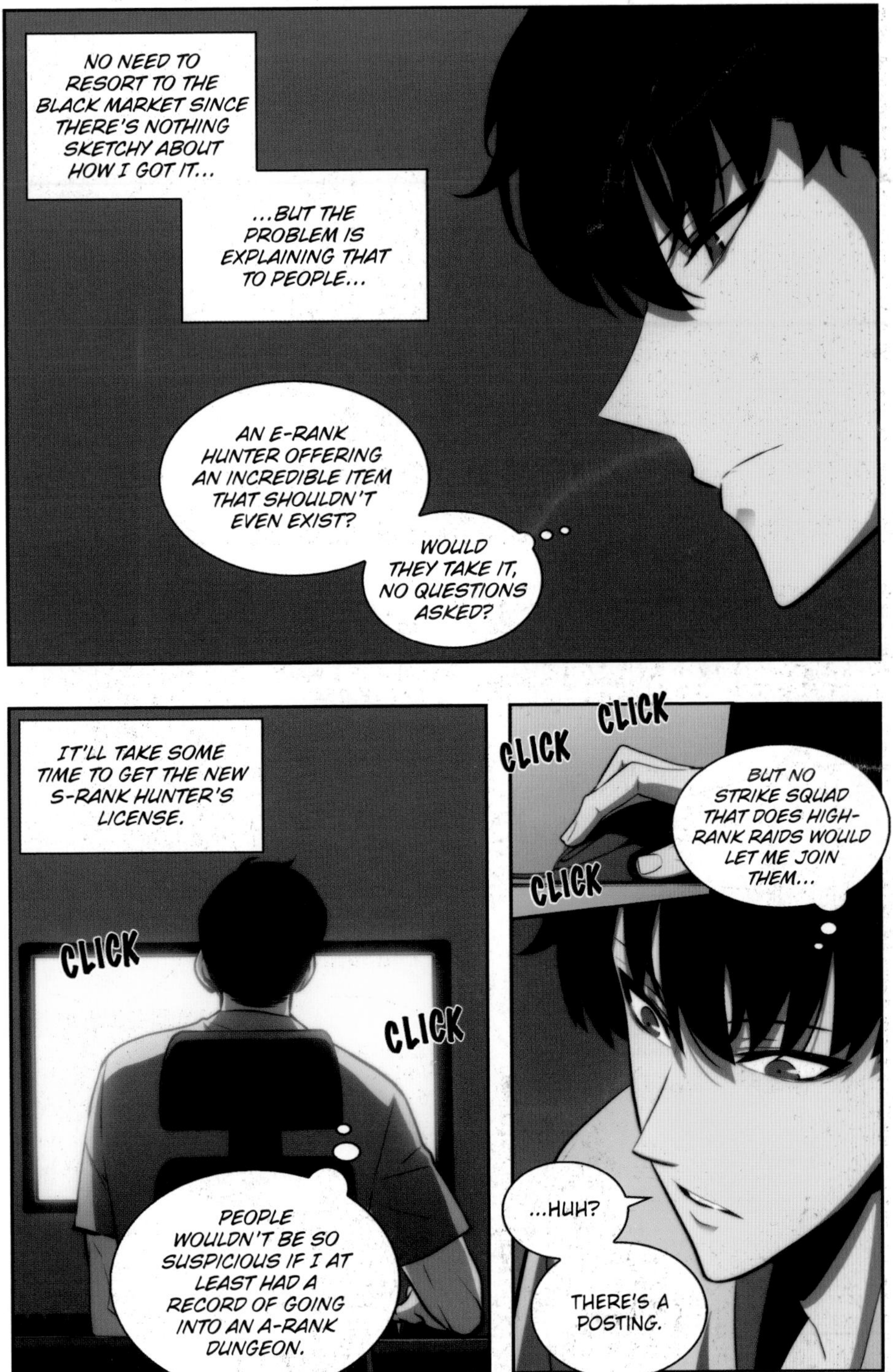
NO NEED TO RESORT TO THE BLACK MARKET SINCE THERE'S NOTHING SKETCHY ABOUT HOW I GOT IT...
...BUT THE PROBLEM IS EXPLAINING THAT TO PEOPLE...
AN E-RANK HUNTER OFFERING AN INCREDIBLE ITEM THAT SHOULDN'T EVEN EXIST?
WOULD THEY TAKE IT, NO QUESTIONS ASKED?
IT'LL TAKE SOME TIME TO GET THE NEW S-RANK HUNTER'S LICENSE.
CLICK
CLICK
PEOPLE WOULDN'T BE SO SUSPICIOUS IF I AT LEAST HAD A RECORD OF GOING INTO AN A-RANK DUNGEON.
CLICK
CLICK
CLICK
BUT NO STRIKE SQUAD THAT DOES HIGH-RANK RAIDS WOULD LET ME JOIN THEM...
...HUH?
THERE'S A POSTING.

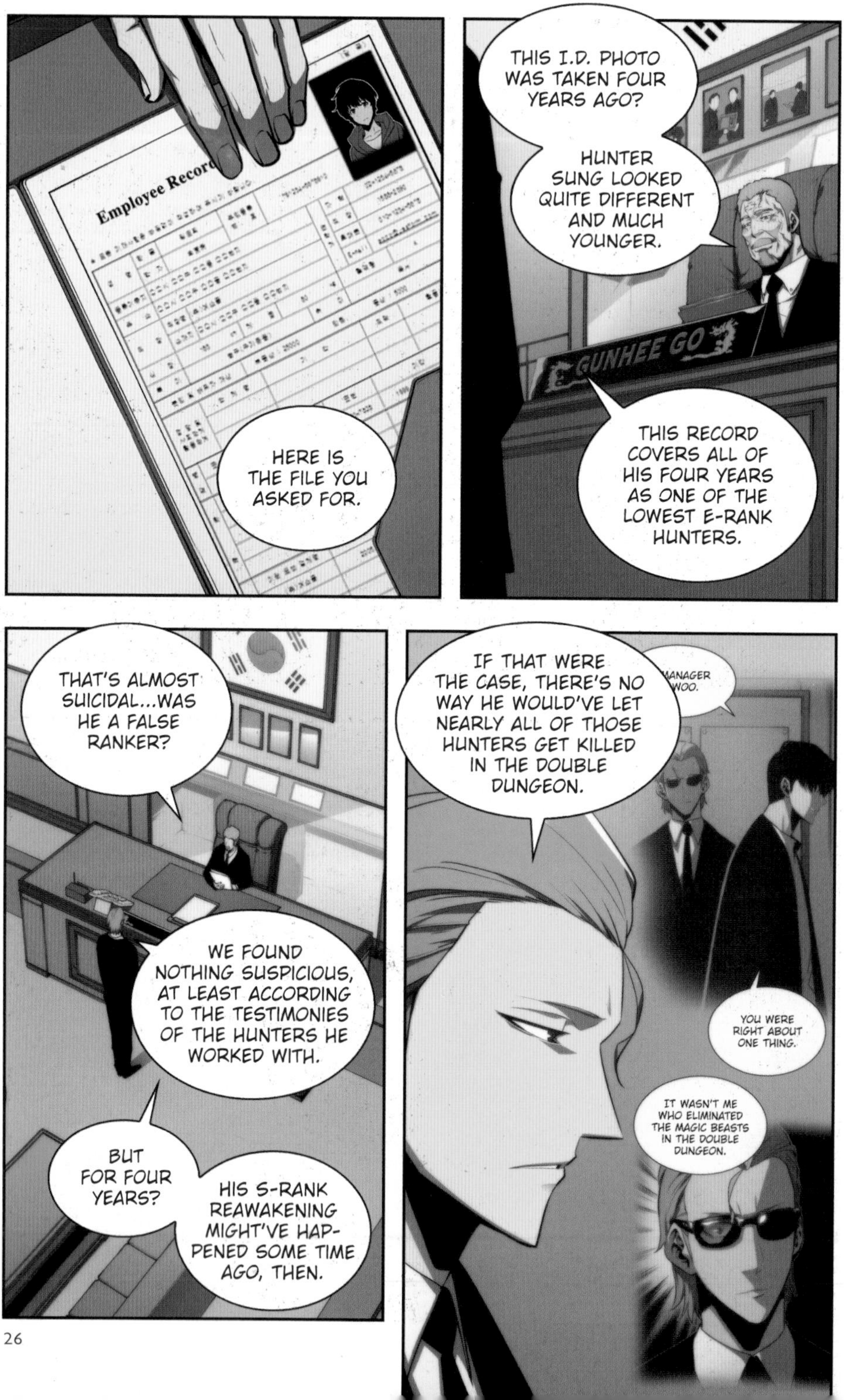
HERE IS THE FILE YOU ASKED FOR.
THIS I.D. PHOTO WAS TAKEN FOUR YEARS AGO?
HUNTER SUNG LOOKED QUITE DIFFERENT AND MUCH YOUNGER.
GUNHEE GO
THIS RECORD COVERS ALL OF HIS FOUR YEARS AS ONE OF THE LOWEST E-RANK HUNTERS.
THAT'S ALMOST SUICIDAL...WAS HE A FALSE RANKER?
WE FOUND NOTHING SUSPICIOUS, AT LEAST ACCORDING TO THE TESTIMONIES OF THE HUNTERS HE WORKED WITH.
BUT FOR FOUR YEARS?
HIS S-RANK REAWAKENING MIGHT'VE HAPPENED SOME TIME AGO, THEN.
IF THAT WERE THE CASE, THERE'S NO WAY HE WOULD'VE LET NEARLY ALL OF THOSE HUNTERS GET KILLED IN THE DOUBLE DUNGEON.
MANAGER WOO.
YOU WERE RIGHT ABOUT ONE THING.
IT WASN'T ME WHO ELIMINATED THE MAGIC BEASTS IN THE DOUBLE DUNGEON.

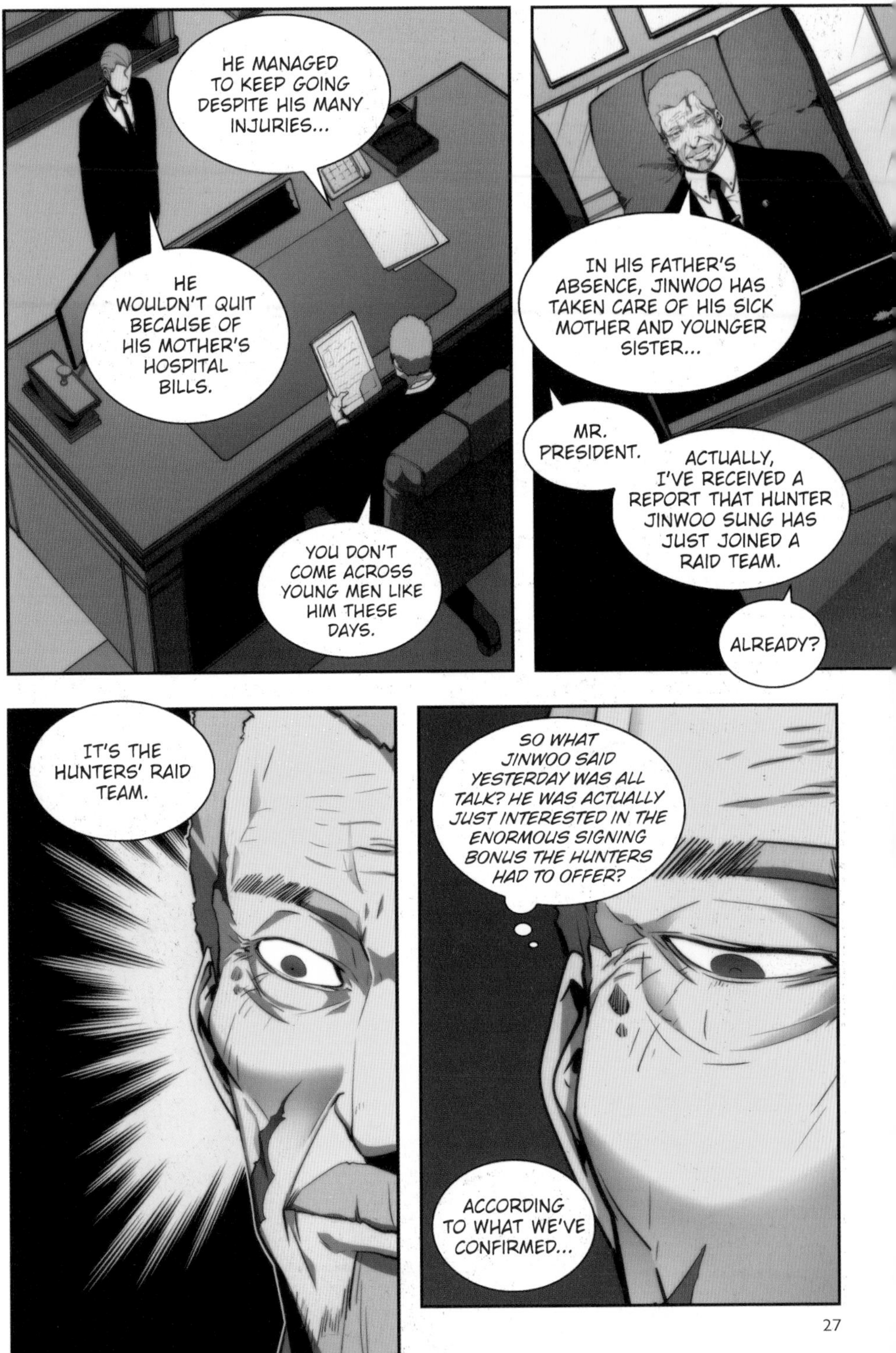
HE MANAGED TO KEEP GOING DESPITE HIS MANY INJURIES...
HE WOULDN'T QUIT BECAUSE OF HIS MOTHER'S HOSPITAL BILLS.
YOU DON'T COME ACROSS YOUNG MEN LIKE HIM THESE DAYS.
IN HIS FATHER'S ABSENCE, JINWOO HAS TAKEN CARE OF HIS SICK MOTHER AND YOUNGER SISTER...
MR. PRESIDENT.
ACTUALLY, I'VE RECEIVED A REPORT THAT HUNTER JINWOO SUNG HAS JUST JOINED A RAID TEAM.
ALREADY?
IT'S THE HUNTERS' RAID TEAM.
SO WHAT JINWOO SAID YESTERDAY WAS ALL TALK? HE WAS ACTUALLY JUST INTERESTED IN THE ENORMOUS SIGNING BONUS THE HUNTERS HAD TO OFFER?
ACCORDING TO WHAT WE'VE CONFIRMED...

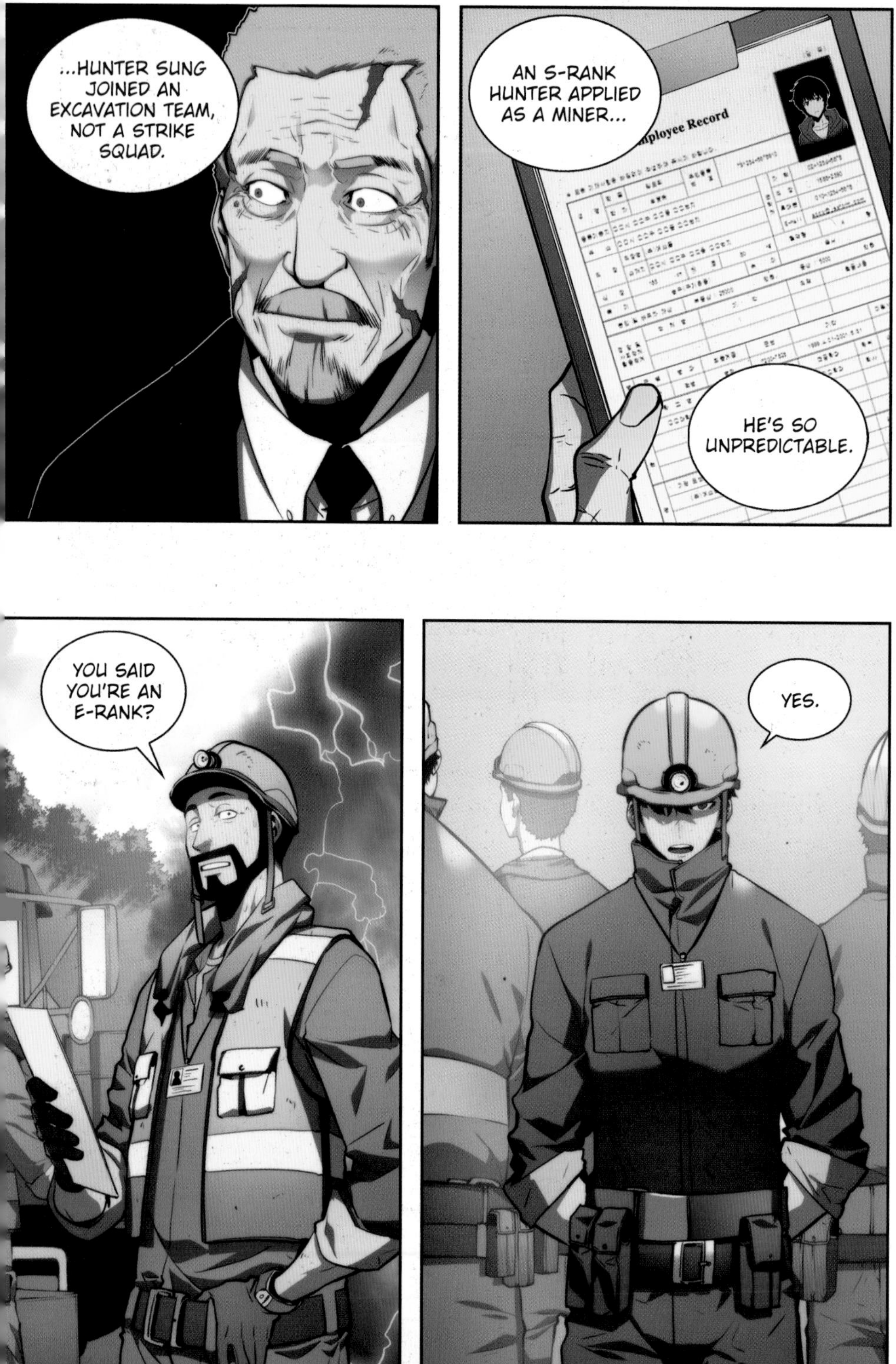
...HUNTER SUNG JOINED AN EXCAVATION TEAM, NOT A STRIKE SQUAD.
AN S-RANK HUNTER APPLIED AS A MINER...
HE'S SO UNPREDICTABLE.
YOU SAID YOU'RE AN E-RANK?
YES.

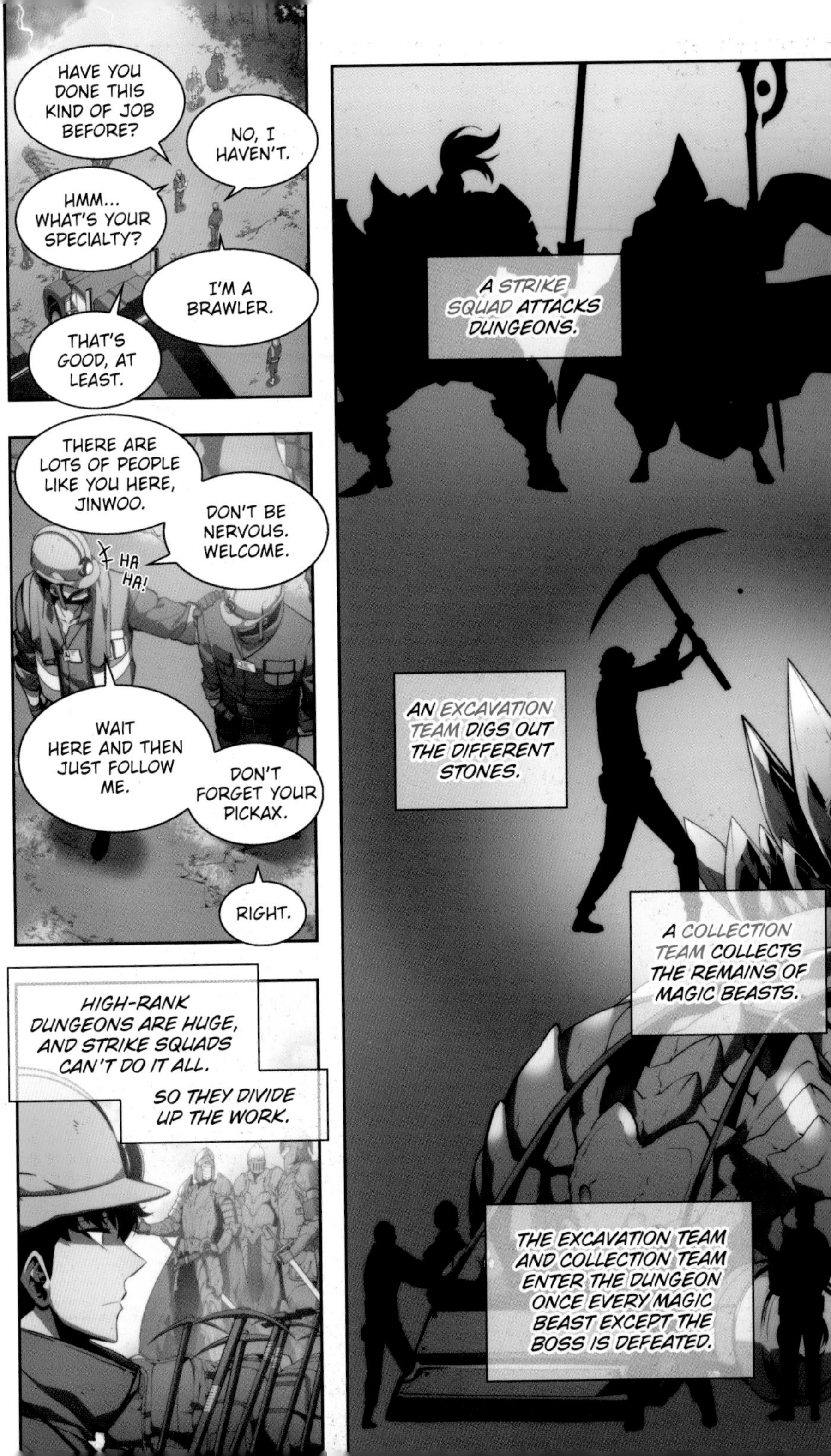
HAVE YOU DONE THIS KIND OF JOB BEFORE?
NO, I HAVEN'T.
HMM... WHAT'S YOUR SPECIALTY?
I'M A BRAWLER.
THAT'S GOOD, AT LEAST.
THERE ARE LOTS OF PEOPLE LIKE YOU HERE, JINWOO.
DON'T BE NERVOUS. WELCOME.
HA HA!
WAIT HERE AND THEN JUST FOLLOW ME.
DON'T FORGET YOUR PICKAX.
RIGHT.
HIGH-RANK DUNGEONS ARE HUGE, AND STRIKE SQUADS CAN'T DO IT ALL.
SO THEY DIVIDE UP THE WORK.
A STRIKE SQUAD ATTACKS DUNGEONS.
AN EXCAVATION TEAM DIGS OUT THE DIFFERENT STONES.
A COLLECTION TEAM COLLECTS THE REMAINS OF MAGIC BEASTS.
THE EXCAVATION TEAM AND COLLECTION TEAM ENTER THE DUNGEON ONCE EVERY MAGIC BEAST EXCEPT THE BOSS IS DEFEATED.

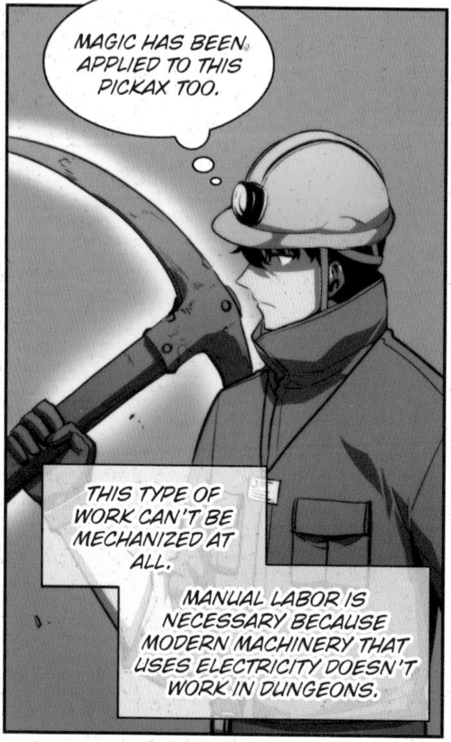
MAGIC HAS BEEN APPLIED TO THIS PICKAX TOO.
THIS TYPE OF WORK CAN'T BE MECHANIZED AT ALL.
MANUAL LABOR IS NECESSARY BECAUSE MODERN MACHINERY THAT USES ELECTRICITY DOESN'T WORK IN DUNGEONS.
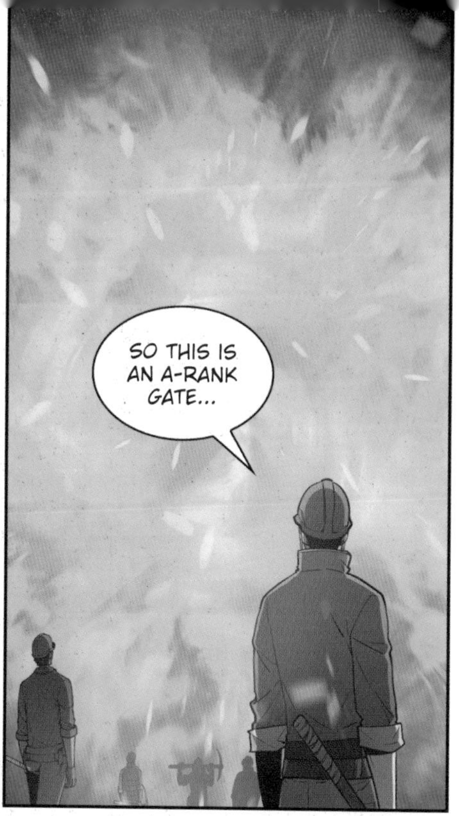
SO THIS IS AN A-RANK GATE...
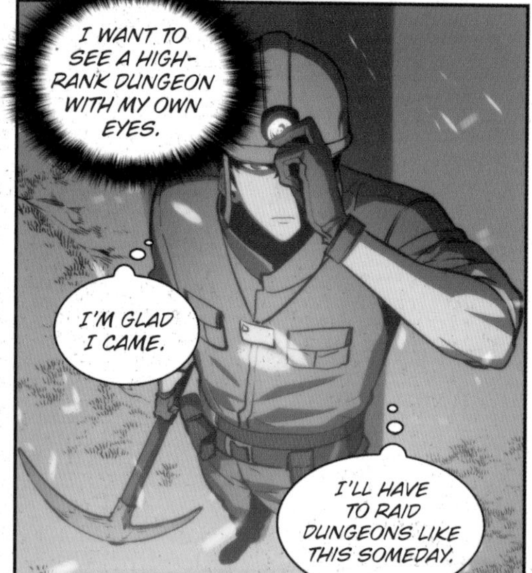
I WANT TO SEE A HIGH-RANK DUNGEON WITH MY OWN EYES.
I'M GLAD I CAME.
I'LL HAVE TO RAID DUNGEONS LIKE THIS SOMEDAY.
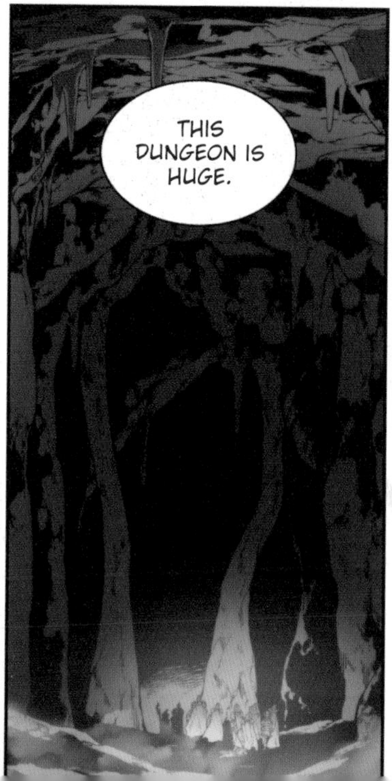
THIS DUNGEON IS HUGE.

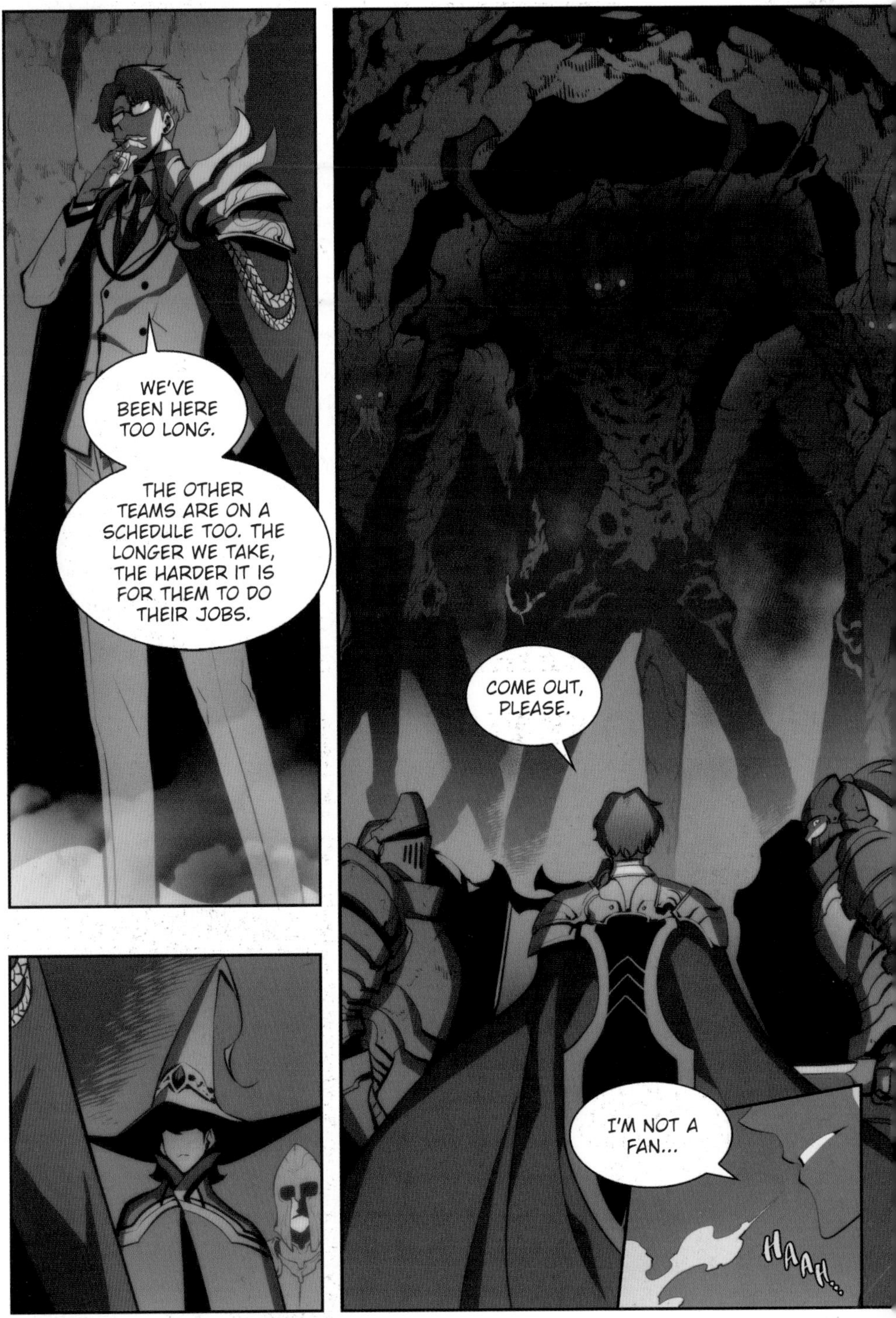
WE'VE BEEN HERE TOO LONG.
THE OTHER TEAMS ARE ON A SCHEDULE TOO. THE LONGER WE TAKE, THE HARDER IT IS FOR THEM TO DO THEIR JOBS.
COME OUT, PLEASE.
I'M NOT A FAN...
HAAAH...

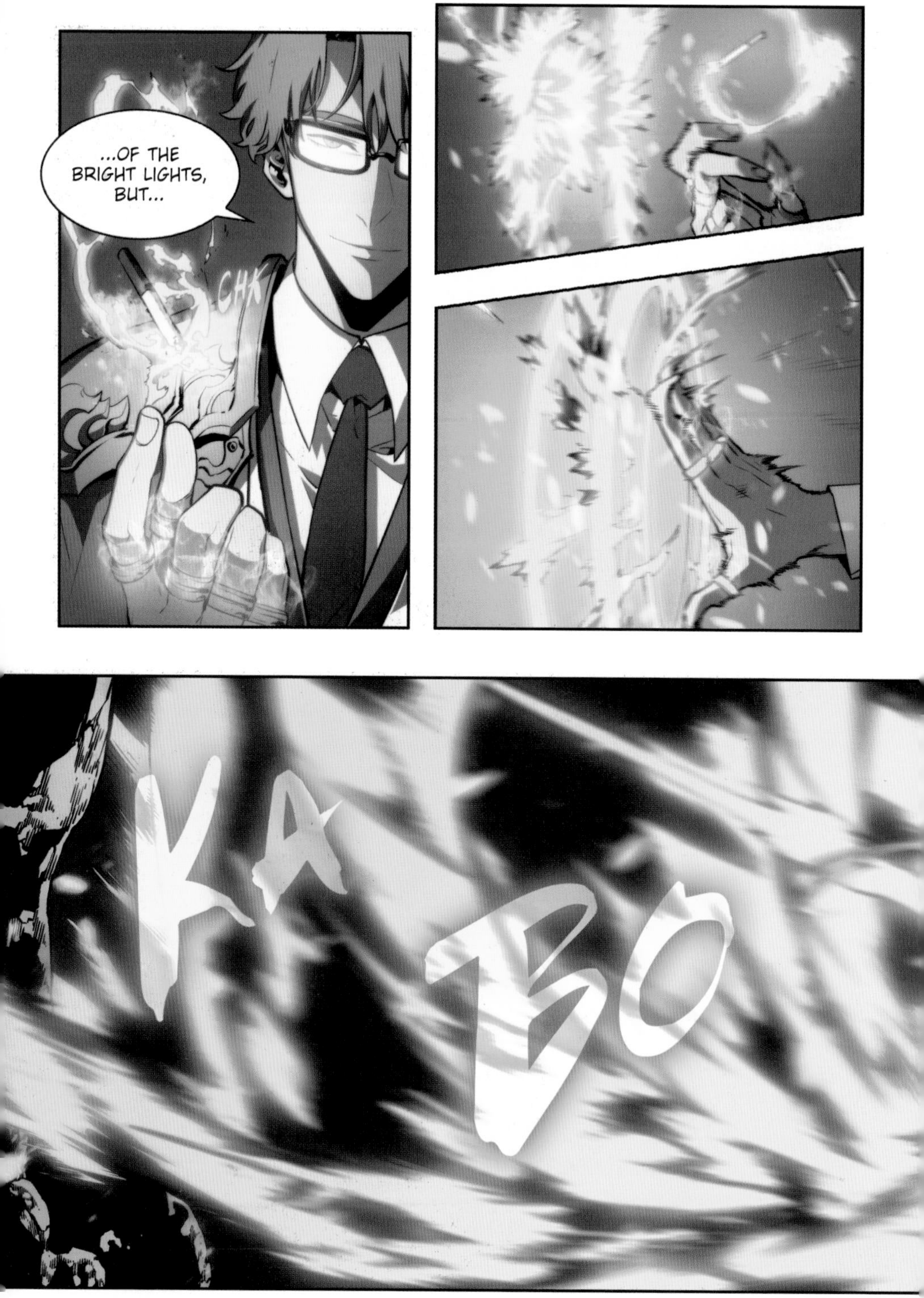
...OF THE BRIGHT LIGHTS, BUT...
CHK
KABO

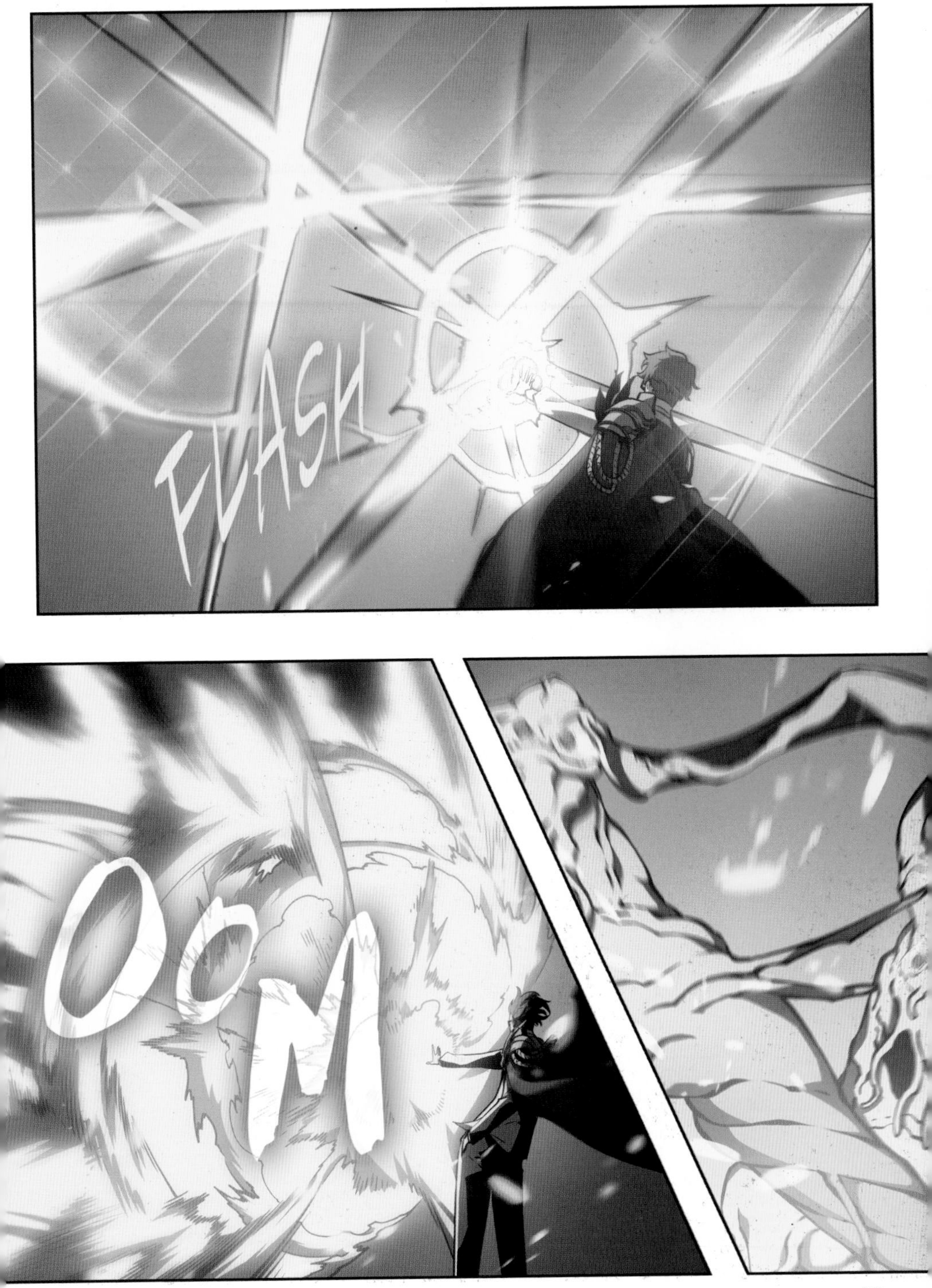
FLASH
OOM

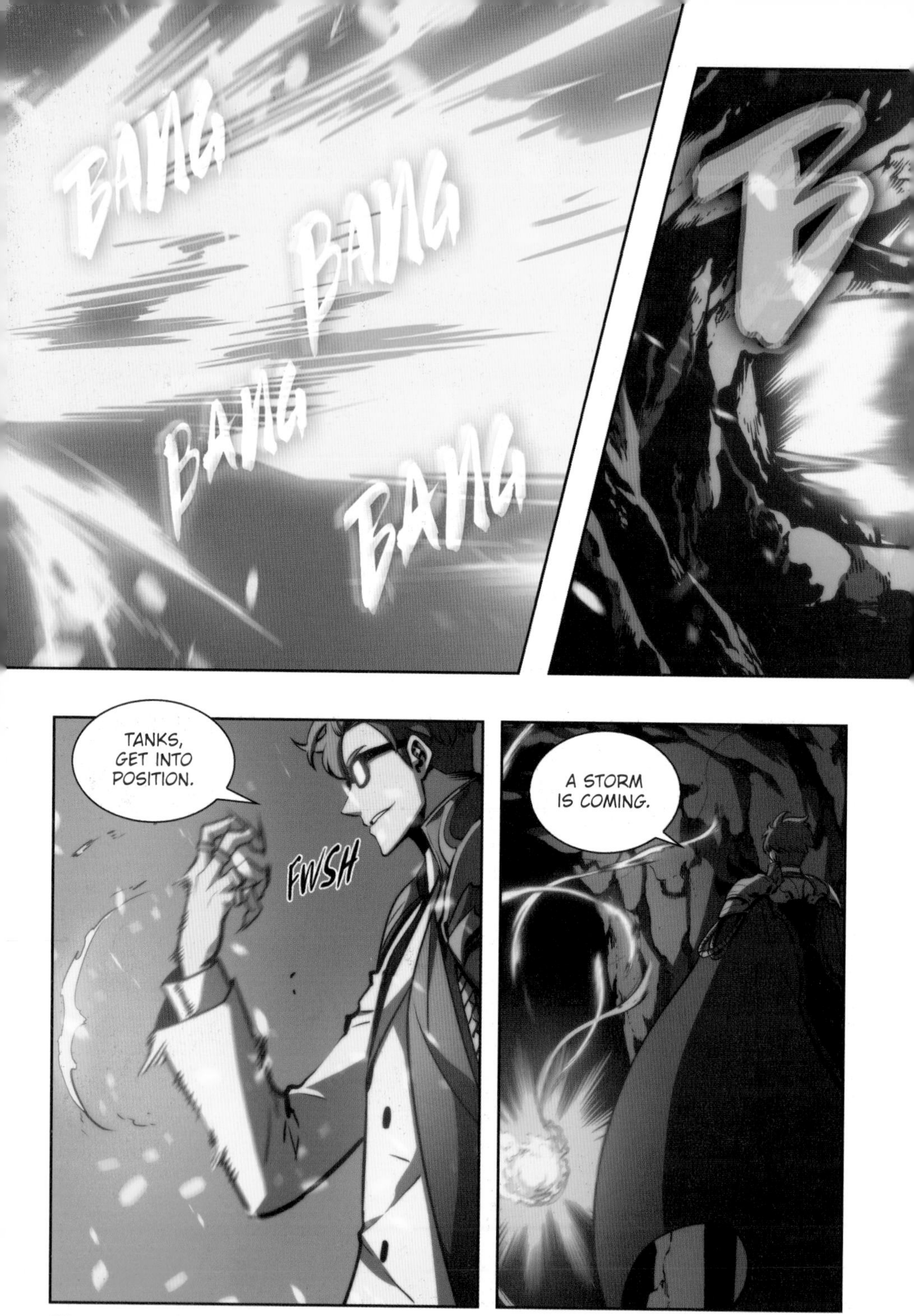
BANG
BANG
BANG
BANG
B
TANKS, GET INTO POSITION.
FWSH
A STORM IS COMING.

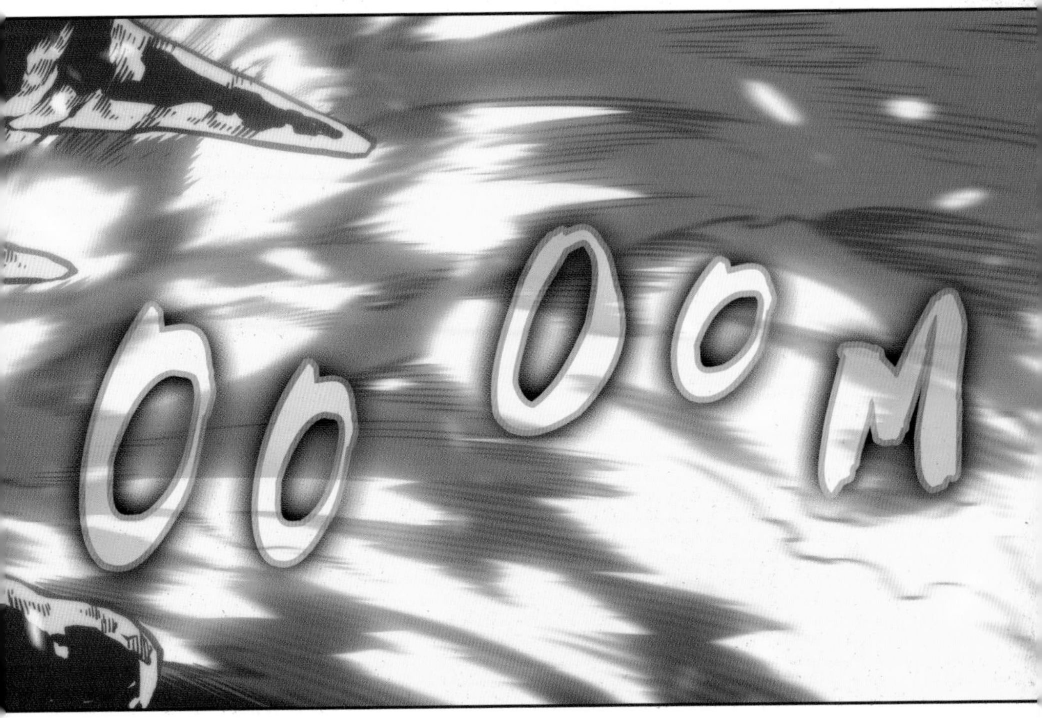
OOOOM

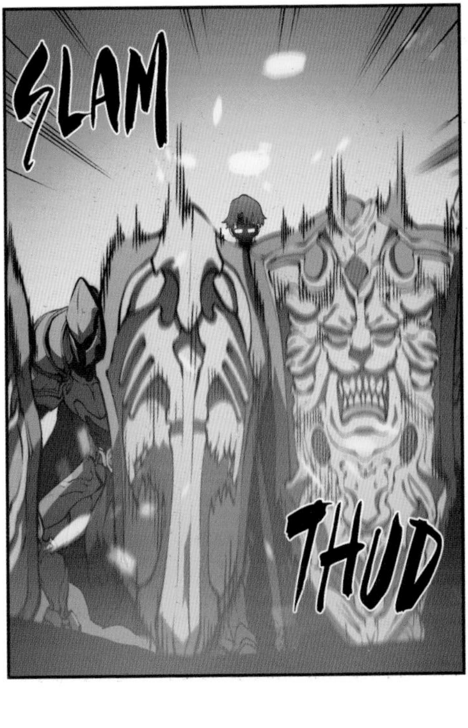
SLAM
THUD

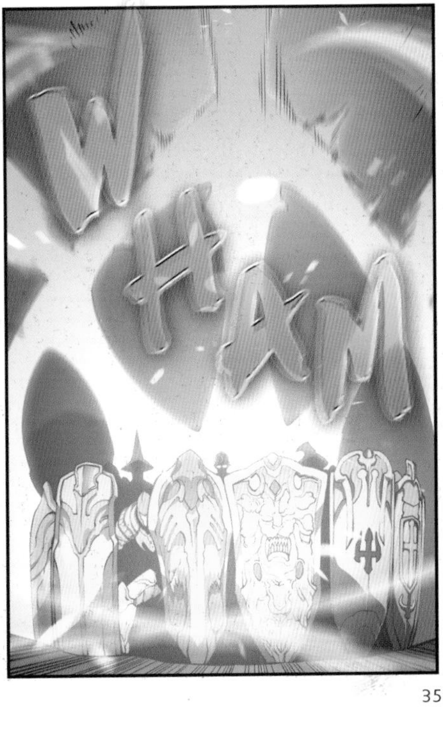
WHAM

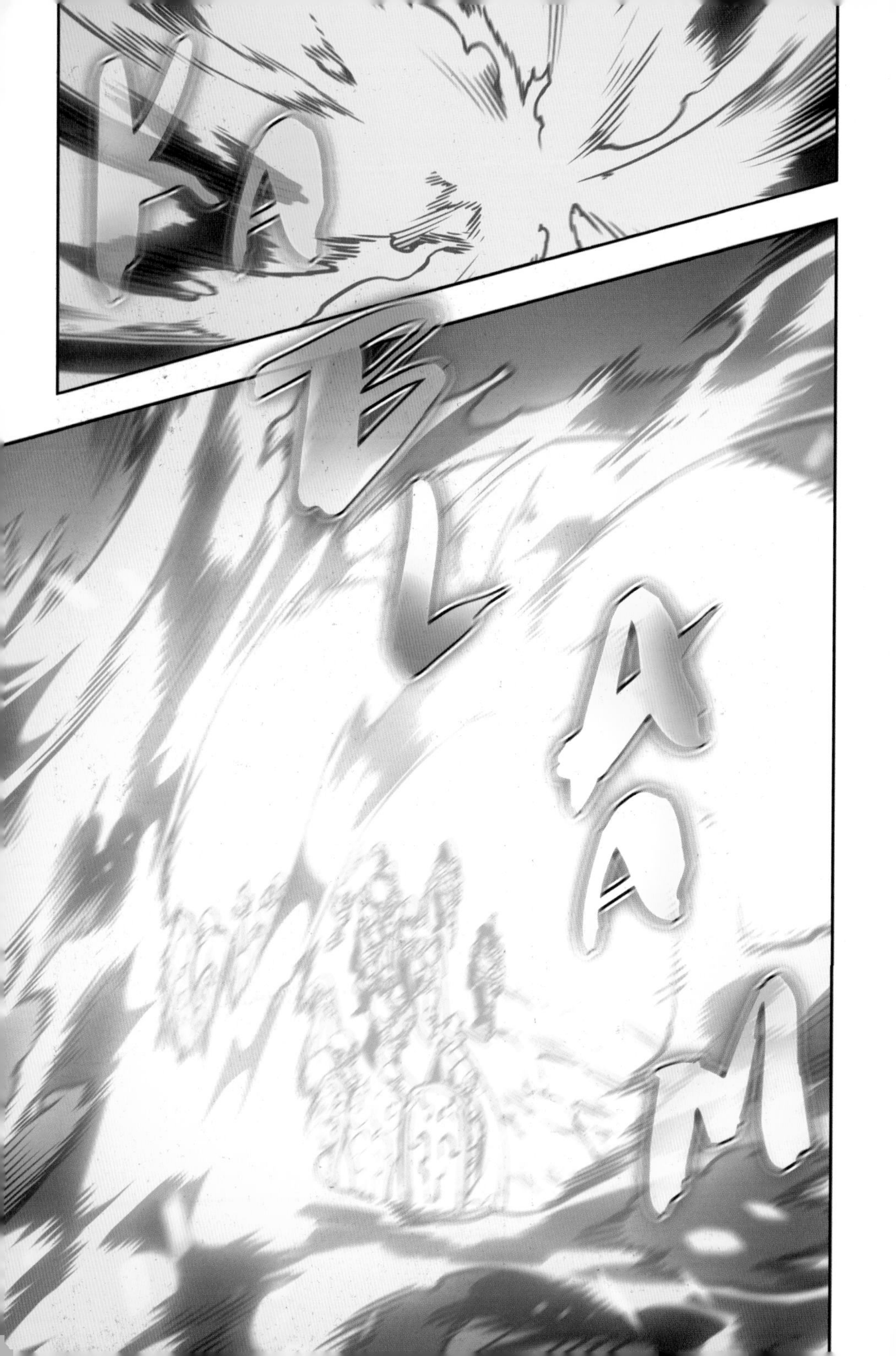
KA
BLAAM

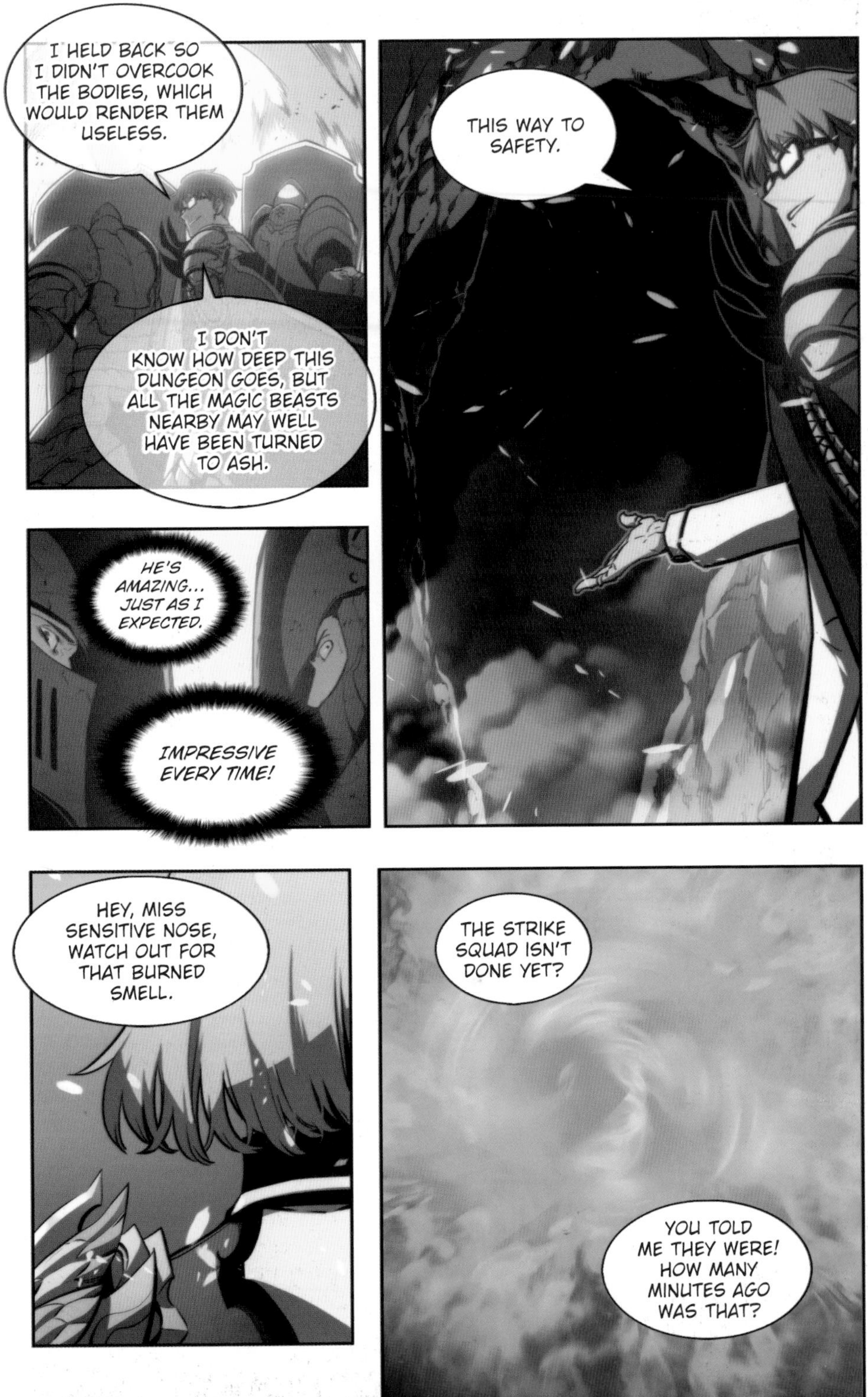
I HELD BACK SO I DIDN'T OVERCOOK THE BODIES, WHICH WOULD RENDER THEM USELESS.
I DON'T KNOW HOW DEEP THIS DUNGEON GOES, BUT ALL THE MAGIC BEASTS NEARBY MAY WELL HAVE BEEN TURNED TO ASH.
HE'S AMAZING... JUST AS I EXPECTED.
IMPRESSIVE EVERY TIME!
THIS WAY TO SAFETY.
HEY, MISS SENSITIVE NOSE, WATCH OUT FOR THAT BURNED SMELL.
THE STRIKE SQUAD ISN'T DONE YET?
YOU TOLD ME THEY WERE! HOW MANY MINUTES AGO WAS THAT?

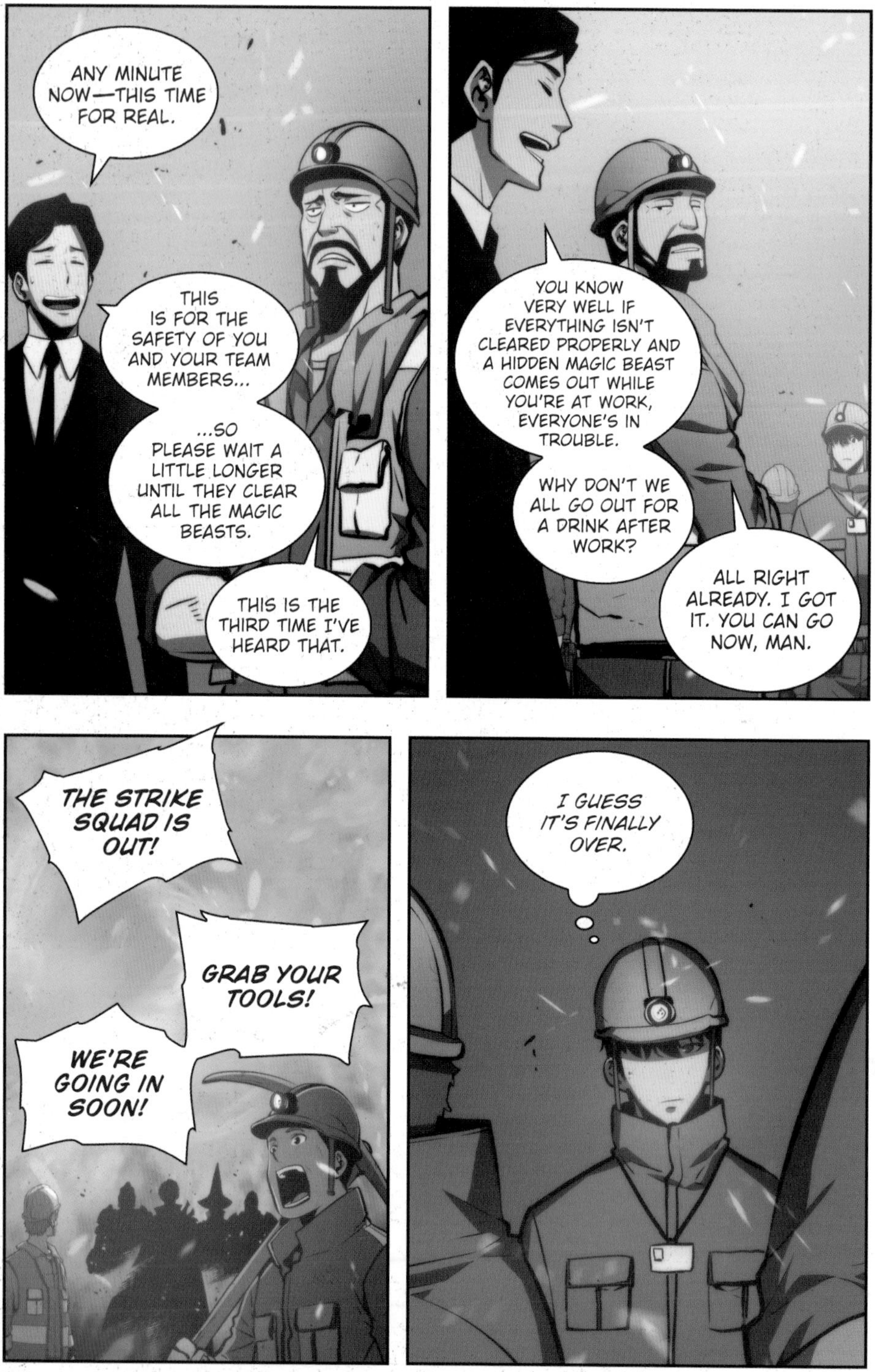
ANY MINUTE NOW—THIS TIME FOR REAL.
THIS IS FOR THE SAFETY OF YOU AND YOUR TEAM MEMBERS...
...SO PLEASE WAIT A LITTLE LONGER UNTIL THEY CLEAR ALL THE MAGIC BEASTS.
THIS IS THE THIRD TIME I'VE HEARD THAT.
YOU KNOW VERY WELL IF EVERYTHING ISN'T CLEARED PROPERLY AND A HIDDEN MAGIC BEAST COMES OUT WHILE YOU'RE AT WORK, EVERYONE'S IN TROUBLE.
WHY DON'T WE ALL GO OUT FOR A DRINK AFTER WORK?
ALL RIGHT ALREADY. I GOT IT. YOU CAN GO NOW, MAN.
THE STRIKE SQUAD IS OUT!
GRAB YOUR TOOLS!
WE'RE GOING IN SOON!
I GUESS IT'S FINALLY OVER.

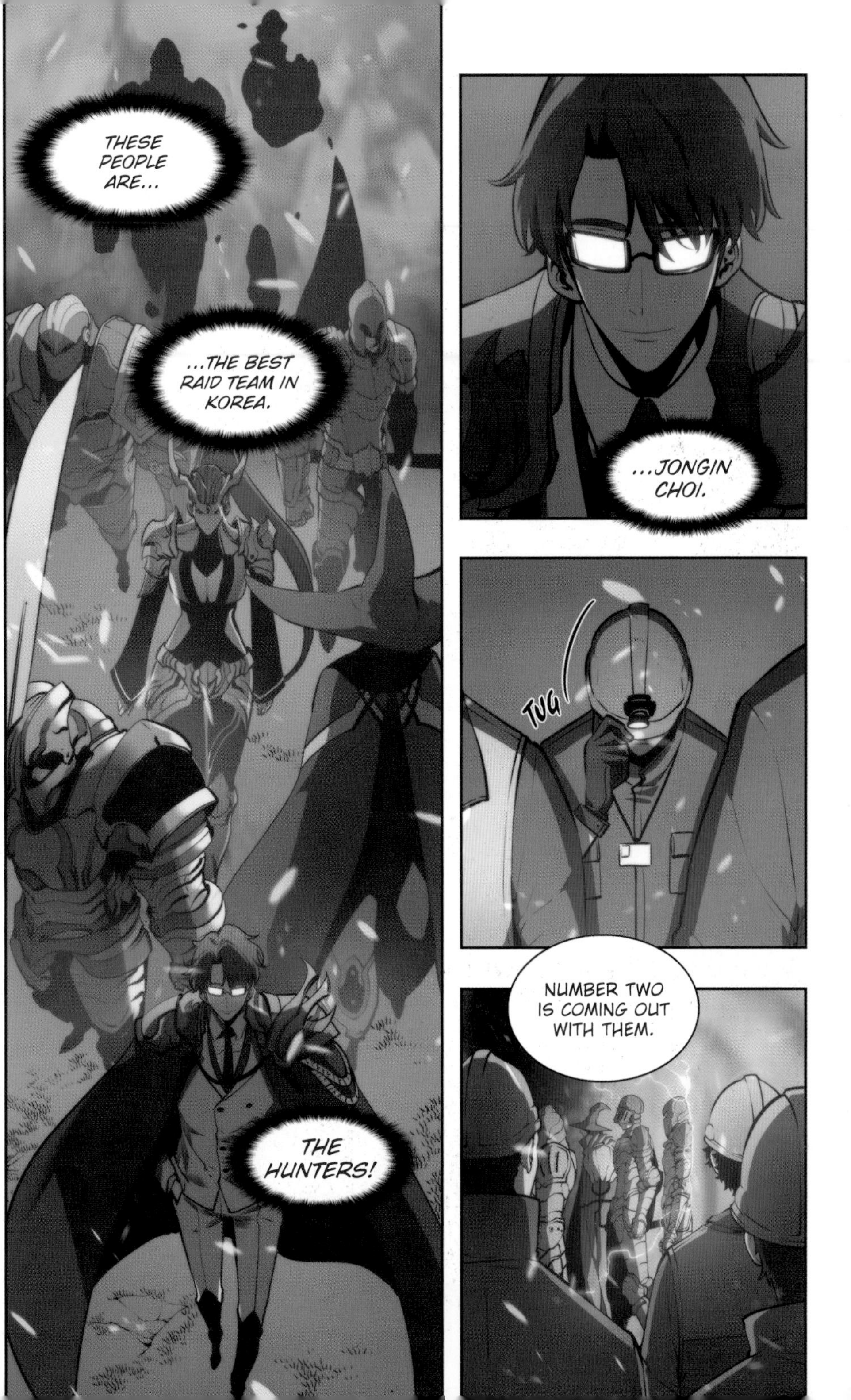
THESE PEOPLE ARE...
...THE BEST RAID TEAM IN KOREA.
THE HUNTERS!
...JONGIN CHOI.
TUG
NUMBER TWO IS COMING OUT WITH THEM.

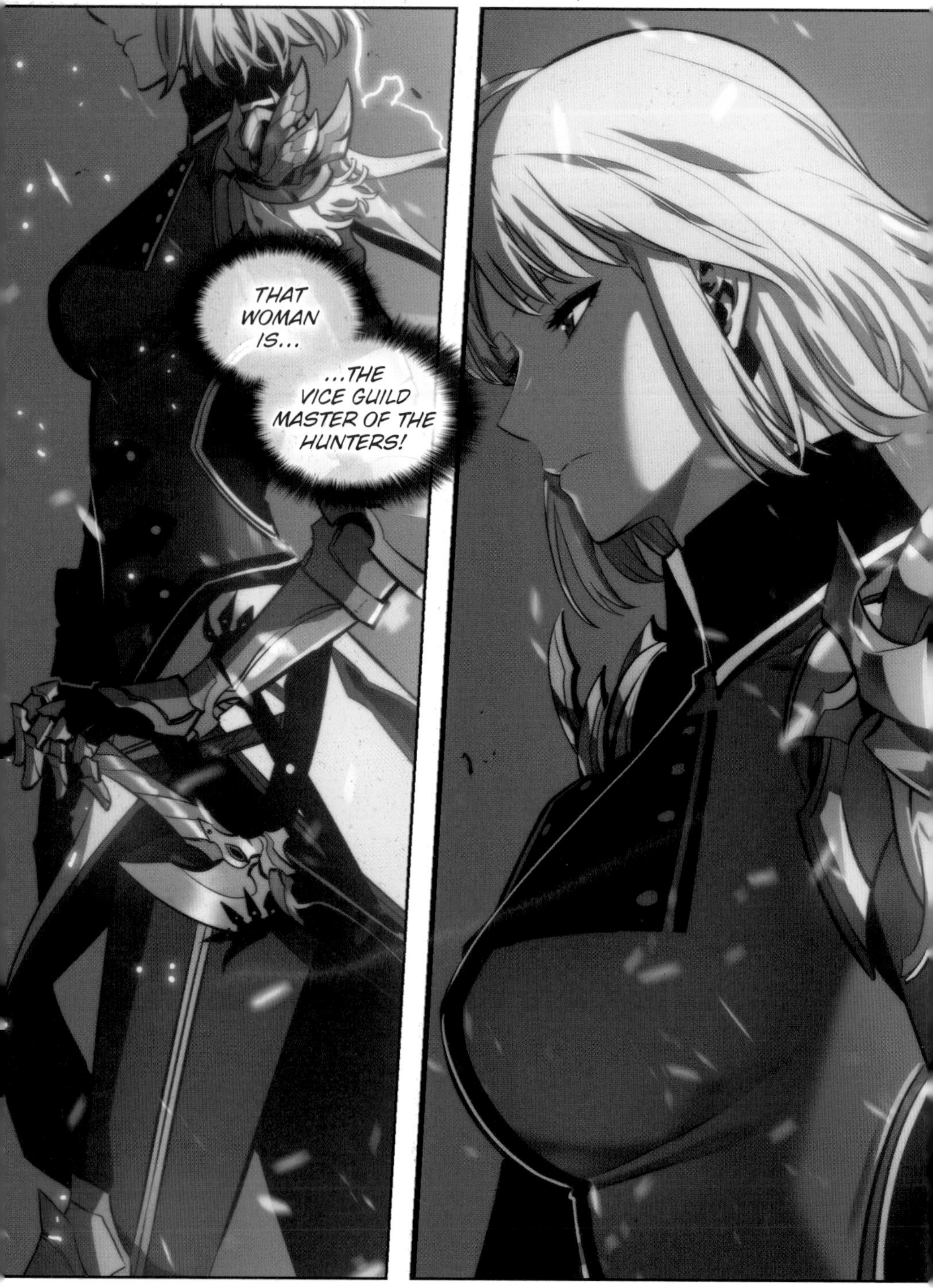
THAT WOMAN IS...
...THE VICE GUILD MASTER OF THE HUNTERS!

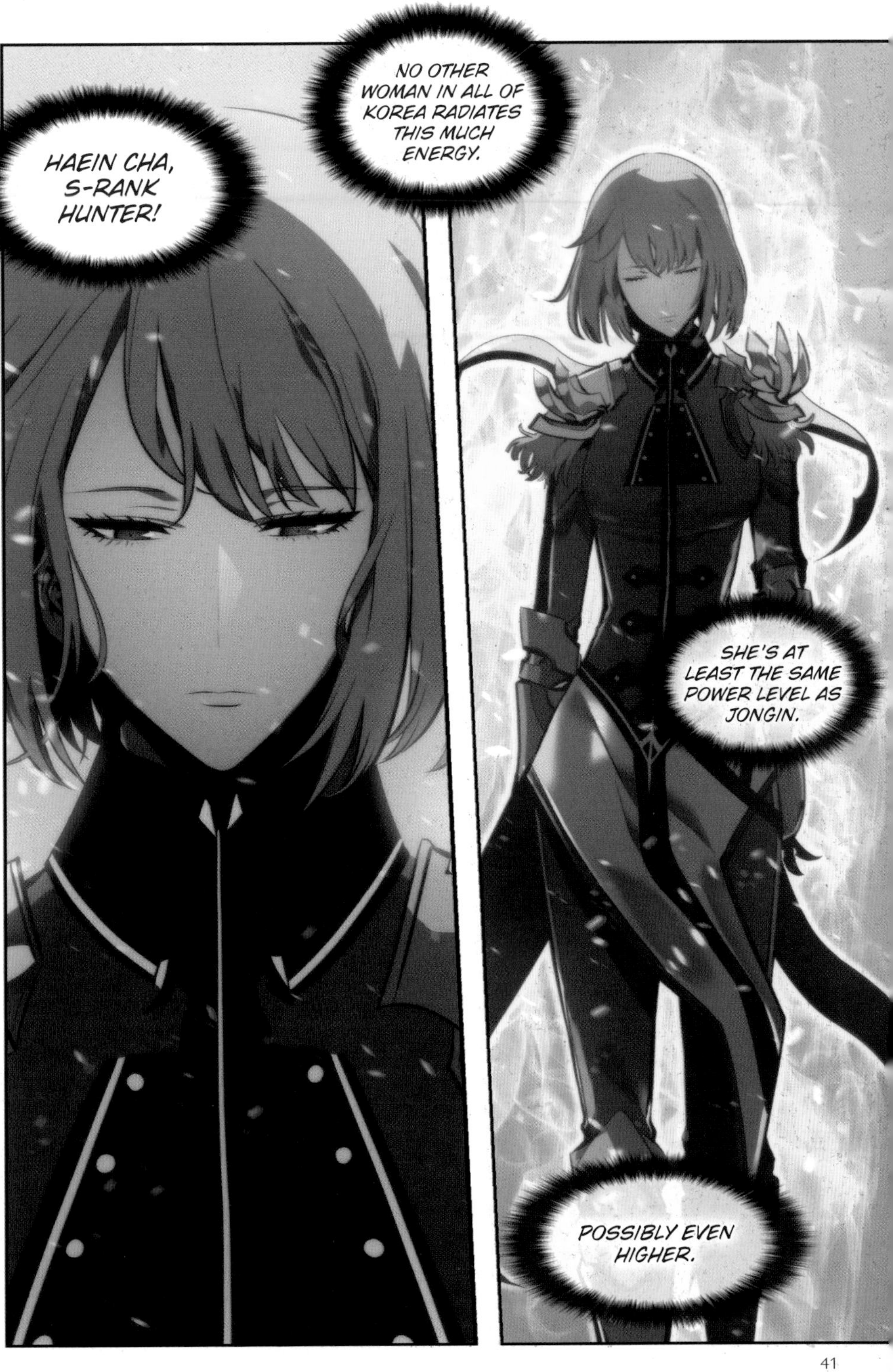
HAEIN CHA, S-RANK HUNTER!
NO OTHER WOMAN IN ALL OF KOREA RADIATES THIS MUCH ENERGY.
SHE'S AT LEAST THE SAME POWER LEVEL AS JONGIN.
POSSIBLY EVEN HIGHER.

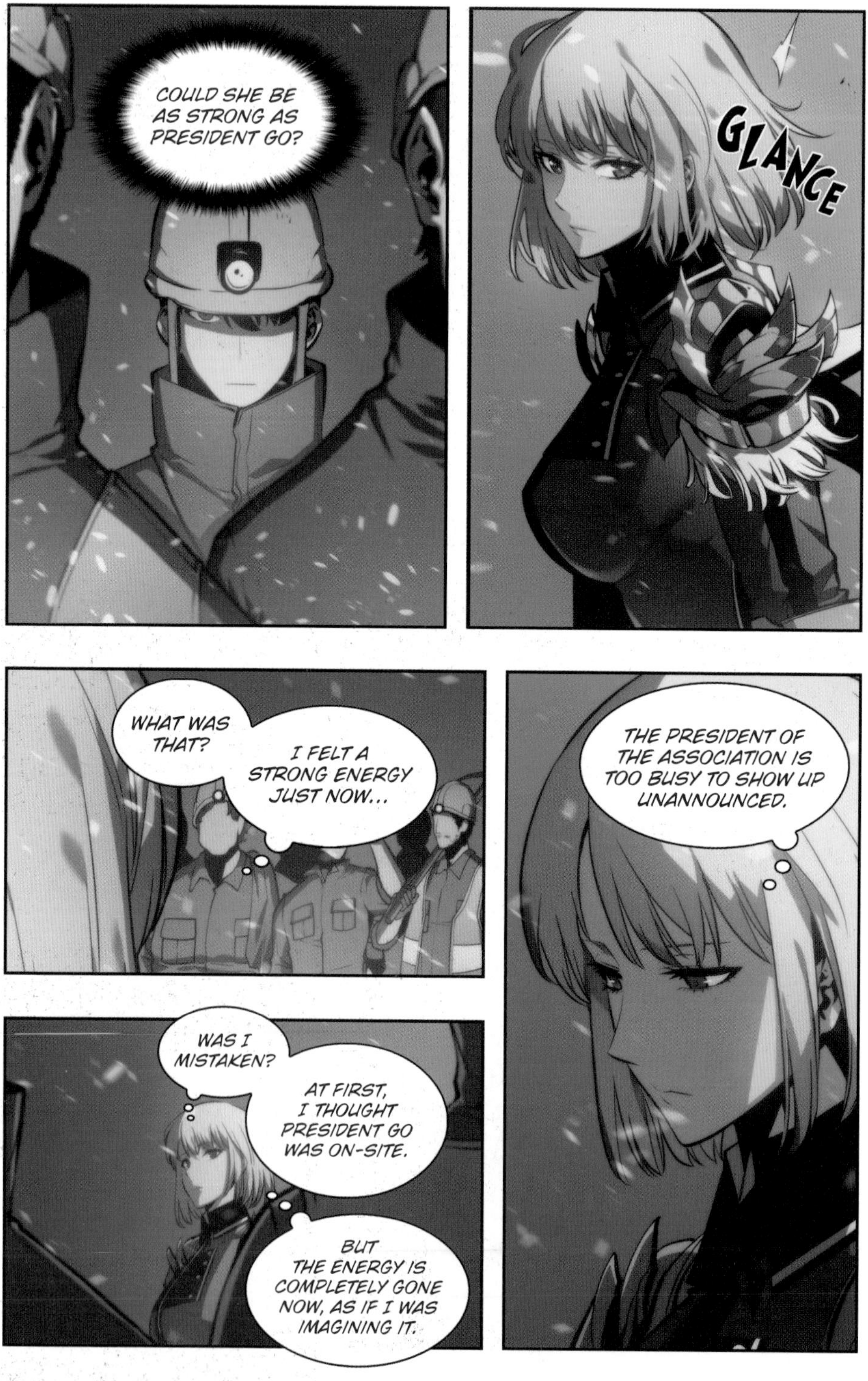
COULD SHE BE AS STRONG AS PRESIDENT GO?
GLANCE
WHAT WAS THAT?
I FELT A STRONG ENERGY JUST NOW...
WAS I MISTAKEN?
AT FIRST, I THOUGHT PRESIDENT GO WAS ON-SITE.
BUT THE ENERGY IS COMPLETELY GONE NOW, AS IF I WAS IMAGINING IT.
THE PRESIDENT OF THE ASSOCIATION IS TOO BUSY TO SHOW UP UNANNOUNCED.

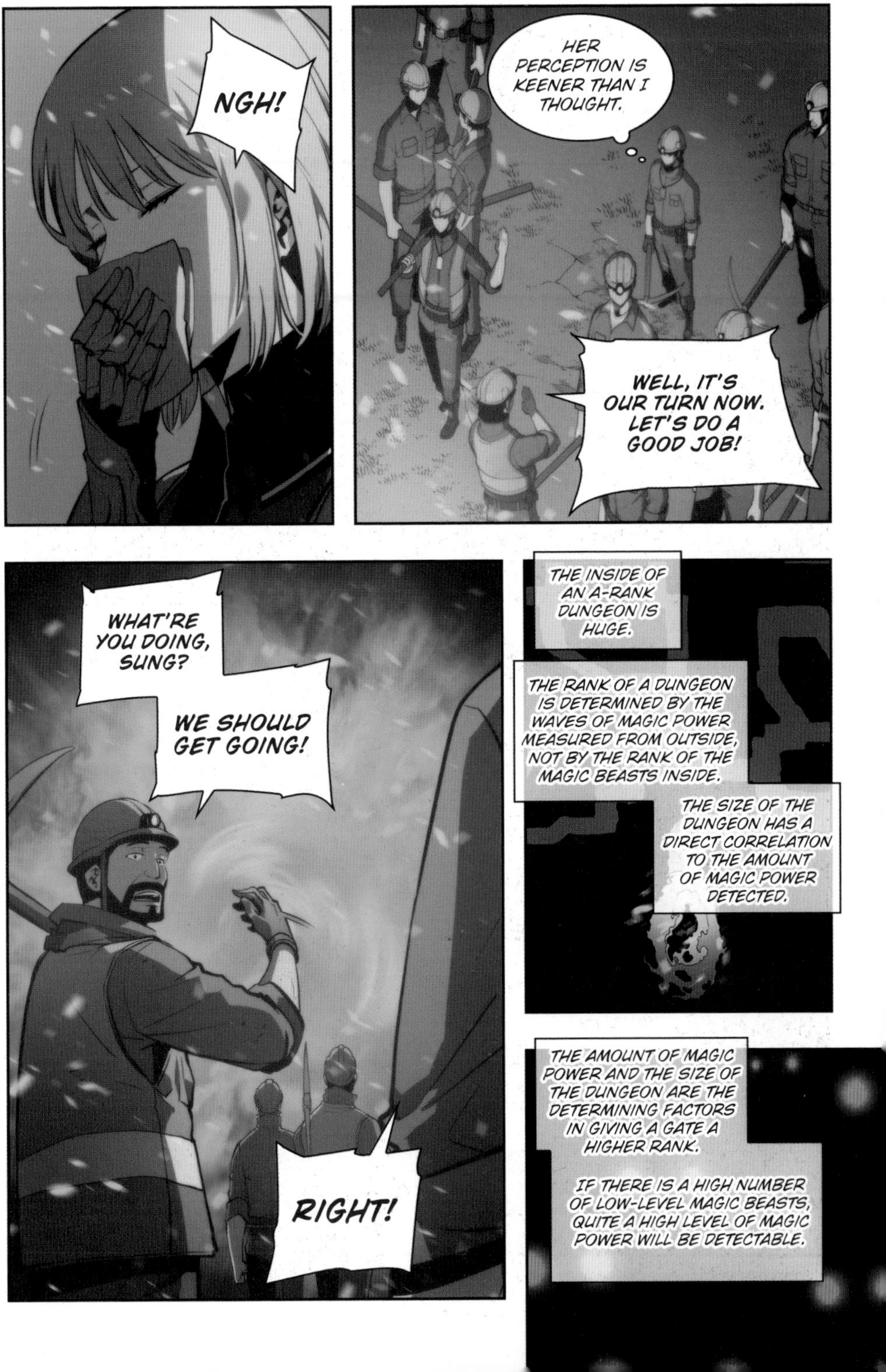
NGH!
HER PERCEPTION IS KEENER THAN I THOUGHT.
WELL, IT'S OUR TURN NOW. LET'S DO A GOOD JOB!
WHAT'RE YOU DOING, SUNG?
WE SHOULD GET GOING!
RIGHT!
THE INSIDE OF AN A-RANK DUNGEON IS HUGE.
THE RANK OF A DUNGEON IS DETERMINED BY THE WAVES OF MAGIC POWER MEASURED FROM OUTSIDE, NOT BY THE RANK OF THE MAGIC BEASTS INSIDE.
THE SIZE OF THE DUNGEON HAS A DIRECT CORRELATION TO THE AMOUNT OF MAGIC POWER DETECTED.
THE AMOUNT OF MAGIC POWER AND THE SIZE OF THE DUNGEON ARE THE DETERMINING FACTORS IN GIVING A GATE A HIGHER RANK.
IF THERE IS A HIGH NUMBER OF LOW-LEVEL MAGIC BEASTS, QUITE A HIGH LEVEL OF MAGIC POWER WILL BE DETECTABLE.

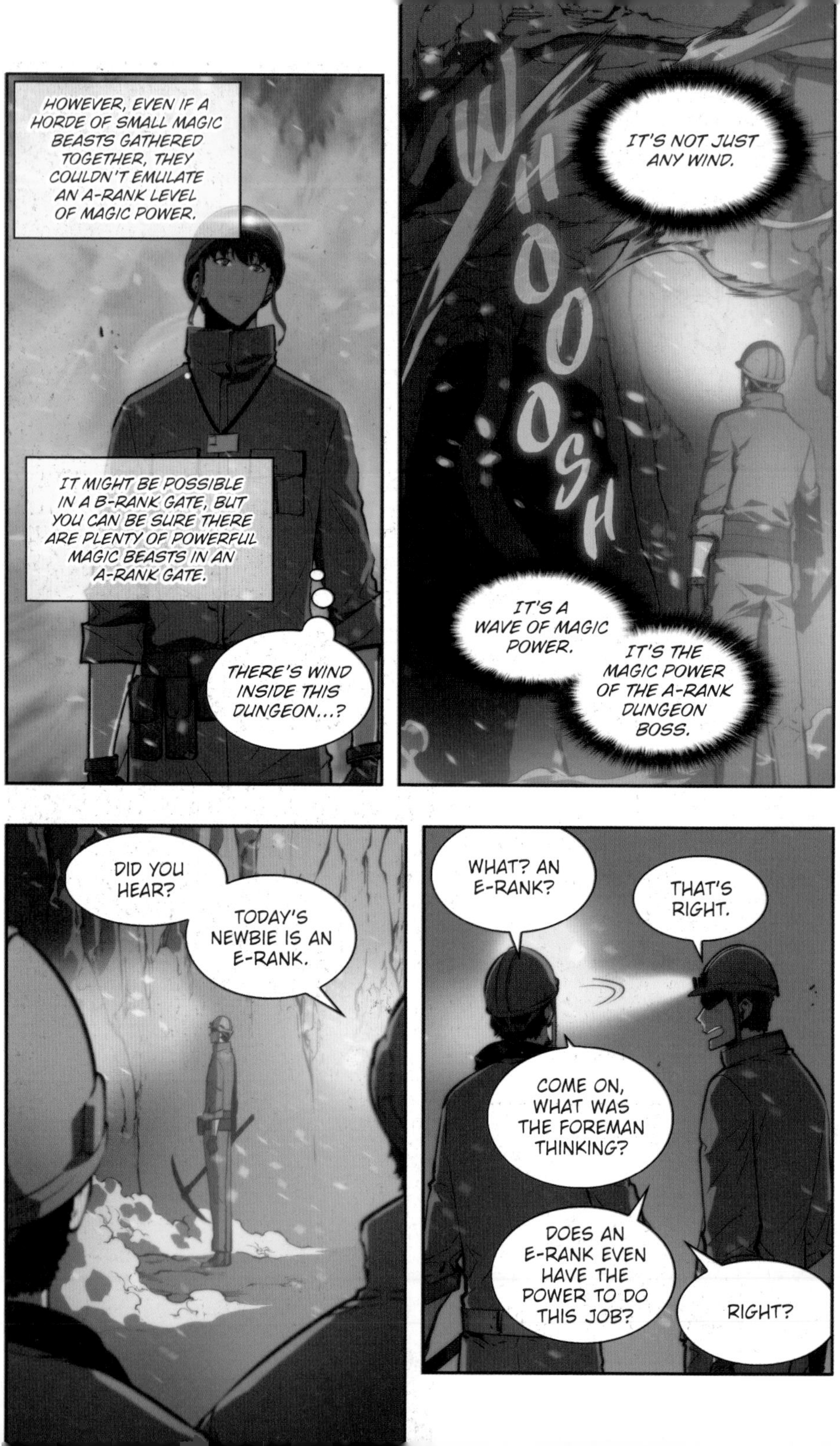
HOWEVER, EVEN IF A HORDE OF SMALL MAGIC BEASTS GATHERED TOGETHER, THEY COULDN'T EMULATE AN A-RANK LEVEL OF MAGIC POWER.
IT MIGHT BE POSSIBLE IN A B-RANK GATE, BUT YOU CAN BE SURE THERE ARE PLENTY OF POWERFUL MAGIC BEASTS IN AN A-RANK GATE.
THERE'S WIND INSIDE THIS DUNGEON...?
WHOOOOSH
IT'S NOT JUST ANY WIND.
IT'S A WAVE OF MAGIC POWER.
IT'S THE MAGIC POWER OF THE A-RANK DUNGEON BOSS.
DID YOU HEAR?
TODAY'S NEWBIE IS AN E-RANK.
WHAT? AN E-RANK?
THAT'S RIGHT.
COME ON, WHAT WAS THE FOREMAN THINKING?
DOES AN E-RANK EVEN HAVE THE POWER TO DO THIS JOB?
RIGHT?

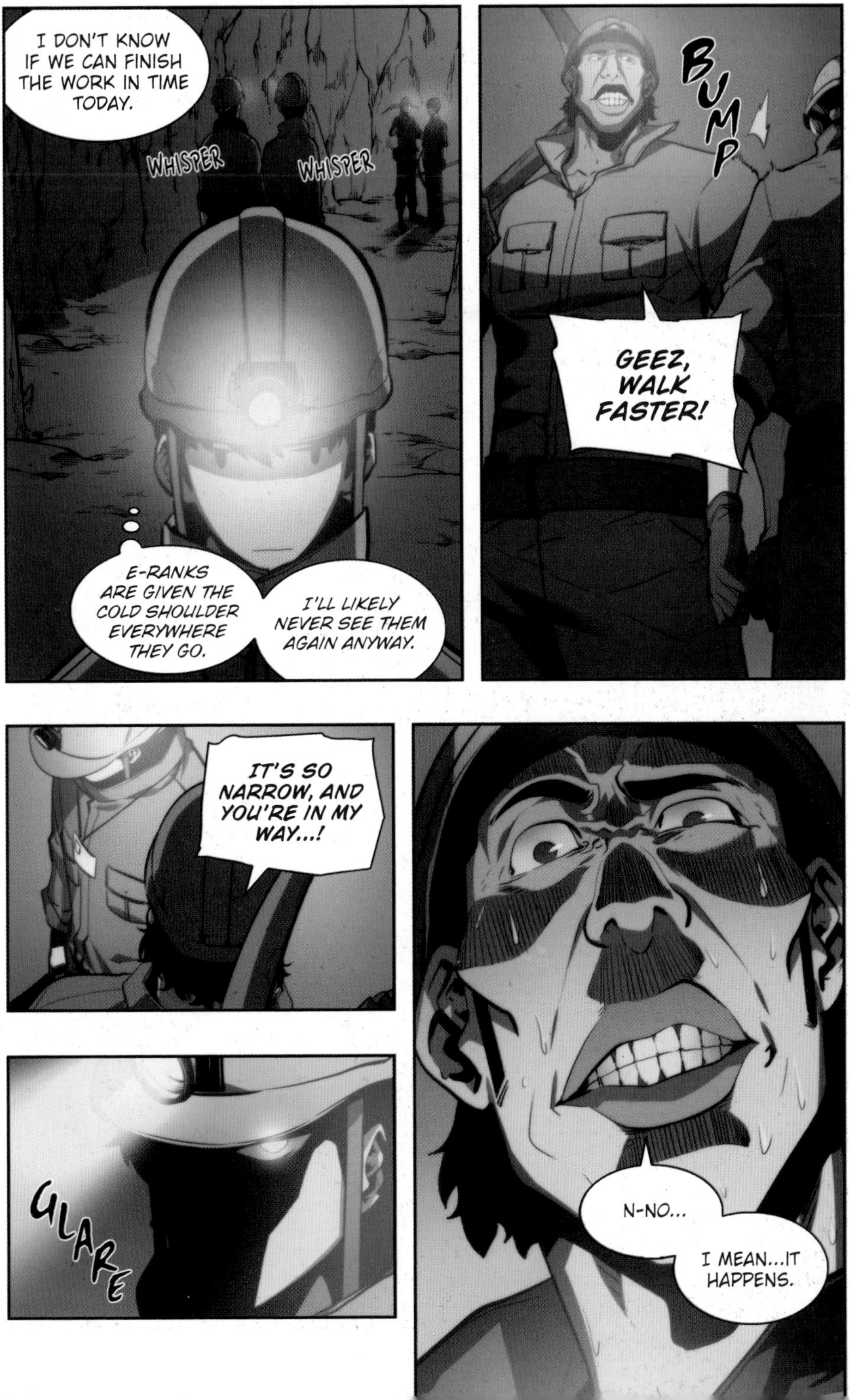
I DON'T KNOW IF WE CAN FINISH THE WORK IN TIME TODAY.
WHISPER
WHISPER
E-RANKS ARE GIVEN THE COLD SHOULDER EVERYWHERE THEY GO.
I'LL LIKELY NEVER SEE THEM AGAIN ANYWAY.
BUMP
GEEZ, WALK FASTER!
IT'S SO NARROW, AND YOU'RE IN MY WAY...!
GLARE
N-NO...
I MEAN...IT HAPPENS.

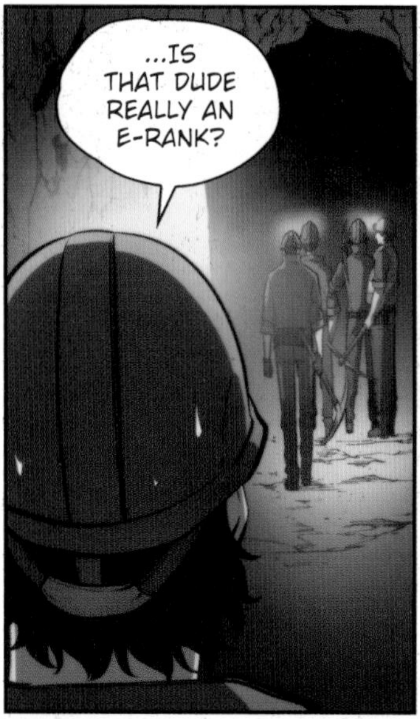
...IS THAT DUDE REALLY AN E-RANK?

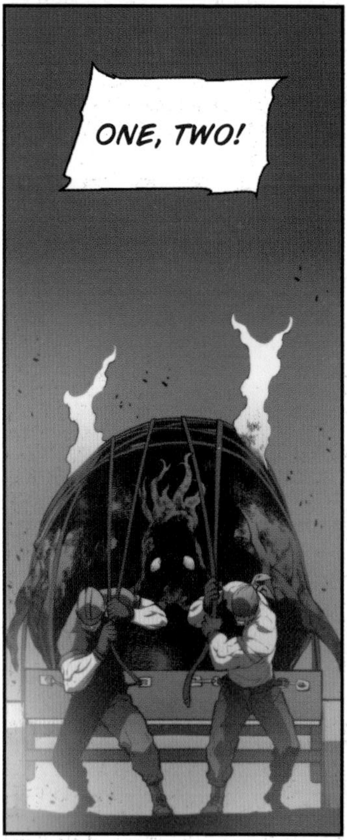
ONE, TWO!

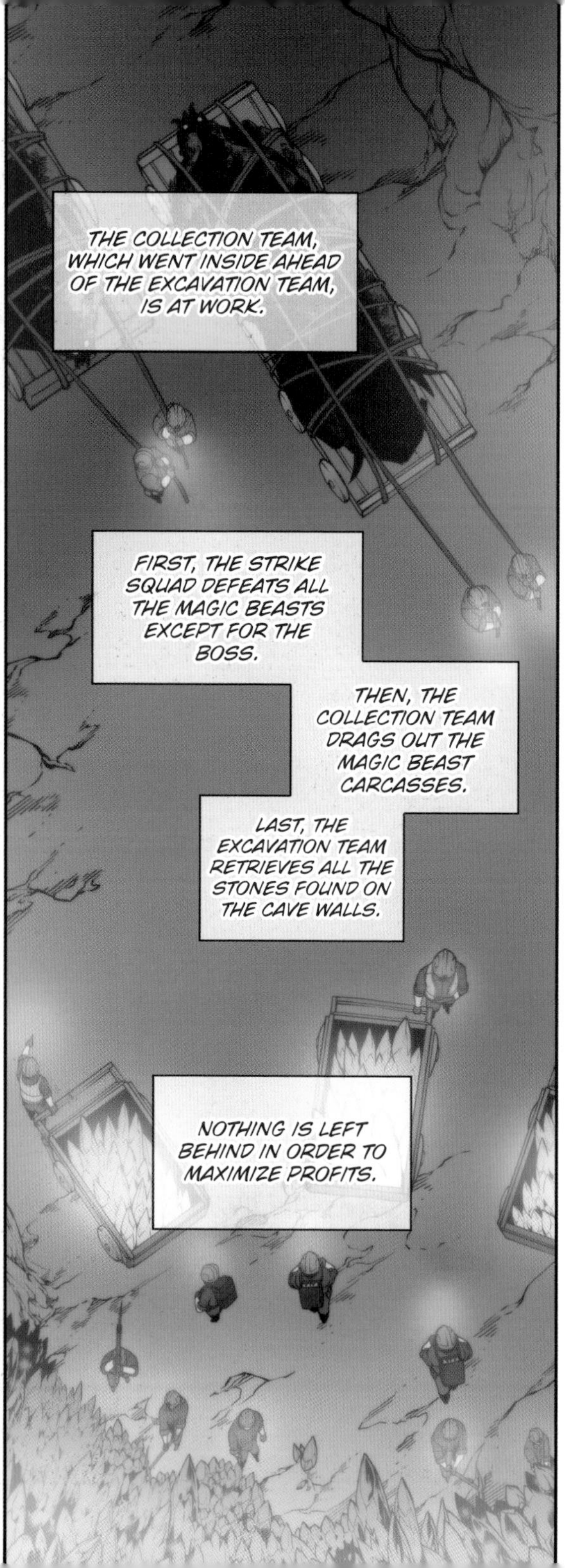
THE COLLECTION TEAM, WHICH WENT INSIDE AHEAD OF THE EXCAVATION TEAM, IS AT WORK.
FIRST, THE STRIKE SQUAD DEFEATS ALL THE MAGIC BEASTS EXCEPT FOR THE BOSS.
THEN, THE COLLECTION TEAM DRAGS OUT THE MAGIC BEAST CARCASSES.
LAST, THE EXCAVATION TEAM RETRIEVES ALL THE STONES FOUND ON THE CAVE WALLS.
NOTHING IS LEFT BEHIND IN ORDER TO MAXIMIZE PROFITS.

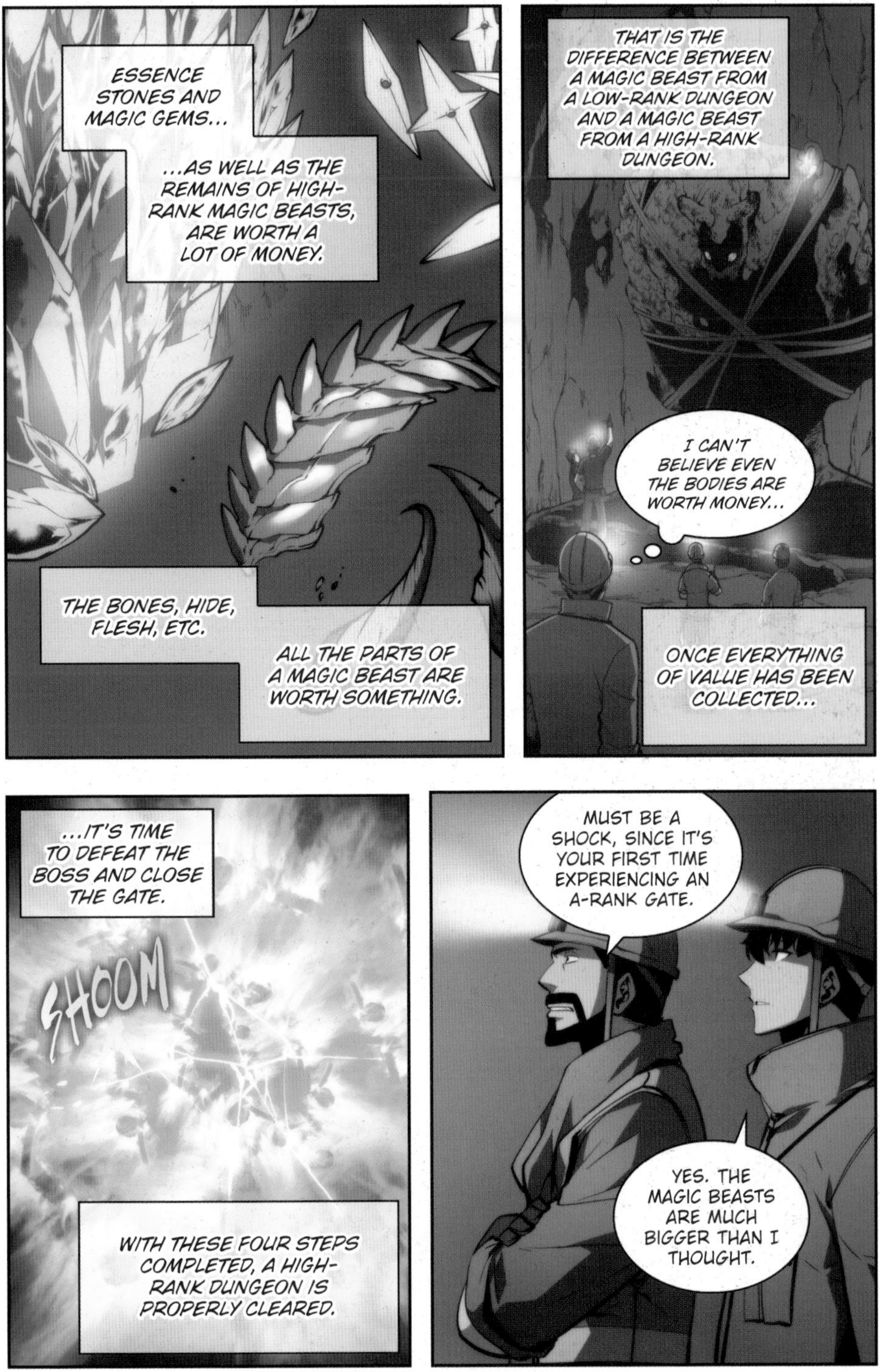
ESSENCE STONES AND MAGIC GEMS...
...AS WELL AS THE REMAINS OF HIGH-RANK MAGIC BEASTS, ARE WORTH A LOT OF MONEY.
THE BONES, HIDE, FLESH, ETC.
ALL THE PARTS OF A MAGIC BEAST ARE WORTH SOMETHING.
THAT IS THE DIFFERENCE BETWEEN A MAGIC BEAST FROM A LOW-RANK DUNGEON AND A MAGIC BEAST FROM A HIGH-RANK DUNGEON.
I CAN'T BELIEVE EVEN THE BODIES ARE WORTH MONEY...
ONCE EVERYTHING OF VALUE HAS BEEN COLLECTED...
...IT'S TIME TO DEFEAT THE BOSS AND CLOSE THE GATE.
SHOOM
WITH THESE FOUR STEPS COMPLETED, A HIGH-RANK DUNGEON IS PROPERLY CLEARED.
MUST BE A SHOCK, SINCE IT'S YOUR FIRST TIME EXPERIENCING AN A-RANK GATE.
YES. THE MAGIC BEASTS ARE MUCH BIGGER THAN I THOUGHT.

EVEN THOUGH ALL THE OTHER MAGIC BEASTS HAVE BEEN KILLED, THE BOSS IS STILL ALIVE, RIGHT?

THAT'S RIGHT. ONCE THE BOSS IS KILLED, THE GATE WILL CLOSE.

WE CAN'T KILL THE BOSS UNTIL ALL THE COLLECTING AND THE MINING IS DONE.

WHAT HAPPENS IF THE BOSS GETS OUT OF ITS LAIR?

THAT RARELY HAPPENS, BUT IF IT DID...

...EVERYONE HERE WOULD BE DEAD.

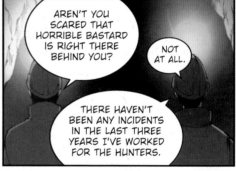

AREN'T YOU SCARED THAT HORRIBLE BASTARD IS RIGHT THERE BEHIND YOU?

NOT AT ALL.

THERE HAVEN'T BEEN ANY INCIDENTS IN THE LAST THREE YEARS I'VE WORKED FOR THE HUNTERS.

PEOPLE SAY IGNORANCE IS BLISS.

THE MAGIC POWER IS STRONG ENOUGH TO VIBRATE THROUGH ME.

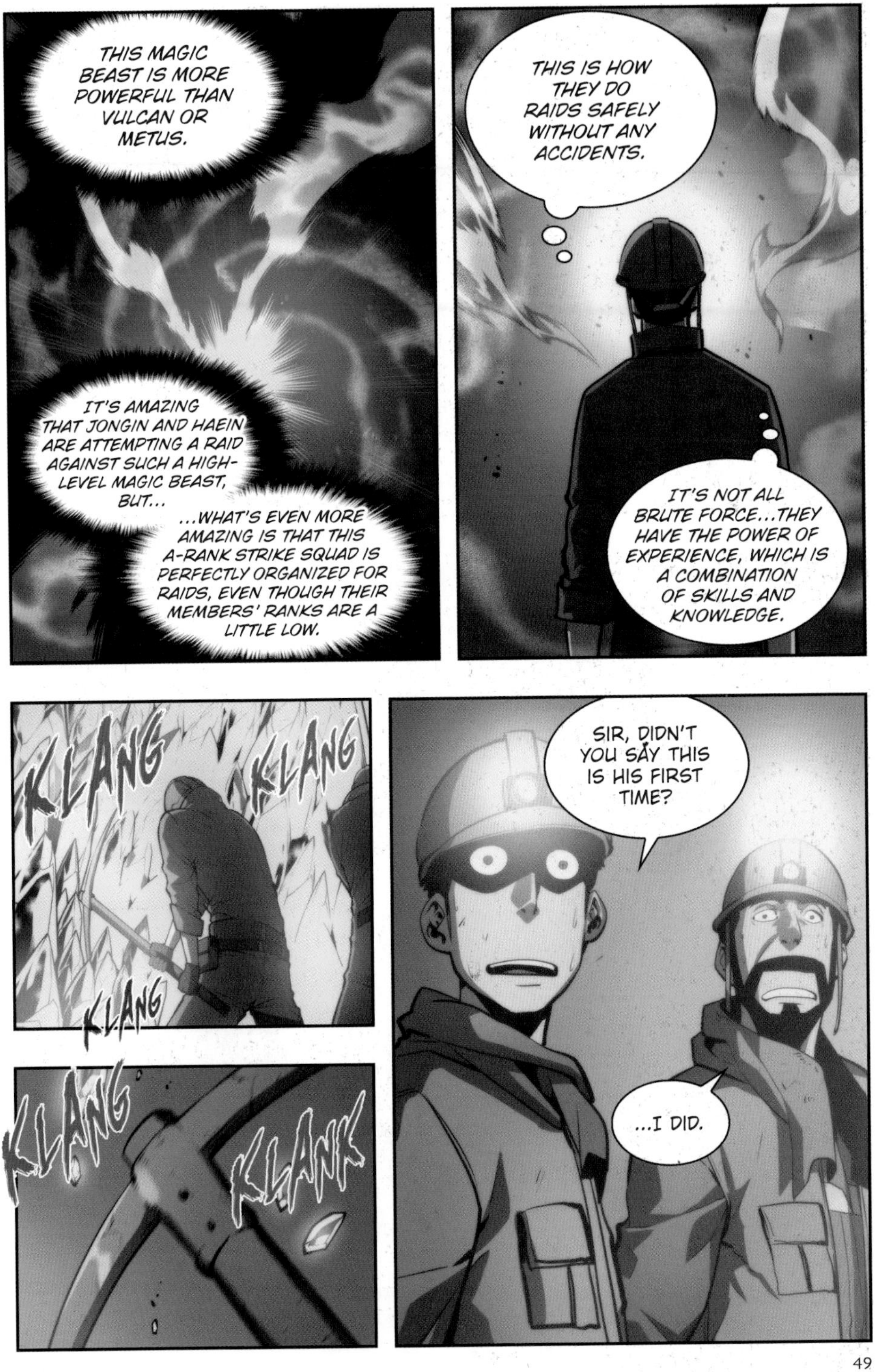
THIS MAGIC BEAST IS MORE POWERFUL THAN VULCAN OR METUS.
IT'S AMAZING THAT JONGIN AND HAEIN ARE ATTEMPTING A RAID AGAINST SUCH A HIGH-LEVEL MAGIC BEAST, BUT...
...WHAT'S EVEN MORE AMAZING IS THAT THIS A-RANK STRIKE SQUAD IS PERFECTLY ORGANIZED FOR RAIDS, EVEN THOUGH THEIR MEMBERS' RANKS ARE A LITTLE LOW.
THIS IS HOW THEY DO RAIDS SAFELY WITHOUT ANY ACCIDENTS.
IT'S NOT ALL BRUTE FORCE...THEY HAVE THE POWER OF EXPERIENCE, WHICH IS A COMBINATION OF SKILLS AND KNOWLEDGE.
KLANG
KLANG
KLANG
SIR, DIDN'T YOU SAY THIS IS HIS FIRST TIME?
KLANG
KLANK
...I DID.

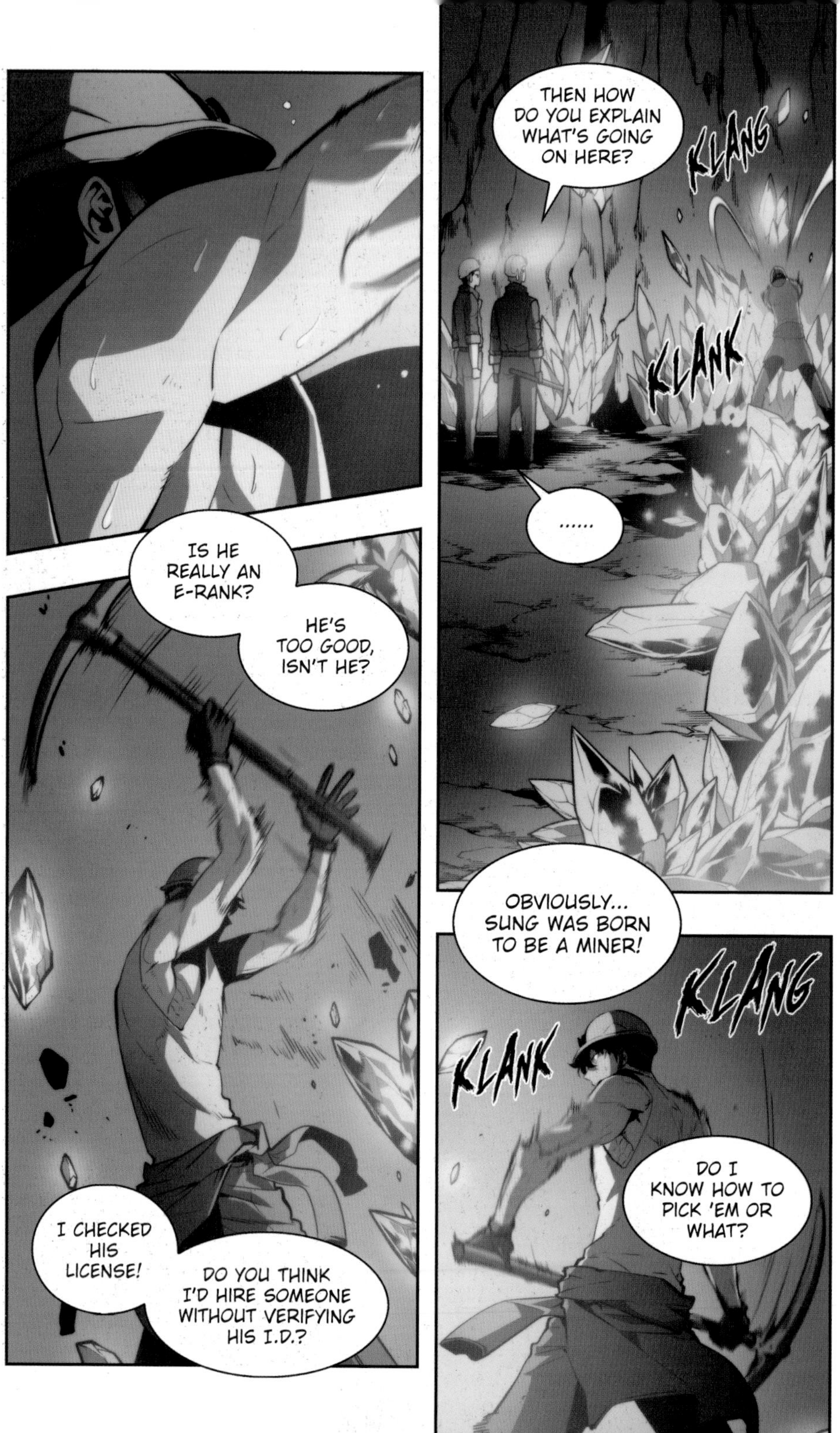
IS HE REALLY AN E-RANK?
HE'S TOO GOOD, ISN'T HE?
I CHECKED HIS LICENSE!
DO YOU THINK I'D HIRE SOMEONE WITHOUT VERIFYING HIS I.D.?
THEN HOW DO YOU EXPLAIN WHAT'S GOING ON HERE?
KLANG
KLANK
......
OBVIOUSLY... SUNG WAS BORN TO BE A MINER!
KLANK
KLANG
DO I KNOW HOW TO PICK 'EM OR WHAT?

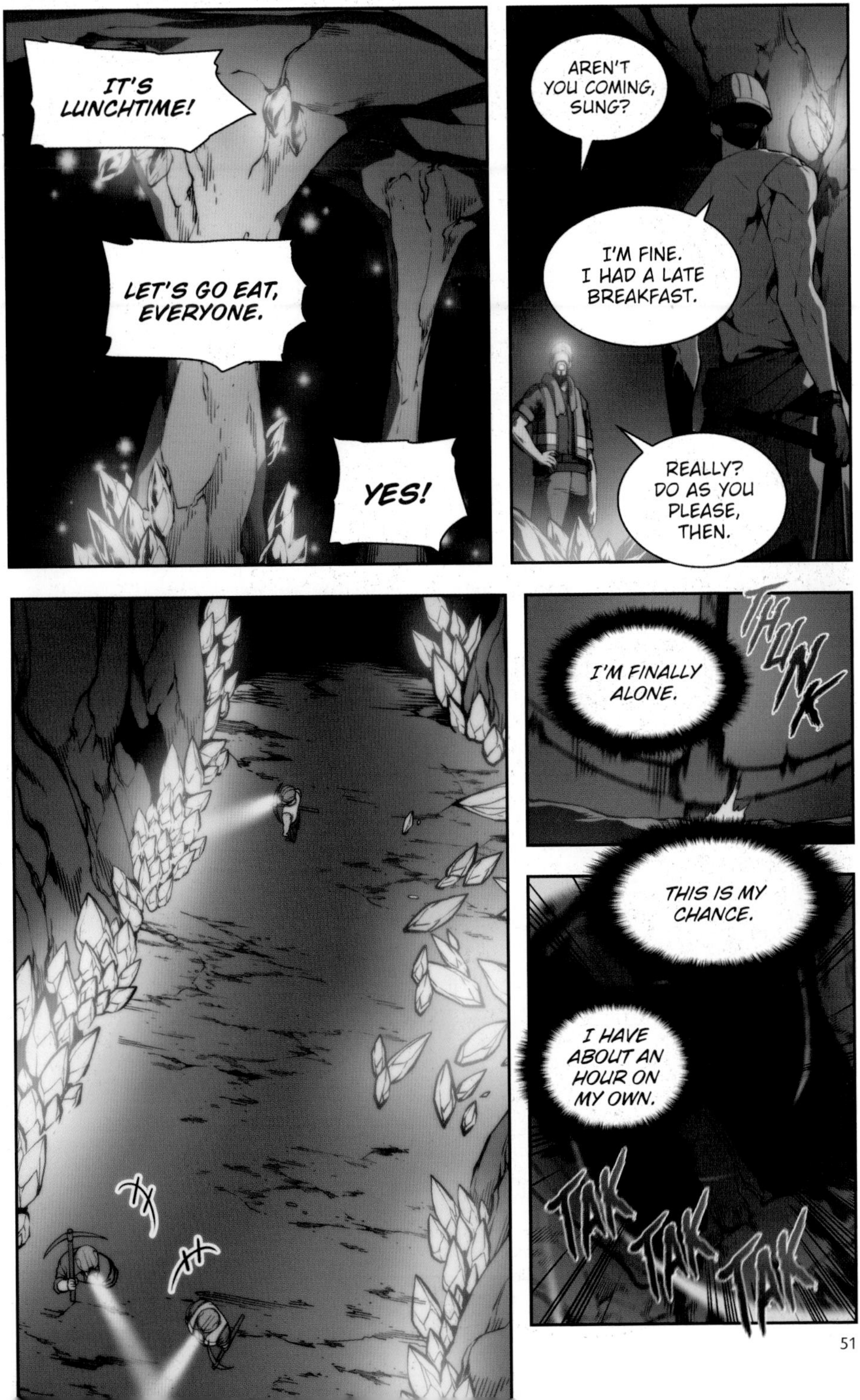
IT'S LUNCHTIME!
LET'S GO EAT, EVERYONE.
YES!
AREN'T YOU COMING, SUNG?
I'M FINE. I HAD A LATE BREAKFAST.
REALLY? DO AS YOU PLEASE, THEN.
I'M FINALLY ALONE.
THUNK
THIS IS MY CHANCE.
I HAVE ABOUT AN HOUR ON MY OWN.
TAK TAK TAK

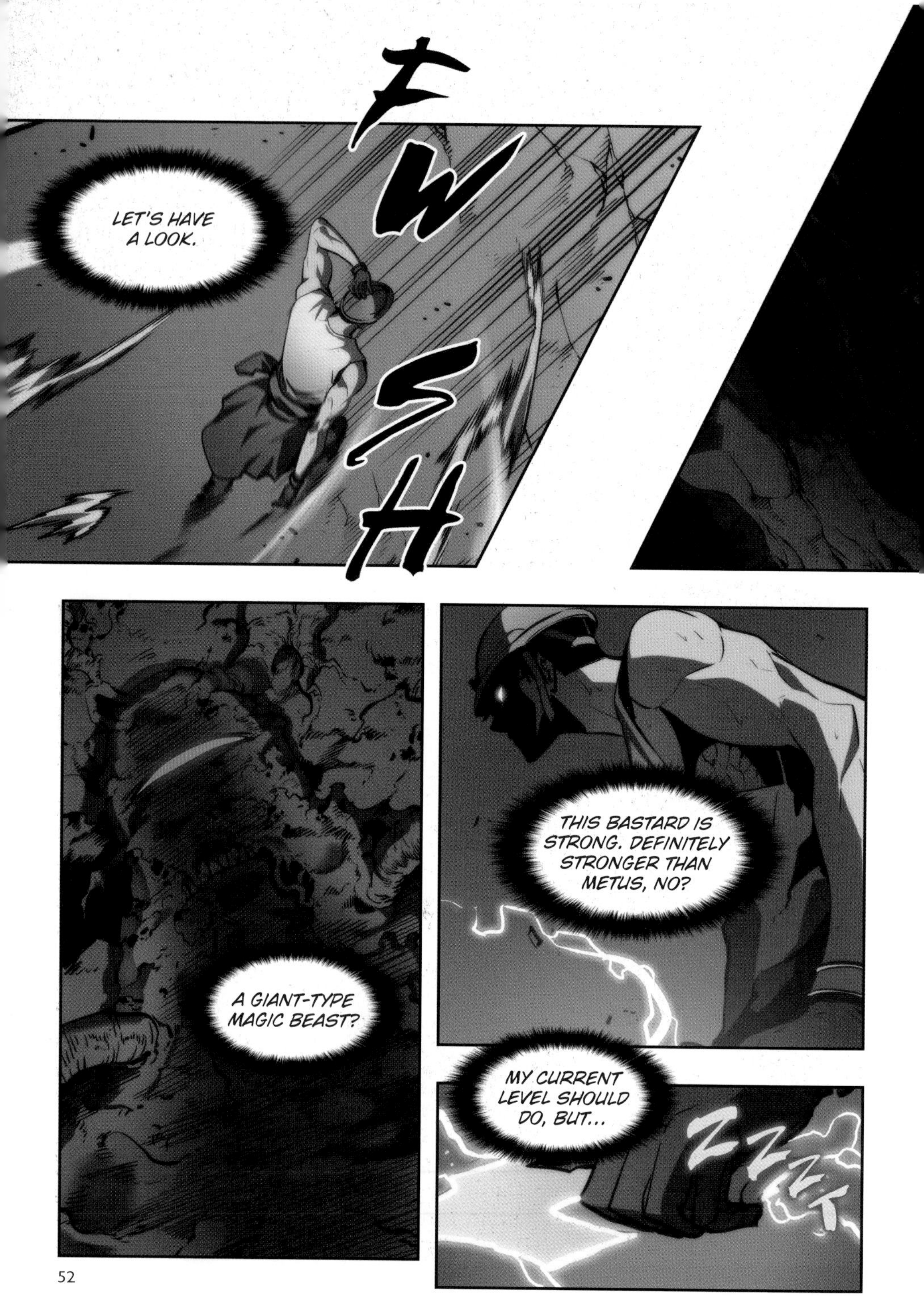
LET'S HAVE A LOOK.
FWSH
A GIANT-TYPE MAGIC BEAST?
THIS BASTARD IS STRONG. DEFINITELY STRONGER THAN METUS, NO?
MY CURRENT LEVEL SHOULD DO, BUT...
ZZZT

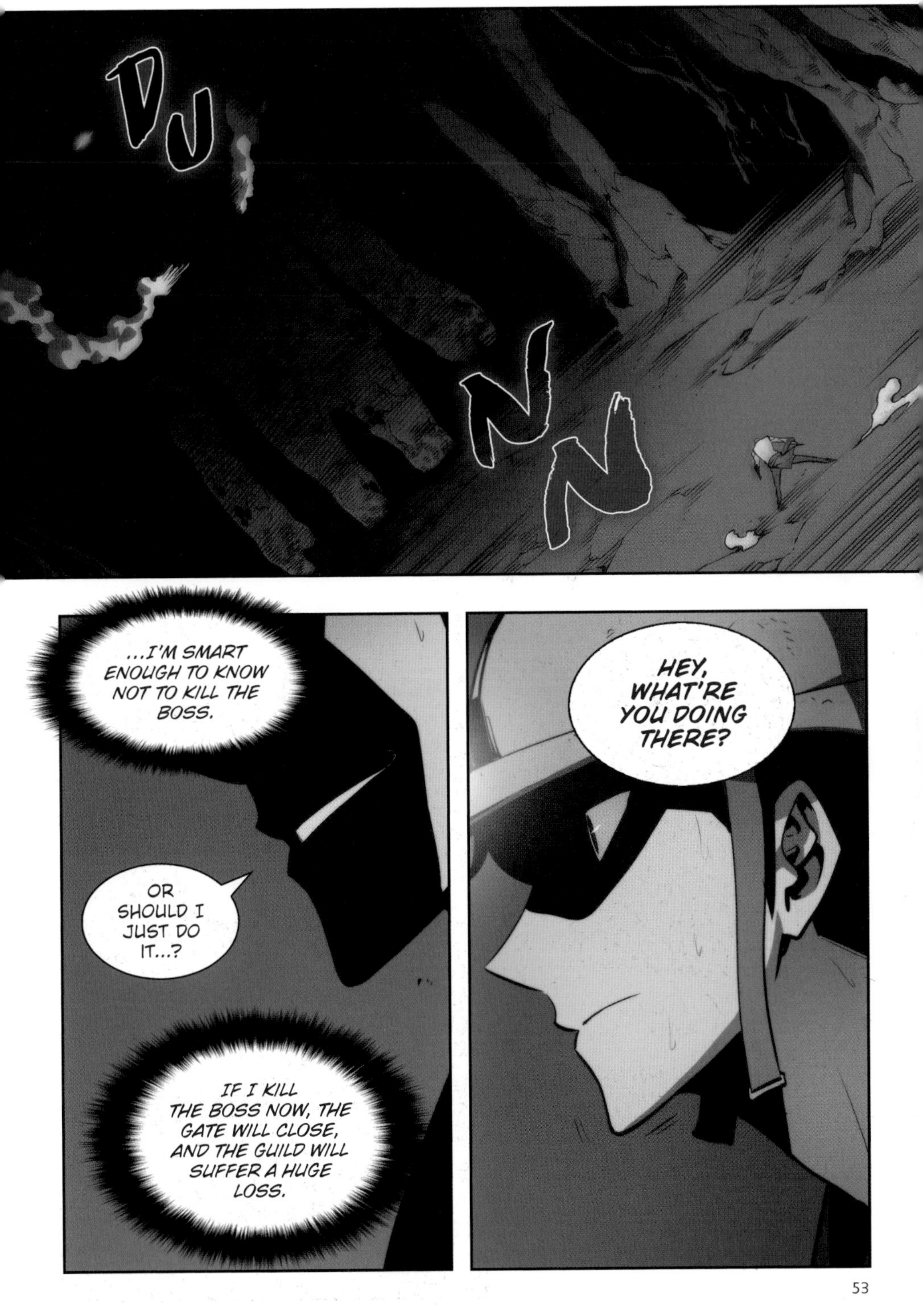
DJ
NN
...I'M SMART ENOUGH TO KNOW NOT TO KILL THE BOSS.
OR SHOULD I JUST DO IT...?
IF I KILL THE BOSS NOW, THE GATE WILL CLOSE, AND THE GUILD WILL SUFFER A HUGE LOSS.
HEY, WHAT'RE YOU DOING THERE?

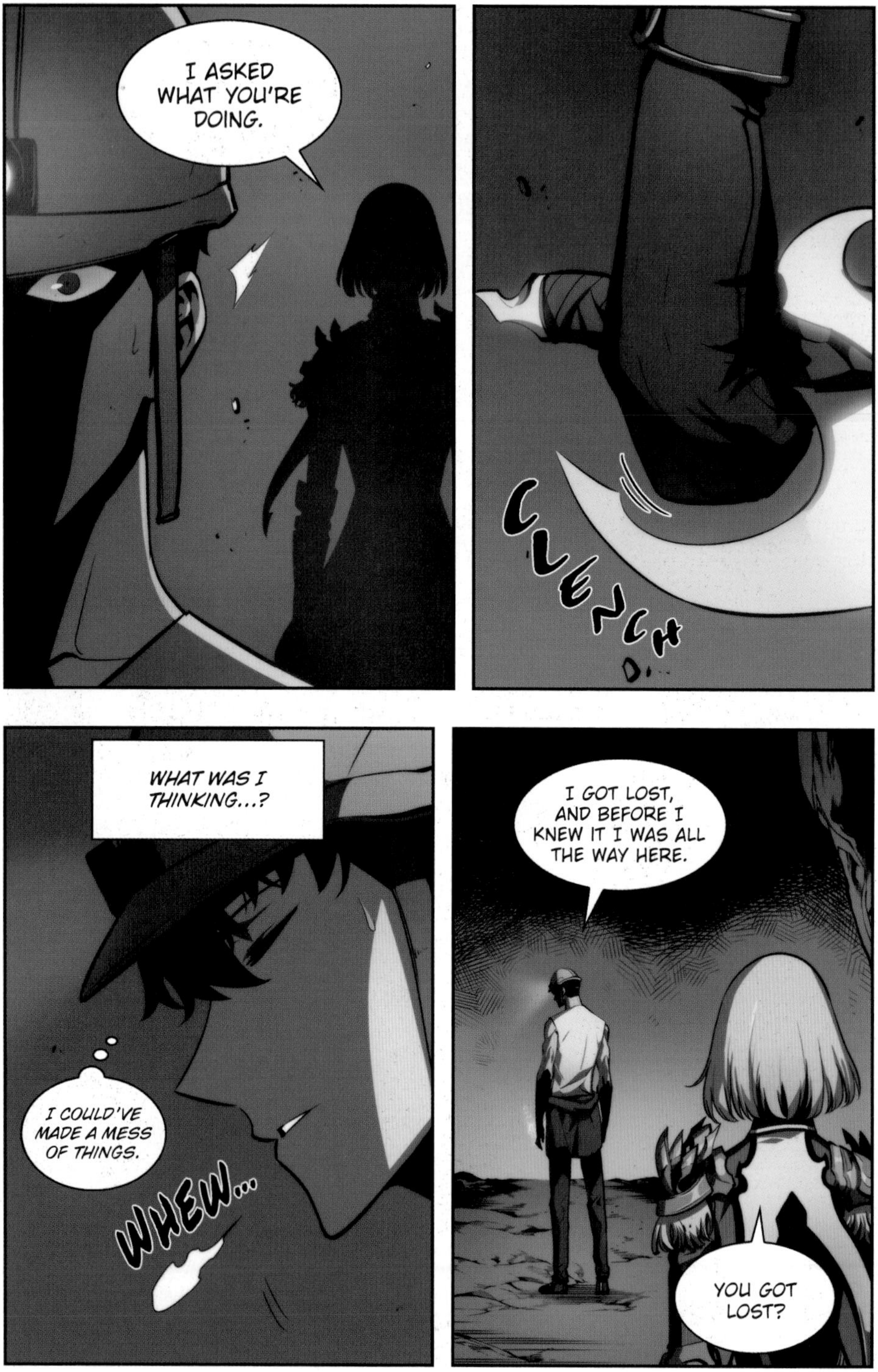
I ASKED WHAT YOU'RE DOING.
CLENCH
WHAT WAS I THINKING...?
I COULD'VE MADE A MESS OF THINGS.
WHEW...
I GOT LOST, AND BEFORE I KNEW IT I WAS ALL THE WAY HERE.
YOU GOT LOST?

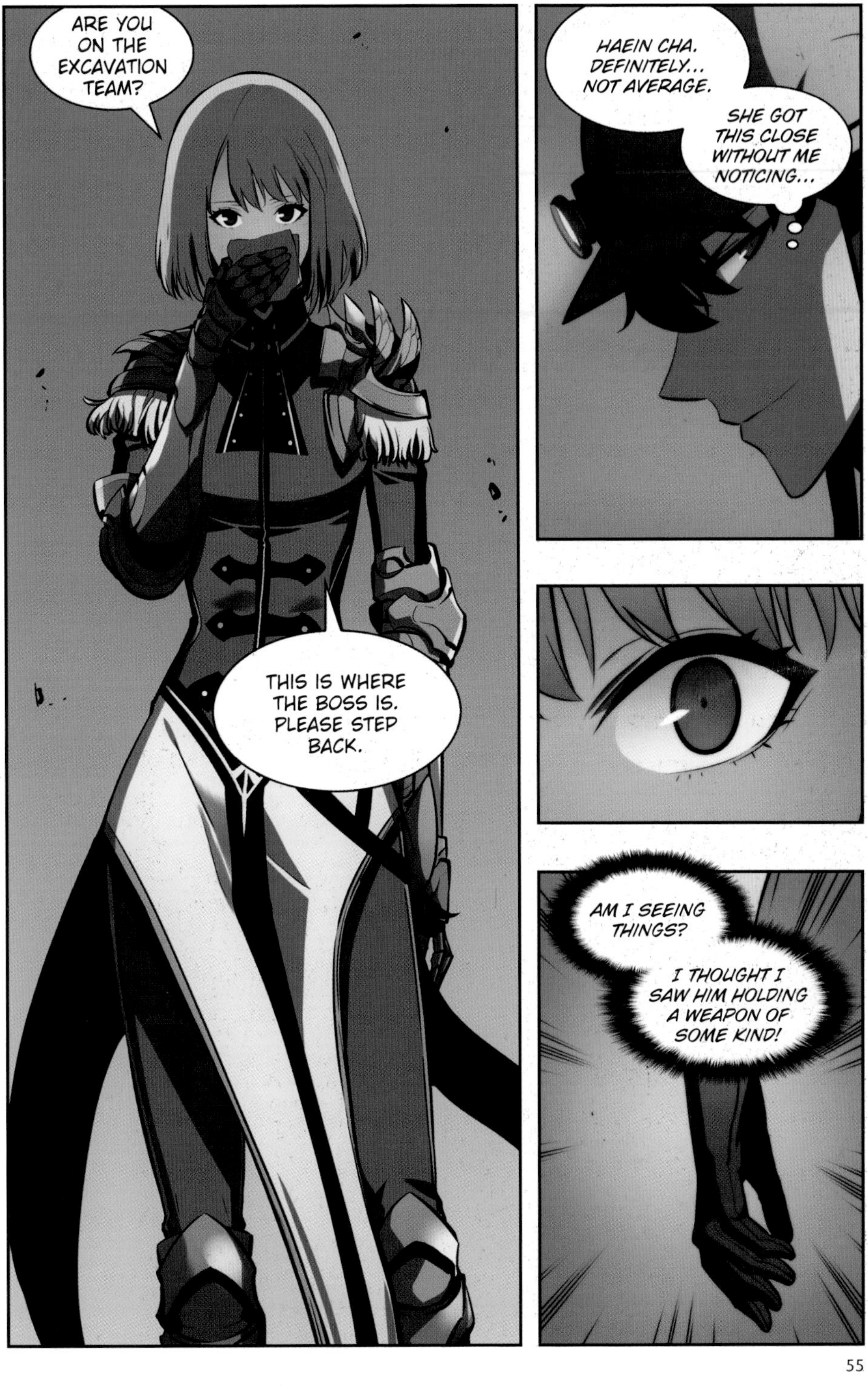
ARE YOU ON THE EXCAVATION TEAM?
THIS IS WHERE THE BOSS IS. PLEASE STEP BACK.
HAEIN CHA. DEFINITELY... NOT AVERAGE.
SHE GOT THIS CLOSE WITHOUT ME NOTICING...
AM I SEEING THINGS?
I THOUGHT I SAW HIM HOLDING A WEAPON OF SOME KIND!

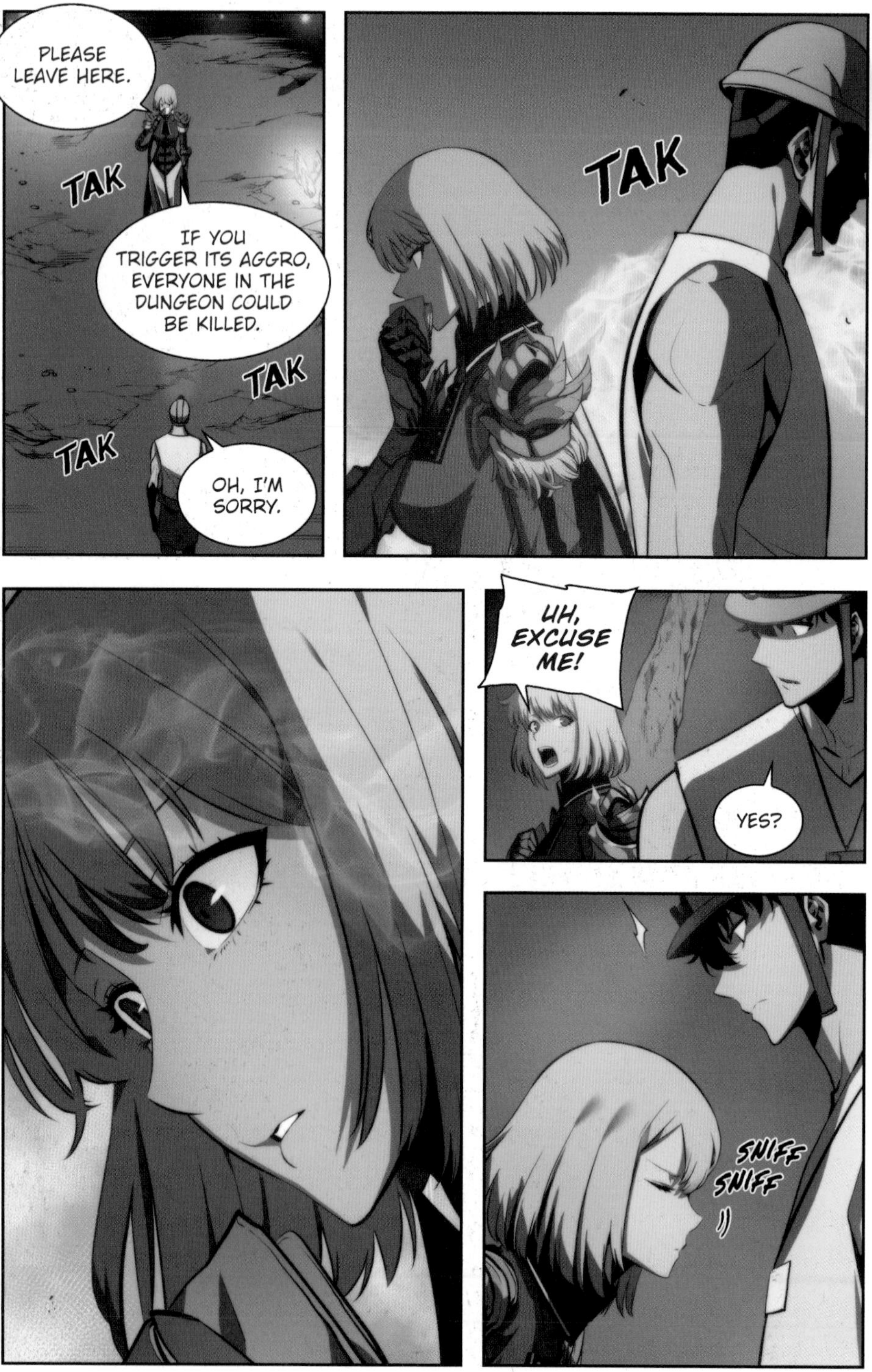
PLEASE LEAVE HERE.
TAK
IF YOU TRIGGER ITS AGGRO, EVERYONE IN THE DUNGEON COULD BE KILLED.
TAK
TAK
OH, I'M SORRY.
TAK
UH, EXCUSE ME!
YES?
SNIFF SNIFF

THERE'S NO...ODOR.

IS THERE A PROBLEM?

GRAB

ARE YOU... REALLY A HUNTER?

E-RANK...

International Hunter's License

Name: Jinwoo Sung
Rank: E-r...
This indi... ...has
been cer... ...to work
as a h... ...unter's
Asso... Korea.

JINWOO SUNG...

...NEVER MIND! PLEASE BE CAREFUL AS YOU HEAD BACK.

THIS DUNGEON IS HUGE.

)) AHEM!

RIGHT. THANK YOU.

IS IT BECAUSE OF HIS LOW RANK?

HE HAD NO STENCH.

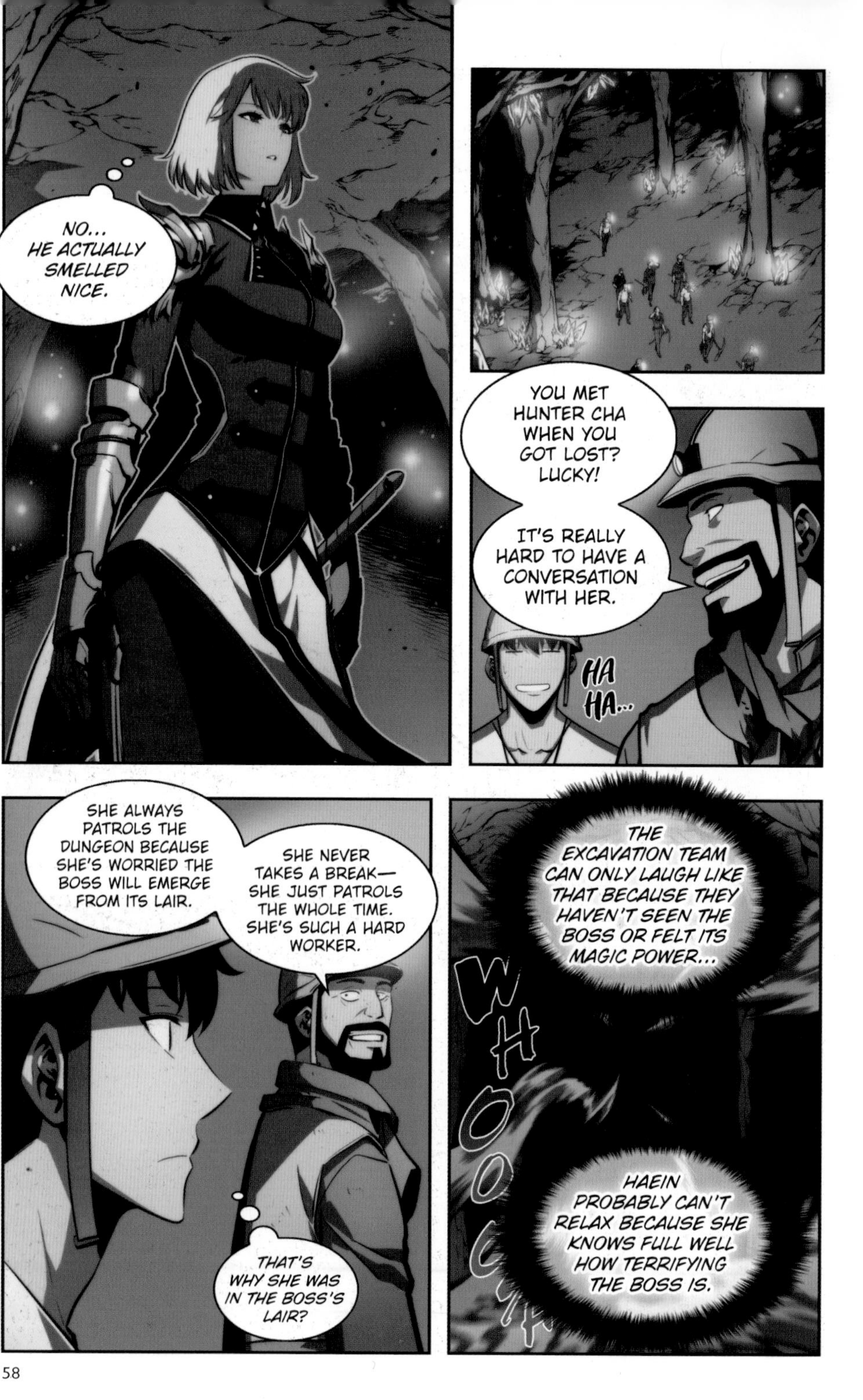
NO... HE ACTUALLY SMELLED NICE.
YOU MET HUNTER CHA WHEN YOU GOT LOST? LUCKY!
IT'S REALLY HARD TO HAVE A CONVERSATION WITH HER.
HA HA...
SHE ALWAYS PATROLS THE DUNGEON BECAUSE SHE'S WORRIED THE BOSS WILL EMERGE FROM ITS LAIR.
SHE NEVER TAKES A BREAK—SHE JUST PATROLS THE WHOLE TIME. SHE'S SUCH A HARD WORKER.
THAT'S WHY SHE WAS IN THE BOSS'S LAIR?
THE EXCAVATION TEAM CAN ONLY LAUGH LIKE THAT BECAUSE THEY HAVEN'T SEEN THE BOSS OR FELT ITS MAGIC POWER...
HAEIN PROBABLY CAN'T RELAX BECAUSE SHE KNOWS FULL WELL HOW TERRIFYING THE BOSS IS.

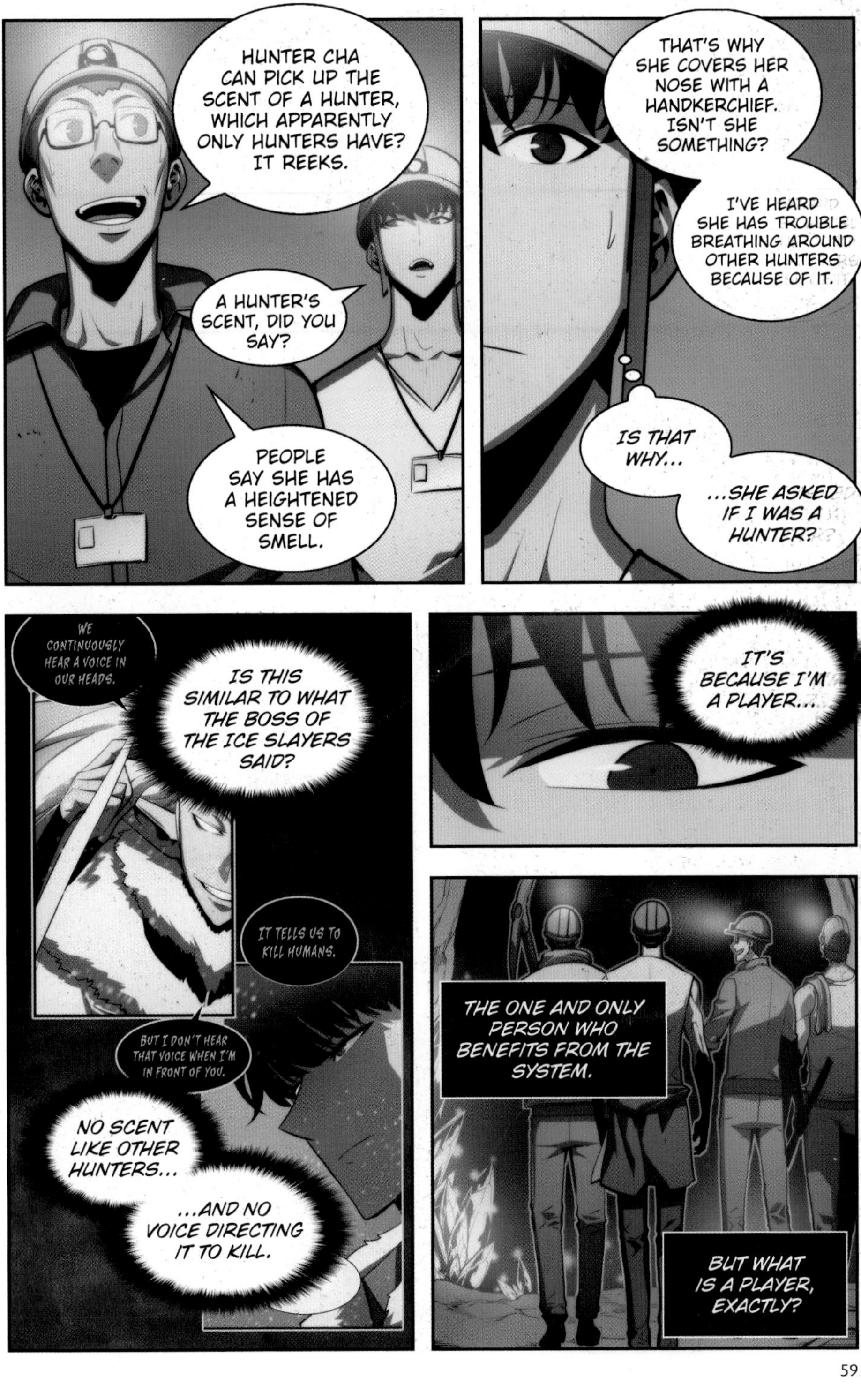
HUNTER CHA CAN PICK UP THE SCENT OF A HUNTER, WHICH APPARENTLY ONLY HUNTERS HAVE? IT REEKS.
A HUNTER'S SCENT, DID YOU SAY?
PEOPLE SAY SHE HAS A HEIGHTENED SENSE OF SMELL.
THAT'S WHY SHE COVERS HER NOSE WITH A HANDKERCHIEF. ISN'T SHE SOMETHING?
I'VE HEARD SHE HAS TROUBLE BREATHING AROUND OTHER HUNTERS BECAUSE OF IT.
IS THAT WHY...
...SHE ASKED IF I WAS A HUNTER?
WE CONTINUOUSLY HEAR A VOICE IN OUR HEADS.
IS THIS SIMILAR TO WHAT THE BOSS OF THE ICE SLAYERS SAID?
IT TELLS US TO KILL HUMANS.
BUT I DON'T HEAR THAT VOICE WHEN I'M IN FRONT OF YOU.
NO SCENT LIKE OTHER HUNTERS...
...AND NO VOICE DIRECTING IT TO KILL.
IT'S BECAUSE I'M A PLAYER...
THE ONE AND ONLY PERSON WHO BENEFITS FROM THE SYSTEM.
BUT WHAT IS A PLAYER, EXACTLY?

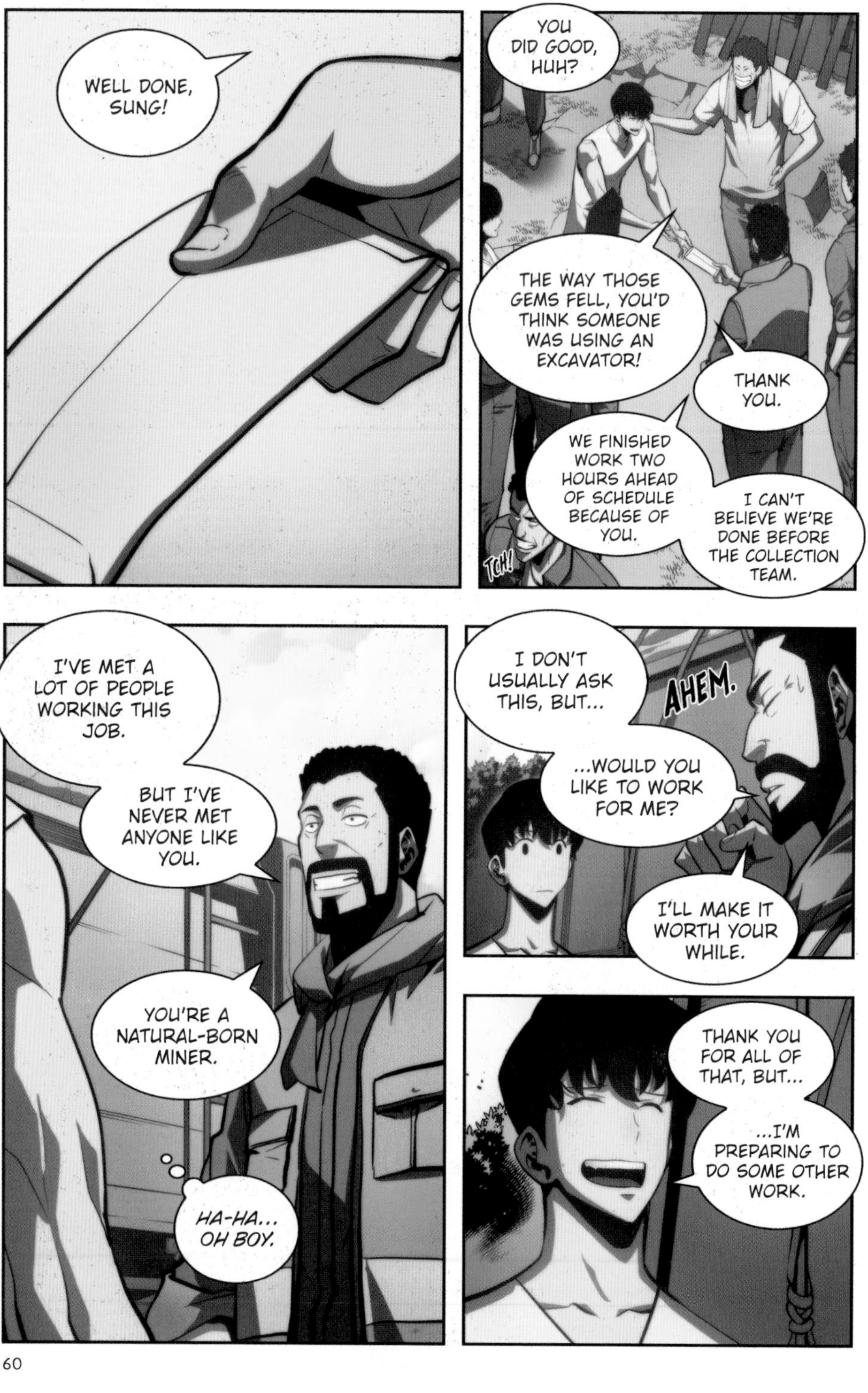
WELL DONE, SUNG!
YOU DID GOOD, HUH?
THE WAY THOSE GEMS FELL, YOU'D THINK SOMEONE WAS USING AN EXCAVATOR!
THANK YOU.
WE FINISHED WORK TWO HOURS AHEAD OF SCHEDULE BECAUSE OF YOU.
TCH!
I CAN'T BELIEVE WE'RE DONE BEFORE THE COLLECTION TEAM.
I'VE MET A LOT OF PEOPLE WORKING THIS JOB.
BUT I'VE NEVER MET ANYONE LIKE YOU.
YOU'RE A NATURAL-BORN MINER.
HA-HA... OH BOY.
I DON'T USUALLY ASK THIS, BUT...
AHEM.
...WOULD YOU LIKE TO WORK FOR ME?
I'LL MAKE IT WORTH YOUR WHILE.
THANK YOU FOR ALL OF THAT, BUT...
...I'M PREPARING TO DO SOME OTHER WORK.

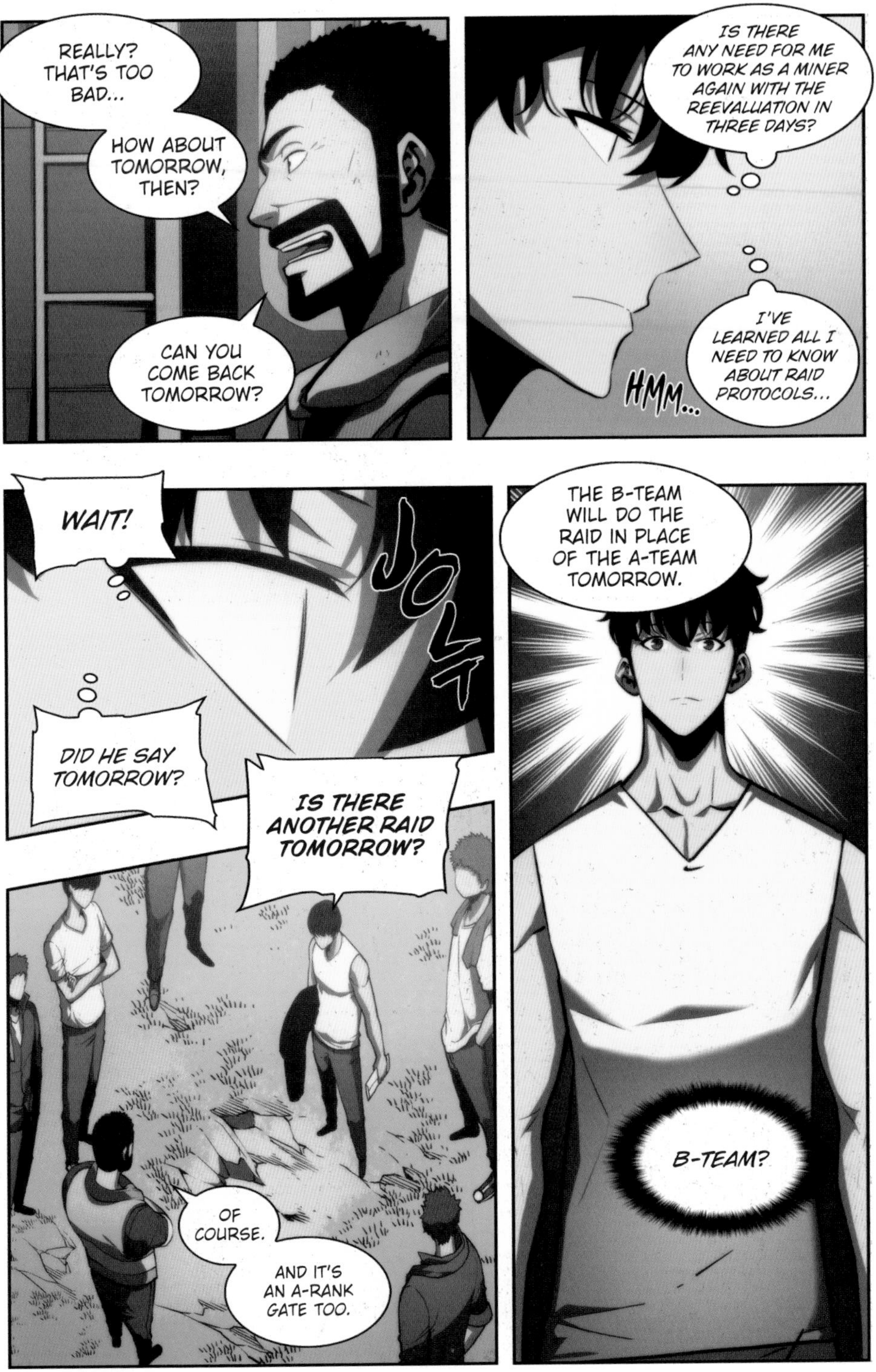
REALLY? THAT'S TOO BAD...
HOW ABOUT TOMORROW, THEN?
CAN YOU COME BACK TOMORROW?
IS THERE ANY NEED FOR ME TO WORK AS A MINER AGAIN WITH THE REEVALUATION IN THREE DAYS?
HMM...
I'VE LEARNED ALL I NEED TO KNOW ABOUT RAID PROTOCOLS...
WAIT!
JOLT
DID HE SAY TOMORROW?
IS THERE ANOTHER RAID TOMORROW?
OF COURSE.
AND IT'S AN A-RANK GATE TOO.
THE B-TEAM WILL DO THE RAID IN PLACE OF THE A-TEAM TOMORROW.
B-TEAM?

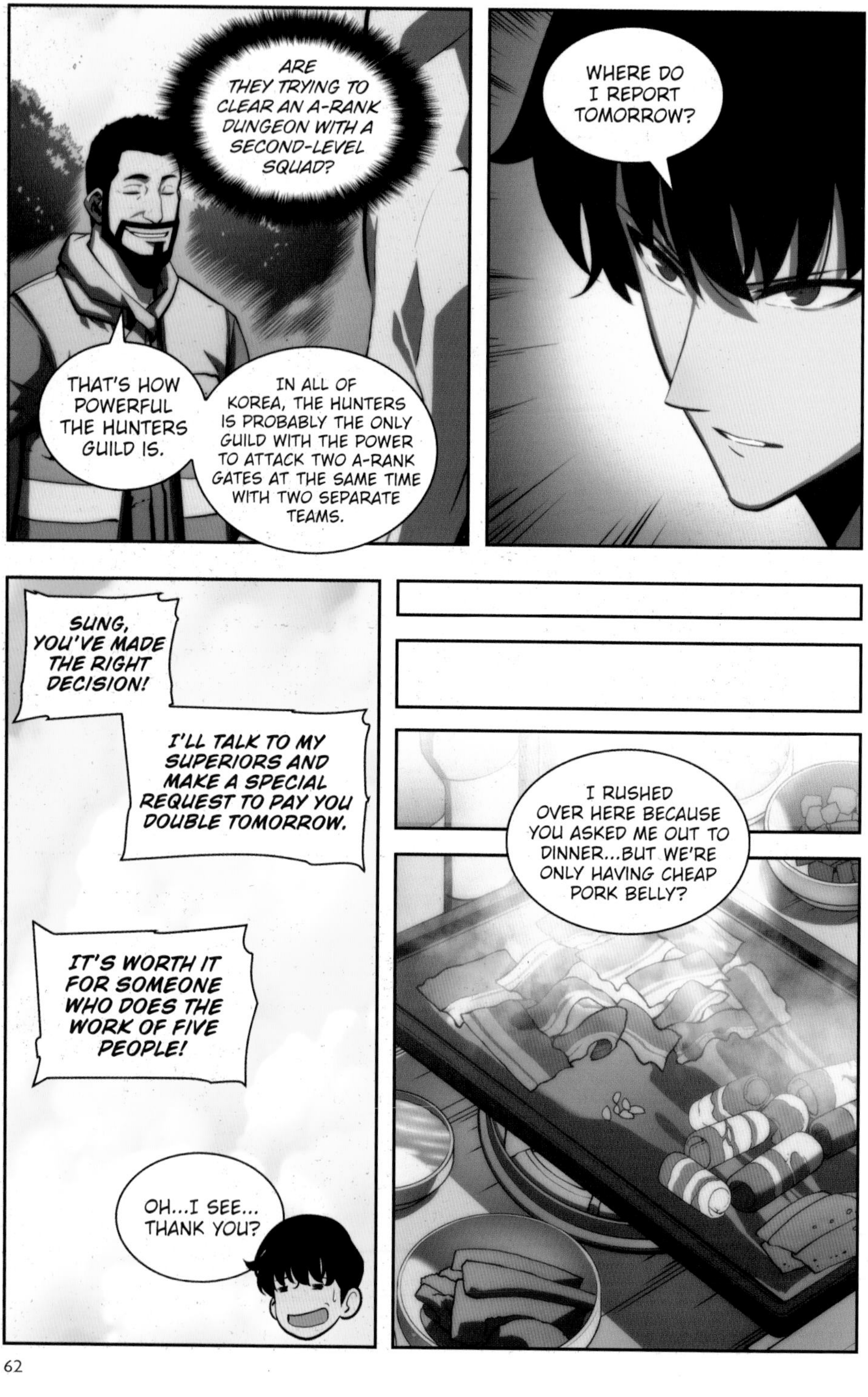
ARE THEY TRYING TO CLEAR AN A-RANK DUNGEON WITH A SECOND-LEVEL SQUAD?
THAT'S HOW POWERFUL THE HUNTERS GUILD IS.
IN ALL OF KOREA, THE HUNTERS IS PROBABLY THE ONLY GUILD WITH THE POWER TO ATTACK TWO A-RANK GATES AT THE SAME TIME WITH TWO SEPARATE TEAMS.
WHERE DO I REPORT TOMORROW?
SUNG, YOU'VE MADE THE RIGHT DECISION!
I'LL TALK TO MY SUPERIORS AND MAKE A SPECIAL REQUEST TO PAY YOU DOUBLE TOMORROW.
IT'S WORTH IT FOR SOMEONE WHO DOES THE WORK OF FIVE PEOPLE!
OH...I SEE... THANK YOU?
I RUSHED OVER HERE BECAUSE YOU ASKED ME OUT TO DINNER...BUT WE'RE ONLY HAVING CHEAP PORK BELLY?

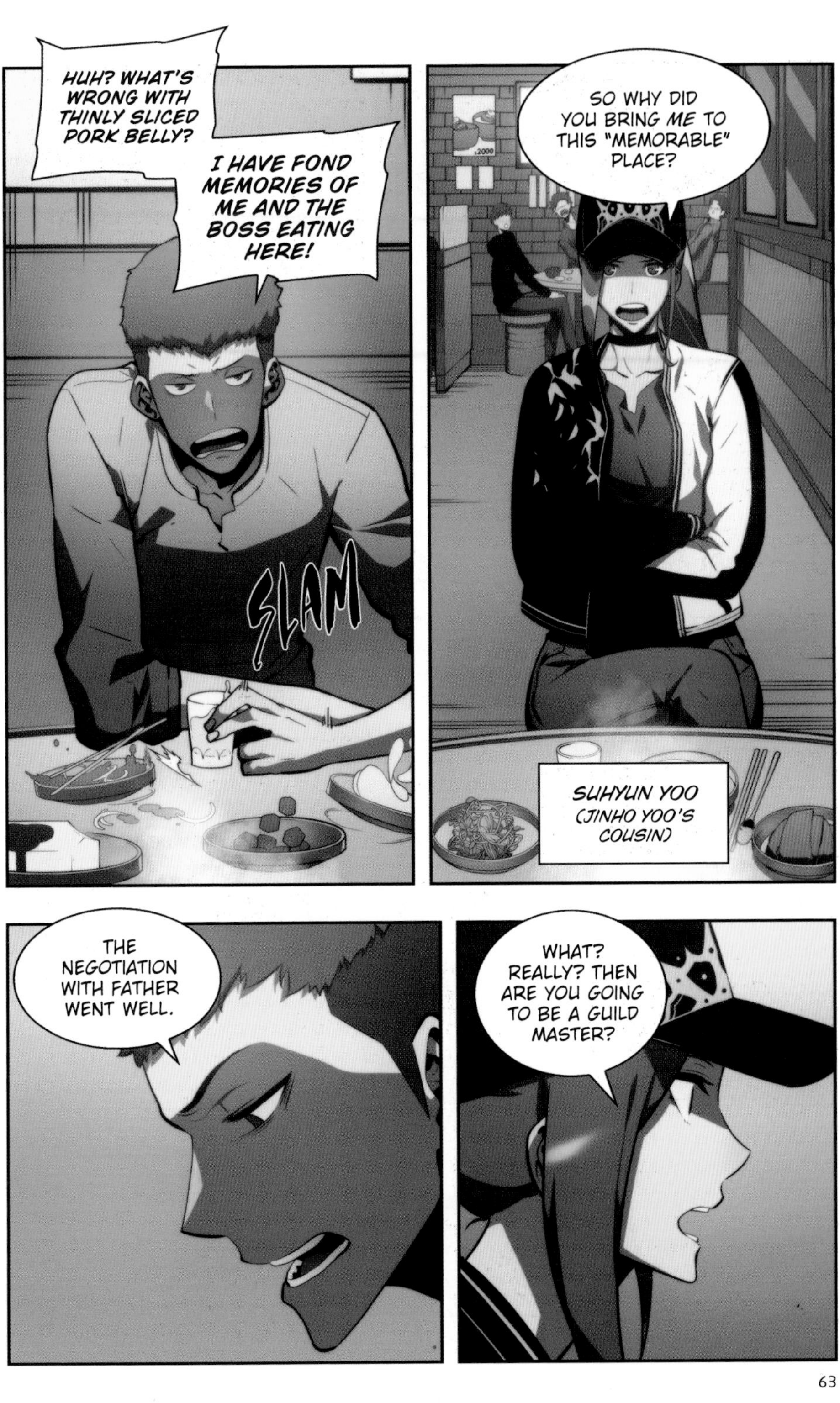
HUH? WHAT'S WRONG WITH THINLY SLICED PORK BELLY?
I HAVE FOND MEMORIES OF ME AND THE BOSS EATING HERE!
SLAM
SO WHY DID YOU BRING ME TO THIS "MEMORABLE" PLACE?
SUHYUN YOO (JINHO YOO'S COUSIN)
THE NEGOTIATION WITH FATHER WENT WELL.
WHAT? REALLY? THEN ARE YOU GOING TO BE A GUILD MASTER?

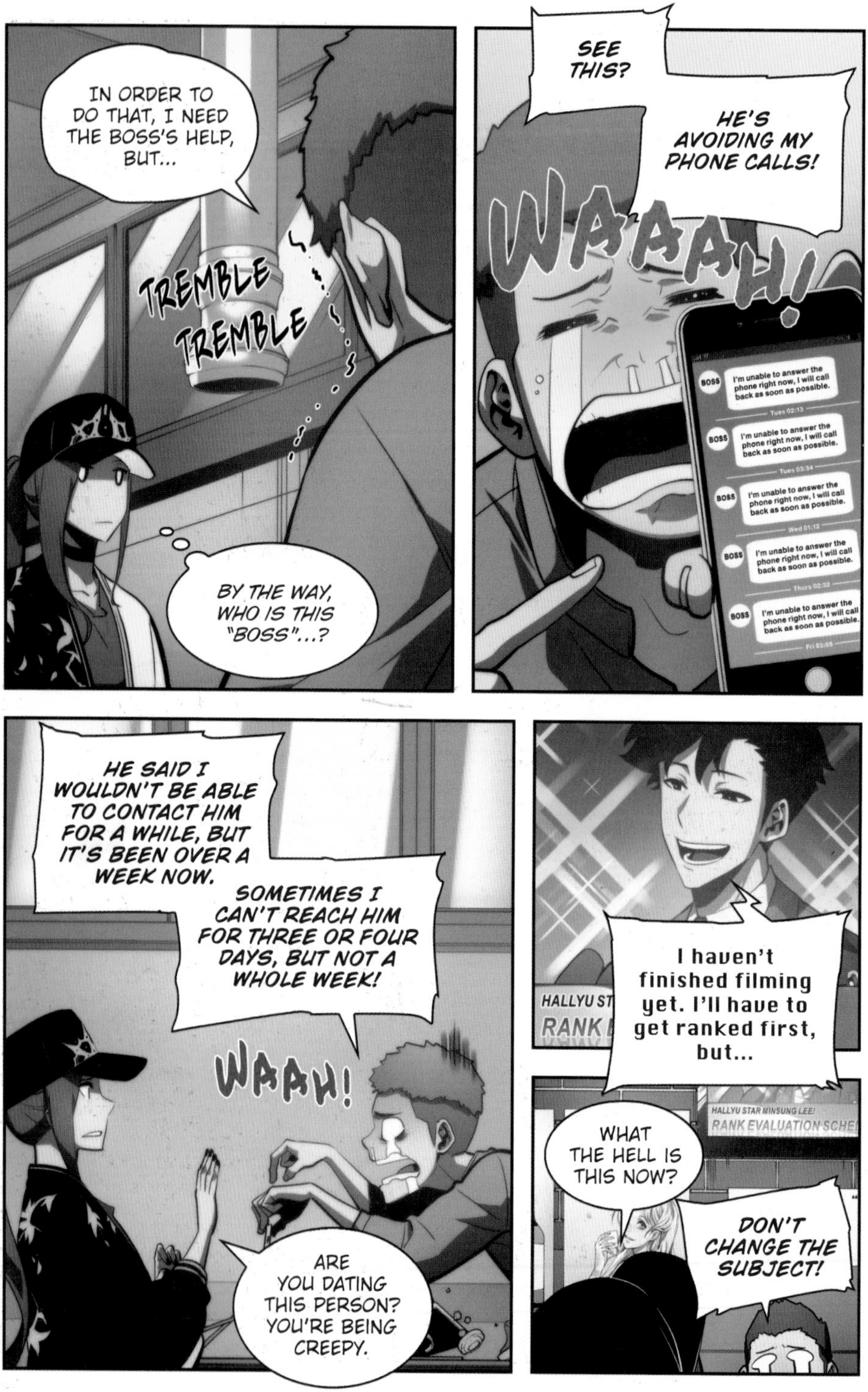
IN ORDER TO DO THAT, I NEED THE BOSS'S HELP, BUT...
TREMBLE TREMBLE
BY THE WAY, WHO IS THIS "BOSS"...?
SEE THIS?
HE'S AVOIDING MY PHONE CALLS!
WAAAH!
BOSS
I'm unable to answer the phone right now, I will call back as soon as possible.
Tues 02:13
BOSS
I'm unable to answer the phone right now, I will call back as soon as possible.
Tues 03:34
BOSS
I'm unable to answer the phone right now, I will call back as soon as possible.
Wed 01:12
BOSS
I'm unable to answer the phone right now, I will call back as soon as possible.
Thurs 02:32
BOSS
I'm unable to answer the phone right now, I will call back as soon as possible.
Fri 03:05
HE SAID I WOULDN'T BE ABLE TO CONTACT HIM FOR A WHILE, BUT IT'S BEEN OVER A WEEK NOW.
SOMETIMES I CAN'T REACH HIM FOR THREE OR FOUR DAYS, BUT NOT A WHOLE WEEK!
WAAH!
ARE YOU DATING THIS PERSON? YOU'RE BEING CREEPY.
I haven't finished filming yet. I'll have to get ranked first, but...
HALLYU STAR MINSUNG LEE!
WHAT THE HELL IS THIS NOW?
DON'T CHANGE THE SUBJECT!

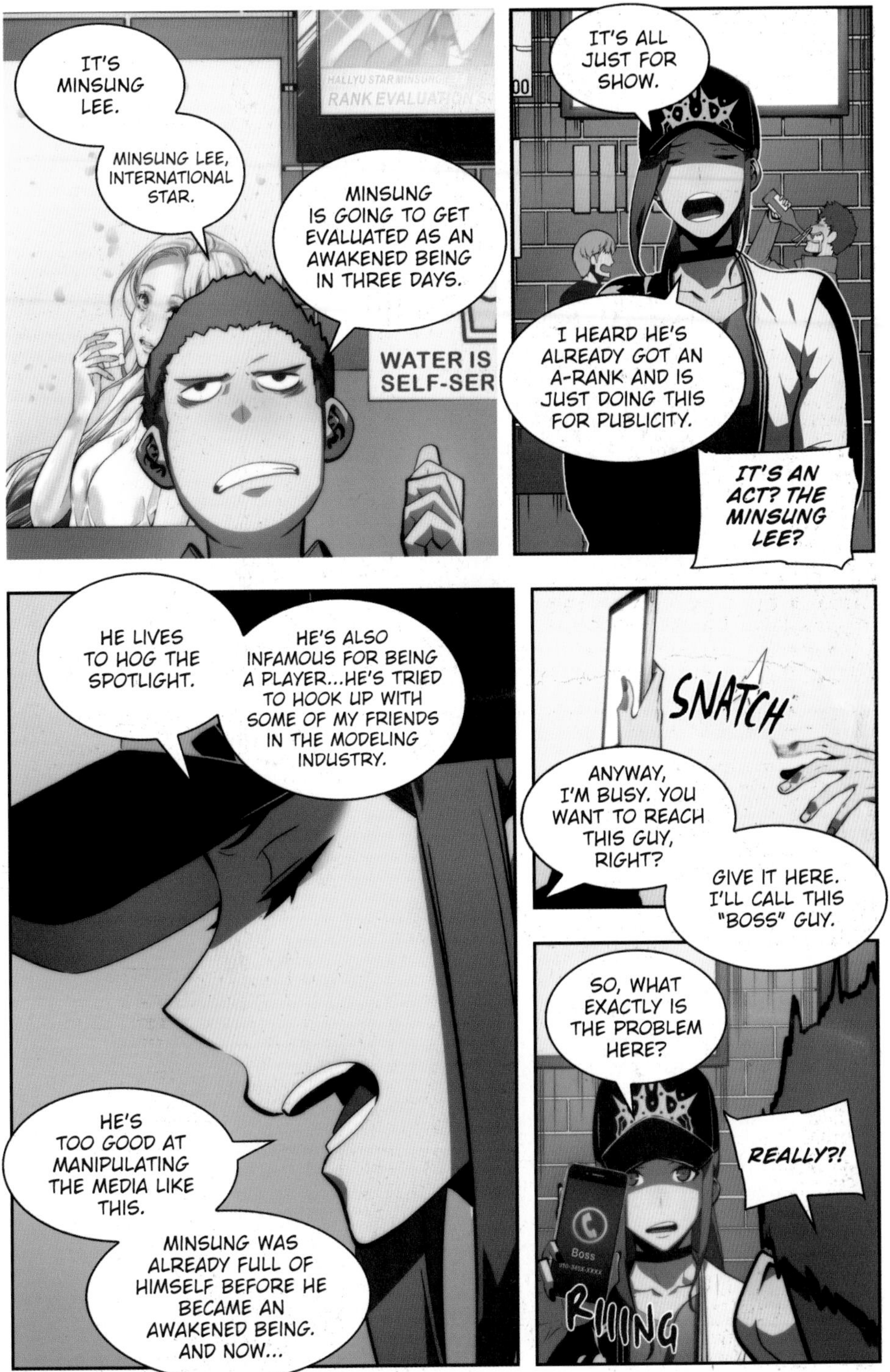
HALLYU STAR MINSUNG
RANK EVALUATION
IT'S MINSUNG LEE.
MINSUNG LEE, INTERNATIONAL STAR.
MINSUNG IS GOING TO GET EVALUATED AS AN AWAKENED BEING IN THREE DAYS.
WATER IS SELF-SER
IT'S ALL JUST FOR SHOW.
I HEARD HE'S ALREADY GOT AN A-RANK AND IS JUST DOING THIS FOR PUBLICITY.
IT'S AN ACT? THE MINSUNG LEE?
HE LIVES TO HOG THE SPOTLIGHT.
HE'S ALSO INFAMOUS FOR BEING A PLAYER...HE'S TRIED TO HOOK UP WITH SOME OF MY FRIENDS IN THE MODELING INDUSTRY.
HE'S TOO GOOD AT MANIPULATING THE MEDIA LIKE THIS.
MINSUNG WAS ALREADY FULL OF HIMSELF BEFORE HE BECAME AN AWAKENED BEING. AND NOW...
SNATCH
ANYWAY, I'M BUSY. YOU WANT TO REACH THIS GUY, RIGHT?
GIVE IT HERE. I'LL CALL THIS "BOSS" GUY.
SO, WHAT EXACTLY IS THE PROBLEM HERE?
REALLY?!
Boss
RIIING

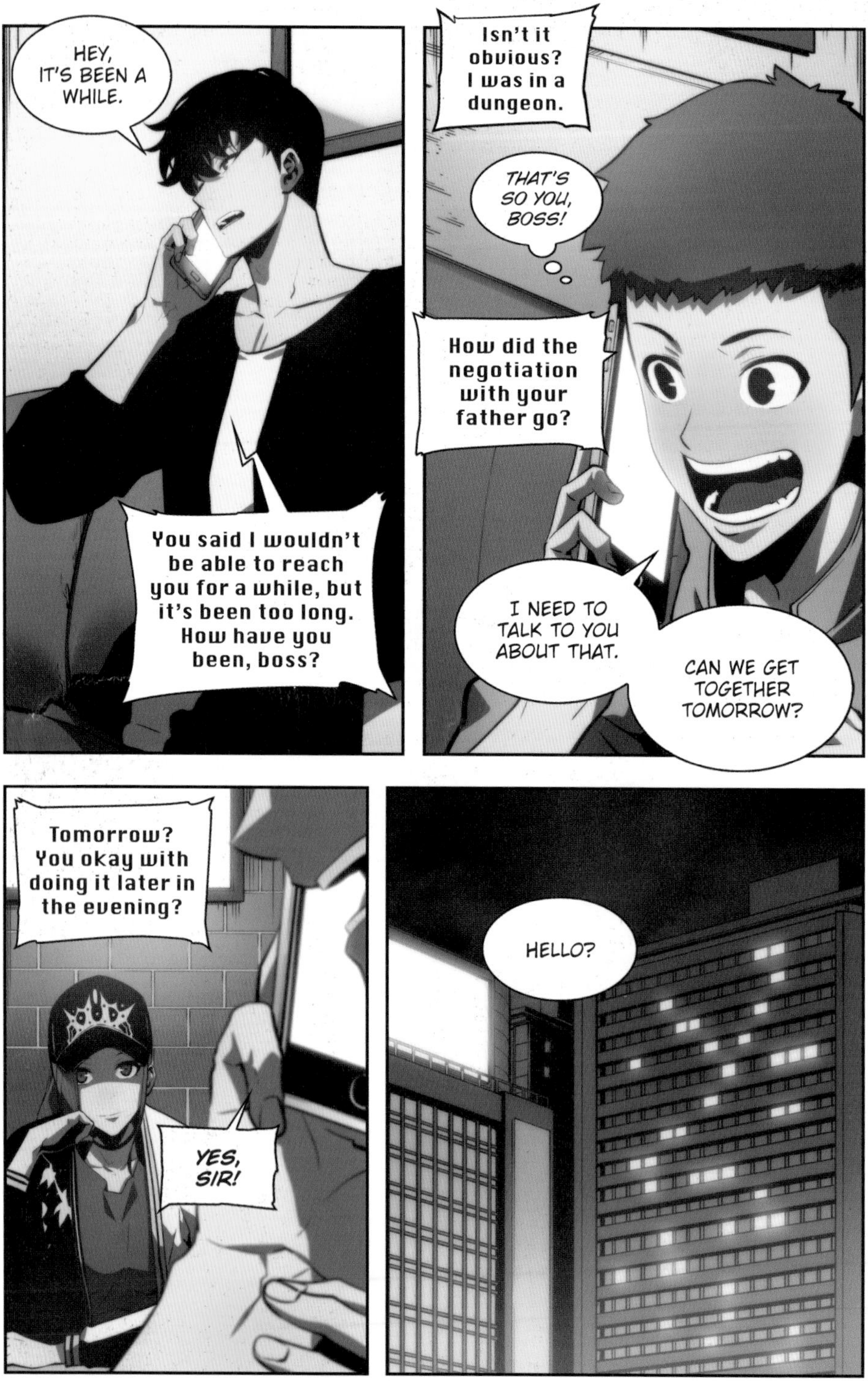
HEY, IT'S BEEN A WHILE.
You said I wouldn't be able to reach you for a while, but it's been too long. How have you been, boss?
Isn't it obvious? I was in a dungeon.
THAT'S SO YOU, BOSS!
How did the negotiation with your father go?
I NEED TO TALK TO YOU ABOUT THAT.
CAN WE GET TOGETHER TOMORROW?
Tomorrow? You okay with doing it later in the evening?
YES, SIR!
HELLO?

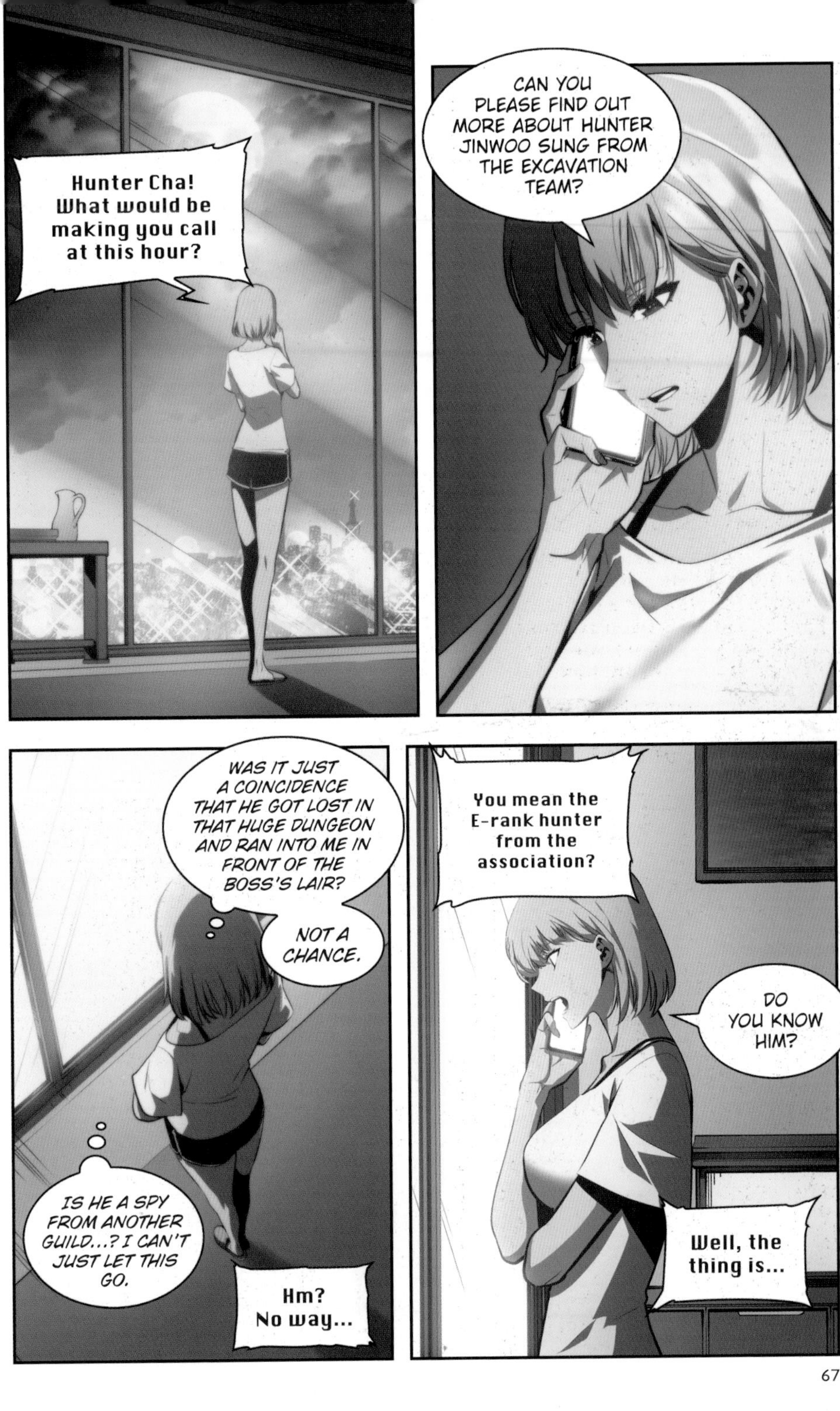
Hunter Cha! What would be making you call at this hour?
CAN YOU PLEASE FIND OUT MORE ABOUT HUNTER JINWOO SUNG FROM THE EXCAVATION TEAM?
WAS IT JUST A COINCIDENCE THAT HE GOT LOST IN THAT HUGE DUNGEON AND RAN INTO ME IN FRONT OF THE BOSS'S LAIR?
NOT A CHANCE.
IS HE A SPY FROM ANOTHER GUILD...? I CAN'T JUST LET THIS GO.
Hm? No way...
You mean the E-rank hunter from the association?
DO YOU KNOW HIM?
Well, the thing is...

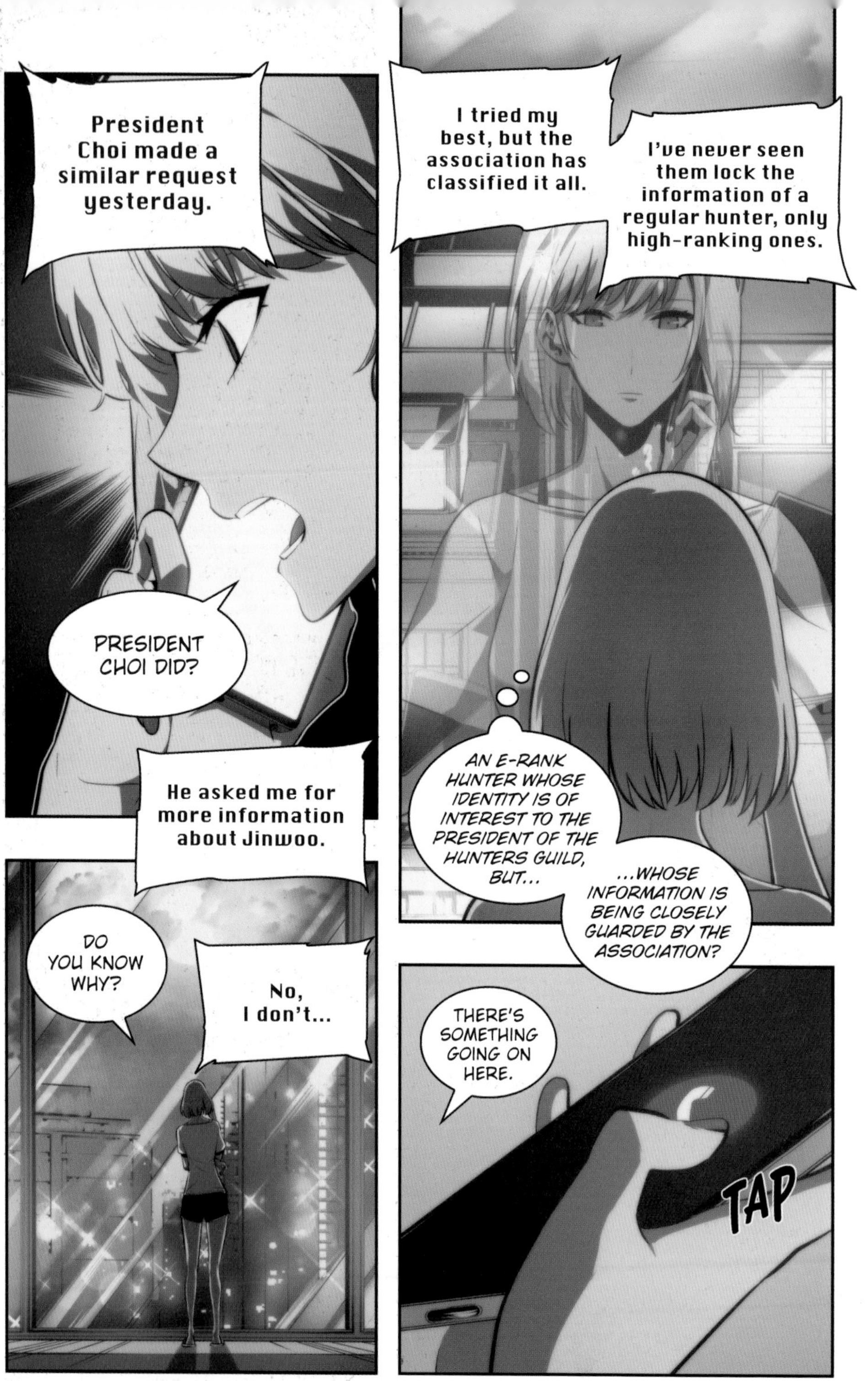
President Choi made a similar request yesterday.
PRESIDENT CHOI DID?
He asked me for more information about Jinwoo.
DO YOU KNOW WHY?
No, I don't...
I tried my best, but the association has classified it all.
I've never seen them lock the information of a regular hunter, only high-ranking ones.
AN E-RANK HUNTER WHOSE IDENTITY IS OF INTEREST TO THE PRESIDENT OF THE HUNTERS GUILD, BUT...
...WHOSE INFORMATION IS BEING CLOSELY GUARDED BY THE ASSOCIATION?
THERE'S SOMETHING GOING ON HERE.
TAP

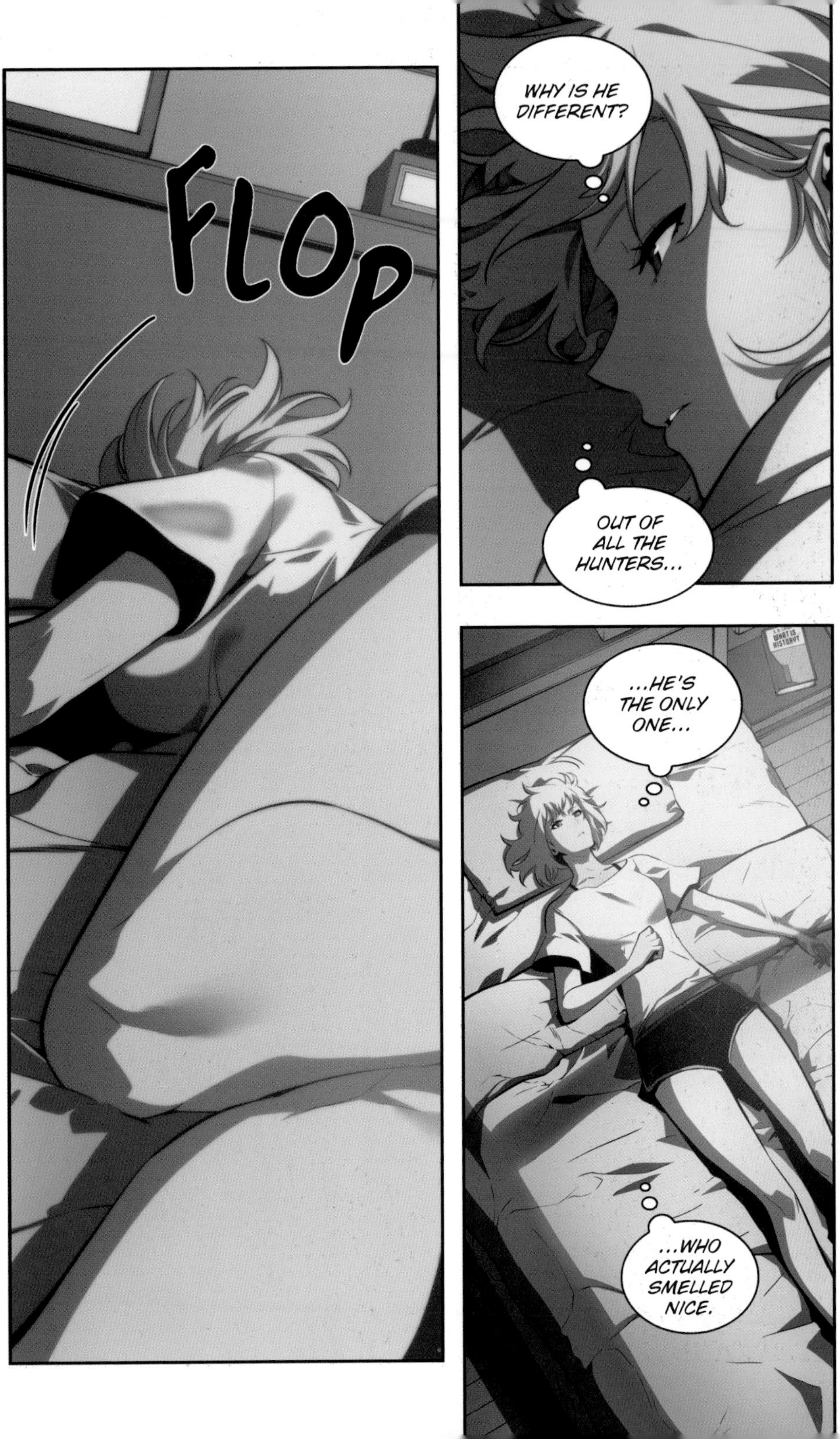
FLOP
WHY IS HE DIFFERENT?
OUT OF ALL THE HUNTERS...
...HE'S THE ONLY ONE...
...WHO ACTUALLY SMELLED NICE.

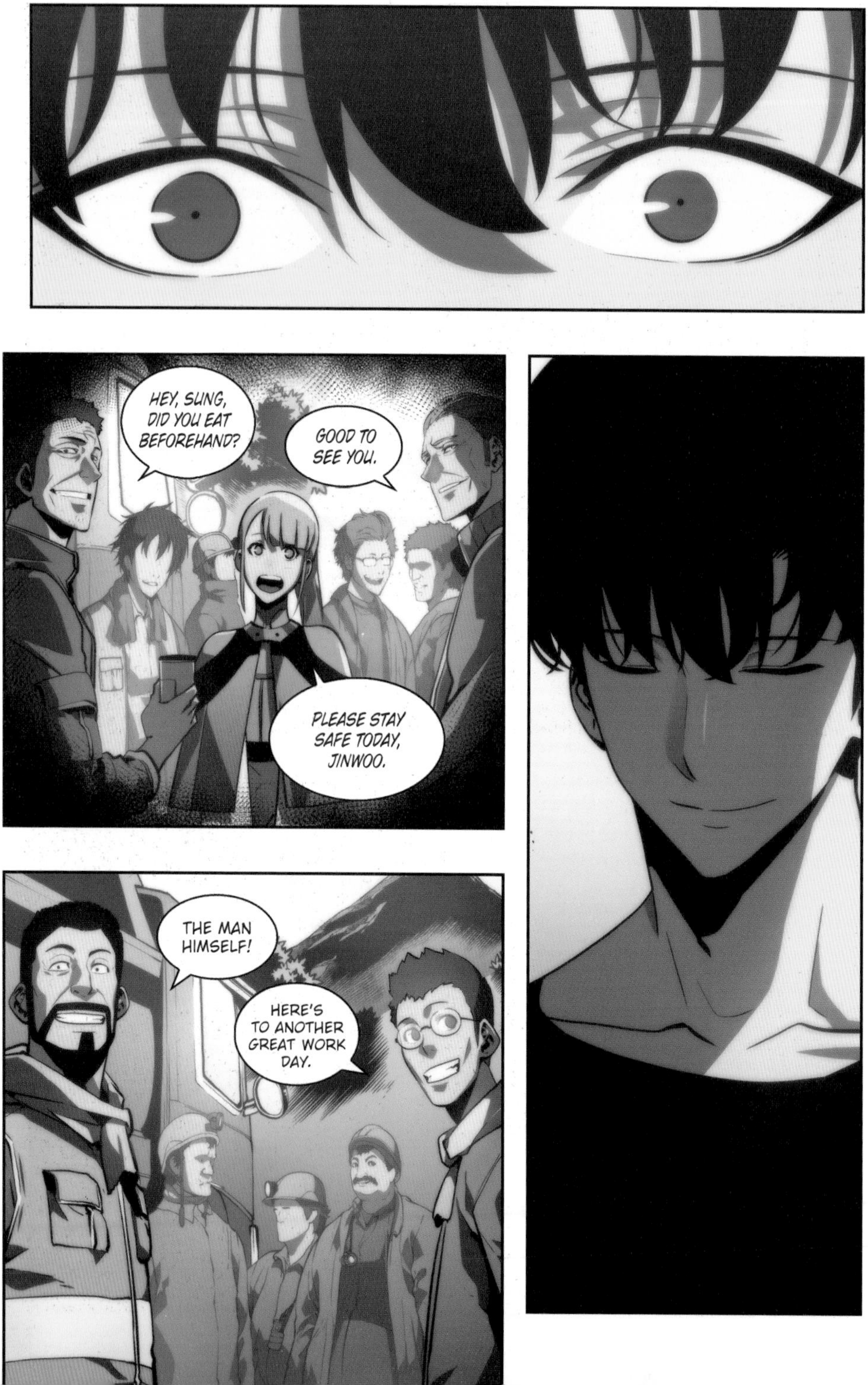
HEY, SUNG, DID YOU EAT BEFOREHAND?
GOOD TO SEE YOU.
PLEASE STAY SAFE TODAY, JINWOO.
THE MAN HIMSELF!
HERE'S TO ANOTHER GREAT WORK DAY.

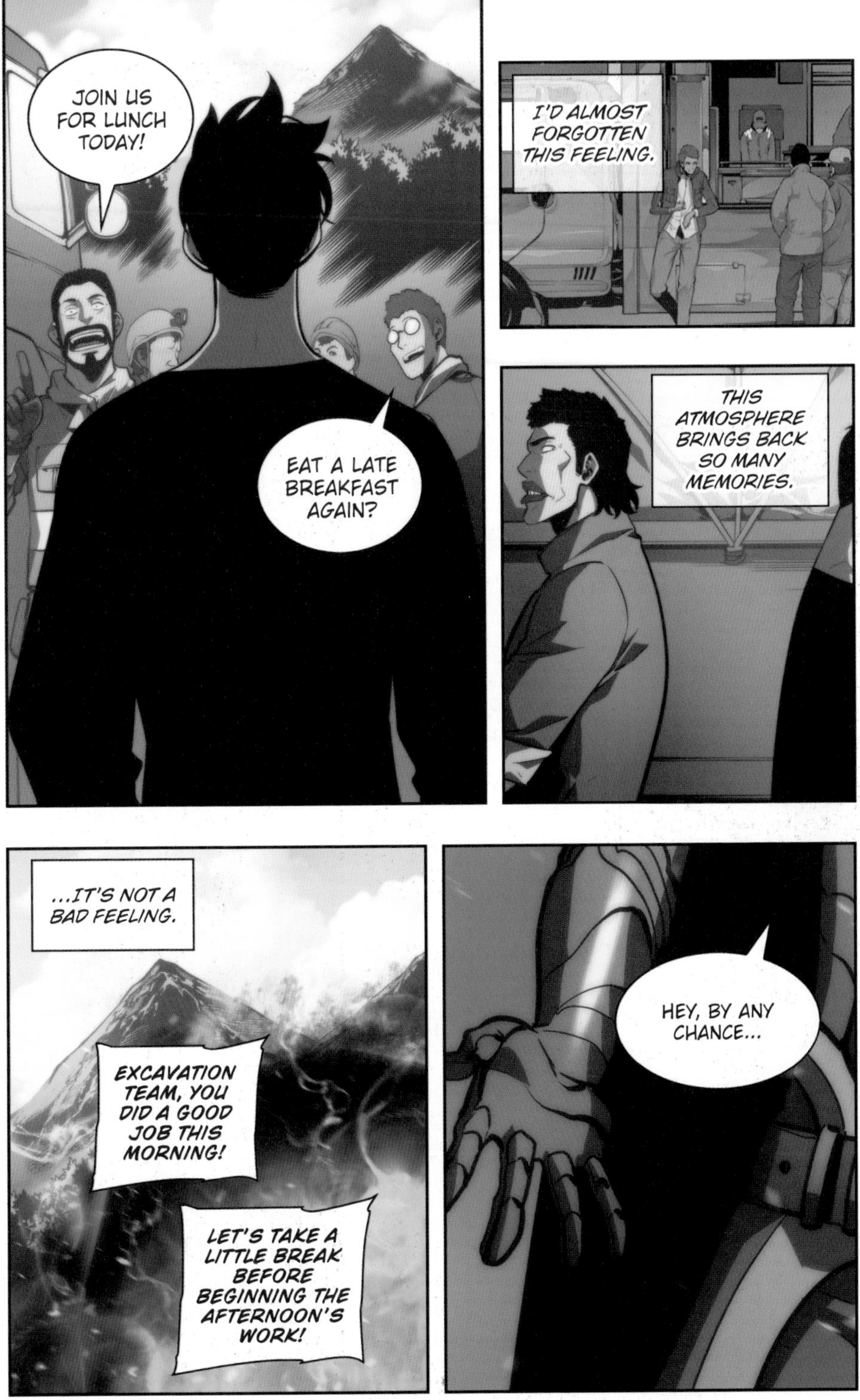
JOIN US FOR LUNCH TODAY!
EAT A LATE BREAKFAST AGAIN?
I'D ALMOST FORGOTTEN THIS FEELING.
THIS ATMOSPHERE BRINGS BACK SO MANY MEMORIES.
...IT'S NOT A BAD FEELING.
EXCAVATION TEAM, YOU DID A GOOD JOB THIS MORNING!
LET'S TAKE A LITTLE BREAK BEFORE BEGINNING THE AFTERNOON'S WORK!
HEY, BY ANY CHANCE...

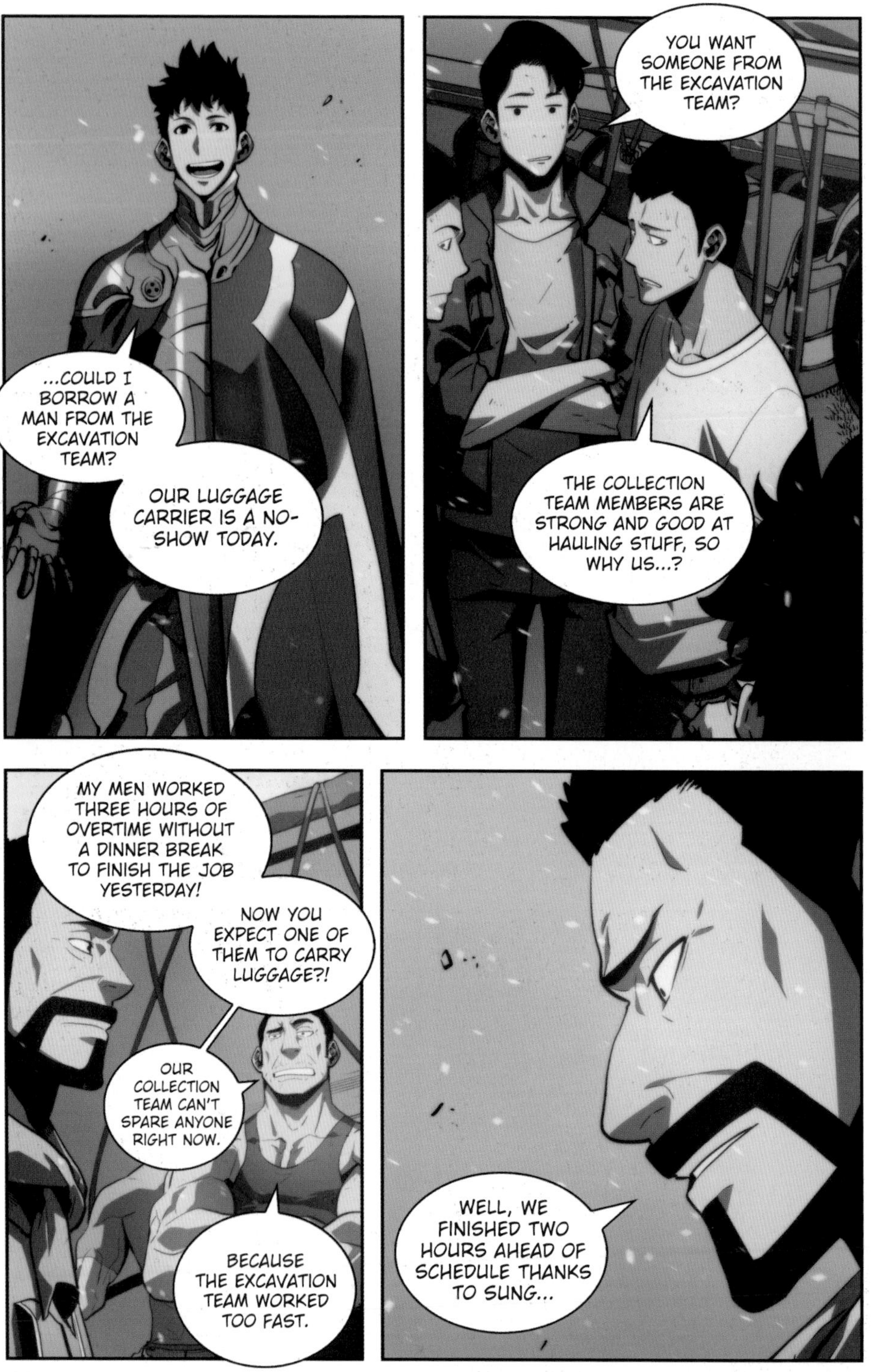
...COULD I BORROW A MAN FROM THE EXCAVATION TEAM?
OUR LUGGAGE CARRIER IS A NO-SHOW TODAY.
YOU WANT SOMEONE FROM THE EXCAVATION TEAM?
THE COLLECTION TEAM MEMBERS ARE STRONG AND GOOD AT HAULING STUFF, SO WHY US...?
MY MEN WORKED THREE HOURS OF OVERTIME WITHOUT A DINNER BREAK TO FINISH THE JOB YESTERDAY!
NOW YOU EXPECT ONE OF THEM TO CARRY LUGGAGE?!
OUR COLLECTION TEAM CAN'T SPARE ANYONE RIGHT NOW.
BECAUSE THE EXCAVATION TEAM WORKED TOO FAST.
WELL, WE FINISHED TWO HOURS AHEAD OF SCHEDULE THANKS TO SUNG...

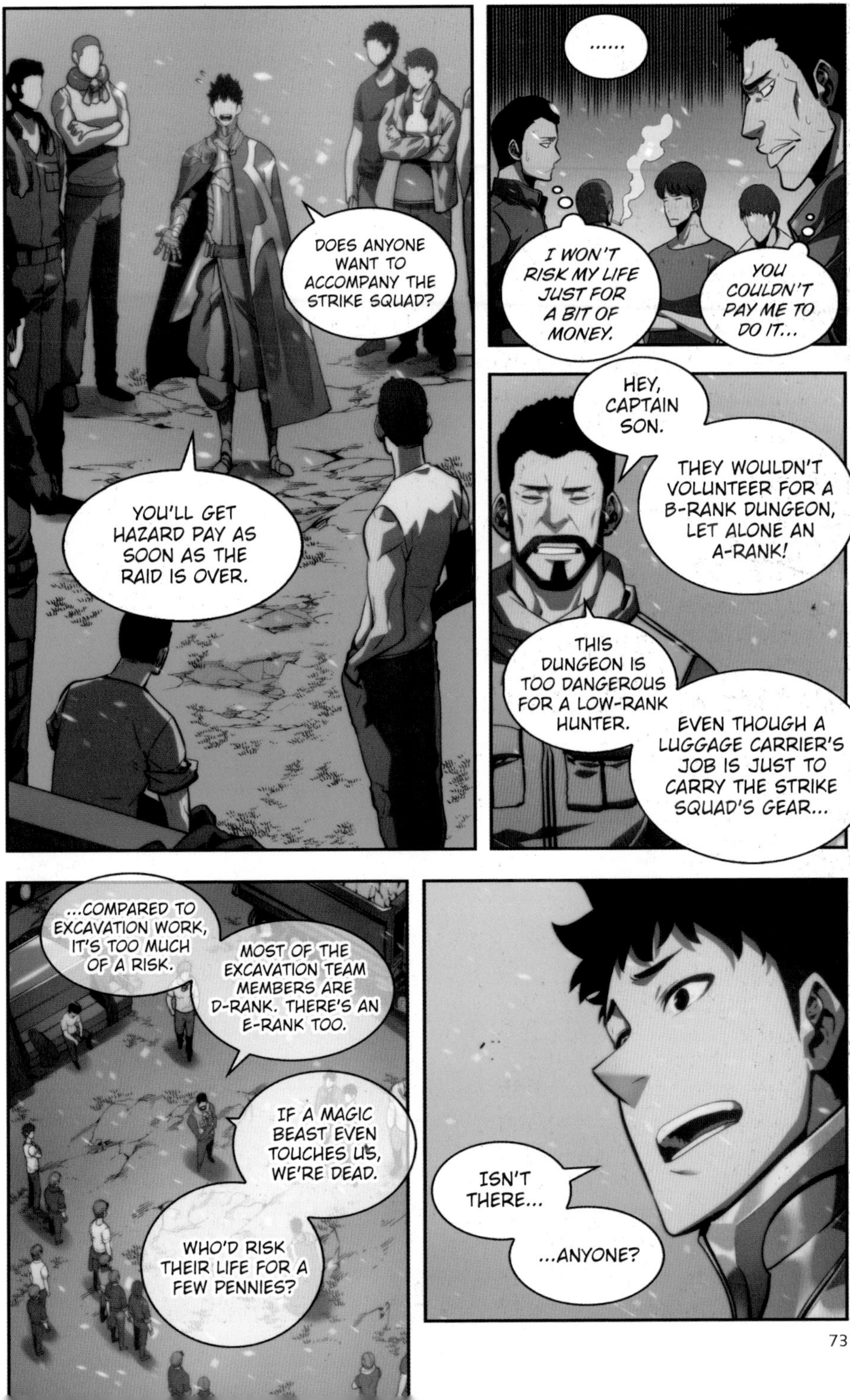
DOES ANYONE WANT TO ACCOMPANY THE STRIKE SQUAD?
YOU'LL GET HAZARD PAY AS SOON AS THE RAID IS OVER.
......
I WON'T RISK MY LIFE JUST FOR A BIT OF MONEY.
YOU COULDN'T PAY ME TO DO IT...
HEY, CAPTAIN SON.
THEY WOULDN'T VOLUNTEER FOR A B-RANK DUNGEON, LET ALONE AN A-RANK!
THIS DUNGEON IS TOO DANGEROUS FOR A LOW-RANK HUNTER.
EVEN THOUGH A LUGGAGE CARRIER'S JOB IS JUST TO CARRY THE STRIKE SQUAD'S GEAR...
...COMPARED TO EXCAVATION WORK, IT'S TOO MUCH OF A RISK.
MOST OF THE EXCAVATION TEAM MEMBERS ARE D-RANK. THERE'S AN E-RANK TOO.
IF A MAGIC BEAST EVEN TOUCHES US, WE'RE DEAD.
WHO'D RISK THEIR LIFE FOR A FEW PENNIES?
ISN'T THERE...
...ANYONE?

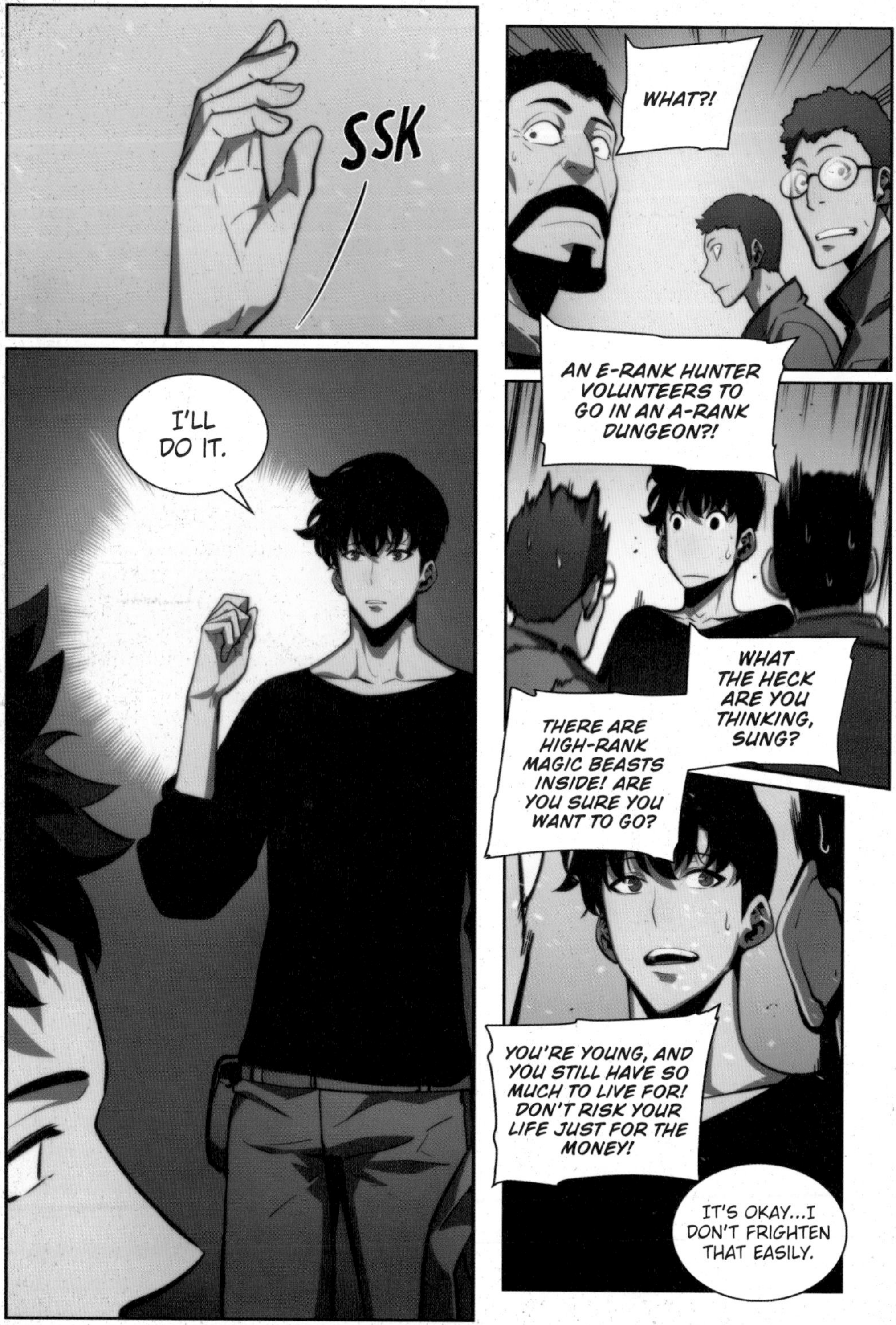
SSK
WHAT?!
I'LL DO IT.
AN E-RANK HUNTER VOLUNTEERS TO GO IN AN A-RANK DUNGEON?!
WHAT THE HECK ARE YOU THINKING, SUNG?
THERE ARE HIGH-RANK MAGIC BEASTS INSIDE! ARE YOU SURE YOU WANT TO GO?
YOU'RE YOUNG, AND YOU STILL HAVE SO MUCH TO LIVE FOR! DON'T RISK YOUR LIFE JUST FOR THE MONEY!
IT'S OKAY...I DON'T FRIGHTEN THAT EASILY.

CHAPTER 12

The S-rank Luggage Carrier

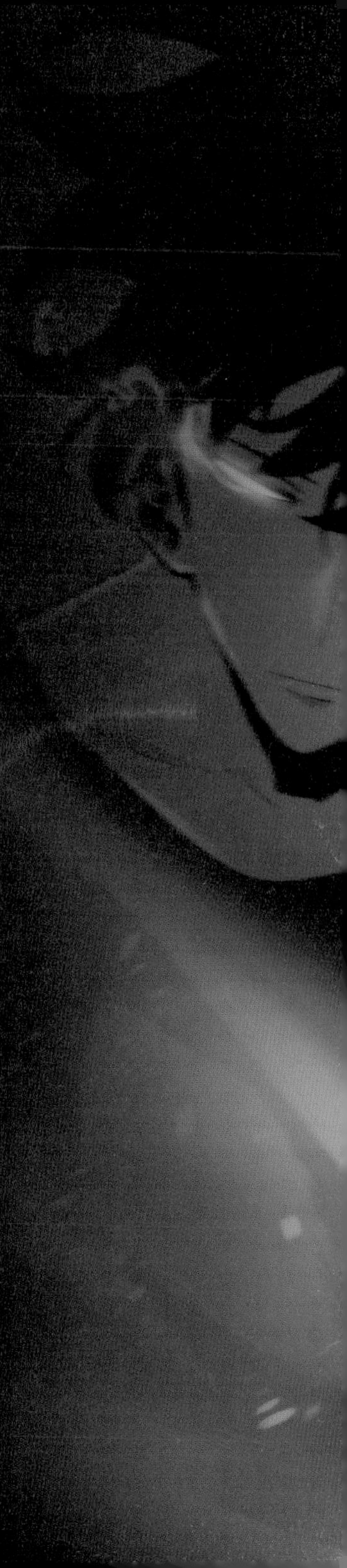

Solo Leveling

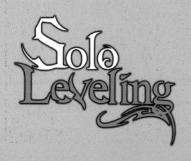

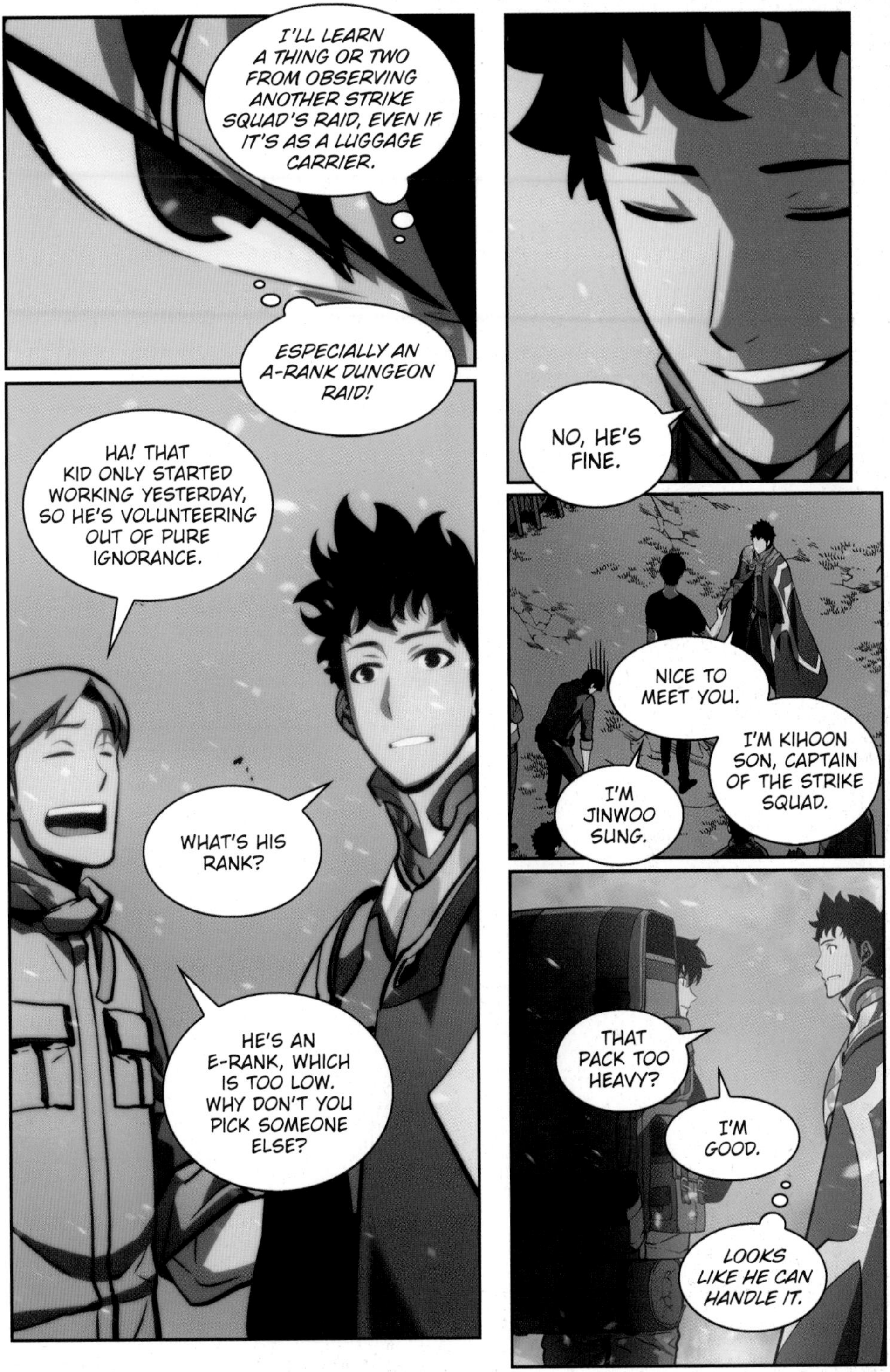
I'LL LEARN A THING OR TWO FROM OBSERVING ANOTHER STRIKE SQUAD'S RAID, EVEN IF IT'S AS A LUGGAGE CARRIER.
ESPECIALLY AN A-RANK DUNGEON RAID!
HA! THAT KID ONLY STARTED WORKING YESTERDAY, SO HE'S VOLUNTEERING OUT OF PURE IGNORANCE.
WHAT'S HIS RANK?
HE'S AN E-RANK, WHICH IS TOO LOW. WHY DON'T YOU PICK SOMEONE ELSE?
NO, HE'S FINE.
NICE TO MEET YOU.
I'M KIHOON SON, CAPTAIN OF THE STRIKE SQUAD.
I'M JINWOO SUNG.
THAT PACK TOO HEAVY?
I'M GOOD.
LOOKS LIKE HE CAN HANDLE IT.

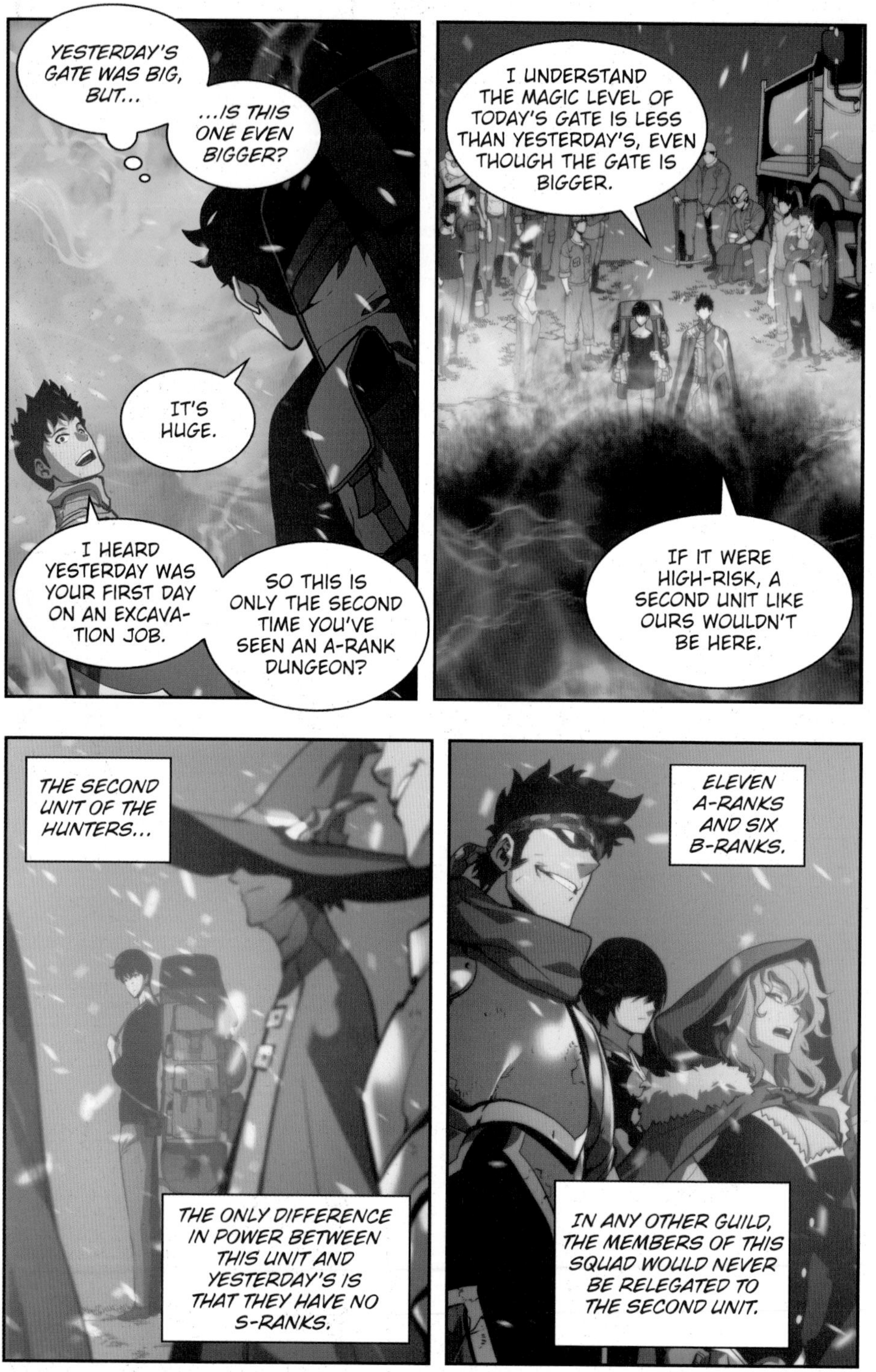
YESTERDAY'S GATE WAS BIG, BUT...
...IS THIS ONE EVEN BIGGER?
IT'S HUGE.
I HEARD YESTERDAY WAS YOUR FIRST DAY ON AN EXCAVATION JOB.
SO THIS IS ONLY THE SECOND TIME YOU'VE SEEN AN A-RANK DUNGEON?
I UNDERSTAND THE MAGIC LEVEL OF TODAY'S GATE IS LESS THAN YESTERDAY'S, EVEN THOUGH THE GATE IS BIGGER.
IF IT WERE HIGH-RISK, A SECOND UNIT LIKE OURS WOULDN'T BE HERE.
THE SECOND UNIT OF THE HUNTERS...
THE ONLY DIFFERENCE IN POWER BETWEEN THIS UNIT AND YESTERDAY'S IS THAT THEY HAVE NO S-RANKS.
ELEVEN A-RANKS AND SIX B-RANKS.
IN ANY OTHER GUILD, THE MEMBERS OF THIS SQUAD WOULD NEVER BE RELEGATED TO THE SECOND UNIT.

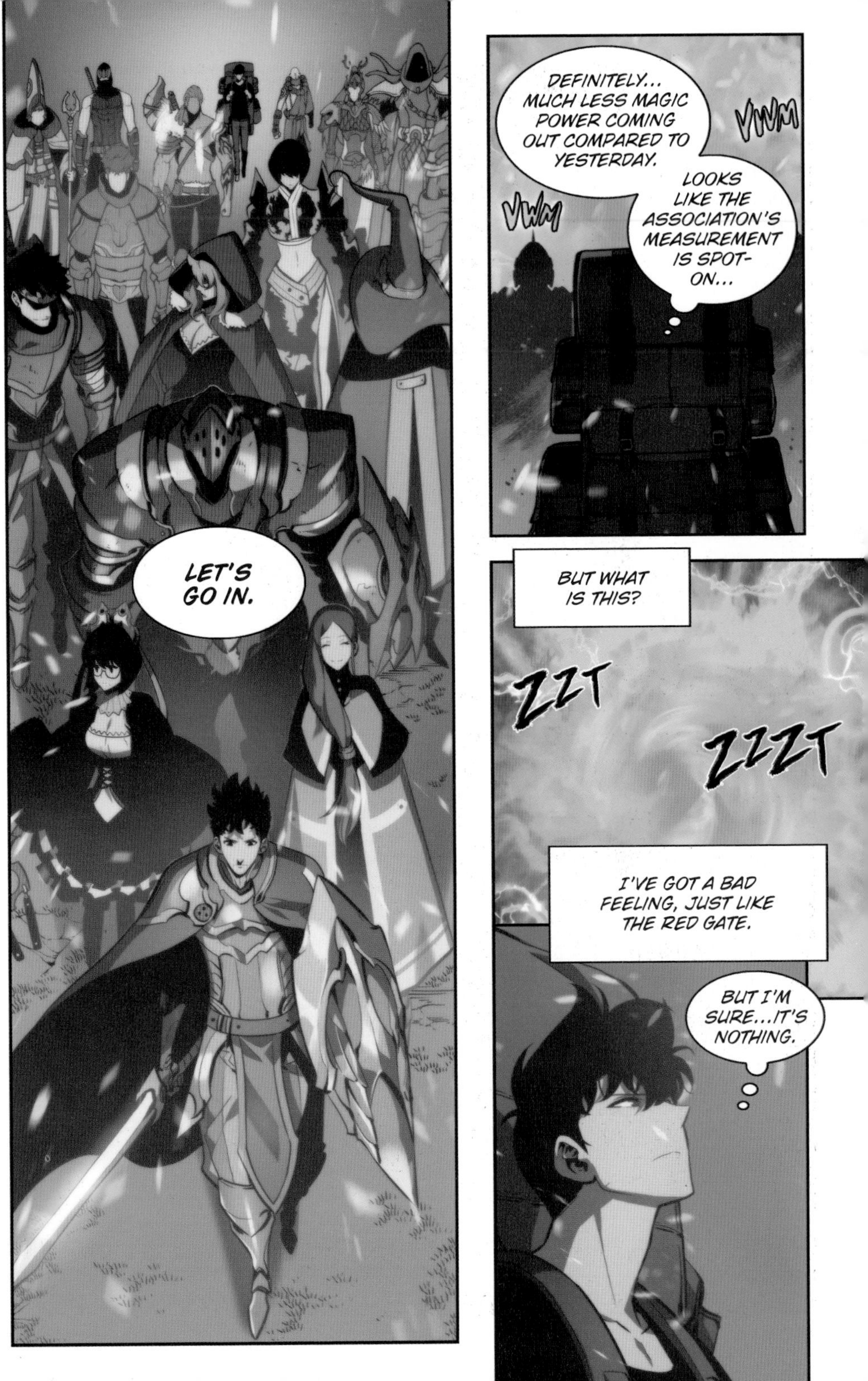
LET'S GO IN.
DEFINITELY... MUCH LESS MAGIC POWER COMING OUT COMPARED TO YESTERDAY.
VWM
LOOKS LIKE THE ASSOCIATION'S MEASUREMENT IS SPOT-ON...
VWM
BUT WHAT IS THIS?
ZZT
ZZZT
I'VE GOT A BAD FEELING, JUST LIKE THE RED GATE.
BUT I'M SURE...IT'S NOTHING.

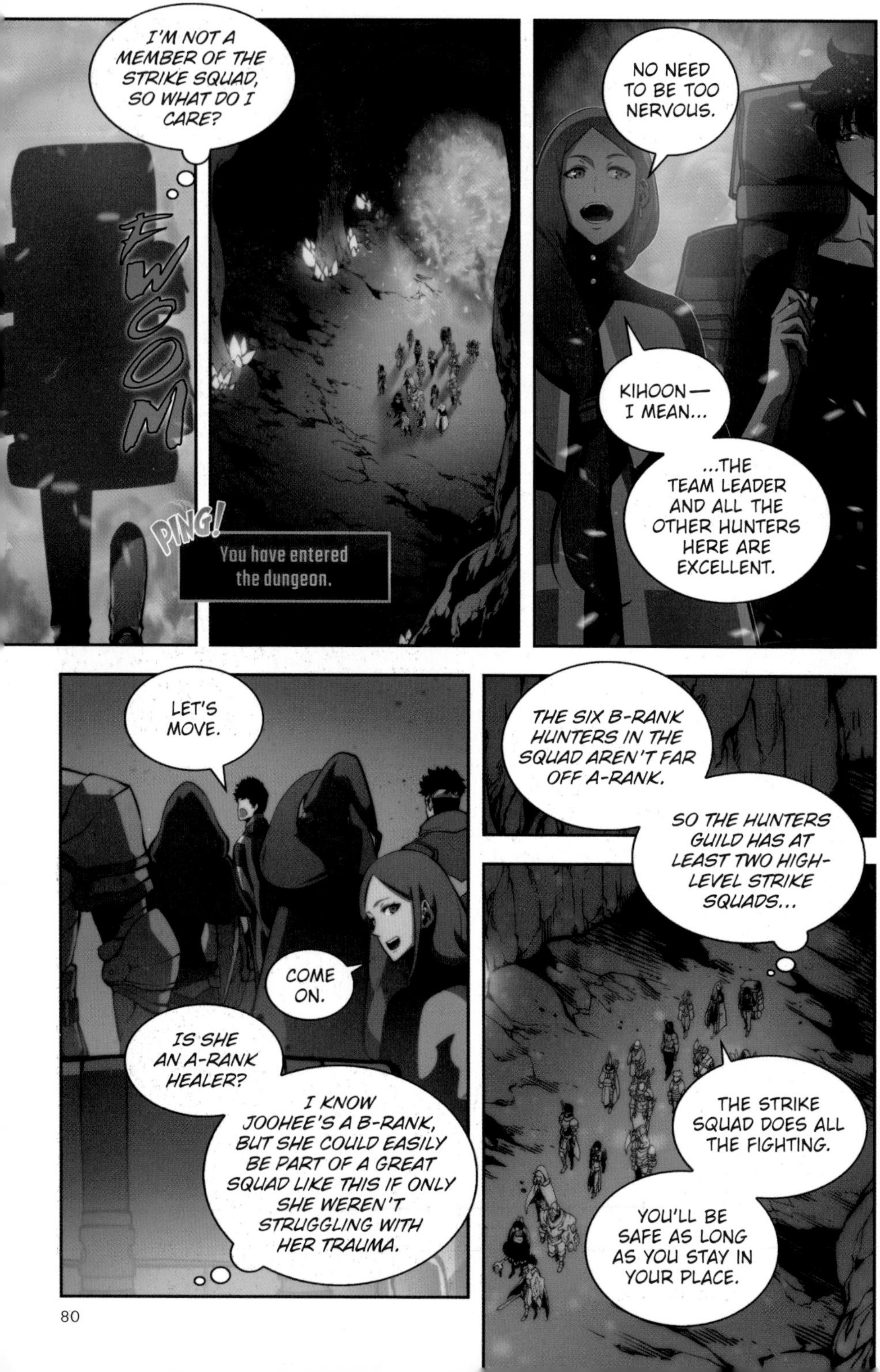
I'M NOT A MEMBER OF THE STRIKE SQUAD, SO WHAT DO I CARE?
FWOOM
PING!
You have entered the dungeon.
NO NEED TO BE TOO NERVOUS.
KIHOON— I MEAN...
...THE TEAM LEADER AND ALL THE OTHER HUNTERS HERE ARE EXCELLENT.
LET'S MOVE.
COME ON.
IS SHE AN A-RANK HEALER?
I KNOW JOOHEE'S A B-RANK, BUT SHE COULD EASILY BE PART OF A GREAT SQUAD LIKE THIS IF ONLY SHE WEREN'T STRUGGLING WITH HER TRAUMA.
THE SIX B-RANK HUNTERS IN THE SQUAD AREN'T FAR OFF A-RANK.
SO THE HUNTERS GUILD HAS AT LEAST TWO HIGH-LEVEL STRIKE SQUADS...
THE STRIKE SQUAD DOES ALL THE FIGHTING.
YOU'LL BE SAFE AS LONG AS YOU STAY IN YOUR PLACE.

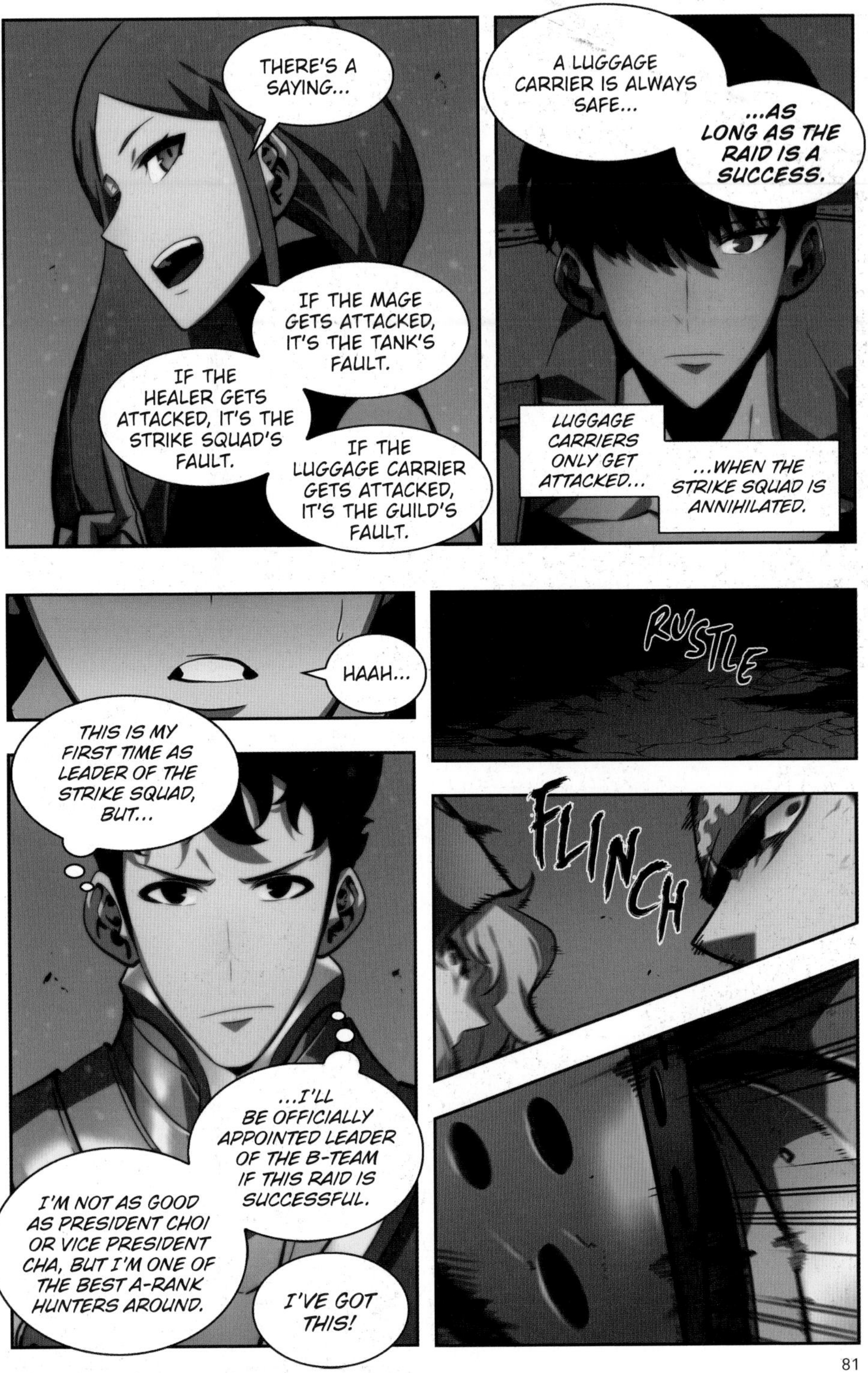
THERE'S A SAYING...
IF THE MAGE GETS ATTACKED, IT'S THE TANK'S FAULT.
IF THE HEALER GETS ATTACKED, IT'S THE STRIKE SQUAD'S FAULT.
IF THE LUGGAGE CARRIER GETS ATTACKED, IT'S THE GUILD'S FAULT.
A LUGGAGE CARRIER IS ALWAYS SAFE...
...AS LONG AS THE RAID IS A SUCCESS.
LUGGAGE CARRIERS ONLY GET ATTACKED...
...WHEN THE STRIKE SQUAD IS ANNIHILATED.
HAAH...
RUSTLE
THIS IS MY FIRST TIME AS LEADER OF THE STRIKE SQUAD, BUT...
...I'LL BE OFFICIALLY APPOINTED LEADER OF THE B-TEAM IF THIS RAID IS SUCCESSFUL.
I'M NOT AS GOOD AS PRESIDENT CHOI OR VICE PRESIDENT CHA, BUT I'M ONE OF THE BEST A-RANK HUNTERS AROUND.
I'VE GOT THIS!
FLINCH

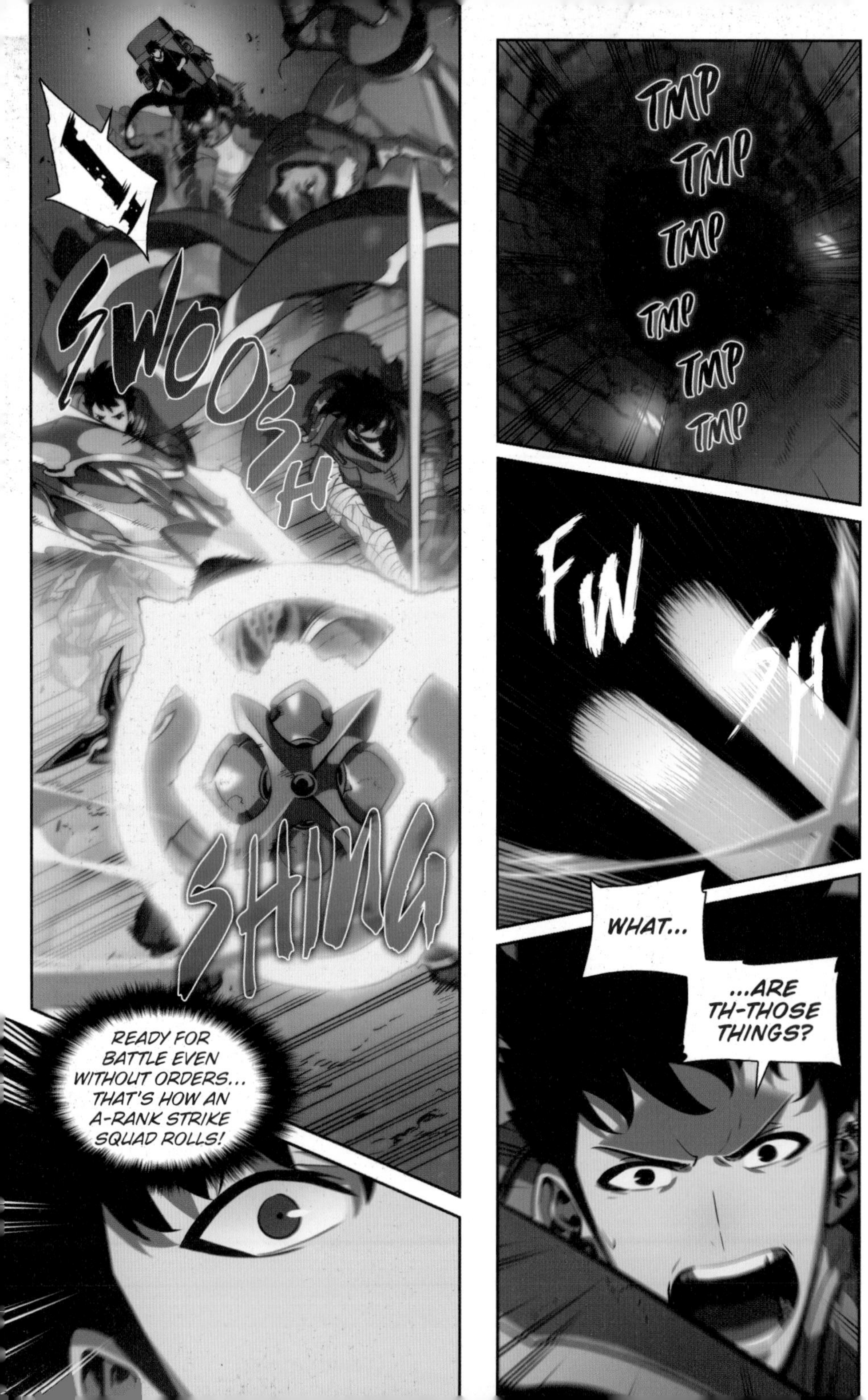
SWOOSH
SHING
READY FOR BATTLE EVEN WITHOUT ORDERS... THAT'S HOW AN A-RANK STRIKE SQUAD ROLLS!
TMP
TMP
TMP
TMP
TMP
TMP
FWSH
WHAT...
...ARE TH-THOSE THINGS?

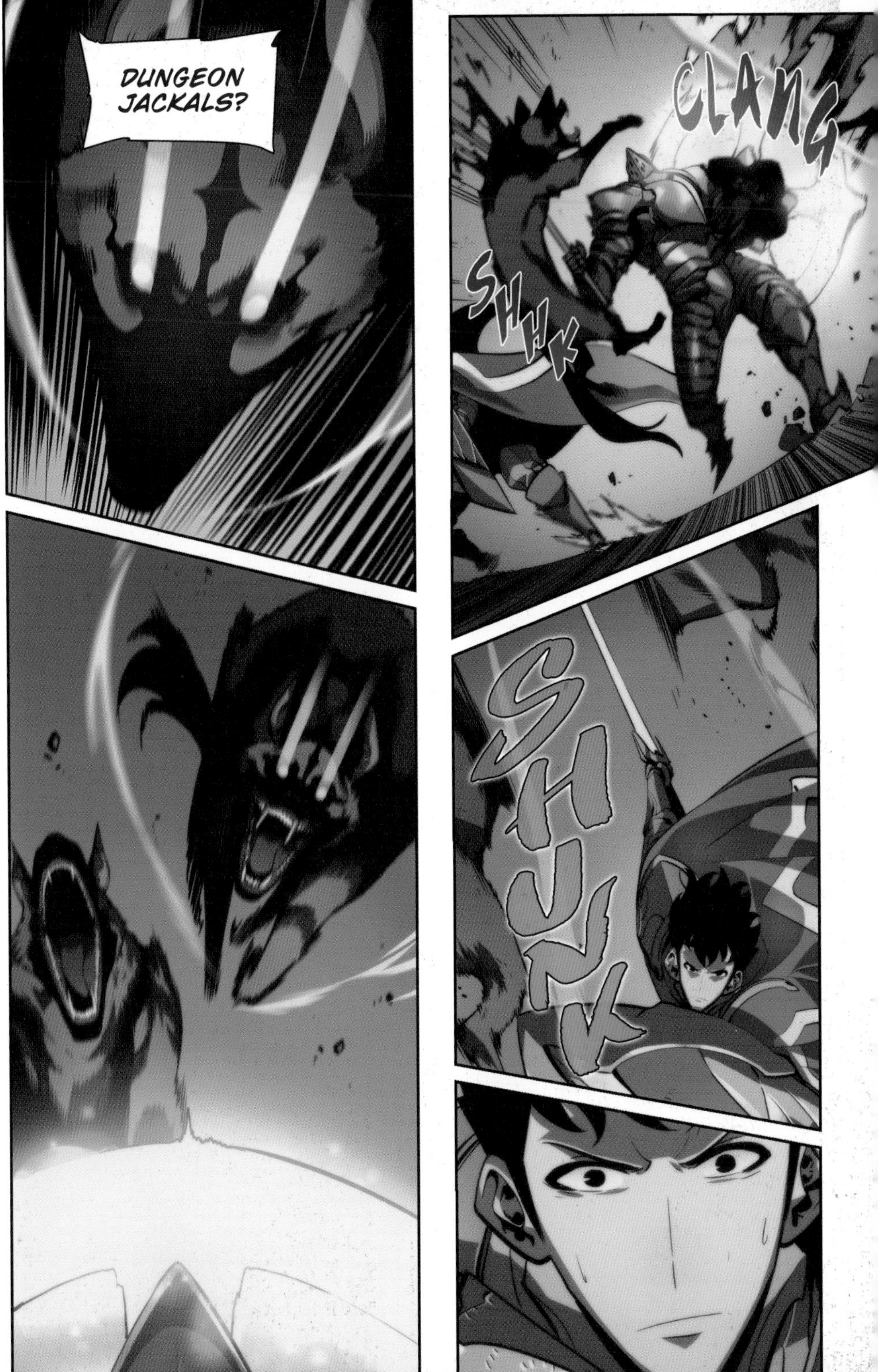
DUNGEON JACKALS?
CLANG
SHHK
SHUNK

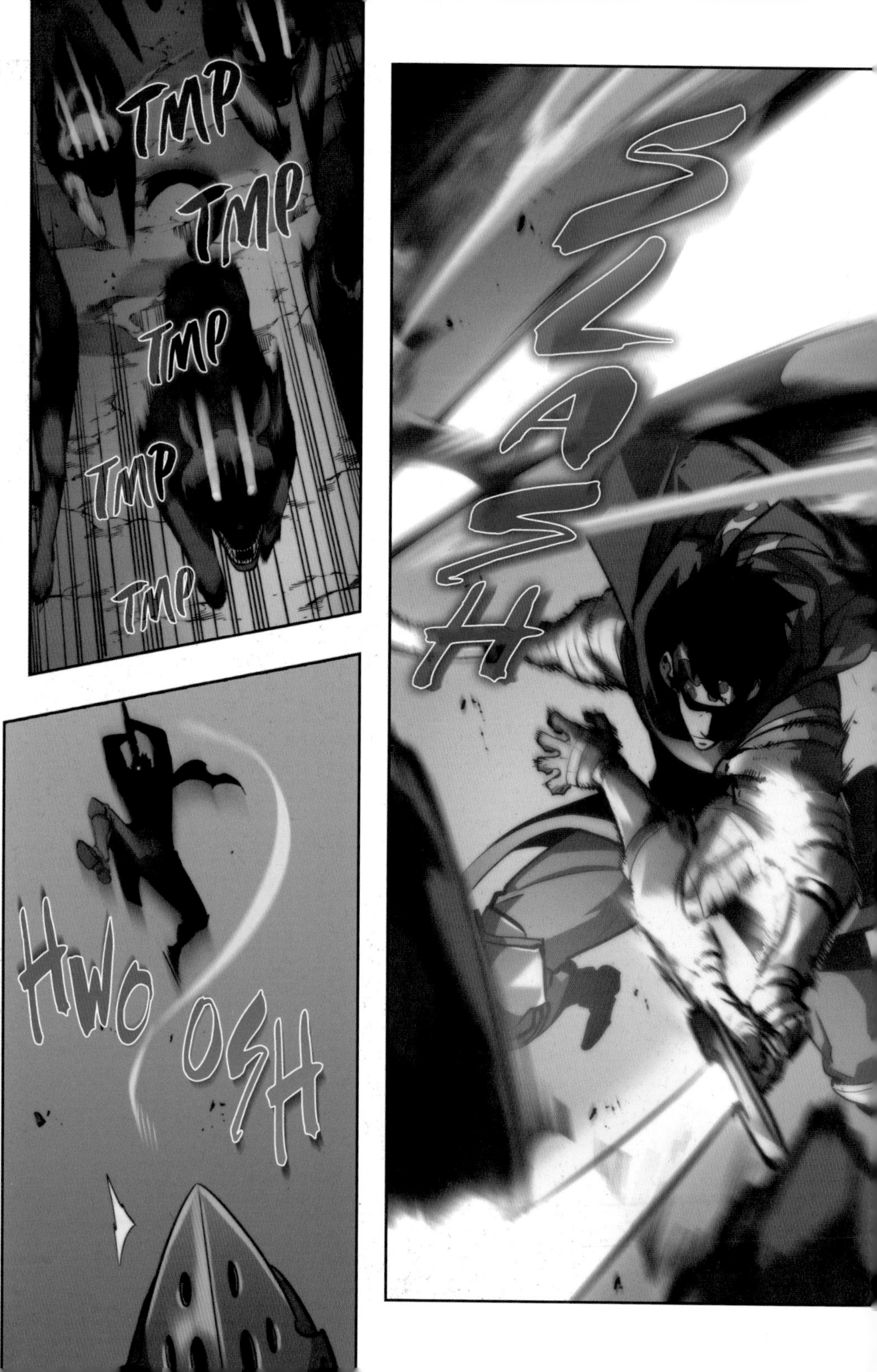
TMP
TMP
TMP
TMP
TMP
HWOOSH
SLASH

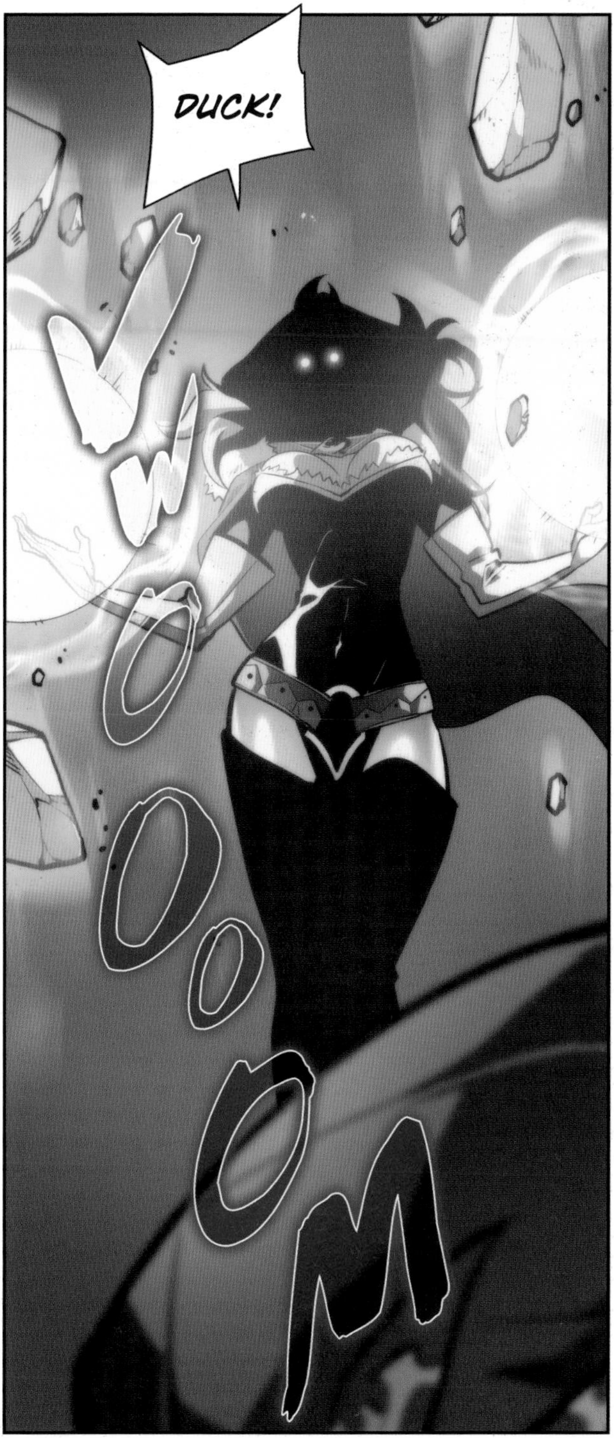
DUCK!
VWOOOOM
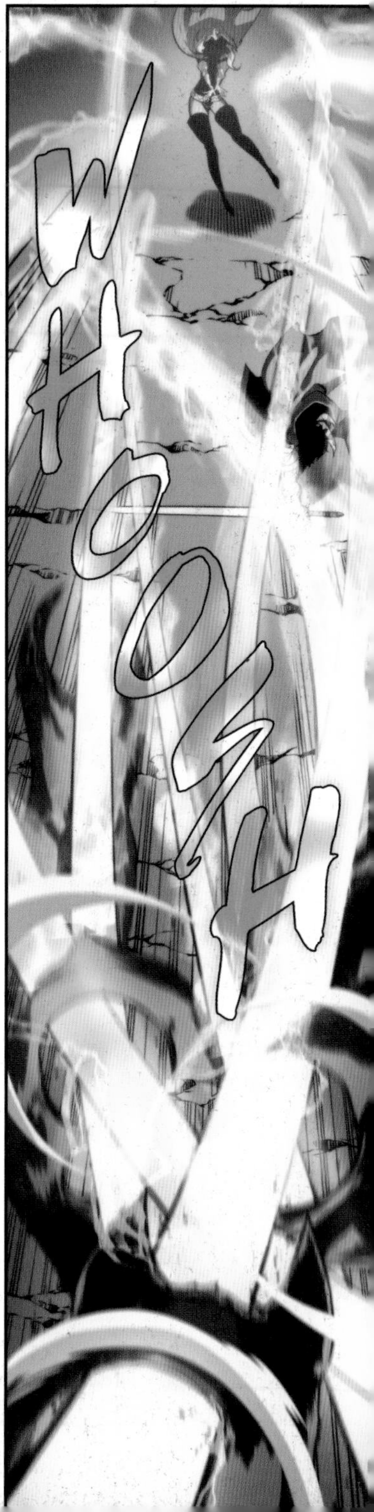
WHOOSH

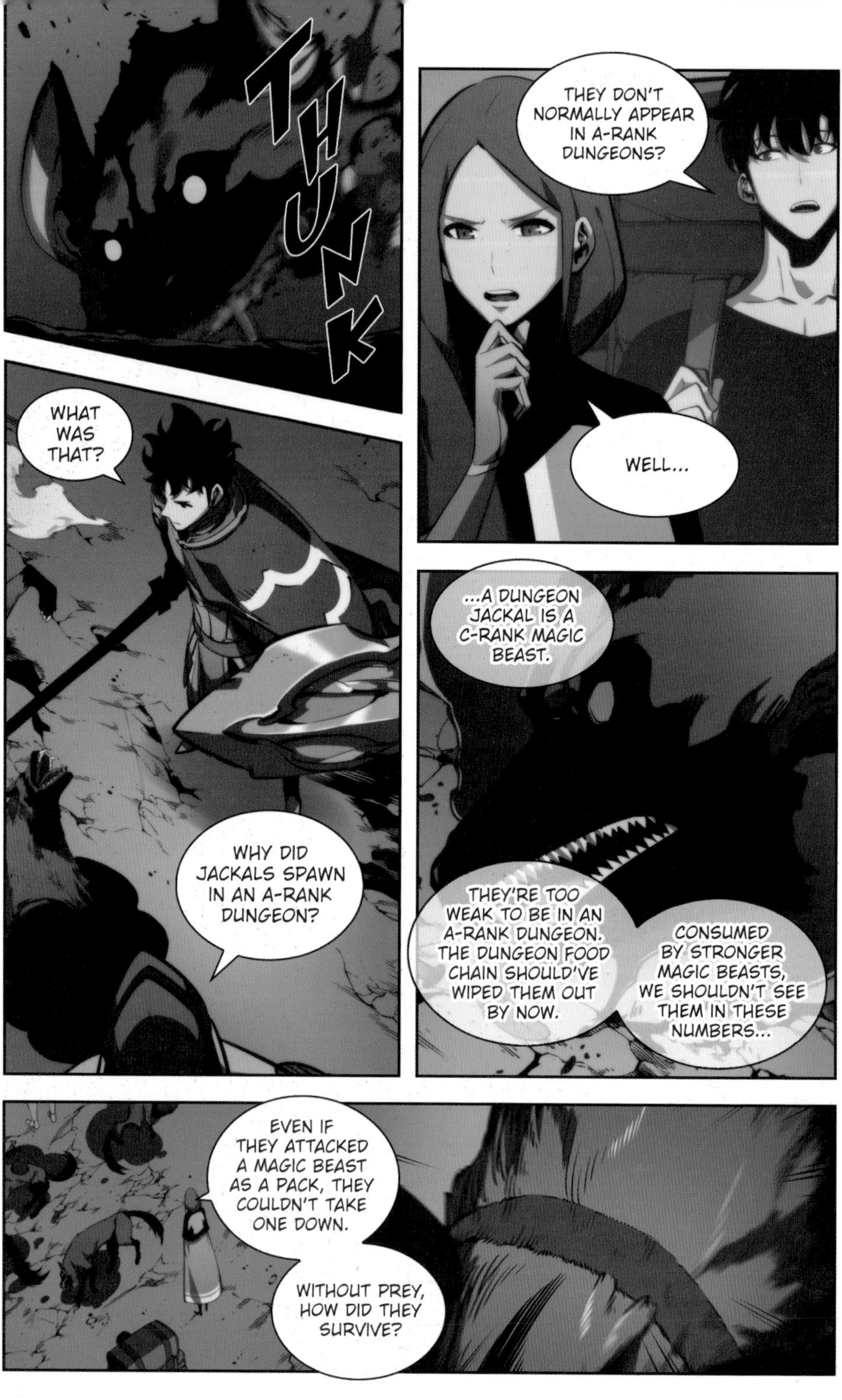
THUNK
WHAT WAS THAT?
WHY DID JACKALS SPAWN IN AN A-RANK DUNGEON?
THEY DON'T NORMALLY APPEAR IN A-RANK DUNGEONS?
WELL...
...A DUNGEON JACKAL IS A C-RANK MAGIC BEAST.
THEY'RE TOO WEAK TO BE IN AN A-RANK DUNGEON. THE DUNGEON FOOD CHAIN SHOULD'VE WIPED THEM OUT BY NOW.
CONSUMED BY STRONGER MAGIC BEASTS, WE SHOULDN'T SEE THEM IN THESE NUMBERS...
EVEN IF THEY ATTACKED A MAGIC BEAST AS A PACK, THEY COULDN'T TAKE ONE DOWN.
WITHOUT PREY, HOW DID THEY SURVIVE?

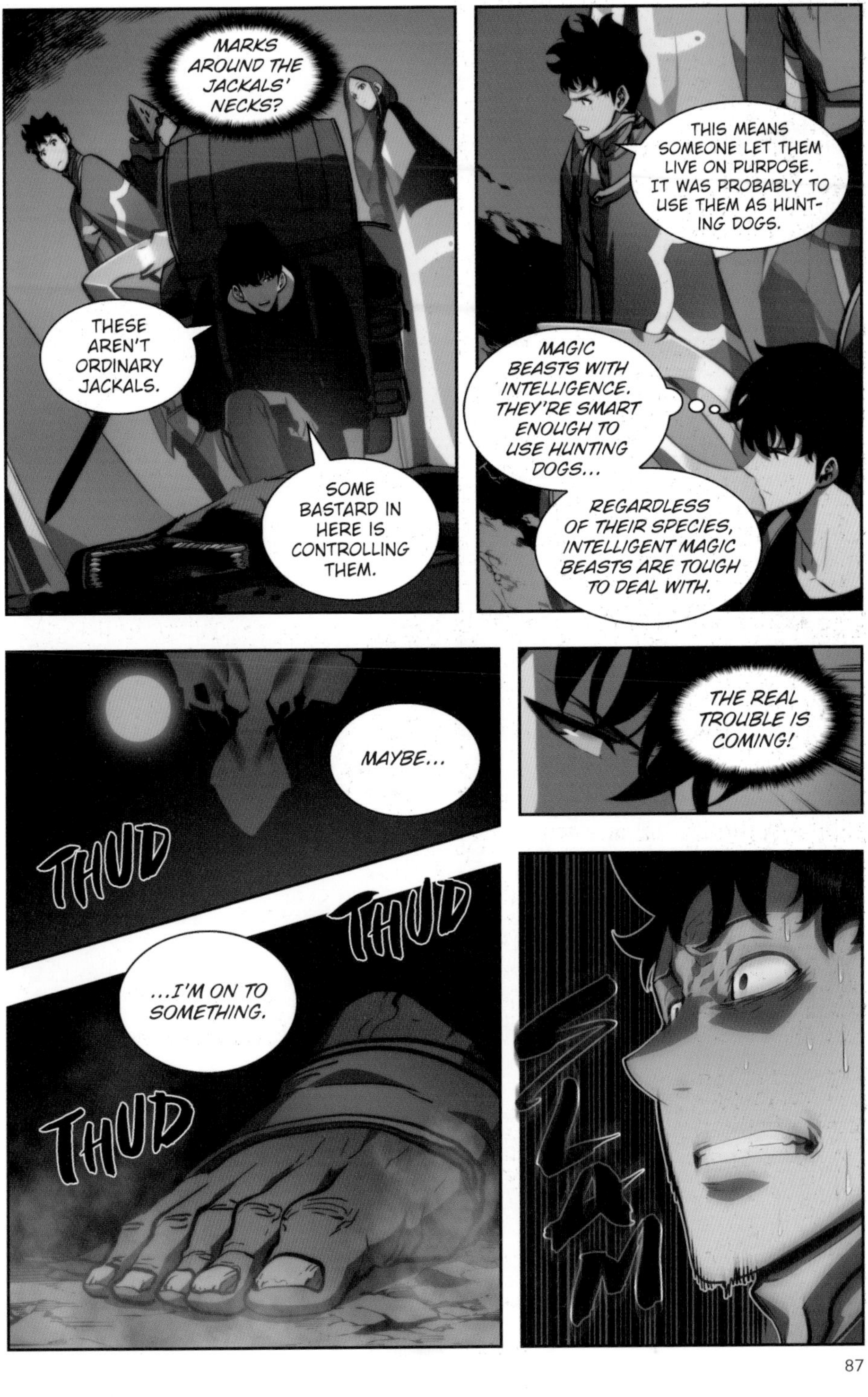
MARKS AROUND THE JACKALS' NECKS?
THESE AREN'T ORDINARY JACKALS.
SOME BASTARD IN HERE IS CONTROLLING THEM.
THIS MEANS SOMEONE LET THEM LIVE ON PURPOSE. IT WAS PROBABLY TO USE THEM AS HUNT-ING DOGS.
MAGIC BEASTS WITH INTELLIGENCE. THEY'RE SMART ENOUGH TO USE HUNTING DOGS...
REGARDLESS OF THEIR SPECIES, INTELLIGENT MAGIC BEASTS ARE TOUGH TO DEAL WITH.
MAYBE...
THUD
THUD
...I'M ON TO SOMETHING.
THUD
THE REAL TROUBLE IS COMING!

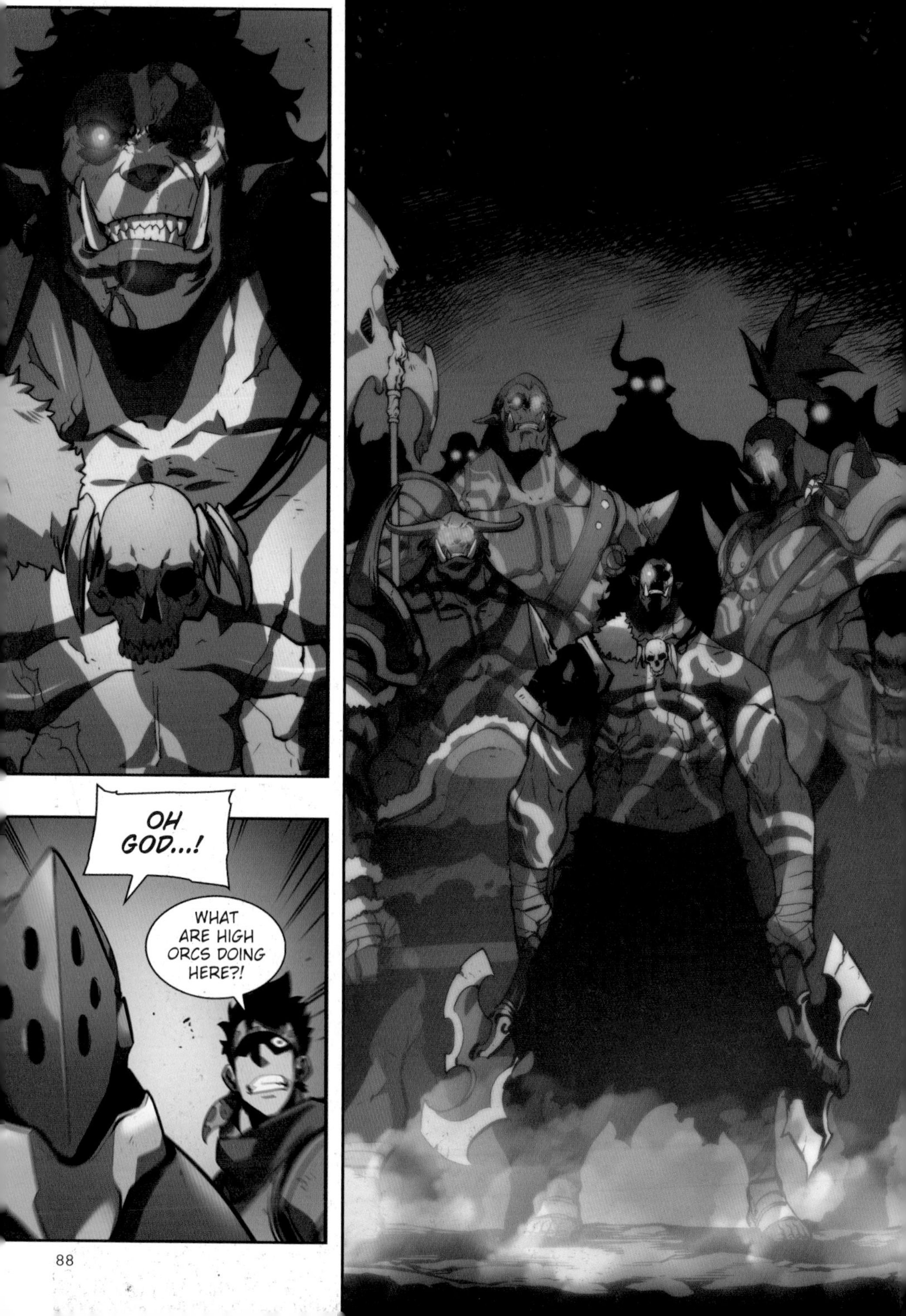
OH GOD...!
WHAT ARE HIGH ORCS DOING HERE?!

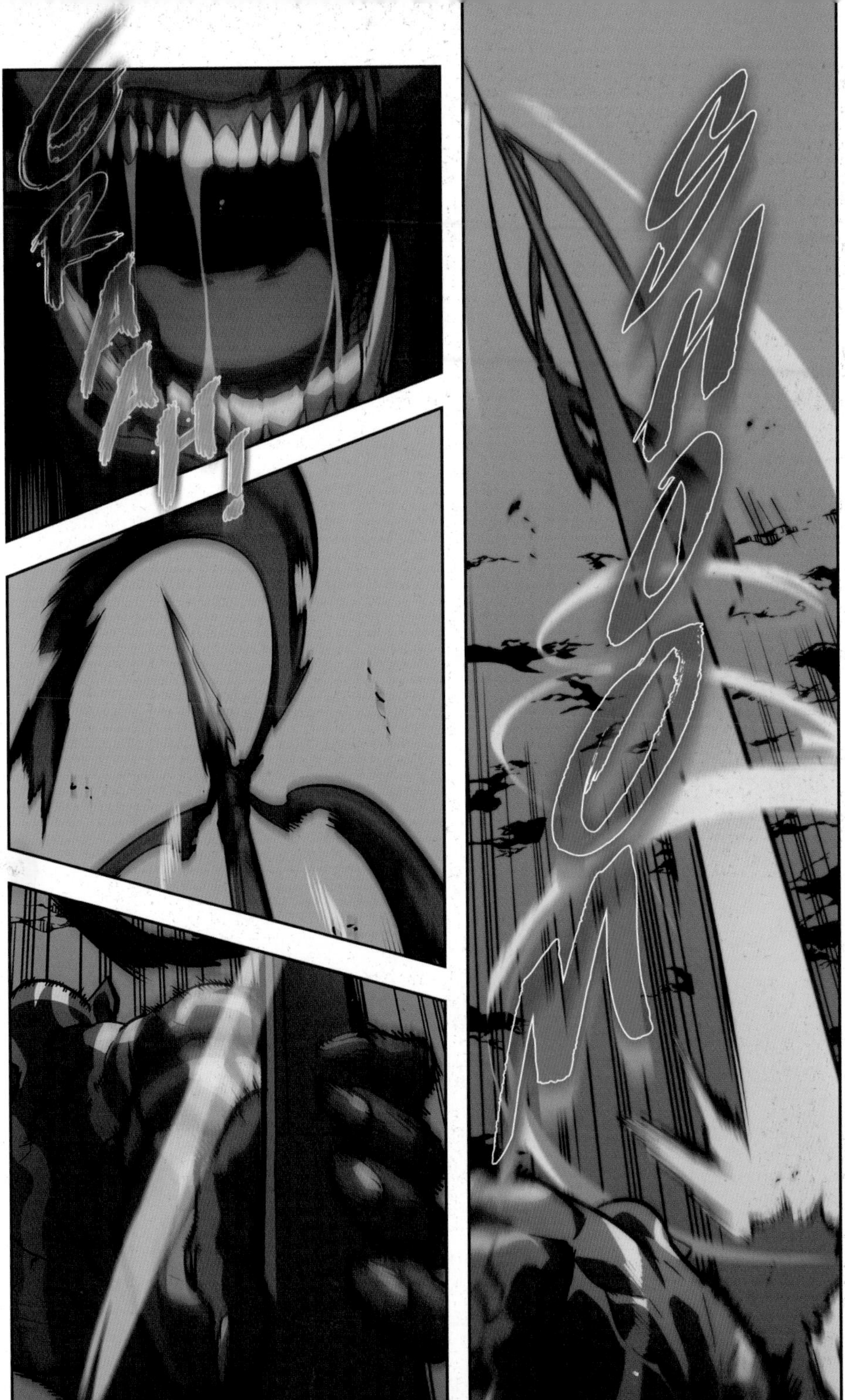
GRAAH!
GHOOM

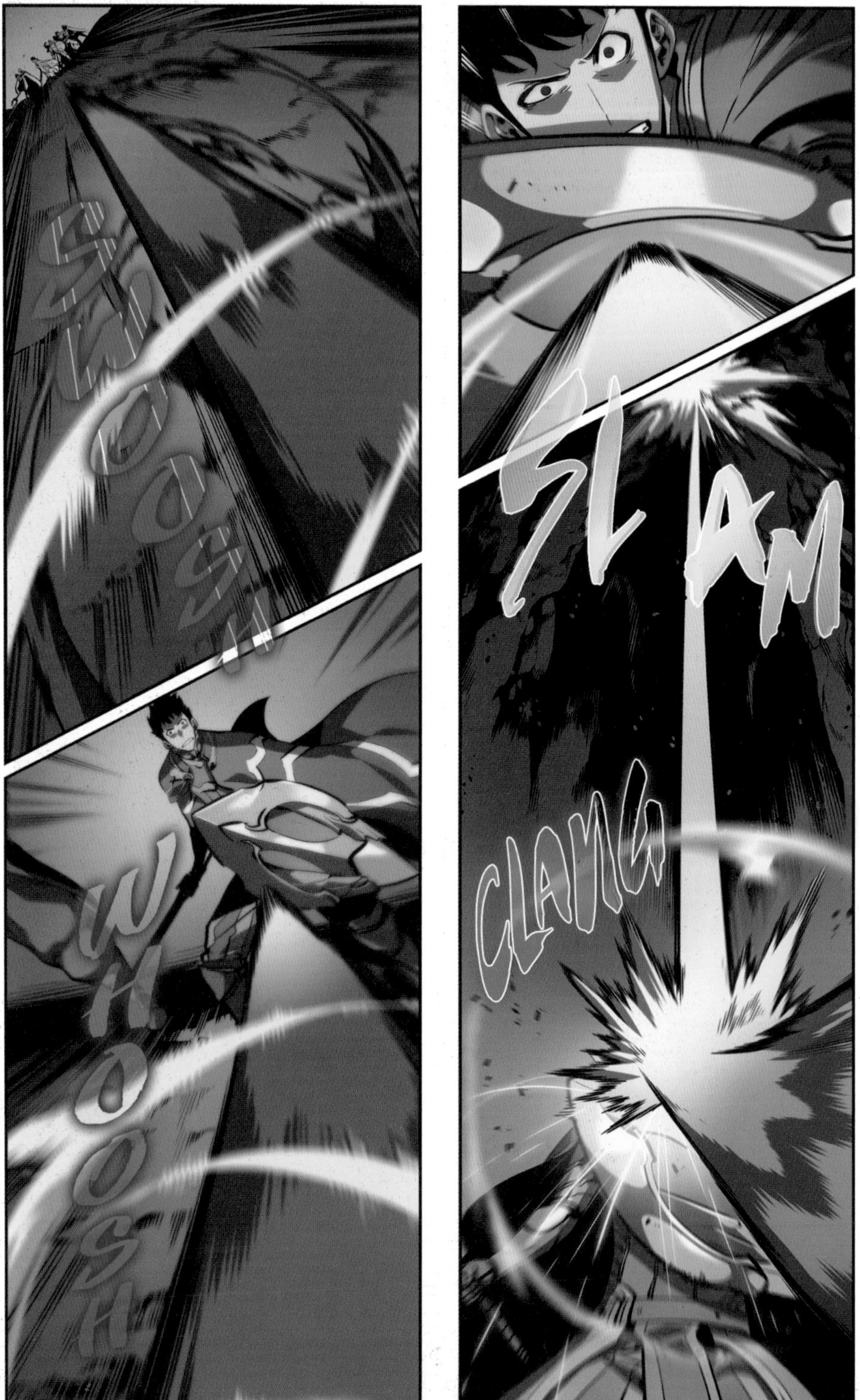
SWOOSH
WHOOOSH
SLAM
CLANG

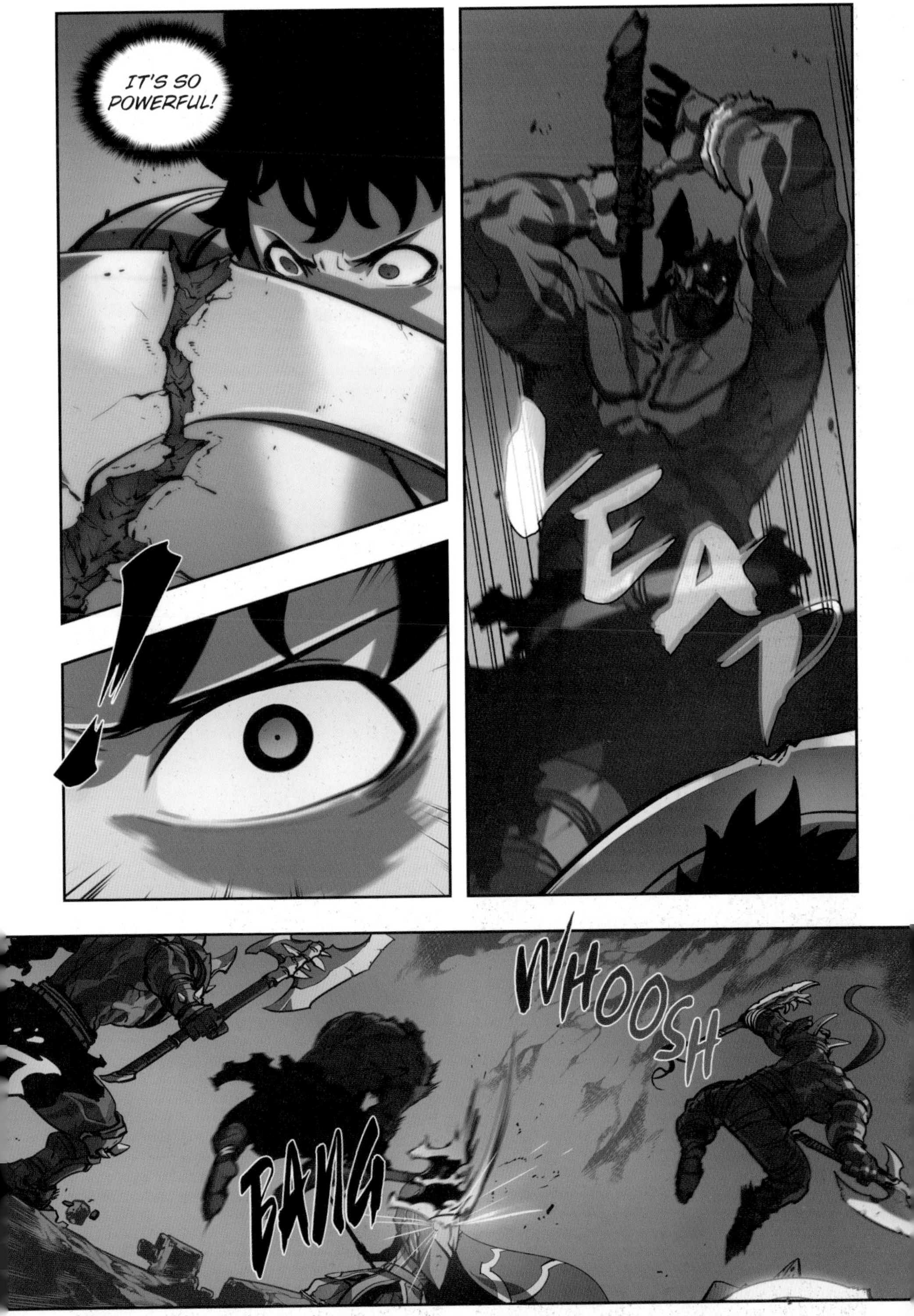
IT'S SO POWERFUL!
!
WHOOSH
BANG

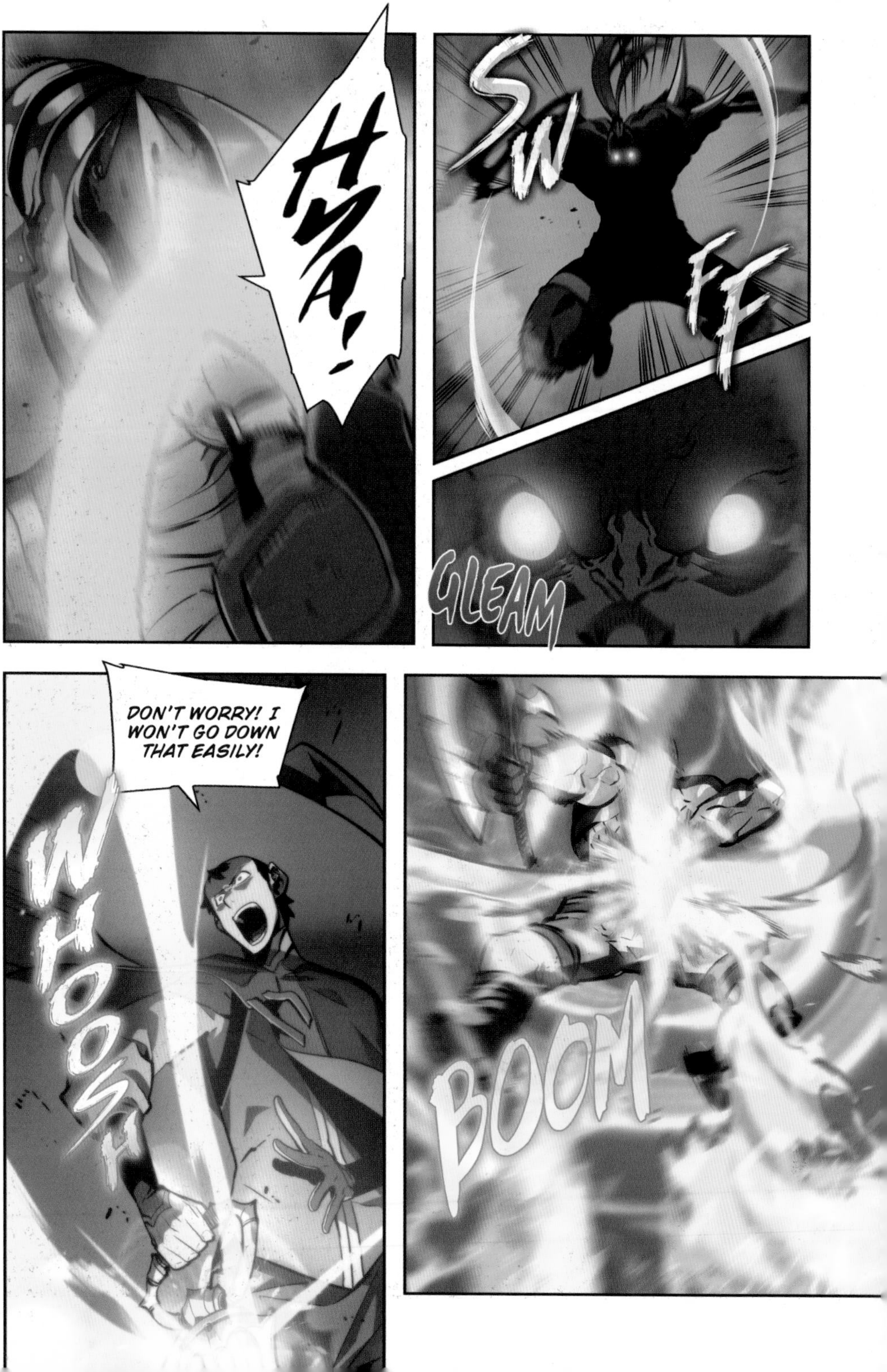
HYA!!
SWFF
GLEAM
DON'T WORRY! I WON'T GO DOWN THAT EASILY!
WHOOSH
BOOM

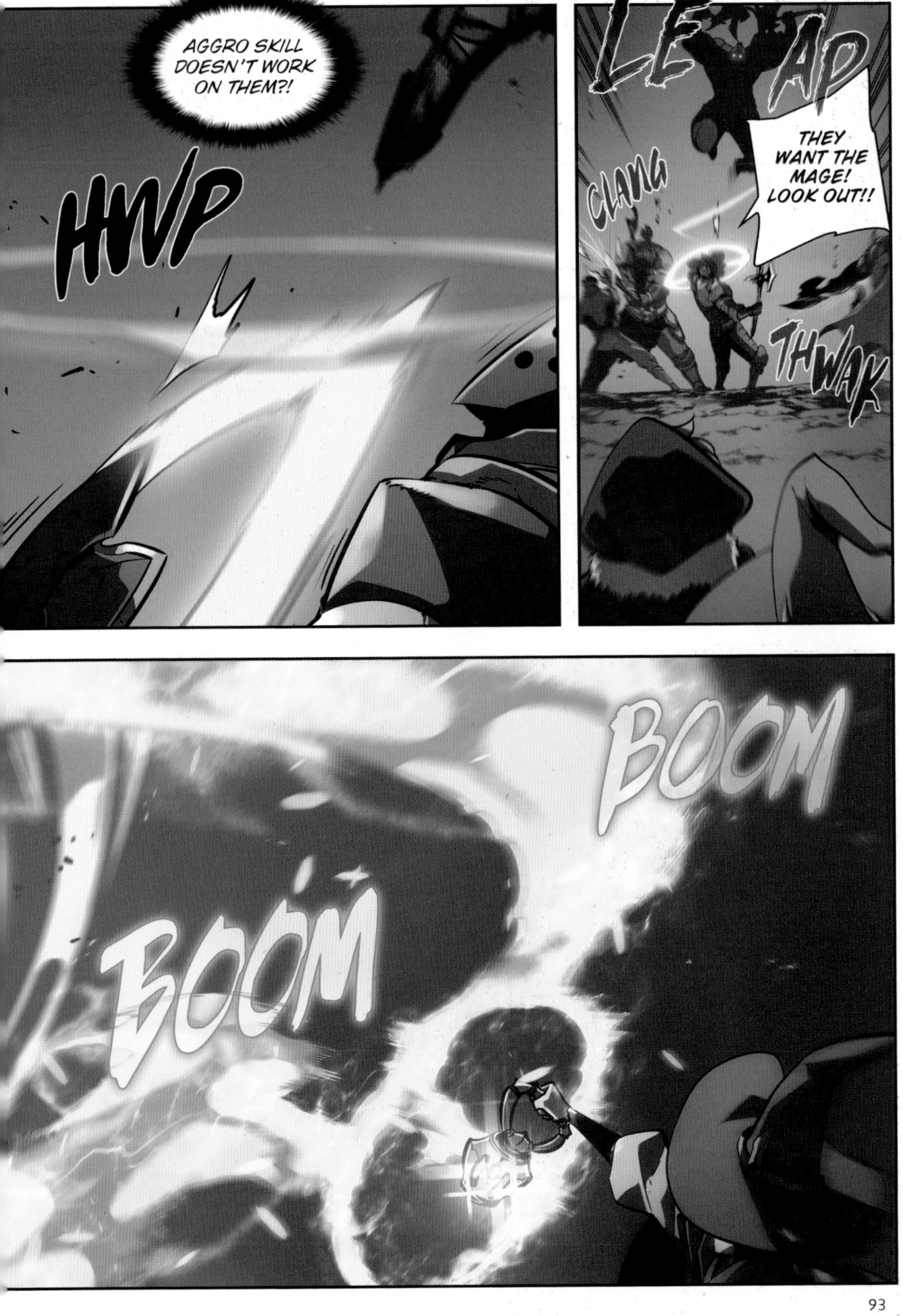
AGGRO SKILL DOESN'T WORK ON THEM?!
HWIP
LEAP
CLANG
THEY WANT THE MAGE! LOOK OUT!!
THWAK
BOOM
BOOM

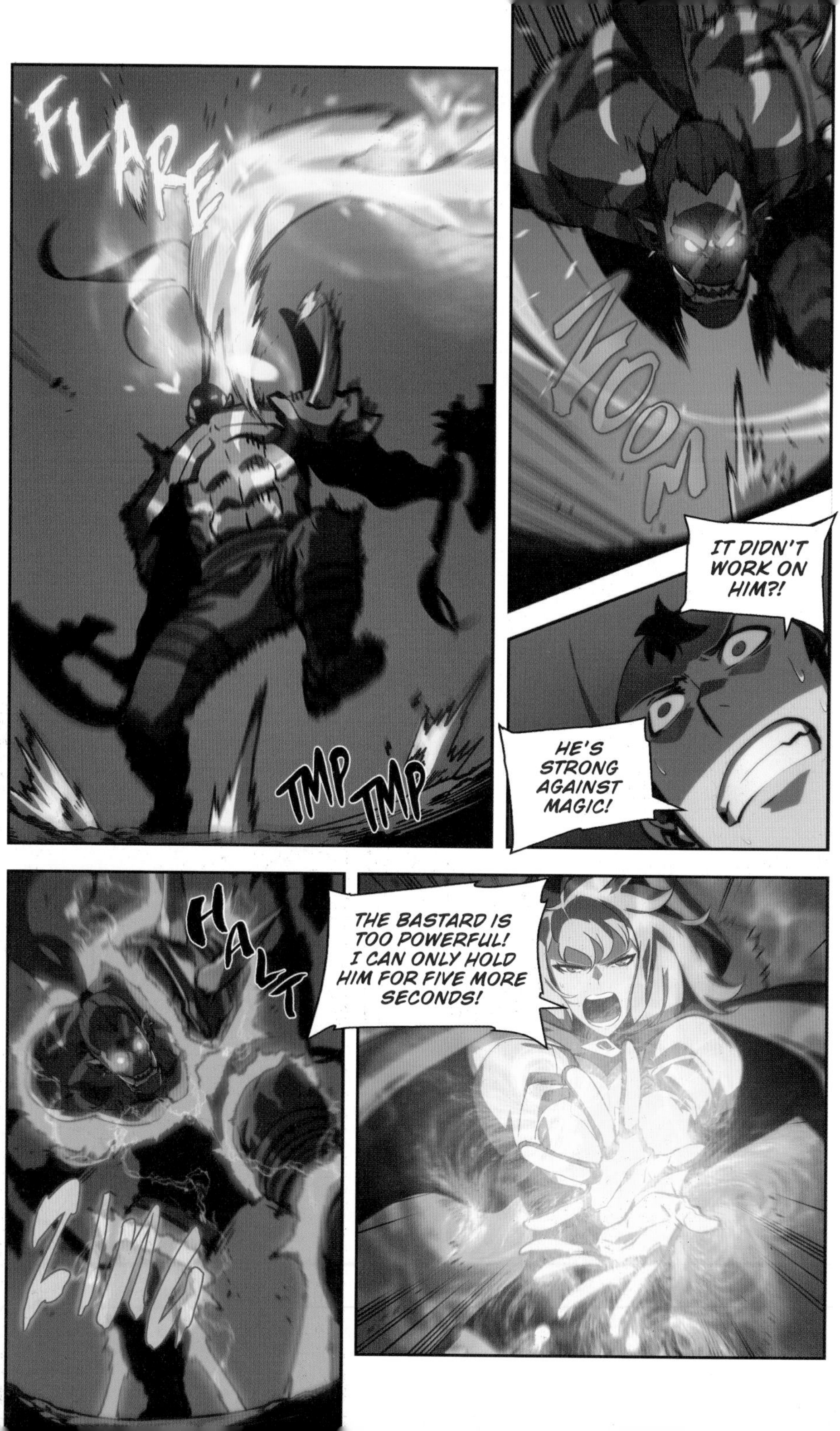
FLARE
TMP TMP
VOOM
IT DIDN'T WORK ON HIM?!
HE'S STRONG AGAINST MAGIC!
HALT
ZING
THE BASTARD IS TOO POWERFUL! I CAN ONLY HOLD HIM FOR FIVE MORE SECONDS!

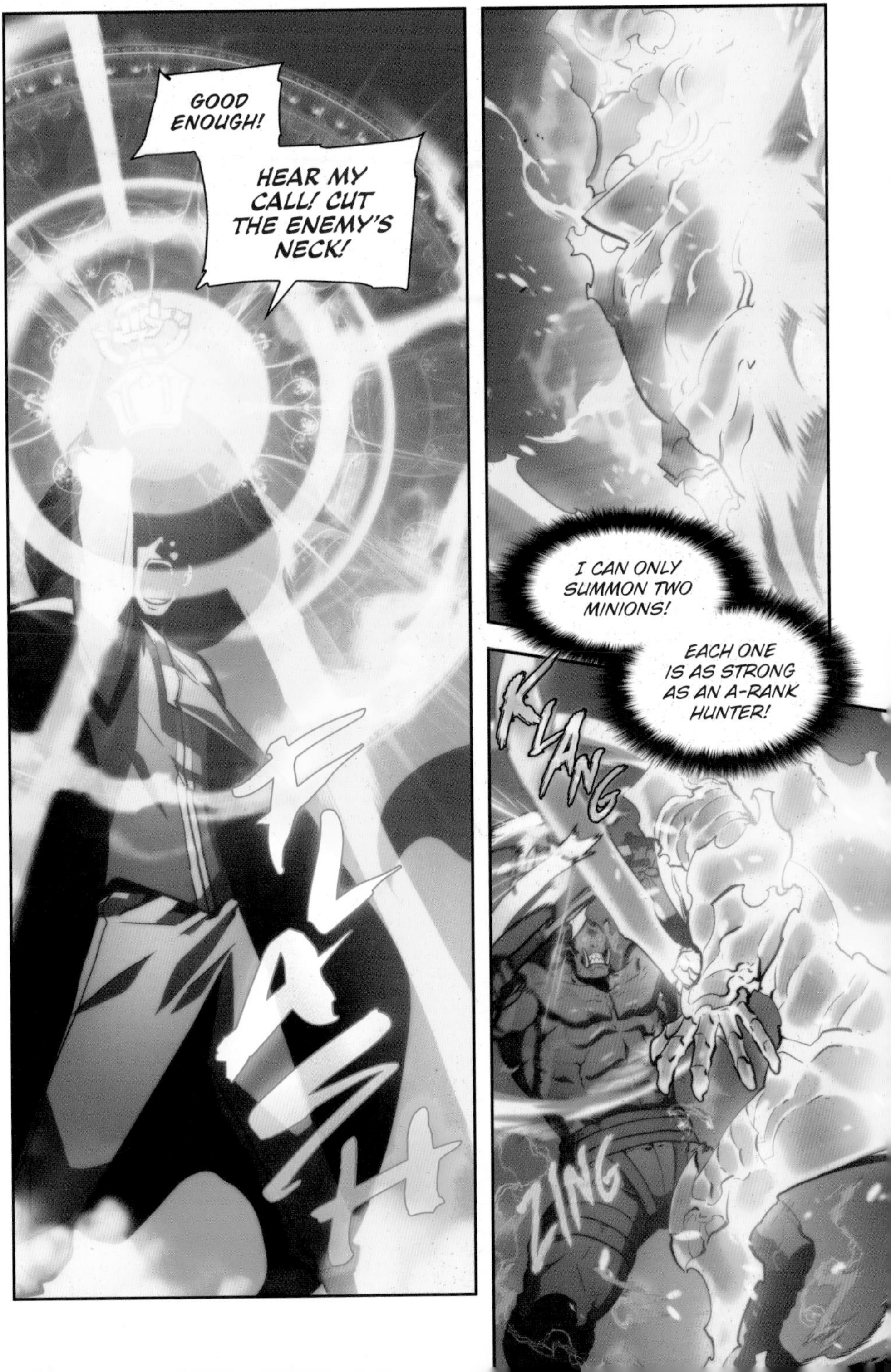
GOOD ENOUGH!
HEAR MY CALL! CUT THE ENEMY'S NECK!
FLASH
I CAN ONLY SUMMON TWO MINIONS!
EACH ONE IS AS STRONG AS AN A-RANK HUNTER!
KLANG
ZING

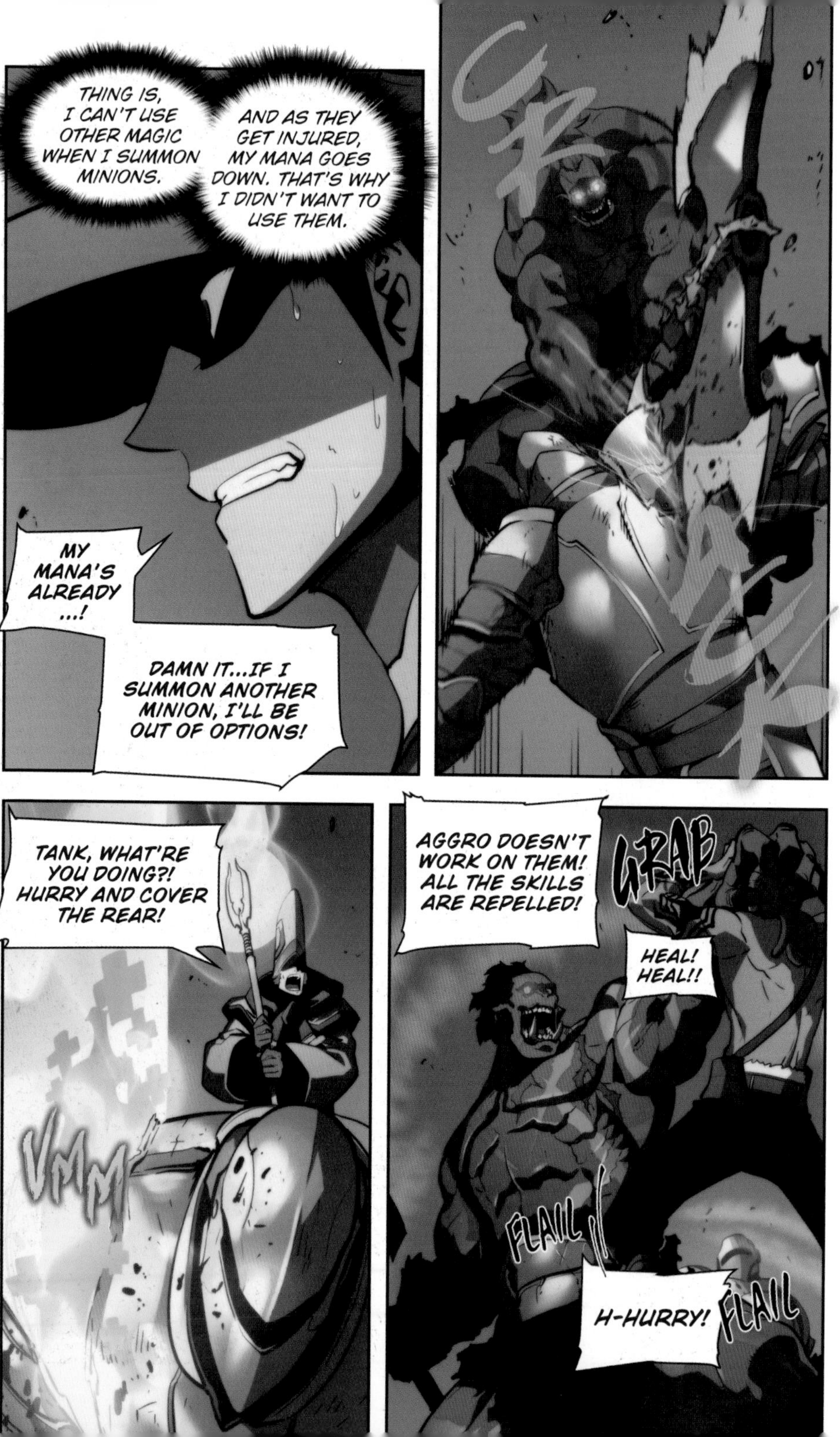
THING IS, I CAN'T USE OTHER MAGIC WHEN I SUMMON MINIONS.
AND AS THEY GET INJURED, MY MANA GOES DOWN. THAT'S WHY I DIDN'T WANT TO USE THEM.
MY MANA'S ALREADY ...!
DAMN IT...IF I SUMMON ANOTHER MINION, I'LL BE OUT OF OPTIONS!
TANK, WHAT'RE YOU DOING?! HURRY AND COVER THE REAR!
VMM
AGGRO DOESN'T WORK ON THEM! ALL THE SKILLS ARE REPELLED!
GRAB
HEAL! HEAL!!
FLAIL
H-HURRY!
FLAIL

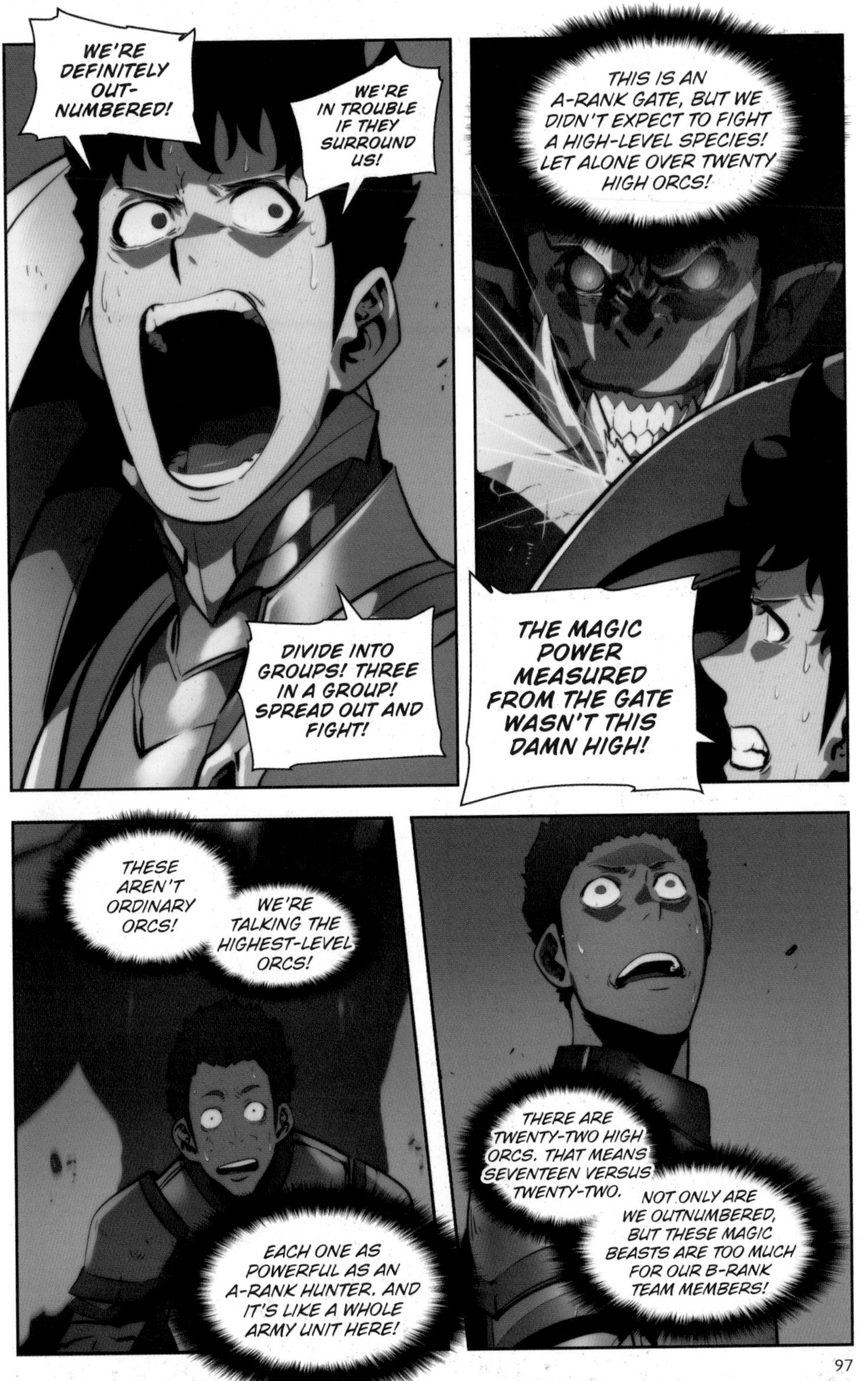
WE'RE DEFINITELY OUT-NUMBERED!
WE'RE IN TROUBLE IF THEY SURROUND US!
DIVIDE INTO GROUPS! THREE IN A GROUP! SPREAD OUT AND FIGHT!
THIS IS AN A-RANK GATE, BUT WE DIDN'T EXPECT TO FIGHT A HIGH-LEVEL SPECIES! LET ALONE OVER TWENTY HIGH ORCS!
THE MAGIC POWER MEASURED FROM THE GATE WASN'T THIS DAMN HIGH!
THESE AREN'T ORDINARY ORCS!
WE'RE TALKING THE HIGHEST-LEVEL ORCS!
EACH ONE AS POWERFUL AS AN A-RANK HUNTER. AND IT'S LIKE A WHOLE ARMY UNIT HERE!
THERE ARE TWENTY-TWO HIGH ORCS. THAT MEANS SEVENTEEN VERSUS TWENTY-TWO.
NOT ONLY ARE WE OUTNUMBERED, BUT THESE MAGIC BEASTS ARE TOO MUCH FOR OUR B-RANK TEAM MEMBERS!

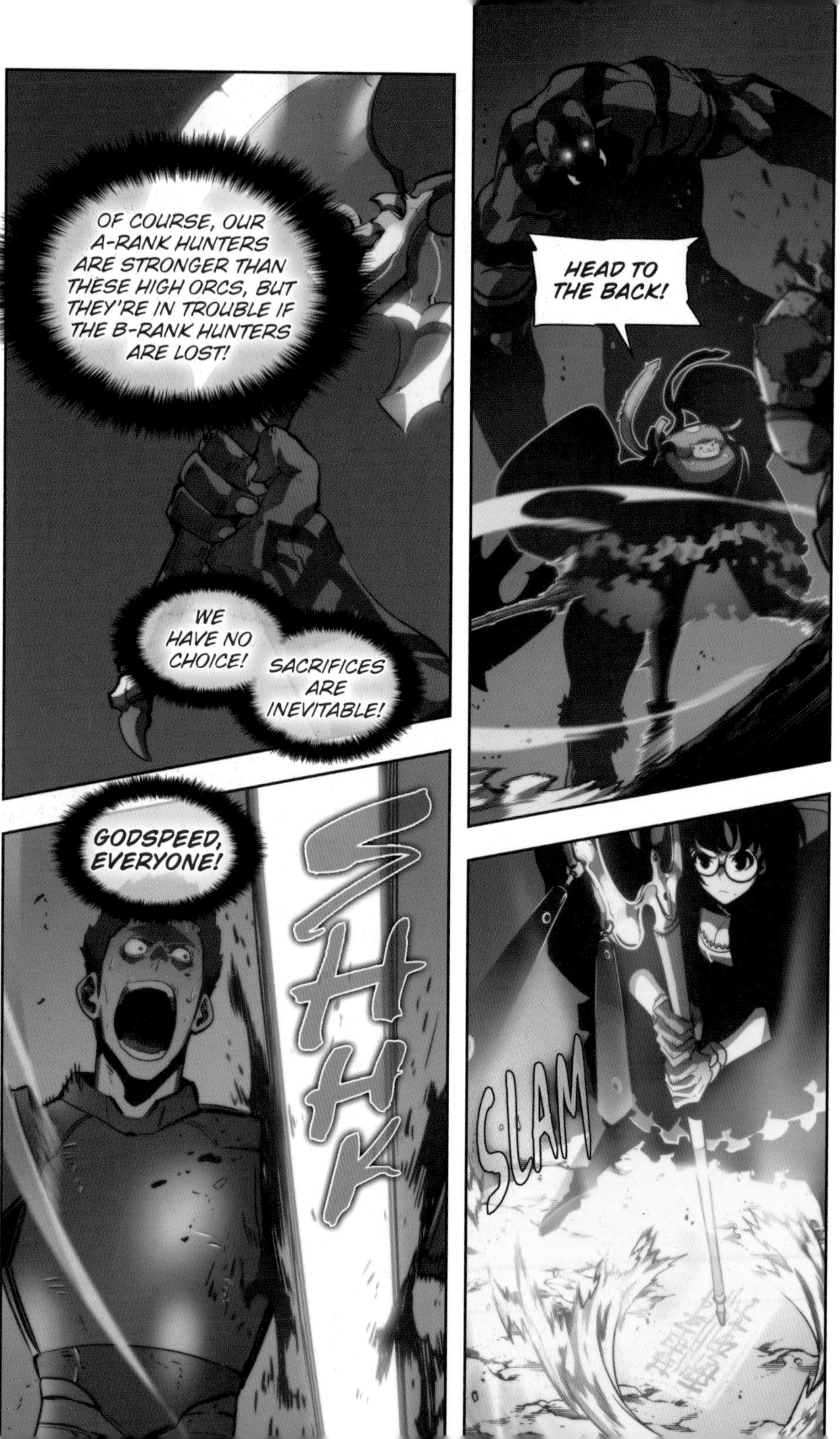
OF COURSE, OUR A-RANK HUNTERS ARE STRONGER THAN THESE HIGH ORCS, BUT THEY'RE IN TROUBLE IF THE B-RANK HUNTERS ARE LOST!
WE HAVE NO CHOICE!
SACRIFICES ARE INEVITABLE!
HEAD TO THE BACK!
GODSPEED, EVERYONE!
SHHK
SLAM

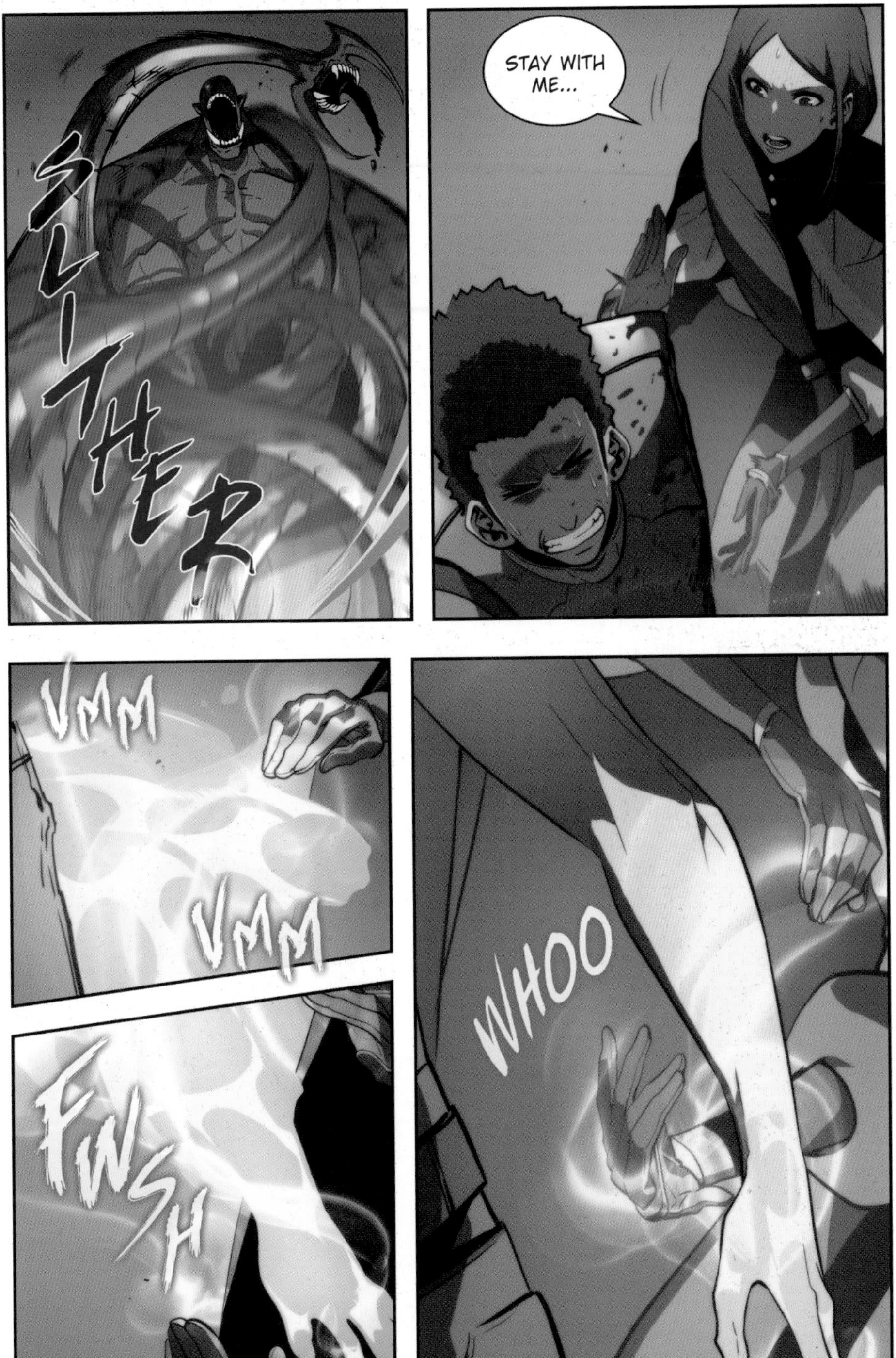
SLITHER
STAY WITH ME...
VMM
VMM
FWSH
WHOO

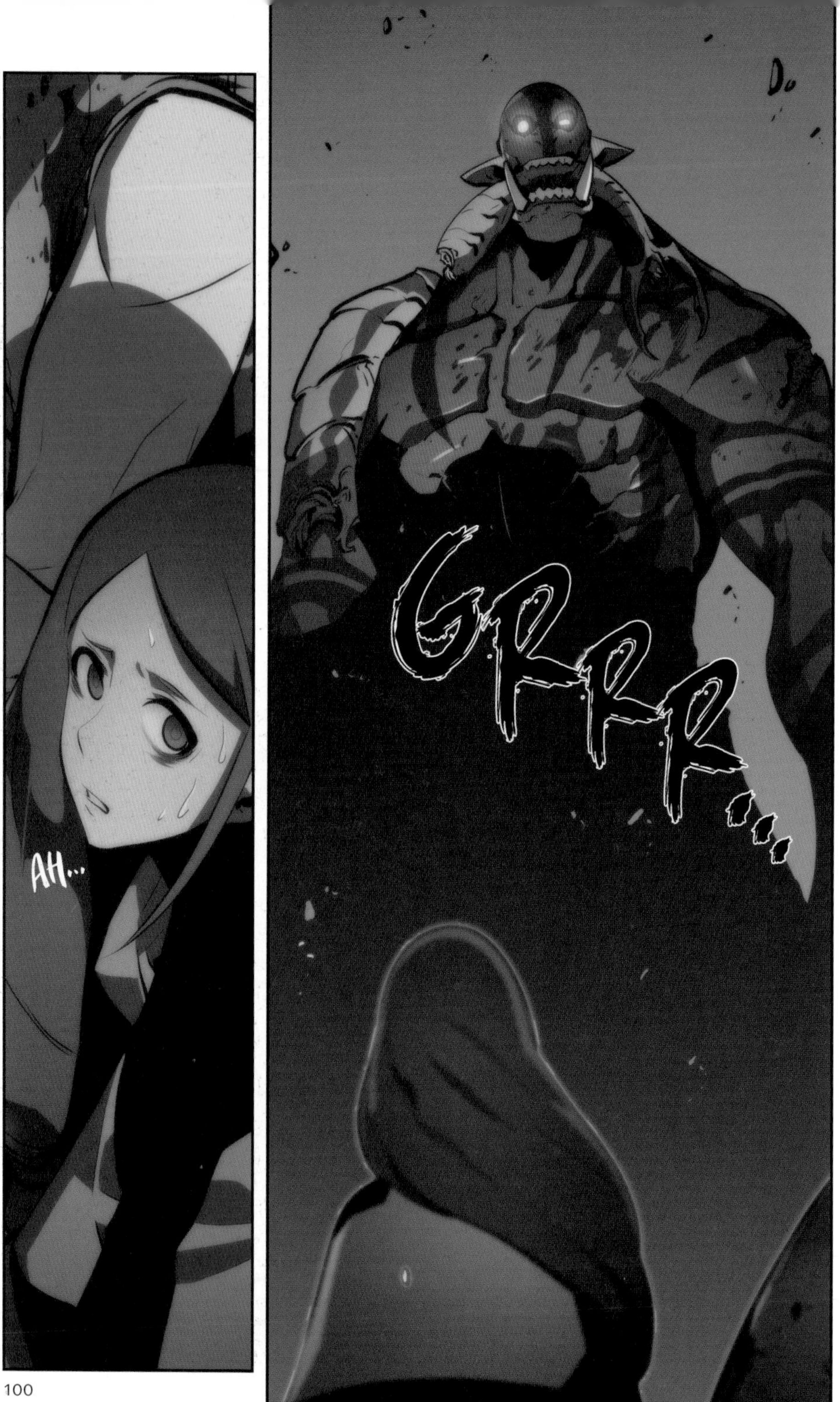
AH...
GRRR...

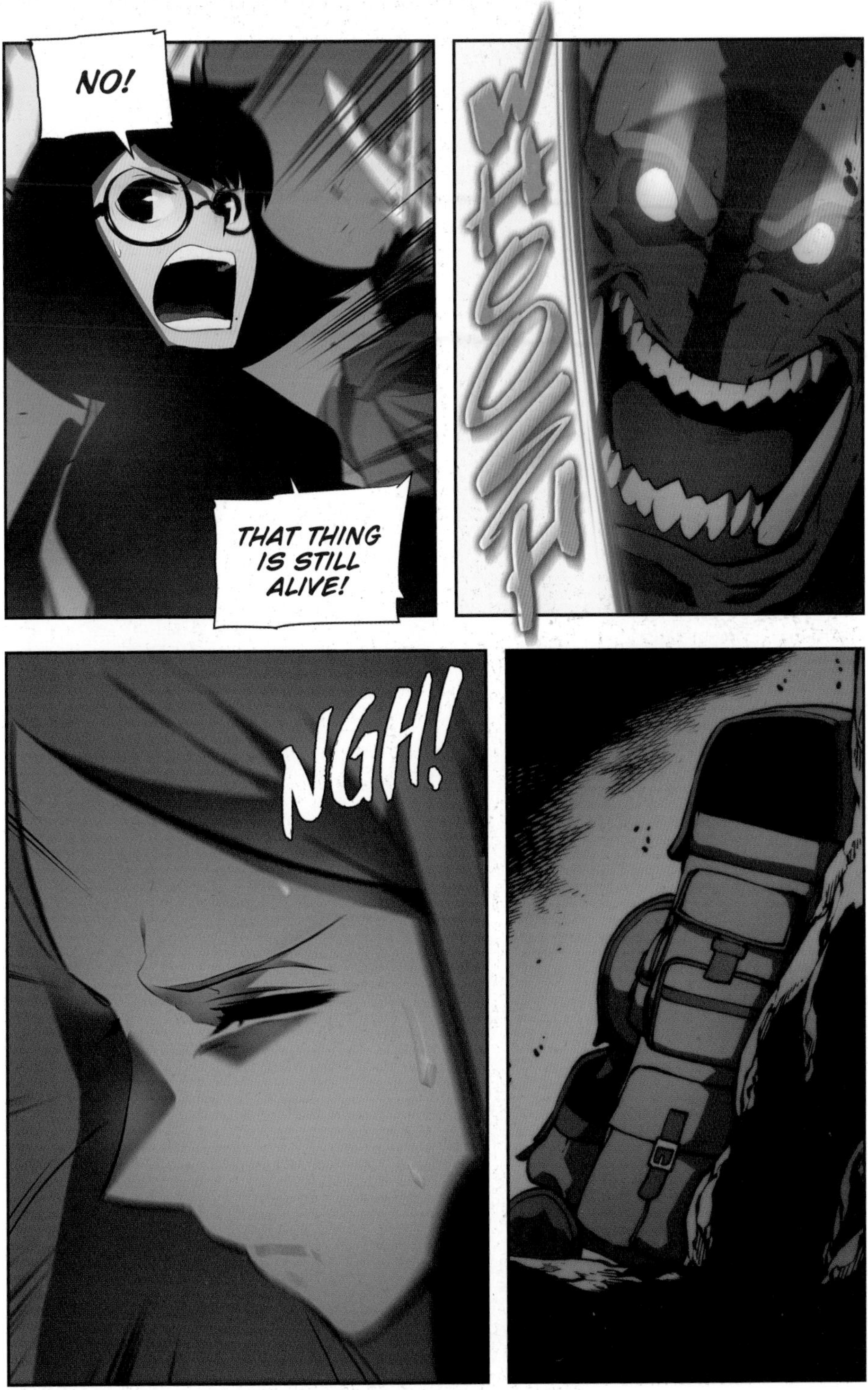
NO!
THAT THING IS STILL ALIVE!
WHOOSH
NGH!

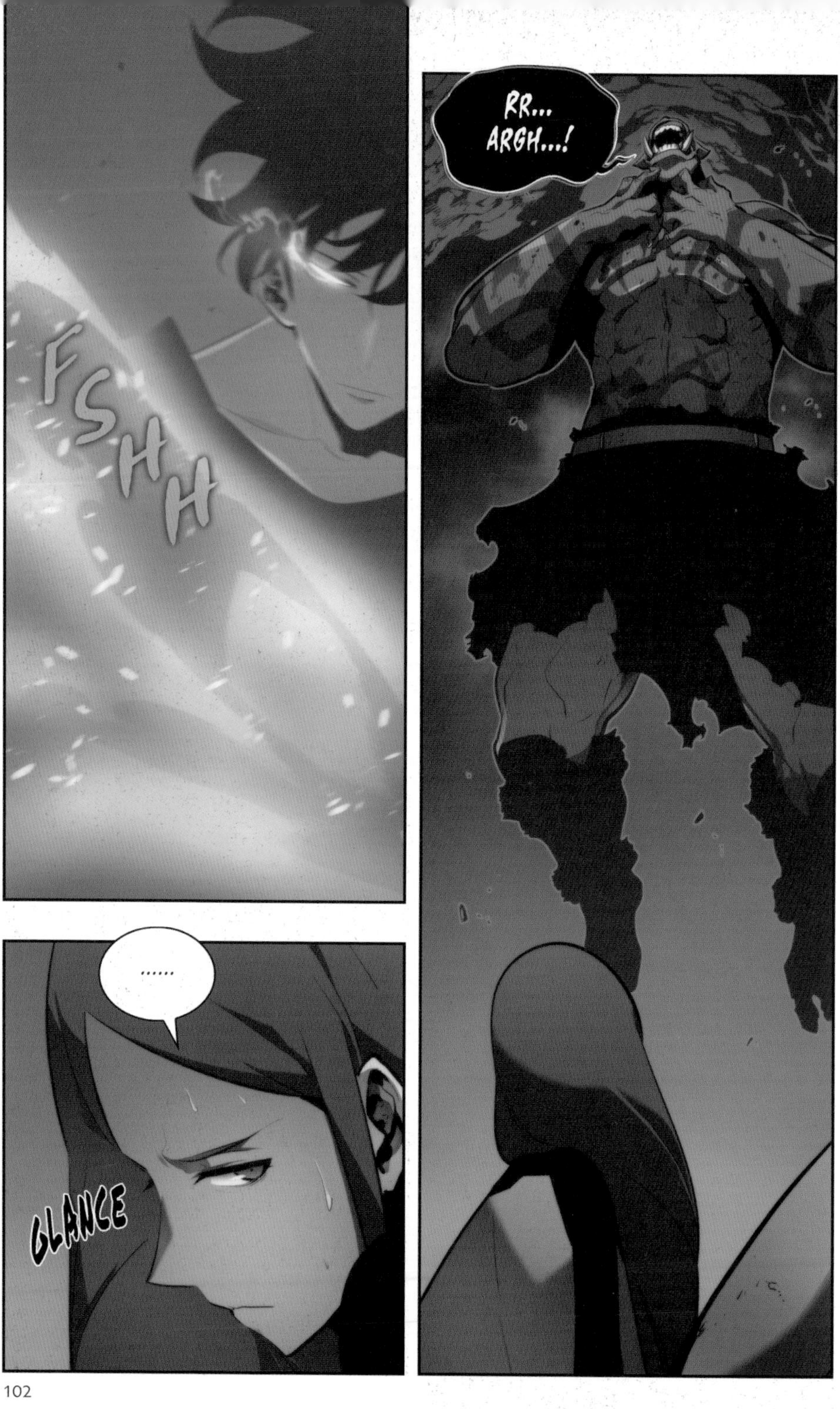
FSHH
......
GLANCE
RR... ARGH...!

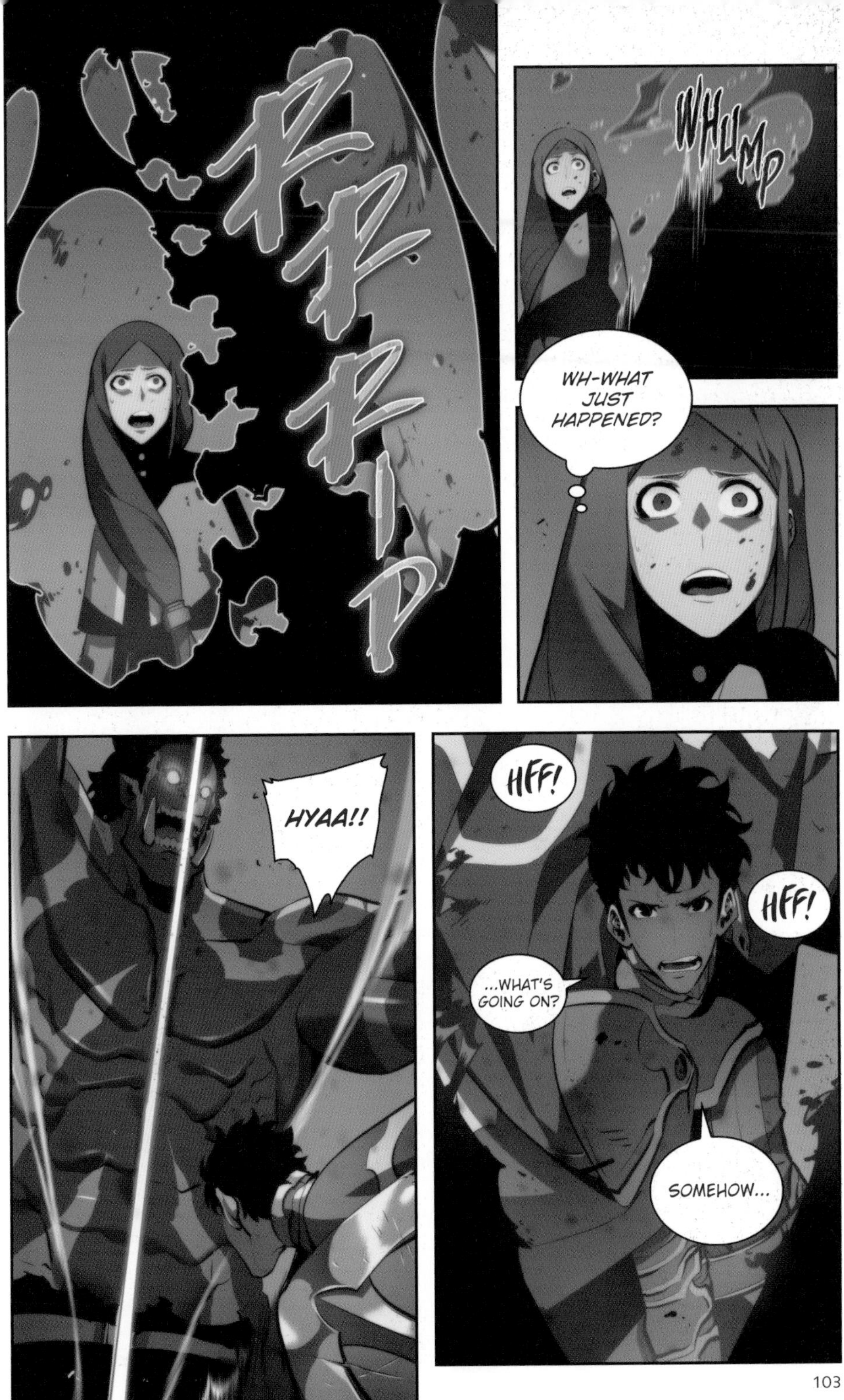
WHUMP
WH-WHAT JUST HAPPENED?
HYAA!!
HFF!
HFF!
...WHAT'S GOING ON?
SOMEHOW...

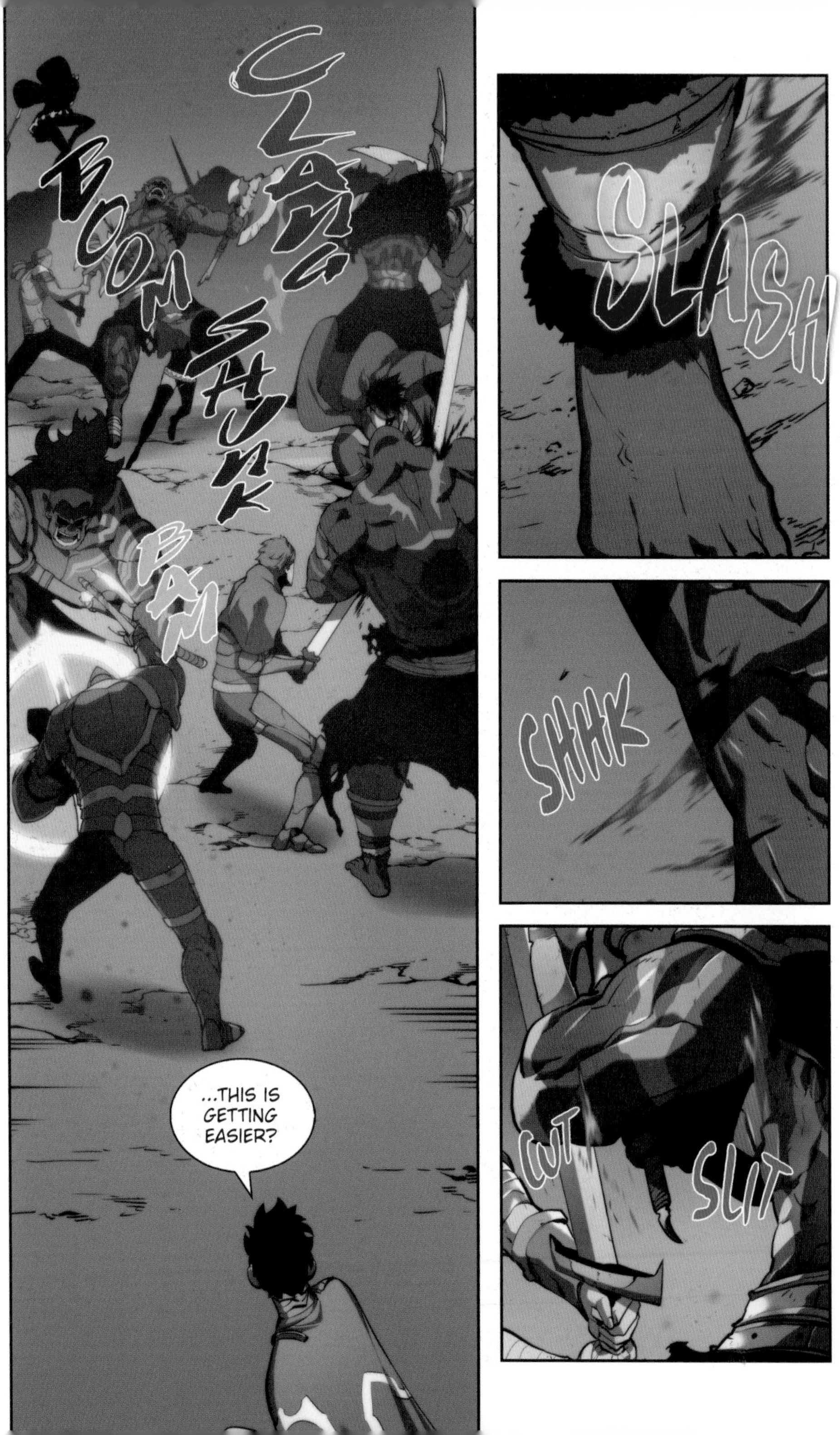
CLANG
BOOM
SHUNK
BAM
...THIS IS GETTING EASIER?
SLASH
SHHK
CUT
SLIT

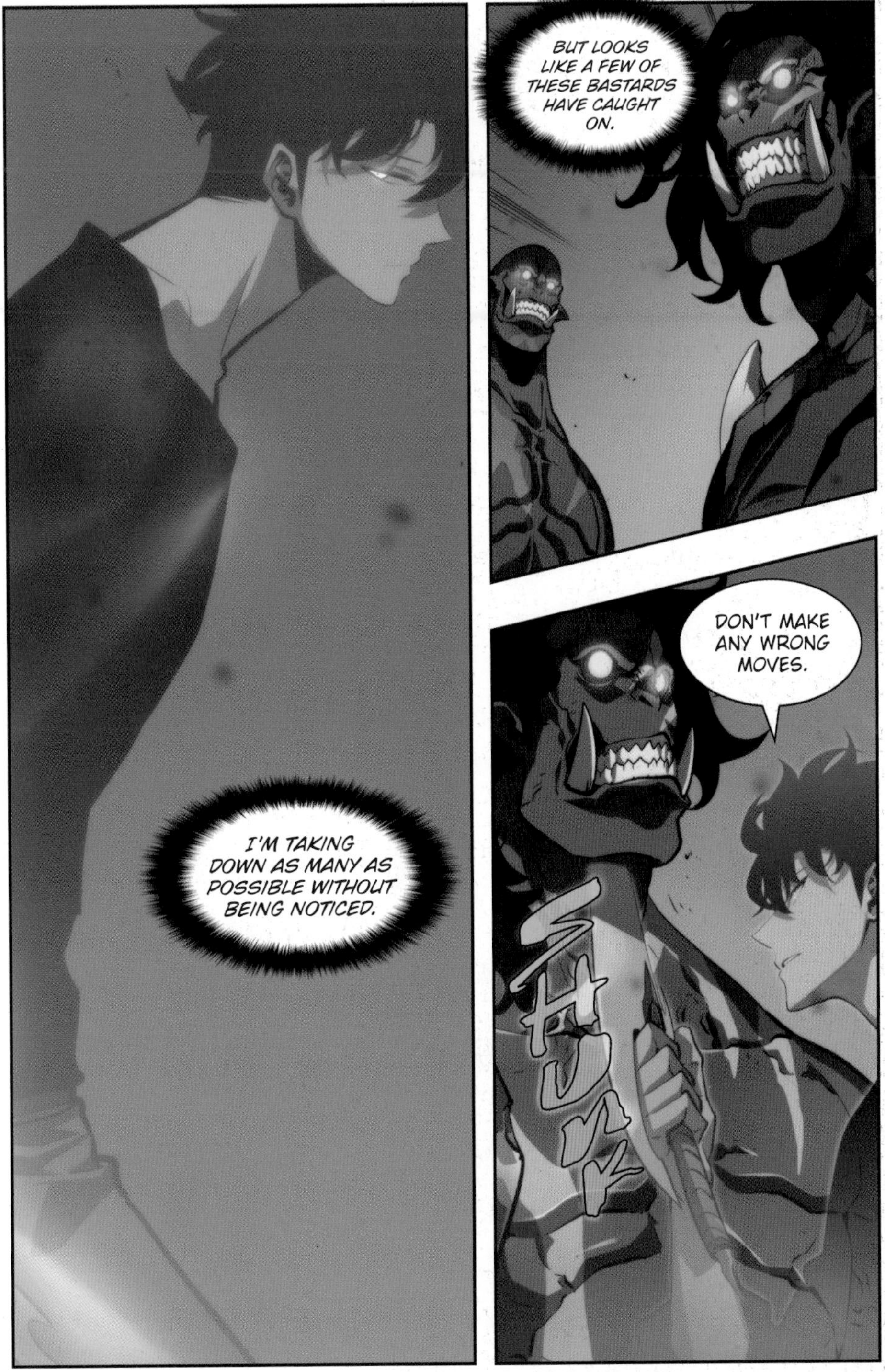
I'M TAKING DOWN AS MANY AS POSSIBLE WITHOUT BEING NOTICED.
BUT LOOKS LIKE A FEW OF THESE BASTARDS HAVE CAUGHT ON.
DON'T MAKE ANY WRONG MOVES.
SHUNK

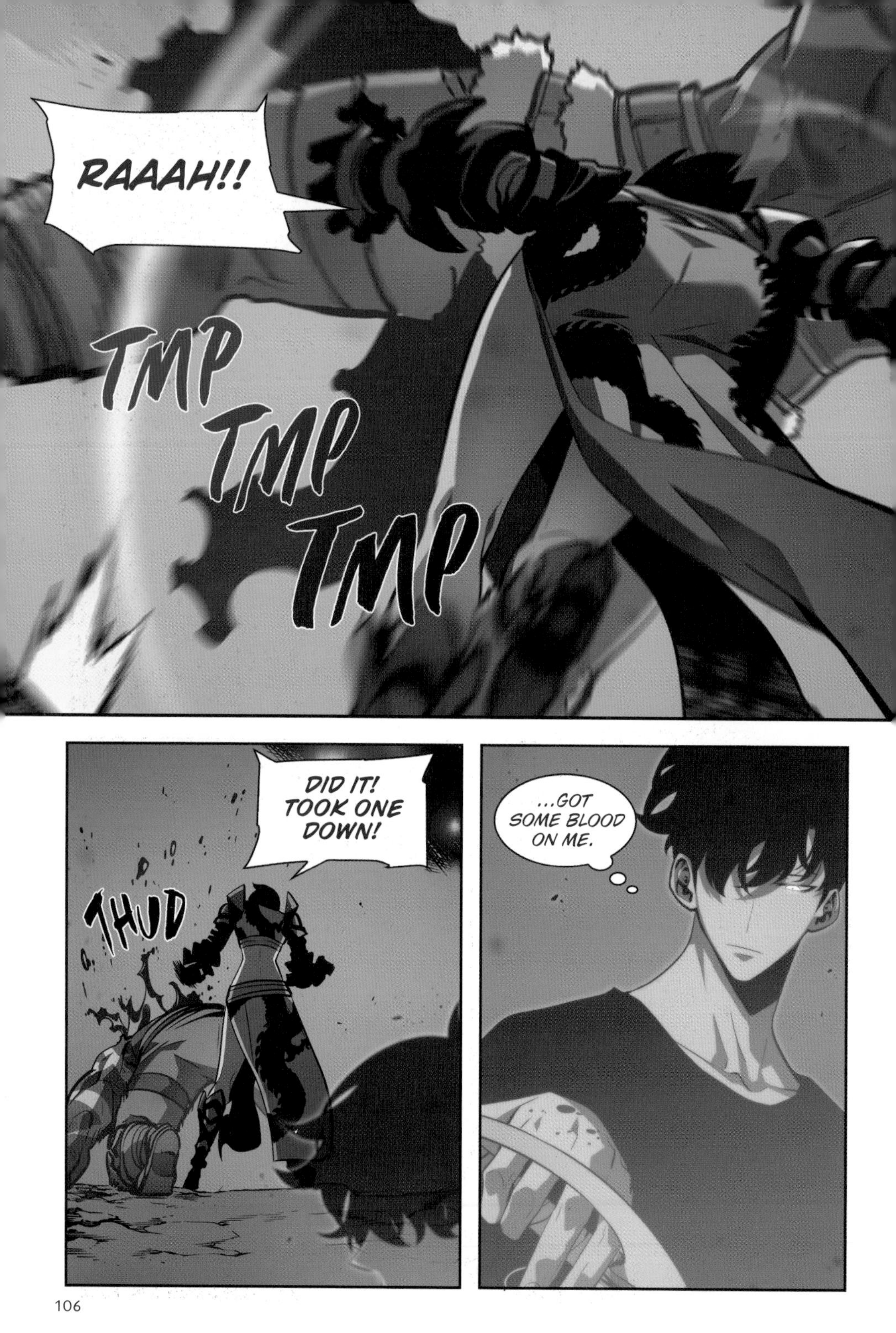
RAAAH!!
TMP
TMP
TMP
DID IT! TOOK ONE DOWN!
THUD
...GOT SOME BLOOD ON ME.

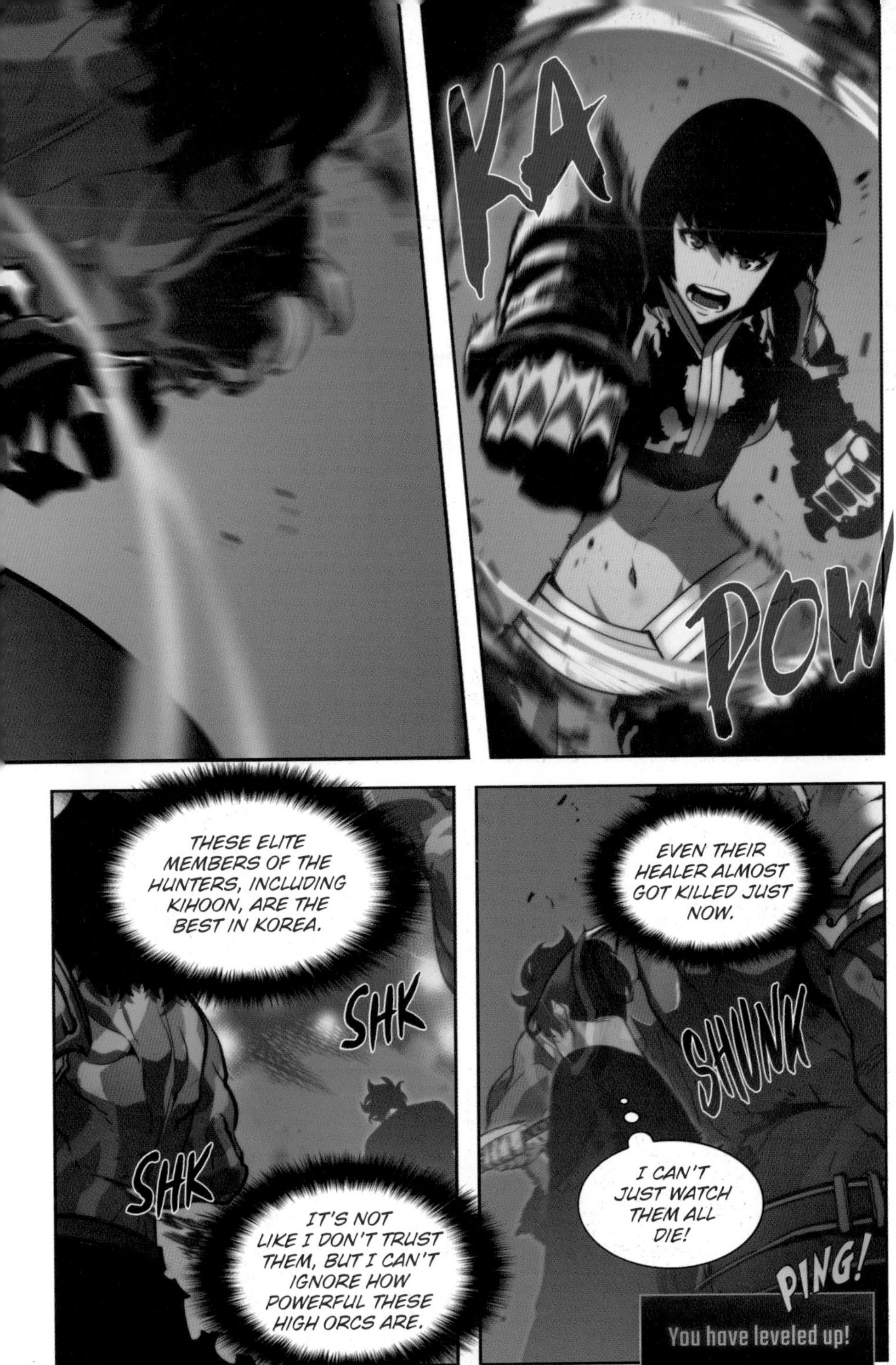
KA
POW
THESE ELITE MEMBERS OF THE HUNTERS, INCLUDING KIHOON, ARE THE BEST IN KOREA.
SHK
SHK
IT'S NOT LIKE I DON'T TRUST THEM, BUT I CAN'T IGNORE HOW POWERFUL THESE HIGH ORCS ARE.
EVEN THEIR HEALER ALMOST GOT KILLED JUST NOW.
SHUNK
I CAN'T JUST WATCH THEM ALL DIE!
PING!
You have leveled up!

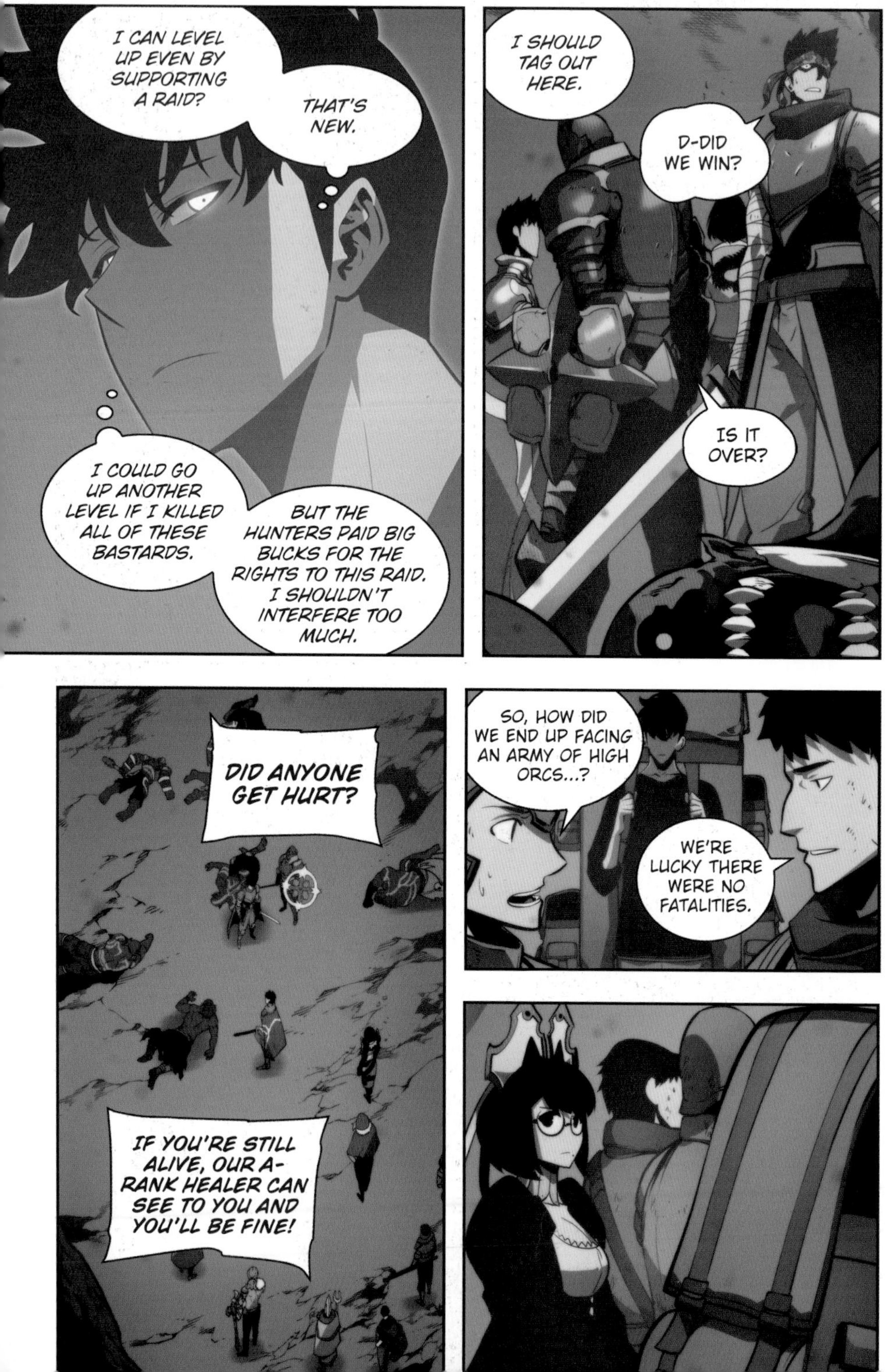
I CAN LEVEL UP EVEN BY SUPPORTING A RAID?
THAT'S NEW.
I COULD GO UP ANOTHER LEVEL IF I KILLED ALL OF THESE BASTARDS.
BUT THE HUNTERS PAID BIG BUCKS FOR THE RIGHTS TO THIS RAID. I SHOULDN'T INTERFERE TOO MUCH.
I SHOULD TAG OUT HERE.
D-DID WE WIN?
IS IT OVER?
DID ANYONE GET HURT?
IF YOU'RE STILL ALIVE, OUR A-RANK HEALER CAN SEE TO YOU AND YOU'LL BE FINE!
SO, HOW DID WE END UP FACING AN ARMY OF HIGH ORCS...?
WE'RE LUCKY THERE WERE NO FATALITIES.

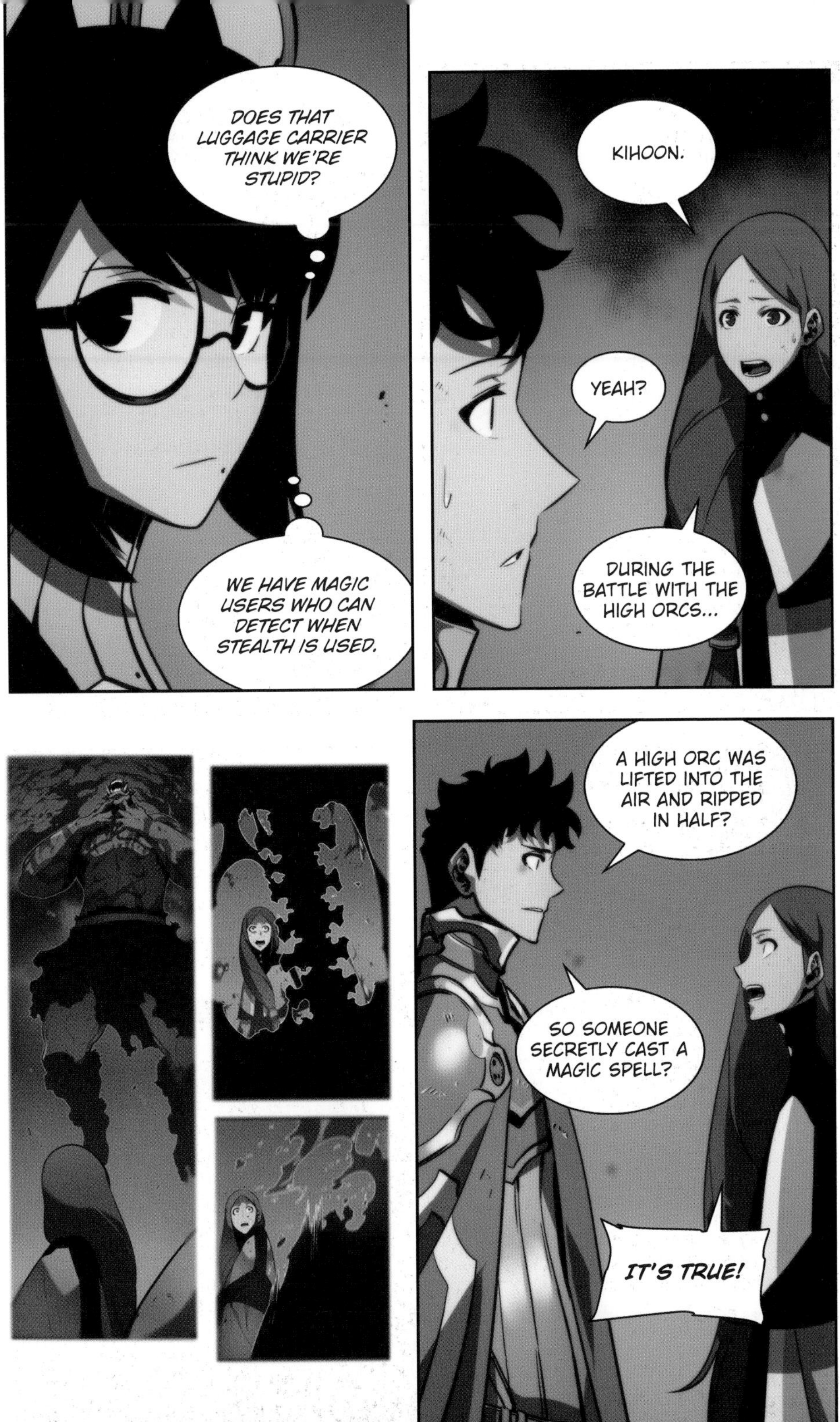
DOES THAT LUGGAGE CARRIER THINK WE'RE STUPID?
WE HAVE MAGIC USERS WHO CAN DETECT WHEN STEALTH IS USED.
KIHOON.
YEAH?
DURING THE BATTLE WITH THE HIGH ORCS...
A HIGH ORC WAS LIFTED INTO THE AIR AND RIPPED IN HALF?
SO SOMEONE SECRETLY CAST A MAGIC SPELL?
IT'S TRUE!

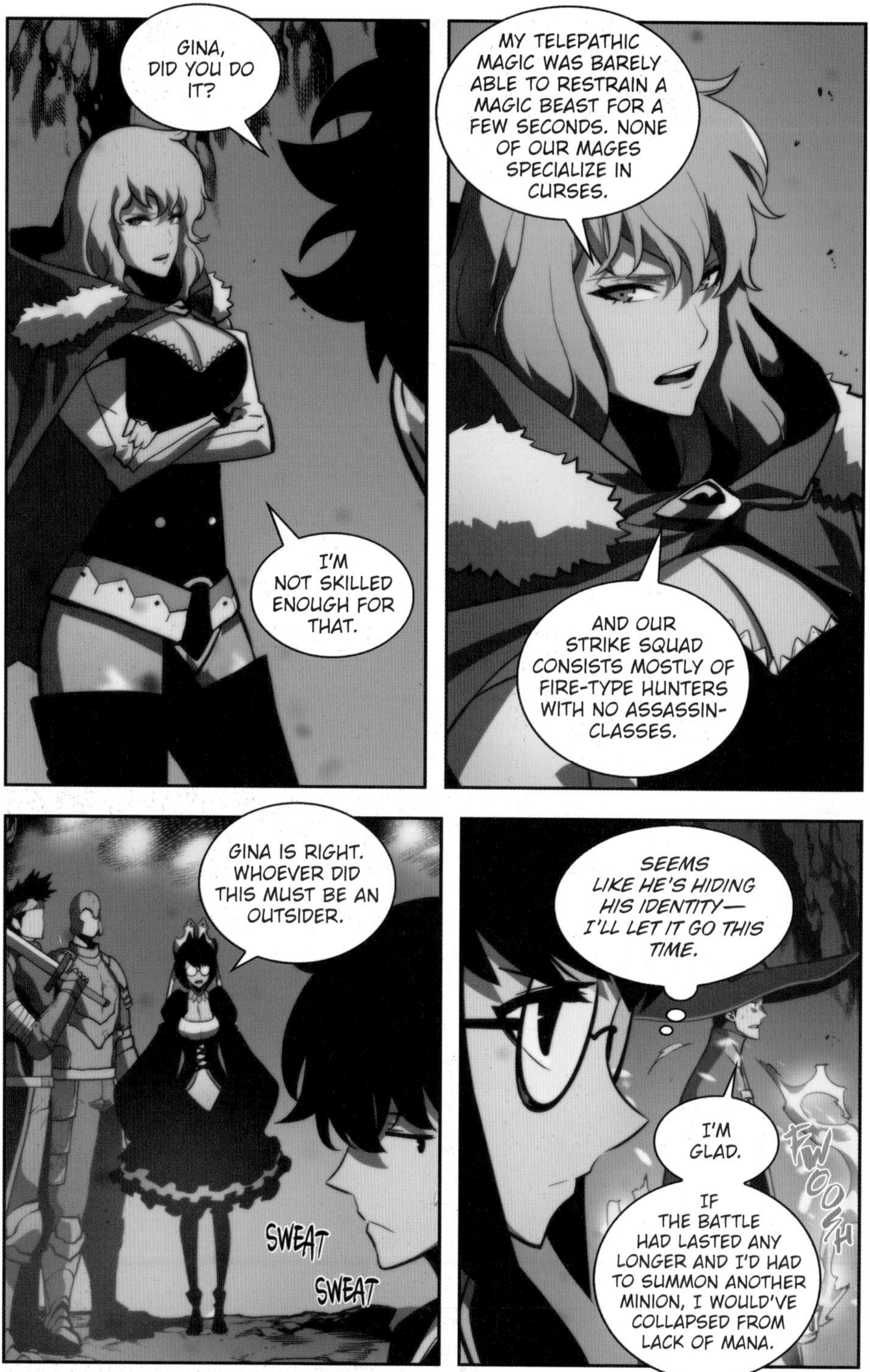
GINA, DID YOU DO IT?
I'M NOT SKILLED ENOUGH FOR THAT.
MY TELEPATHIC MAGIC WAS BARELY ABLE TO RESTRAIN A MAGIC BEAST FOR A FEW SECONDS. NONE OF OUR MAGES SPECIALIZE IN CURSES.
AND OUR STRIKE SQUAD CONSISTS MOSTLY OF FIRE-TYPE HUNTERS WITH NO ASSASSIN-CLASSES.
GINA IS RIGHT. WHOEVER DID THIS MUST BE AN OUTSIDER.
SWEAT
SWEAT
SEEMS LIKE HE'S HIDING HIS IDENTITY— I'LL LET IT GO THIS TIME.
I'M GLAD.
IF THE BATTLE HAD LASTED ANY LONGER AND I'D HAD TO SUMMON ANOTHER MINION, I WOULD'VE COLLAPSED FROM LACK OF MANA.
FWOOSH

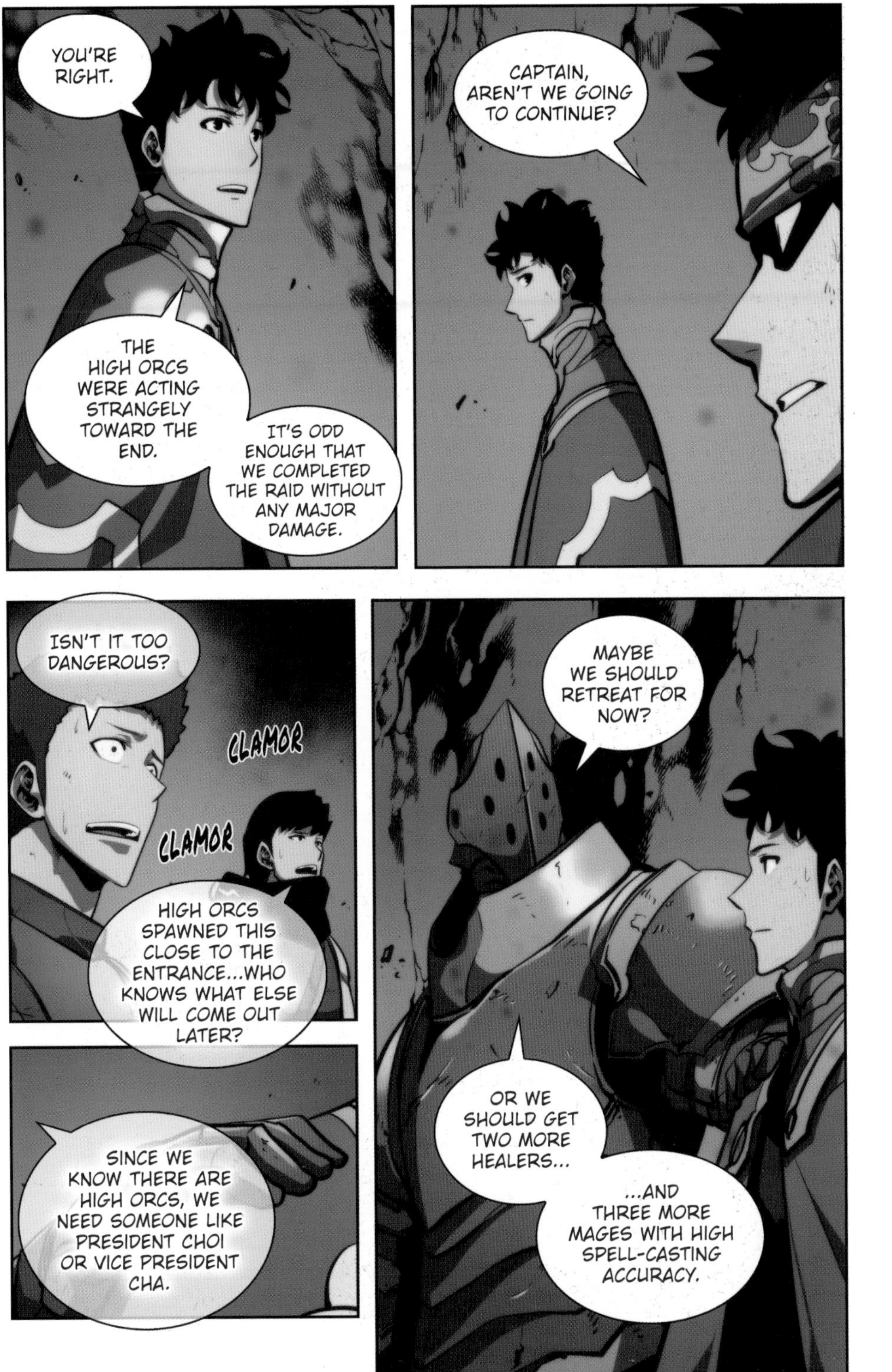
YOU'RE RIGHT.
THE HIGH ORCS WERE ACTING STRANGELY TOWARD THE END.
IT'S ODD ENOUGH THAT WE COMPLETED THE RAID WITHOUT ANY MAJOR DAMAGE.
CAPTAIN, AREN'T WE GOING TO CONTINUE?
ISN'T IT TOO DANGEROUS?
CLAMOR
CLAMOR
HIGH ORCS SPAWNED THIS CLOSE TO THE ENTRANCE...WHO KNOWS WHAT ELSE WILL COME OUT LATER?
SINCE WE KNOW THERE ARE HIGH ORCS, WE NEED SOMEONE LIKE PRESIDENT CHOI OR VICE PRESIDENT CHA.
MAYBE WE SHOULD RETREAT FOR NOW?
OR WE SHOULD GET TWO MORE HEALERS...
...AND THREE MORE MAGES WITH HIGH SPELL-CASTING ACCURACY.

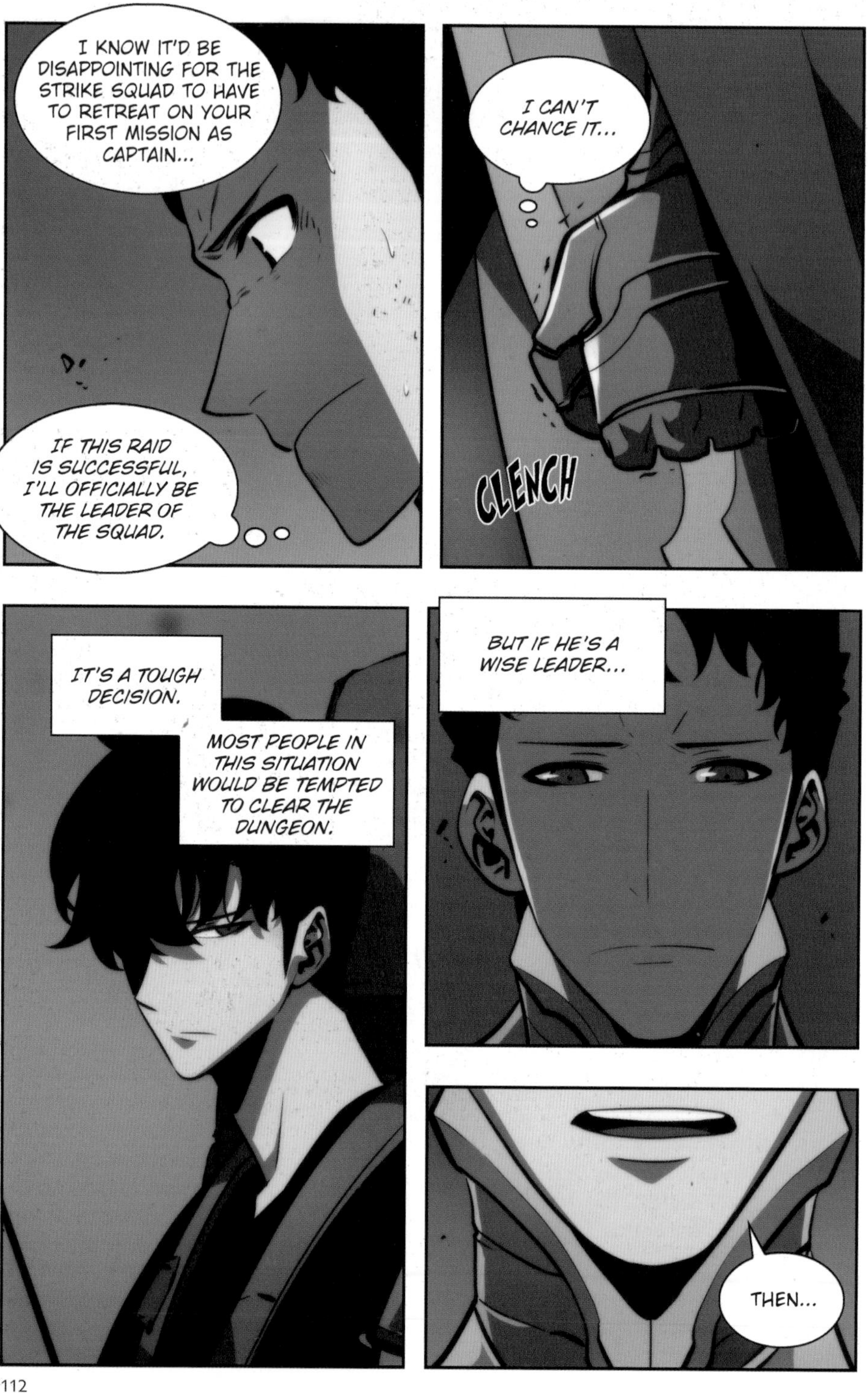
I KNOW IT'D BE DISAPPOINTING FOR THE STRIKE SQUAD TO HAVE TO RETREAT ON YOUR FIRST MISSION AS CAPTAIN...
IF THIS RAID IS SUCCESSFUL, I'LL OFFICIALLY BE THE LEADER OF THE SQUAD.
I CAN'T CHANCE IT...
CLENCH
IT'S A TOUGH DECISION.
MOST PEOPLE IN THIS SITUATION WOULD BE TEMPTED TO CLEAR THE DUNGEON.
BUT IF HE'S A WISE LEADER...
THEN...

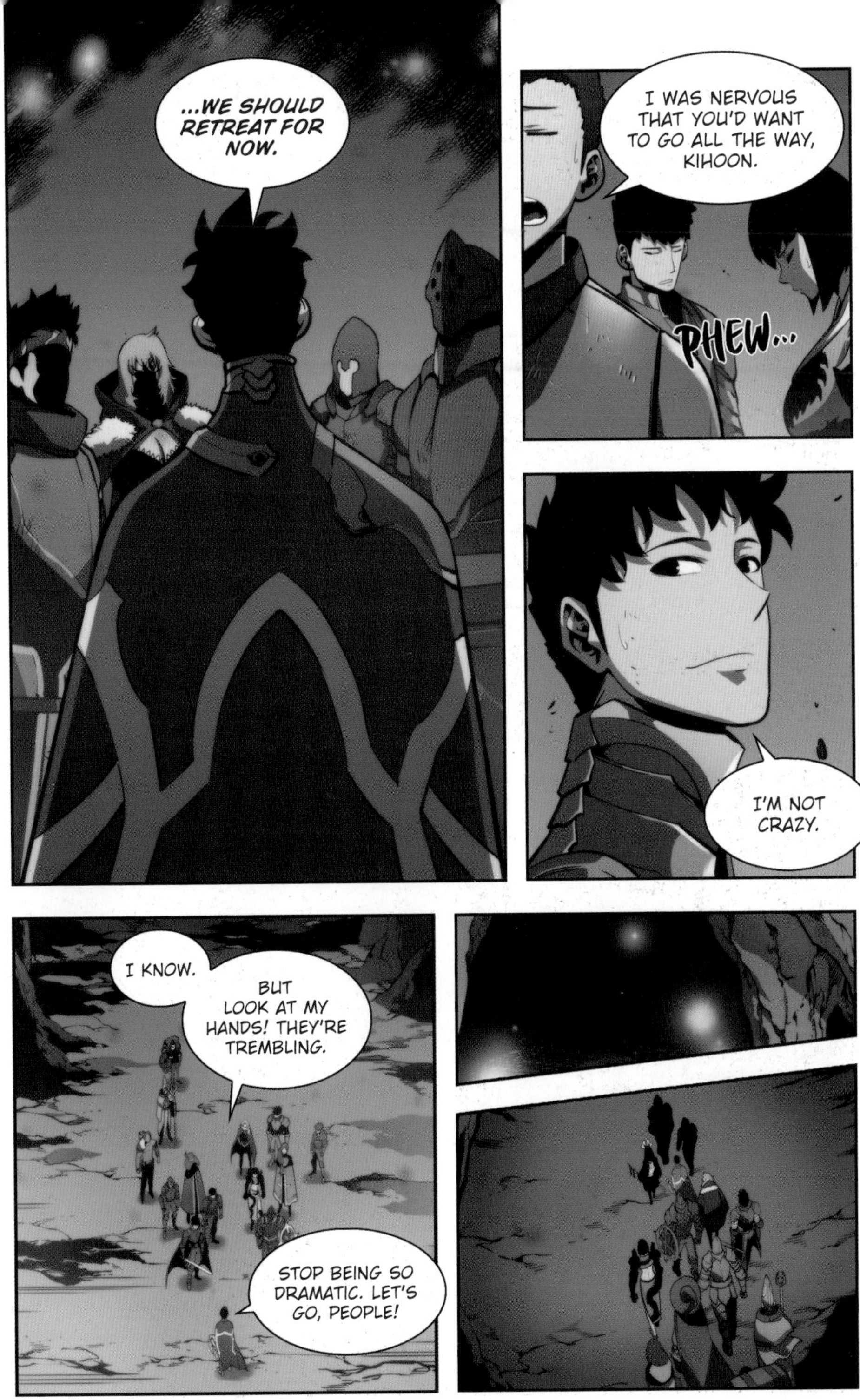
...WE SHOULD RETREAT FOR NOW.
I WAS NERVOUS THAT YOU'D WANT TO GO ALL THE WAY, KIHOON.
PHEW...
I'M NOT CRAZY.
I KNOW.
BUT LOOK AT MY HANDS! THEY'RE TREMBLING.
STOP BEING SO DRAMATIC. LET'S GO, PEOPLE!

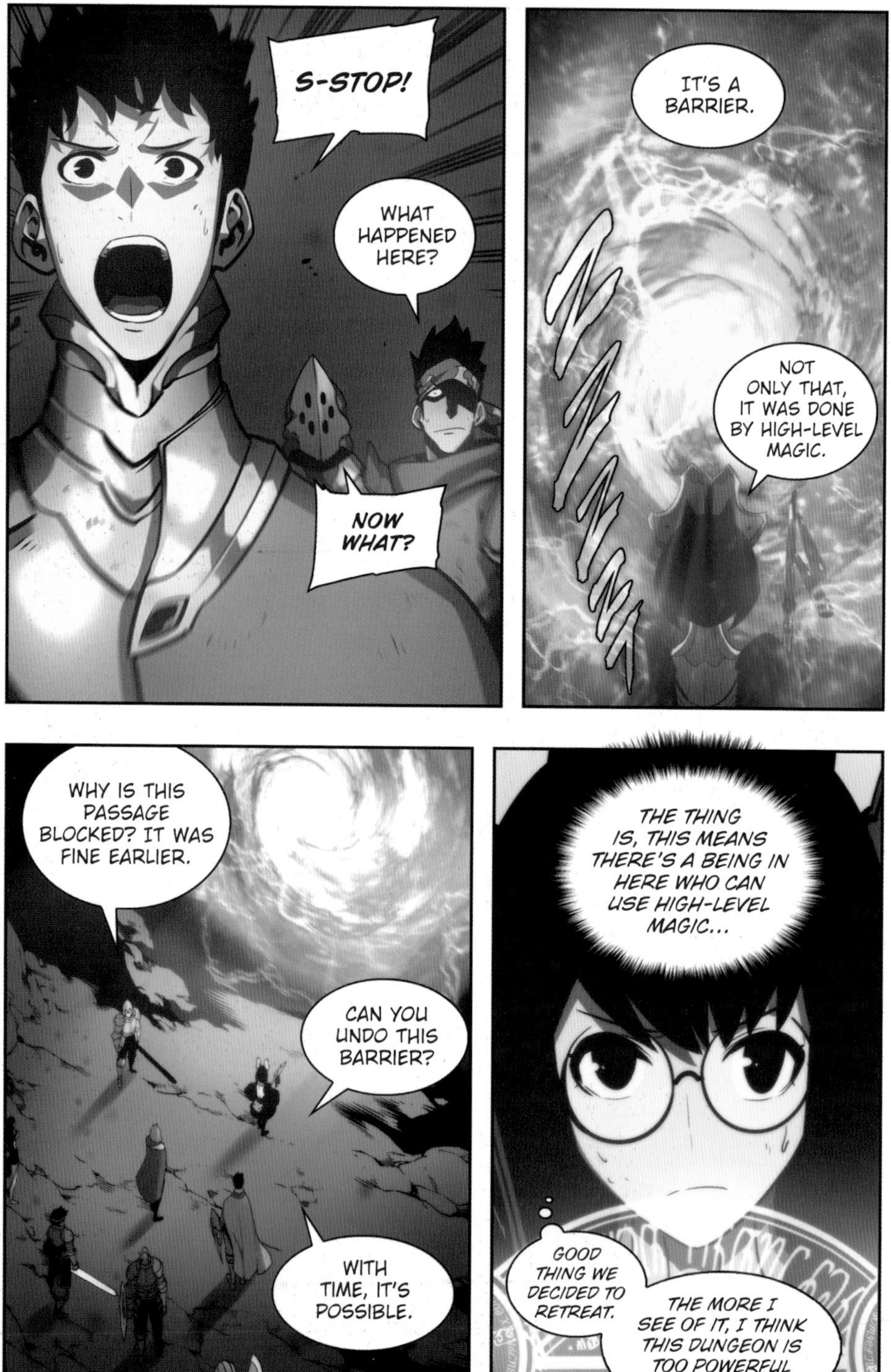
S-STOP!
WHAT HAPPENED HERE?
NOW WHAT?
IT'S A BARRIER.
NOT ONLY THAT, IT WAS DONE BY HIGH-LEVEL MAGIC.
WHY IS THIS PASSAGE BLOCKED? IT WAS FINE EARLIER.
CAN YOU UNDO THIS BARRIER?
WITH TIME, IT'S POSSIBLE.
THE THING IS, THIS MEANS THERE'S A BEING IN HERE WHO CAN USE HIGH-LEVEL MAGIC...
GOOD THING WE DECIDED TO RETREAT.
THE MORE I SEE OF IT, I THINK THIS DUNGEON IS TOO POWERFUL FOR US.

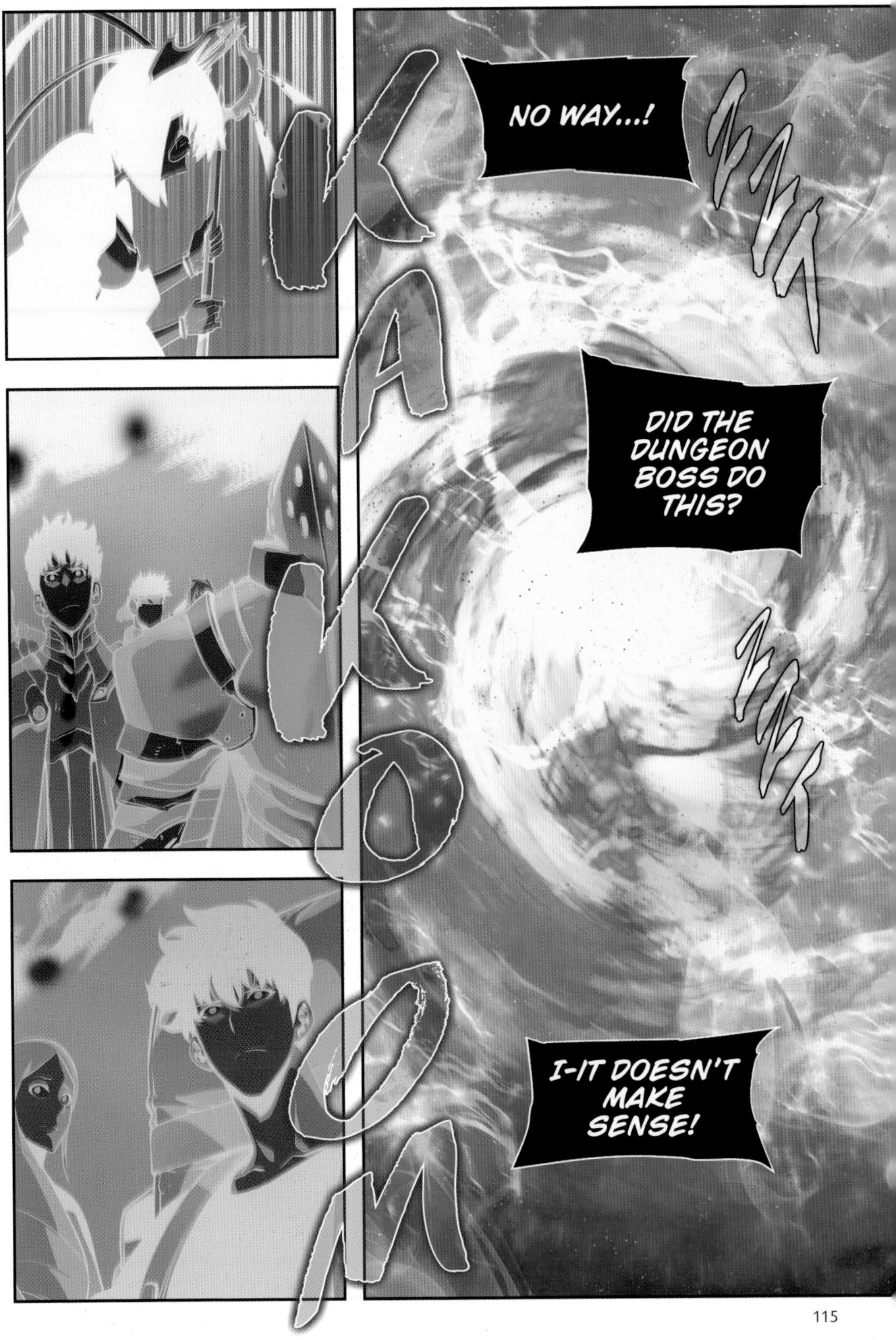
WAKOOM
NO WAY...!
ZZZT
DID THE DUNGEON BOSS DO THIS?
ZZZZT
I-IT DOESN'T MAKE SENSE!

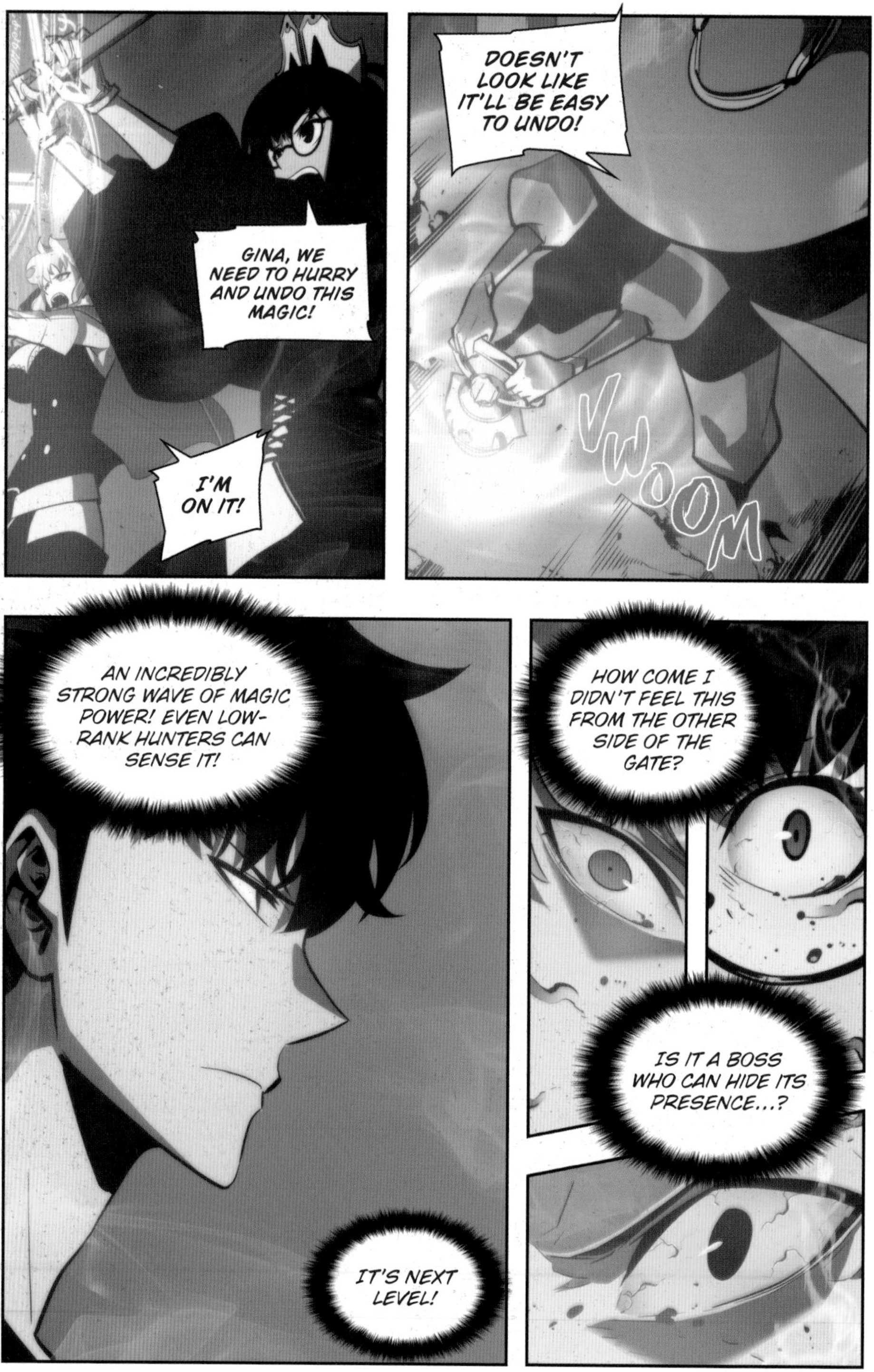
GINA, WE NEED TO HURRY AND UNDO THIS MAGIC!
I'M ON IT!
DOESN'T LOOK LIKE IT'LL BE EASY TO UNDO!
VWOOM
AN INCREDIBLY STRONG WAVE OF MAGIC POWER! EVEN LOW-RANK HUNTERS CAN SENSE IT!
IT'S NEXT LEVEL!
HOW COME I DIDN'T FEEL THIS FROM THE OTHER SIDE OF THE GATE?
IS IT A BOSS WHO CAN HIDE ITS PRESENCE...?

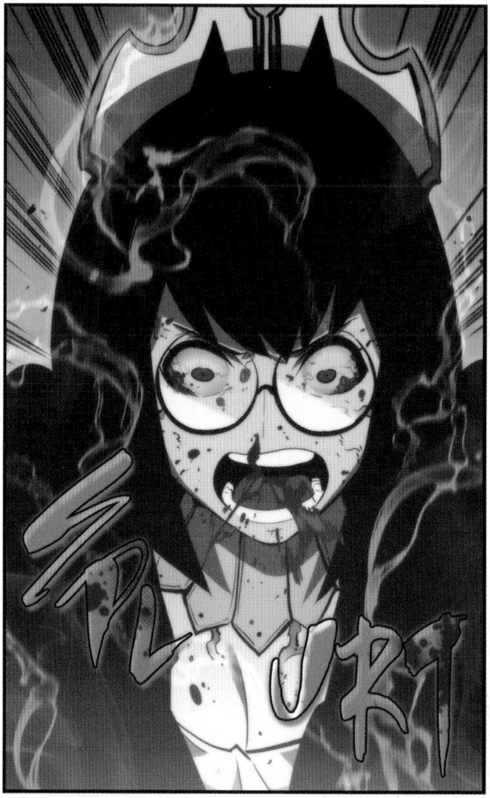
SPLURT

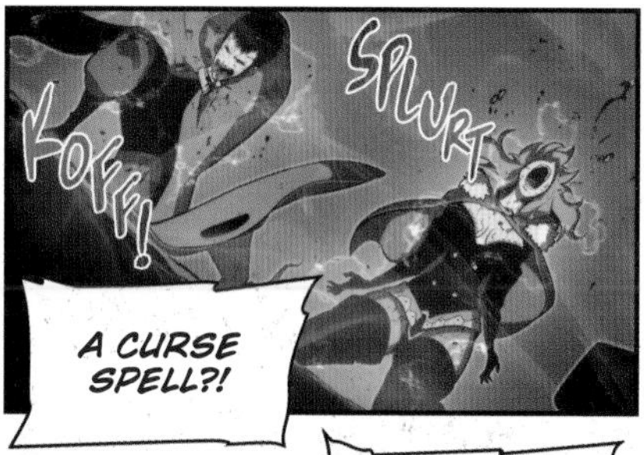
KOFF!
SPLURT
A CURSE SPELL?!

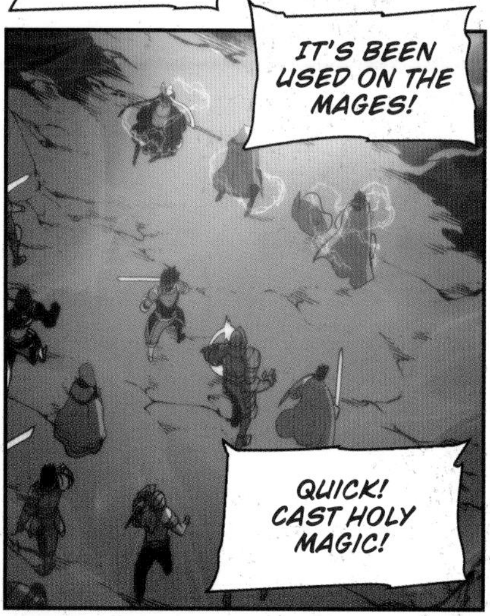
IT'S BEEN USED ON THE MAGES!
QUICK! CAST HOLY MAGIC!

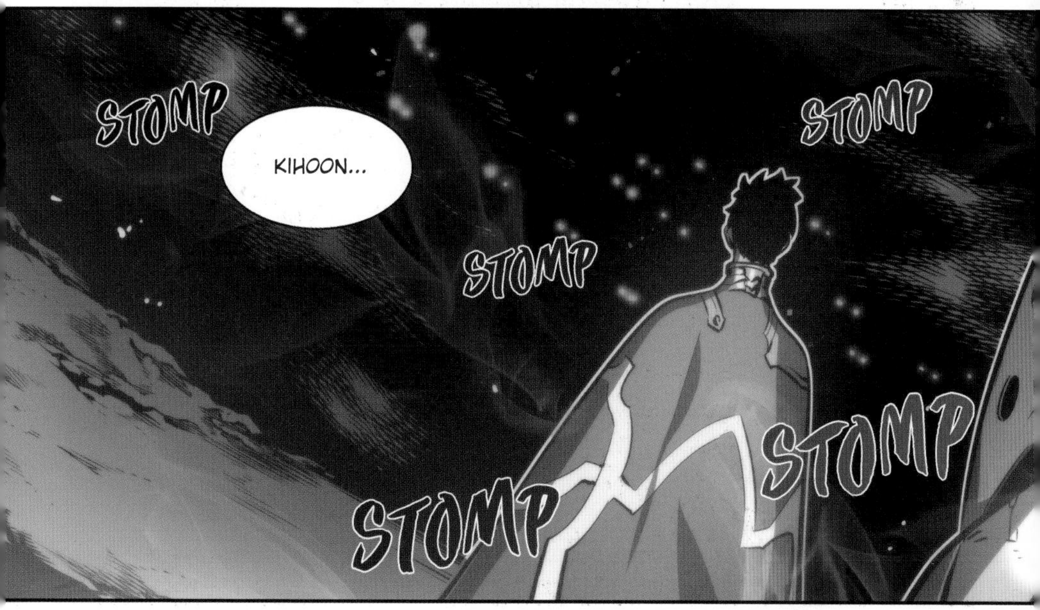
STOMP
KIHOON...
STOMP
STOMP
STOMP
STOMP

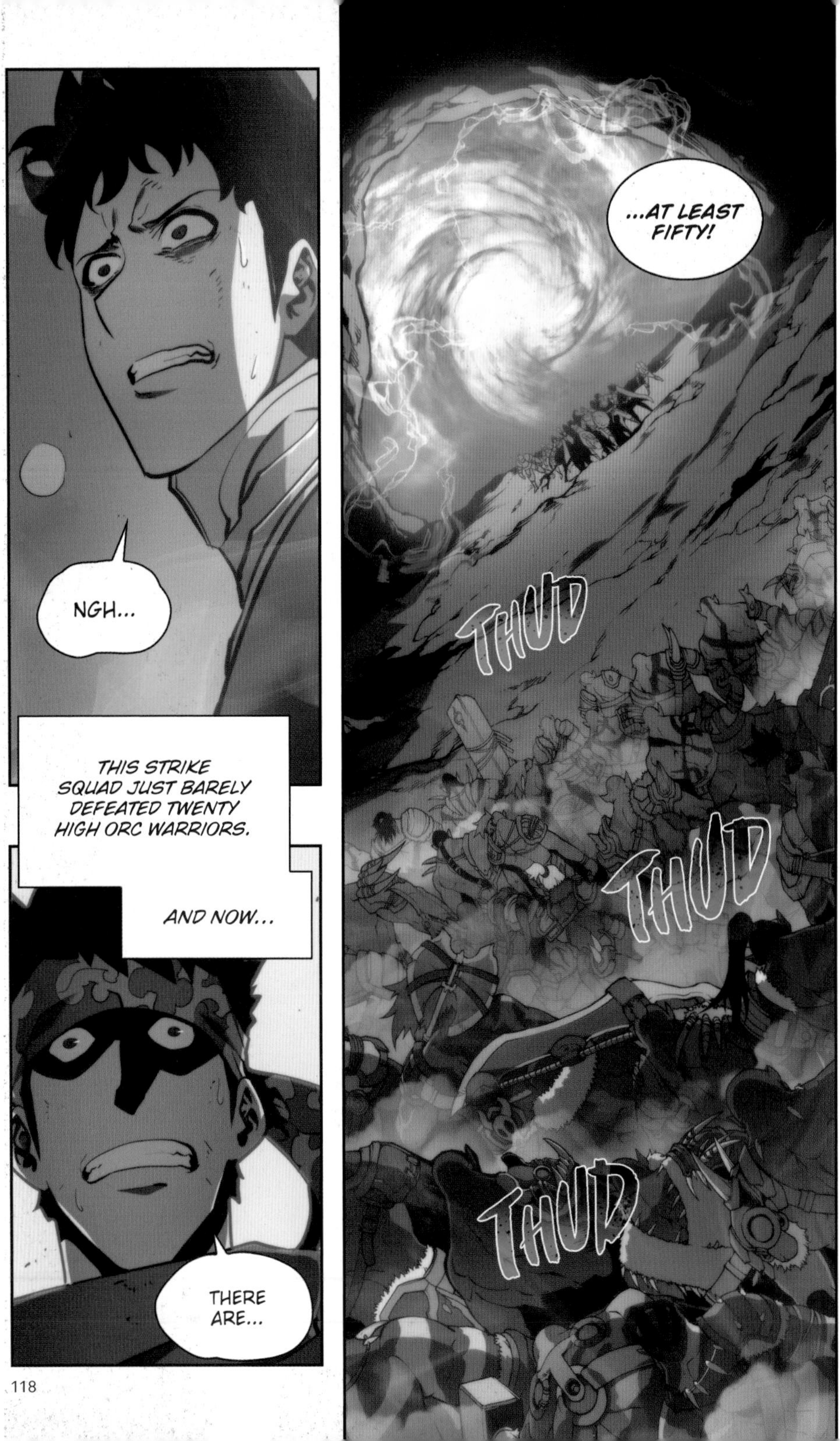
NGH...
THIS STRIKE SQUAD JUST BARELY DEFEATED TWENTY HIGH ORC WARRIORS.
AND NOW...
THERE ARE...
...AT LEAST FIFTY!
THUD
THUD
THUD

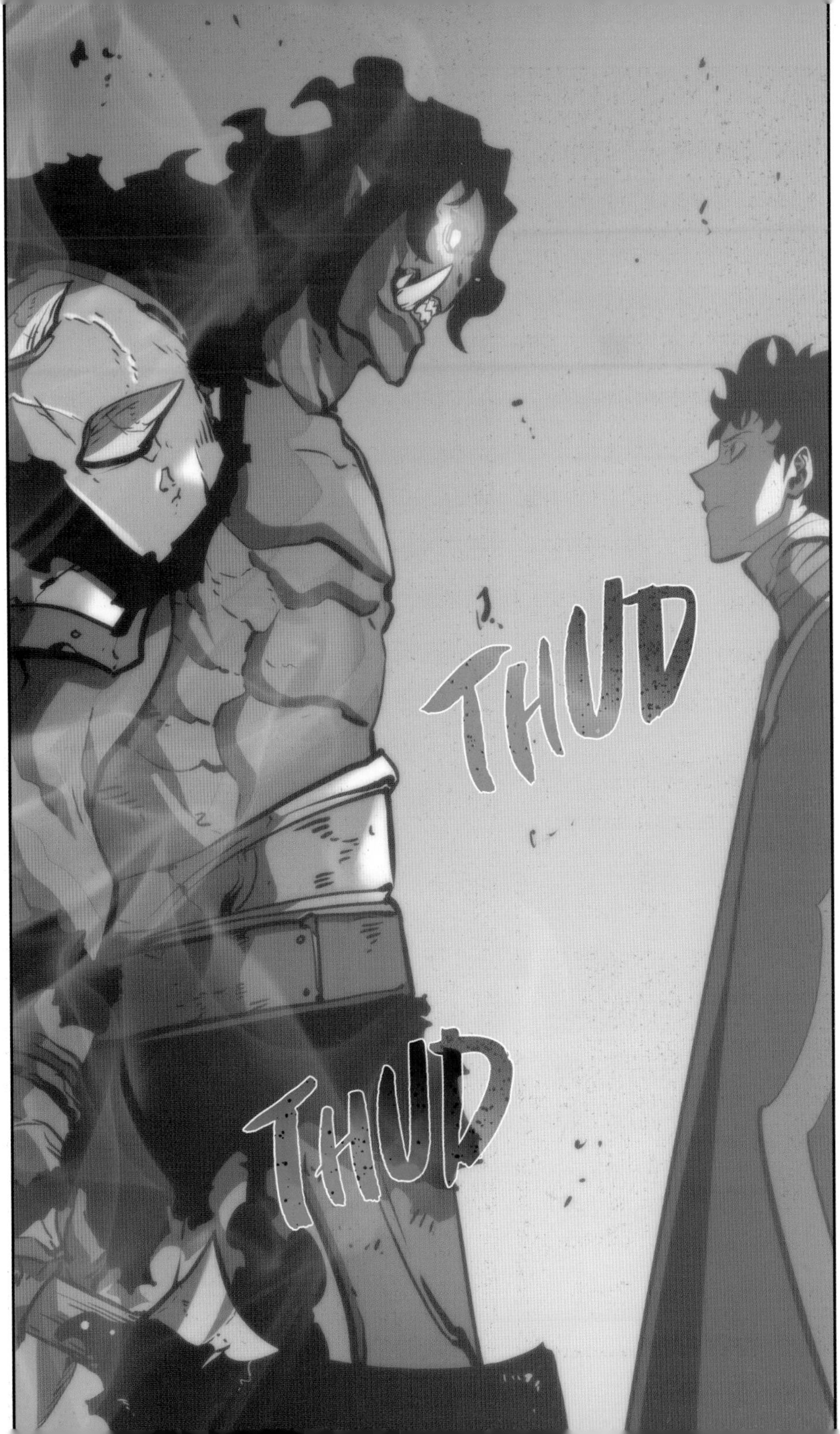
THUD
THUD

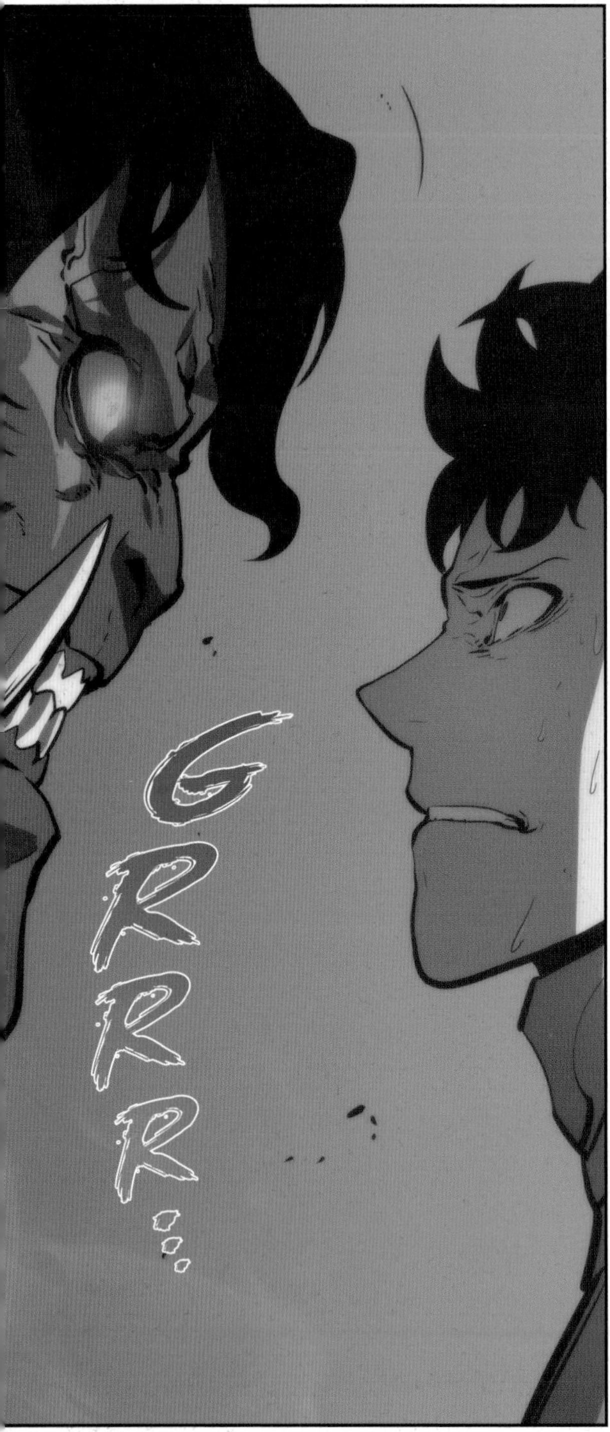
GRRRR...

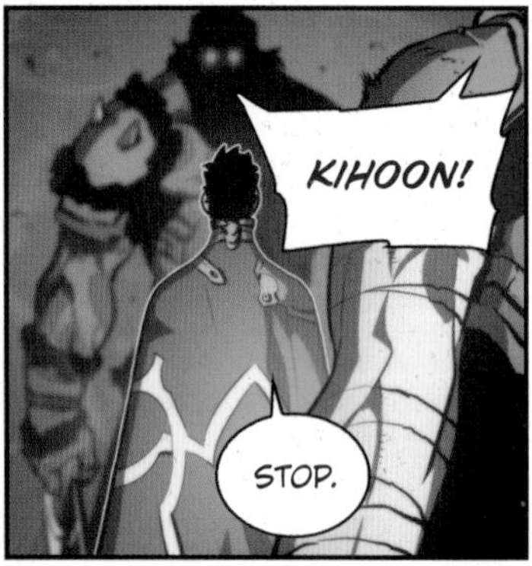
KIHOON!
STOP.

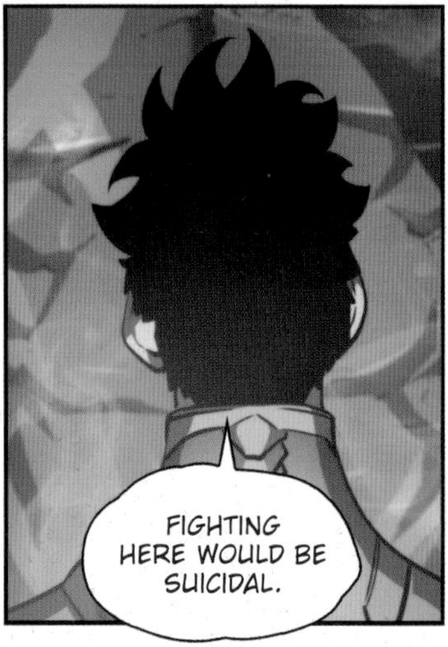
FIGHTING HERE WOULD BE SUICIDAL.

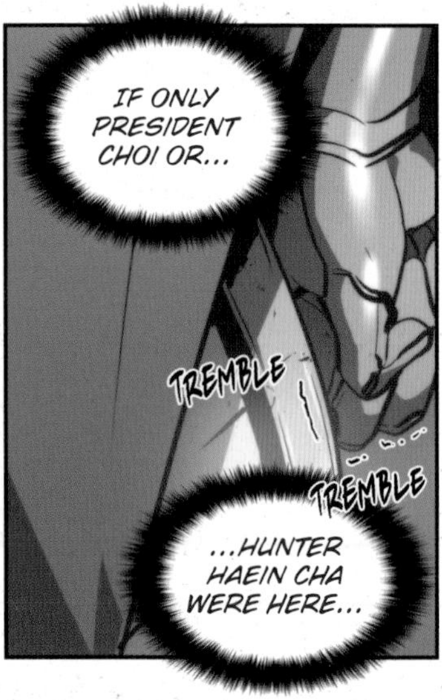
IF ONLY PRESIDENT CHOI OR...
TREMBLE
TREMBLE
...HUNTER HAEIN CHA WERE HERE...

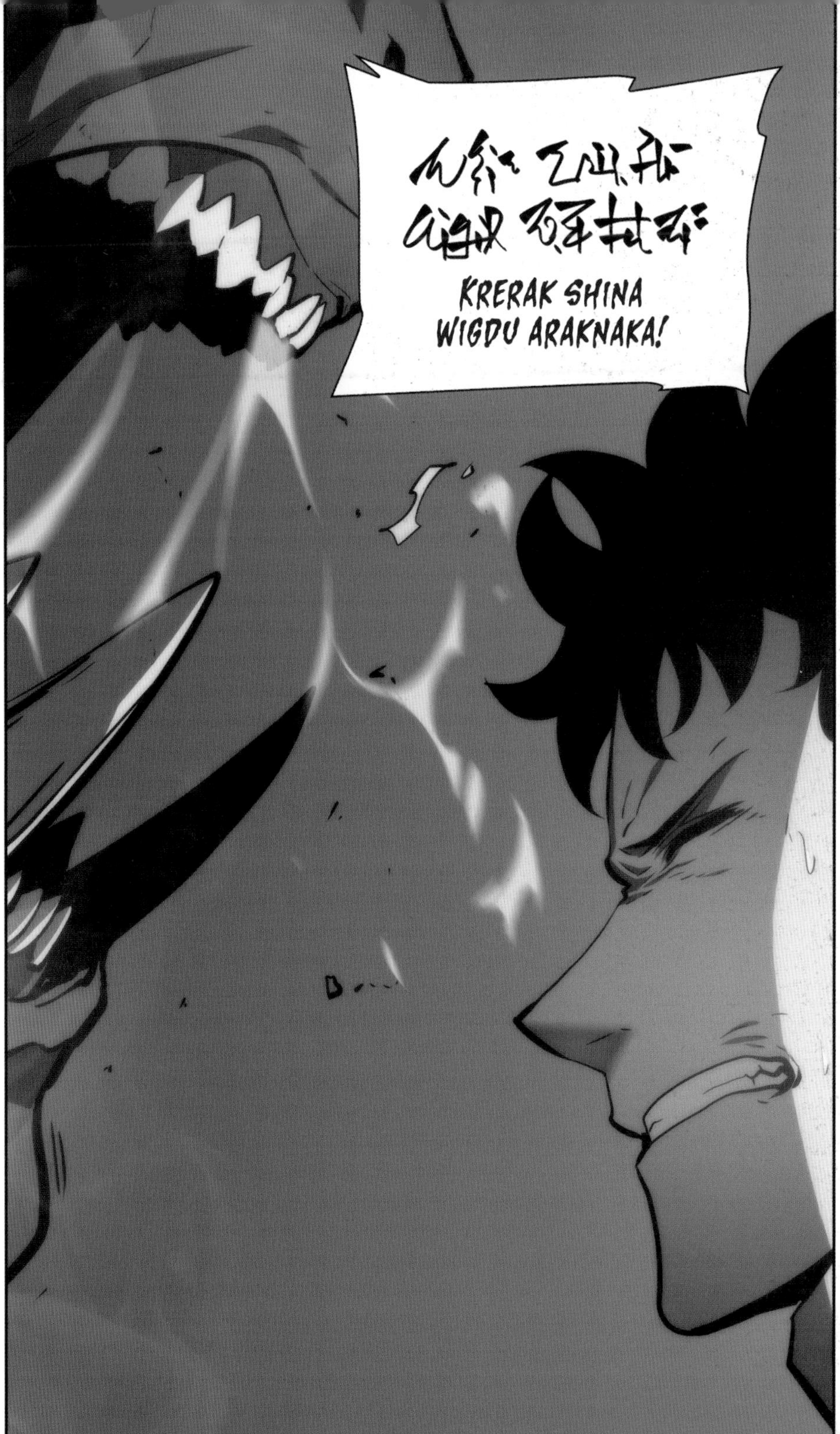
KRERAK SHINA
WIGDU ARAKNAKA!

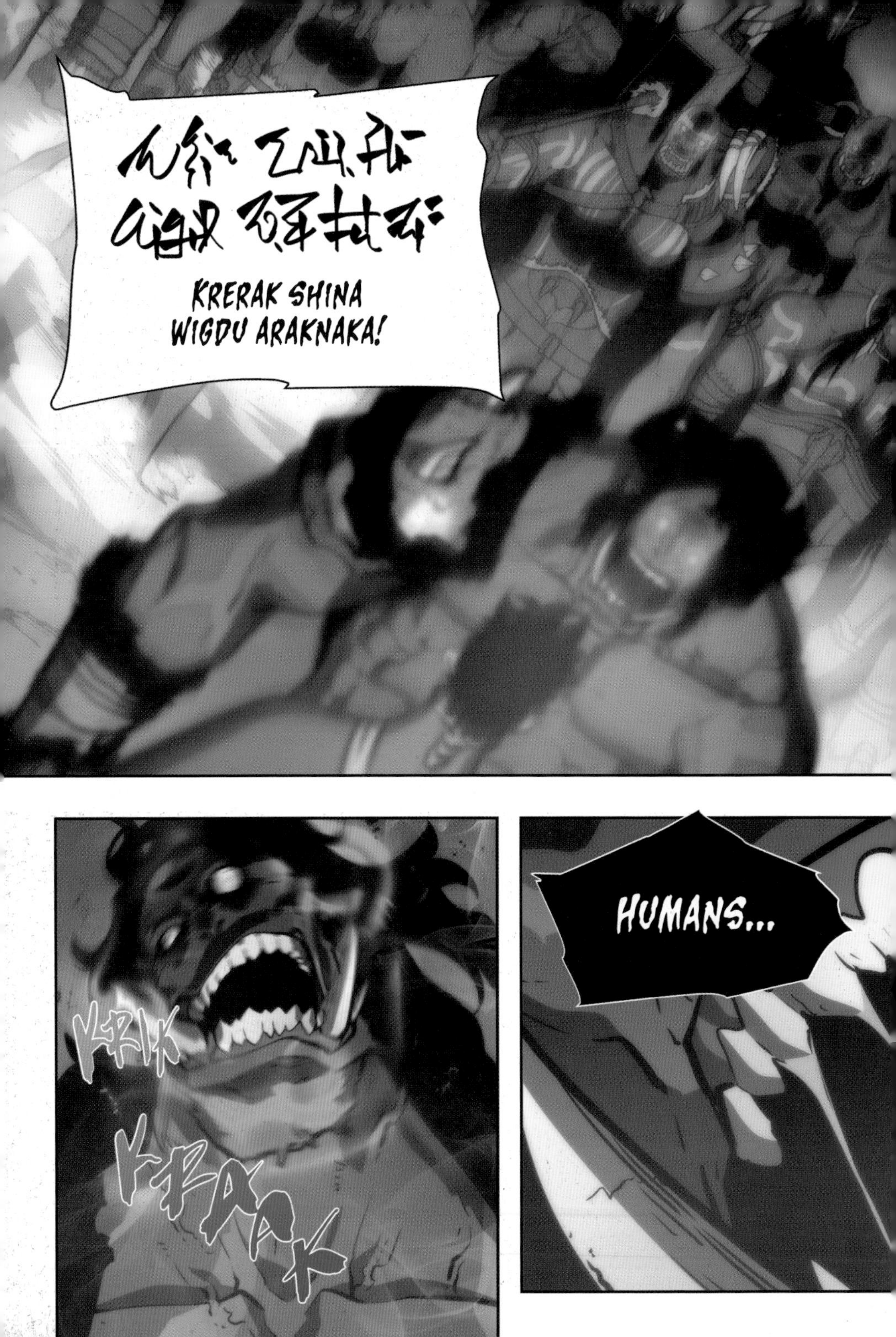
KRERAK SHINA WIGDU ARAKNAKA!
KRIK
KRAAK
HUMANS...

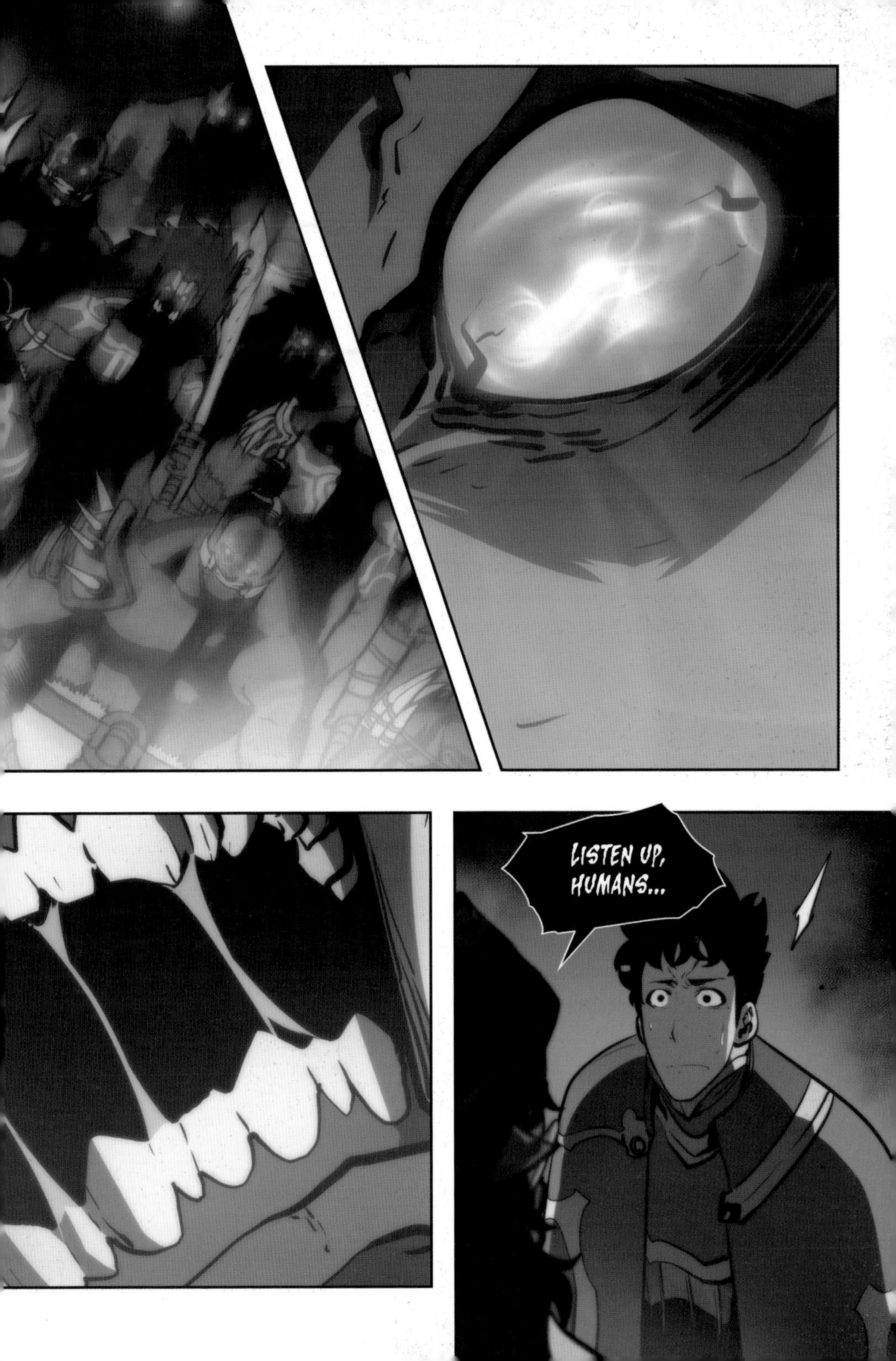
LISTEN UP,
HUMANS...

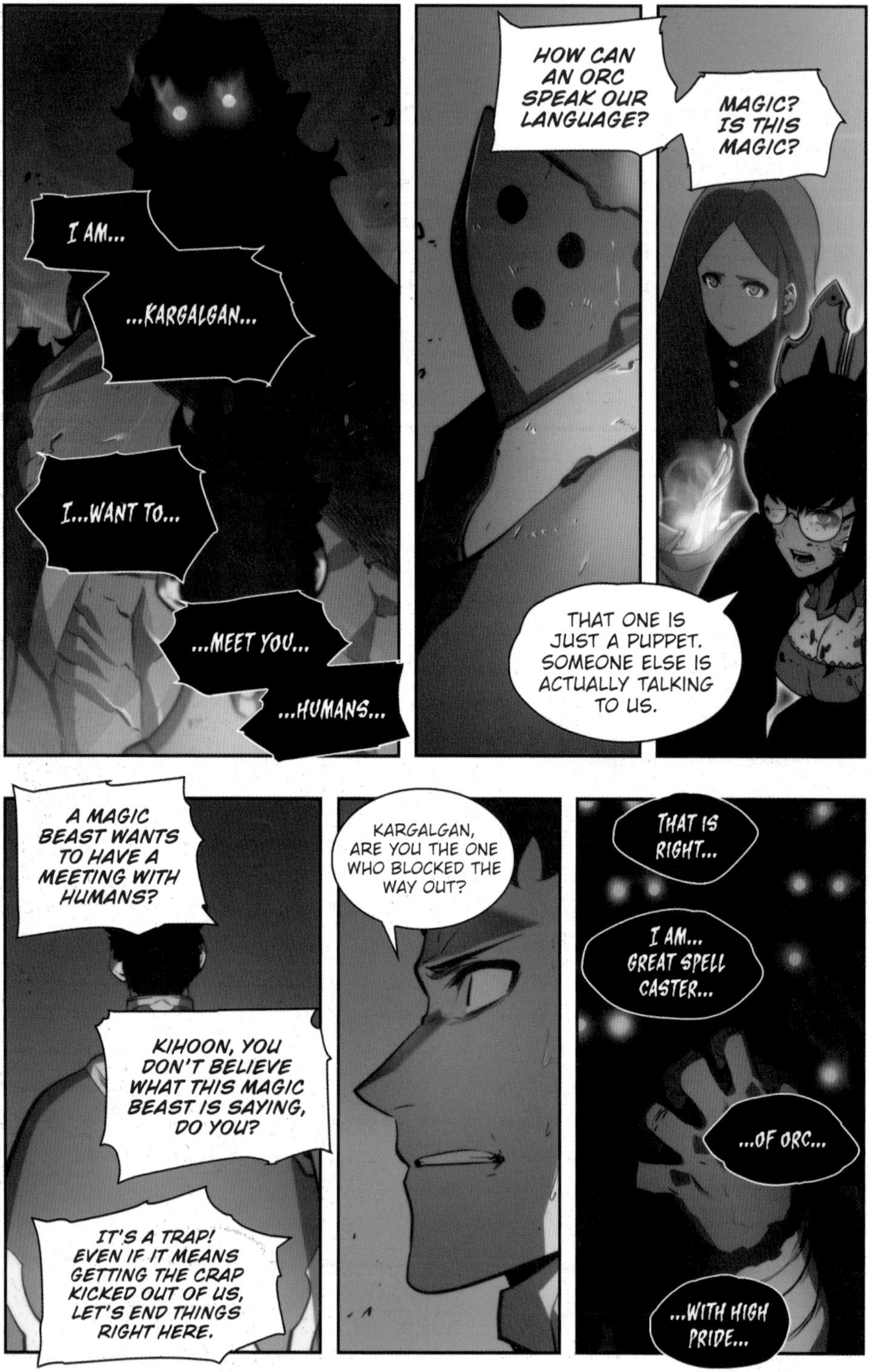
I AM...
...KARGALGAN...
I...WANT TO...
...MEET YOU...
...HUMANS...
HOW CAN AN ORC SPEAK OUR LANGUAGE?
MAGIC? IS THIS MAGIC?
THAT ONE IS JUST A PUPPET. SOMEONE ELSE IS ACTUALLY TALKING TO US.
A MAGIC BEAST WANTS TO HAVE A MEETING WITH HUMANS?
KIHOON, YOU DON'T BELIEVE WHAT THIS MAGIC BEAST IS SAYING, DO YOU?
IT'S A TRAP! EVEN IF IT MEANS GETTING THE CRAP KICKED OUT OF US, LET'S END THINGS RIGHT HERE.
KARGALGAN, ARE YOU THE ONE WHO BLOCKED THE WAY OUT?
THAT IS RIGHT...
I AM... GREAT SPELL CASTER...
...OF ORC...
...WITH HIGH PRIDE...

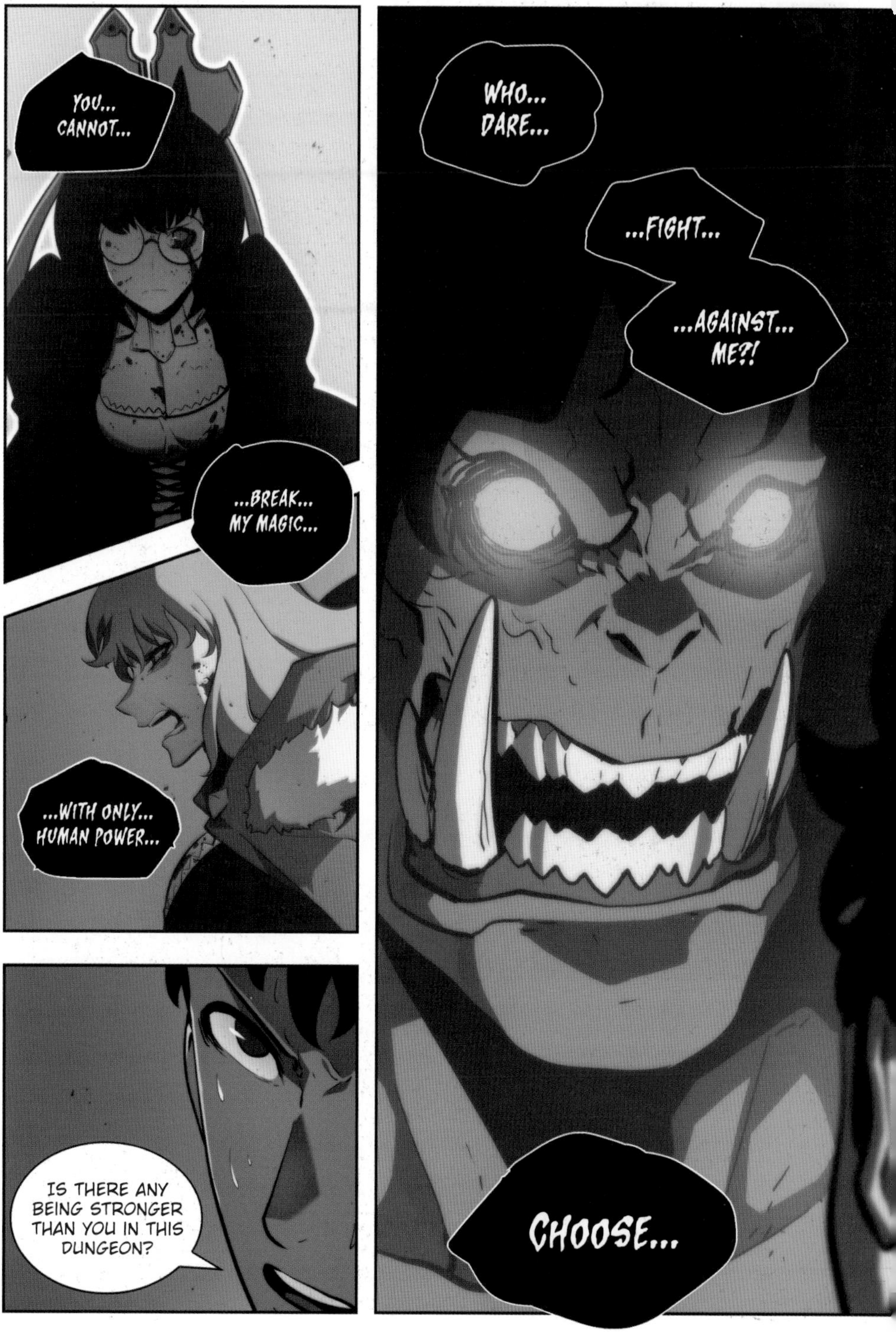
YOU... CANNOT...
...BREAK... MY MAGIC...
...WITH ONLY... HUMAN POWER...
IS THERE ANY BEING STRONGER THAN YOU IN THIS DUNGEON?
WHO... DARE...
...FIGHT...
...AGAINST... ME?!
CHOOSE...

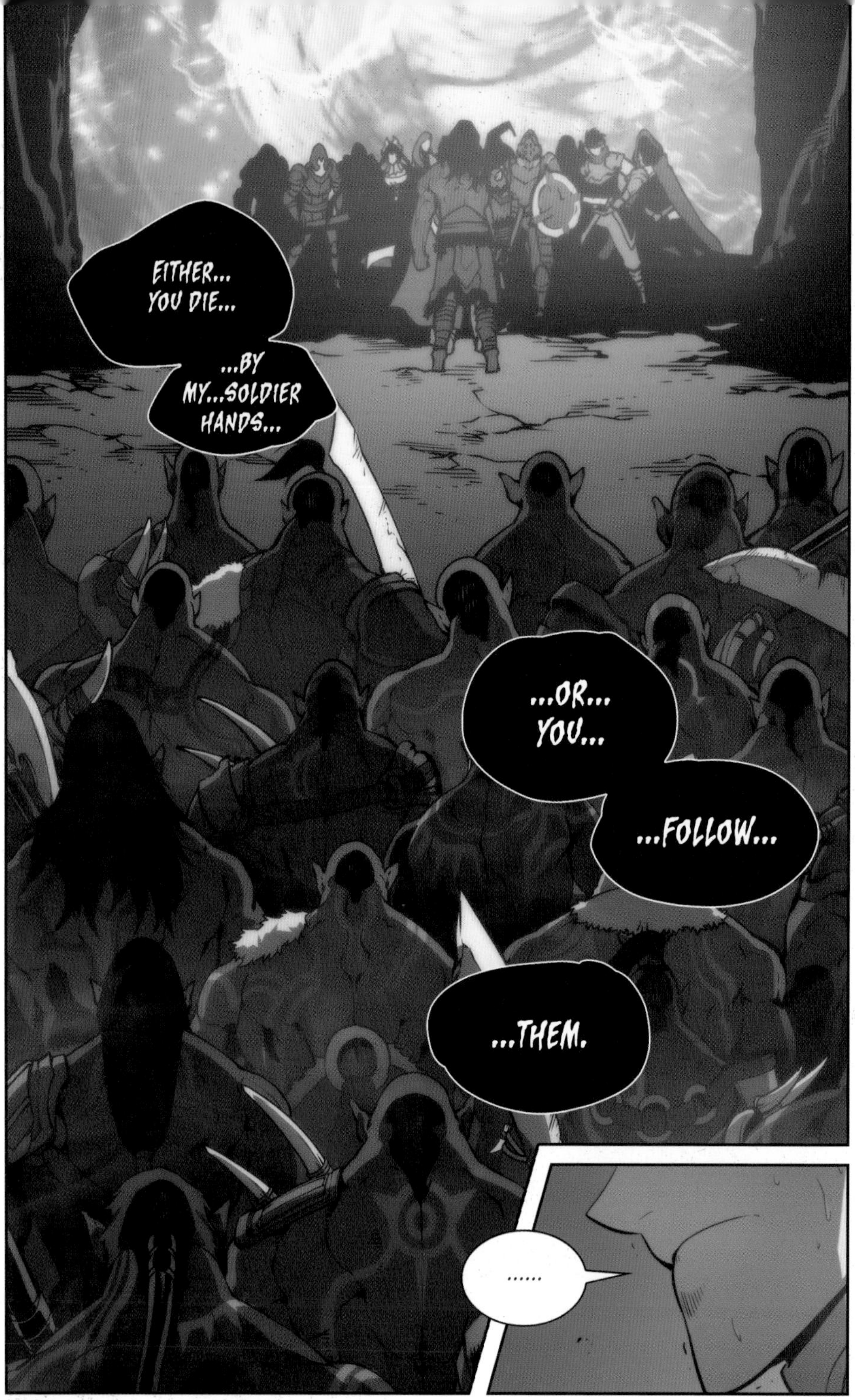
EITHER... YOU DIE...
...BY MY...SOLDIER HANDS...
...OR... YOU...
...FOLLOW...
...THEM.
......

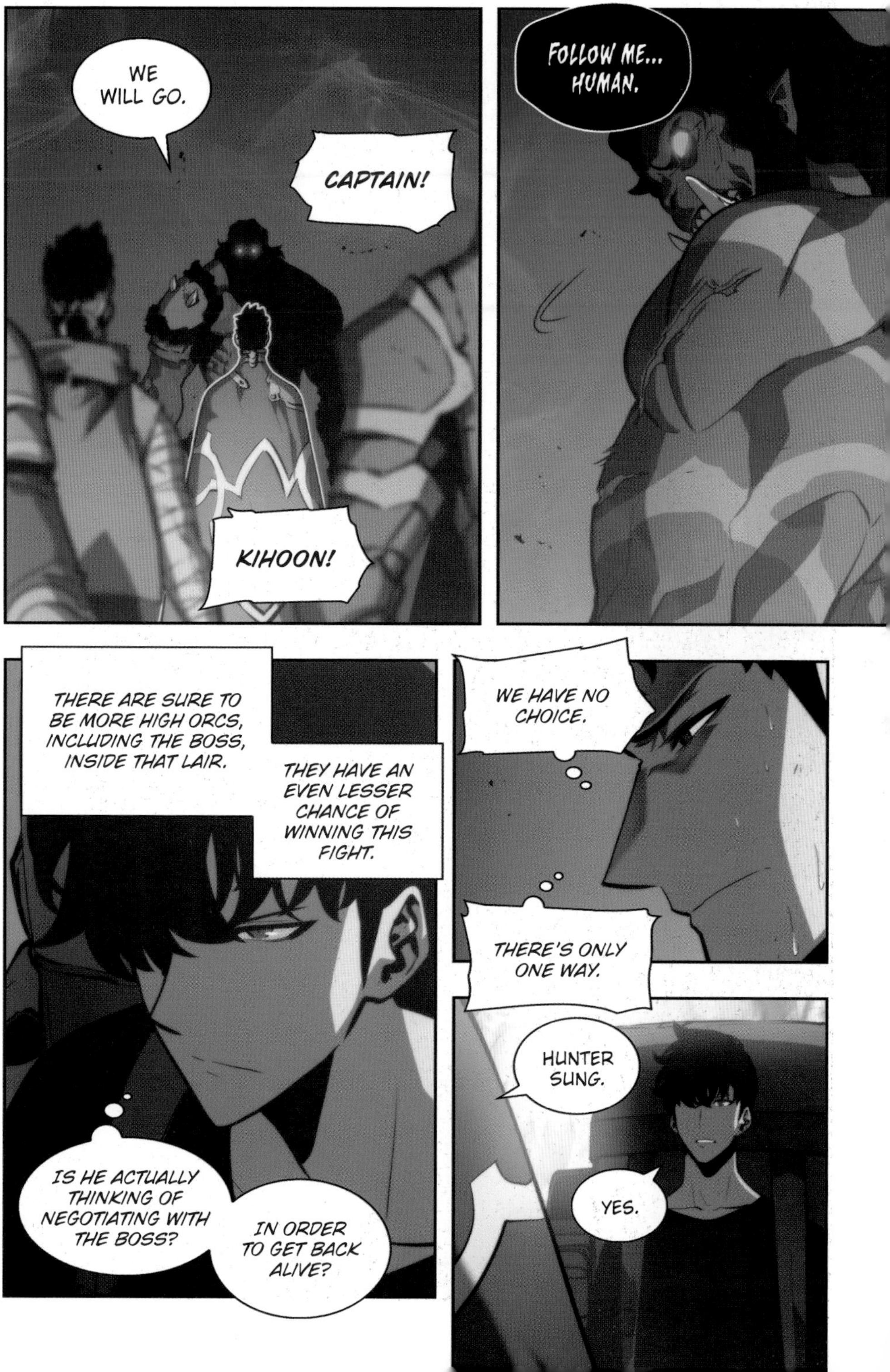
WE WILL GO.
CAPTAIN!
KIHOON!
FOLLOW ME... HUMAN.
THERE ARE SURE TO BE MORE HIGH ORCS, INCLUDING THE BOSS, INSIDE THAT LAIR.
THEY HAVE AN EVEN LESSER CHANCE OF WINNING THIS FIGHT.
IS HE ACTUALLY THINKING OF NEGOTIATING WITH THE BOSS?
IN ORDER TO GET BACK ALIVE?
WE HAVE NO CHOICE.
THERE'S ONLY ONE WAY.
HUNTER SUNG.
YES.

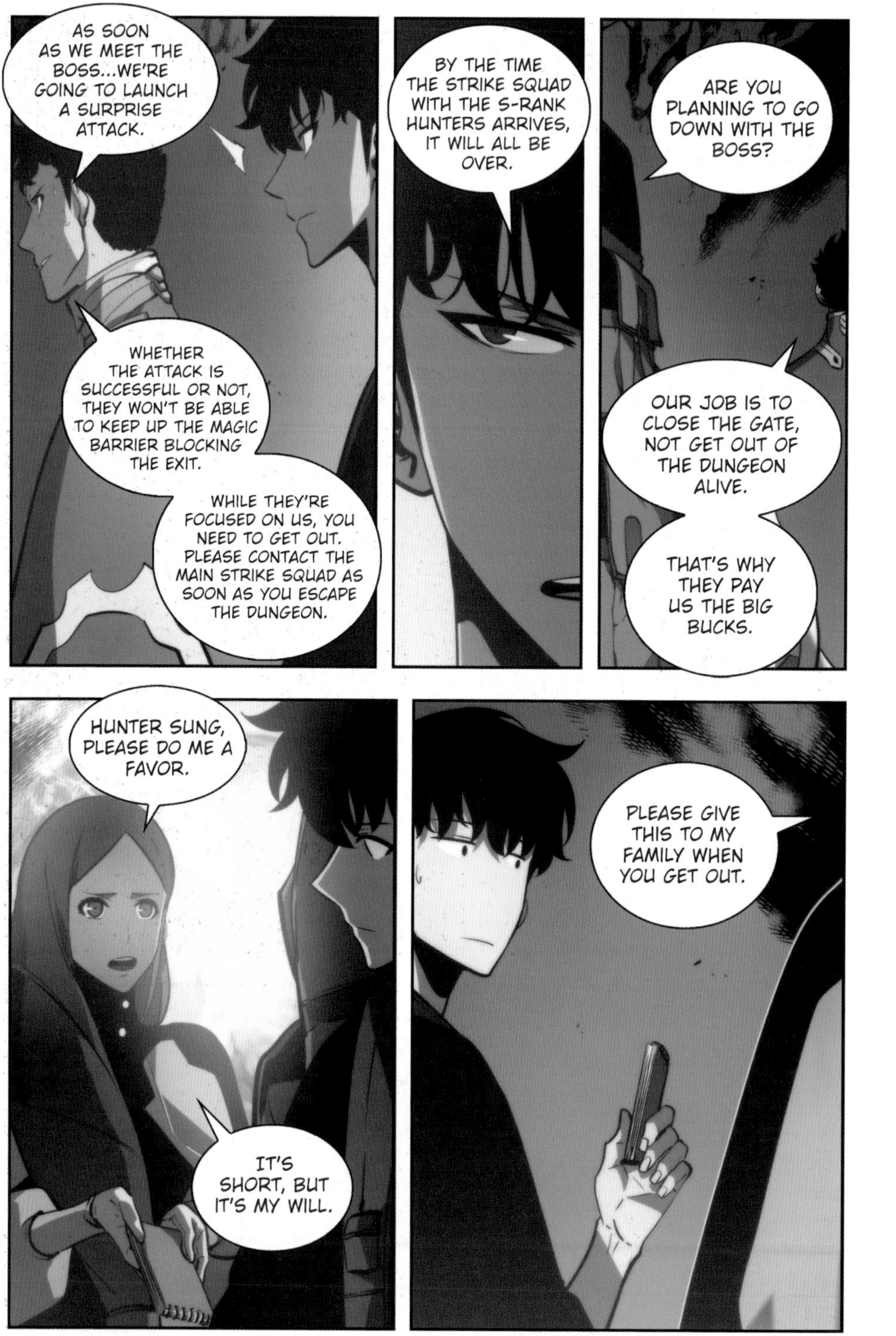
AS SOON AS WE MEET THE BOSS...WE'RE GOING TO LAUNCH A SURPRISE ATTACK.
WHETHER THE ATTACK IS SUCCESSFUL OR NOT, THEY WON'T BE ABLE TO KEEP UP THE MAGIC BARRIER BLOCKING THE EXIT.
WHILE THEY'RE FOCUSED ON US, YOU NEED TO GET OUT. PLEASE CONTACT THE MAIN STRIKE SQUAD AS SOON AS YOU ESCAPE THE DUNGEON.
BY THE TIME THE STRIKE SQUAD WITH THE S-RANK HUNTERS ARRIVES, IT WILL ALL BE OVER.
ARE YOU PLANNING TO GO DOWN WITH THE BOSS?
OUR JOB IS TO CLOSE THE GATE, NOT GET OUT OF THE DUNGEON ALIVE.
THAT'S WHY THEY PAY US THE BIG BUCKS.
HUNTER SUNG, PLEASE DO ME A FAVOR.
IT'S SHORT, BUT IT'S MY WILL.
PLEASE GIVE THIS TO MY FAMILY WHEN YOU GET OUT.

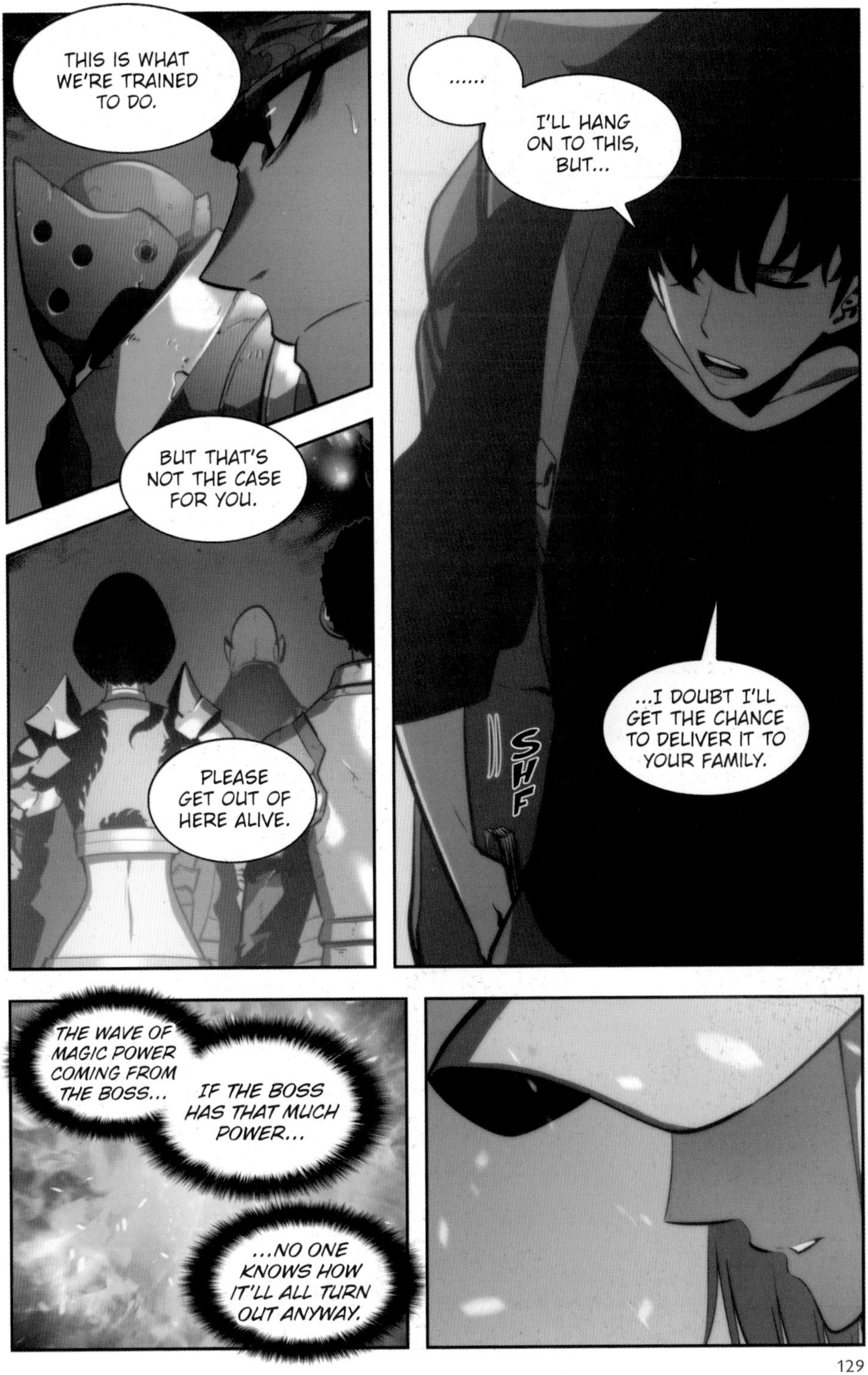
THIS IS WHAT WE'RE TRAINED TO DO.
BUT THAT'S NOT THE CASE FOR YOU.
PLEASE GET OUT OF HERE ALIVE.
......
I'LL HANG ON TO THIS, BUT...
SHF
...I DOUBT I'LL GET THE CHANCE TO DELIVER IT TO YOUR FAMILY.
THE WAVE OF MAGIC POWER COMING FROM THE BOSS...
IF THE BOSS HAS THAT MUCH POWER...
...NO ONE KNOWS HOW IT'LL ALL TURN OUT ANYWAY.

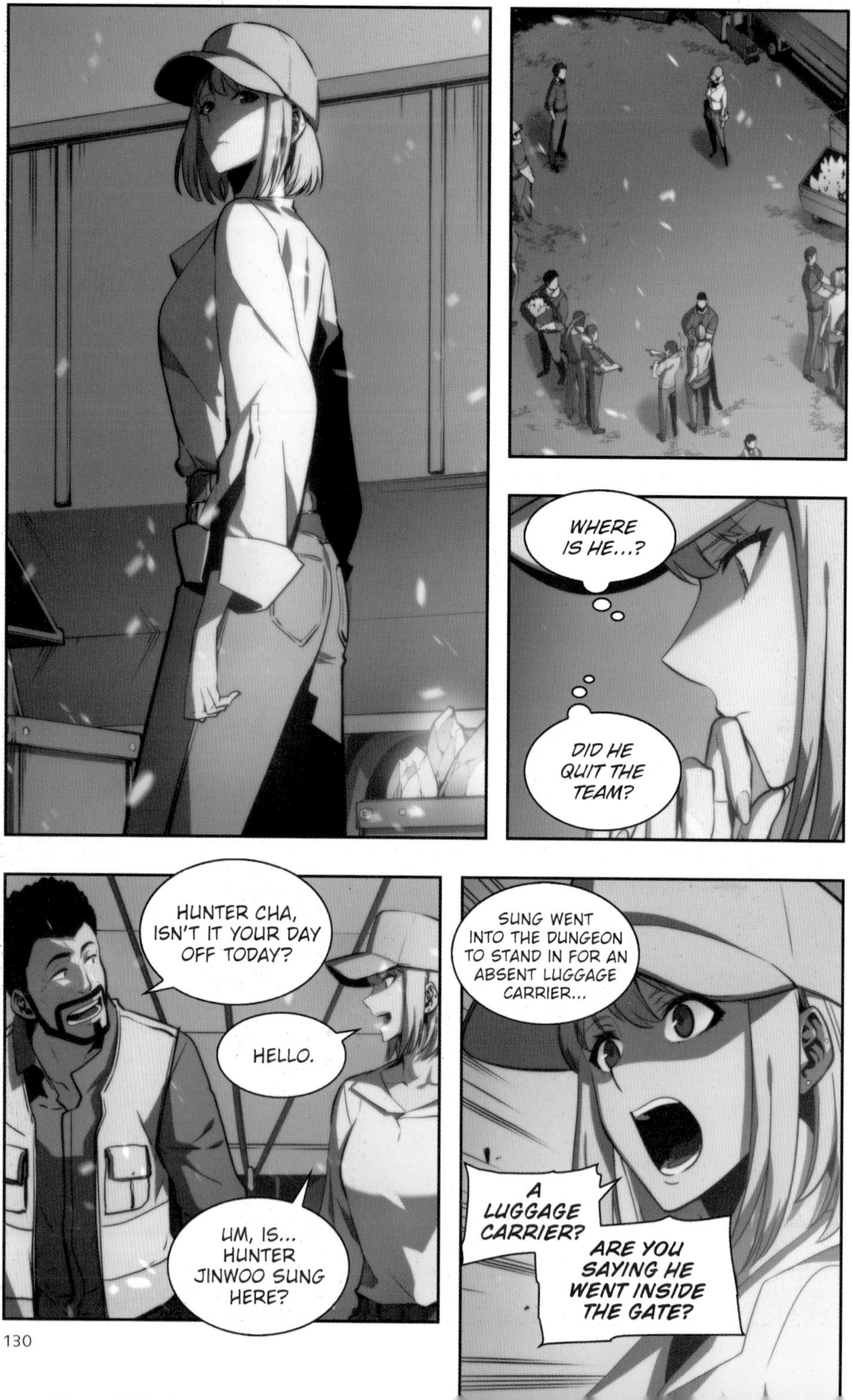
WHERE IS HE...?
DID HE QUIT THE TEAM?
HUNTER CHA, ISN'T IT YOUR DAY OFF TODAY?
HELLO.
UM, IS... HUNTER JINWOO SUNG HERE?
SUNG WENT INTO THE DUNGEON TO STAND IN FOR AN ABSENT LUGGAGE CARRIER...
A LUGGAGE CARRIER?
ARE YOU SAYING HE WENT INSIDE THE GATE?

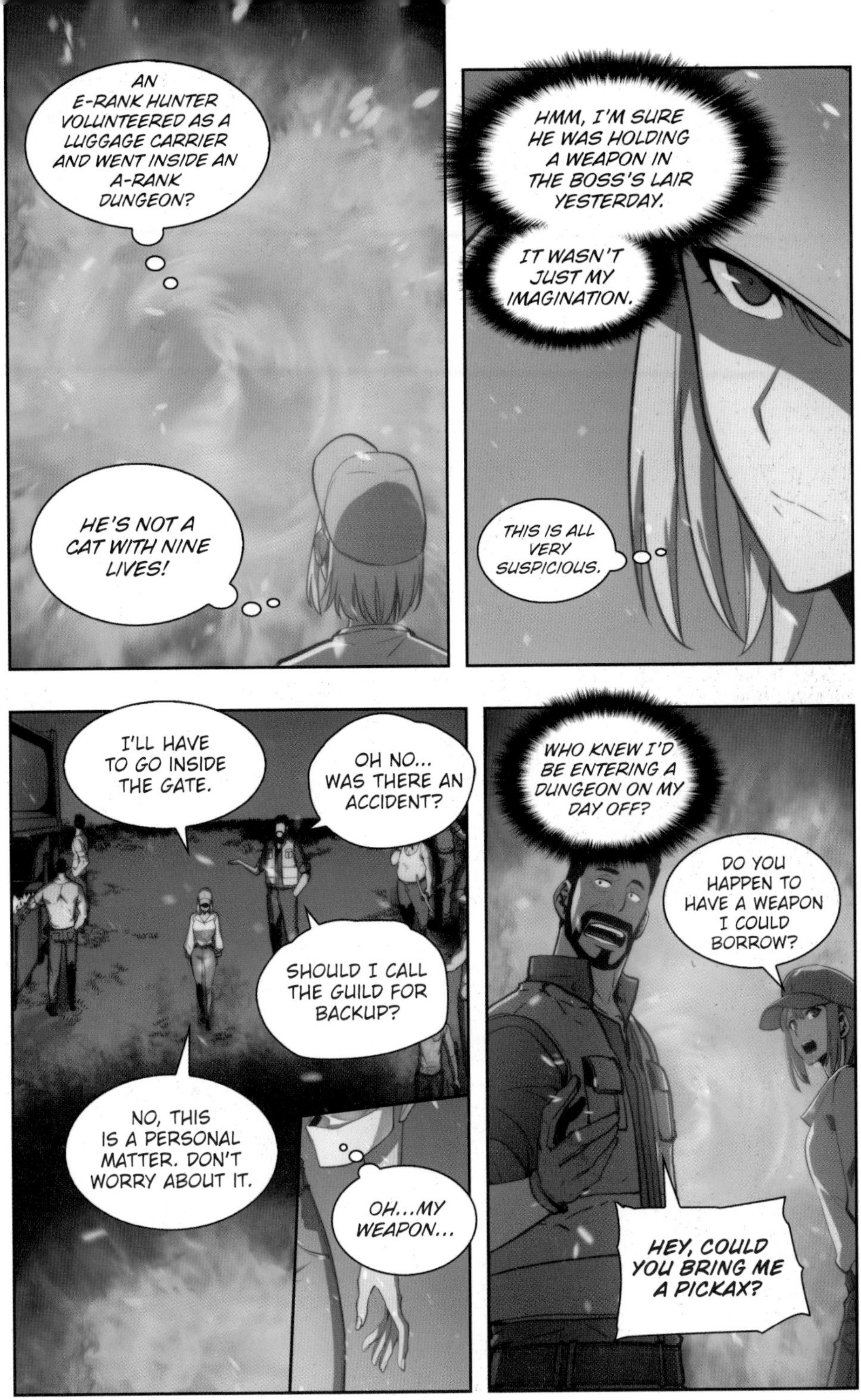
AN E-RANK HUNTER VOLUNTEERED AS A LUGGAGE CARRIER AND WENT INSIDE AN A-RANK DUNGEON?
HE'S NOT A CAT WITH NINE LIVES!
HMM, I'M SURE HE WAS HOLDING A WEAPON IN THE BOSS'S LAIR YESTERDAY.
IT WASN'T JUST MY IMAGINATION.
THIS IS ALL VERY SUSPICIOUS.
I'LL HAVE TO GO INSIDE THE GATE.
OH NO... WAS THERE AN ACCIDENT?
SHOULD I CALL THE GUILD FOR BACKUP?
NO, THIS IS A PERSONAL MATTER. DON'T WORRY ABOUT IT.
OH...MY WEAPON...
WHO KNEW I'D BE ENTERING A DUNGEON ON MY DAY OFF?
DO YOU HAPPEN TO HAVE A WEAPON I COULD BORROW?
HEY, COULD YOU BRING ME A PICKAX?

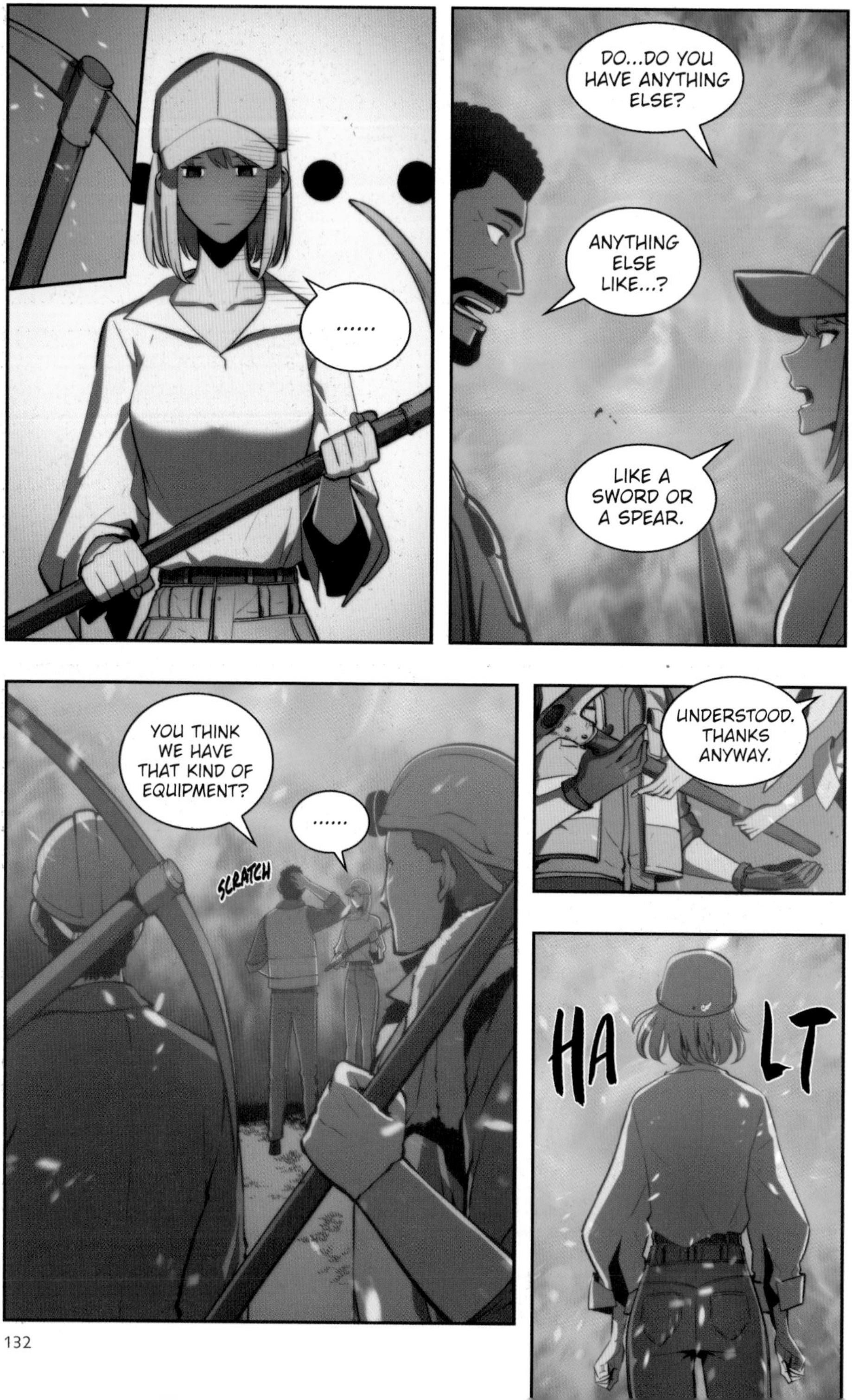
......
DO...DO YOU HAVE ANYTHING ELSE?
ANYTHING ELSE LIKE...?
LIKE A SWORD OR A SPEAR.
YOU THINK WE HAVE THAT KIND OF EQUIPMENT?
......
SCRATCH
UNDERSTOOD. THANKS ANYWAY.
HALT

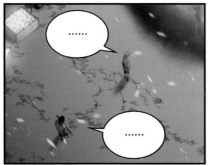

......

......

HUNTER
CHA, YOU SURE IT'S OKAY TO GO IN THERE UNARMED?

TREMBLE

TREMBLE

GRAB

GOOD THINKING! IT'S NEVER A SMART IDEA TO GO IN THERE EMPTY-HANDED.

WELL, THEN...

DASH

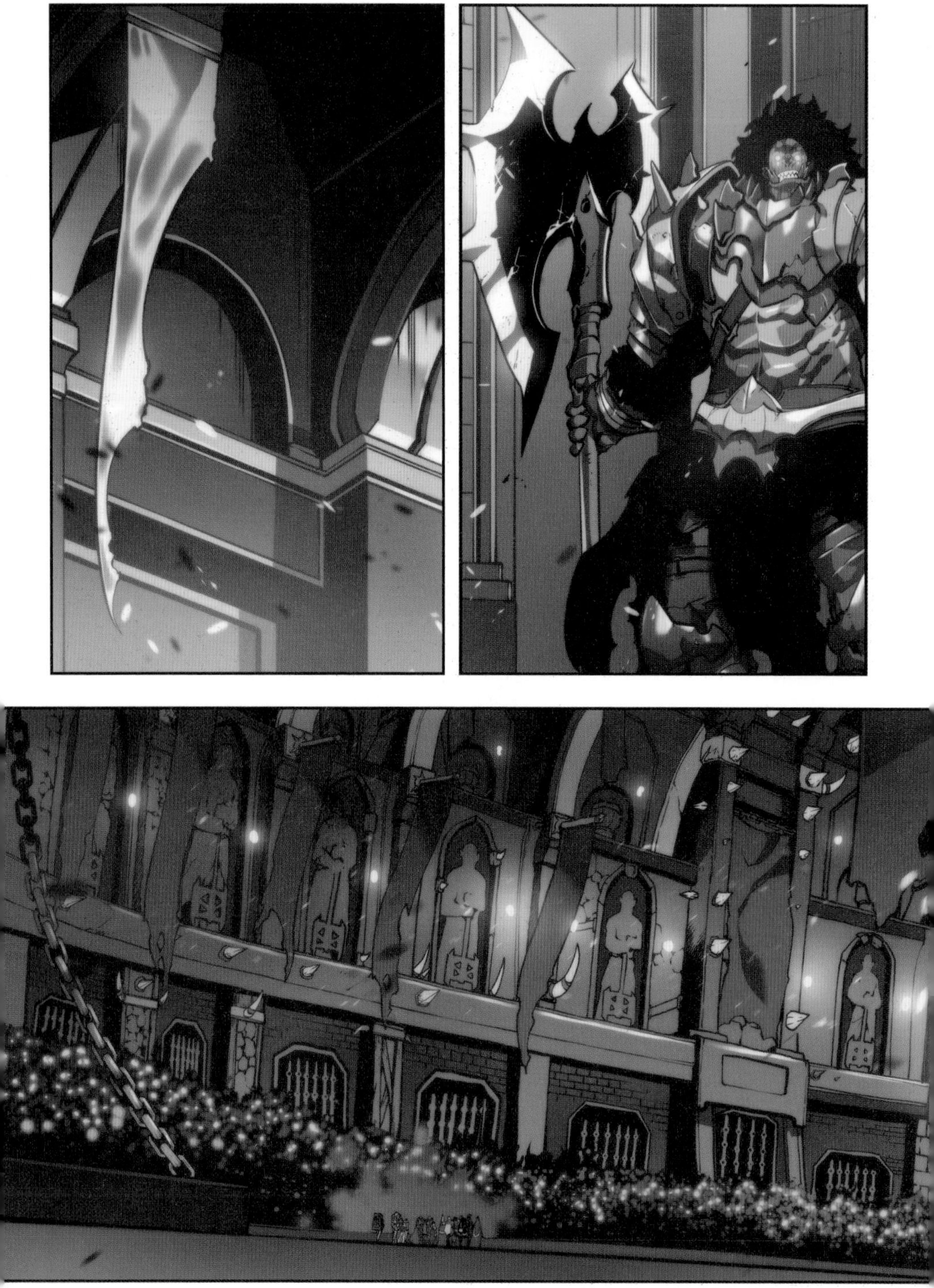

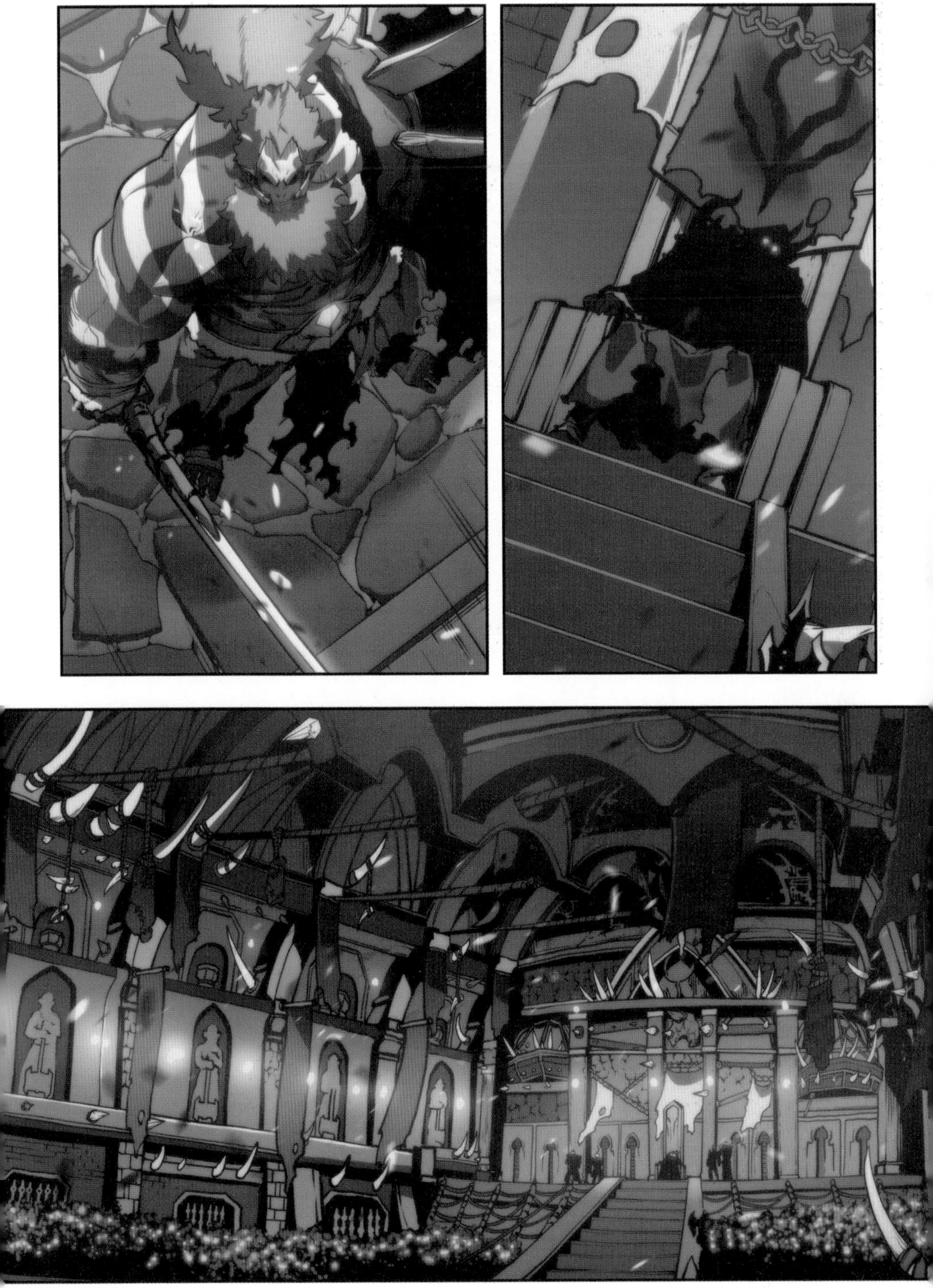

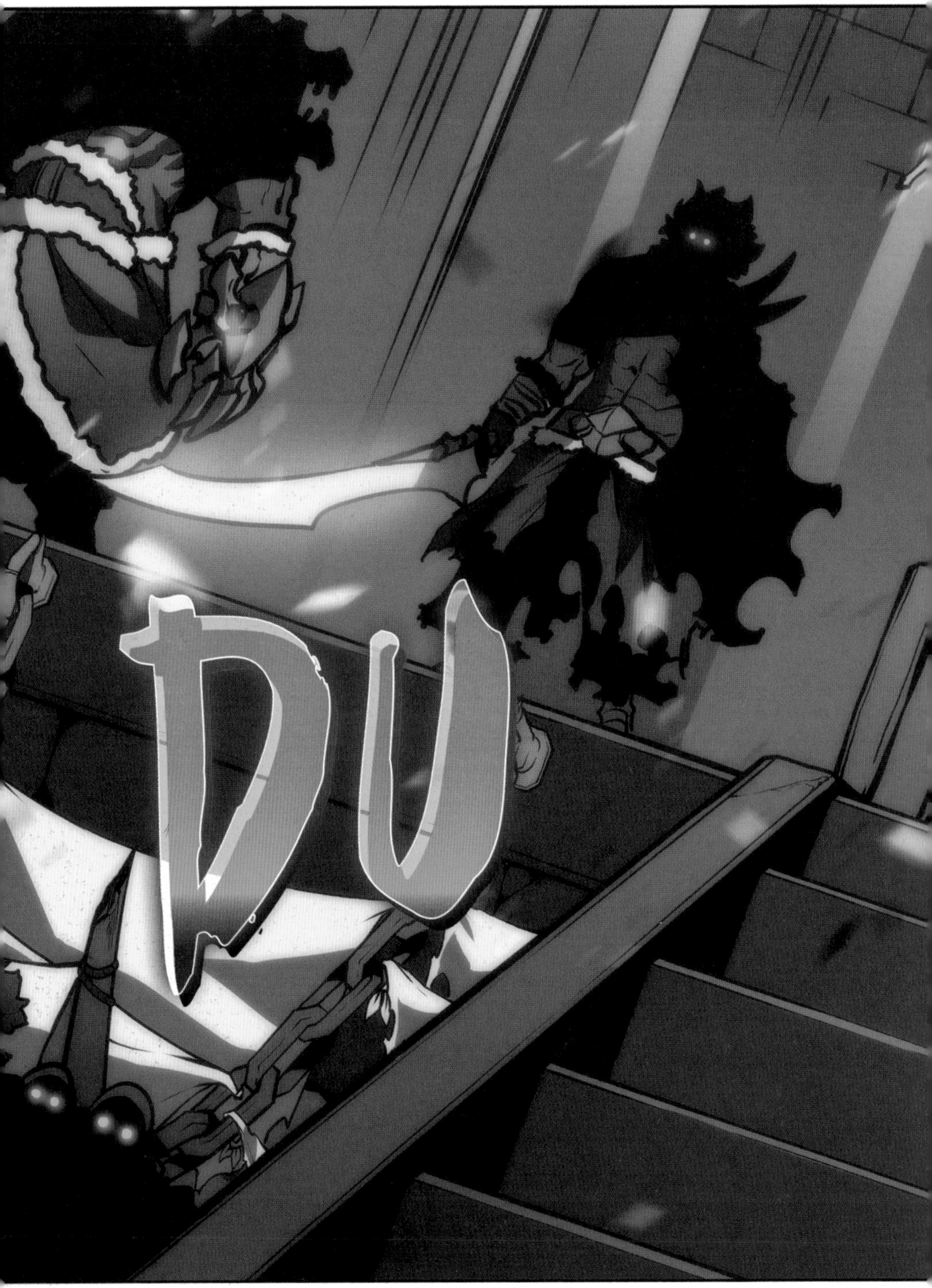
DU

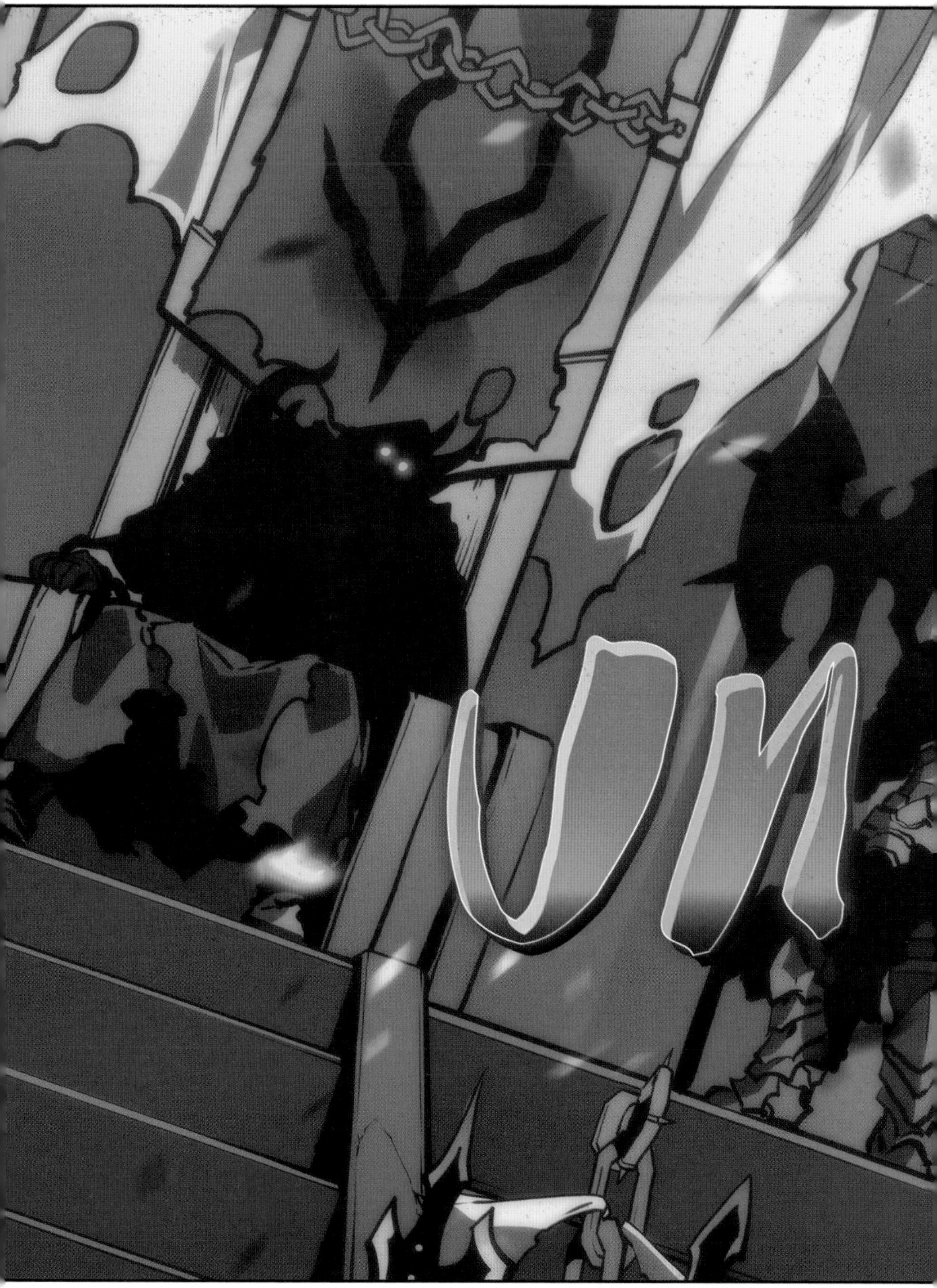
UN

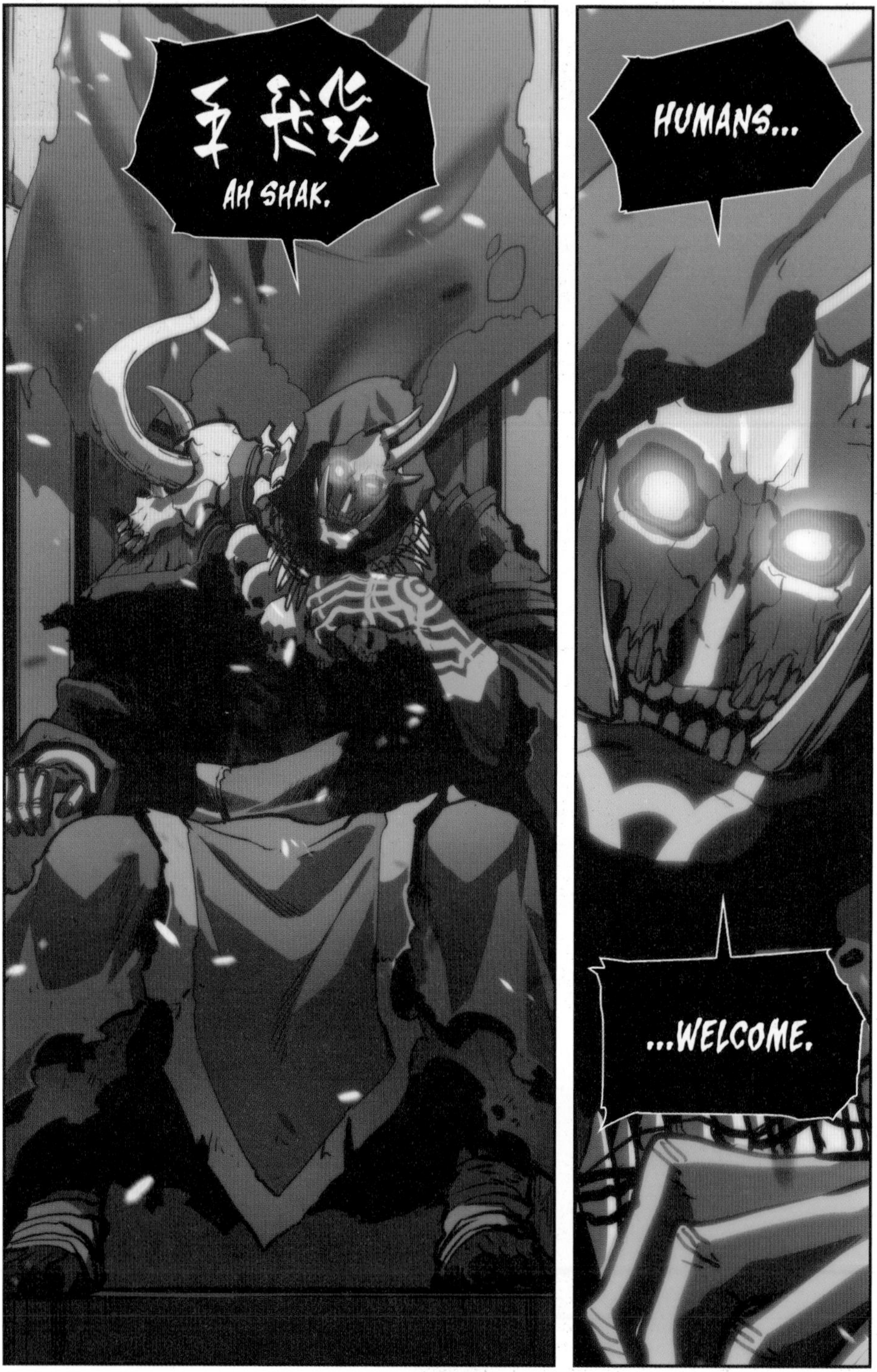
AH SHAK.
HUMANS...
...WELCOME.

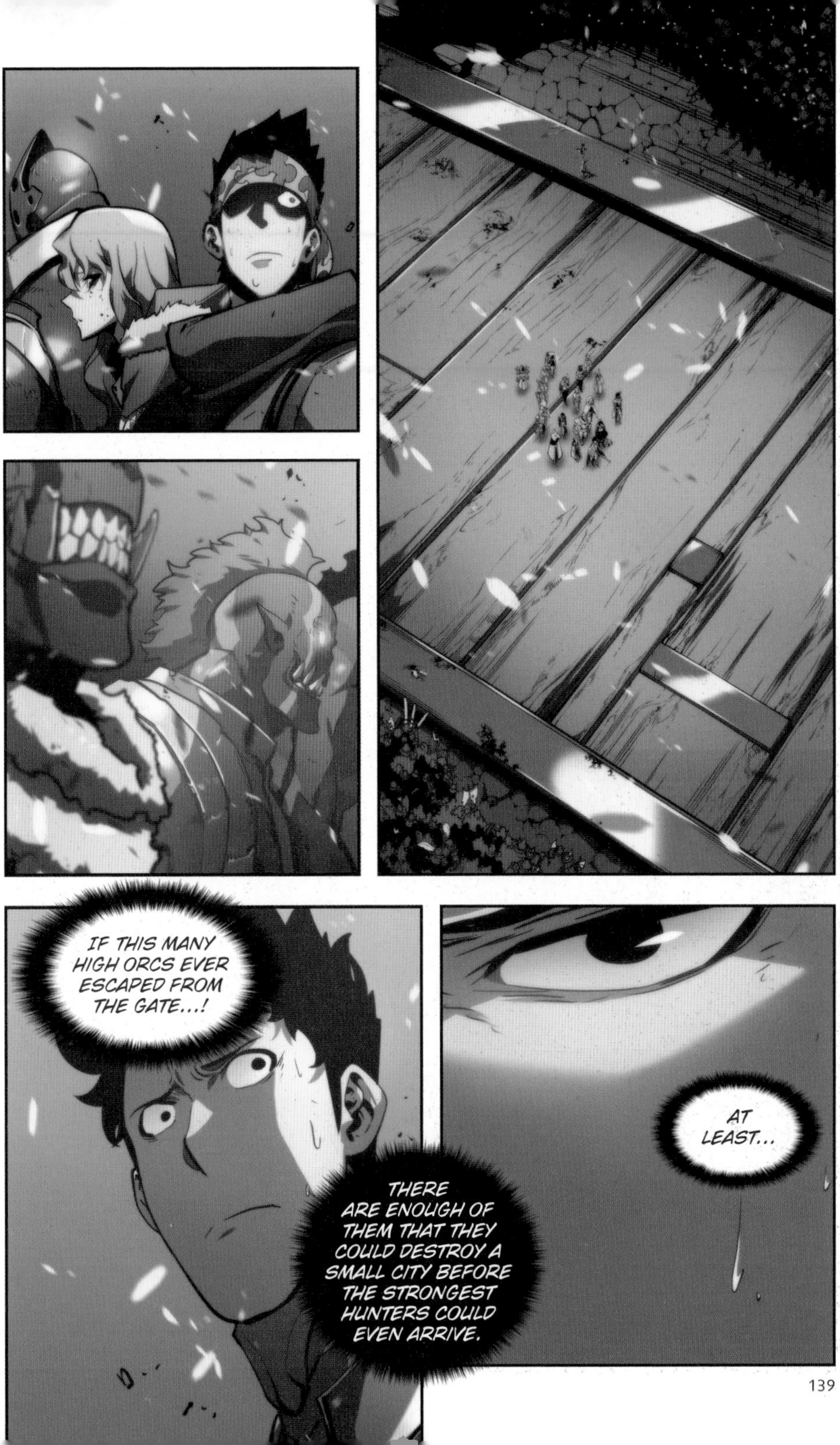
IF THIS MANY HIGH ORCS EVER ESCAPED FROM THE GATE...!
THERE ARE ENOUGH OF THEM THAT THEY COULD DESTROY A SMALL CITY BEFORE THE STRONGEST HUNTERS COULD EVEN ARRIVE.
AT LEAST...

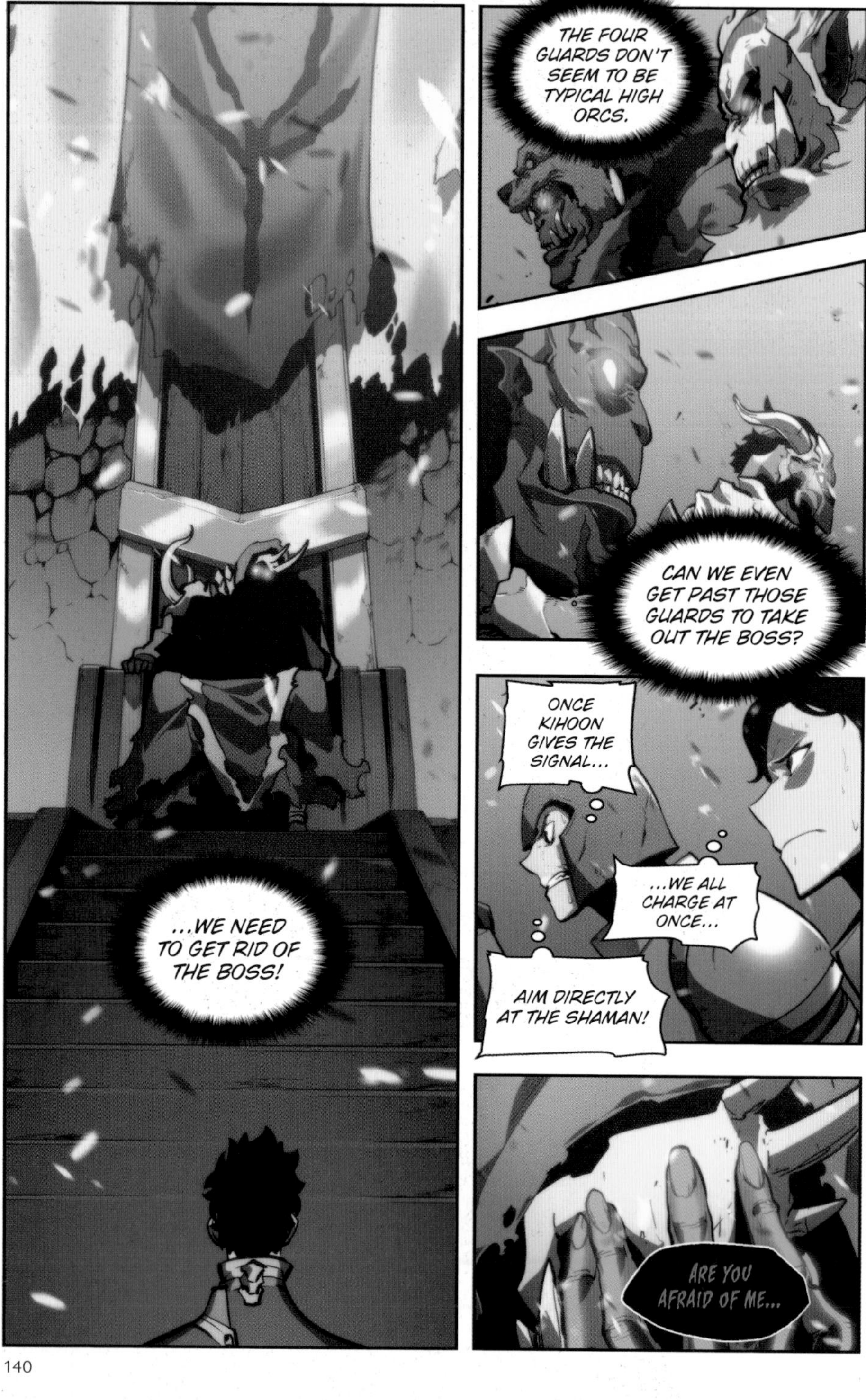
...WE NEED TO GET RID OF THE BOSS!
THE FOUR GUARDS DON'T SEEM TO BE TYPICAL HIGH ORCS.
CAN WE EVEN GET PAST THOSE GUARDS TO TAKE OUT THE BOSS?
ONCE KIHOON GIVES THE SIGNAL...
...WE ALL CHARGE AT ONCE...
AIM DIRECTLY AT THE SHAMAN!
ARE YOU AFRAID OF ME...

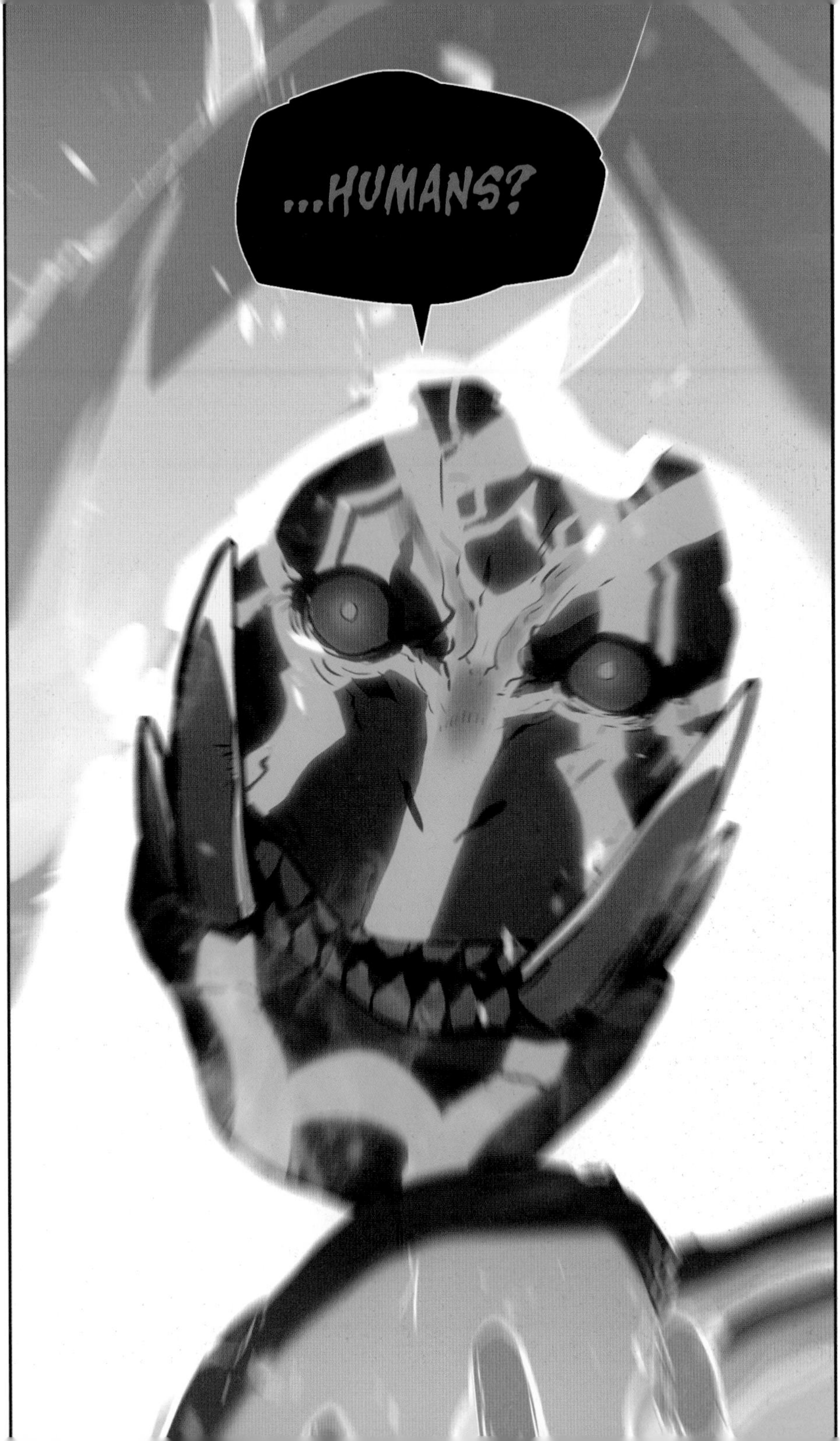
...HUMANS?

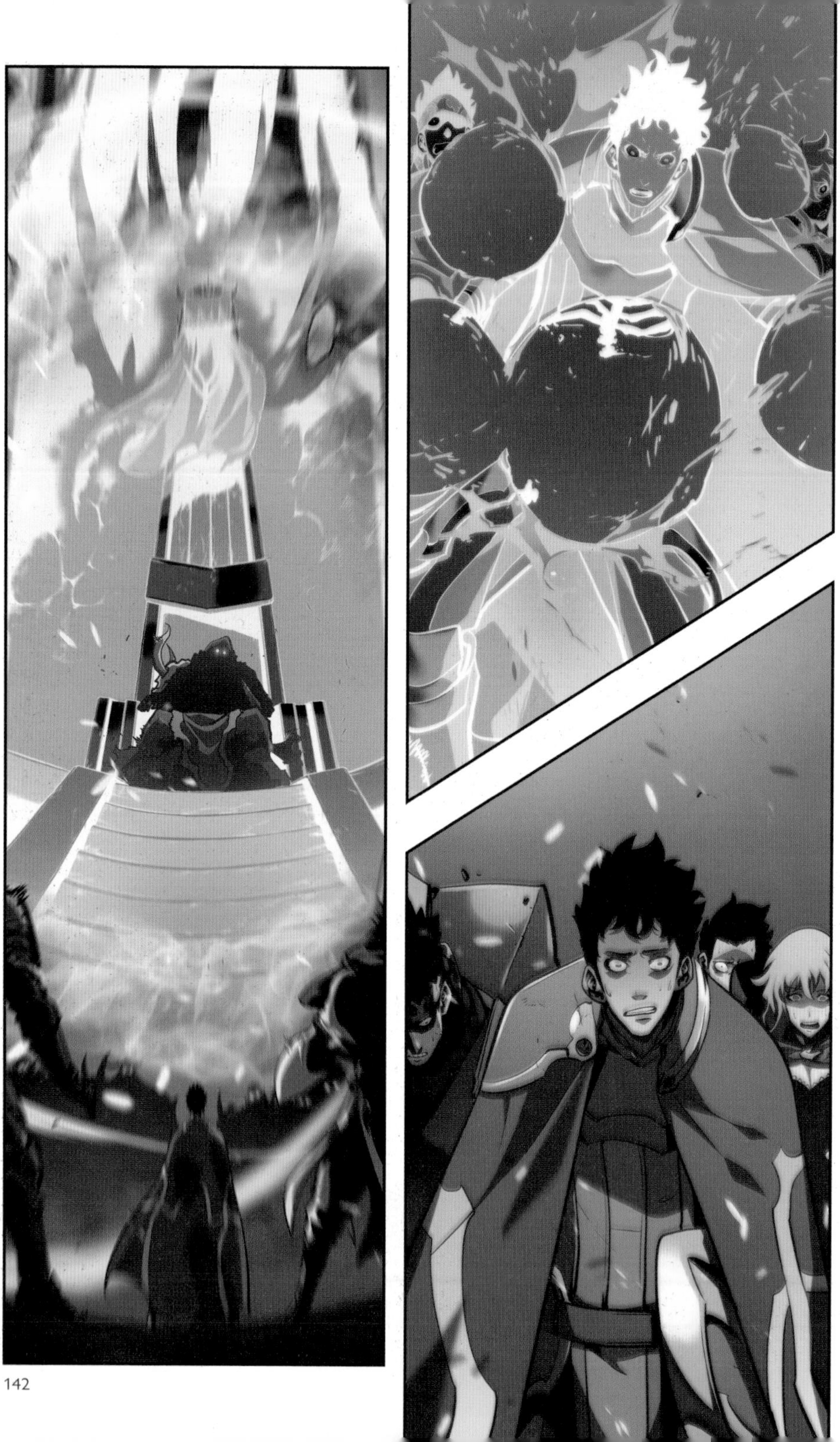

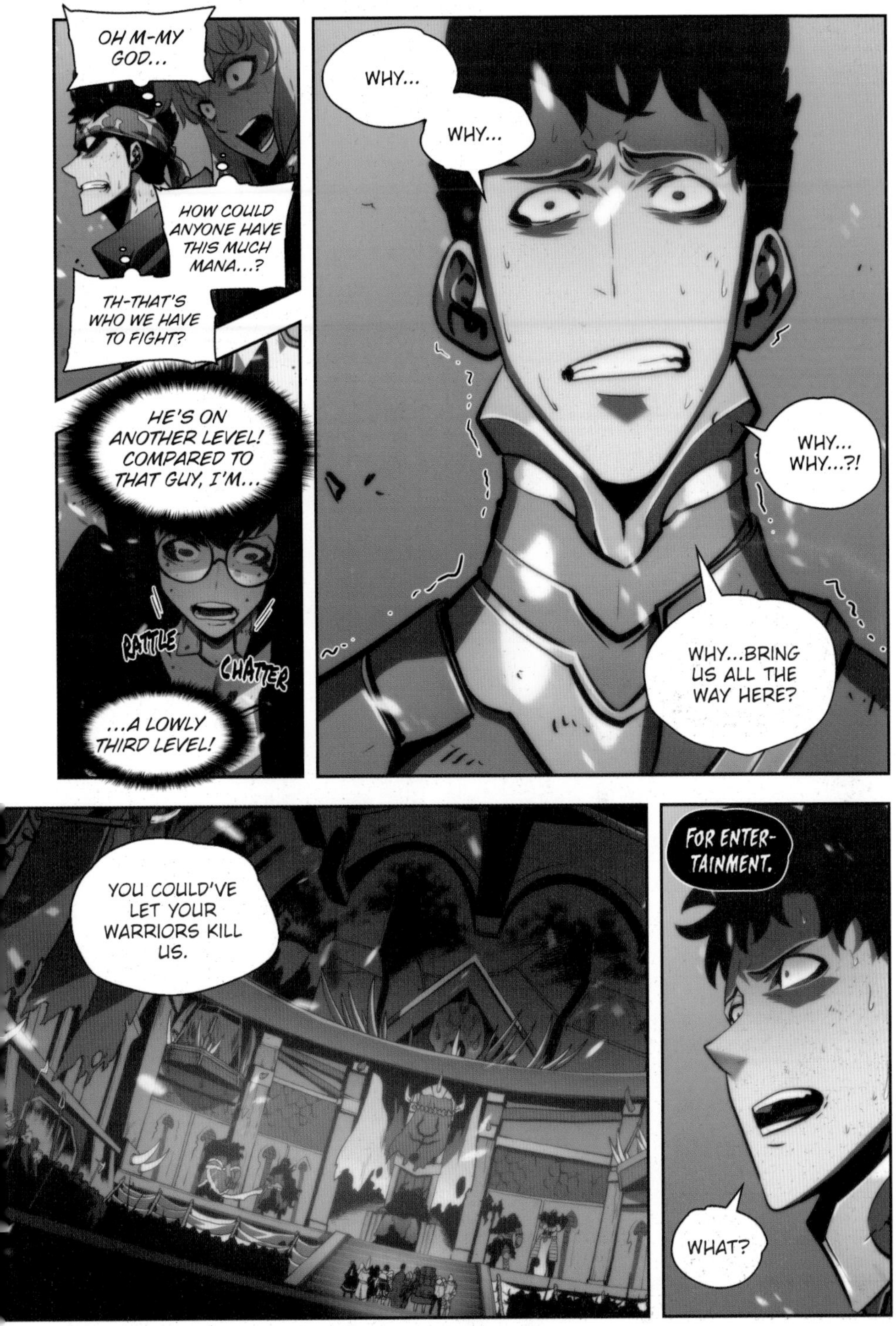
OH M-MY GOD...
HOW COULD ANYONE HAVE THIS MUCH MANA...?
TH-THAT'S WHO WE HAVE TO FIGHT?
HE'S ON ANOTHER LEVEL! COMPARED TO THAT GUY, I'M...
RATTLE
CHATTER
...A LOWLY THIRD LEVEL!
WHY...
WHY...
WHY... WHY...?!
WHY...BRING US ALL THE WAY HERE?
YOU COULD'VE LET YOUR WARRIORS KILL US.
FOR ENTER-TAINMENT.
WHAT?

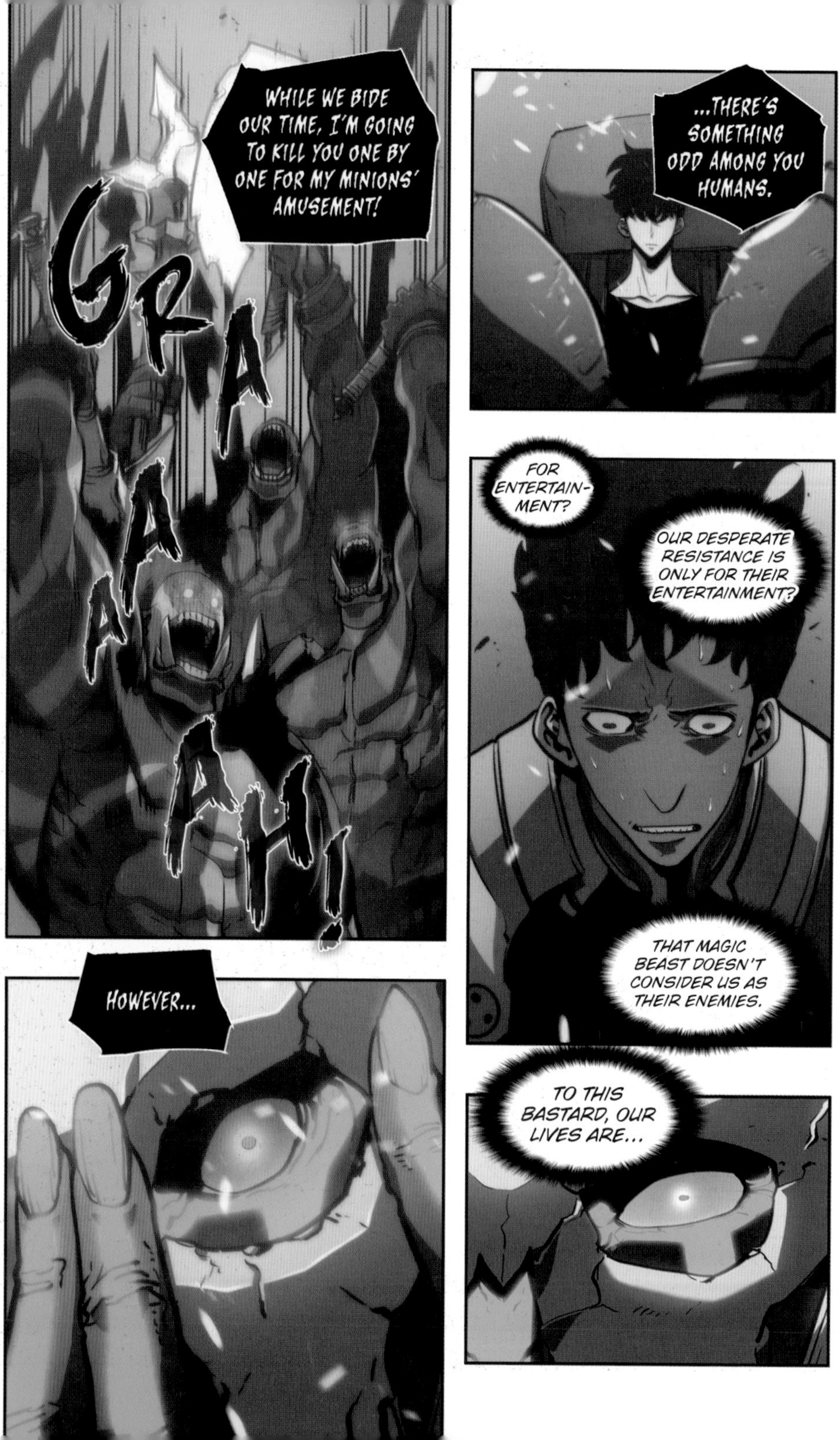

WHILE WE BIDE OUR TIME, I'M GOING TO KILL YOU ONE BY ONE FOR MY MINIONS' AMUSEMENT!
GRAAAAAH!
...THERE'S SOMETHING ODD AMONG YOU HUMANS.
FOR ENTERTAIN-MENT?
OUR DESPERATE RESISTANCE IS ONLY FOR THEIR ENTERTAINMENT?
THAT MAGIC BEAST DOESN'T CONSIDER US AS THEIR ENEMIES.
HOWEVER...
TO THIS BASTARD, OUR LIVES ARE...

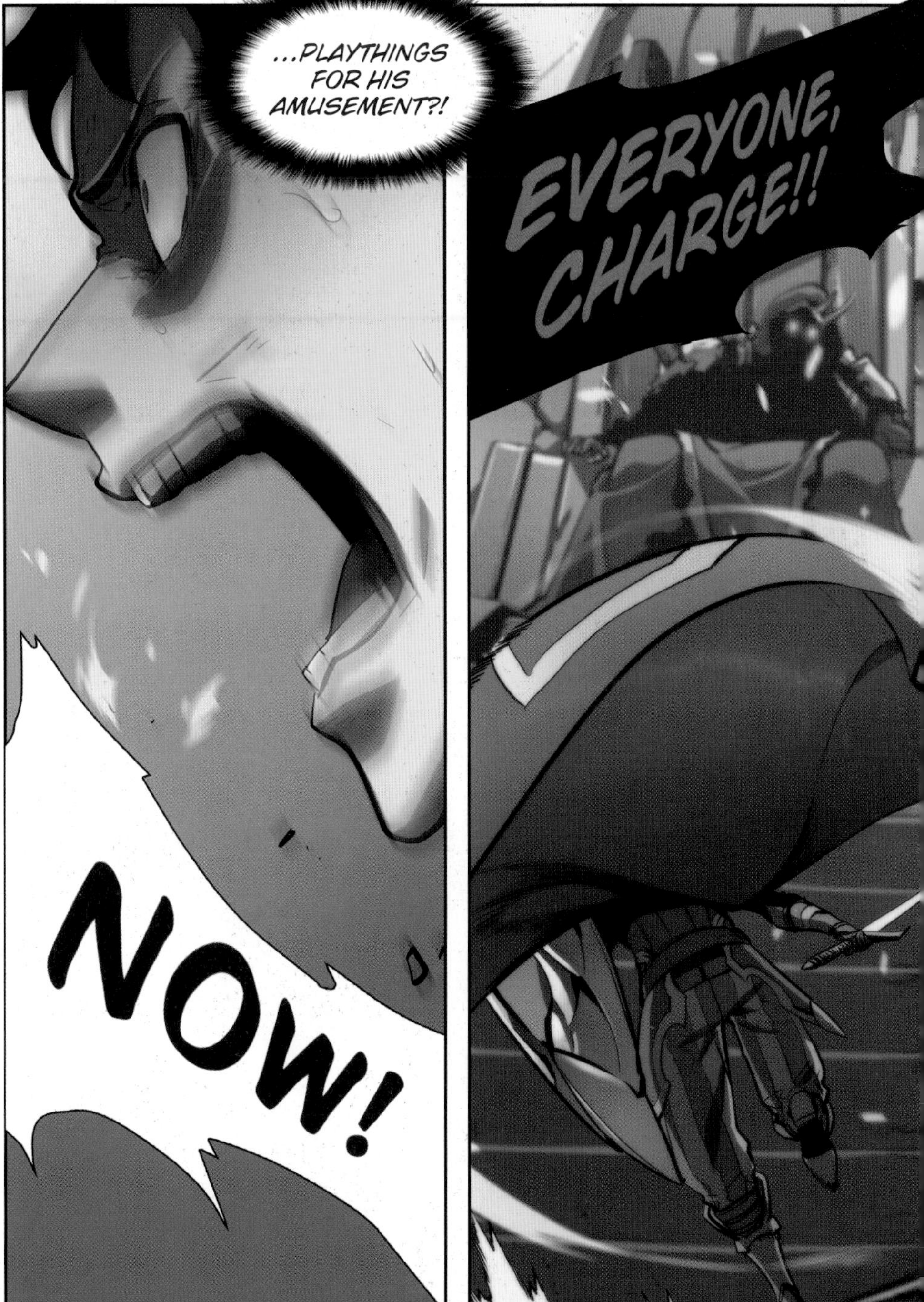
...PLAYTHINGS FOR HIS AMUSEMENT?!
NOW!
EVERYONE, CHARGE!!

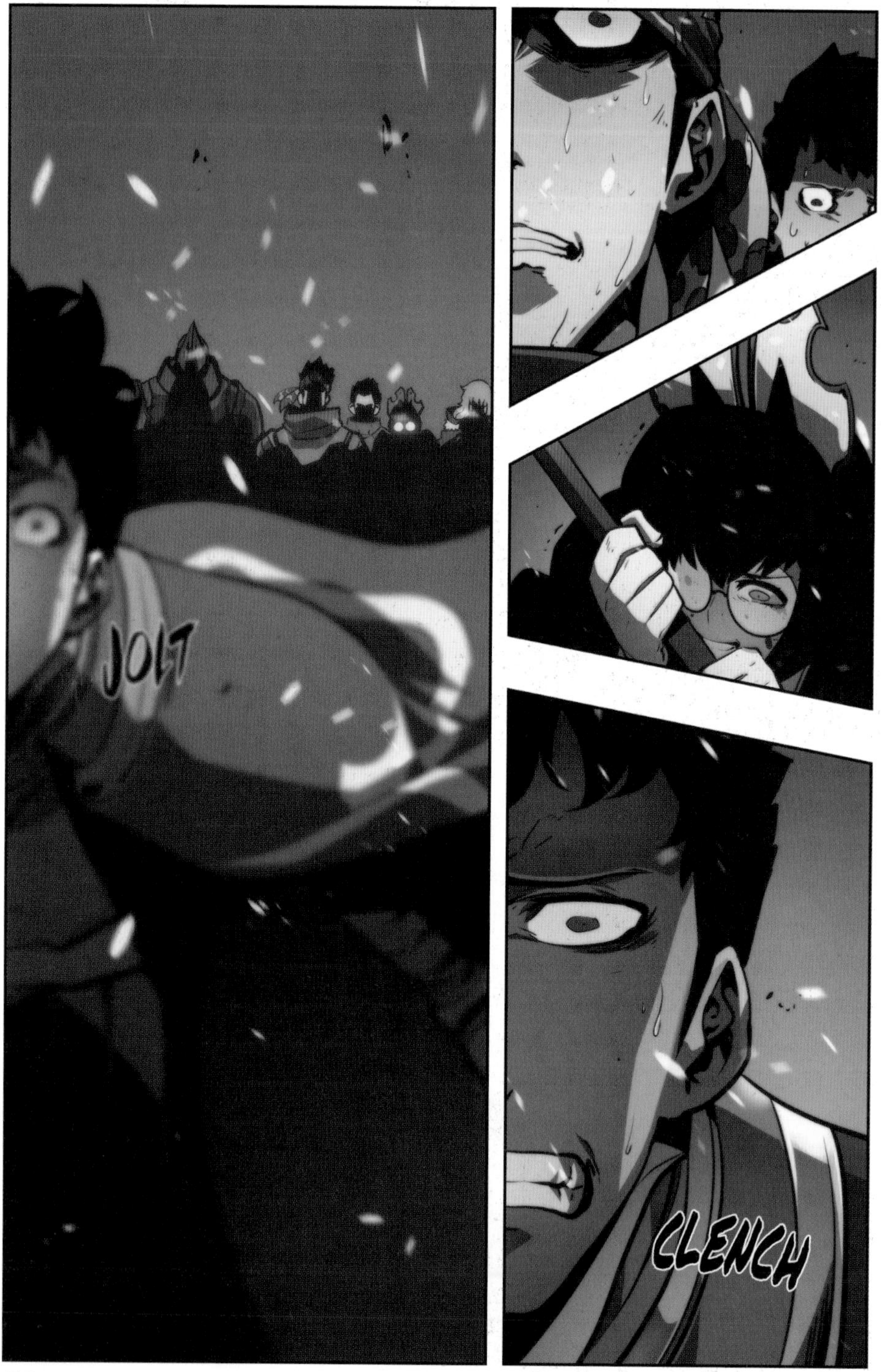
JOLT
CLENCH

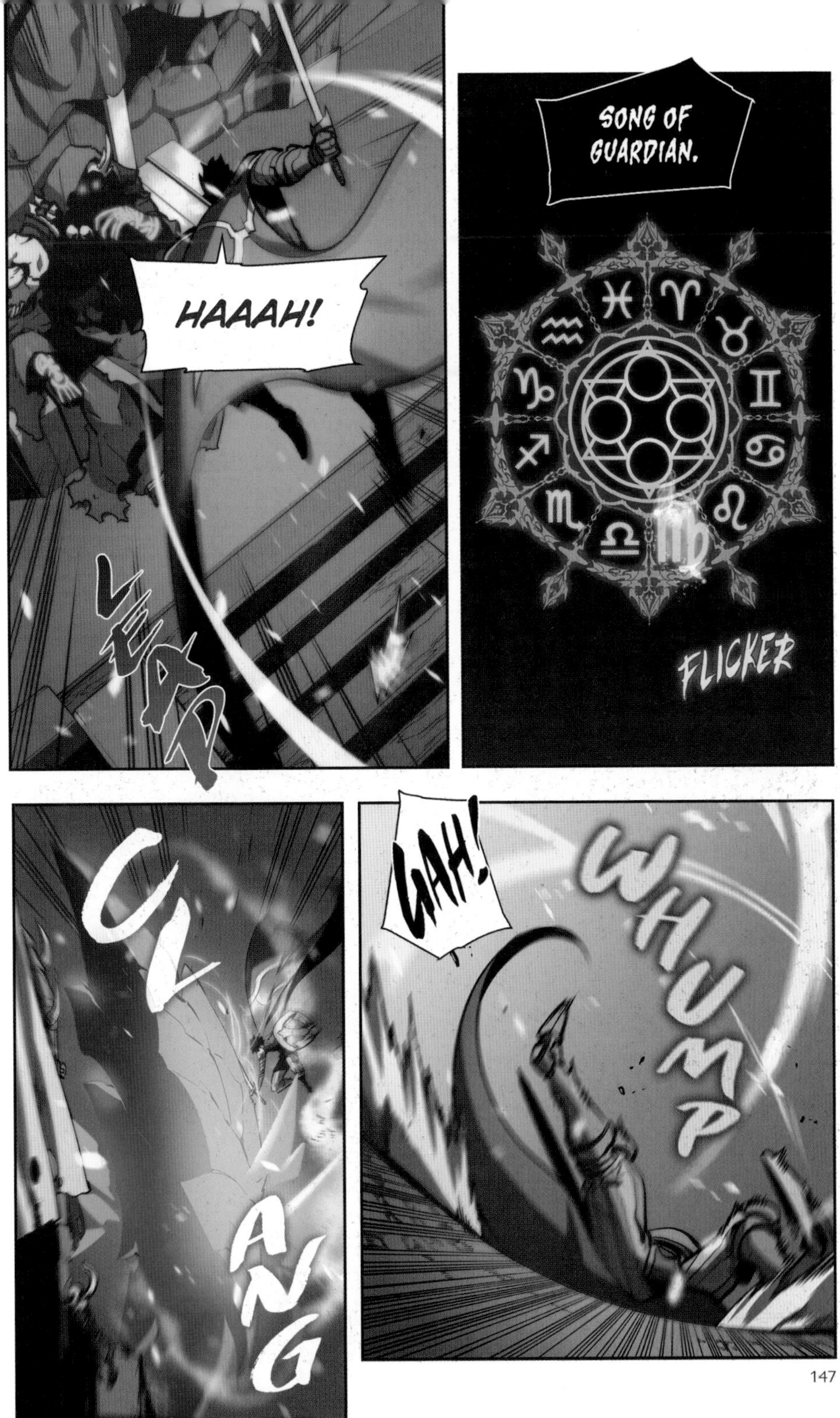

HAAAH!
LEAP
SONG OF GUARDIAN.
FLICKER
CLANG
GAH!
WHUMP

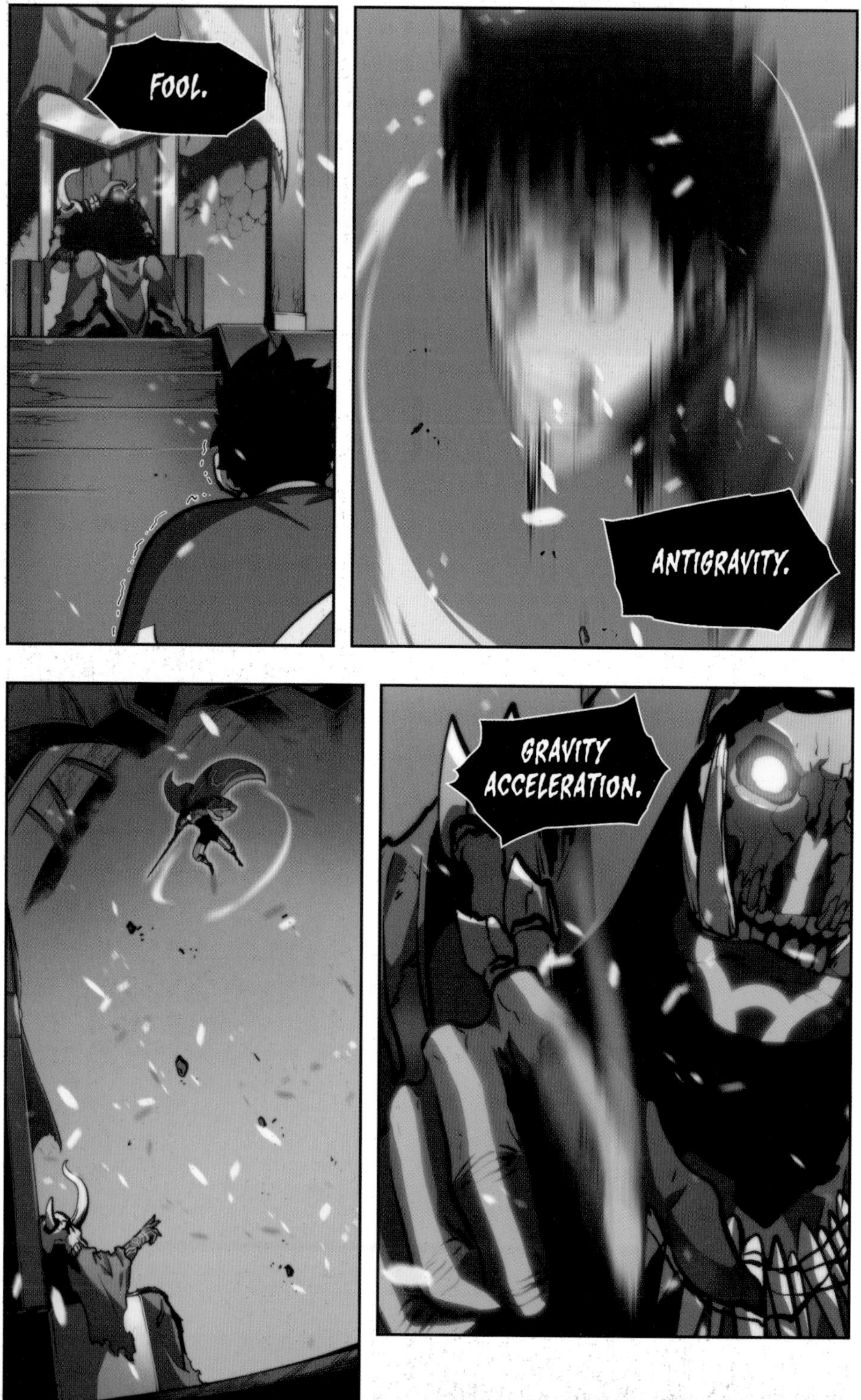
FOOL.
ANTIGRAVITY.
GRAVITY ACCELERATION.

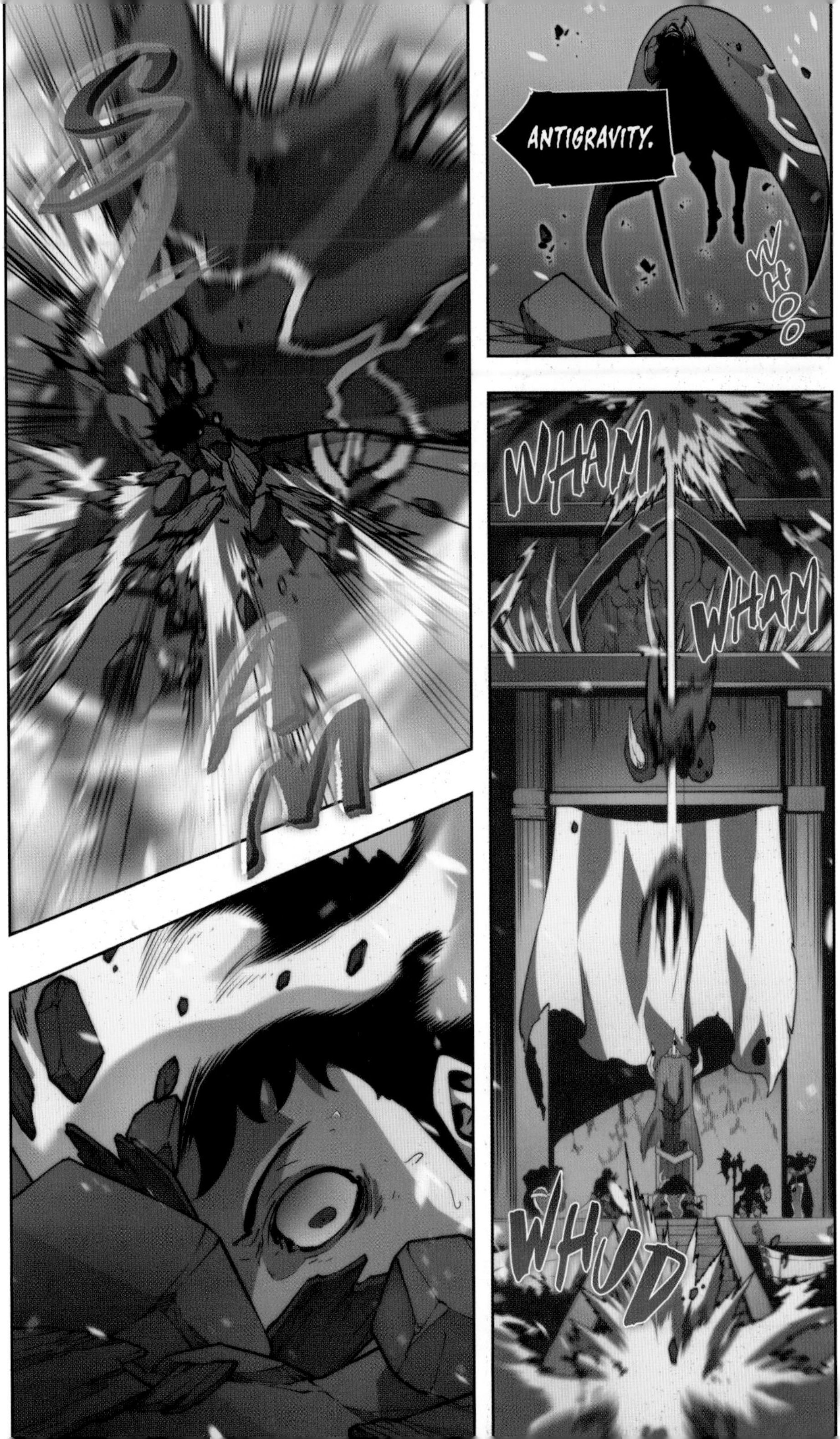
ANTIGRAVITY.
WHOO
WHAM
WHAM
WHUD

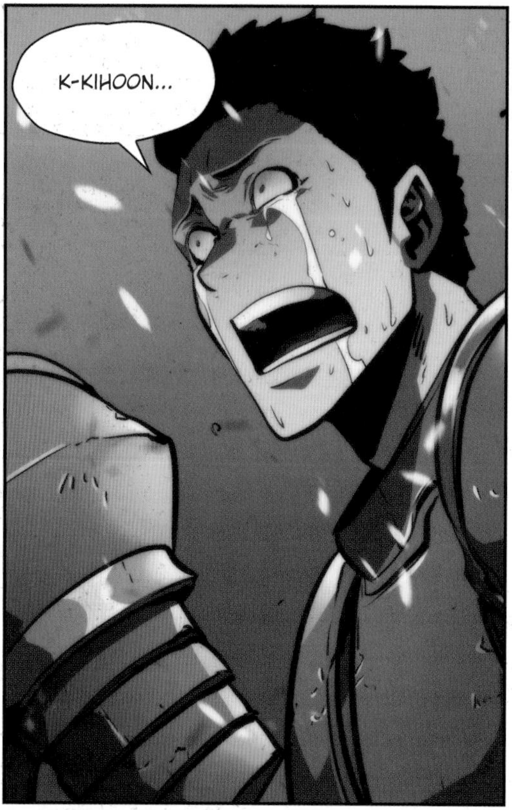
K-KIHOON...
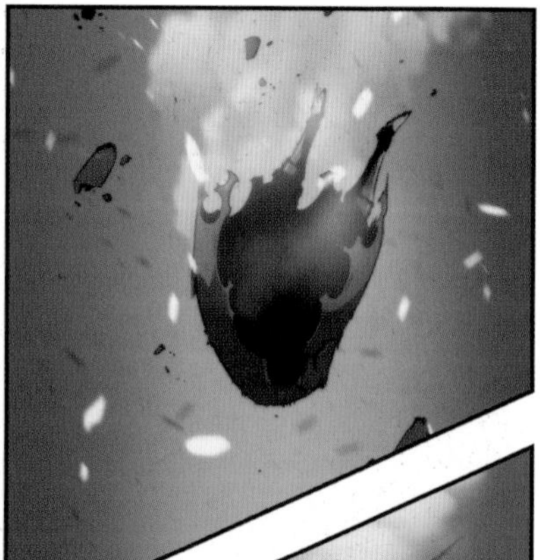
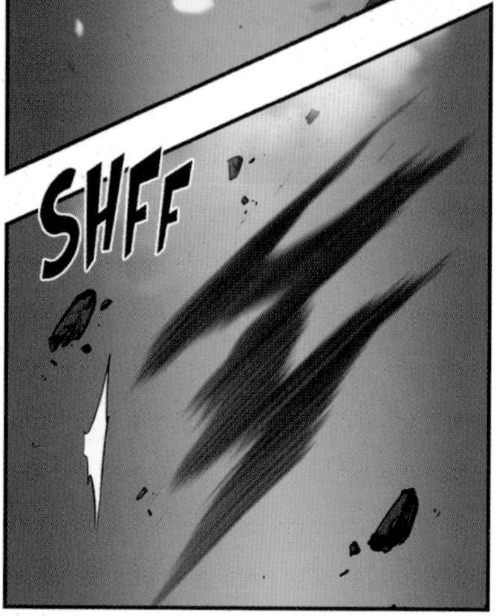
SHFF
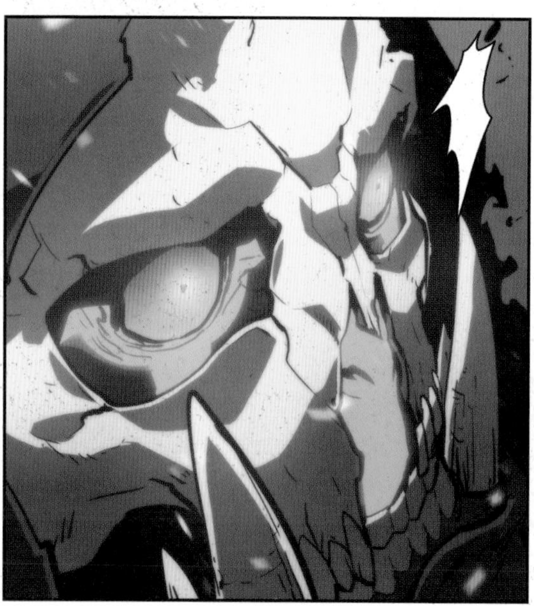
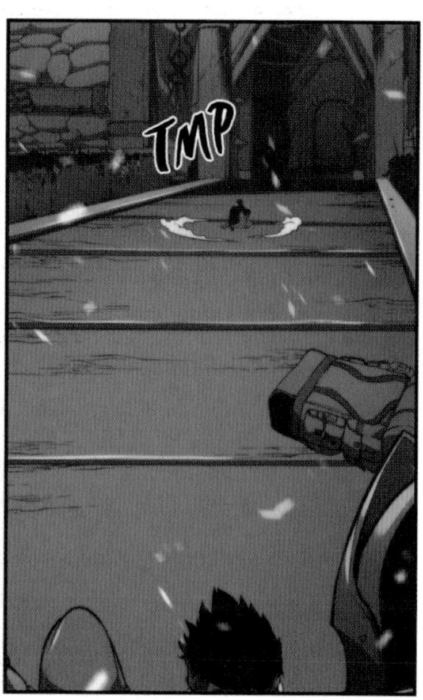
TMP

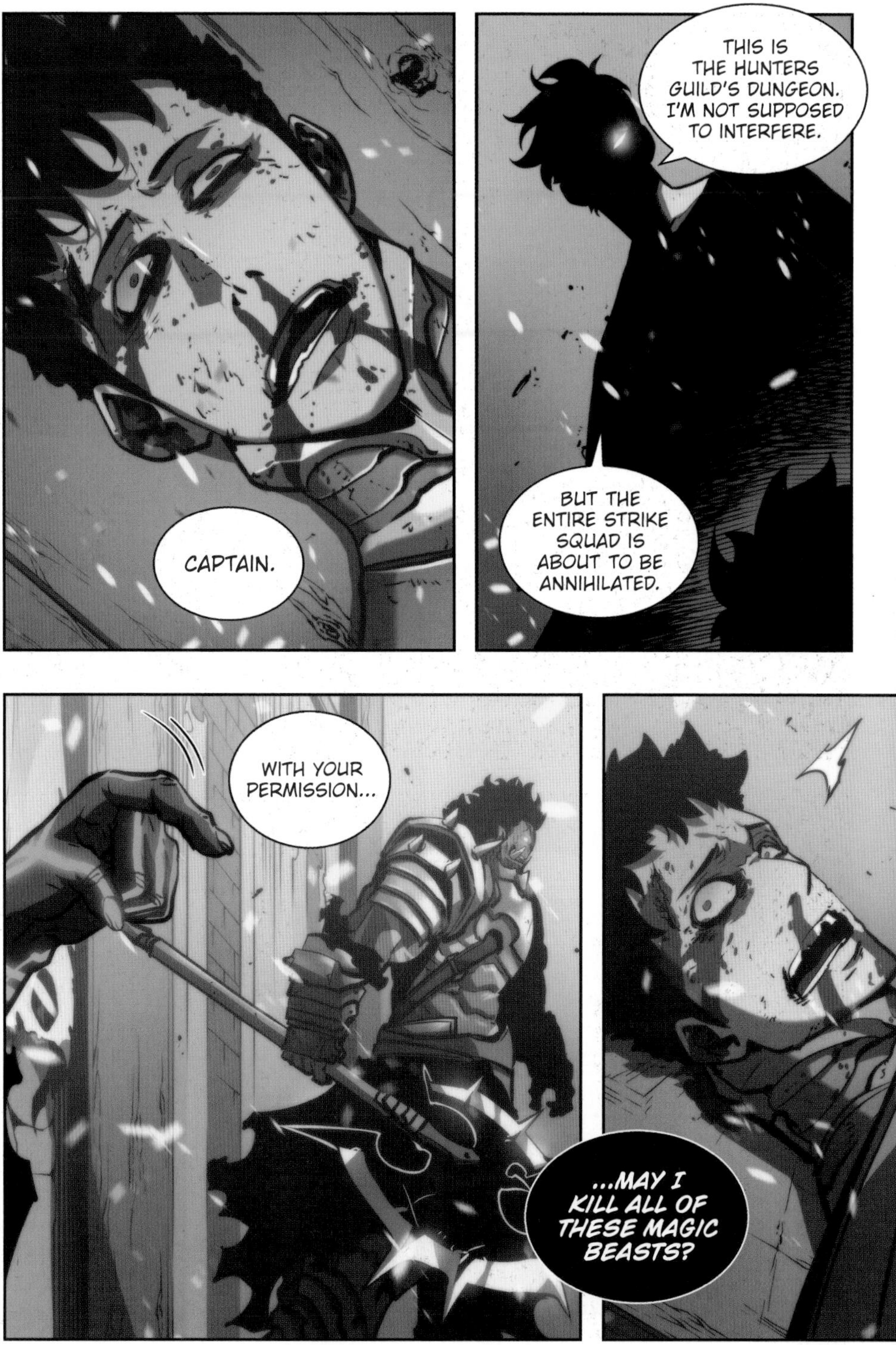
CAPTAIN.
THIS IS THE HUNTERS GUILD'S DUNGEON. I'M NOT SUPPOSED TO INTERFERE.
BUT THE ENTIRE STRIKE SQUAD IS ABOUT TO BE ANNIHILATED.
WITH YOUR PERMISSION...
...MAY I KILL ALL OF THESE MAGIC BEASTS?

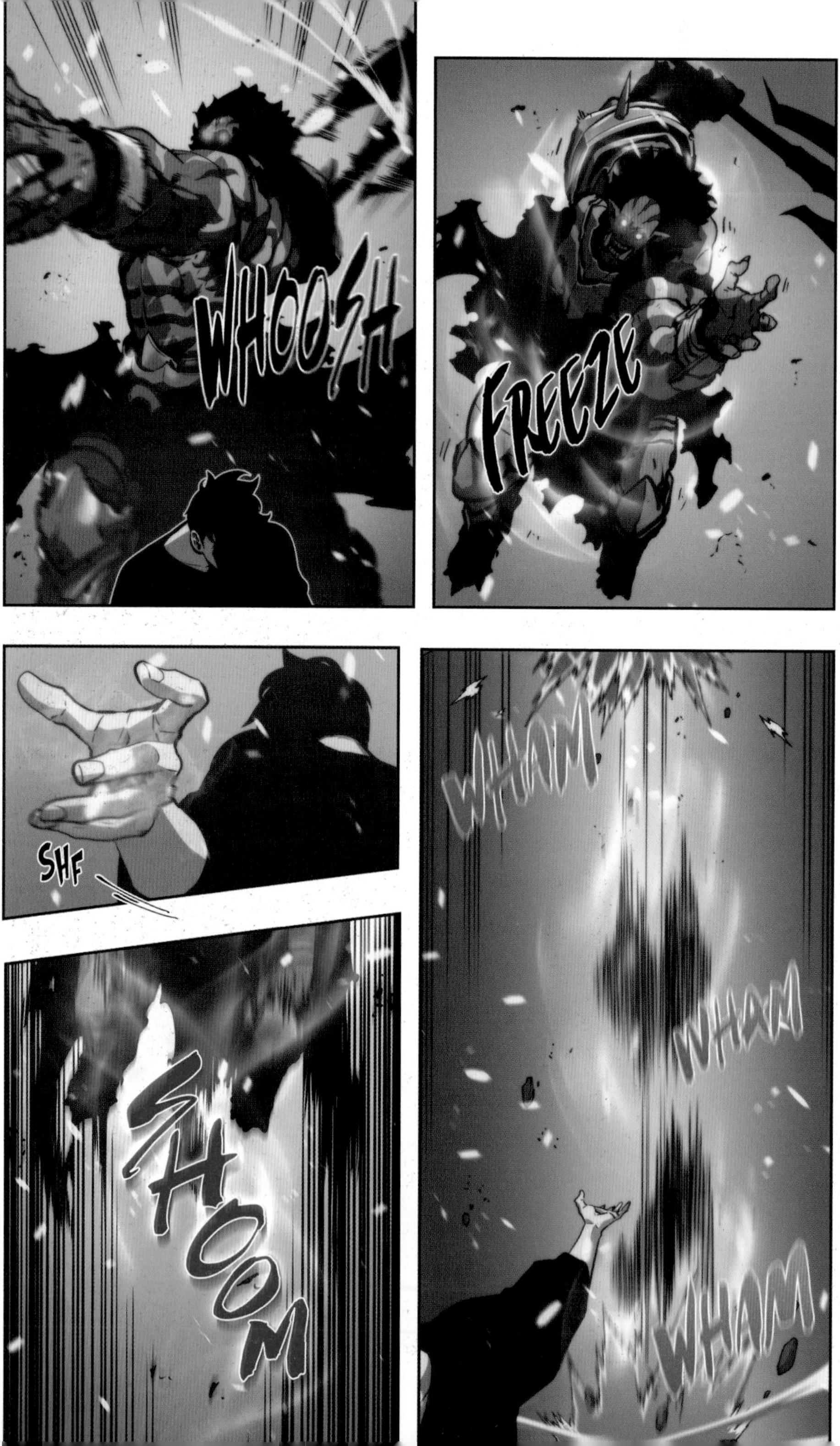
WHOOSH
FREEZE
SHF
SHOOM
WHAM
WHAM
WHAM

WHAM

WHAM

WHAM

WHAM

I'LL ASK YOU AGAIN.

MAY I...

...TAKE ALL OF THESE MAGIC BEASTS?

WHAM

PLEASE...

...PLEASE, GO AHEAD.

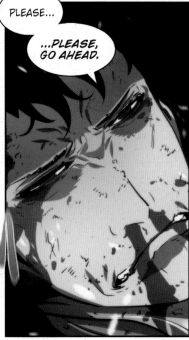

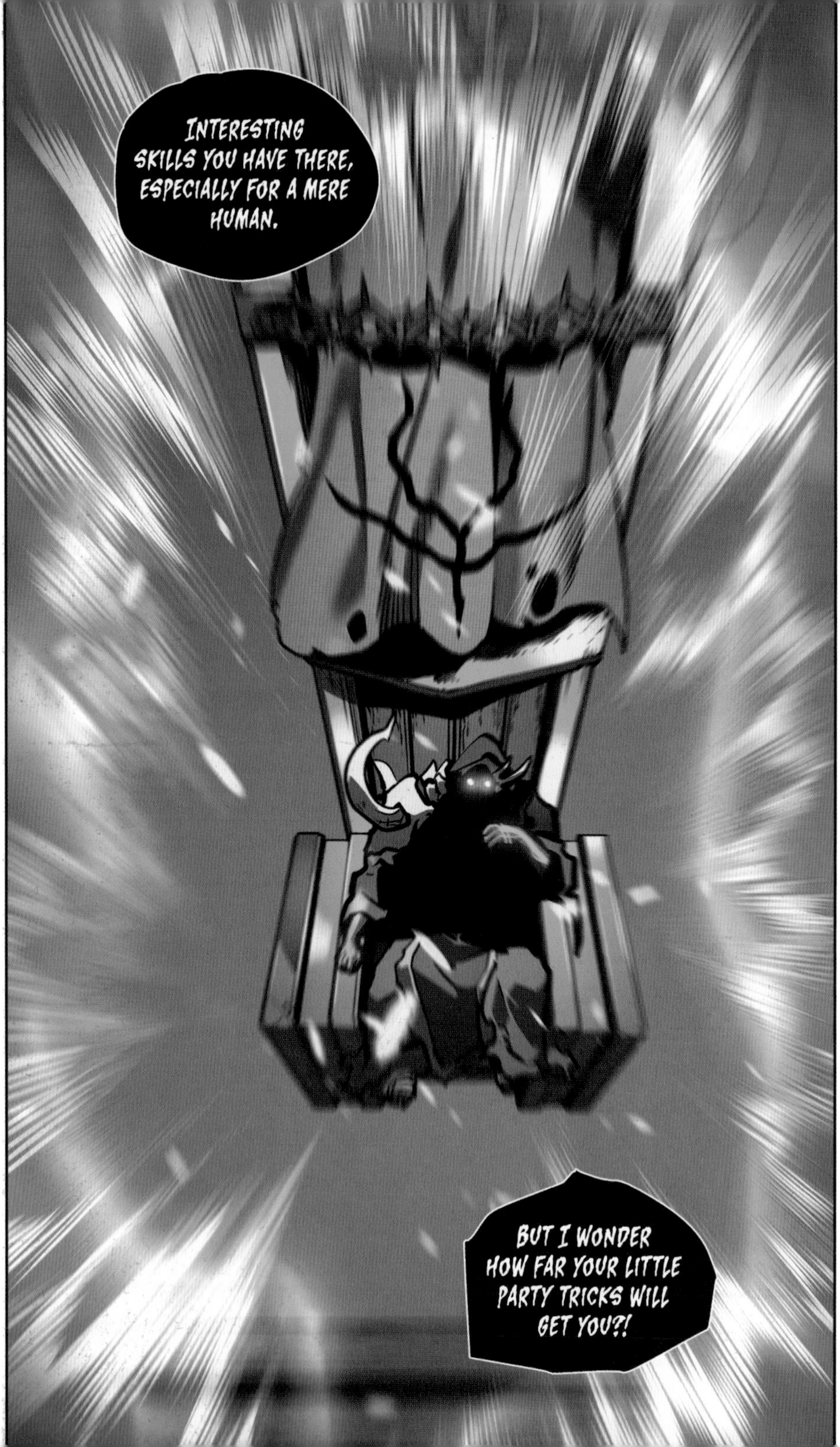
INTERESTING SKILLS YOU HAVE THERE, ESPECIALLY FOR A MERE HUMAN.
BUT I WONDER HOW FAR YOUR LITTLE PARTY TRICKS WILL GET YOU?!

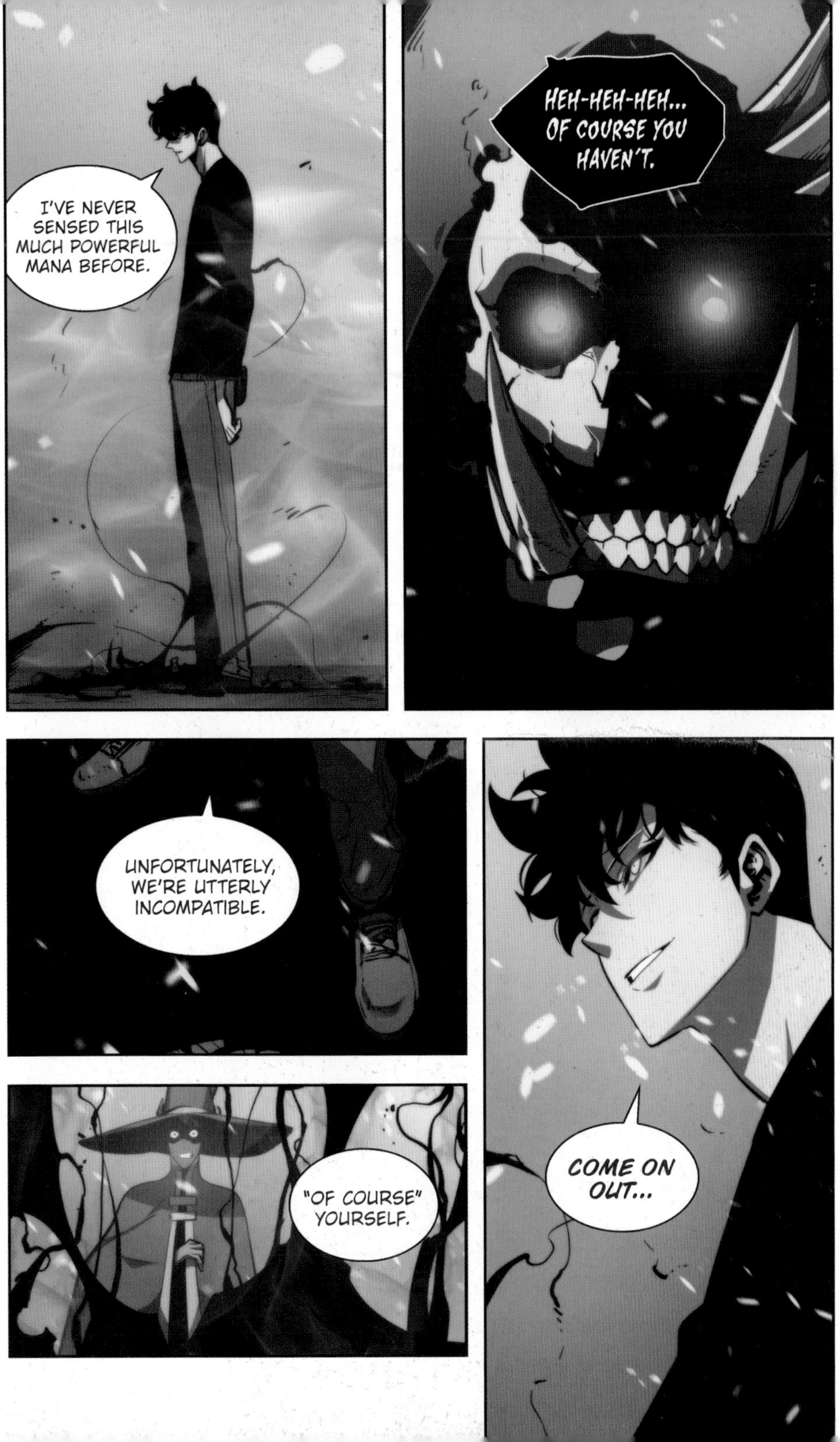
I'VE NEVER SENSED THIS MUCH POWERFUL MANA BEFORE.
HEH-HEH-HEH... OF COURSE YOU HAVEN'T.
UNFORTUNATELY, WE'RE UTTERLY INCOMPATIBLE.
"OF COURSE" YOURSELF.
COME ON OUT...

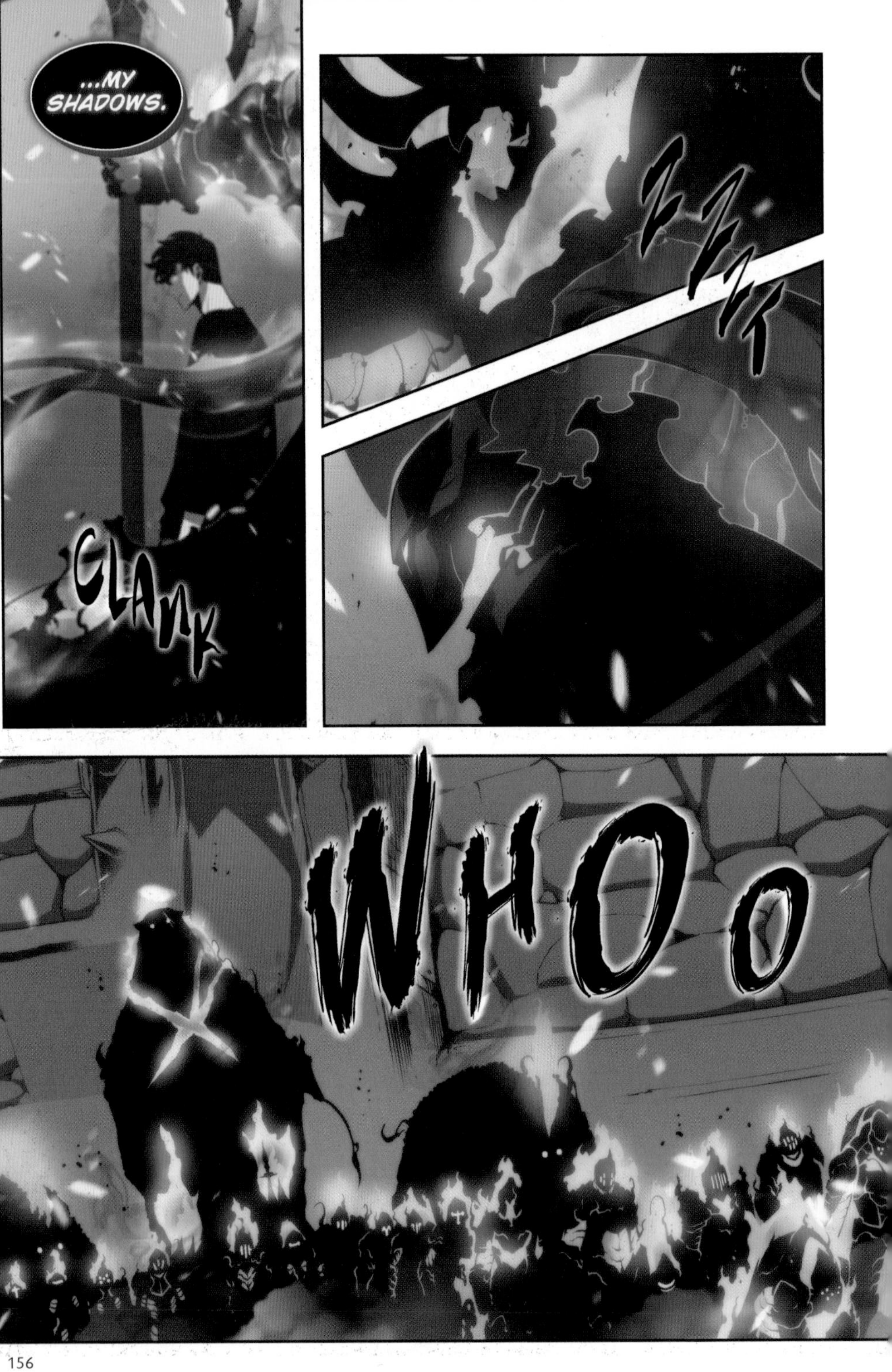
...MY SHADOWS.
CLANK
ZZZZK
WHOOO

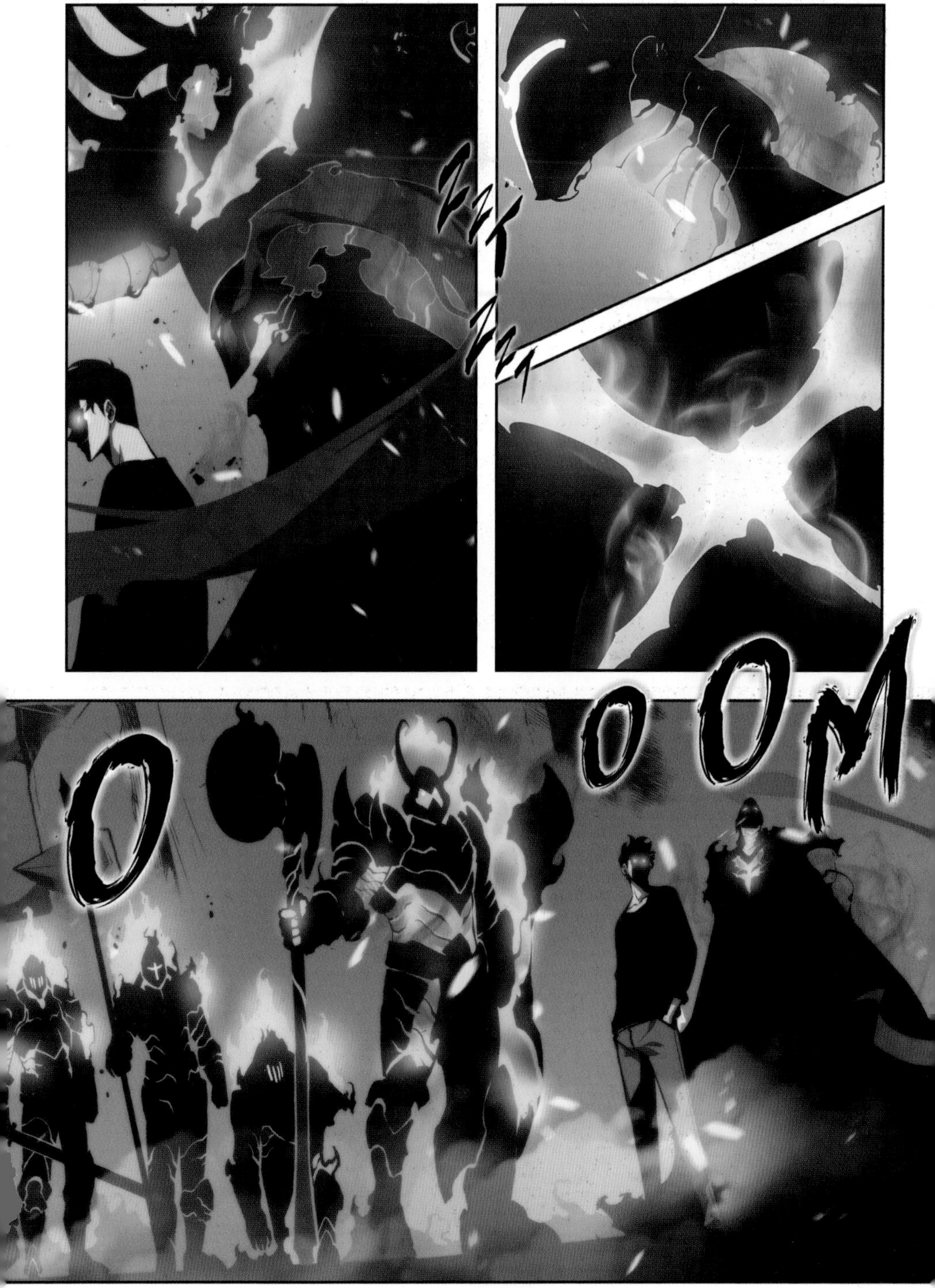
ZZT
ZZT
OOOM

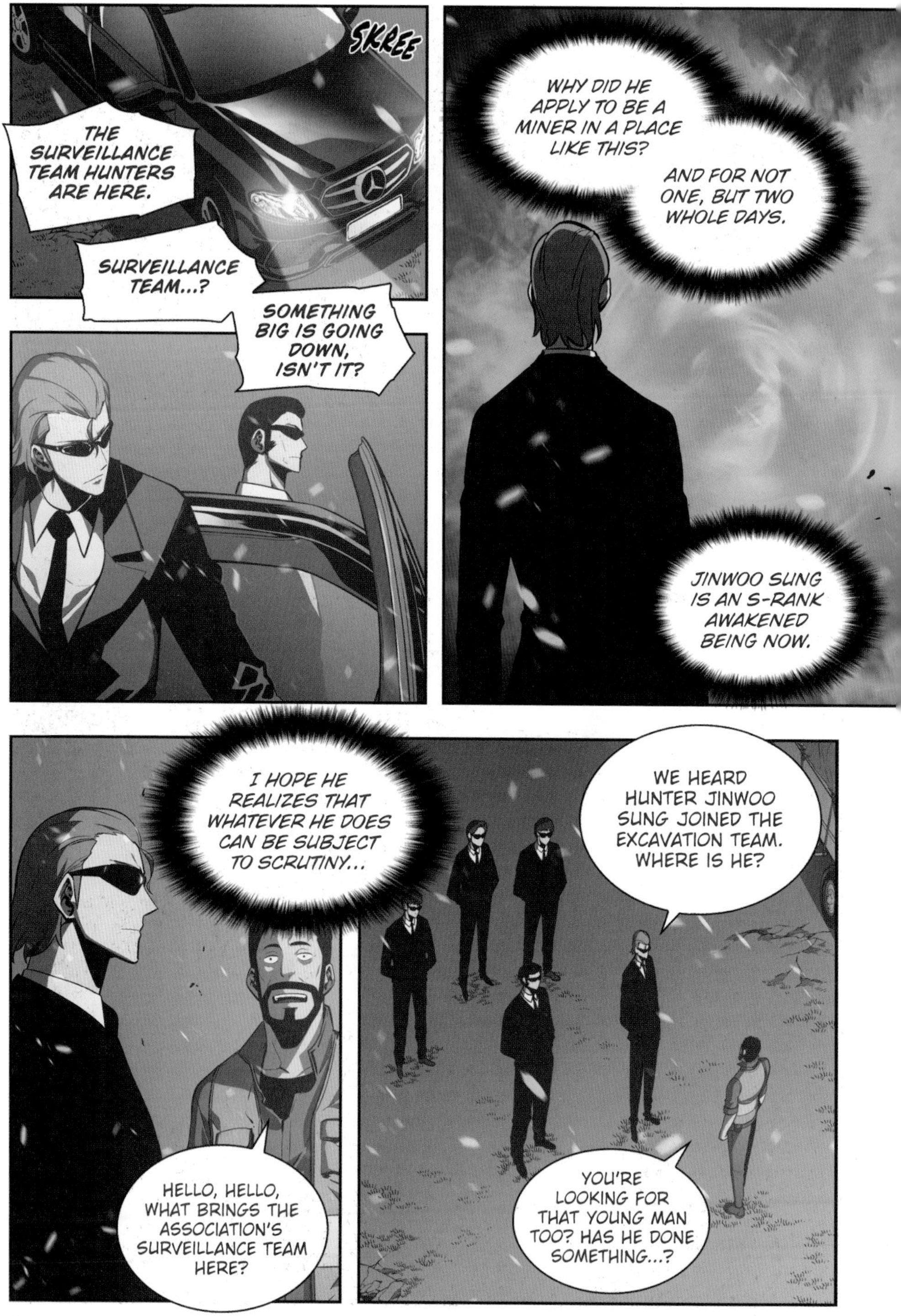
SKREE
THE SURVEILLANCE TEAM HUNTERS ARE HERE.
SURVEILLANCE TEAM...?
SOMETHING BIG IS GOING DOWN, ISN'T IT?
WHY DID HE APPLY TO BE A MINER IN A PLACE LIKE THIS?
AND FOR NOT ONE, BUT TWO WHOLE DAYS.
JINWOO SUNG IS AN S-RANK AWAKENED BEING NOW.
I HOPE HE REALIZES THAT WHATEVER HE DOES CAN BE SUBJECT TO SCRUTINY...
HELLO, HELLO, WHAT BRINGS THE ASSOCIATION'S SURVEILLANCE TEAM HERE?
WE HEARD HUNTER JINWOO SUNG JOINED THE EXCAVATION TEAM. WHERE IS HE?
YOU'RE LOOKING FOR THAT YOUNG MAN TOO? HAS HE DONE SOMETHING...?

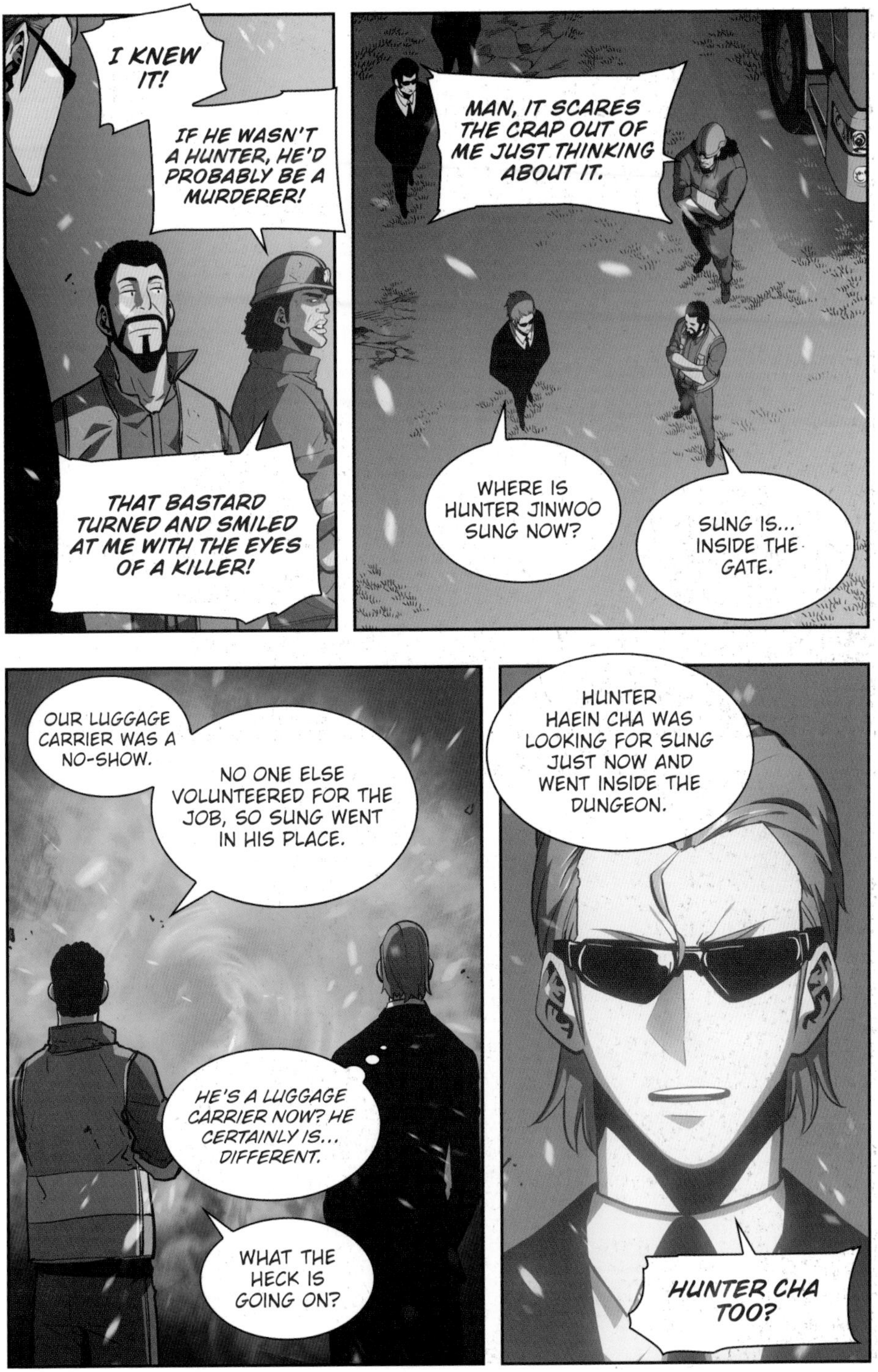

I KNEW IT!
IF HE WASN'T A HUNTER, HE'D PROBABLY BE A MURDERER!
THAT BASTARD TURNED AND SMILED AT ME WITH THE EYES OF A KILLER!
MAN, IT SCARES THE CRAP OUT OF ME JUST THINKING ABOUT IT.
WHERE IS HUNTER JINWOO SUNG NOW?
SUNG IS... INSIDE THE GATE.
OUR LUGGAGE CARRIER WAS A NO-SHOW.
NO ONE ELSE VOLUNTEERED FOR THE JOB, SO SUNG WENT IN HIS PLACE.
HE'S A LUGGAGE CARRIER NOW? HE CERTAINLY IS... DIFFERENT.
WHAT THE HECK IS GOING ON?
HUNTER HAEIN CHA WAS LOOKING FOR SUNG JUST NOW AND WENT INSIDE THE DUNGEON.
HUNTER CHA TOO?

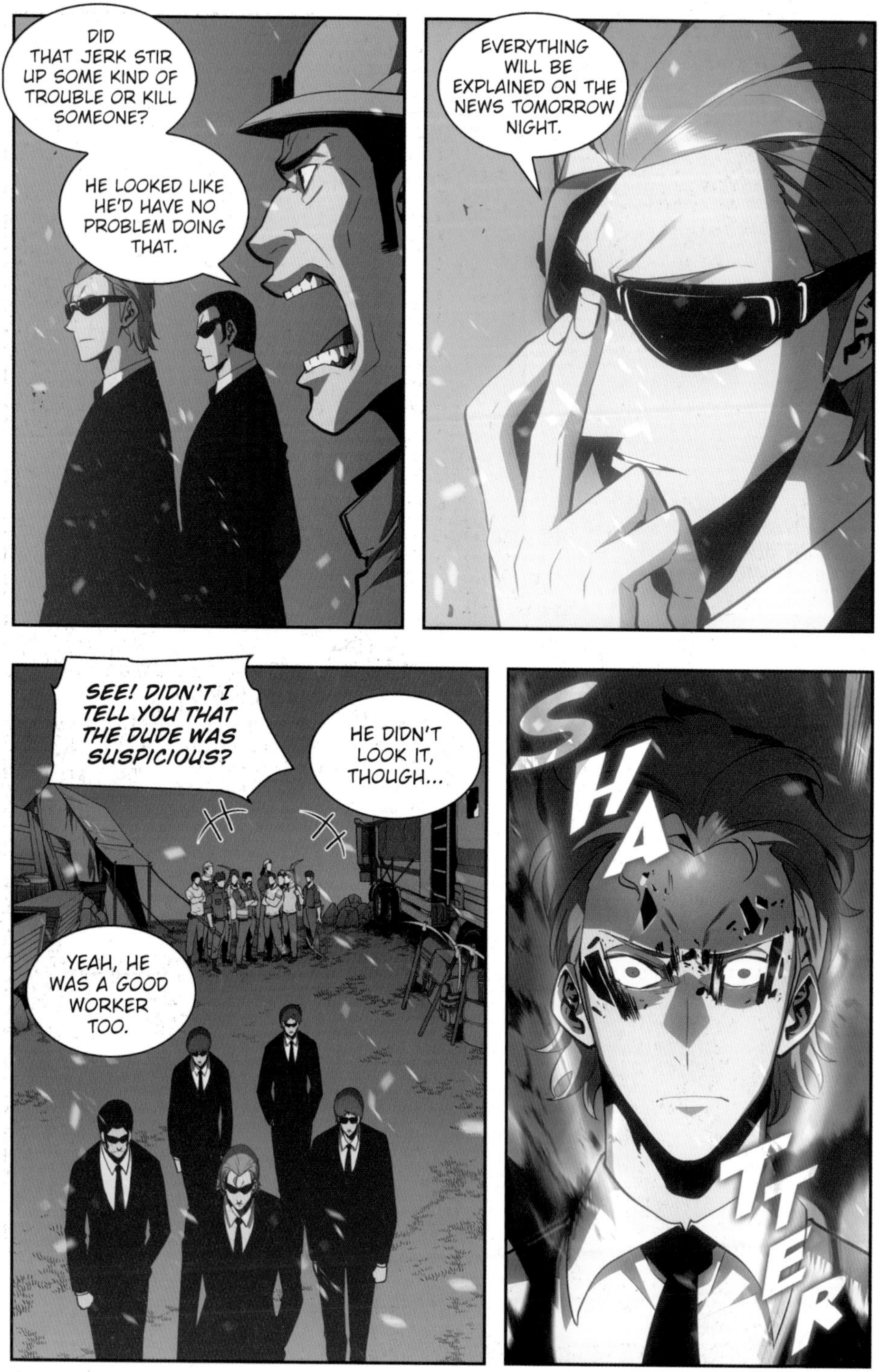
DID THAT JERK STIR UP SOME KIND OF TROUBLE OR KILL SOMEONE?
HE LOOKED LIKE HE'D HAVE NO PROBLEM DOING THAT.
EVERYTHING WILL BE EXPLAINED ON THE NEWS TOMORROW NIGHT.
SEE! DIDN'T I TELL YOU THAT THE DUDE WAS SUSPICIOUS?
HE DIDN'T LOOK IT, THOUGH...
YEAH, HE WAS A GOOD WORKER TOO.
SHATTER

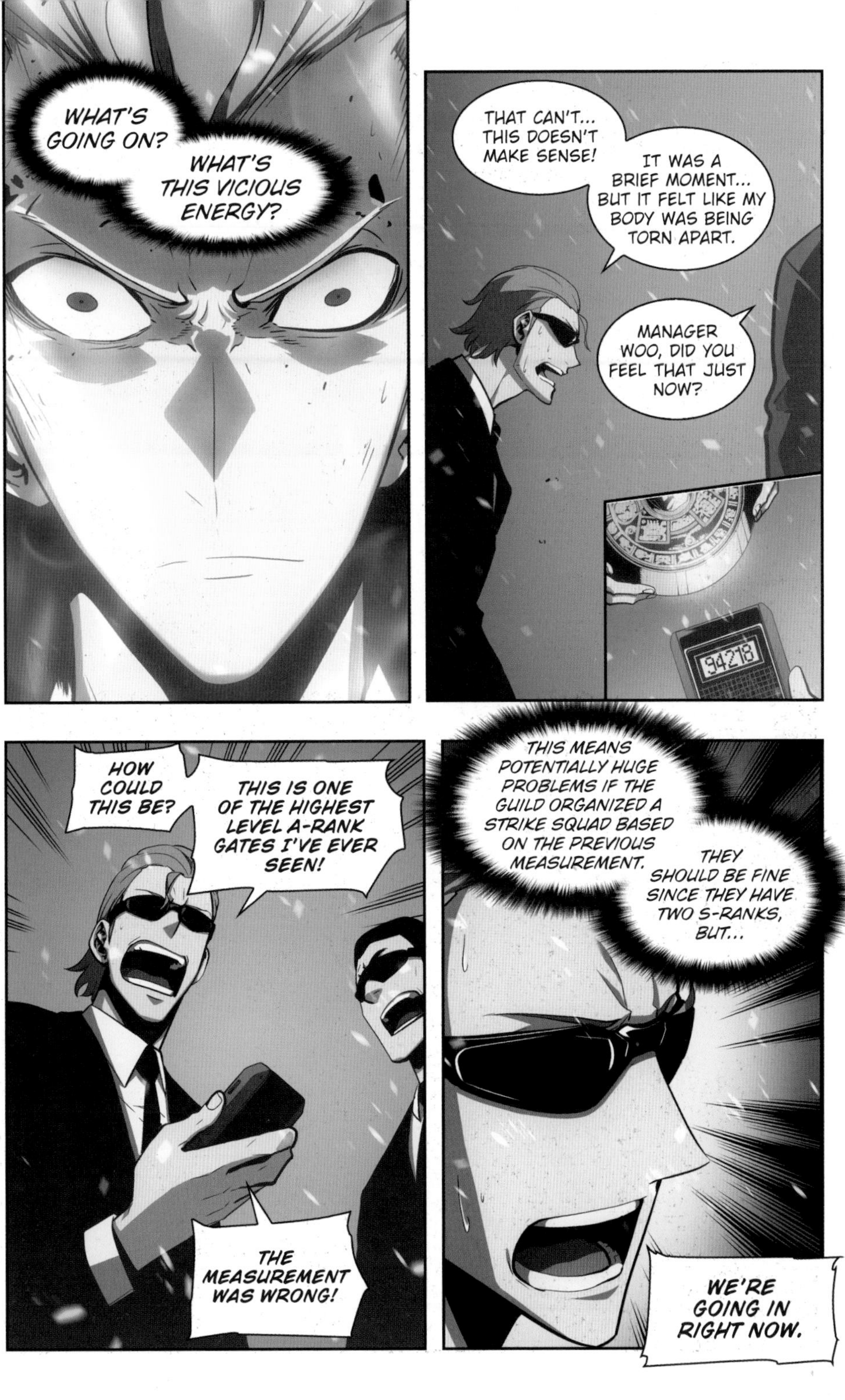

WHAT'S GOING ON?
WHAT'S THIS VICIOUS ENERGY?
THAT CAN'T... THIS DOESN'T MAKE SENSE!
IT WAS A BRIEF MOMENT... BUT IT FELT LIKE MY BODY WAS BEING TORN APART.
MANAGER WOO, DID YOU FEEL THAT JUST NOW?
94218
HOW COULD THIS BE?
THIS IS ONE OF THE HIGHEST LEVEL A-RANK GATES I'VE EVER SEEN!
THE MEASUREMENT WAS WRONG!
THIS MEANS POTENTIALLY HUGE PROBLEMS IF THE GUILD ORGANIZED A STRIKE SQUAD BASED ON THE PREVIOUS MEASUREMENT.
THEY SHOULD BE FINE SINCE THEY HAVE TWO S-RANKS, BUT...
WE'RE GOING IN RIGHT NOW.

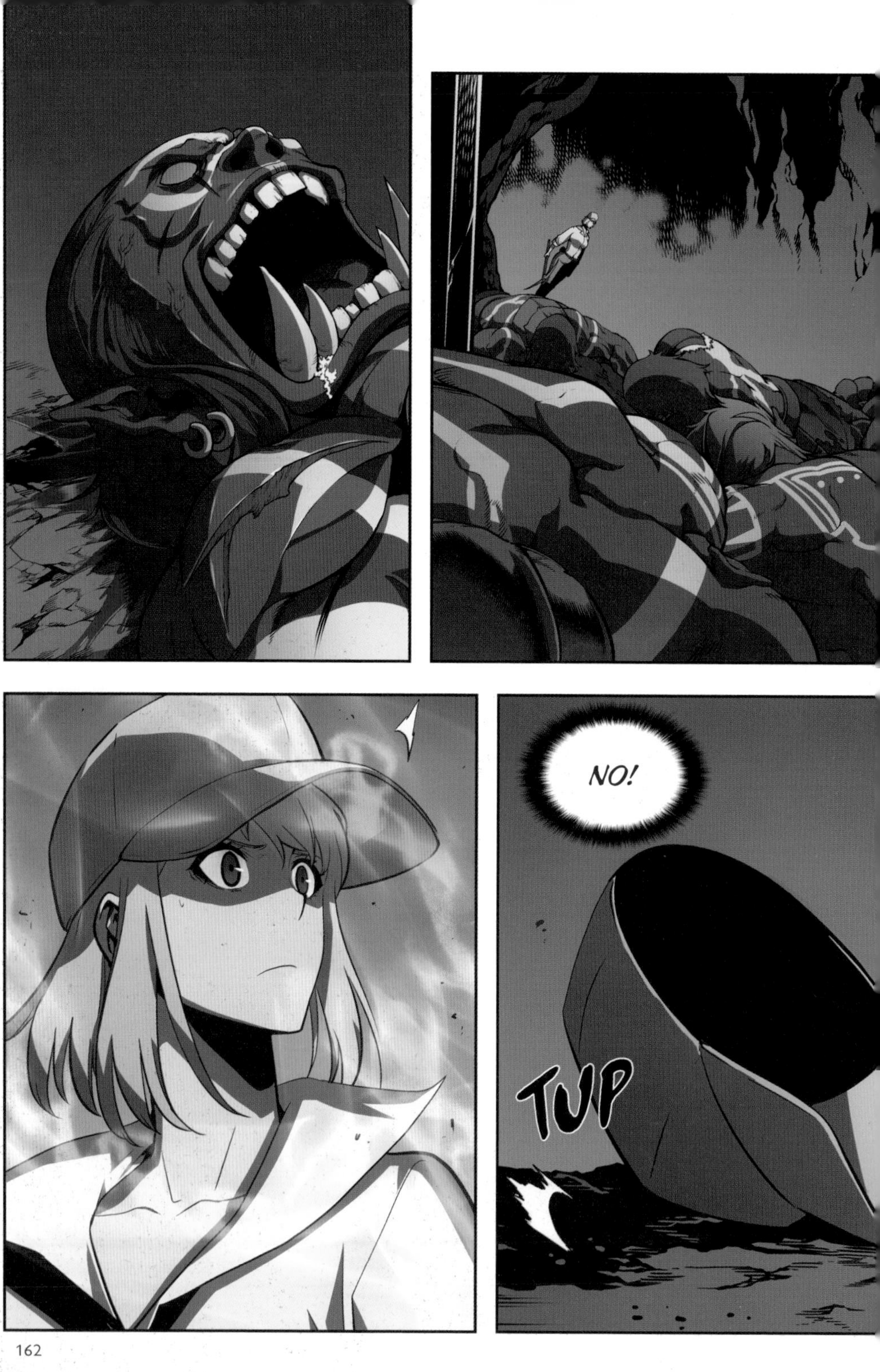
NO!
TUP

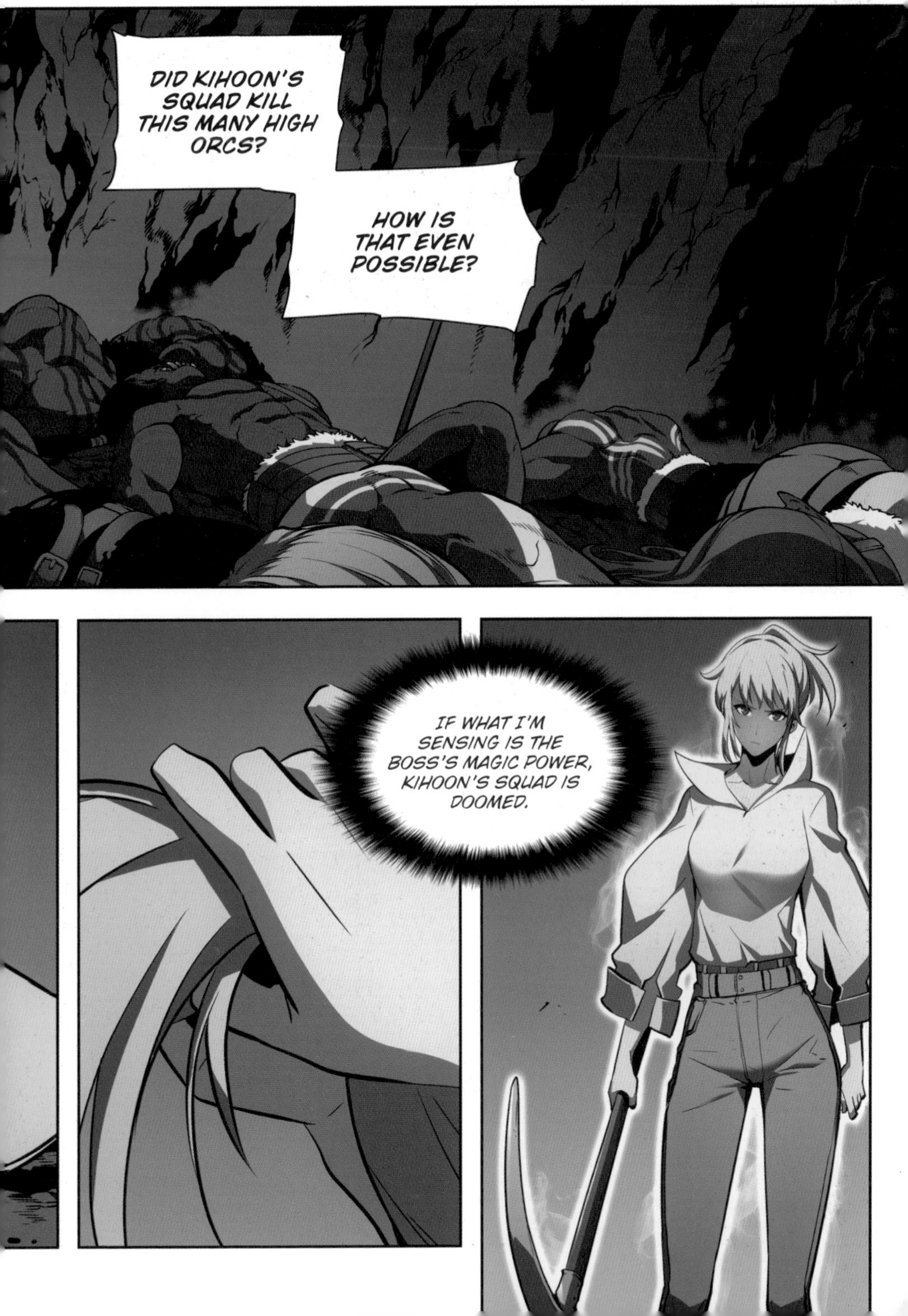
DID KIHOON'S SQUAD KILL THIS MANY HIGH ORCS?
HOW IS THAT EVEN POSSIBLE?
IF WHAT I'M SENSING IS THE BOSS'S MAGIC POWER, KIHOON'S SQUAD IS DOOMED.

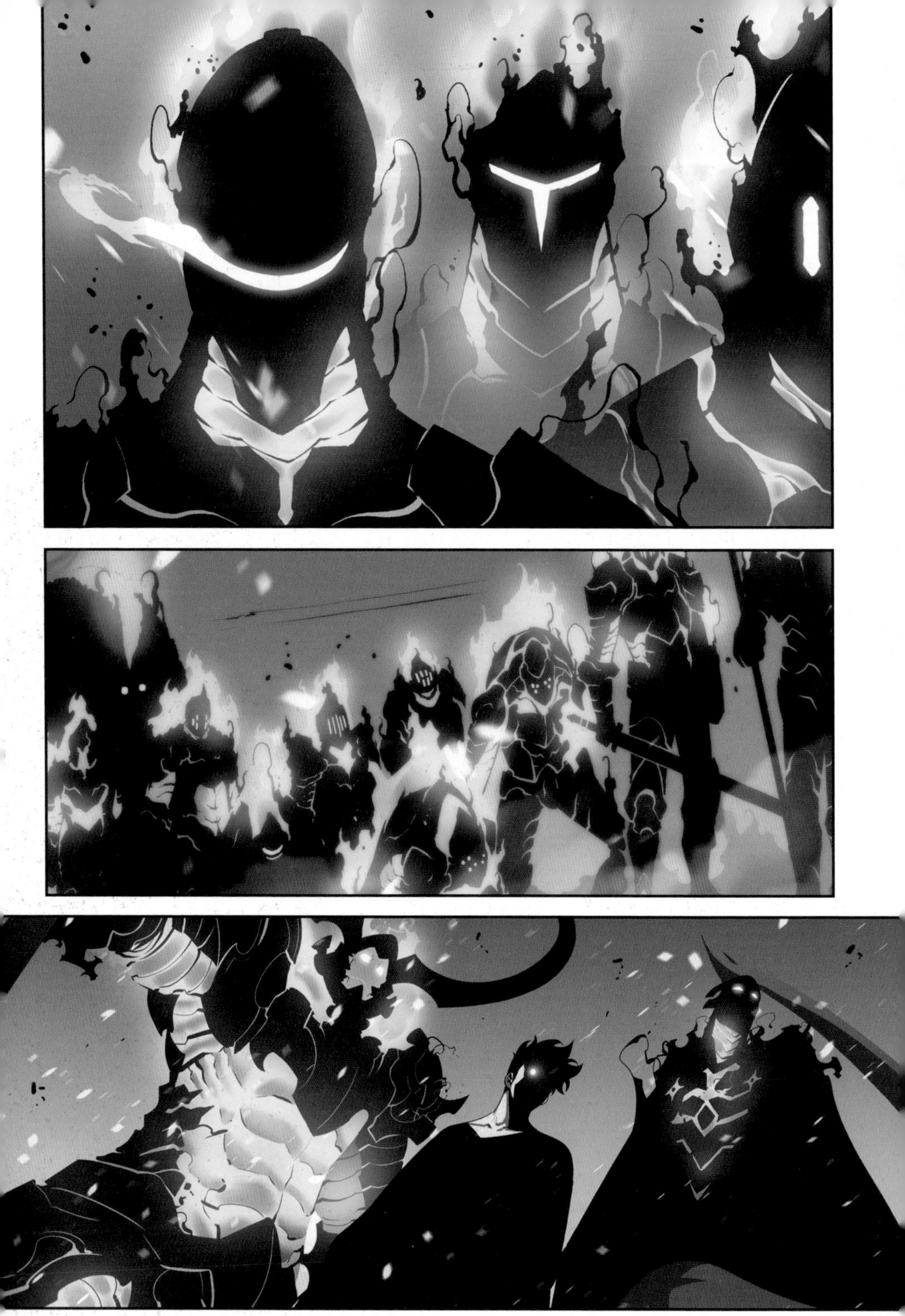

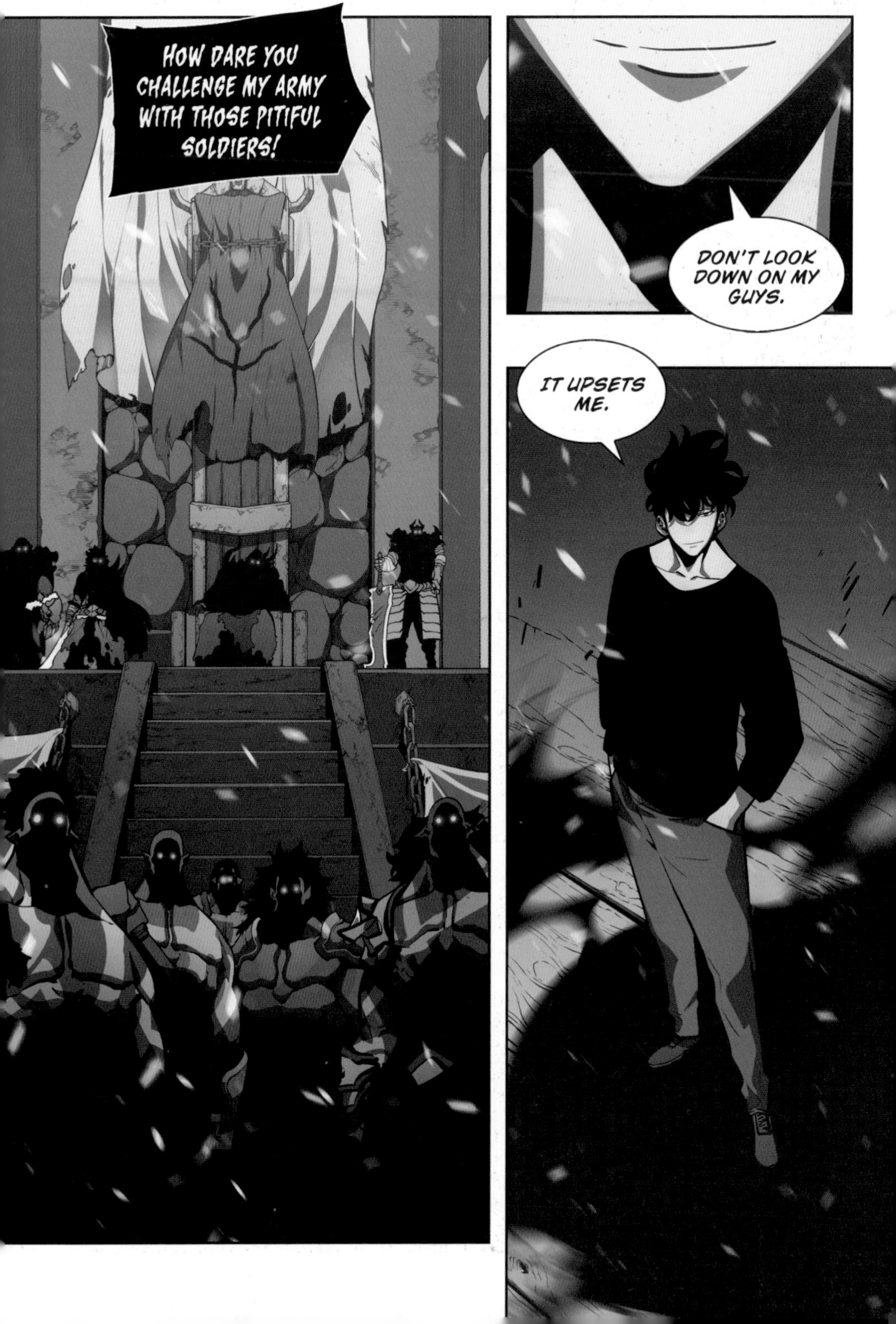
HOW DARE YOU CHALLENGE MY ARMY WITH THOSE PITIFUL SOLDIERS!
DON'T LOOK DOWN ON MY GUYS.
IT UPSETS ME.

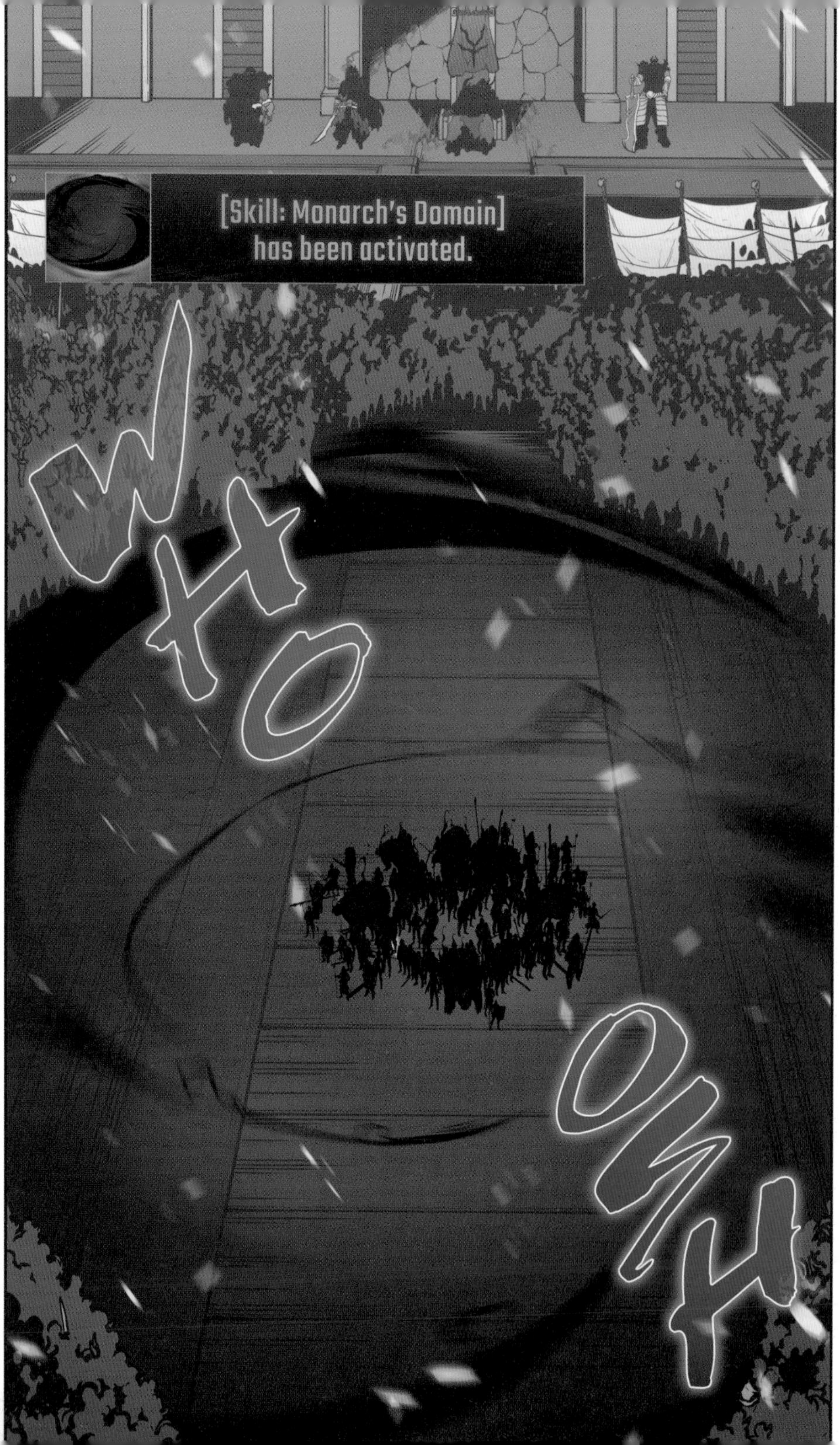
[Skill: Monarch's Domain] has been activated.
WHOOOM

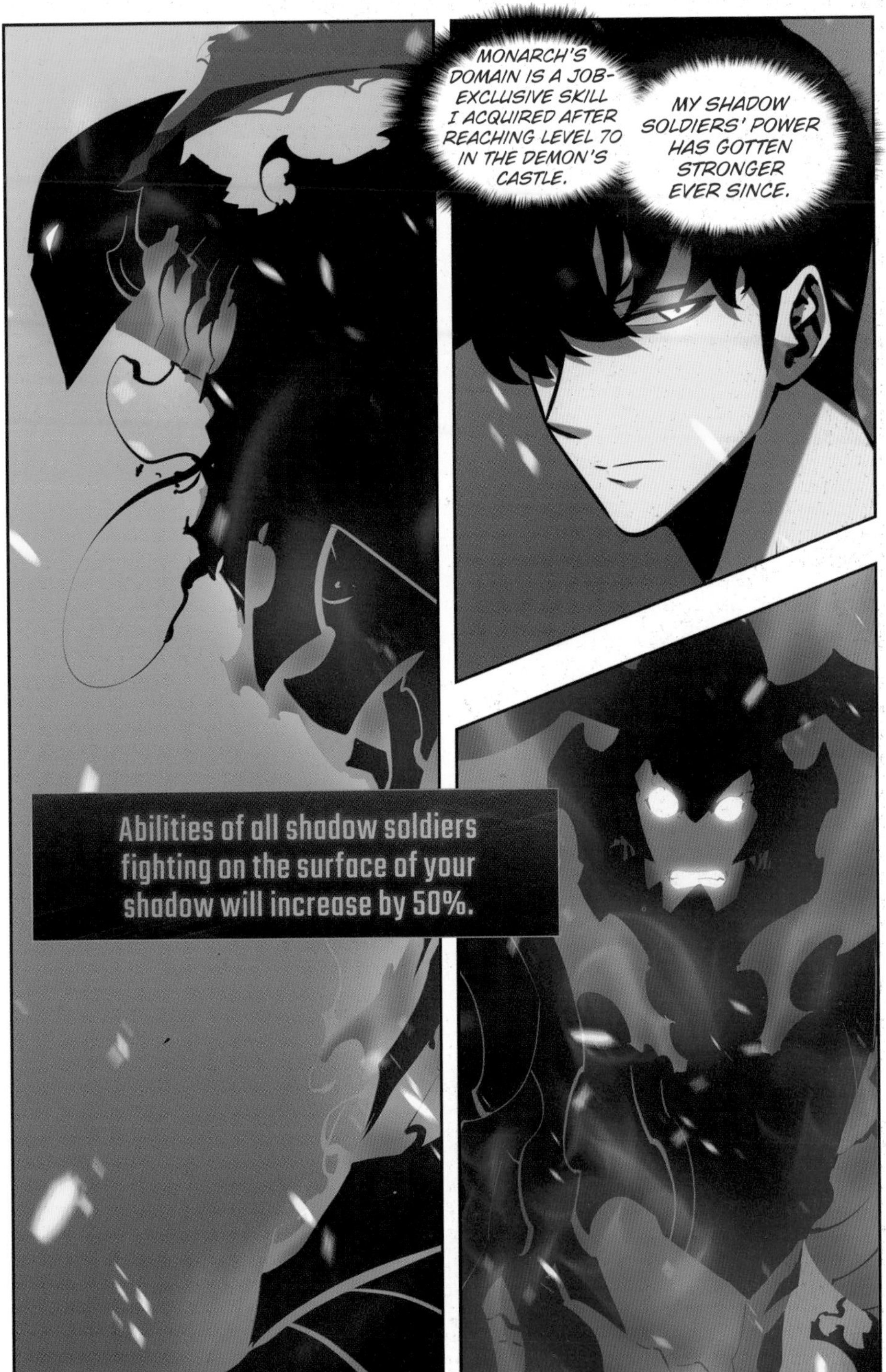
MONARCH'S DOMAIN IS A JOB-EXCLUSIVE SKILL I ACQUIRED AFTER REACHING LEVEL 70 IN THE DEMON'S CASTLE.
MY SHADOW SOLDIERS' POWER HAS GOTTEN STRONGER EVER SINCE.
Abilities of all shadow soldiers fighting on the surface of your shadow will increase by 50%.

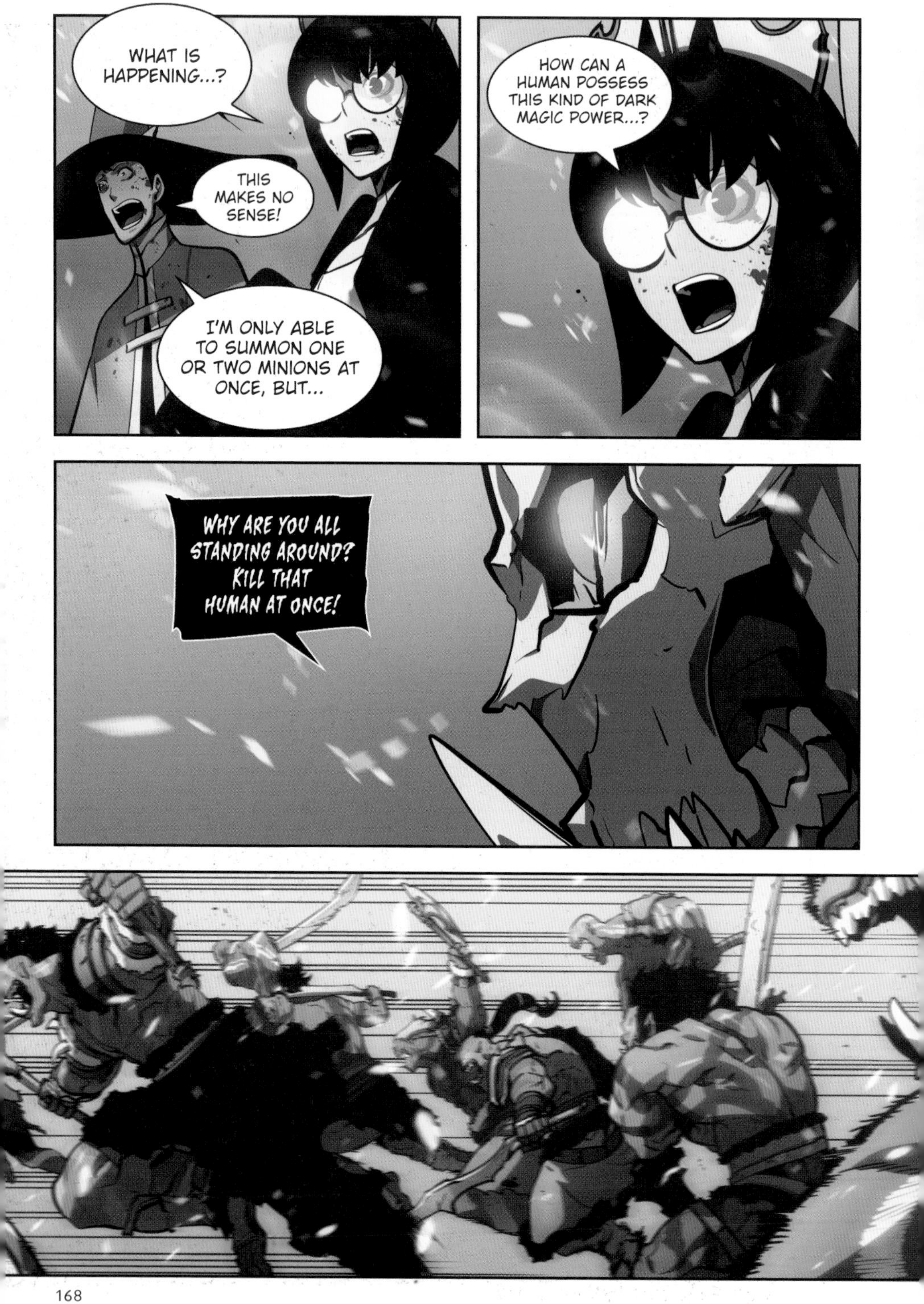
WHAT IS HAPPENING...?
THIS MAKES NO SENSE!
I'M ONLY ABLE TO SUMMON ONE OR TWO MINIONS AT ONCE, BUT...
HOW CAN A HUMAN POSSESS THIS KIND OF DARK MAGIC POWER...?
WHY ARE YOU ALL STANDING AROUND? KILL THAT HUMAN AT ONCE!

Iron is using
[Skill: Epic Taunt].

The debuff has been canceled
out by the opponent's high
resistance level.

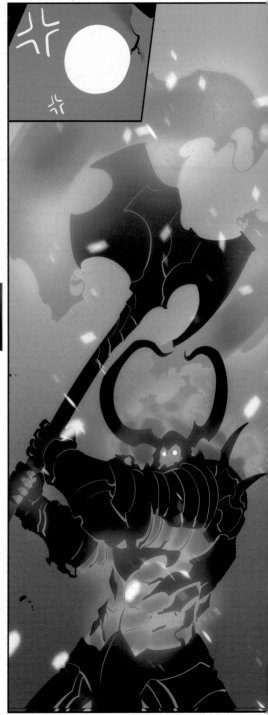

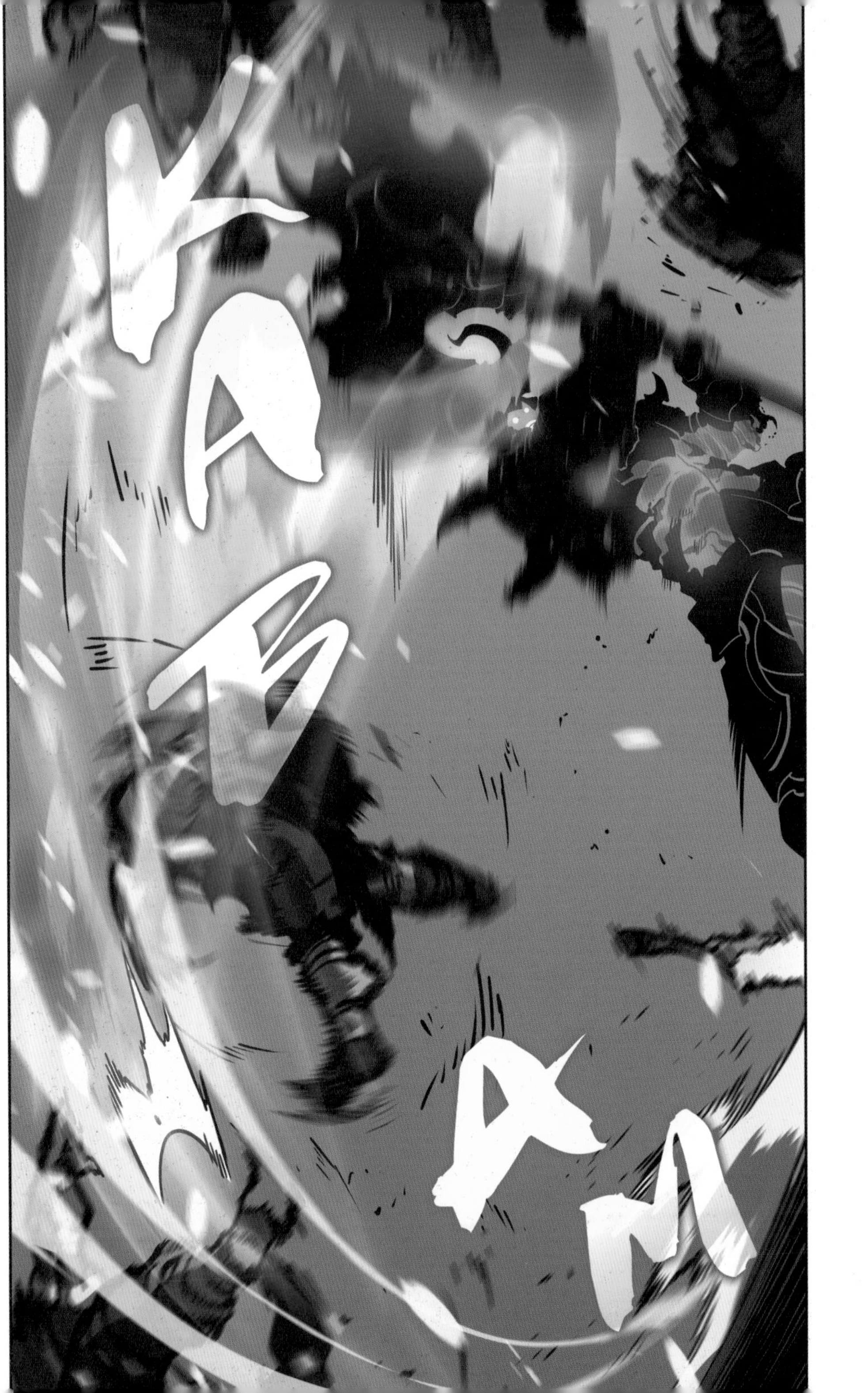
KABAM

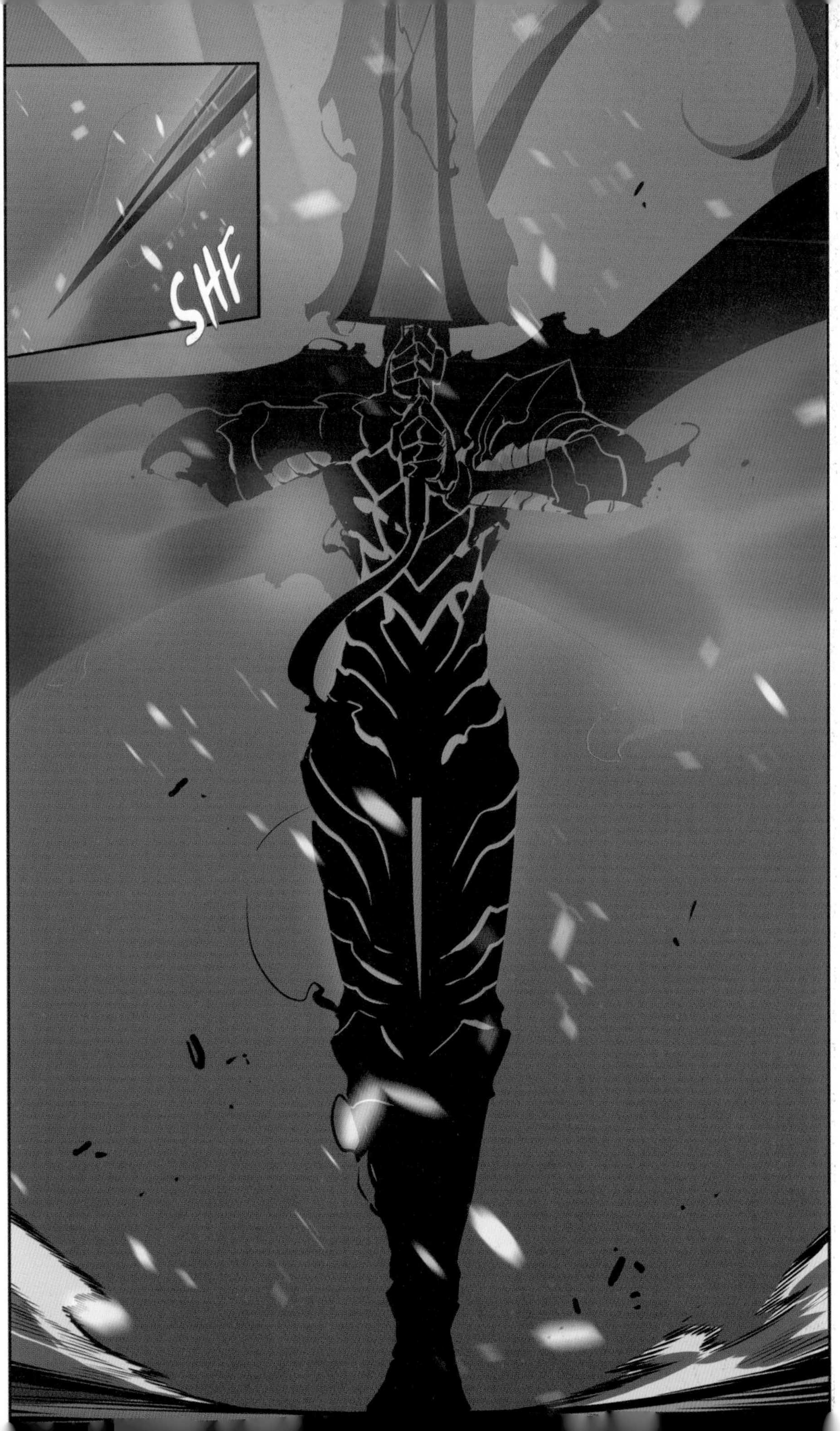
SHF

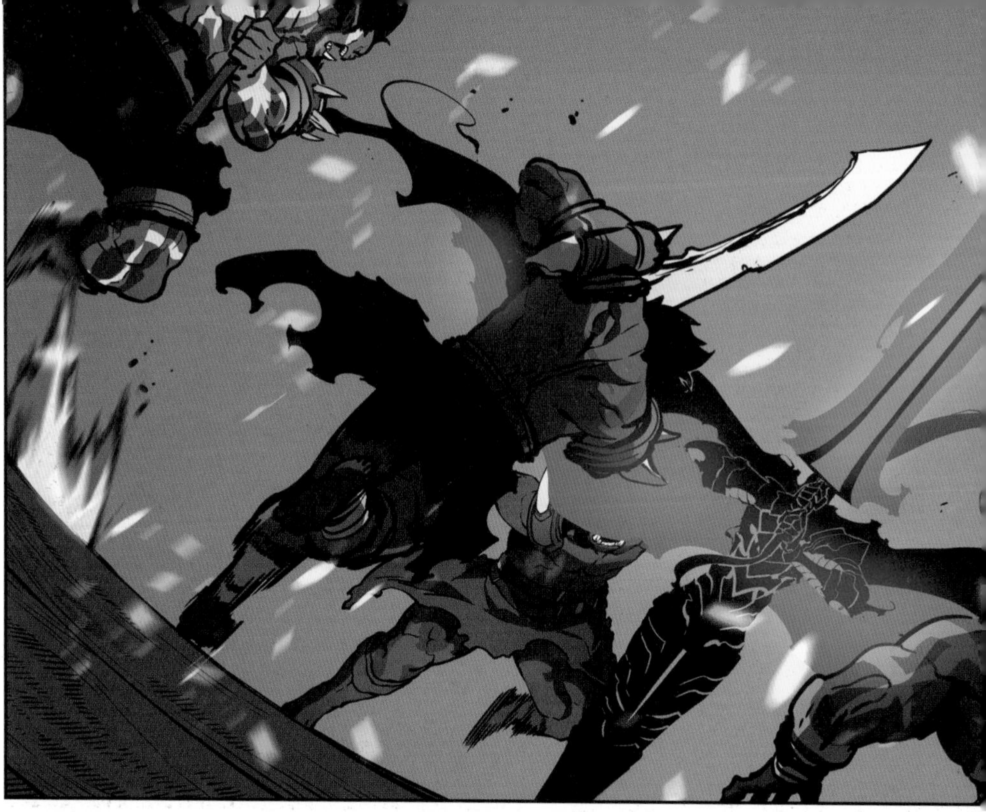

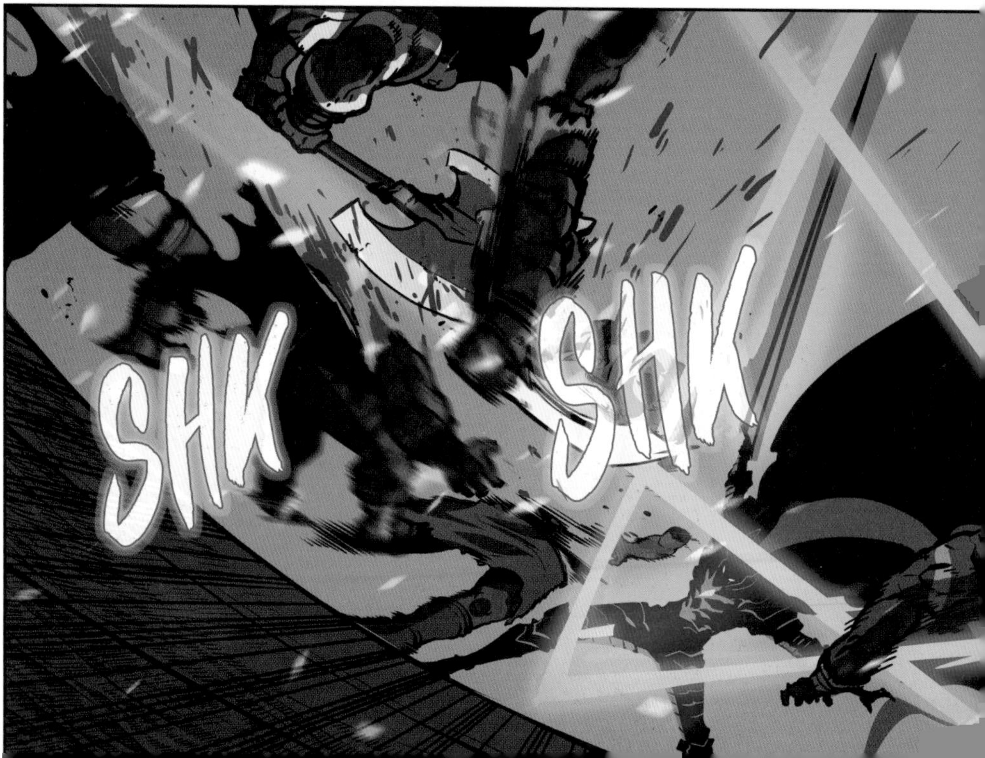
SHK
SHK

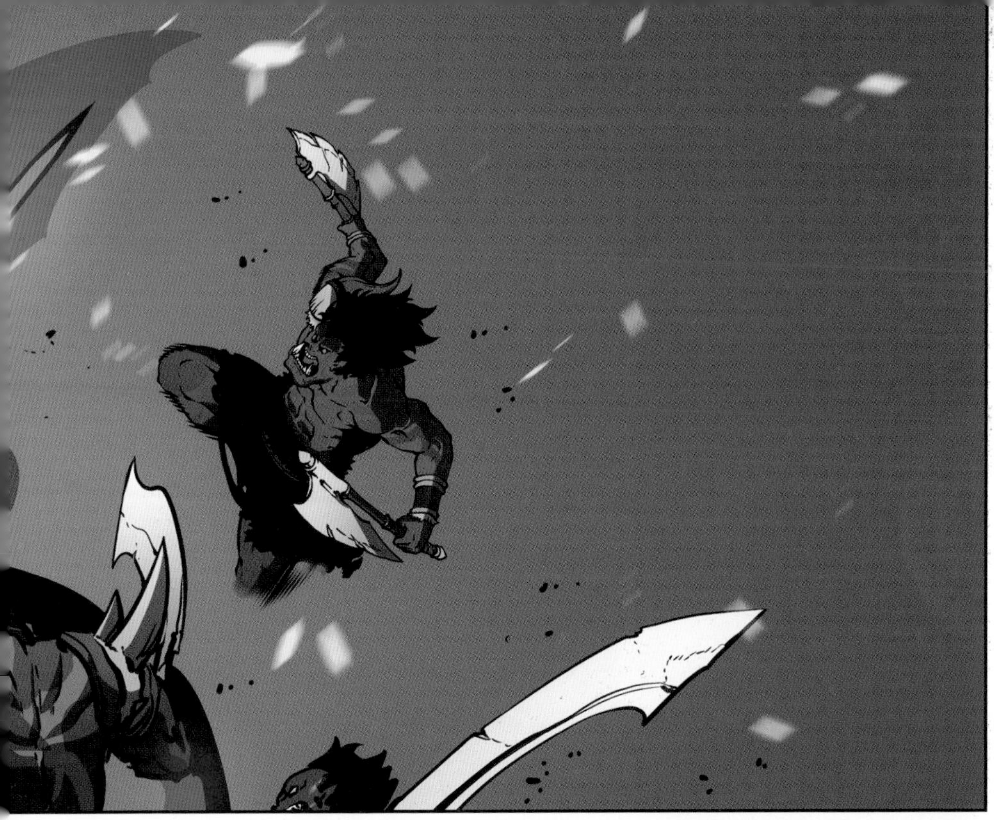

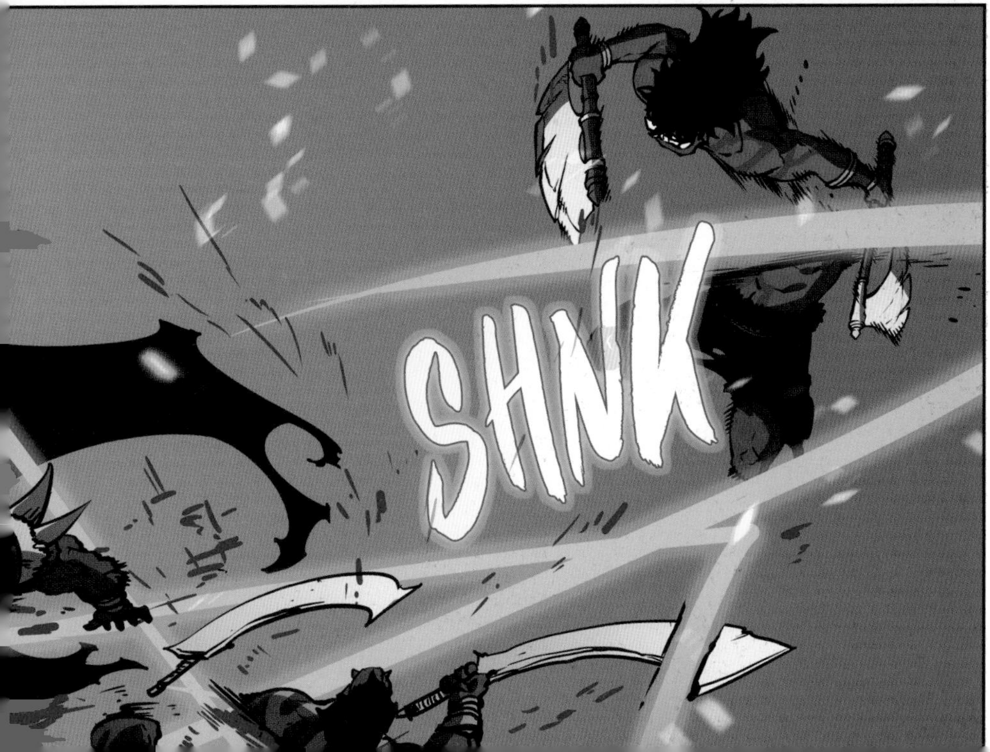
SHNK

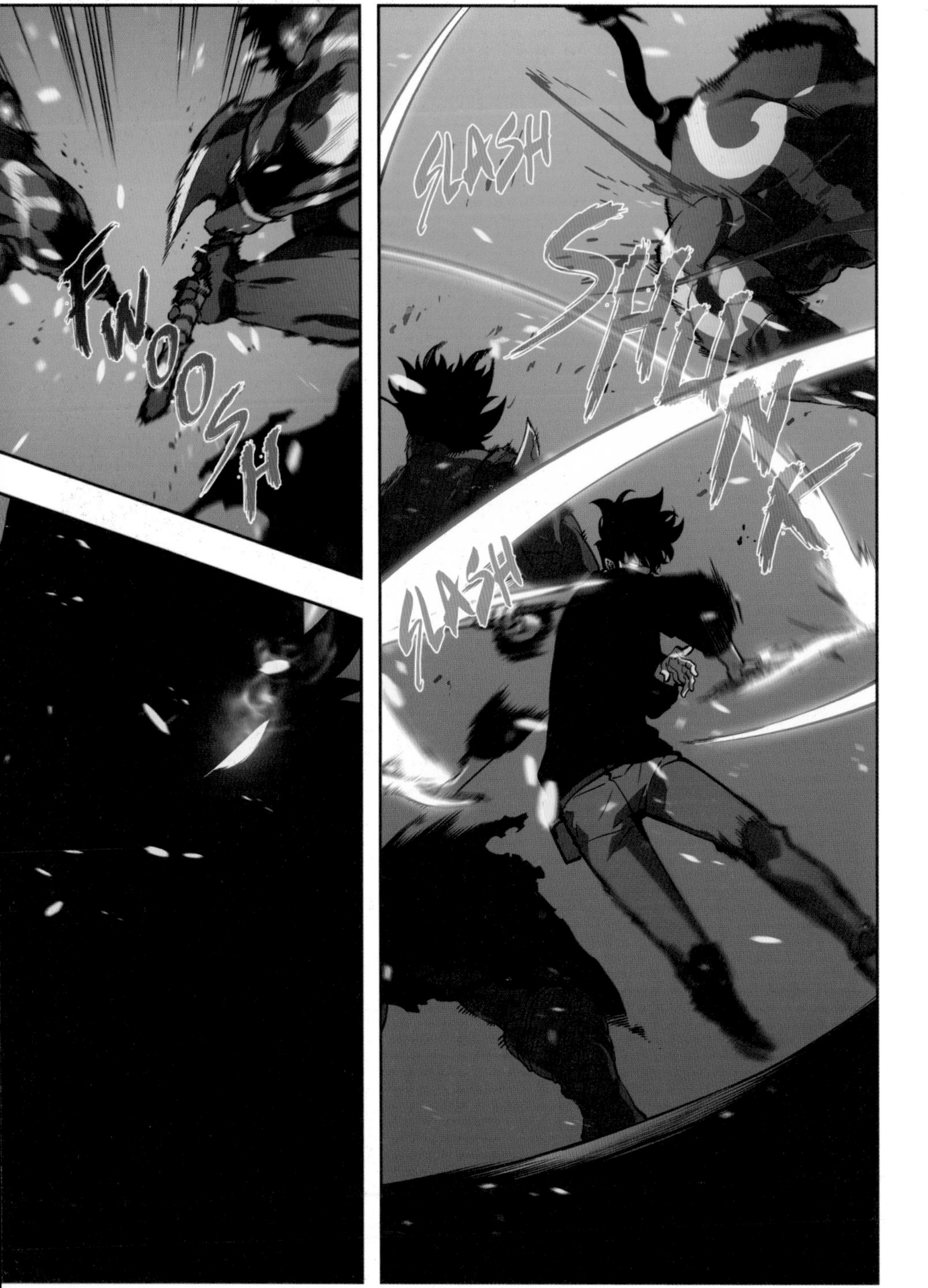
FWOOSH
SLASH
SHUNK
SLASH

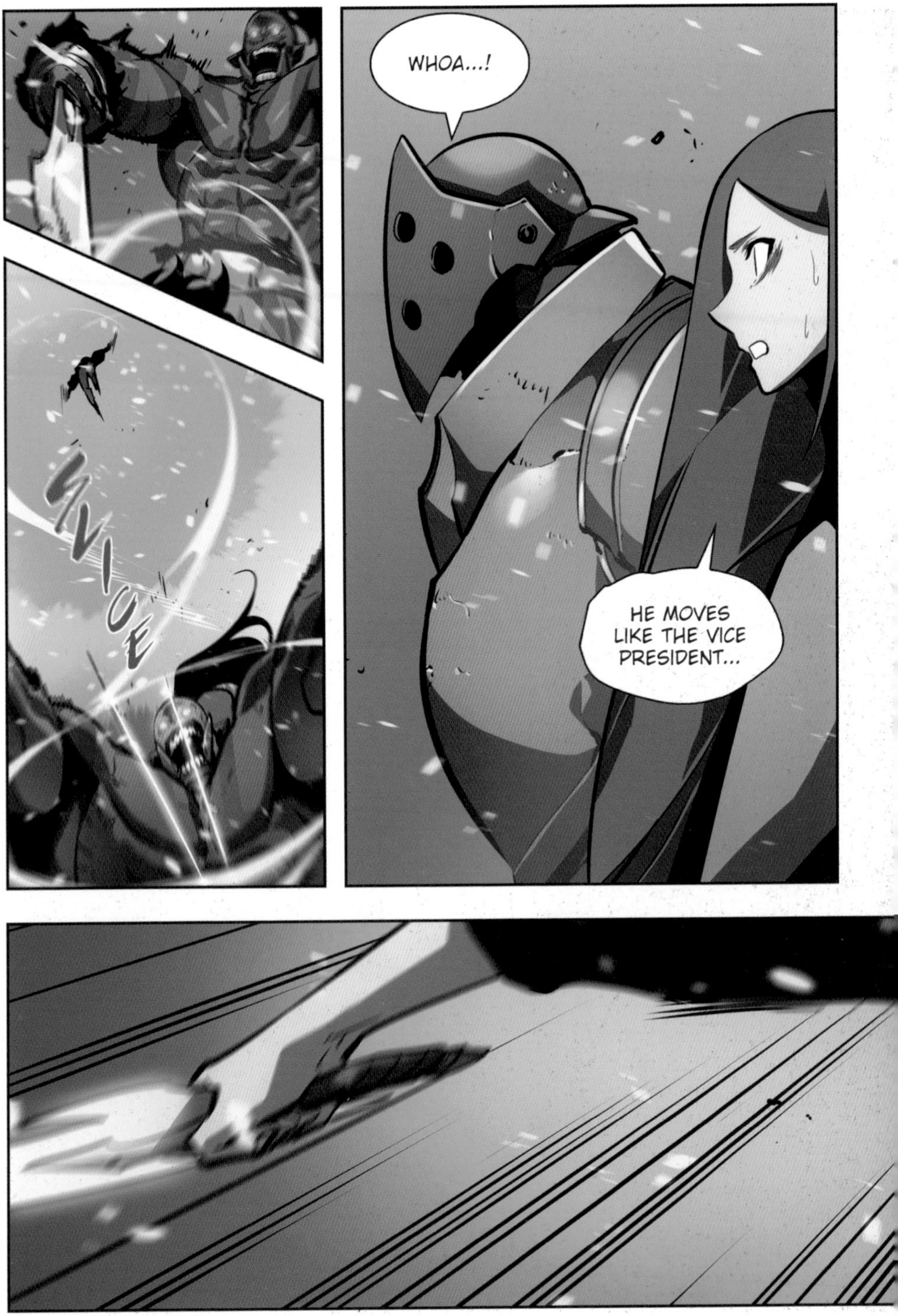
SVICE
WHOA...!
HE MOVES LIKE THE VICE PRESIDENT...

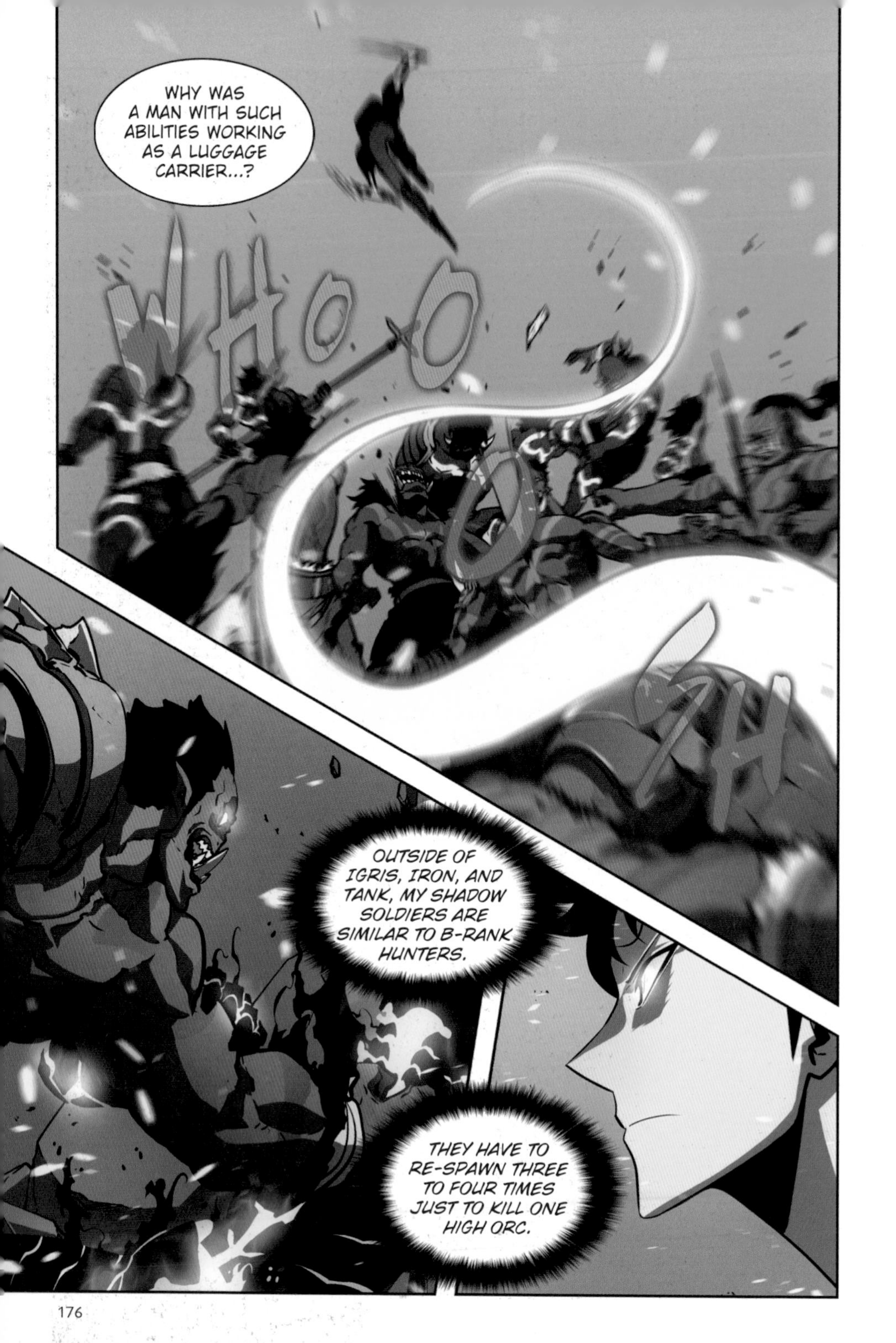
WHY WAS A MAN WITH SUCH ABILITIES WORKING AS A LUGGAGE CARRIER...?
WHOOOSH
OUTSIDE OF IGRIS, IRON, AND TANK, MY SHADOW SOLDIERS ARE SIMILAR TO B-RANK HUNTERS.
THEY HAVE TO RE-SPAWN THREE TO FOUR TIMES JUST TO KILL ONE HIGH ORC.

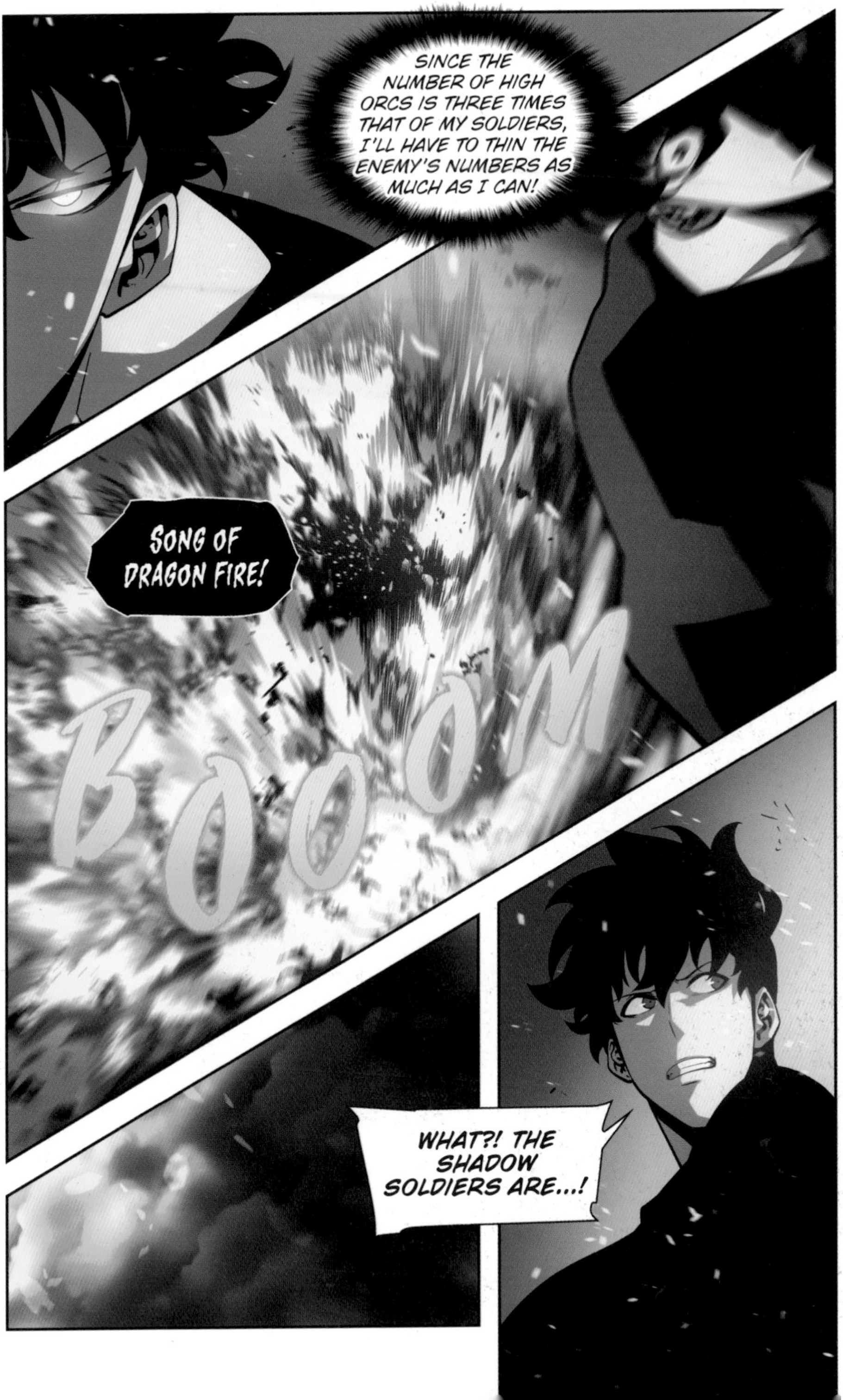
SINCE THE NUMBER OF HIGH ORCS IS THREE TIMES THAT OF MY SOLDIERS, I'LL HAVE TO THIN THE ENEMY'S NUMBERS AS MUCH AS I CAN!
SONG OF DRAGON FIRE!
BOOOM
WHAT?! THE SHADOW SOLDIERS ARE...!

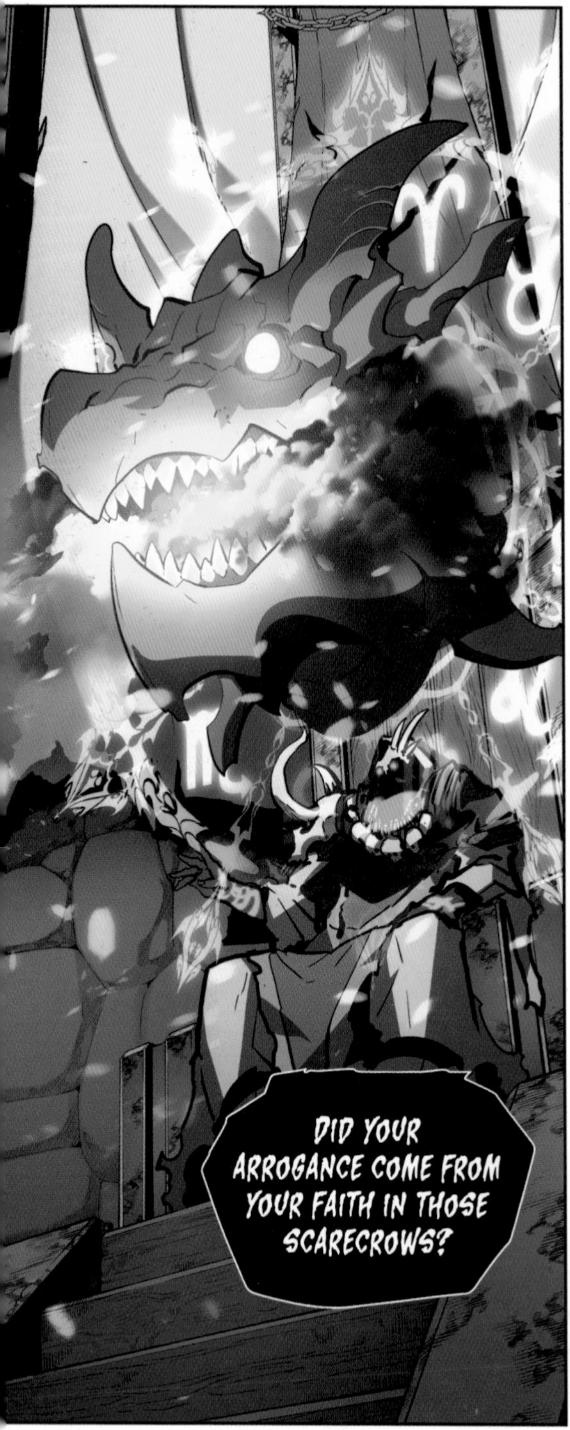
DID YOUR ARROGANCE COME FROM YOUR FAITH IN THOSE SCARECROWS?

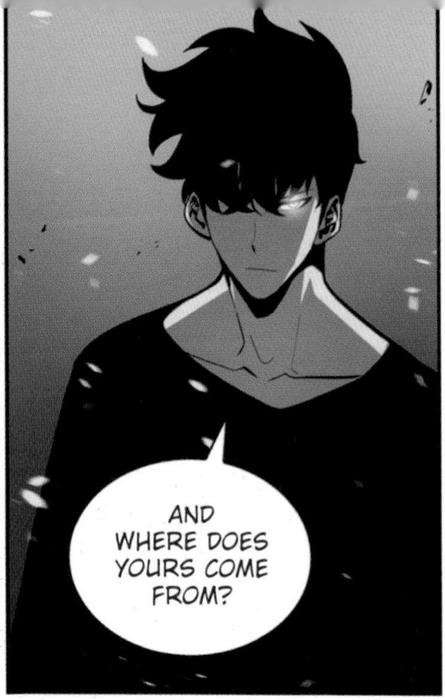
AND WHERE DOES YOURS COME FROM?

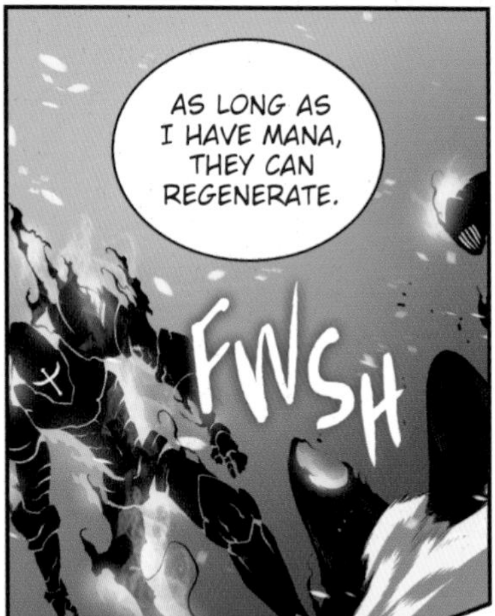
AS LONG AS I HAVE MANA, THEY CAN REGENERATE.
FWSH

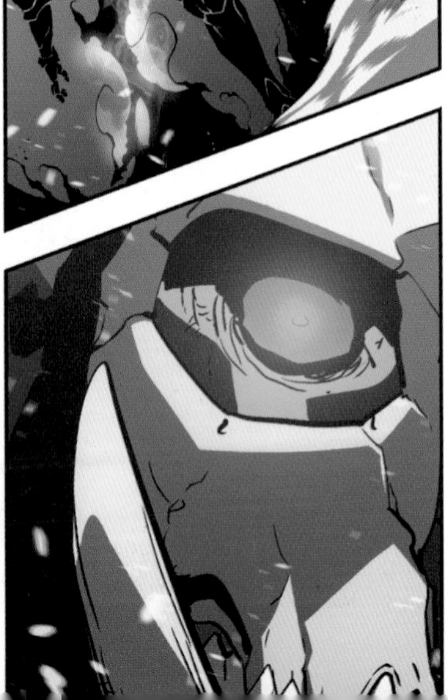

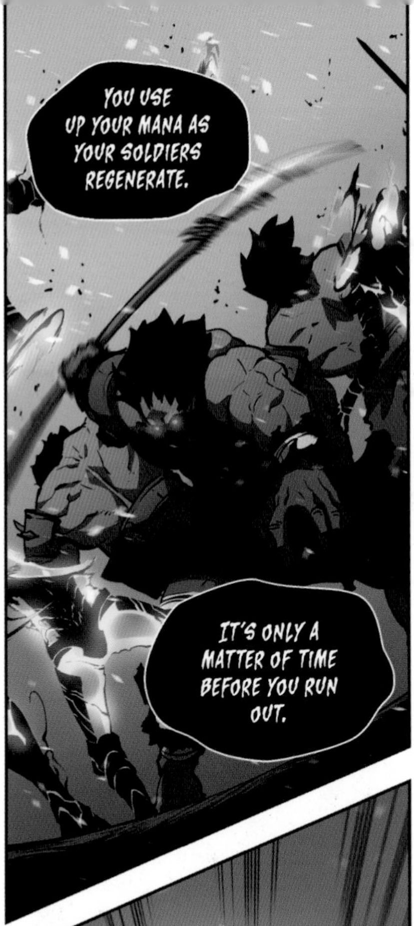
YOU USE UP YOUR MANA AS YOUR SOLDIERS REGENERATE.
IT'S ONLY A MATTER OF TIME BEFORE YOU RUN OUT.

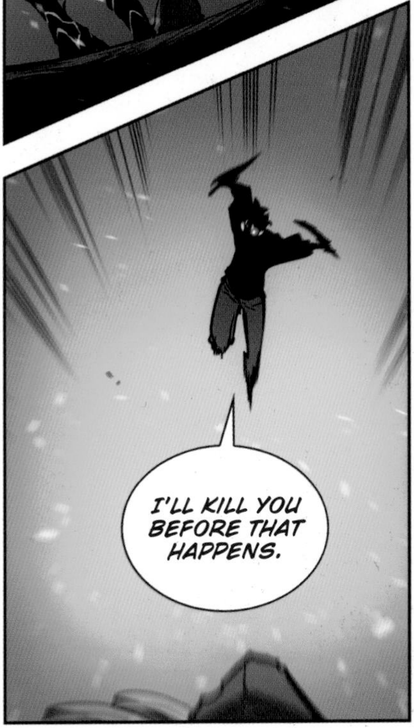
I'LL KILL YOU BEFORE THAT HAPPENS.

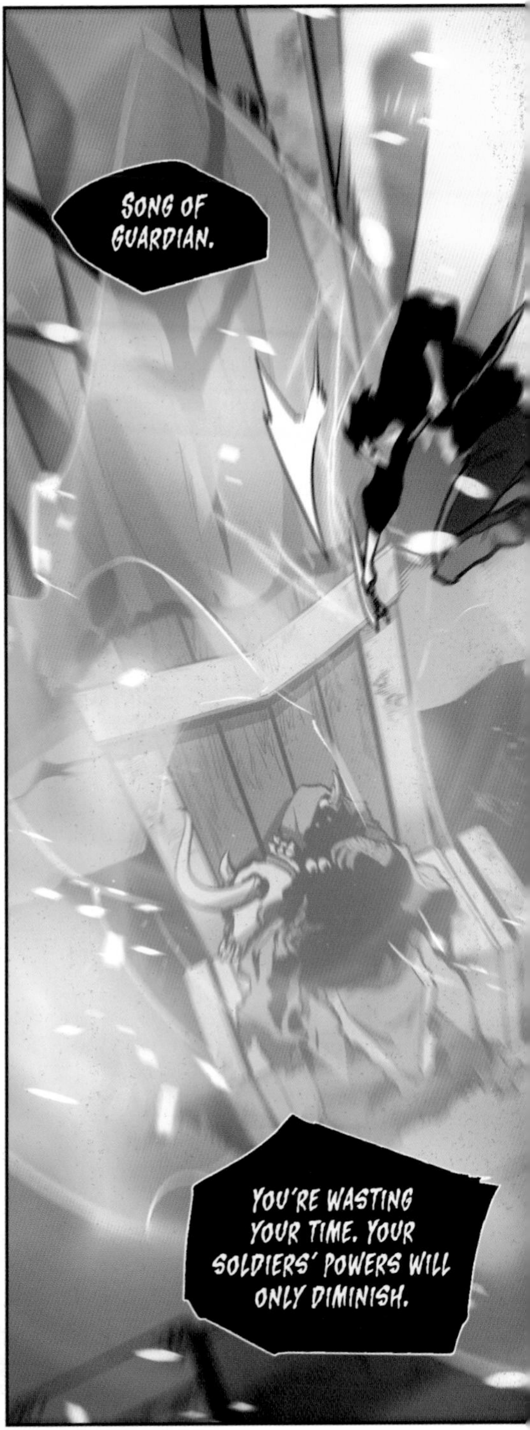
SONG OF GUARDIAN.
YOU'RE WASTING YOUR TIME. YOUR SOLDIERS' POWERS WILL ONLY DIMINISH.

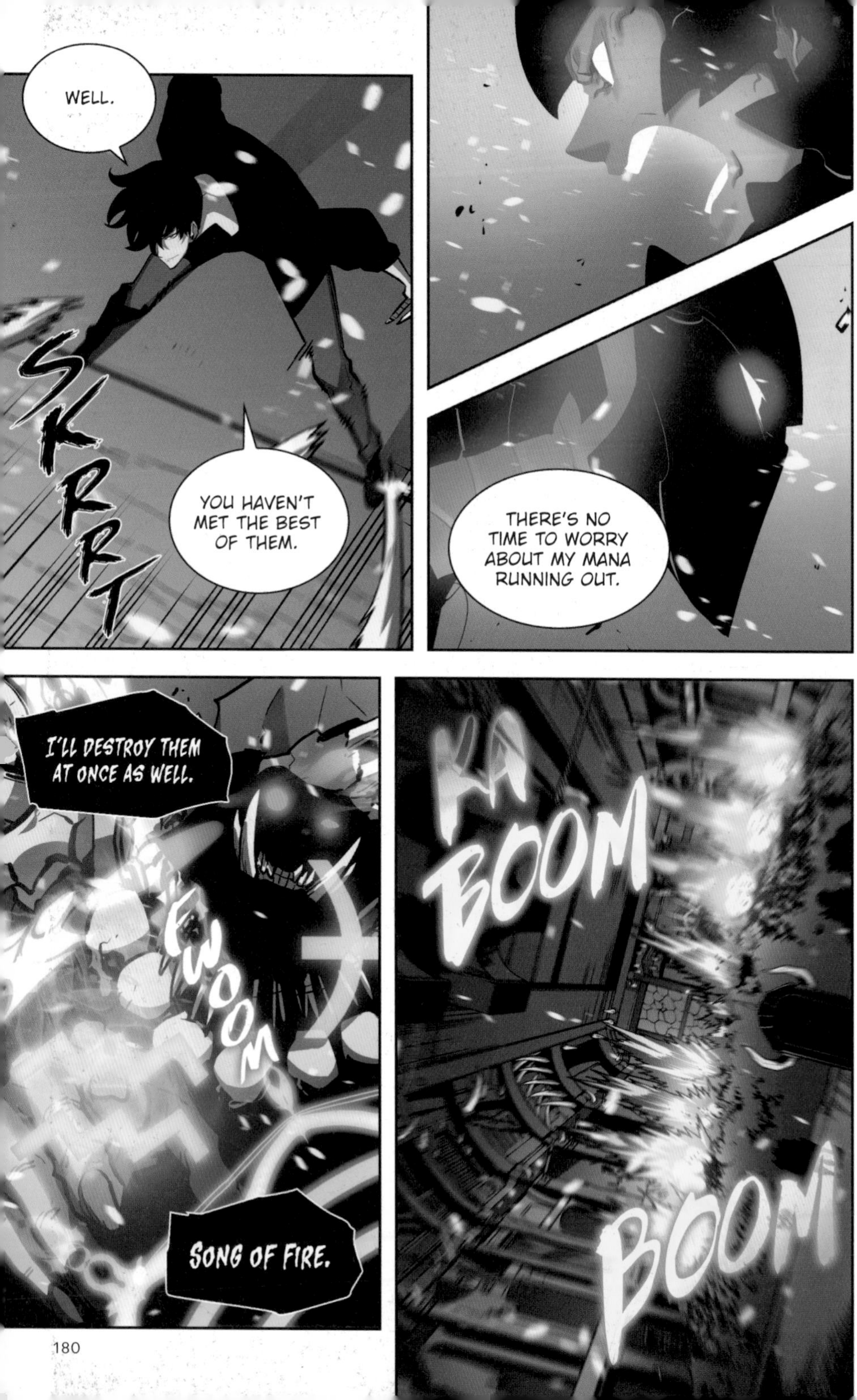
WELL.
SKRRT
YOU HAVEN'T MET THE BEST OF THEM.
THERE'S NO TIME TO WORRY ABOUT MY MANA RUNNING OUT.
I'LL DESTROY THEM AT ONCE AS WELL.
FWOOM
SONG OF FIRE.
KA BOOM
BOOM

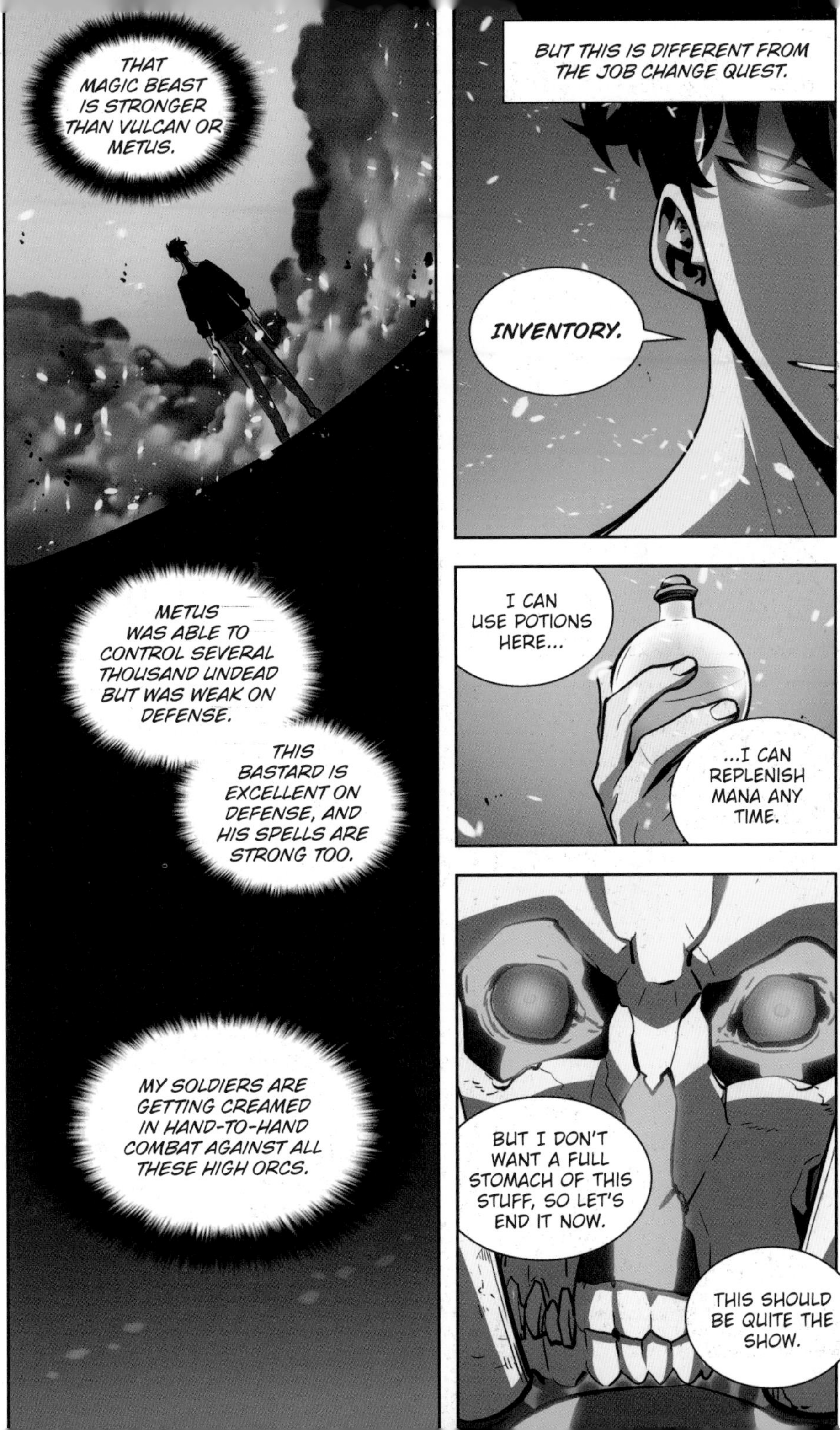
THAT MAGIC BEAST IS STRONGER THAN VULCAN OR METUS.
METUS WAS ABLE TO CONTROL SEVERAL THOUSAND UNDEAD BUT WAS WEAK ON DEFENSE.
THIS BASTARD IS EXCELLENT ON DEFENSE, AND HIS SPELLS ARE STRONG TOO.
MY SOLDIERS ARE GETTING CREAMED IN HAND-TO-HAND COMBAT AGAINST ALL THESE HIGH ORCS.
BUT THIS IS DIFFERENT FROM THE JOB CHANGE QUEST.
INVENTORY.
I CAN USE POTIONS HERE...
...I CAN REPLENISH MANA ANY TIME.
BUT I DON'T WANT A FULL STOMACH OF THIS STUFF, SO LET'S END IT NOW.
THIS SHOULD BE QUITE THE SHOW.

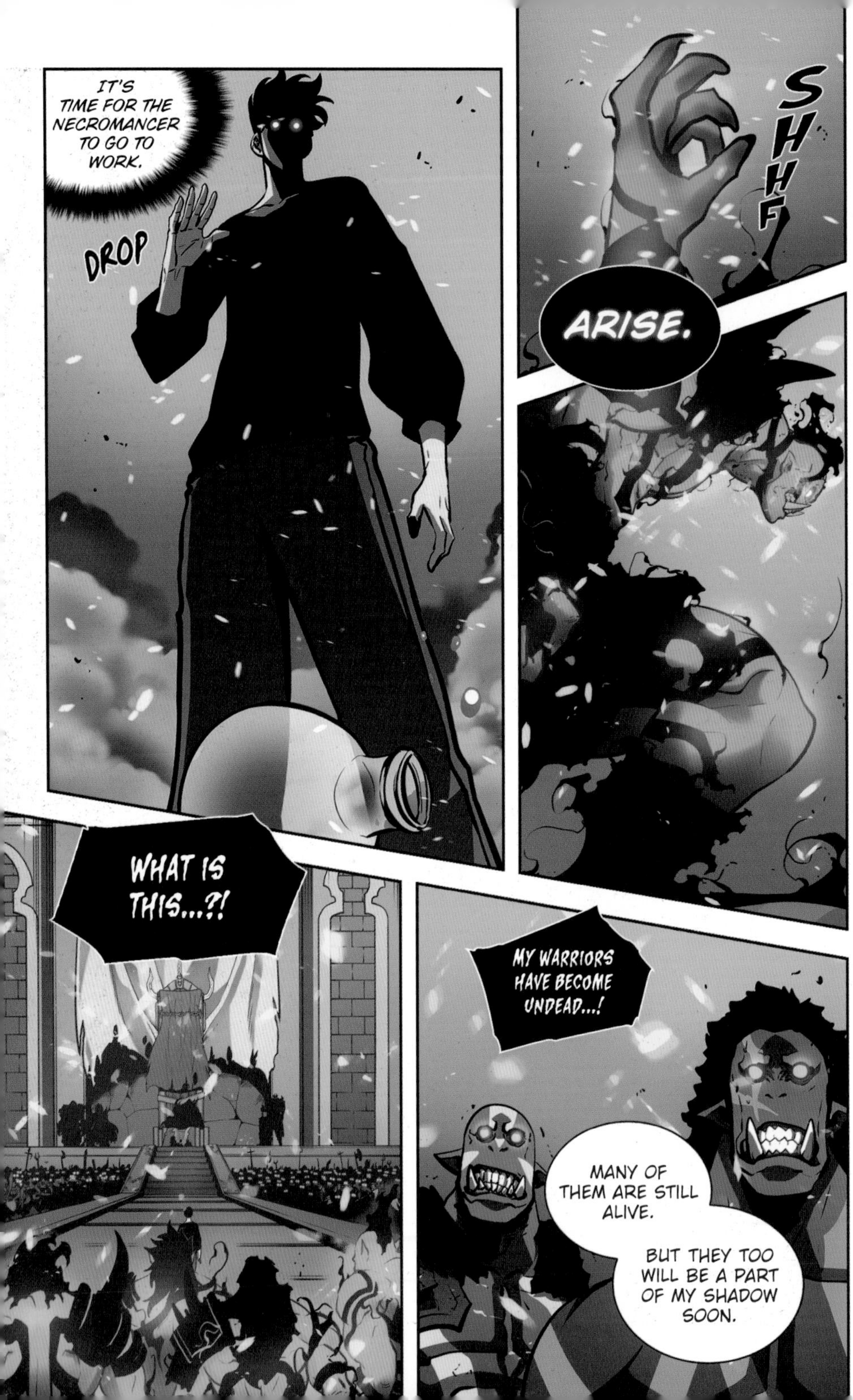
IT'S TIME FOR THE NECROMANCER TO GO TO WORK.
DROP
SHHF
ARISE.
WHAT IS THIS...?!
MY WARRIORS HAVE BECOME UNDEAD...!
MANY OF THEM ARE STILL ALIVE.
BUT THEY TOO WILL BE A PART OF MY SHADOW SOON.

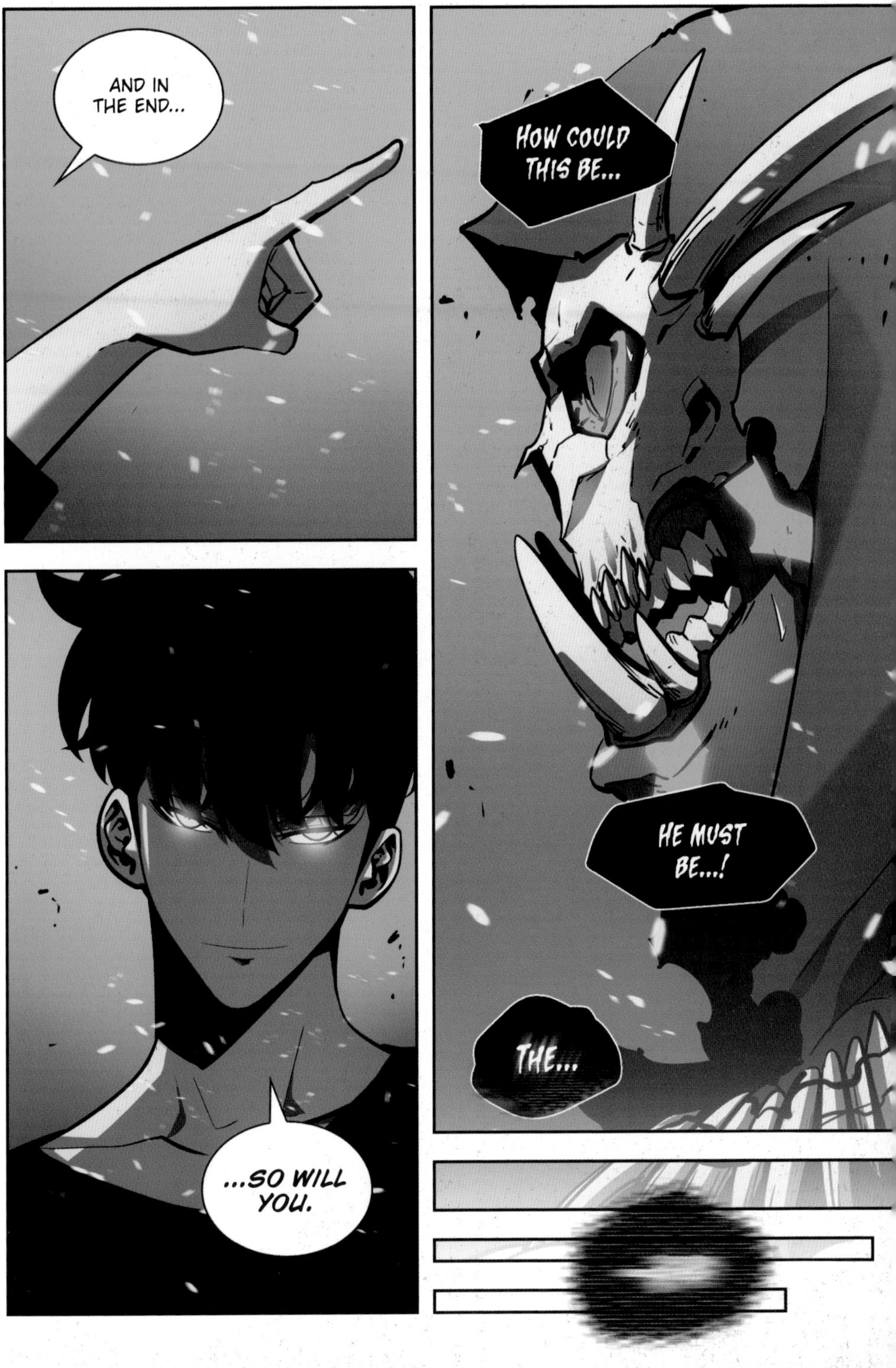
AND IN THE END...
...SO WILL YOU.
HOW COULD THIS BE...
HE MUST BE...!
THE...

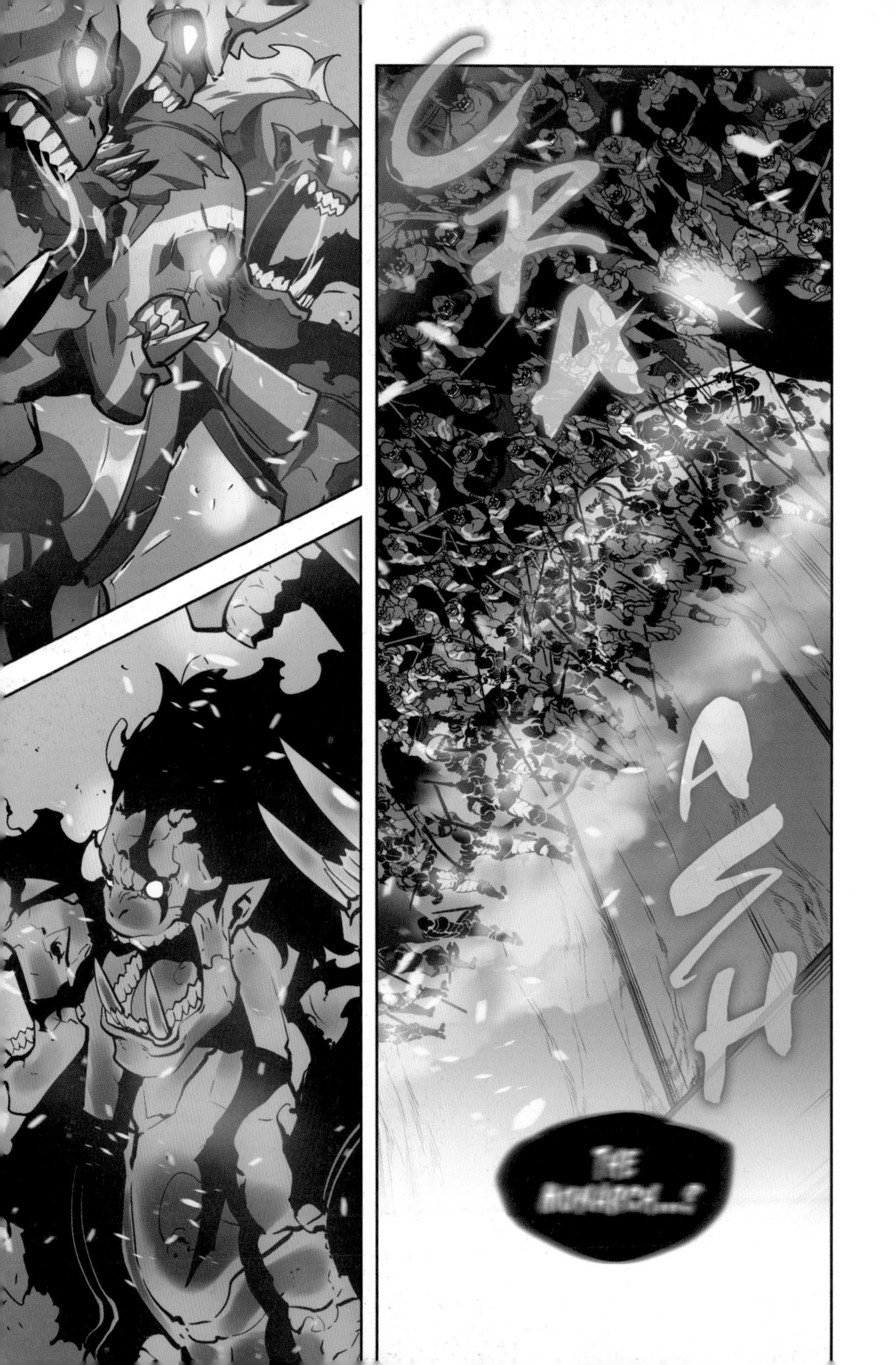
CRAASH

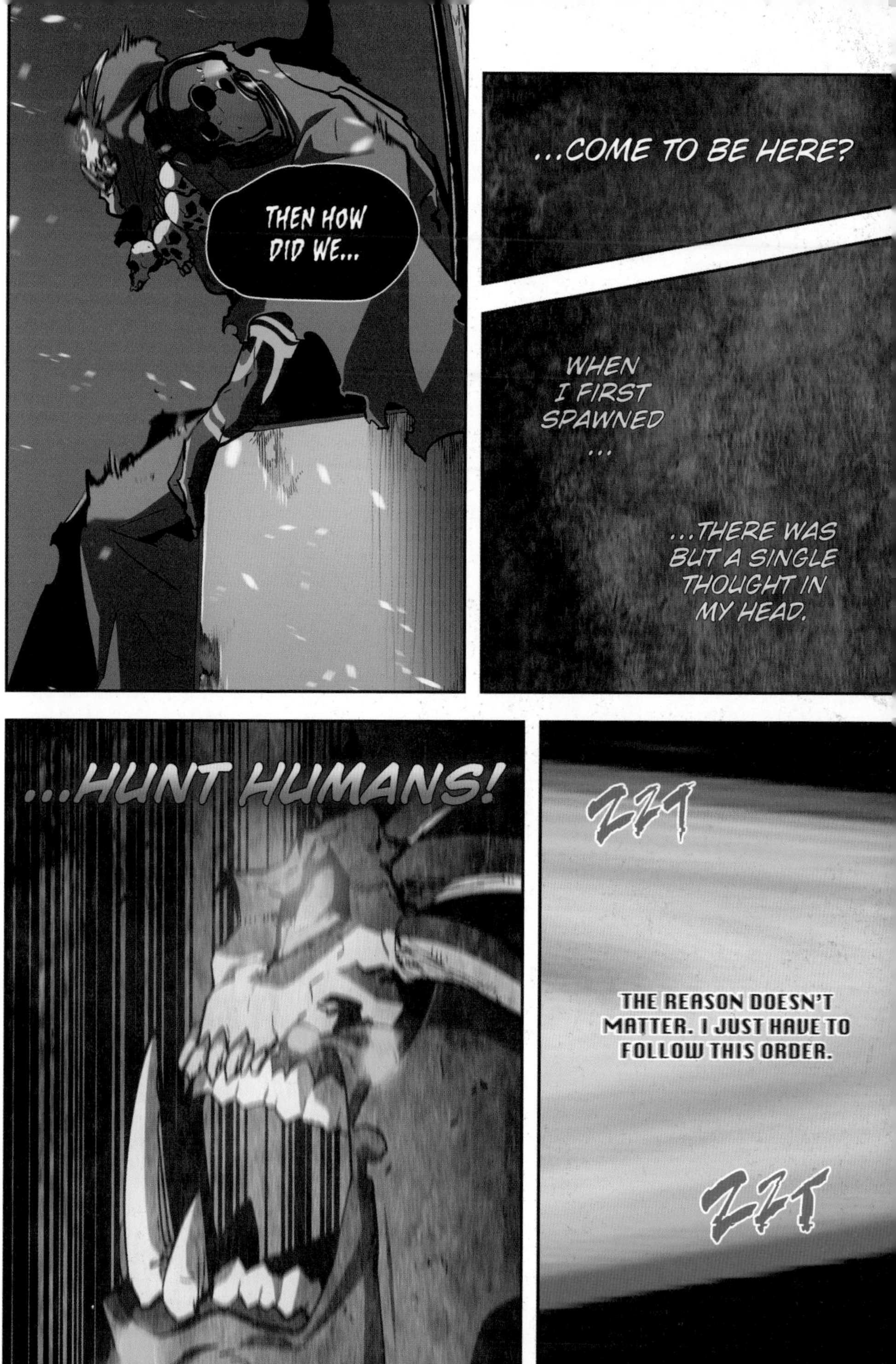
THEN HOW DID WE...
...COME TO BE HERE?
WHEN I FIRST SPAWNED ...
...THERE WAS BUT A SINGLE THOUGHT IN MY HEAD.
...HUNT HUMANS!
ZZT
THE REASON DOESN'T MATTER. I JUST HAVE TO FOLLOW THIS ORDER.
ZZT

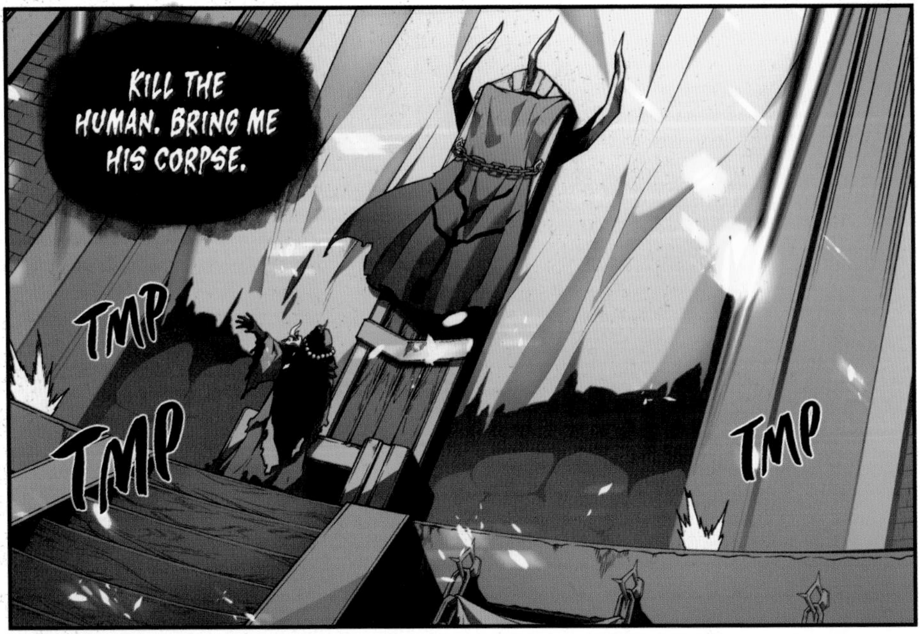
KILL THE HUMAN. BRING ME HIS CORPSE.
TMP
TMP
TMP

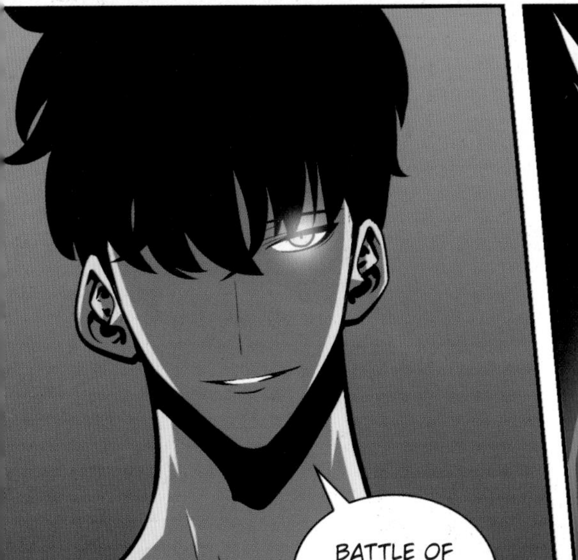
BATTLE OF THE GENERALS NOW, IS IT?

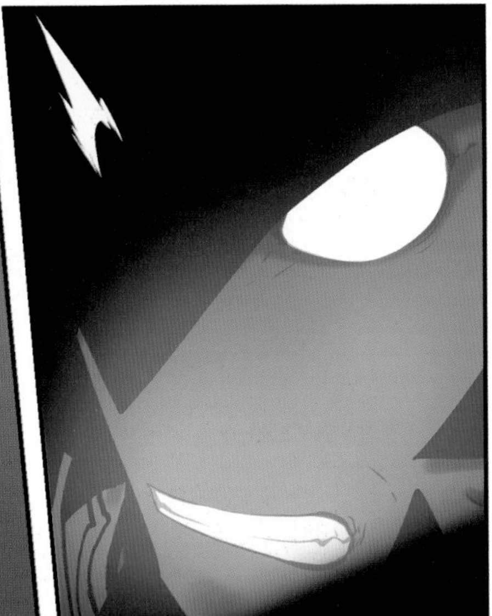
GRR...

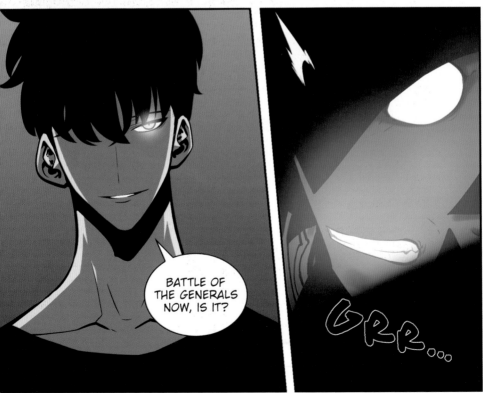

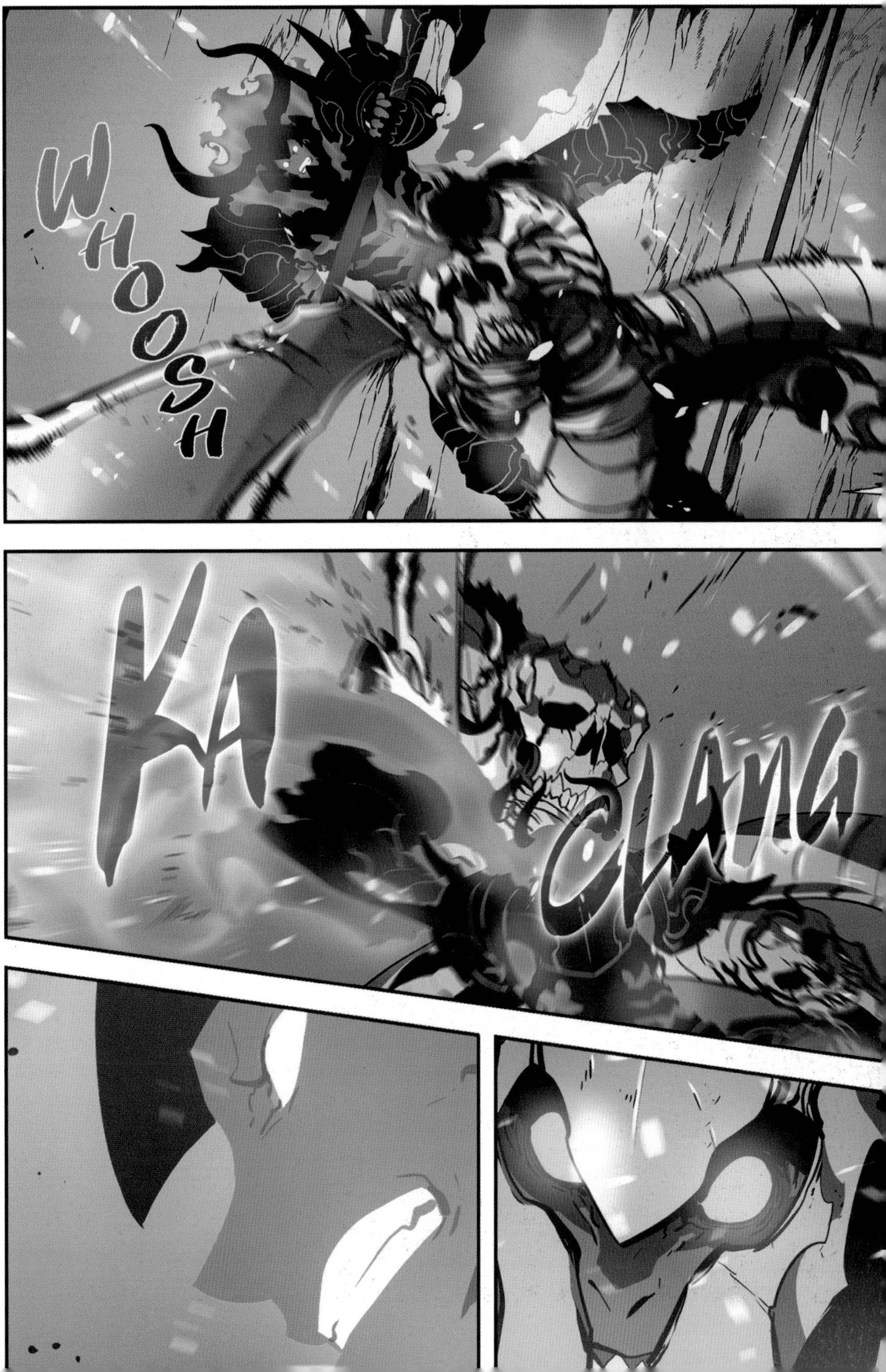
WHOOSH
KA-CLANG

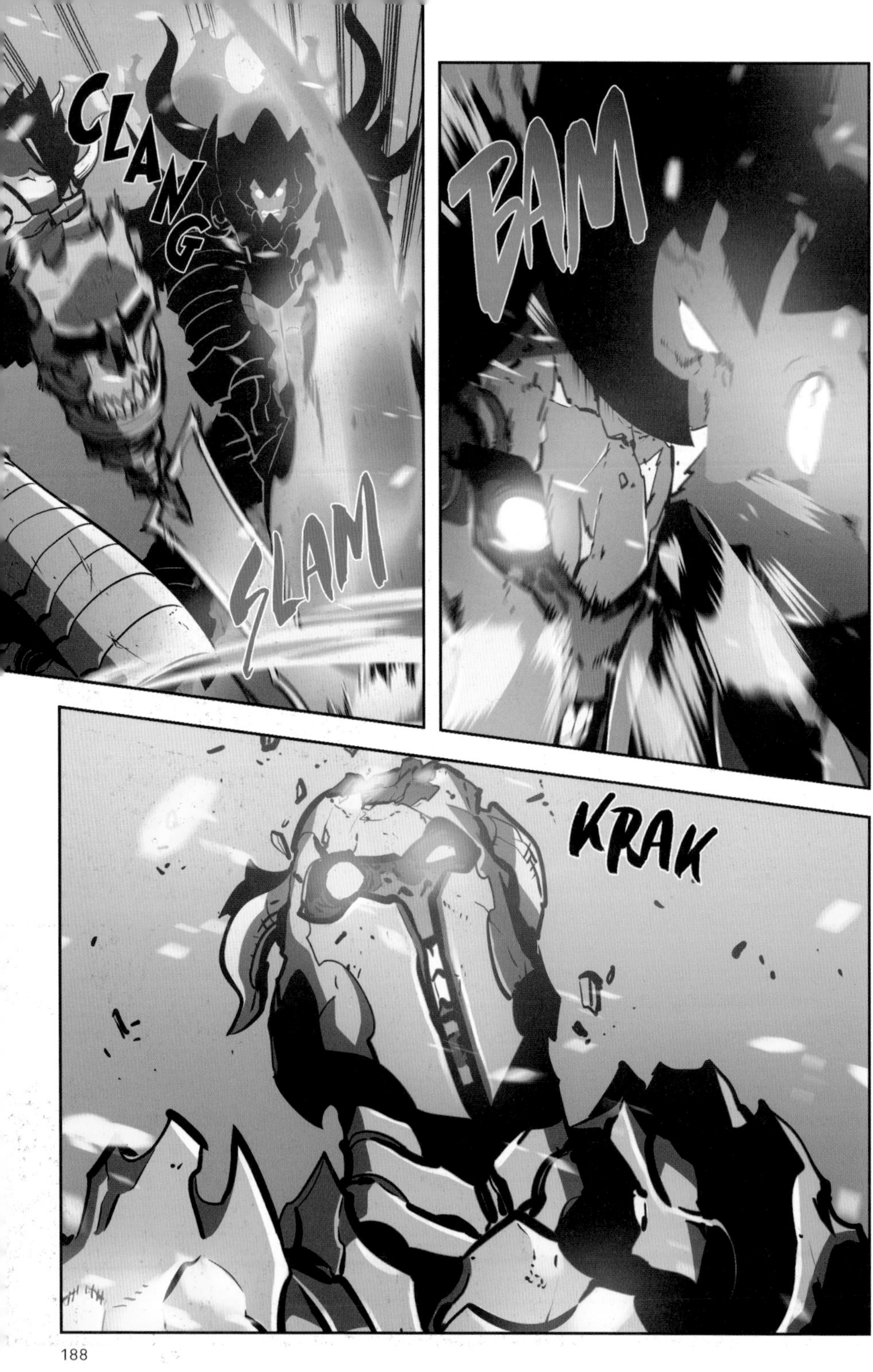
CLANG
SLAM
BAM
KRAK

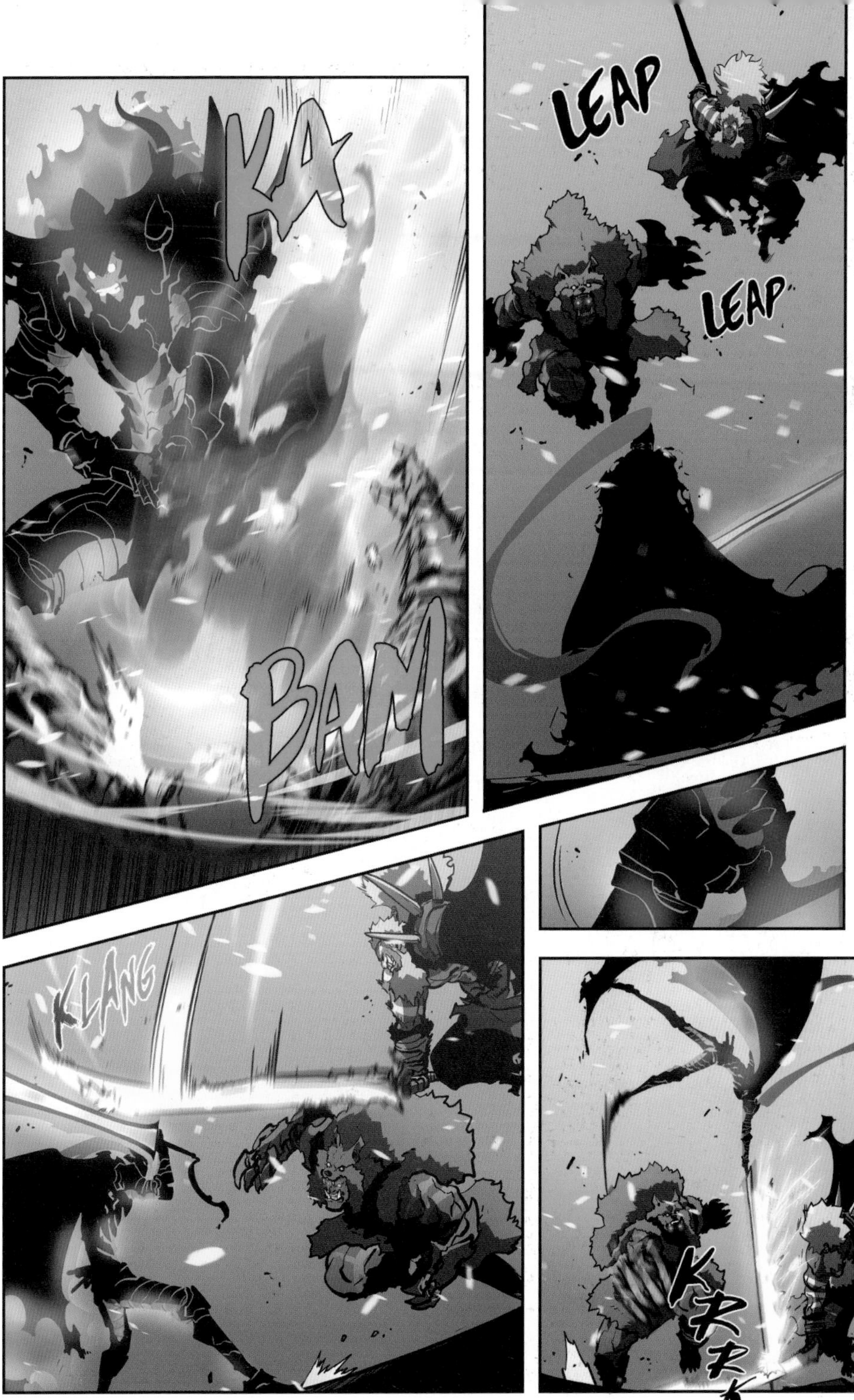
KA
BAM
LEAP
LEAP
KLANG
KRRK

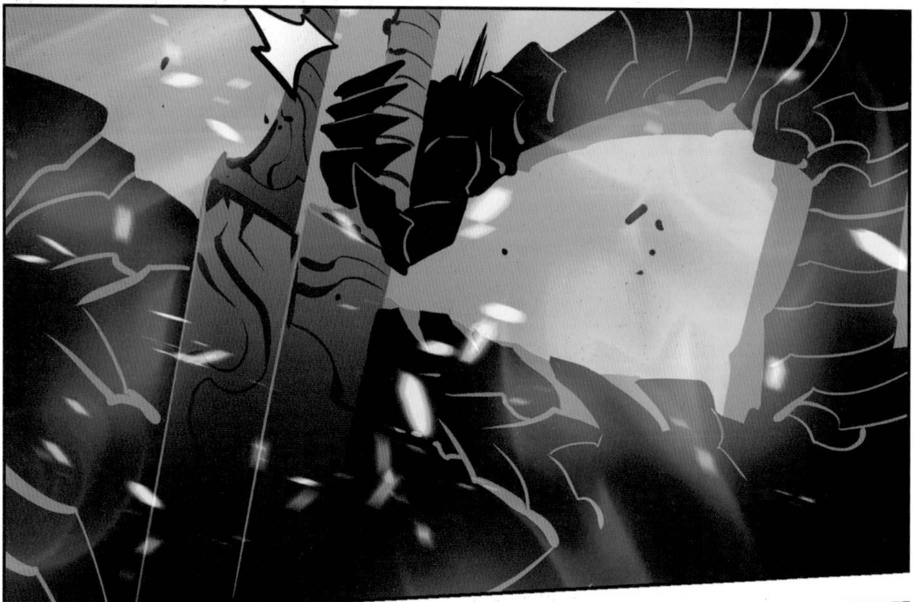

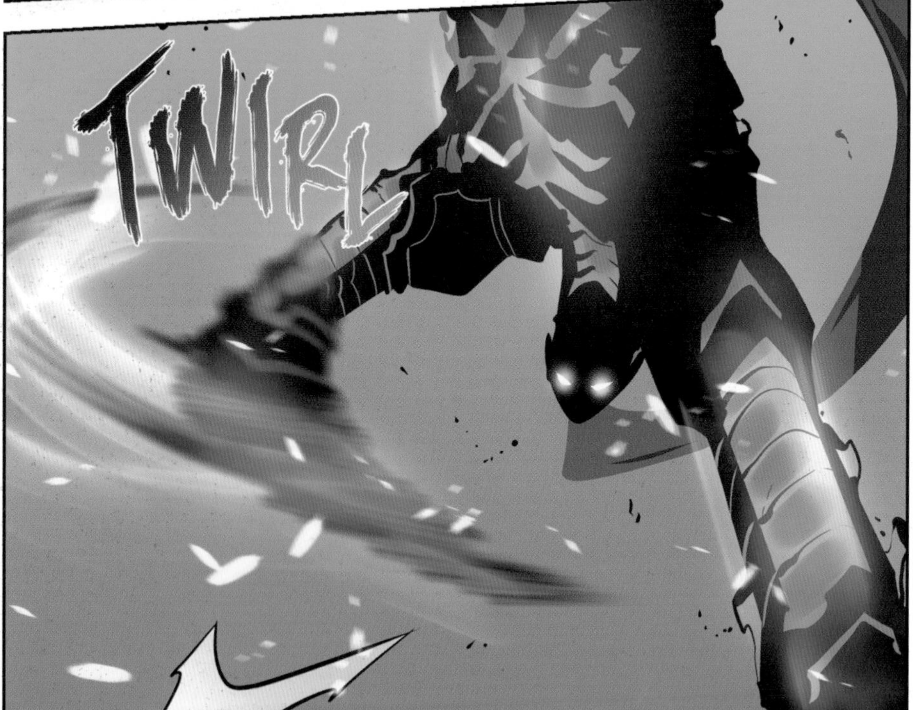
TWIRL

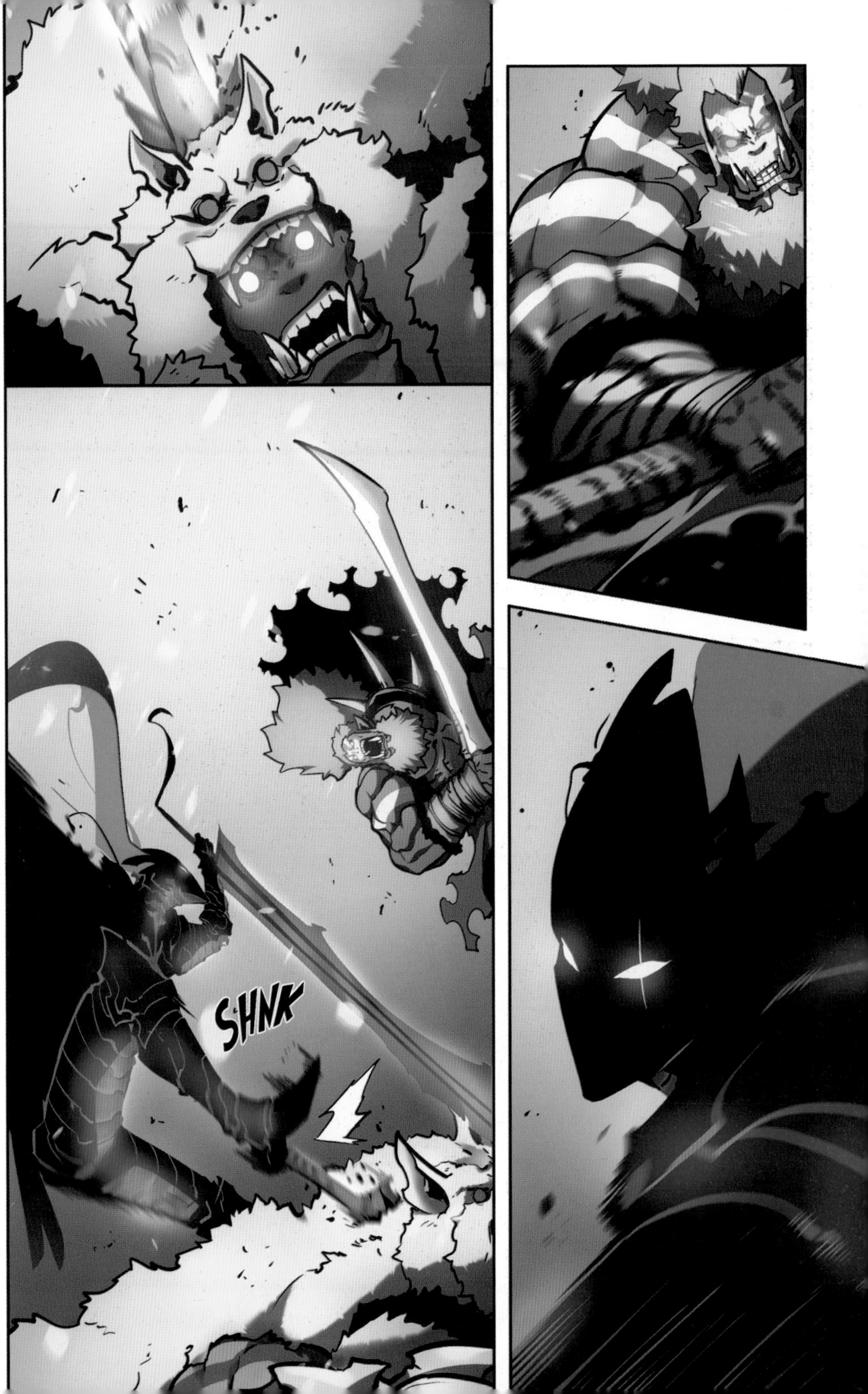
SHNK

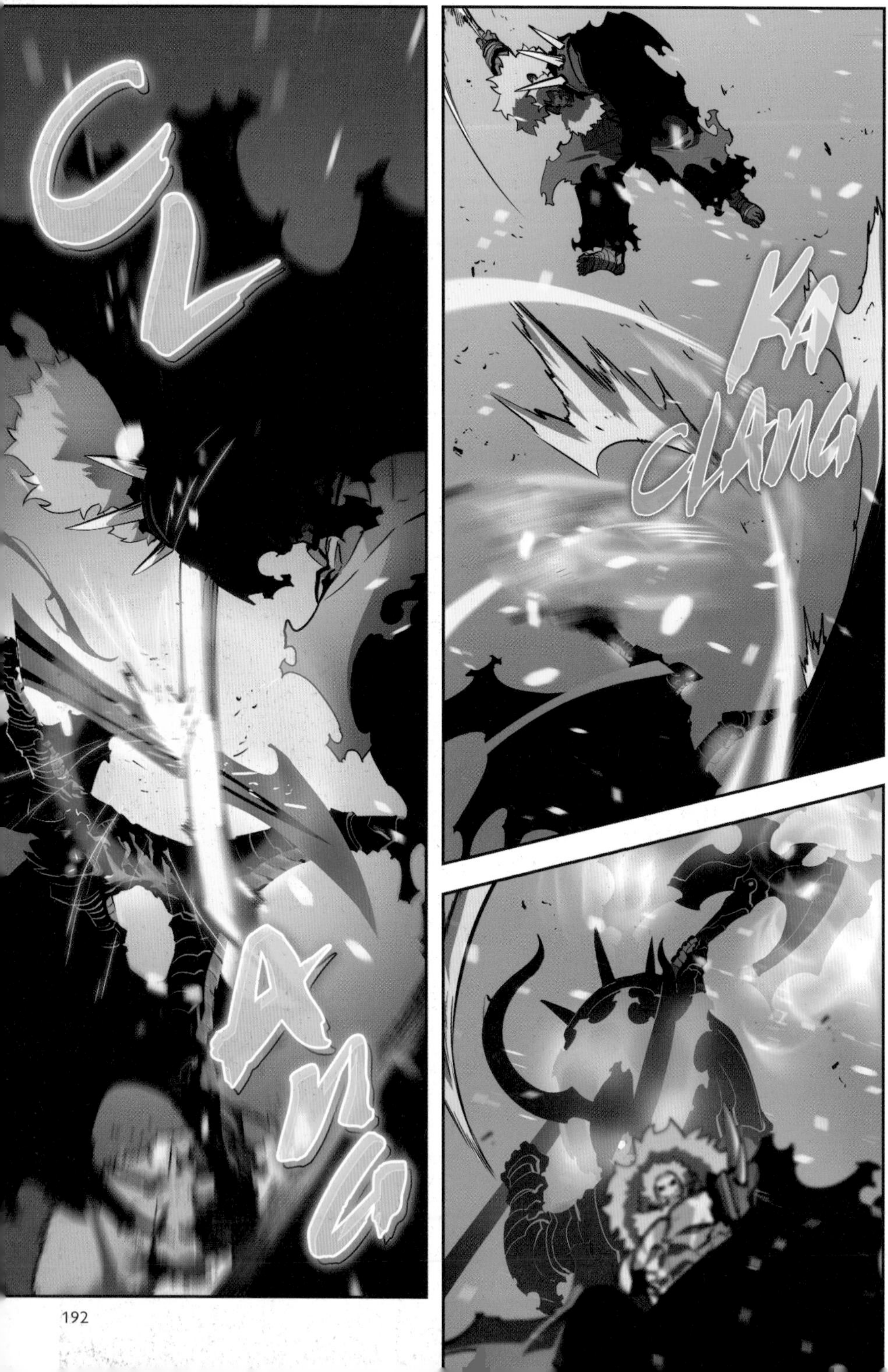
CLANG
KA CLANG

WHAM

THWAK

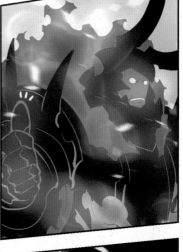

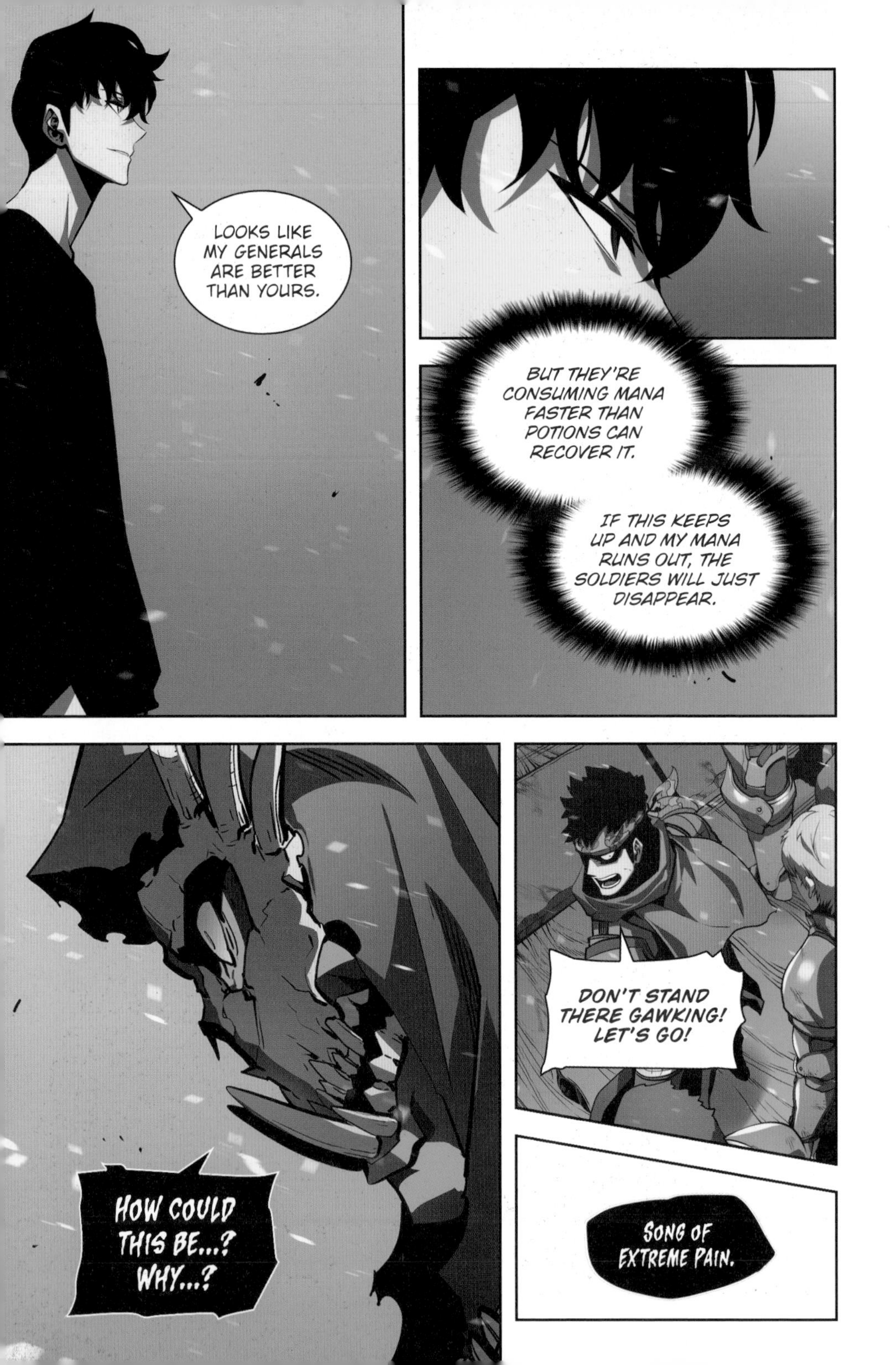
LOOKS LIKE MY GENERALS ARE BETTER THAN YOURS.
BUT THEY'RE CONSUMING MANA FASTER THAN POTIONS CAN RECOVER IT.
IF THIS KEEPS UP AND MY MANA RUNS OUT, THE SOLDIERS WILL JUST DISAPPEAR.
HOW COULD THIS BE...? WHY...?
DON'T STAND THERE GAWKING! LET'S GO!
SONG OF EXTREME PAIN.

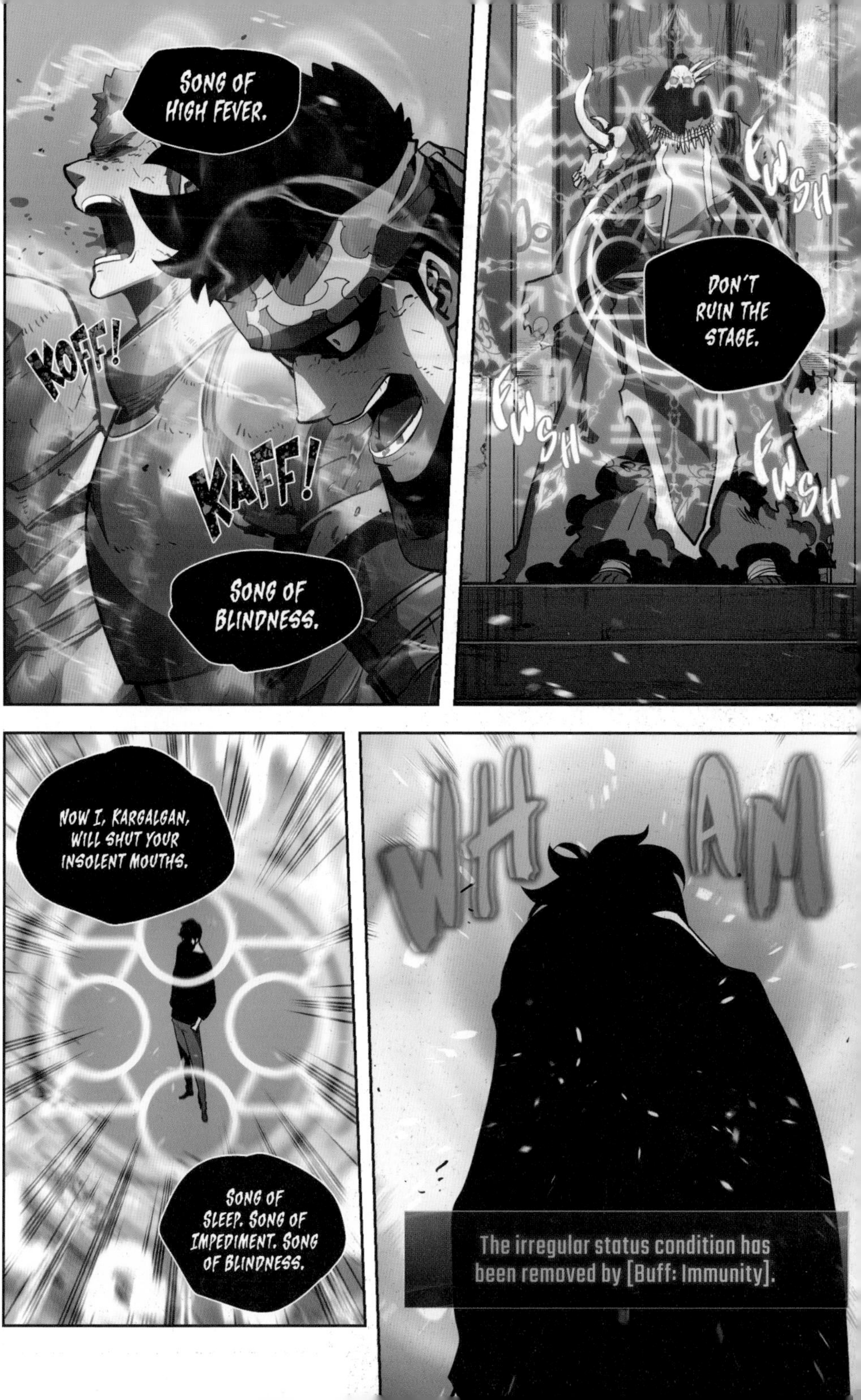
SONG OF HIGH FEVER.
KOFF!
KAFF!
SONG OF BLINDNESS.
DON'T RUIN THE STAGE.
FWSH
FWSH
FWSH
NOW I, KARGALGAN, WILL SHUT YOUR INSOLENT MOUTHS.
SONG OF SLEEP. SONG OF IMPEDIMENT. SONG OF BLINDNESS.
WHAM
The irregular status condition has been removed by [Buff: Immunity].

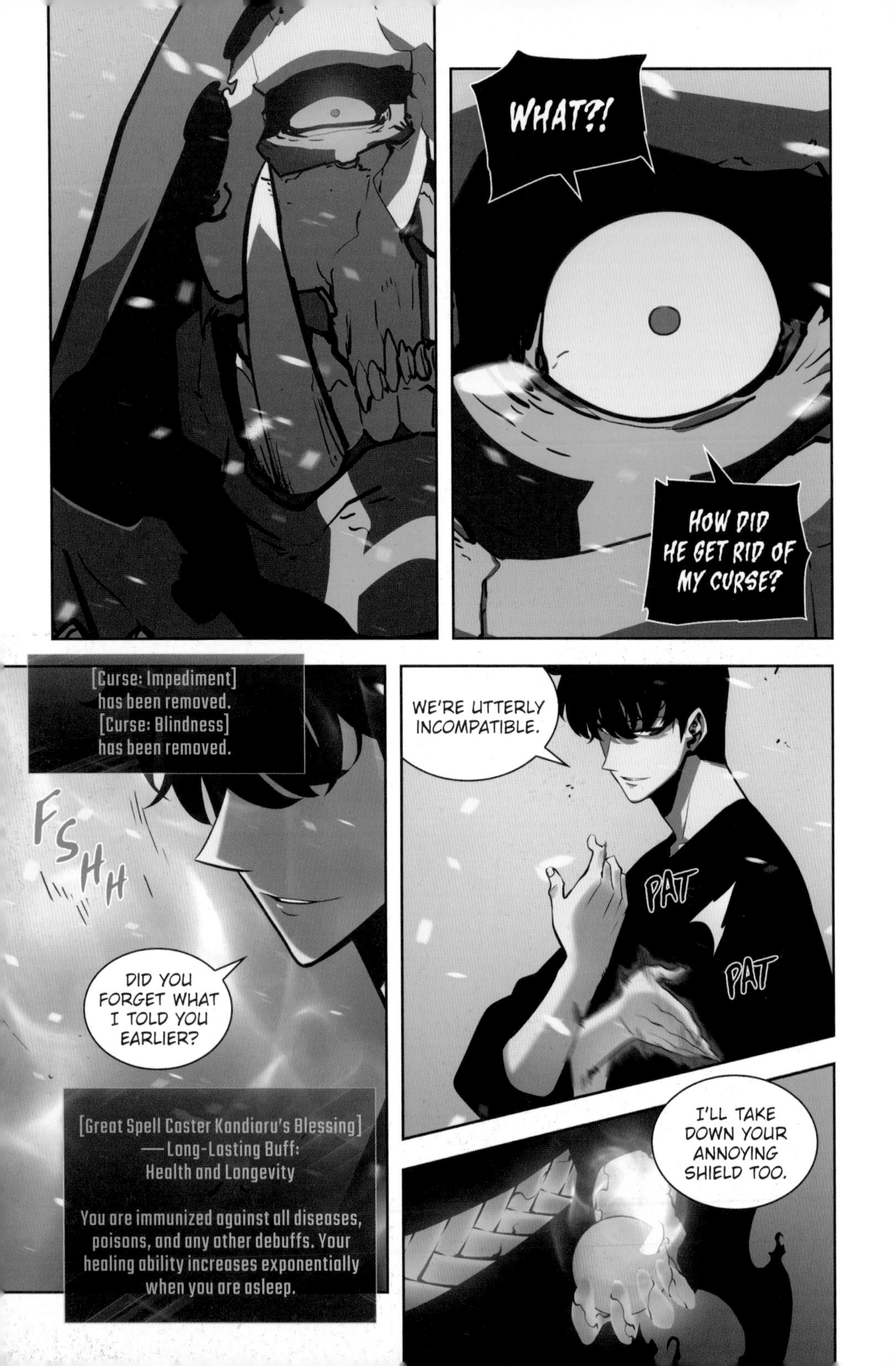
WHAT?!
HOW DID HE GET RID OF MY CURSE?
[Curse: Impediment] has been removed.
[Curse: Blindness] has been removed.
FSHH
DID YOU FORGET WHAT I TOLD YOU EARLIER?
[Great Spell Caster Kandiaru's Blessing] —Long-Lasting Buff: Health and Longevity
You are immunized against all diseases, poisons, and any other debuffs. Your healing ability increases exponentially when you are asleep.
WE'RE UTTERLY INCOMPATIBLE.
PAT
PAT
I'LL TAKE DOWN YOUR ANNOYING SHIELD TOO.

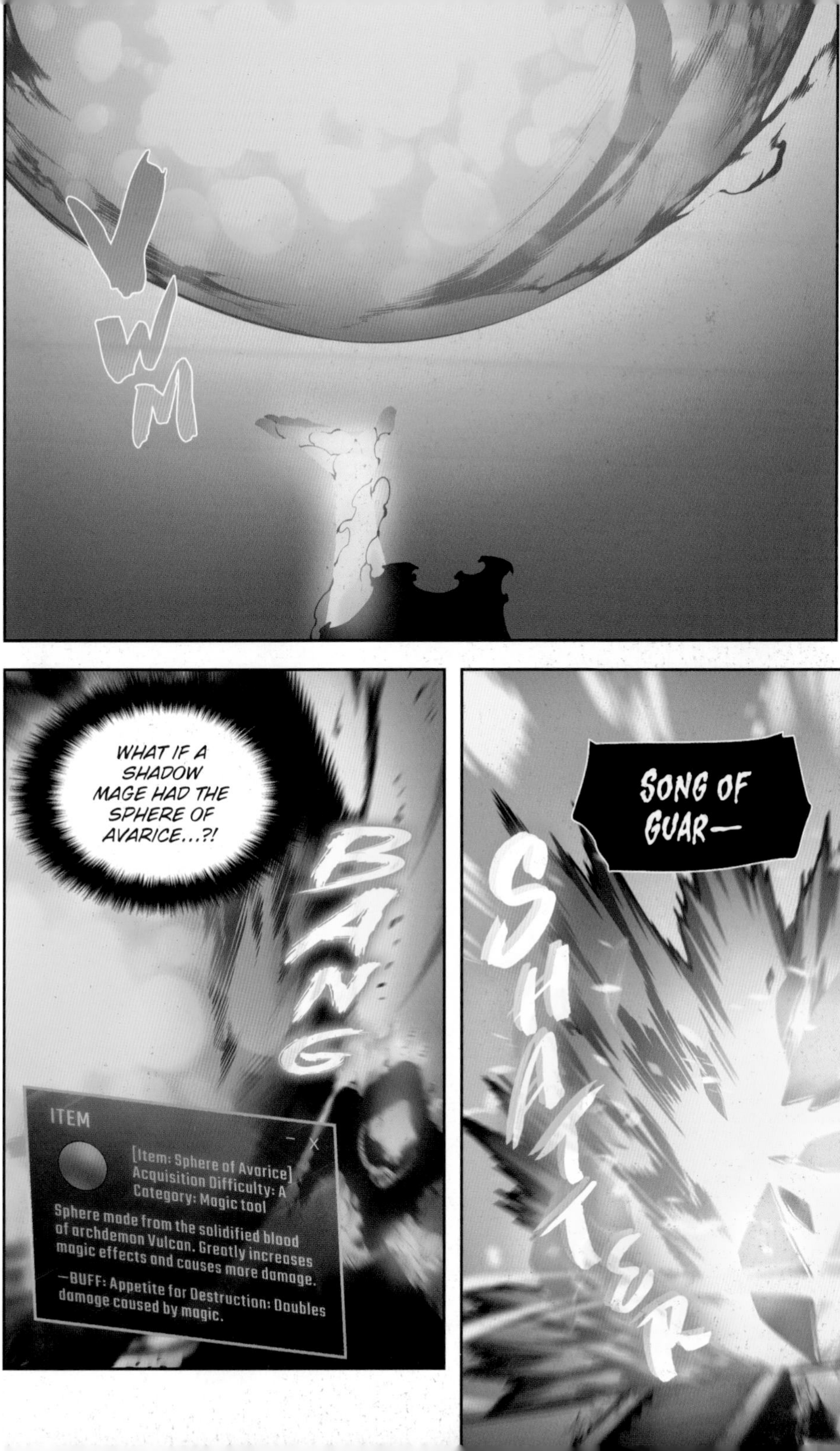
VWM
WHAT IF A SHADOW MAGE HAD THE SPHERE OF AVARICE...?!
BANG
ITEM
[Item: Sphere of Avarice]
Acquisition Difficulty: A
Category: Magic tool
Sphere made from the solidified blood of archdemon Vulcan. Greatly increases magic effects and causes more damage.
—BUFF: Appetite for Destruction: Doubles damage caused by magic.
SONG OF GUAR—
SHATTER

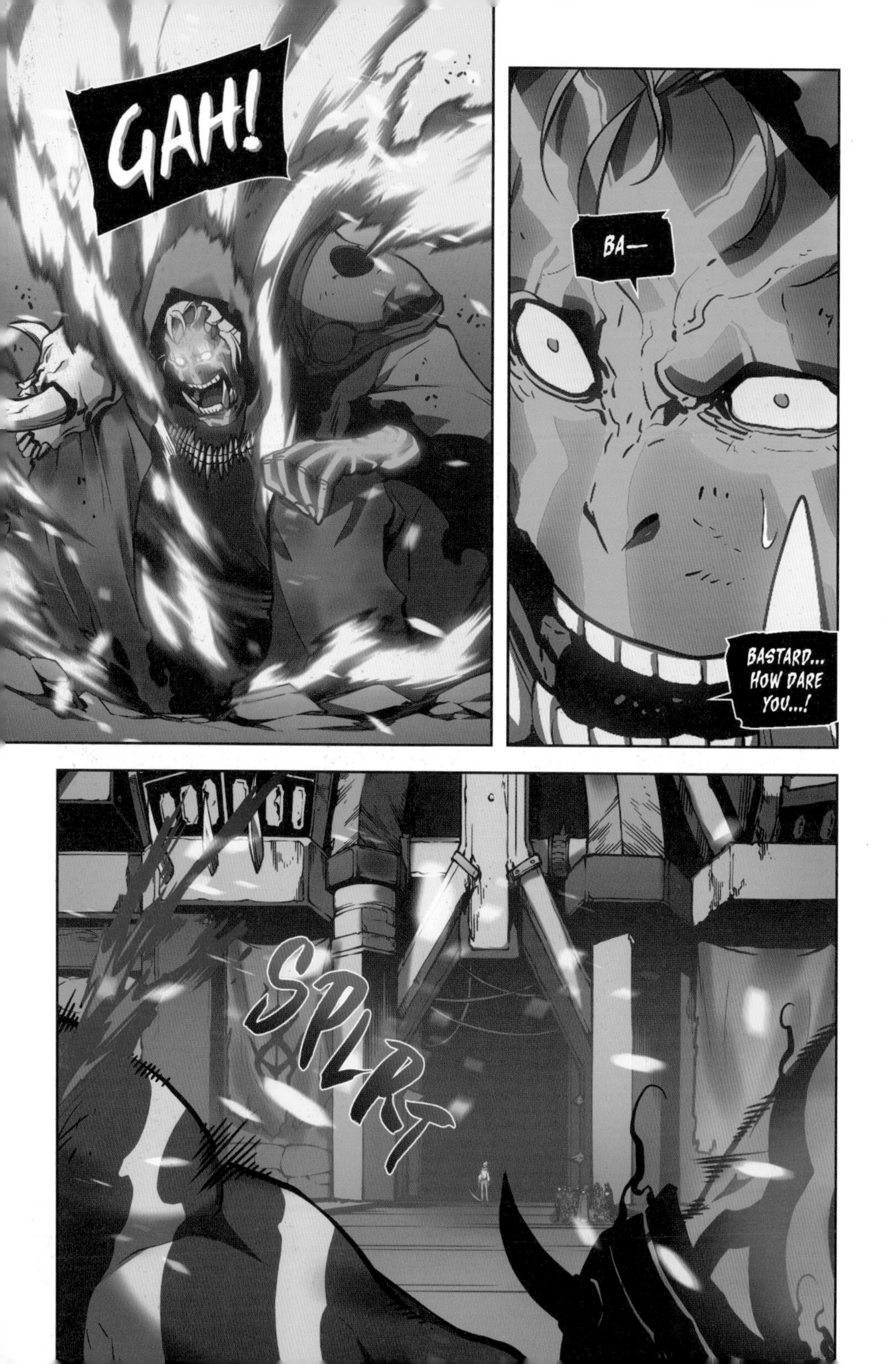
GAH!
BA—
BASTARD... HOW DARE YOU...!
SPLRT

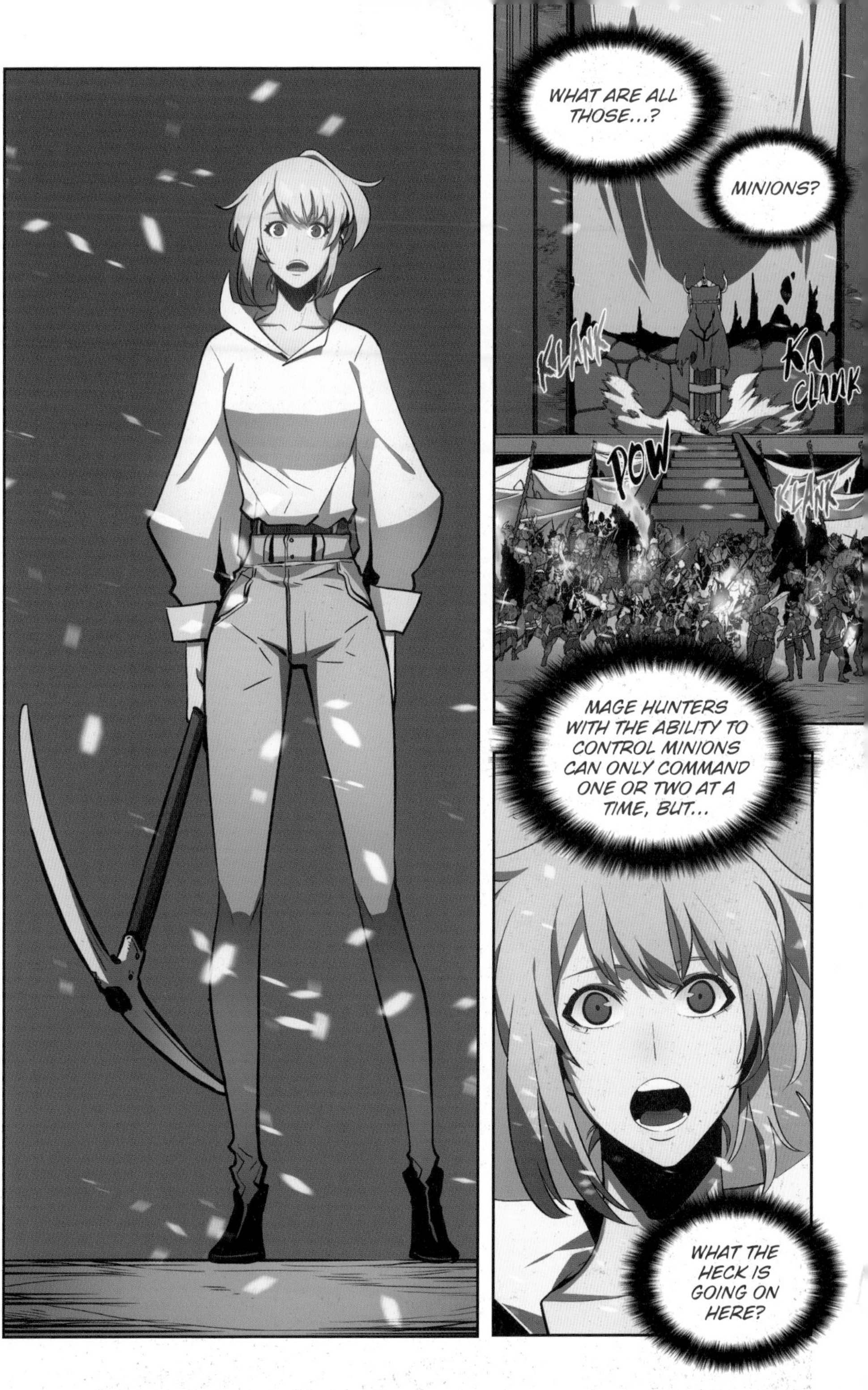
WHAT ARE ALL THOSE...?
MINIONS?
KLANK
KA CLANK
POW
KLANK
MAGE HUNTERS WITH THE ABILITY TO CONTROL MINIONS CAN ONLY COMMAND ONE OR TWO AT A TIME, BUT...
WHAT THE HECK IS GOING ON HERE?

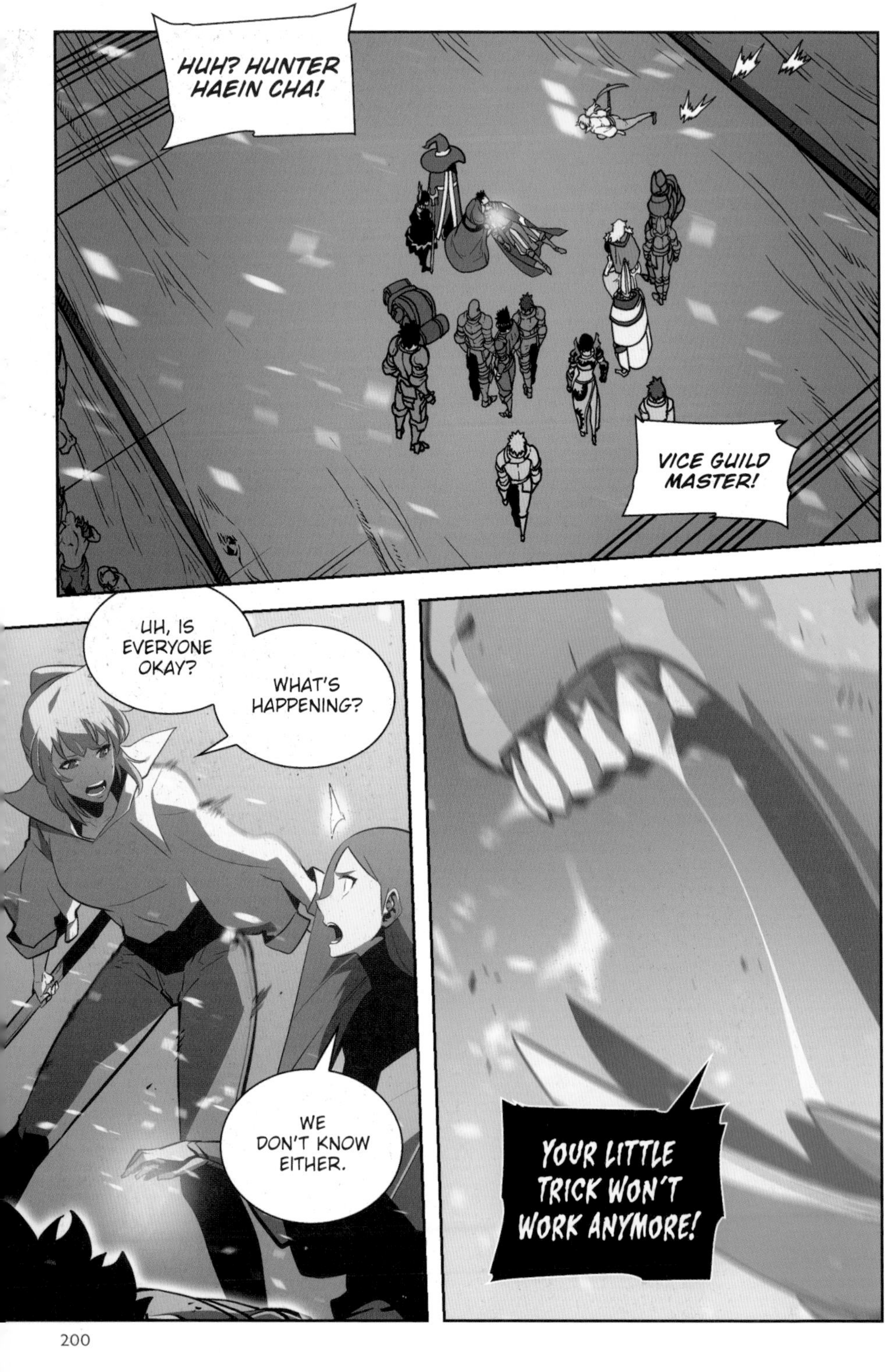
HUH? HUNTER HAEIN CHA!
VICE GUILD MASTER!
UH, IS EVERYONE OKAY?
WHAT'S HAPPENING?
WE DON'T KNOW EITHER.
YOUR LITTLE TRICK WON'T WORK ANYMORE!

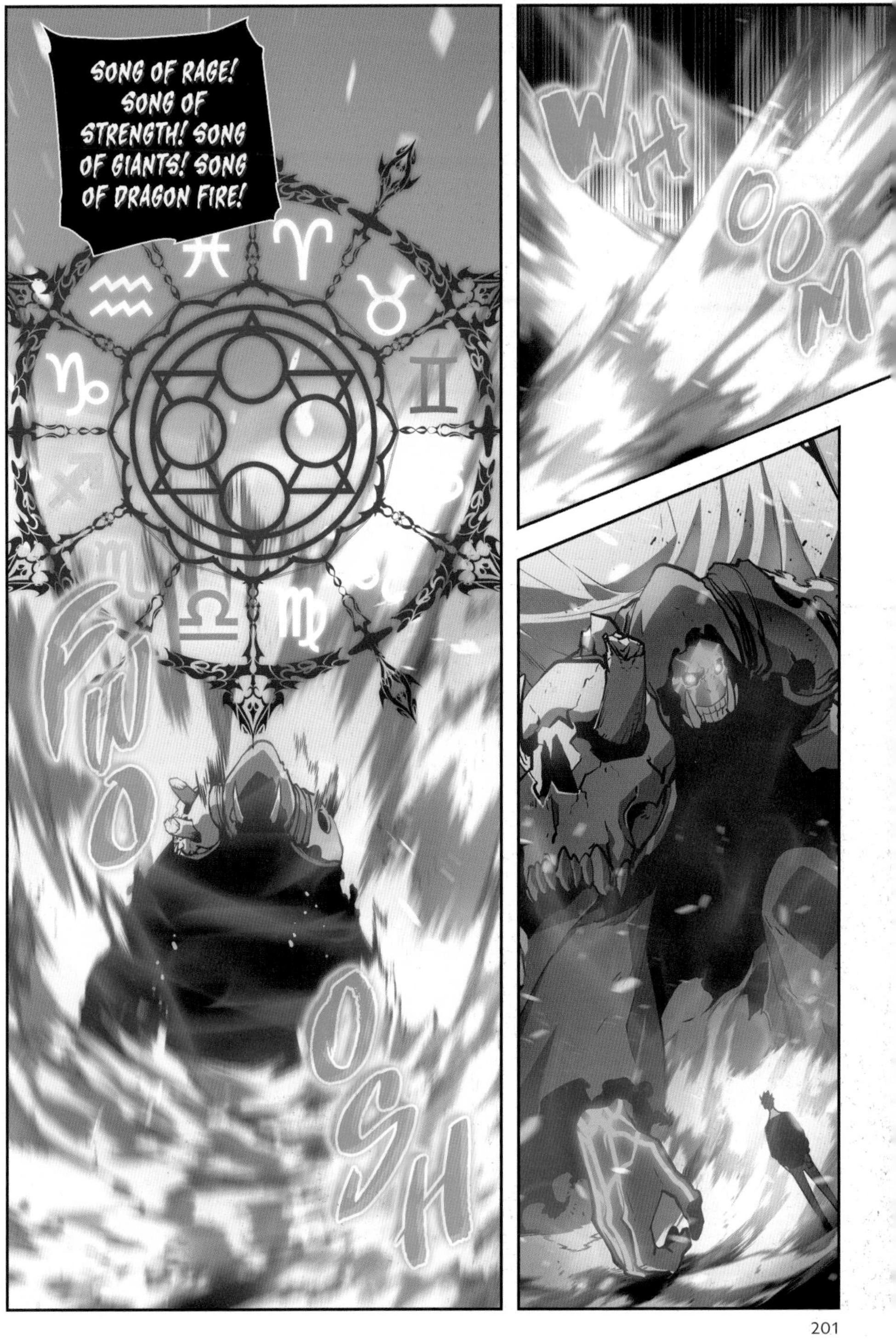
SONG OF RAGE! SONG OF STRENGTH! SONG OF GIANTS! SONG OF DRAGON FIRE!
FWOOSH
WHOOOM

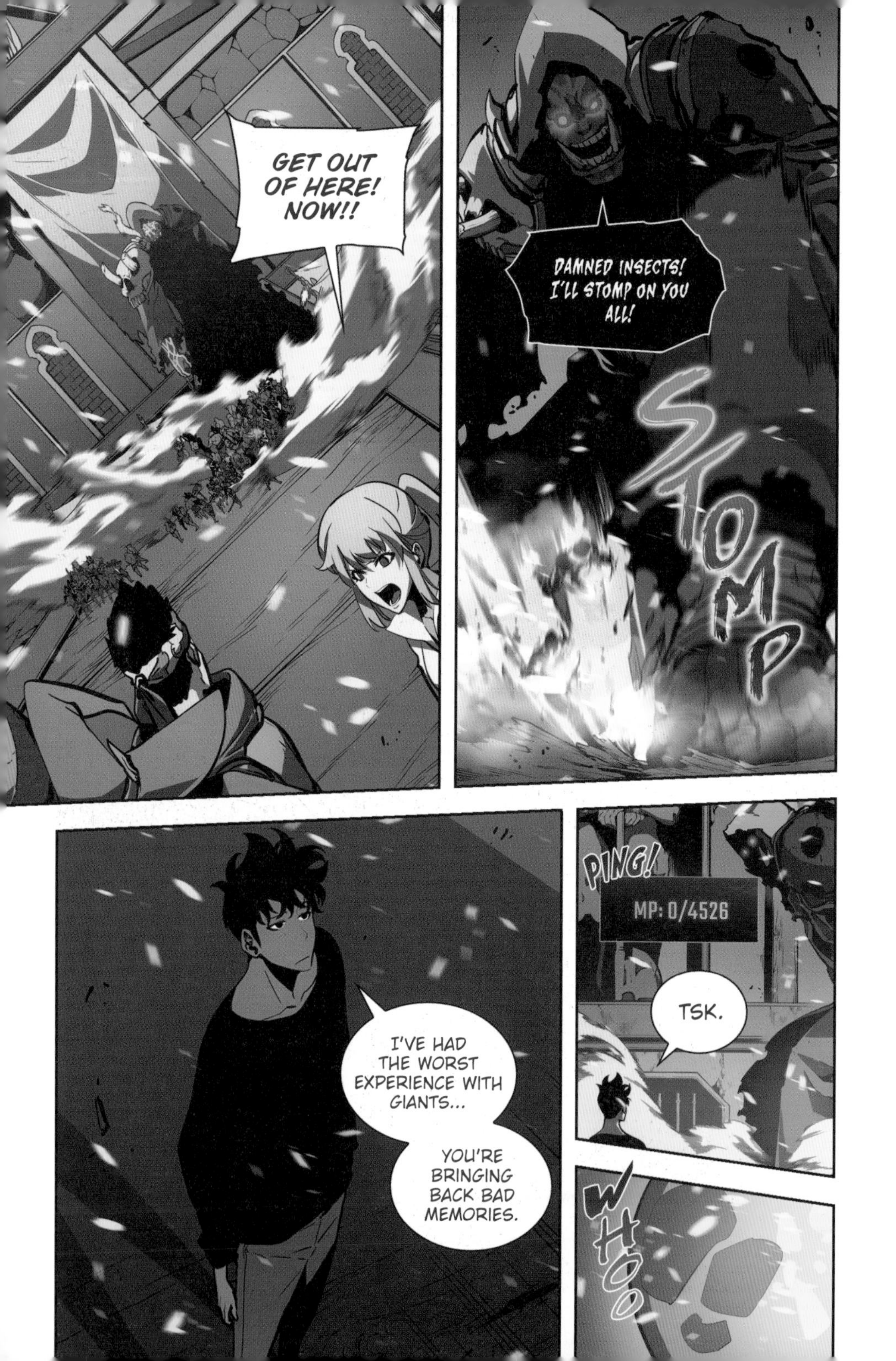
GET OUT OF HERE! NOW!!
DAMNED INSECTS! I'LL STOMP ON YOU ALL!
STOMP
I'VE HAD THE WORST EXPERIENCE WITH GIANTS...
YOU'RE BRINGING BACK BAD MEMORIES.
PING!
MP: 0/4526
TSK.
WHOO

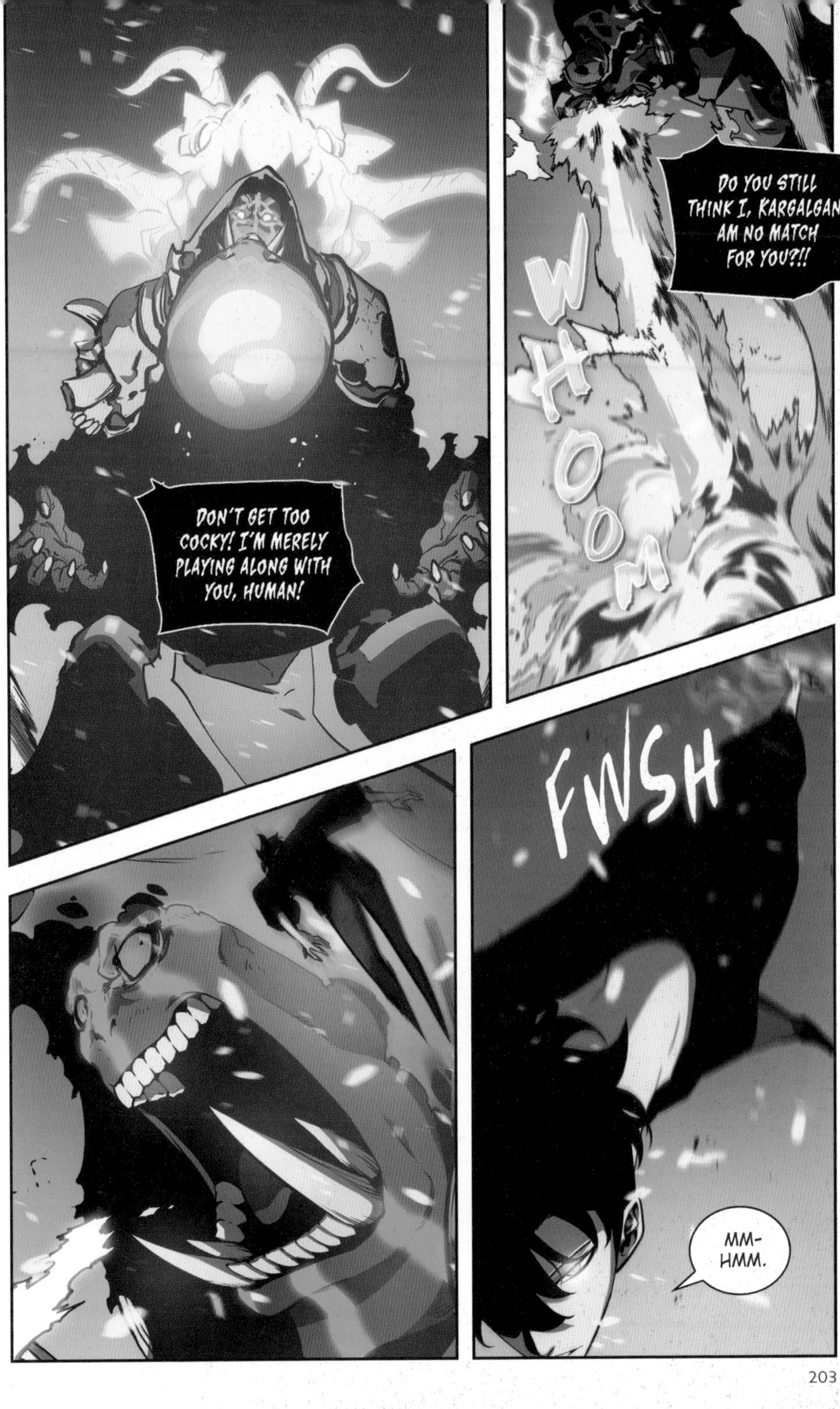
DON'T GET TOO COCKY! I'M MERELY PLAYING ALONG WITH YOU, HUMAN!
DO YOU STILL THINK I, KARGALGAN, AM NO MATCH FOR YOU?!!
WHOOOM
FWSH
MM-HMM.

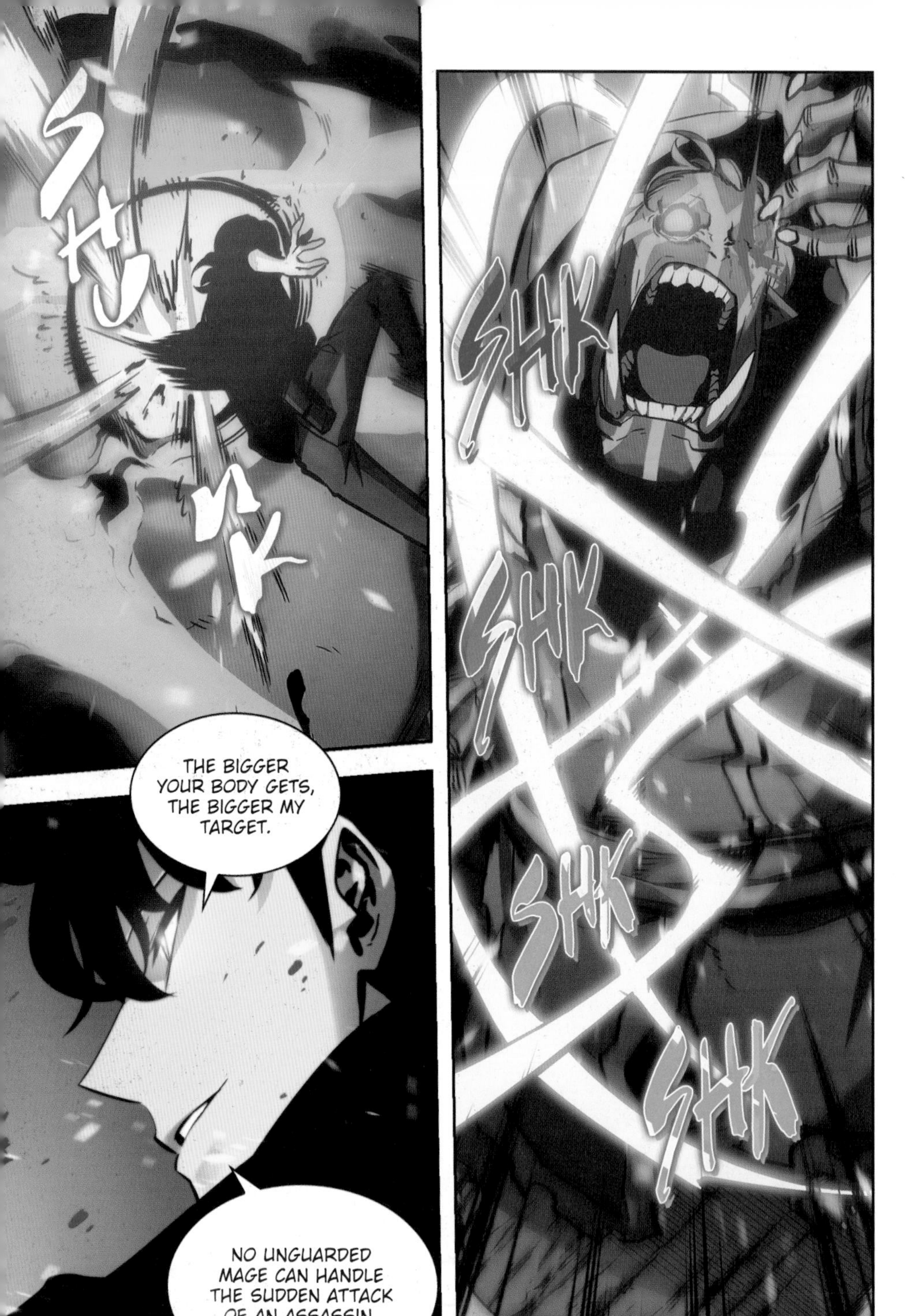
SHUNK
THE BIGGER YOUR BODY GETS, THE BIGGER MY TARGET.
NO UNGUARDED MAGE CAN HANDLE THE SUDDEN ATTACK OF AN ASSASSIN.
SHK
SHK
SHK
SHK

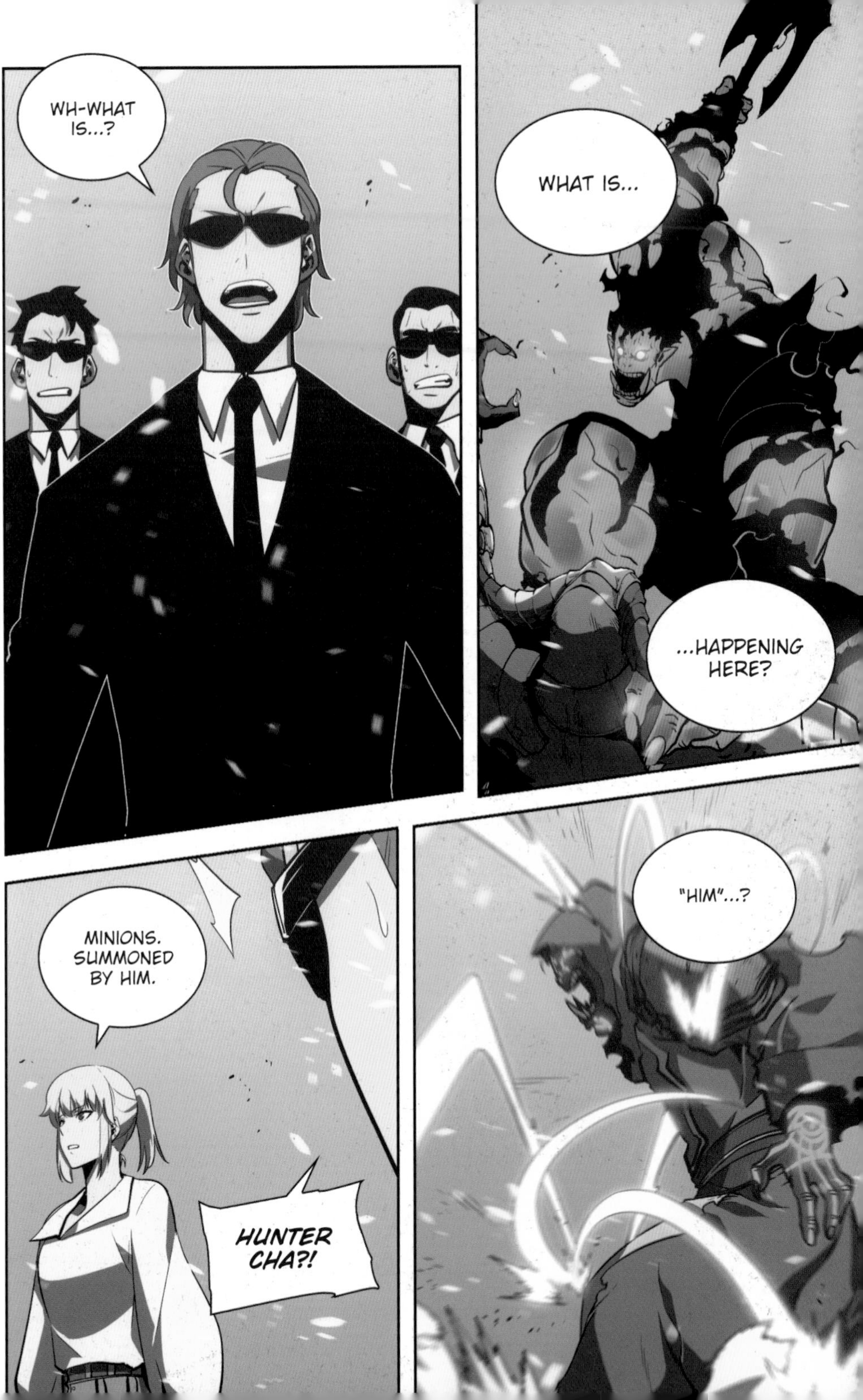
WH-WHAT IS...?
WHAT IS...
...HAPPENING HERE?
MINIONS. SUMMONED BY HIM.
HUNTER CHA?!
"HIM"...?

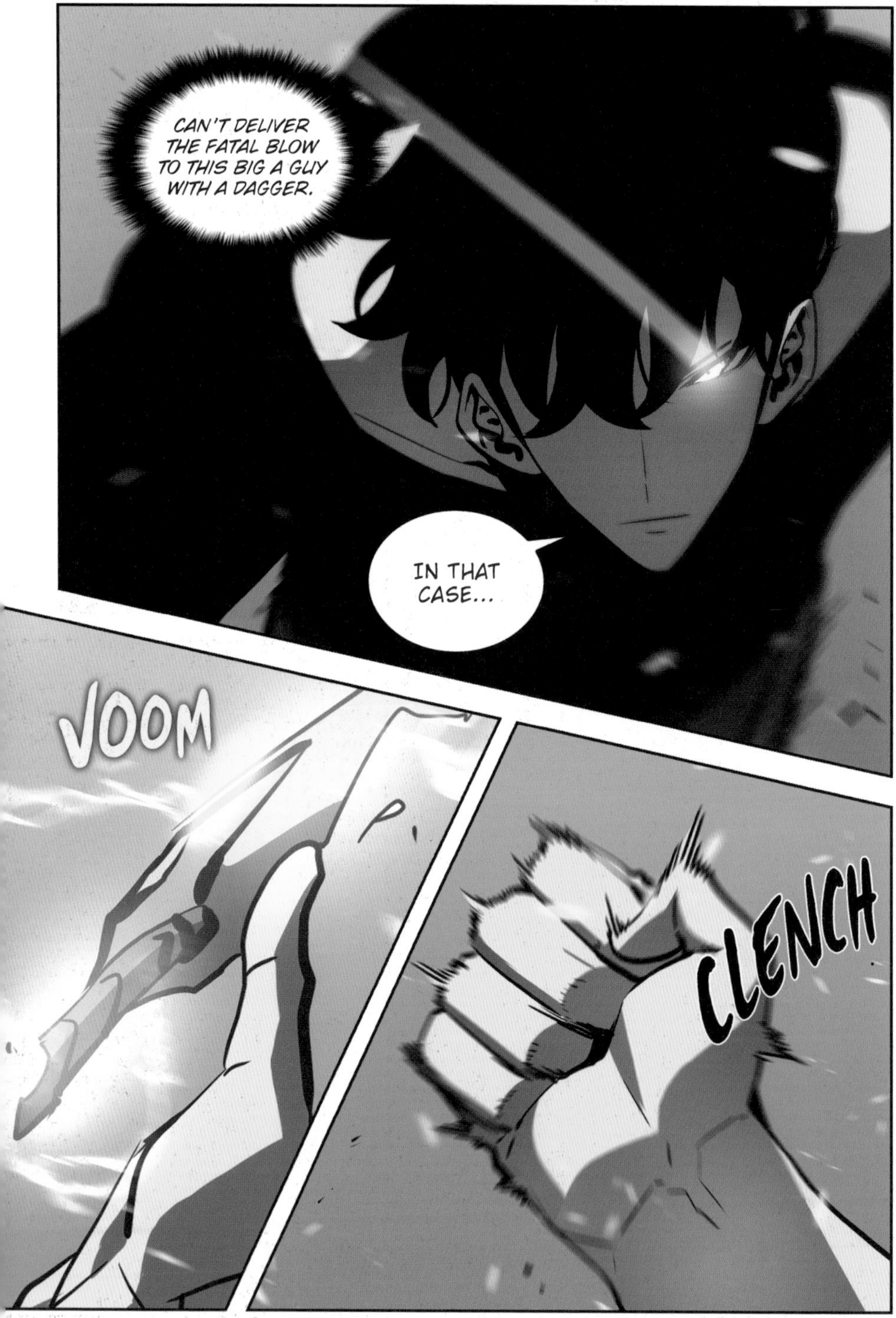
CAN'T DELIVER THE FATAL BLOW TO THIS BIG A GUY WITH A DAGGER.
IN THAT CASE...
VOOM
CLENCH

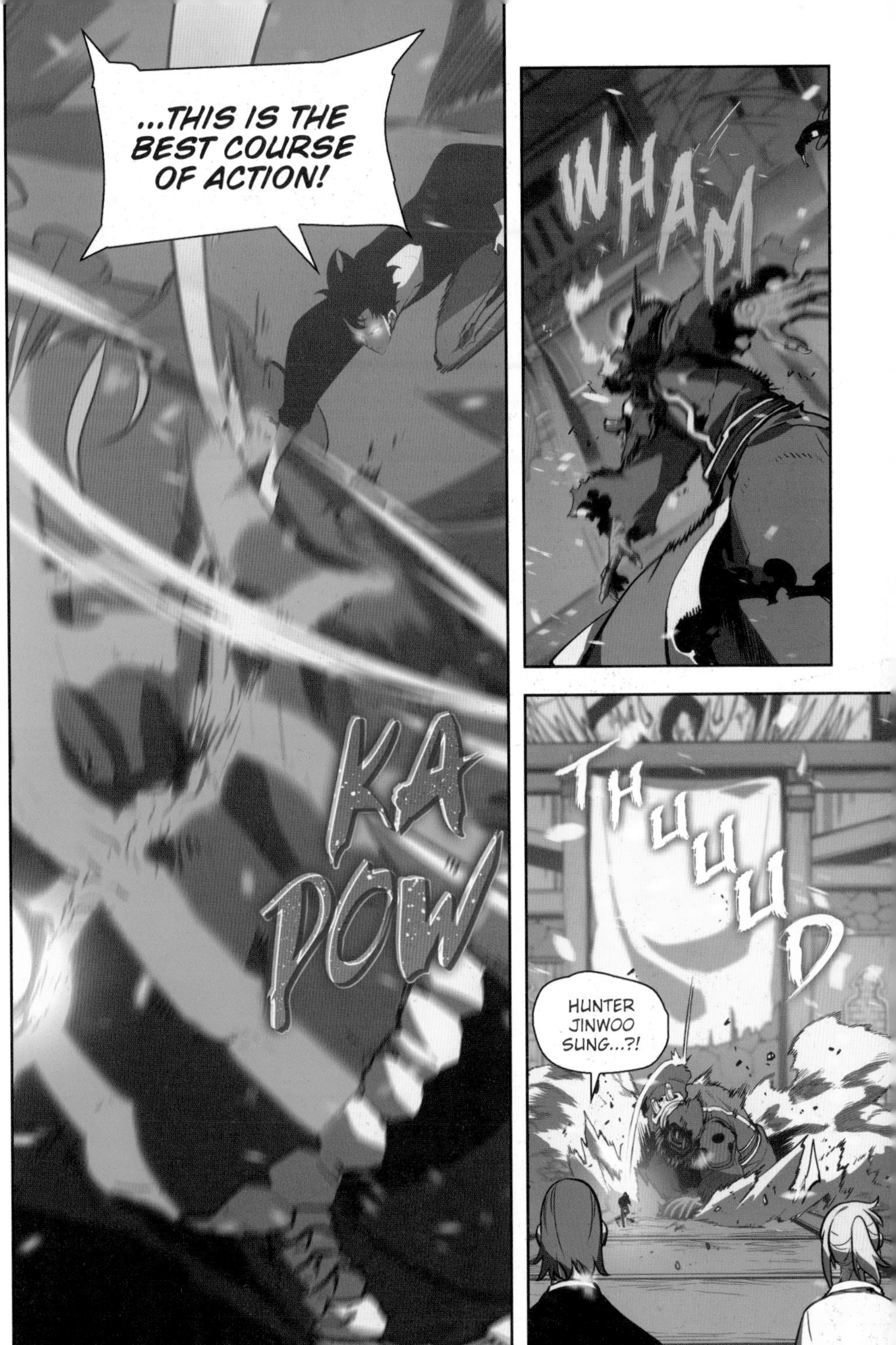
...THIS IS THE BEST COURSE OF ACTION!
KA POW
WHAM
THUUUUD
HUNTER JINWOO SUNG...?!

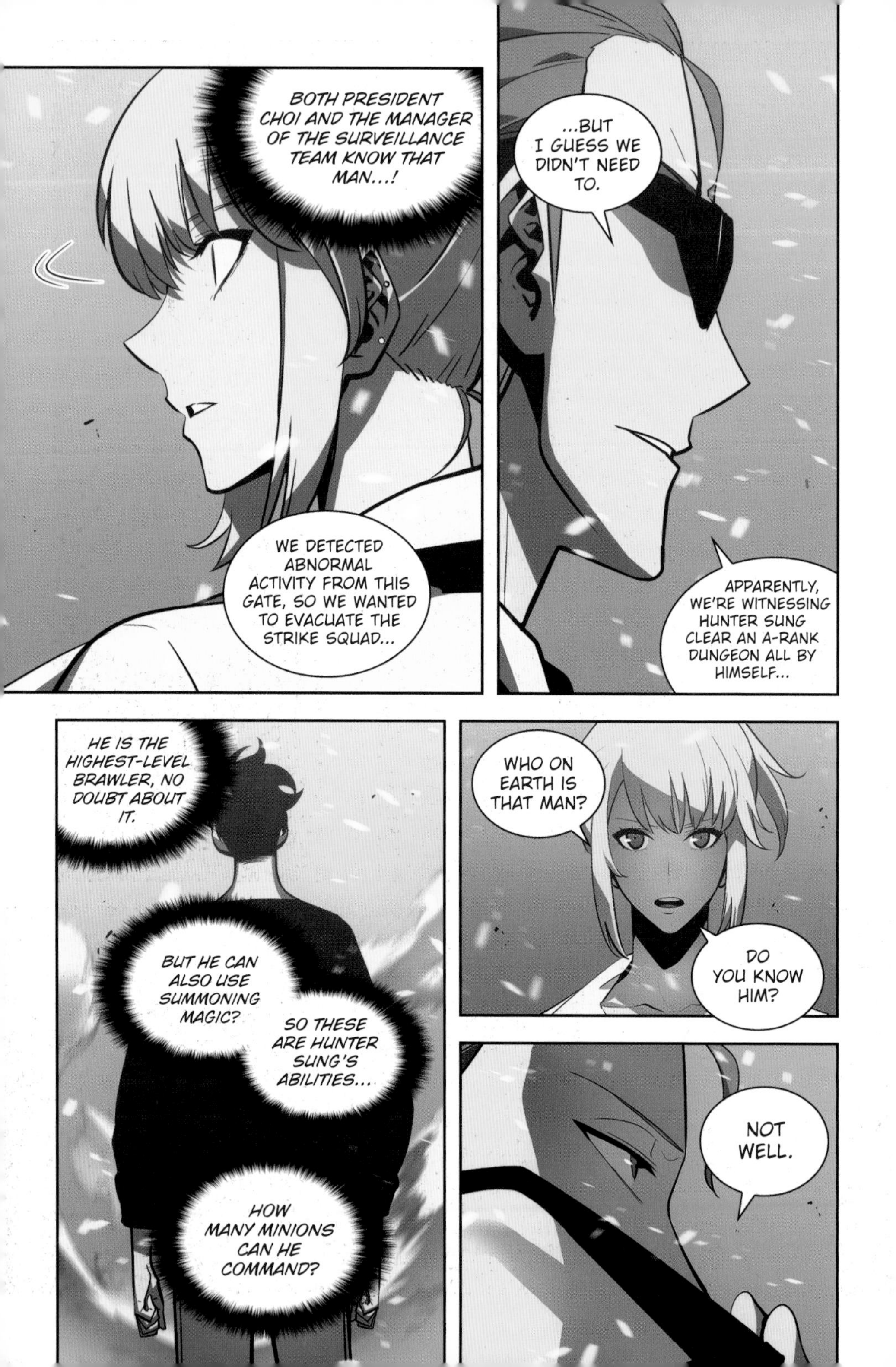
BOTH PRESIDENT CHOI AND THE MANAGER OF THE SURVEILLANCE TEAM KNOW THAT MAN...!
WE DETECTED ABNORMAL ACTIVITY FROM THIS GATE, SO WE WANTED TO EVACUATE THE STRIKE SQUAD...
...BUT I GUESS WE DIDN'T NEED TO.
APPARENTLY, WE'RE WITNESSING HUNTER SUNG CLEAR AN A-RANK DUNGEON ALL BY HIMSELF...
HE IS THE HIGHEST-LEVEL BRAWLER, NO DOUBT ABOUT IT.
BUT HE CAN ALSO USE SUMMONING MAGIC?
SO THESE ARE HUNTER SUNG'S ABILITIES...
HOW MANY MINIONS CAN HE COMMAND?
WHO ON EARTH IS THAT MAN?
DO YOU KNOW HIM?
NOT WELL.

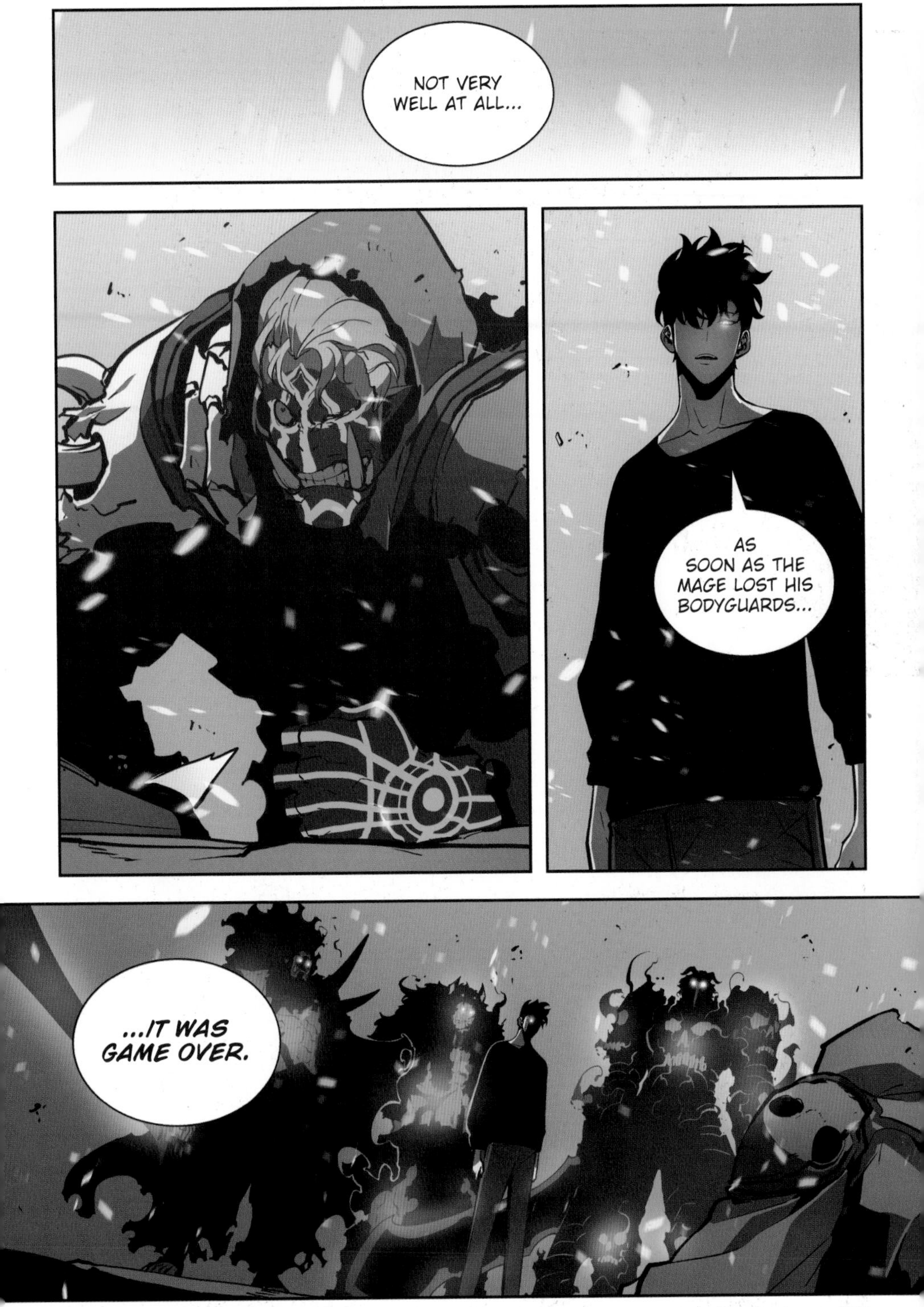
NOT VERY WELL AT ALL...
AS SOON AS THE MAGE LOST HIS BODYGUARDS...
...IT WAS GAME OVER.

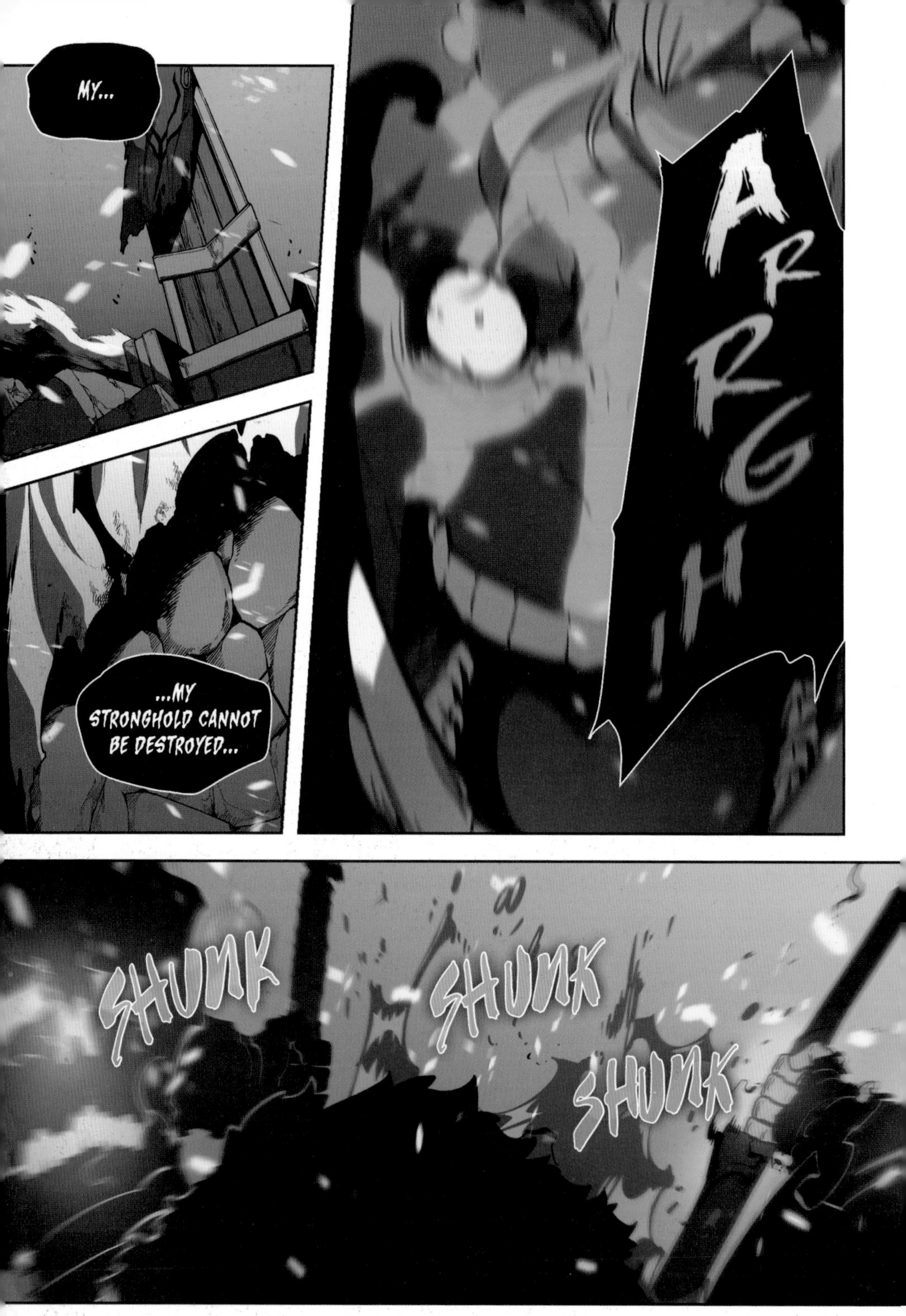
MY...
...MY STRONGHOLD CANNOT BE DESTROYED...
ARRGH!
SHUNK
SHUNK
SHUNK

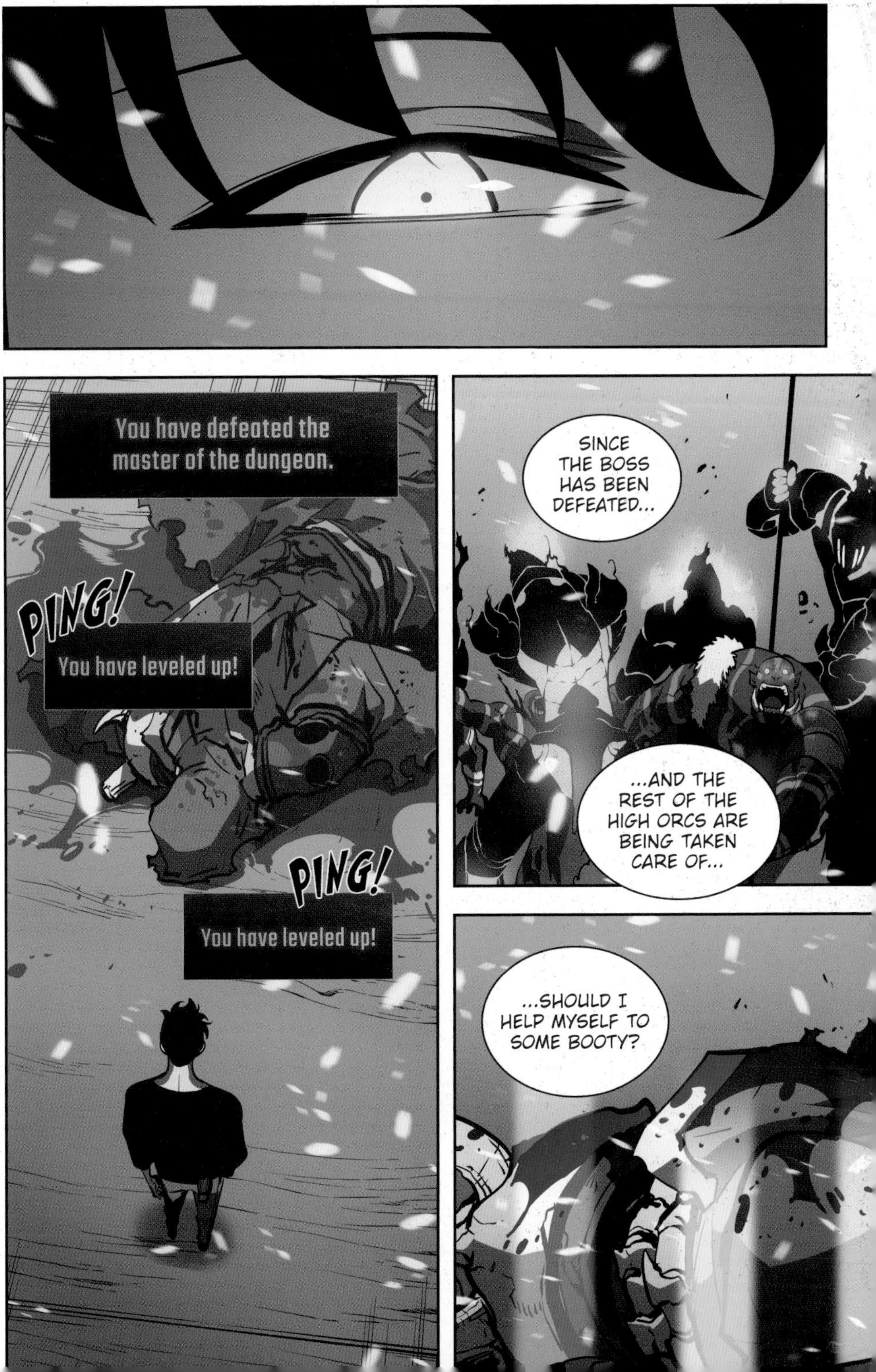
You have defeated the master of the dungeon.
PING!
You have leveled up!
PING!
You have leveled up!
SINCE THE BOSS HAS BEEN DEFEATED...
...AND THE REST OF THE HIGH ORCS ARE BEING TAKEN CARE OF...
...SHOULD I HELP MYSELF TO SOME BOOTY?

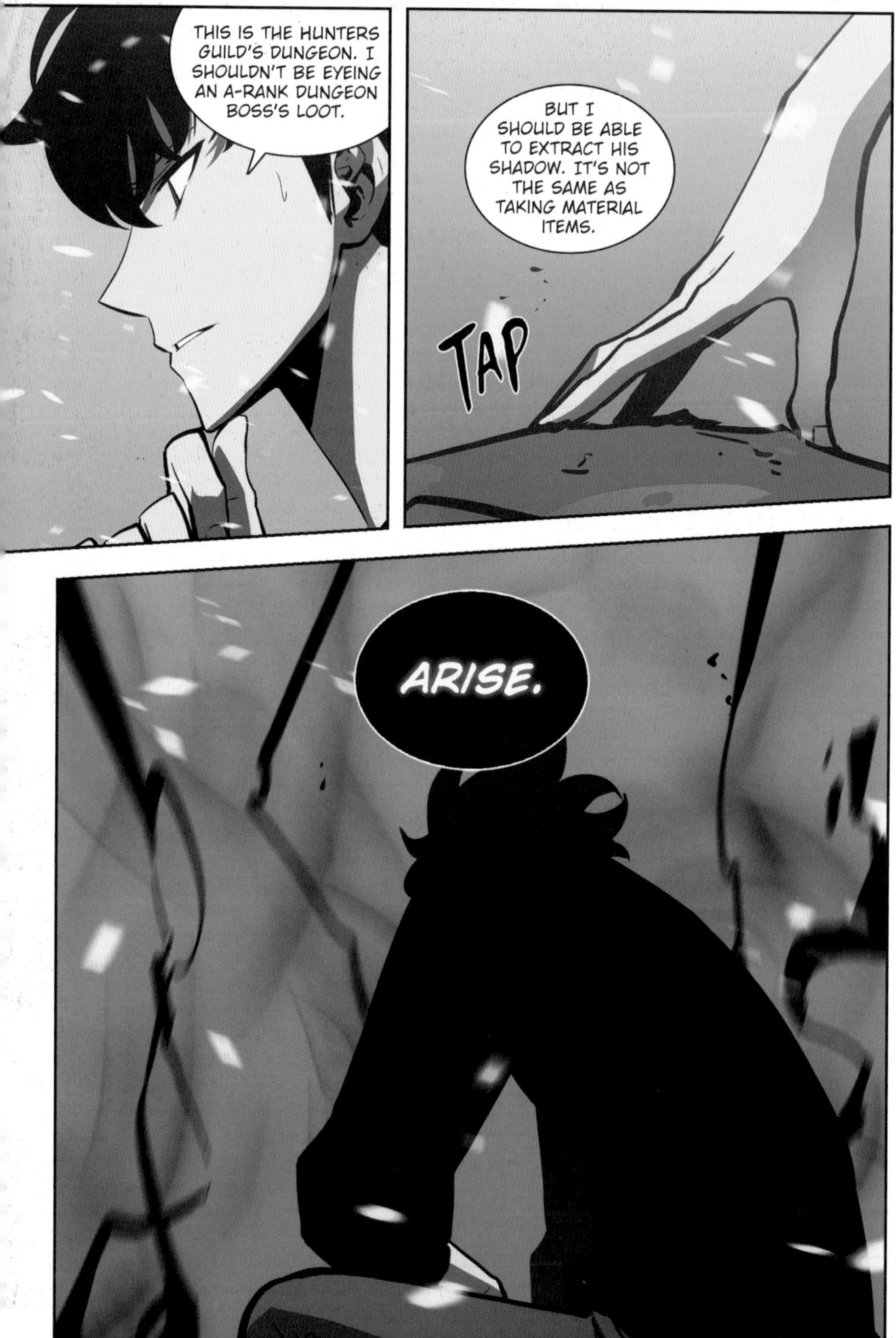
THIS IS THE HUNTERS GUILD'S DUNGEON. I SHOULDN'T BE EYEING AN A-RANK DUNGEON BOSS'S LOOT.
BUT I SHOULD BE ABLE TO EXTRACT HIS SHADOW. IT'S NOT THE SAME AS TAKING MATERIAL ITEMS.
TAP
ARISE.

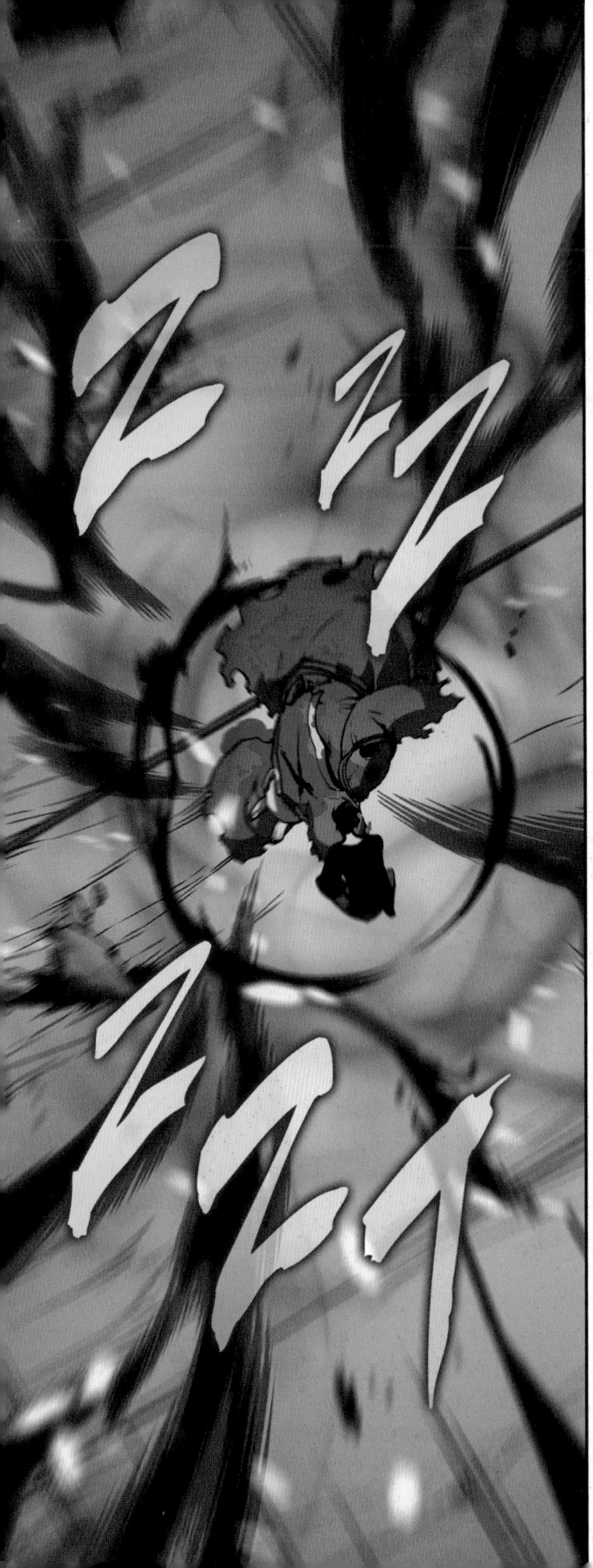

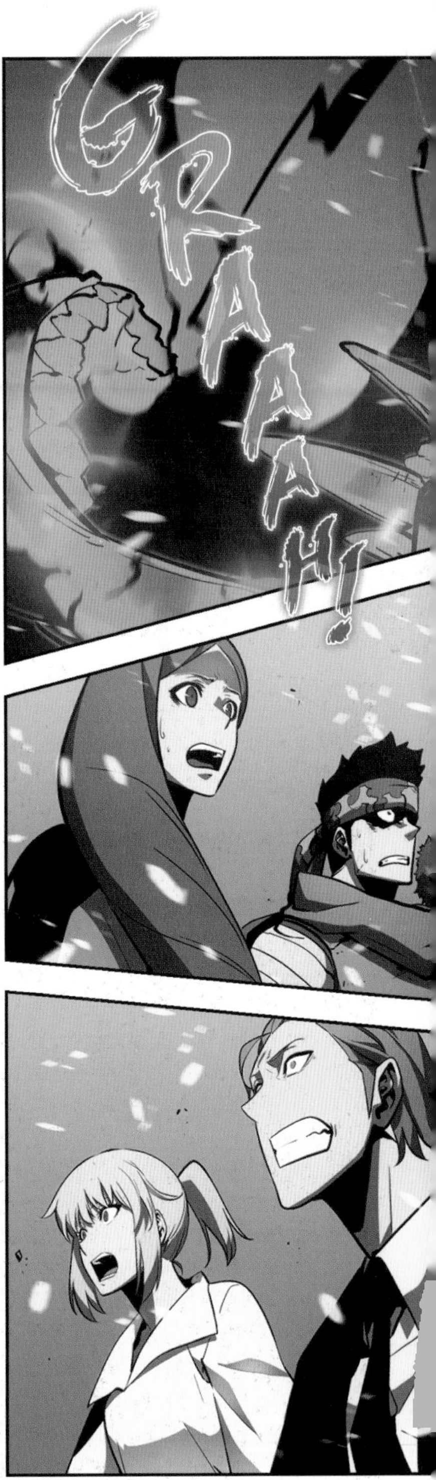
GRAAAAH!

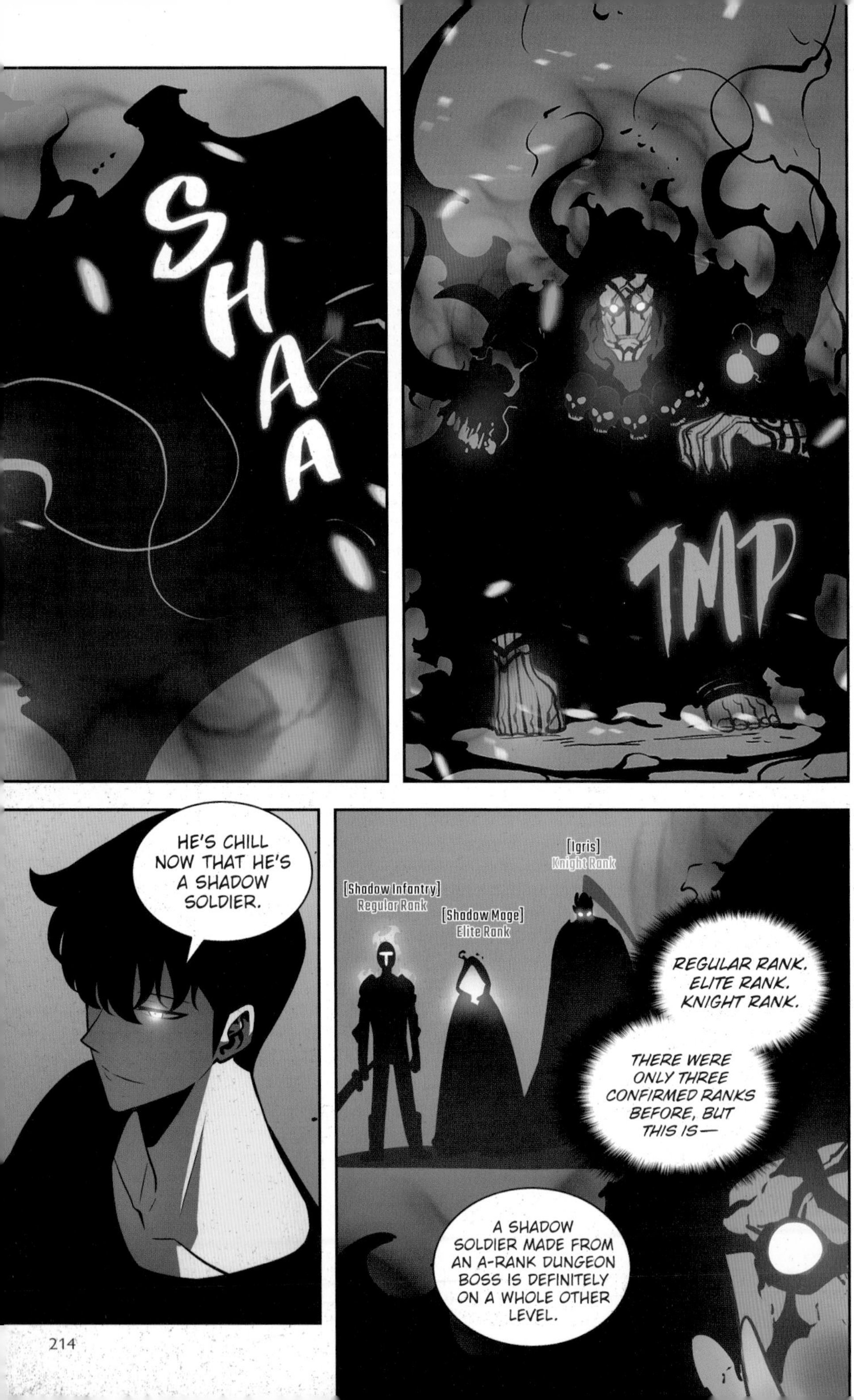
SHAAA
TMP
HE'S CHILL NOW THAT HE'S A SHADOW SOLDIER.
[Shadow Infantry] Regular Rank
[Shadow Mage] Elite Rank
[Igris] Knight Rank
REGULAR RANK. ELITE RANK. KNIGHT RANK.
THERE WERE ONLY THREE CONFIRMED RANKS BEFORE, BUT THIS IS—
A SHADOW SOLDIER MADE FROM AN A-RANK DUNGEON BOSS IS DEFINITELY ON A WHOLE OTHER LEVEL.

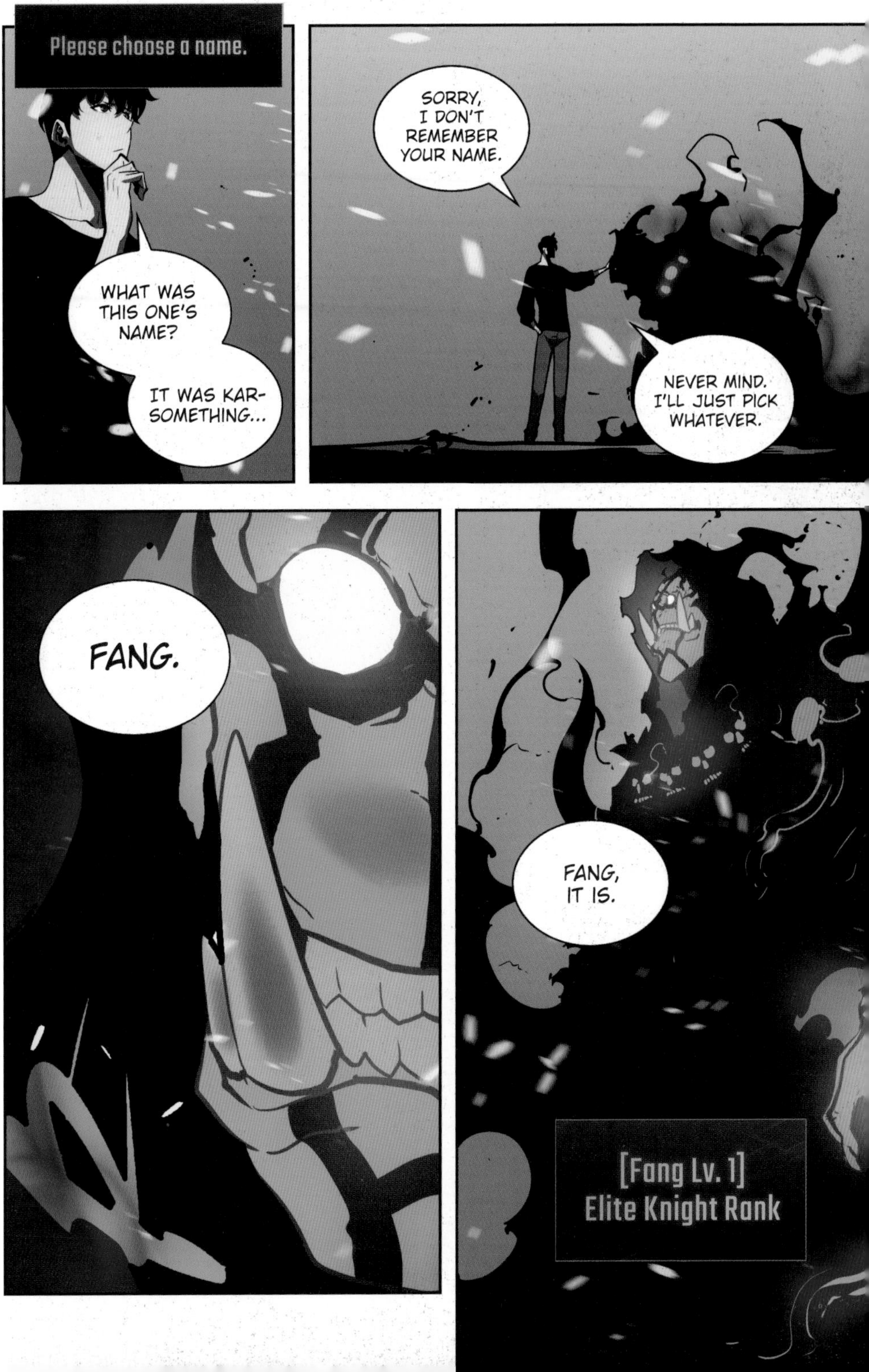
Please choose a name.
WHAT WAS THIS ONE'S NAME?
IT WAS KAR-SOMETHING...
SORRY, I DON'T REMEMBER YOUR NAME.
NEVER MIND. I'LL JUST PICK WHATEVER.
FANG.
FANG, IT IS.
[Fang Lv. 1]
Elite Knight Rank

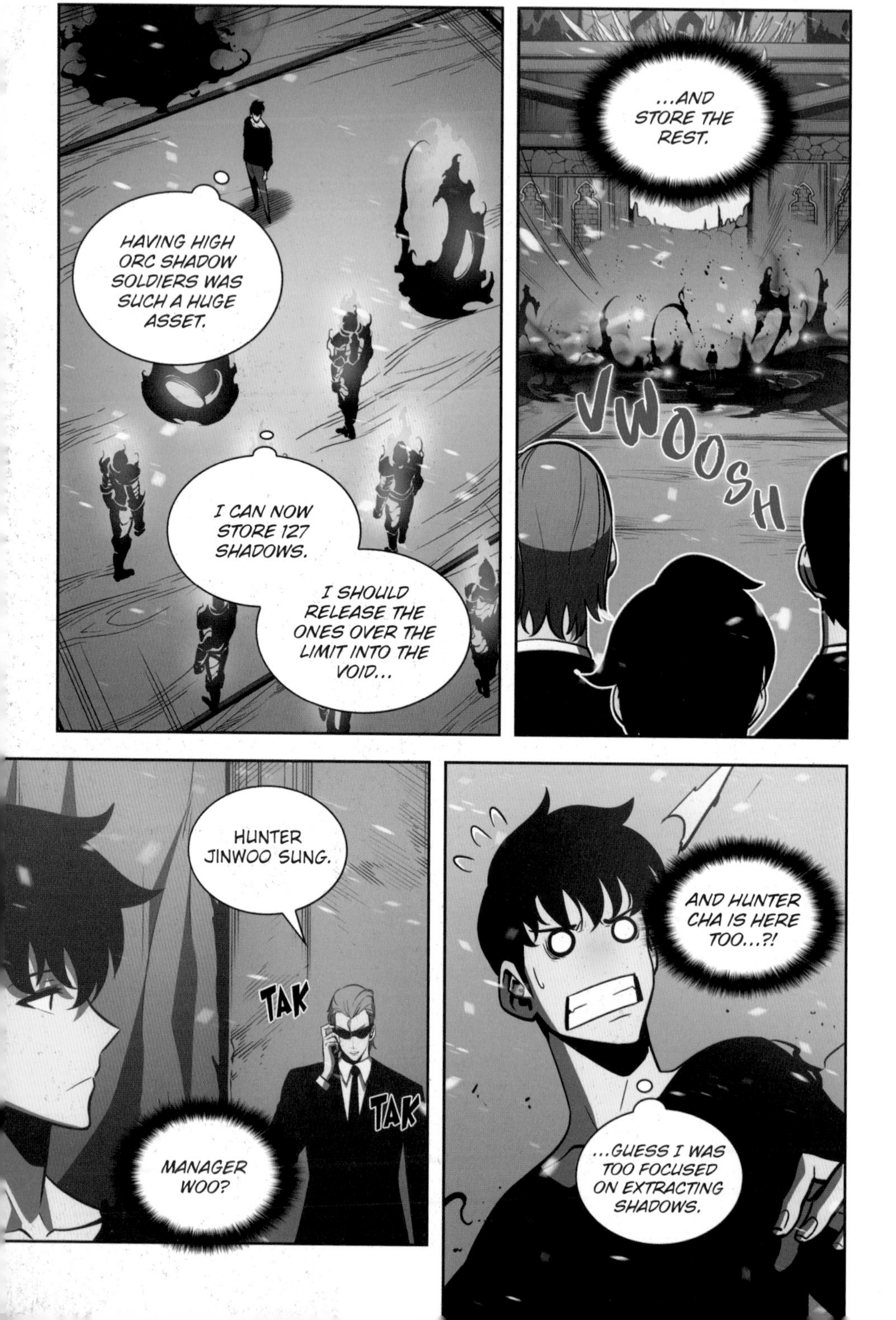
HAVING HIGH ORC SHADOW SOLDIERS WAS SUCH A HUGE ASSET.
I CAN NOW STORE 127 SHADOWS.
I SHOULD RELEASE THE ONES OVER THE LIMIT INTO THE VOID...
...AND STORE THE REST.
VWOOSH
HUNTER JINWOO SUNG.
TAK
TAK
MANAGER WOO?
AND HUNTER CHA IS HERE TOO...?!
...GUESS I WAS TOO FOCUSED ON EXTRACTING SHADOWS.

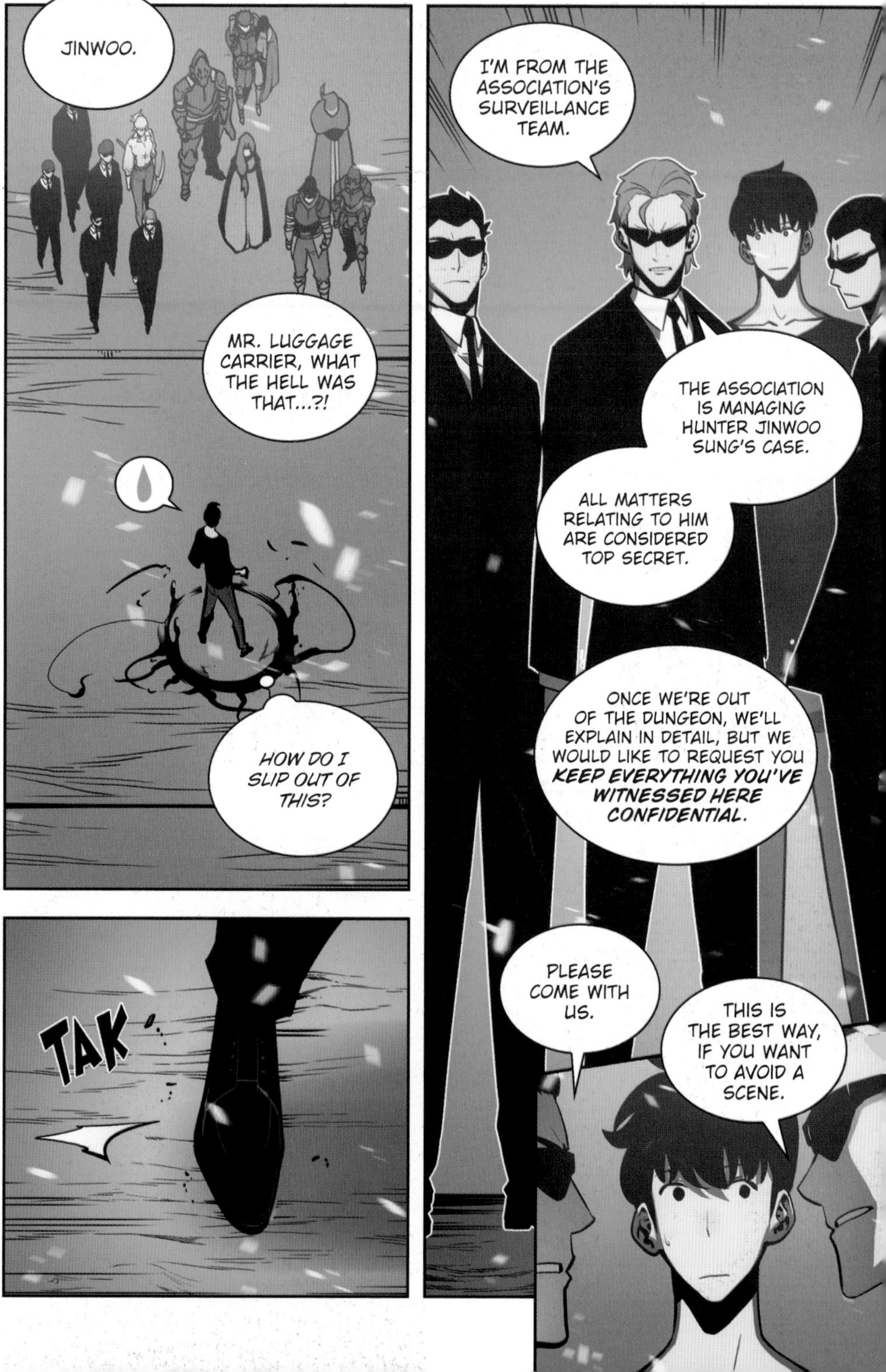
JINWOO.
MR. LUGGAGE CARRIER, WHAT THE HELL WAS THAT...?!
HOW DO I SLIP OUT OF THIS?
TAK
I'M FROM THE ASSOCIATION'S SURVEILLANCE TEAM.
THE ASSOCIATION IS MANAGING HUNTER JINWOO SUNG'S CASE.
ALL MATTERS RELATING TO HIM ARE CONSIDERED TOP SECRET.
ONCE WE'RE OUT OF THE DUNGEON, WE'LL EXPLAIN IN DETAIL, BUT WE WOULD LIKE TO REQUEST YOU KEEP EVERYTHING YOU'VE WITNESSED HERE CONFIDENTIAL.
PLEASE COME WITH US.
THIS IS THE BEST WAY, IF YOU WANT TO AVOID A SCENE.

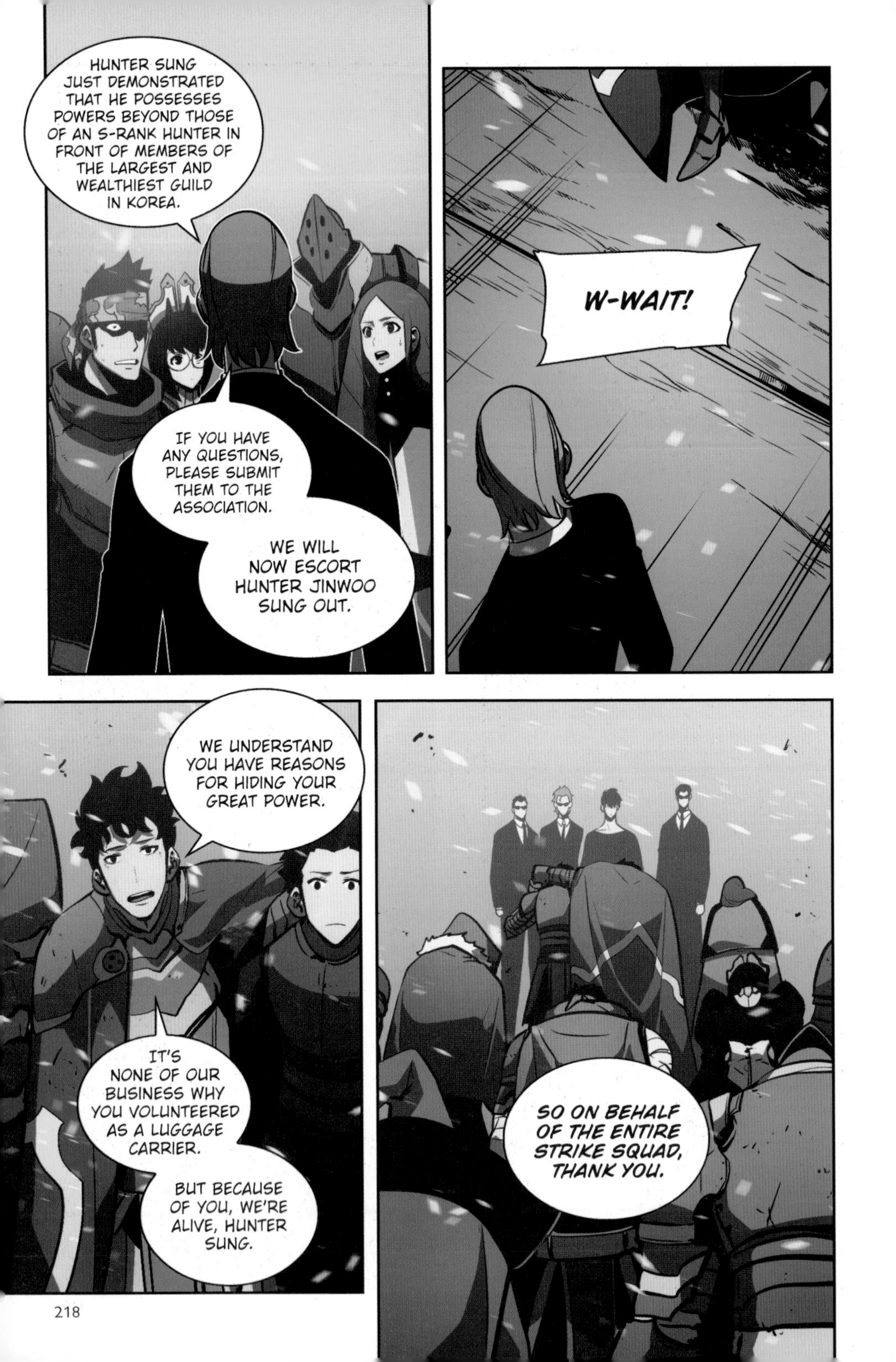
HUNTER SUNG JUST DEMONSTRATED THAT HE POSSESSES POWERS BEYOND THOSE OF AN S-RANK HUNTER IN FRONT OF MEMBERS OF THE LARGEST AND WEALTHIEST GUILD IN KOREA.
IF YOU HAVE ANY QUESTIONS, PLEASE SUBMIT THEM TO THE ASSOCIATION.
WE WILL NOW ESCORT HUNTER JINWOO SUNG OUT.
W-WAIT!
WE UNDERSTAND YOU HAVE REASONS FOR HIDING YOUR GREAT POWER.
IT'S NONE OF OUR BUSINESS WHY YOU VOLUNTEERED AS A LUGGAGE CARRIER.
BUT BECAUSE OF YOU, WE'RE ALIVE, HUNTER SUNG.
SO ON BEHALF OF THE ENTIRE STRIKE SQUAD, THANK YOU.

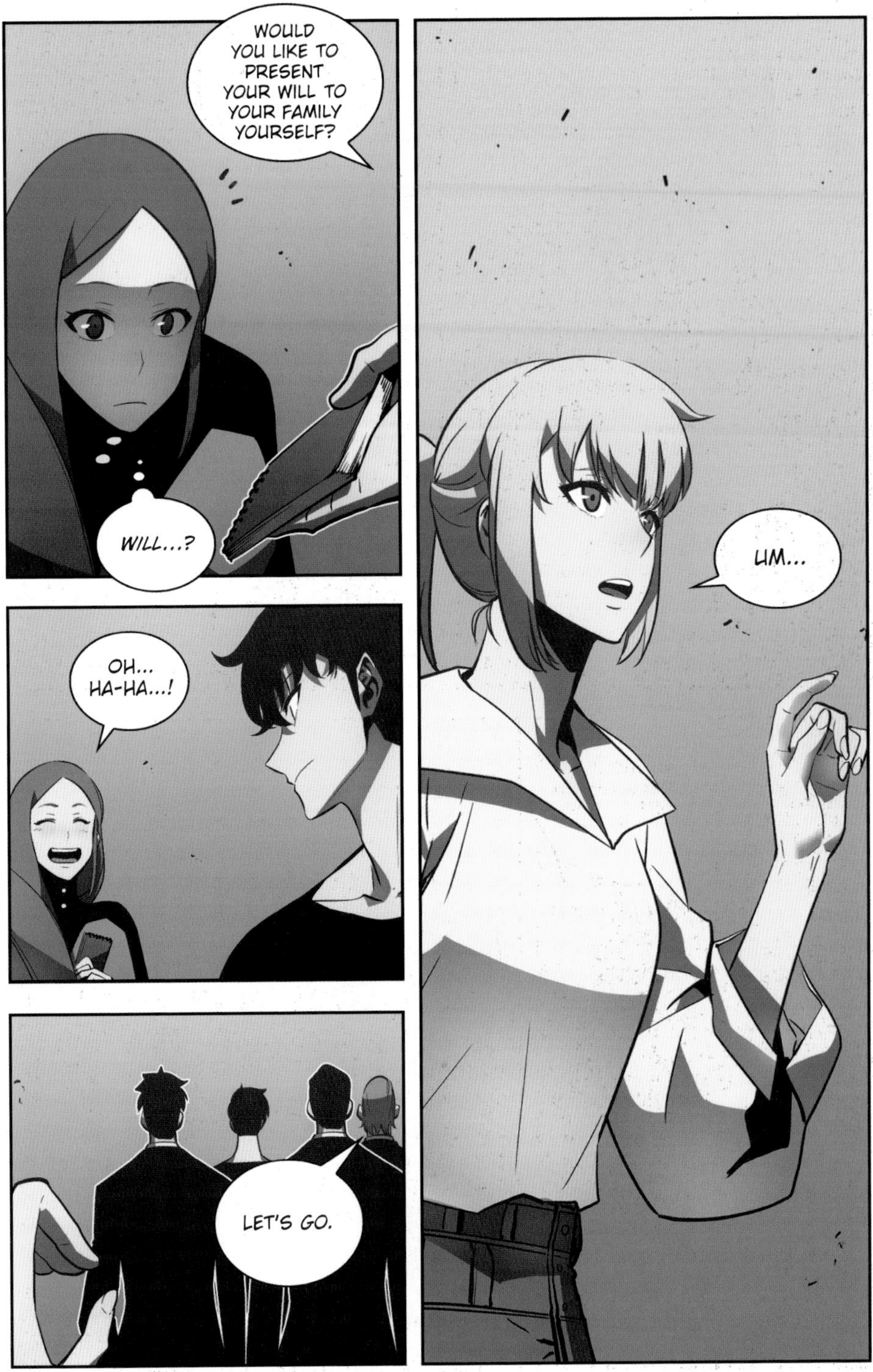
WOULD YOU LIKE TO PRESENT YOUR WILL TO YOUR FAMILY YOURSELF?
WILL...?
OH... HA-HA...!
LET'S GO.
UM...

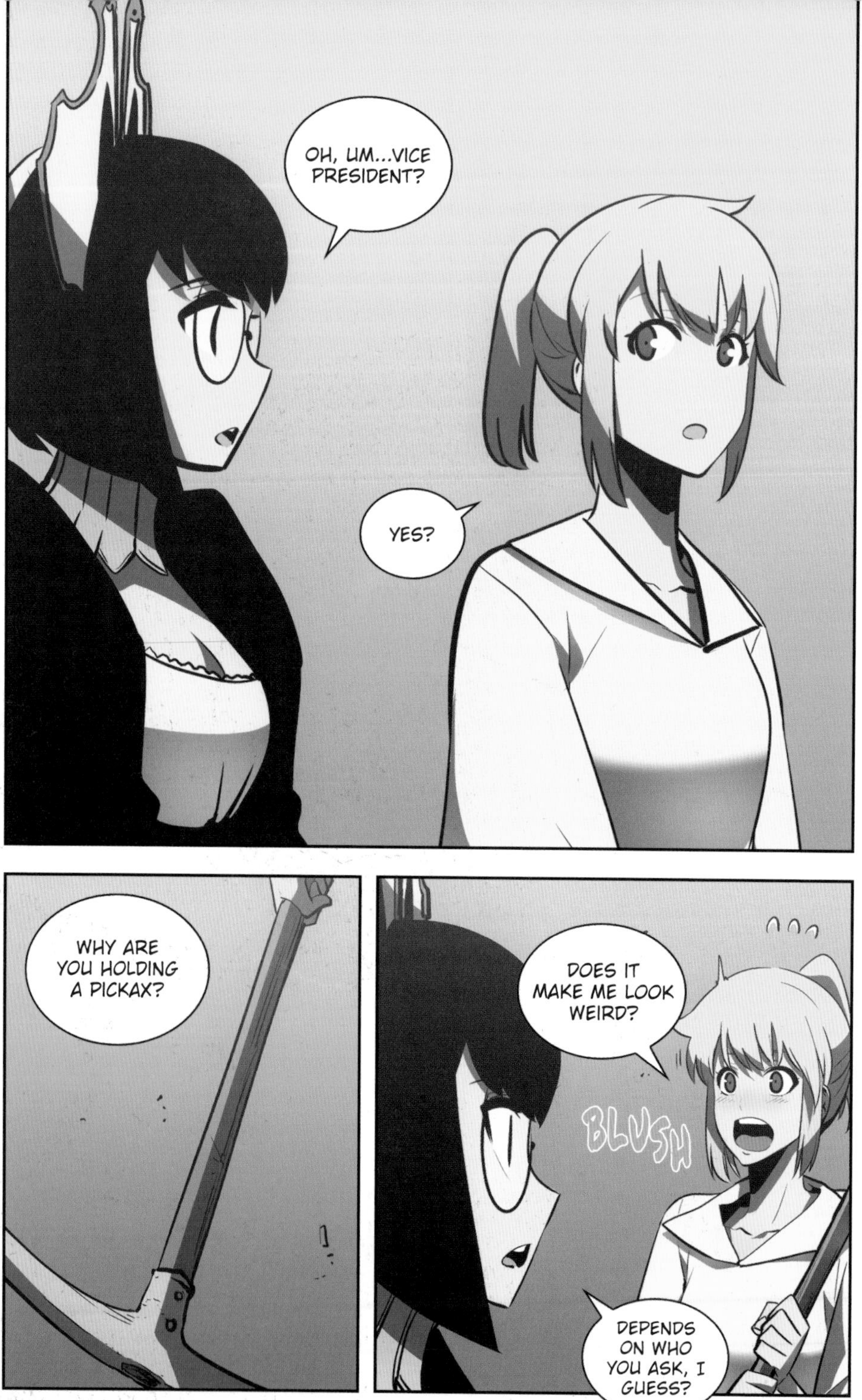
OH, UM...VICE PRESIDENT?
YES?
WHY ARE YOU HOLDING A PICKAX?
DOES IT MAKE ME LOOK WEIRD?
BLUSH
DEPENDS ON WHO YOU ASK, I GUESS?

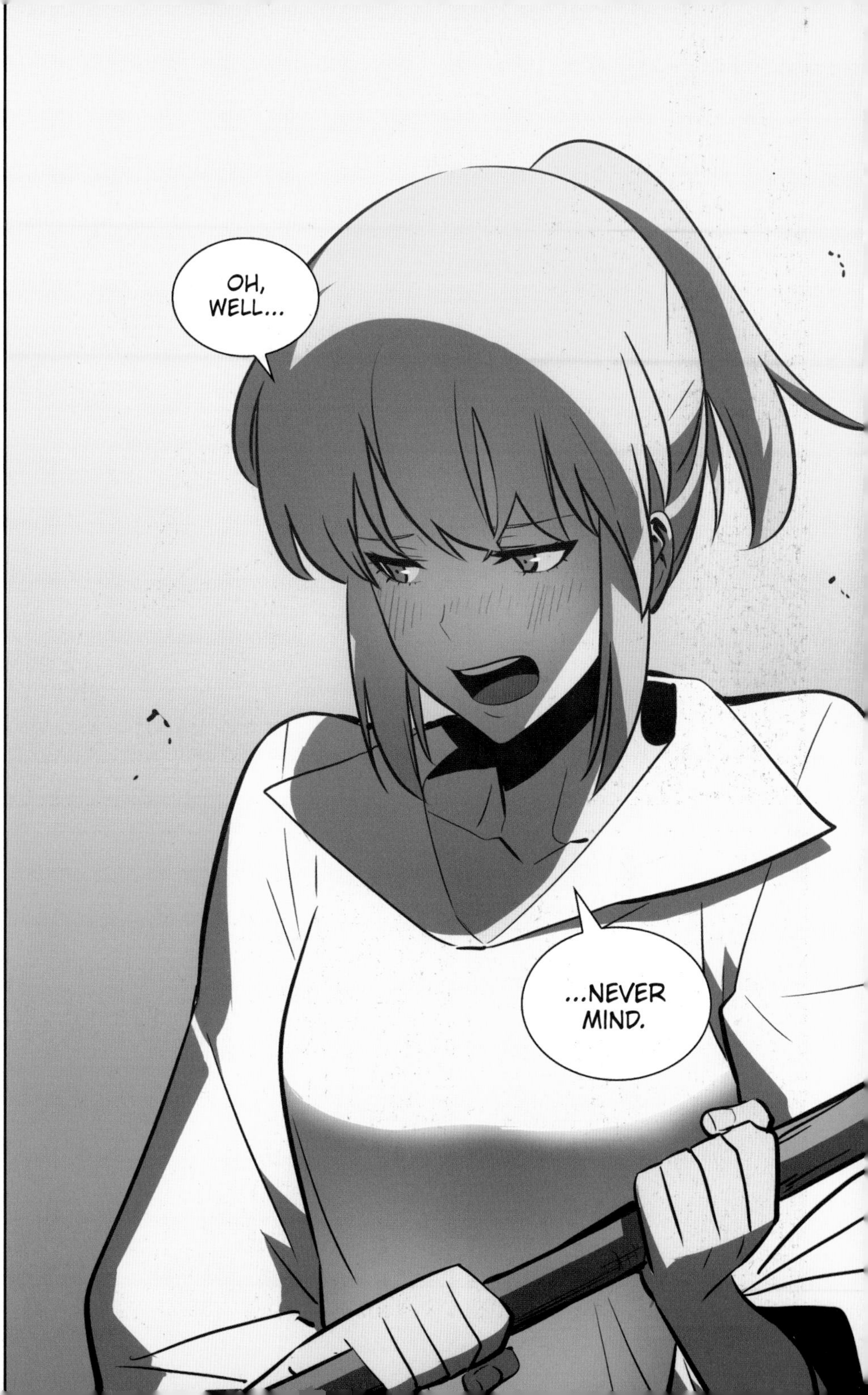
OH, WELL...
...NEVER MIND.

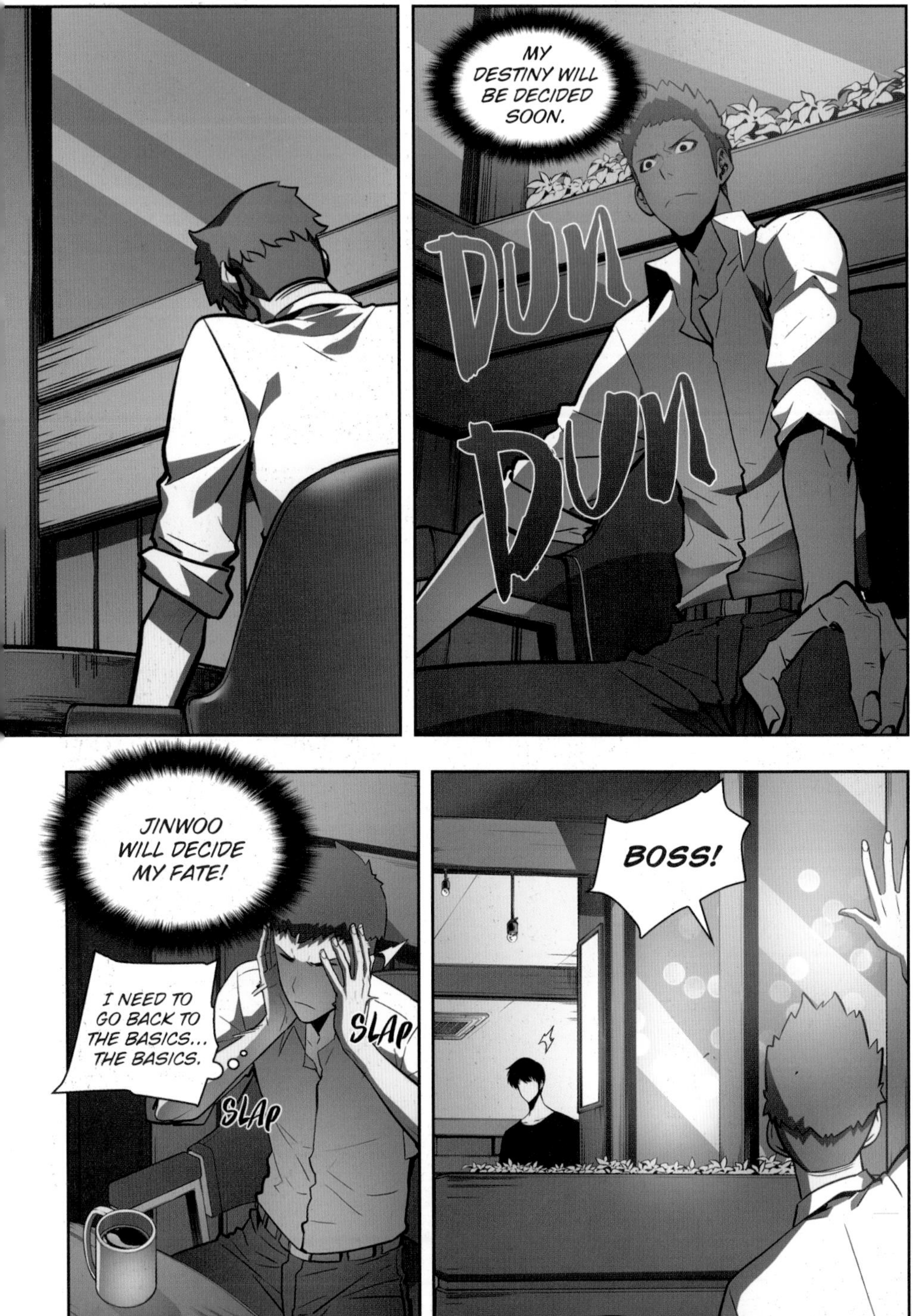
MY DESTINY WILL BE DECIDED SOON.
DUN
DUN
JINWOO WILL DECIDE MY FATE!
I NEED TO GO BACK TO THE BASICS... THE BASICS.
SLAP
SLAP
BOSS!

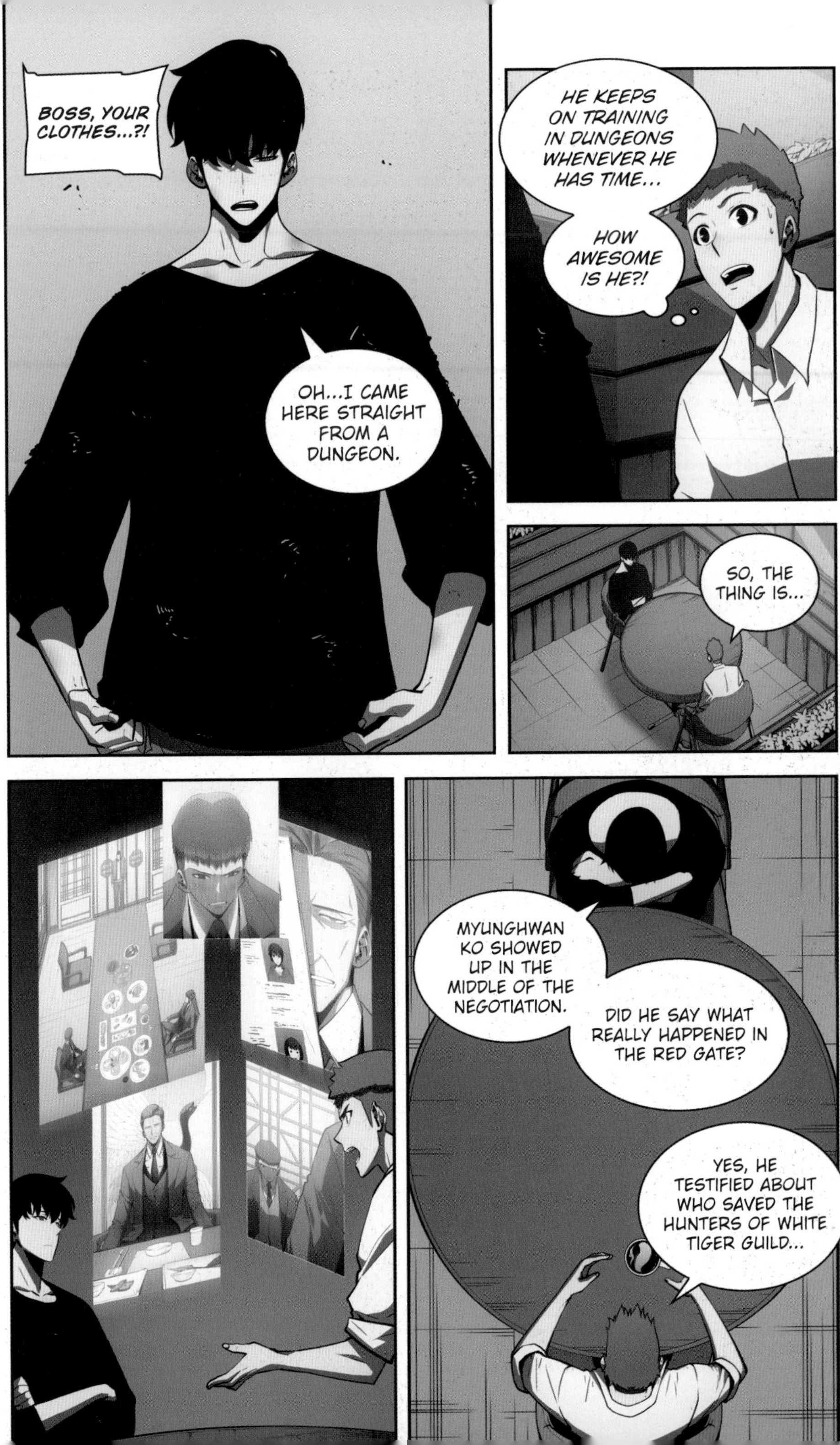
BOSS, YOUR CLOTHES...?!
OH...I CAME HERE STRAIGHT FROM A DUNGEON.
HE KEEPS ON TRAINING IN DUNGEONS WHENEVER HE HAS TIME...
HOW AWESOME IS HE?!
SO, THE THING IS...
MYUNGHWAN KO SHOWED UP IN THE MIDDLE OF THE NEGOTIATION.
DID HE SAY WHAT REALLY HAPPENED IN THE RED GATE?
YES, HE TESTIFIED ABOUT WHO SAVED THE HUNTERS OF WHITE TIGER GUILD...

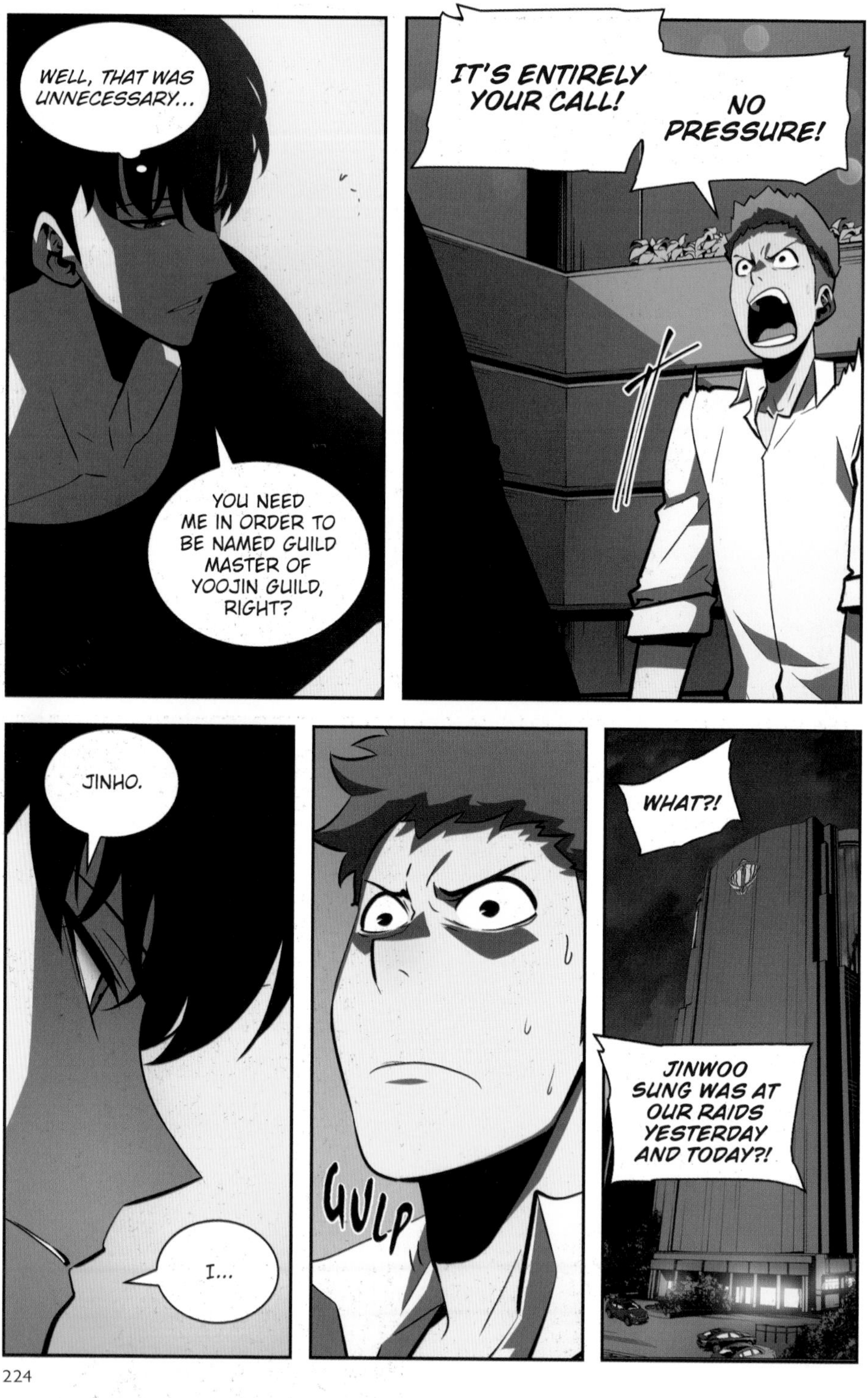
WELL, THAT WAS UNNECESSARY...
YOU NEED ME IN ORDER TO BE NAMED GUILD MASTER OF YOOJIN GUILD, RIGHT?
IT'S ENTIRELY YOUR CALL!
NO PRESSURE!
JINHO.
I...
GULP
WHAT?!
JINWOO SUNG WAS AT OUR RAIDS YESTERDAY AND TODAY?!

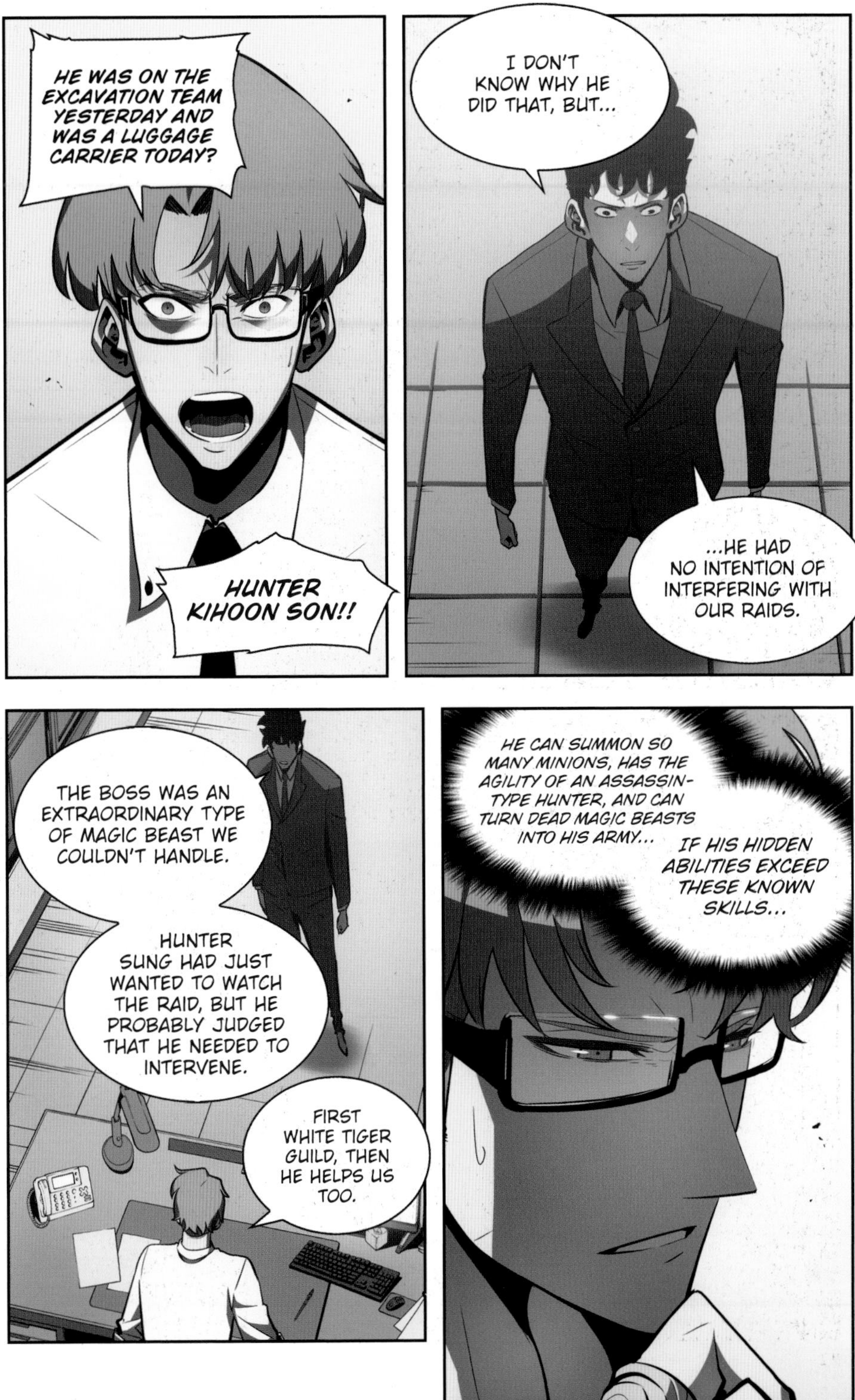
HE WAS ON THE EXCAVATION TEAM YESTERDAY AND WAS A LUGGAGE CARRIER TODAY?
HUNTER KIHOON SON!!
I DON'T KNOW WHY HE DID THAT, BUT...
...HE HAD NO INTENTION OF INTERFERING WITH OUR RAIDS.
THE BOSS WAS AN EXTRAORDINARY TYPE OF MAGIC BEAST WE COULDN'T HANDLE.
HUNTER SUNG HAD JUST WANTED TO WATCH THE RAID, BUT HE PROBABLY JUDGED THAT HE NEEDED TO INTERVENE.
FIRST WHITE TIGER GUILD, THEN HE HELPS US TOO.
HE CAN SUMMON SO MANY MINIONS, HAS THE AGILITY OF AN ASSASSIN-TYPE HUNTER, AND CAN TURN DEAD MAGIC BEASTS INTO HIS ARMY...
IF HIS HIDDEN ABILITIES EXCEED THESE KNOWN SKILLS...

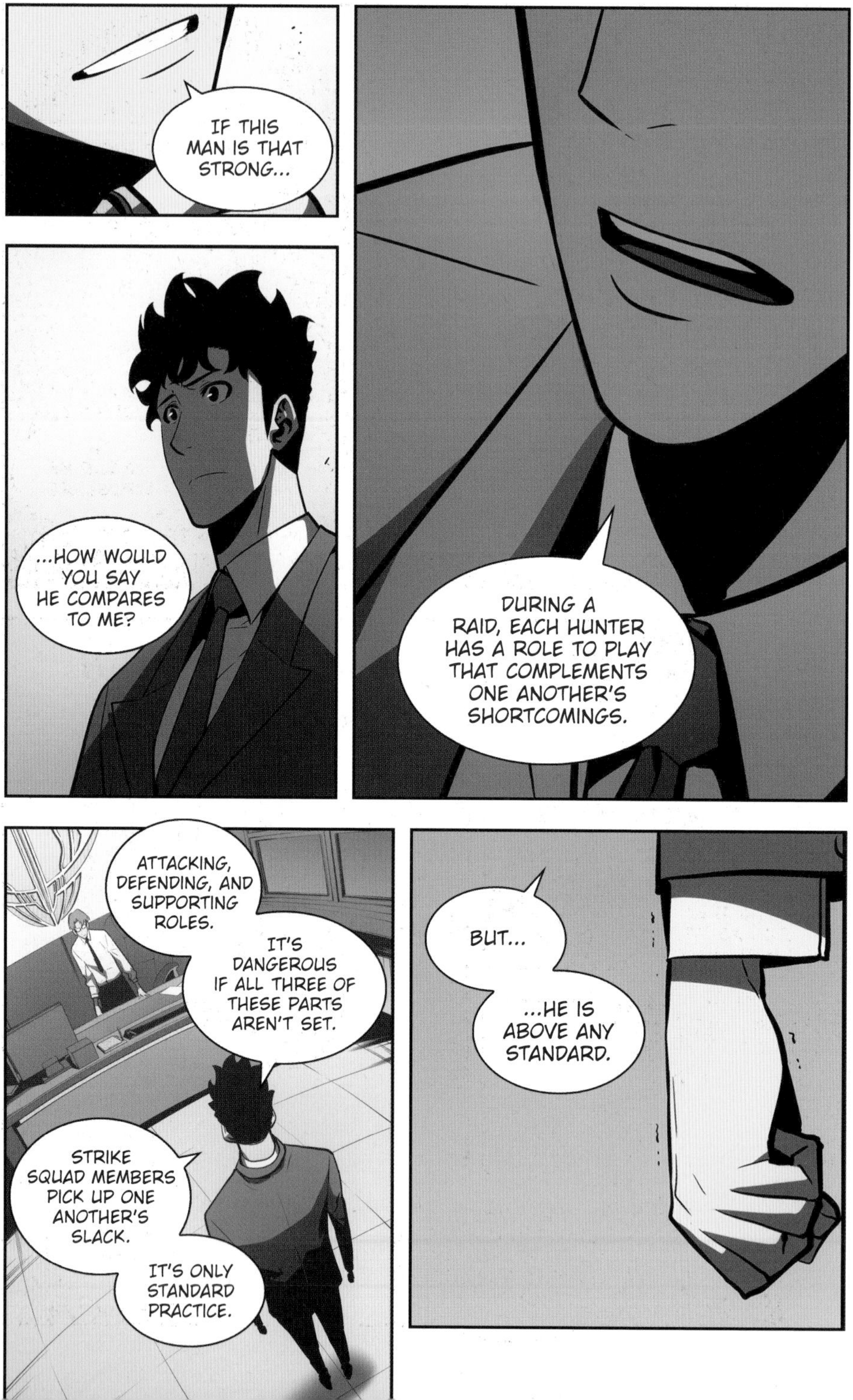
IF THIS MAN IS THAT STRONG...
...HOW WOULD YOU SAY HE COMPARES TO ME?
DURING A RAID, EACH HUNTER HAS A ROLE TO PLAY THAT COMPLEMENTS ONE ANOTHER'S SHORTCOMINGS.
ATTACKING, DEFENDING, AND SUPPORTING ROLES.
IT'S DANGEROUS IF ALL THREE OF THESE PARTS AREN'T SET.
STRIKE SQUAD MEMBERS PICK UP ONE ANOTHER'S SLACK.
IT'S ONLY STANDARD PRACTICE.
BUT...
...HE IS ABOVE ANY STANDARD.

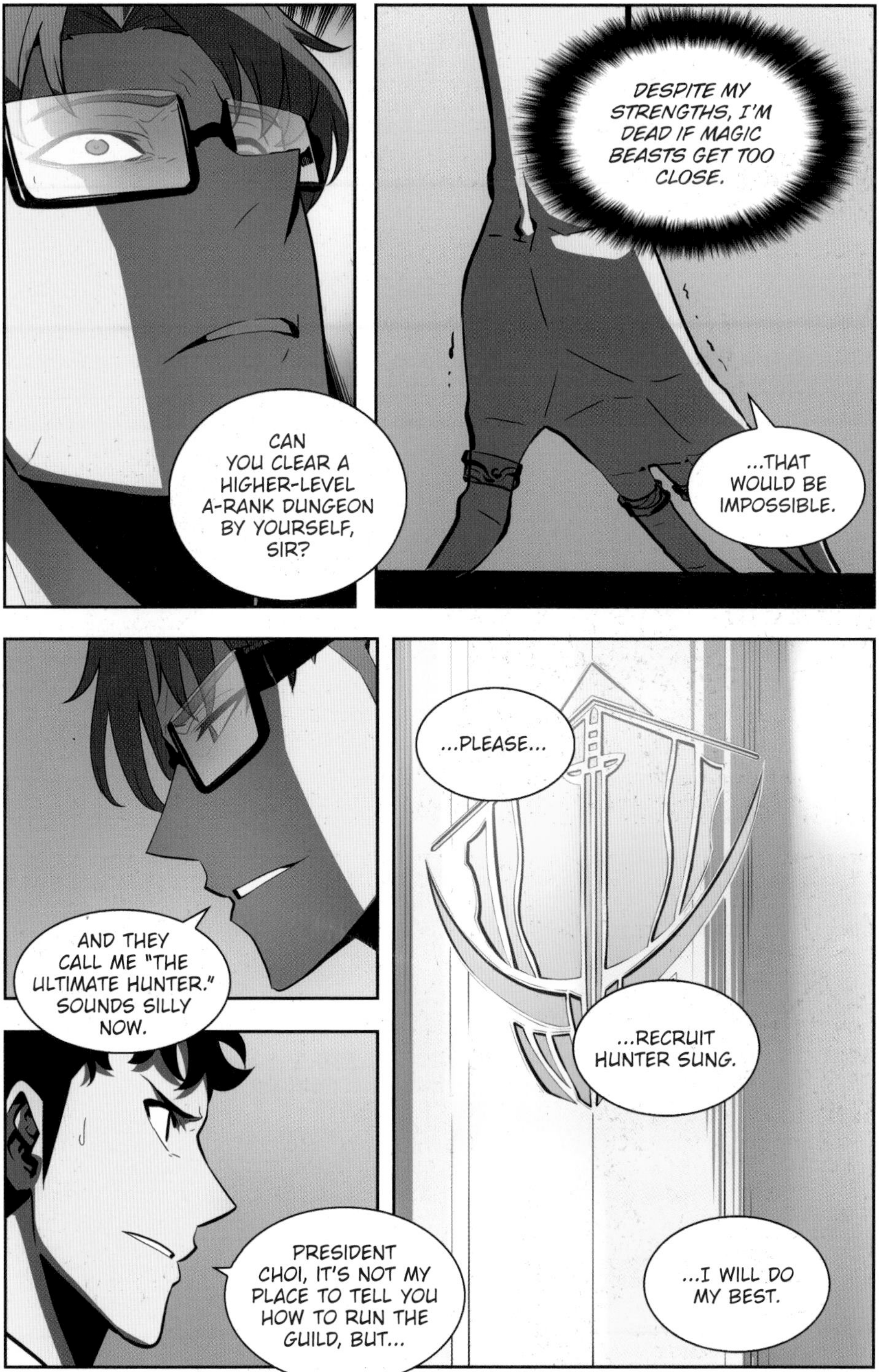
CAN YOU CLEAR A HIGHER-LEVEL A-RANK DUNGEON BY YOURSELF, SIR?
DESPITE MY STRENGTHS, I'M DEAD IF MAGIC BEASTS GET TOO CLOSE.
...THAT WOULD BE IMPOSSIBLE.
AND THEY CALL ME "THE ULTIMATE HUNTER." SOUNDS SILLY NOW.
PRESIDENT CHOI, IT'S NOT MY PLACE TO TELL YOU HOW TO RUN THE GUILD, BUT...
...PLEASE...
...RECRUIT HUNTER SUNG.
...I WILL DO MY BEST.

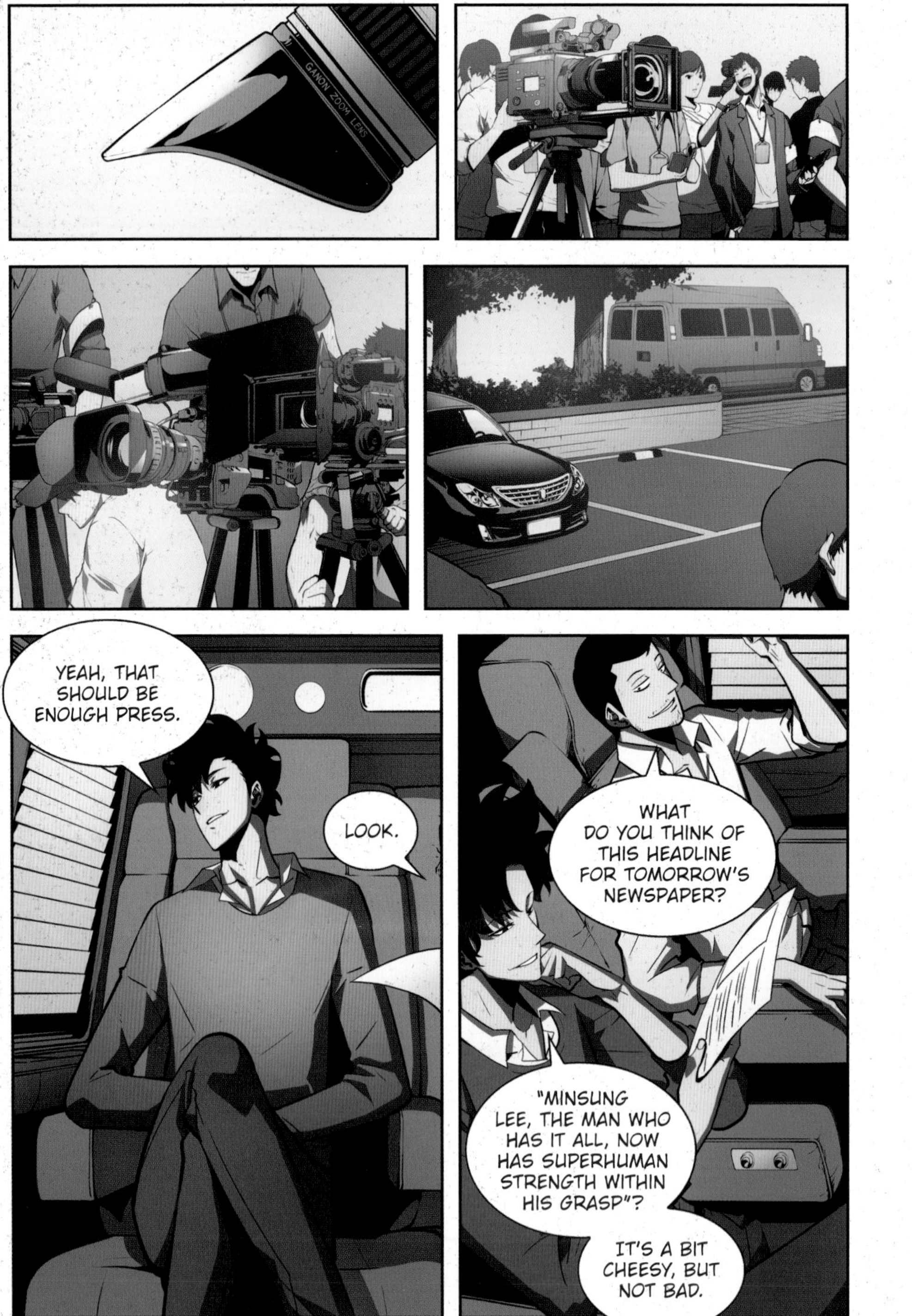
GANON ZOOM LENS
YEAH, THAT SHOULD BE ENOUGH PRESS.
LOOK.
WHAT DO YOU THINK OF THIS HEADLINE FOR TOMORROW'S NEWSPAPER?
"MINSUNG LEE, THE MAN WHO HAS IT ALL, NOW HAS SUPERHUMAN STRENGTH WITHIN HIS GRASP"?
IT'S A BIT CHEESY, BUT NOT BAD.

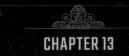

CHAPTER 13

The Tenth S-rank Hunter

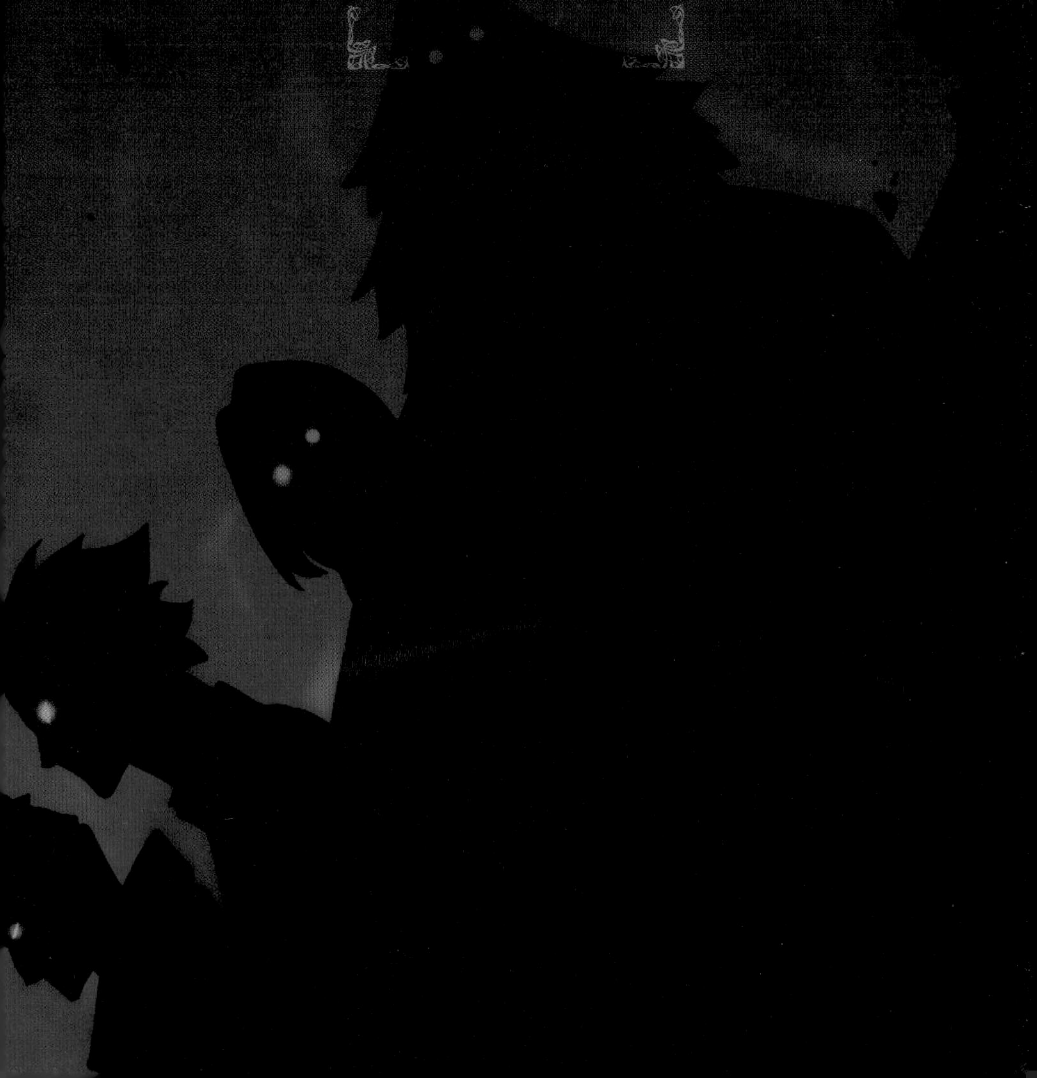

Solo Leveling

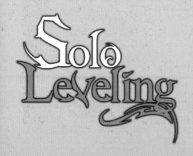

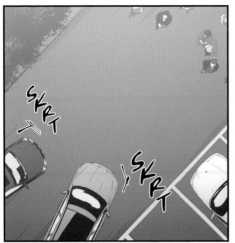

SKRT

SKRT

HUH? SOMEONE'S HERE!

IT'S YOONHO BAEK!

JONGIN CHOI IS HERE TOO!

WHO ARE THESE PEOPLE? REPORTERS?

WHY ARE THERE SO MANY PEOPLE HERE TODAY?

ARE YOU TWO HERE TO RECRUIT MINSUNG LEE FOR YOUR GUILDS?

SNAP

FLASH

AS HUNTERS WHO REPRESENT KOREA, WHAT RANK DO YOU THINK MINSUNG WILL GET?

DO YOU THINK MINSUNG WILL RETIRE FROM ACTING?

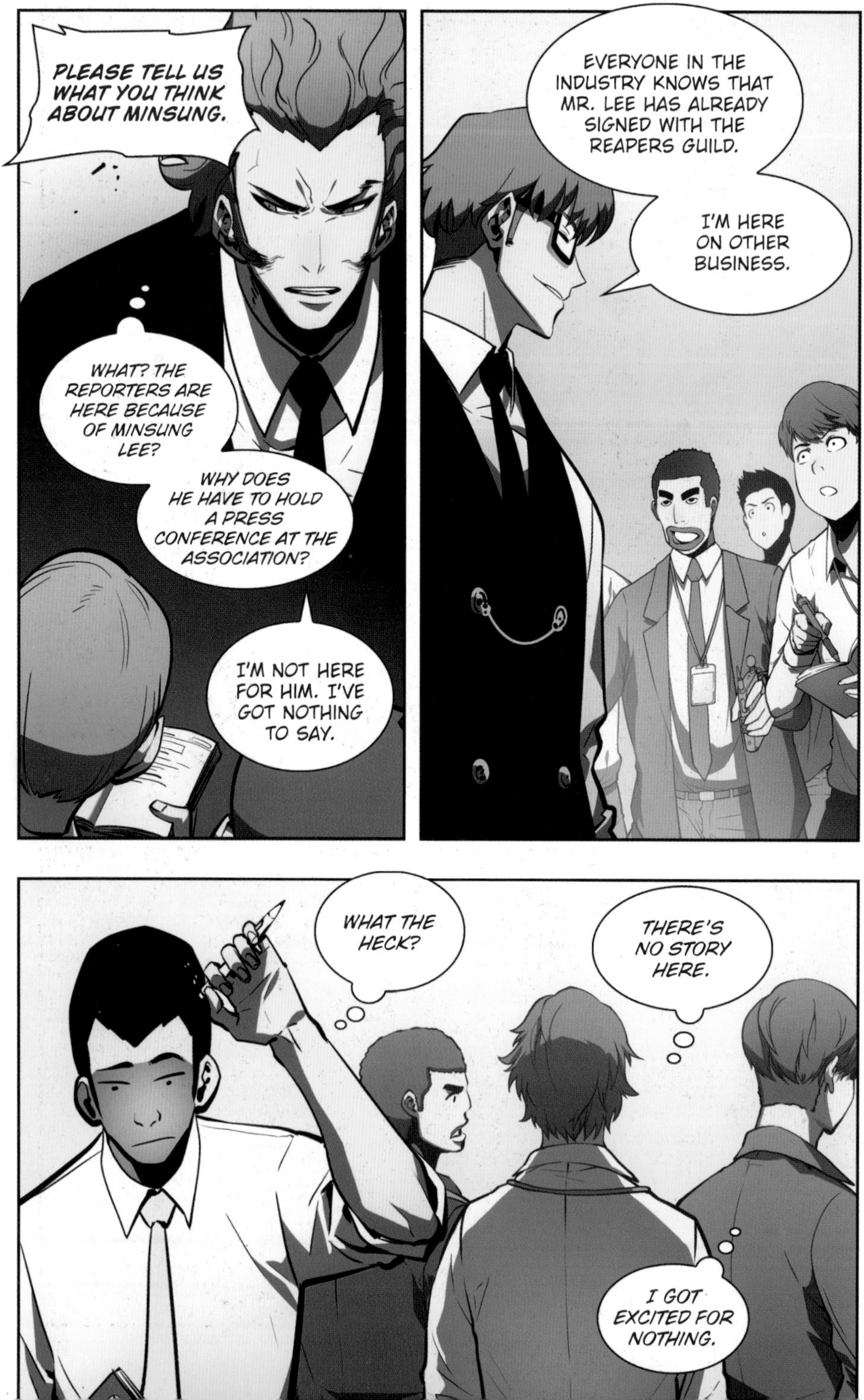
PLEASE TELL US WHAT YOU THINK ABOUT MINSUNG.
WHAT? THE REPORTERS ARE HERE BECAUSE OF MINSUNG LEE?
WHY DOES HE HAVE TO HOLD A PRESS CONFERENCE AT THE ASSOCIATION?
I'M NOT HERE FOR HIM. I'VE GOT NOTHING TO SAY.
EVERYONE IN THE INDUSTRY KNOWS THAT MR. LEE HAS ALREADY SIGNED WITH THE REAPERS GUILD.
I'M HERE ON OTHER BUSINESS.
WHAT THE HECK?
THERE'S NO STORY HERE.
I GOT EXCITED FOR NOTHING.

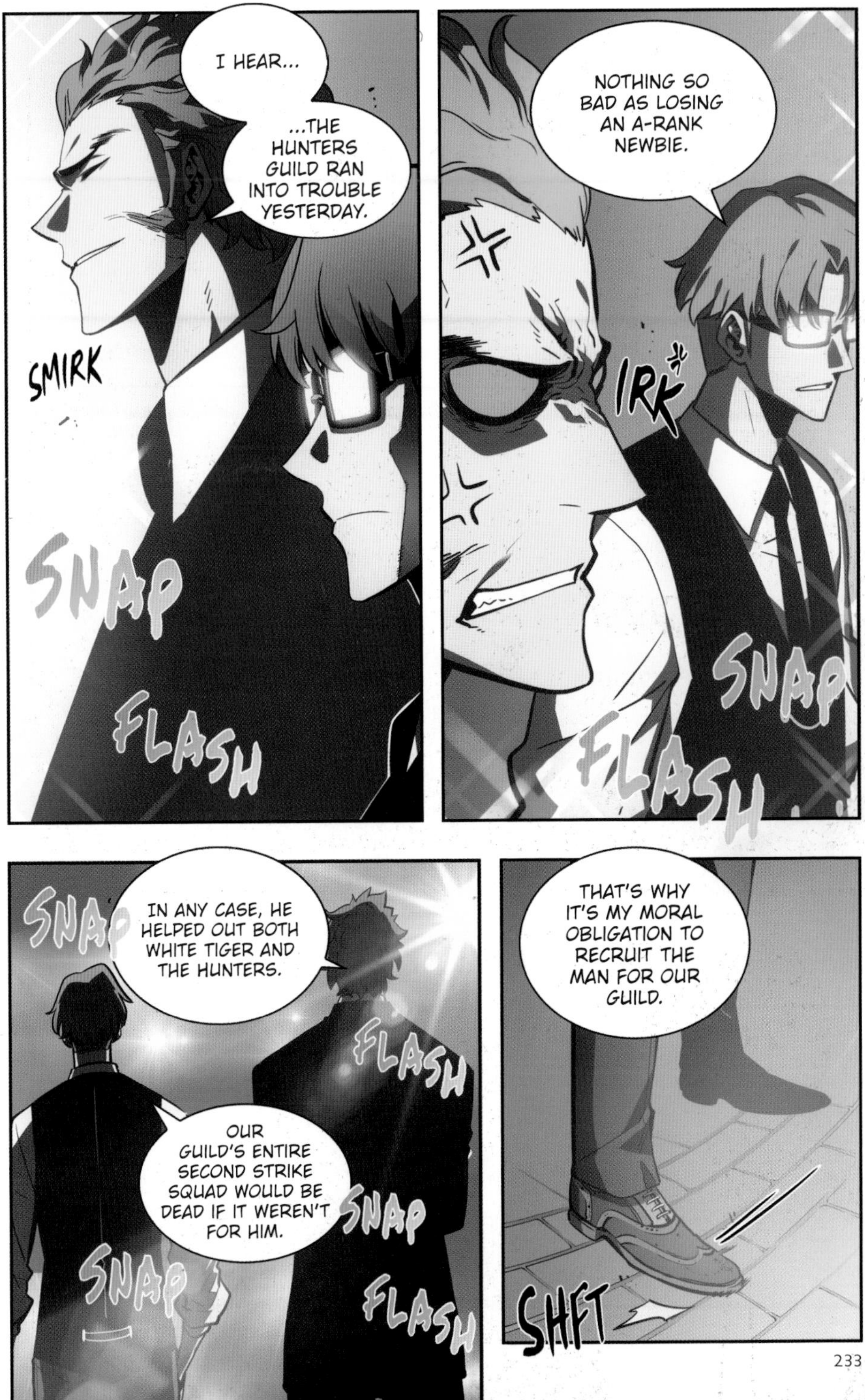
I HEAR...
...THE HUNTERS GUILD RAN INTO TROUBLE YESTERDAY.
SMIRK
SNAP
FLASH
NOTHING SO BAD AS LOSING AN A-RANK NEWBIE.
IRK
SNAP
FLASH
SNAP
IN ANY CASE, HE HELPED OUT BOTH WHITE TIGER AND THE HUNTERS.
FLASH
OUR GUILD'S ENTIRE SECOND STRIKE SQUAD WOULD BE DEAD IF IT WEREN'T FOR HIM.
SNAP
SNAP
FLASH
THAT'S WHY IT'S MY MORAL OBLIGATION TO RECRUIT THE MAN FOR OUR GUILD.
SHFT

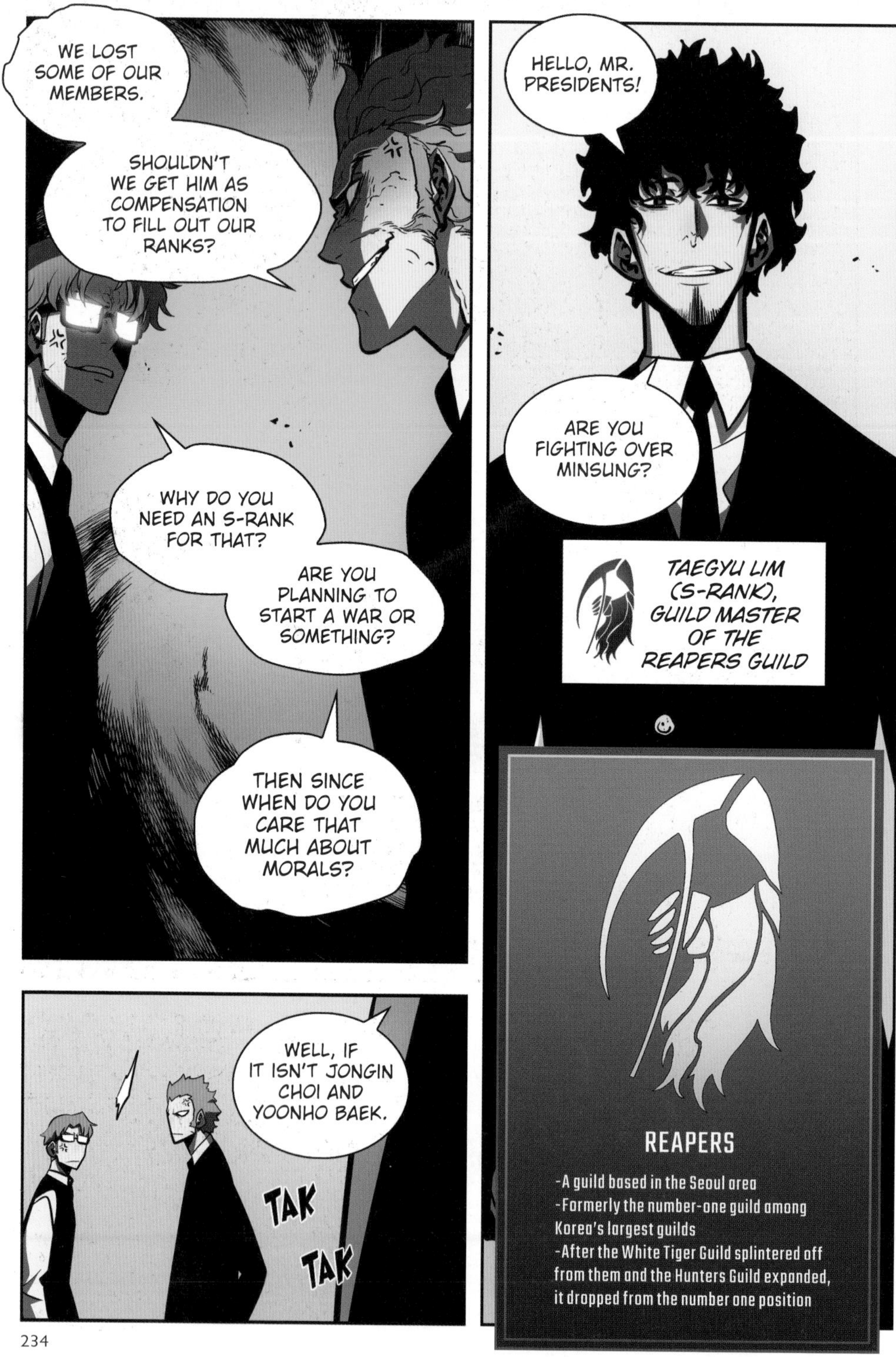

WE LOST SOME OF OUR MEMBERS.
SHOULDN'T WE GET HIM AS COMPENSATION TO FILL OUT OUR RANKS?
WHY DO YOU NEED AN S-RANK FOR THAT?
ARE YOU PLANNING TO START A WAR OR SOMETHING?
THEN SINCE WHEN DO YOU CARE THAT MUCH ABOUT MORALS?
WELL, IF IT ISN'T JONGIN CHOI AND YOONHO BAEK.
TAK
TAK
HELLO, MR. PRESIDENTS!
ARE YOU FIGHTING OVER MINSUNG?
TAEGYU LIM (S-RANK), GUILD MASTER OF THE REAPERS GUILD
REAPERS
-A guild based in the Seoul area
-Formerly the number-one guild among Korea's largest guilds
-After the White Tiger Guild splintered off from them and the Hunters Guild expanded, it dropped from the number one position

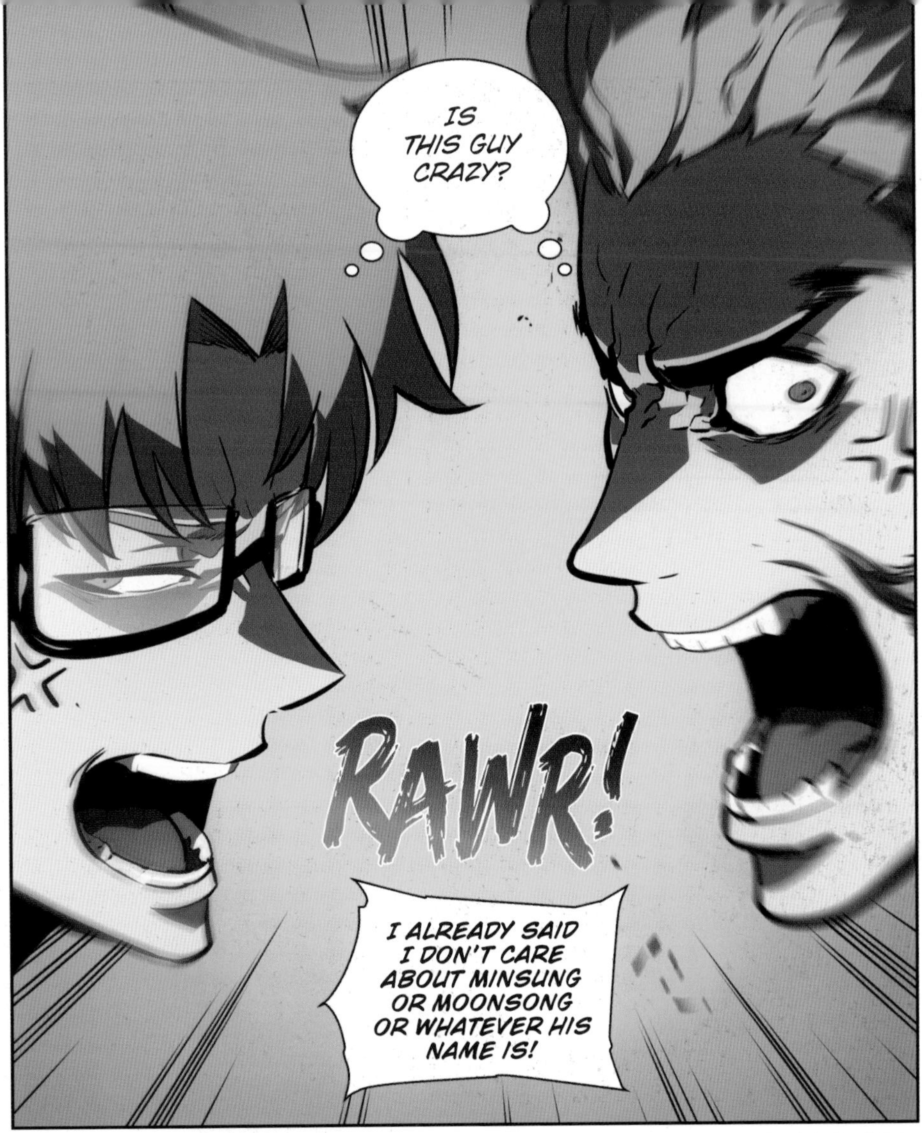
IS THIS GUY CRAZY?
RAWR!
I ALREADY SAID I DON'T CARE ABOUT MINSUNG OR MOONSONG OR WHATEVER HIS NAME IS!
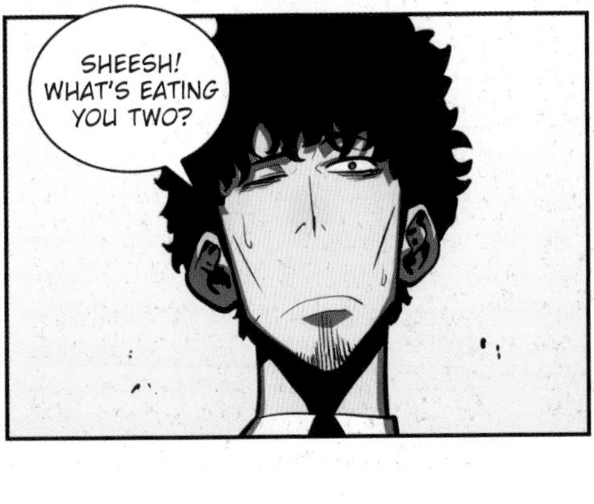
SHEESH! WHAT'S EATING YOU TWO?
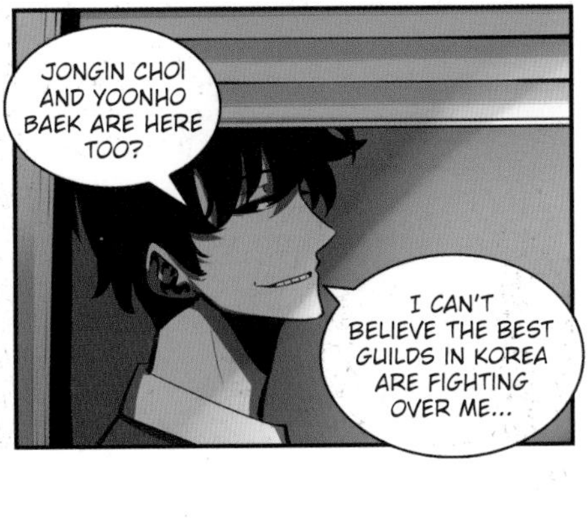
JONGIN CHOI AND YOONHO BAEK ARE HERE TOO?
I CAN'T BELIEVE THE BEST GUILDS IN KOREA ARE FIGHTING OVER ME...

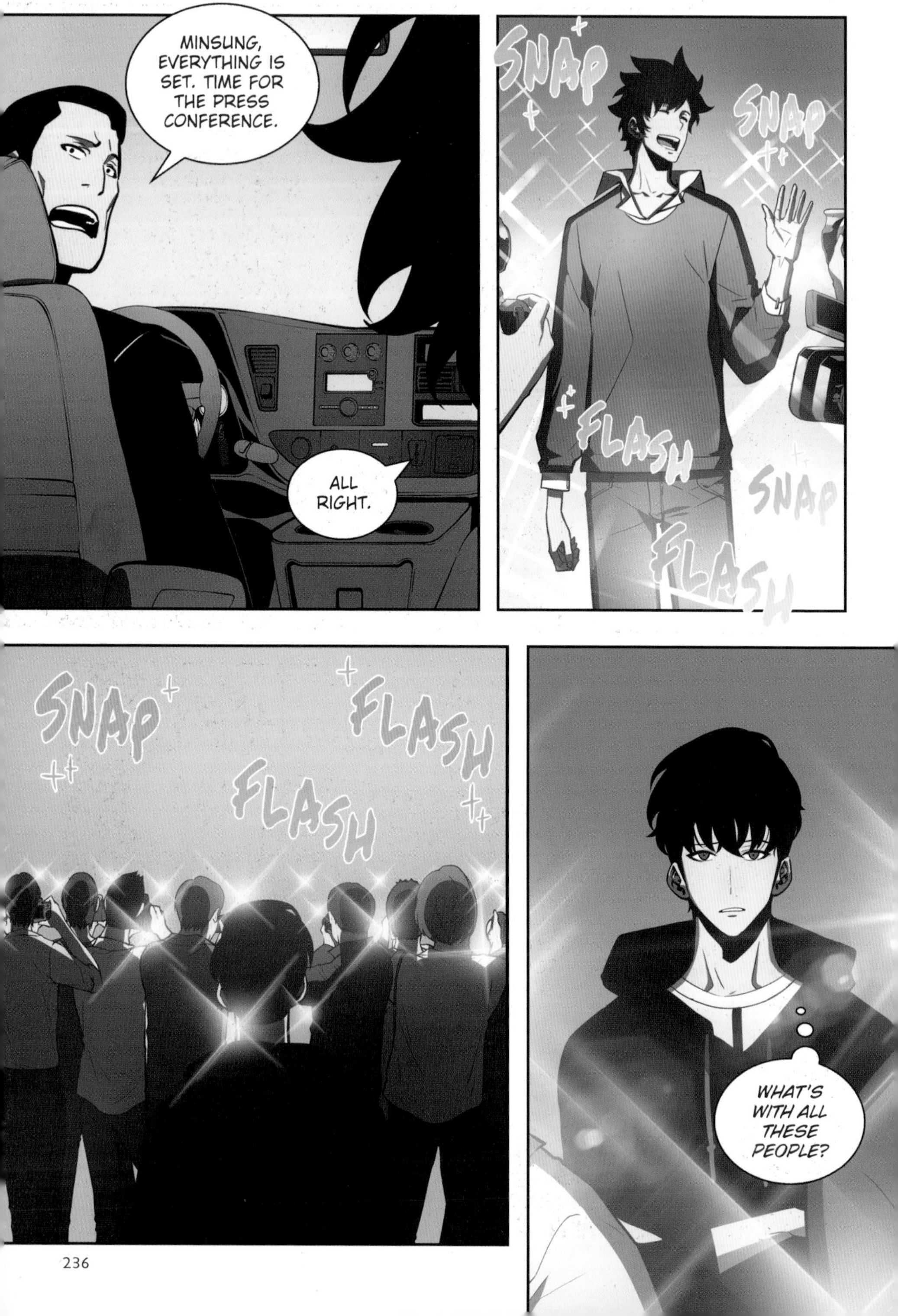
MINSUNG, EVERYTHING IS SET. TIME FOR THE PRESS CONFERENCE.
ALL RIGHT.
SNAP
SNAP
FLASH
SNAP
FLASH
SNAP
FLASH
FLASH
WHAT'S WITH ALL THESE PEOPLE?

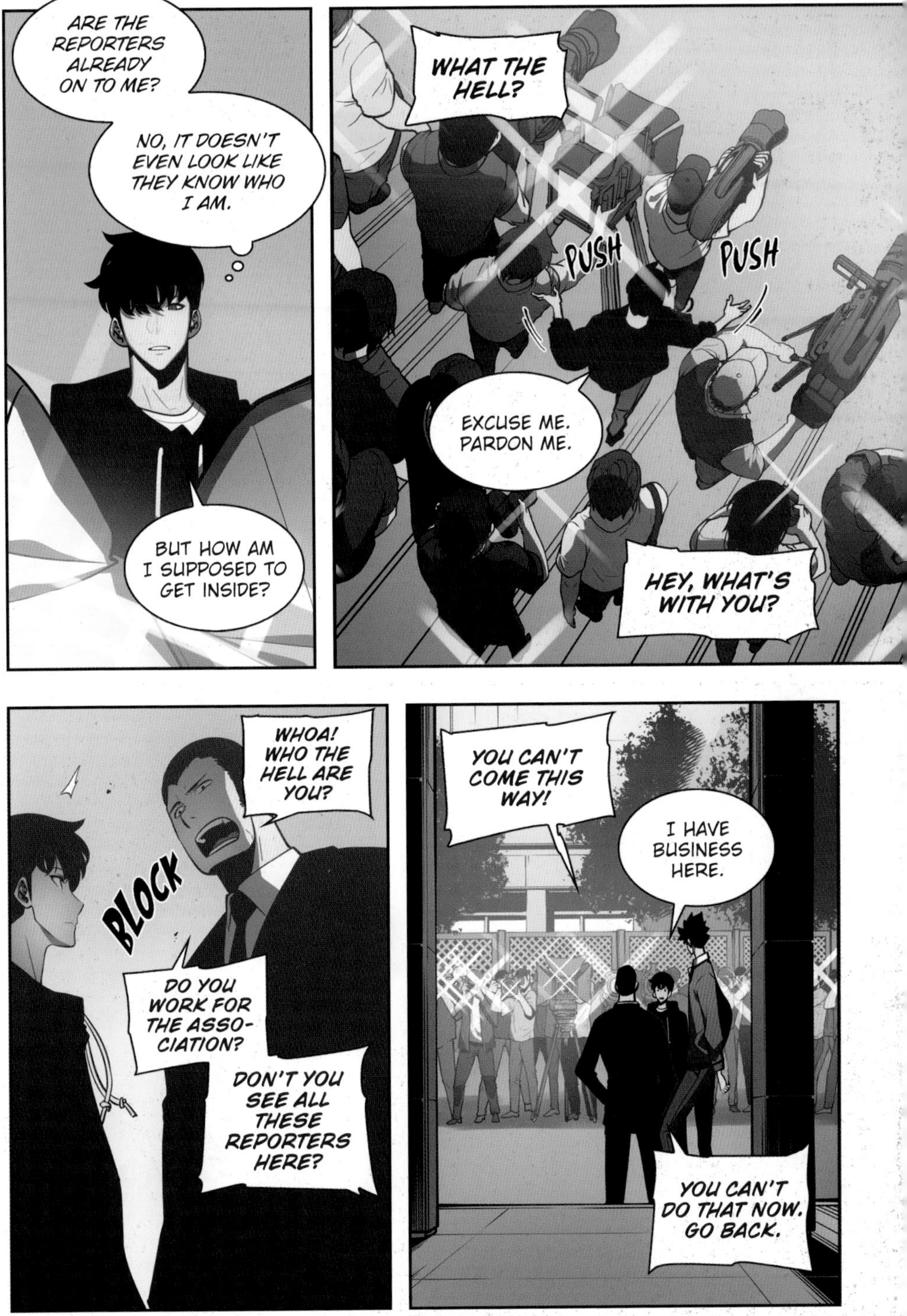
ARE THE REPORTERS ALREADY ON TO ME?
NO, IT DOESN'T EVEN LOOK LIKE THEY KNOW WHO I AM.
BUT HOW AM I SUPPOSED TO GET INSIDE?
WHAT THE HELL?
PUSH
PUSH
EXCUSE ME. PARDON ME.
HEY, WHAT'S WITH YOU?
WHOA! WHO THE HELL ARE YOU?
BLOCK
DO YOU WORK FOR THE ASSO-CIATION?
DON'T YOU SEE ALL THESE REPORTERS HERE?
YOU CAN'T COME THIS WAY!
I HAVE BUSINESS HERE.
YOU CAN'T DO THAT NOW. GO BACK.

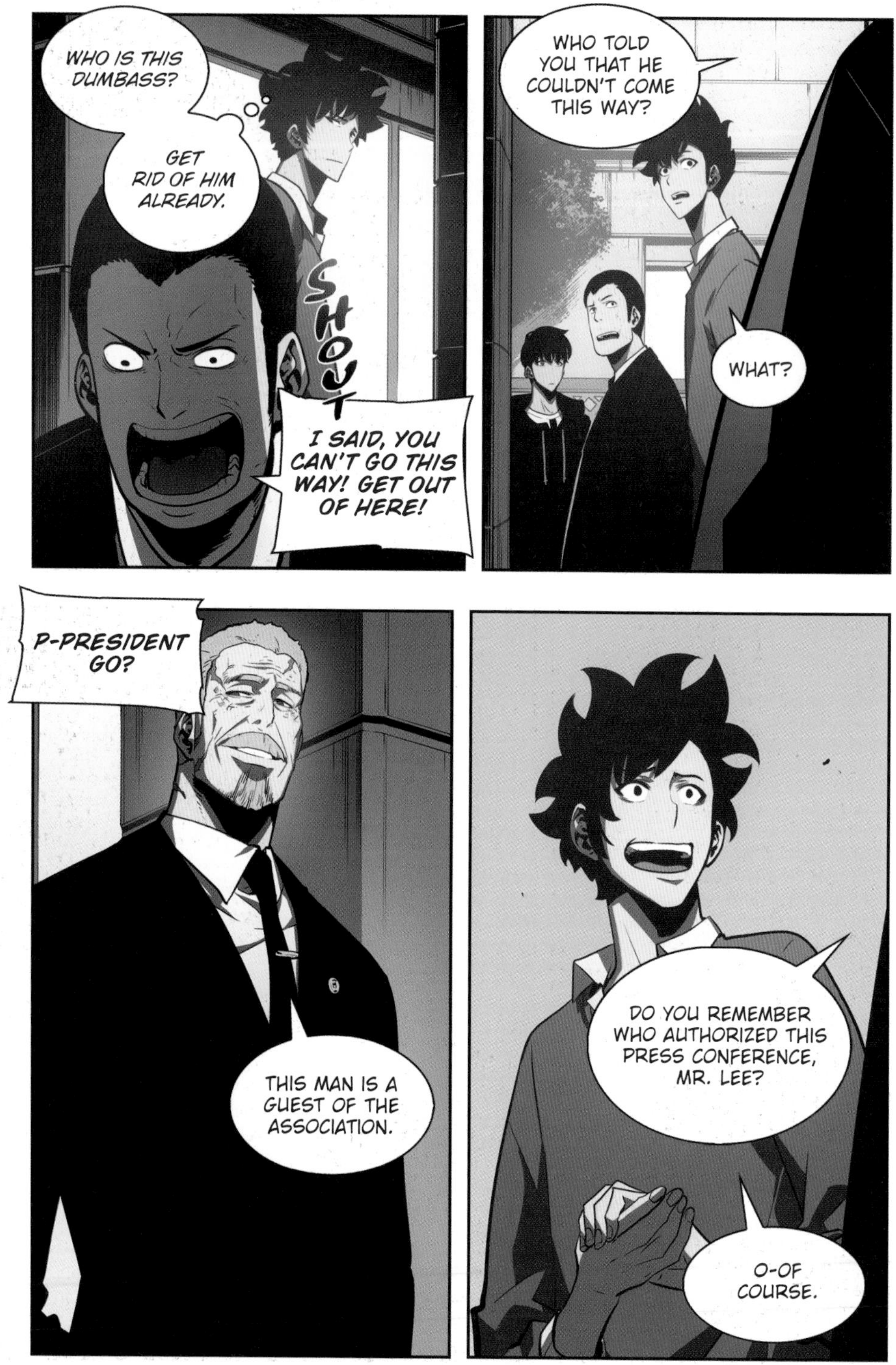
WHO IS THIS DUMBASS?
GET RID OF HIM ALREADY.
SHOUT
I SAID, YOU CAN'T GO THIS WAY! GET OUT OF HERE!
WHO TOLD YOU THAT HE COULDN'T COME THIS WAY?
WHAT?
P-PRESIDENT GO?
THIS MAN IS A GUEST OF THE ASSOCIATION.
DO YOU REMEMBER WHO AUTHORIZED THIS PRESS CONFERENCE, MR. LEE?
O-OF COURSE.

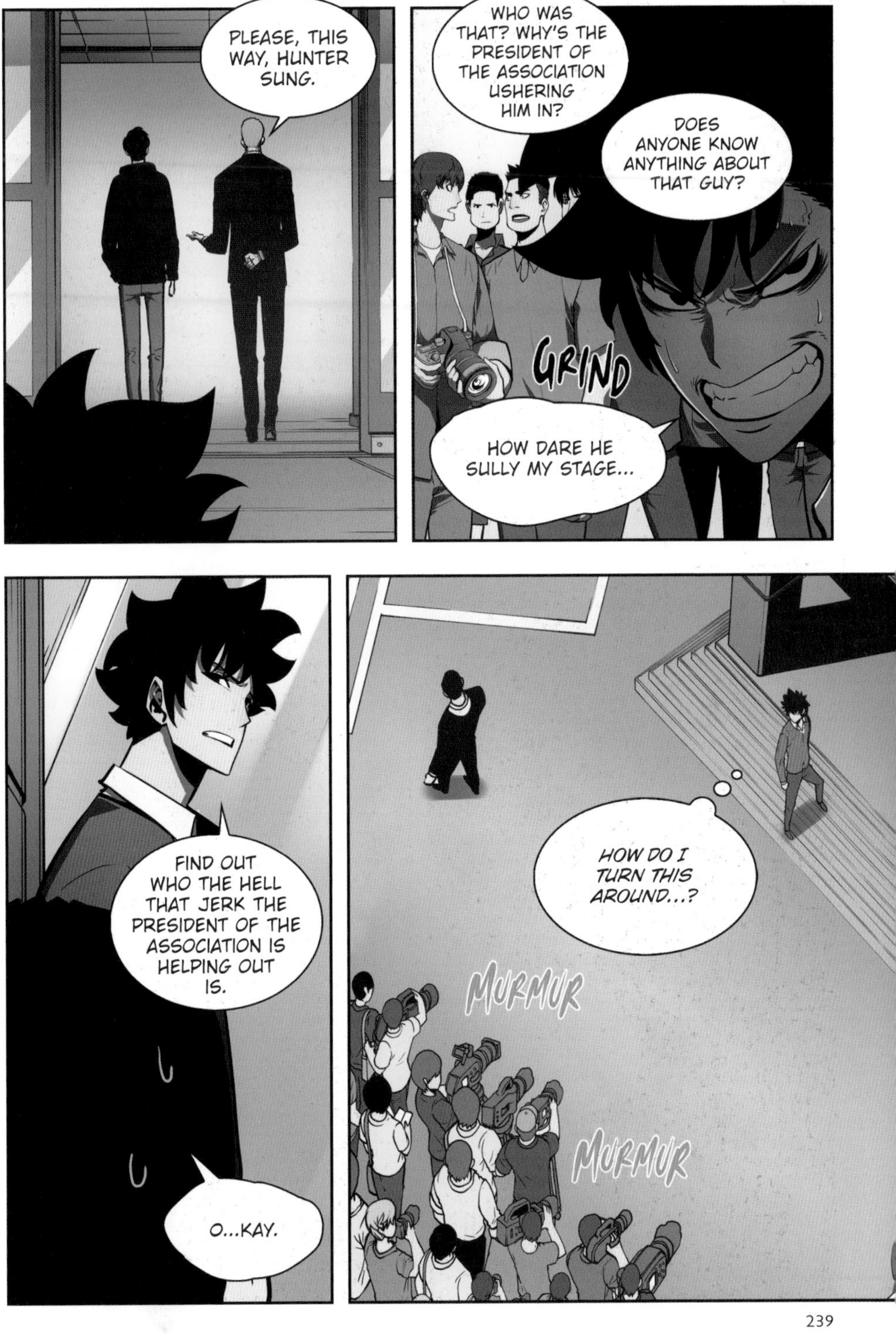
PLEASE, THIS WAY, HUNTER SUNG.
WHO WAS THAT? WHY'S THE PRESIDENT OF THE ASSOCIATION USHERING HIM IN?
DOES ANYONE KNOW ANYTHING ABOUT THAT GUY?
GRIND
HOW DARE HE SULLY MY STAGE...
FIND OUT WHO THE HELL THAT JERK THE PRESIDENT OF THE ASSOCIATION IS HELPING OUT IS.
O...KAY.
HOW DO I TURN THIS AROUND...?
MURMUR
MURMUR

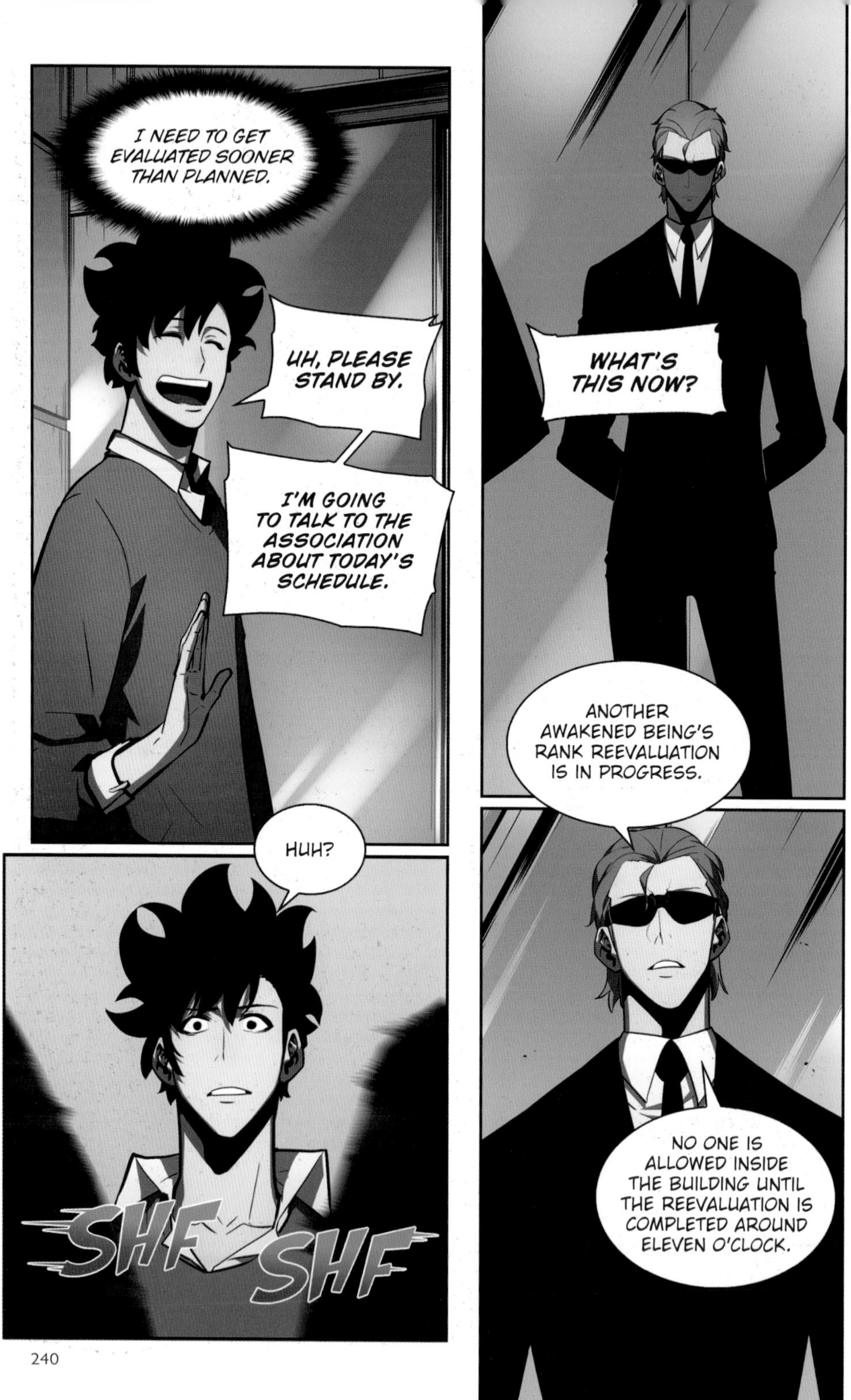
I NEED TO GET EVALUATED SOONER THAN PLANNED.
UH, PLEASE STAND BY.
I'M GOING TO TALK TO THE ASSOCIATION ABOUT TODAY'S SCHEDULE.
WHAT'S THIS NOW?
ANOTHER AWAKENED BEING'S RANK REEVALUATION IS IN PROGRESS.
HUH?
SHF SHF
NO ONE IS ALLOWED INSIDE THE BUILDING UNTIL THE REEVALUATION IS COMPLETED AROUND ELEVEN O'CLOCK.

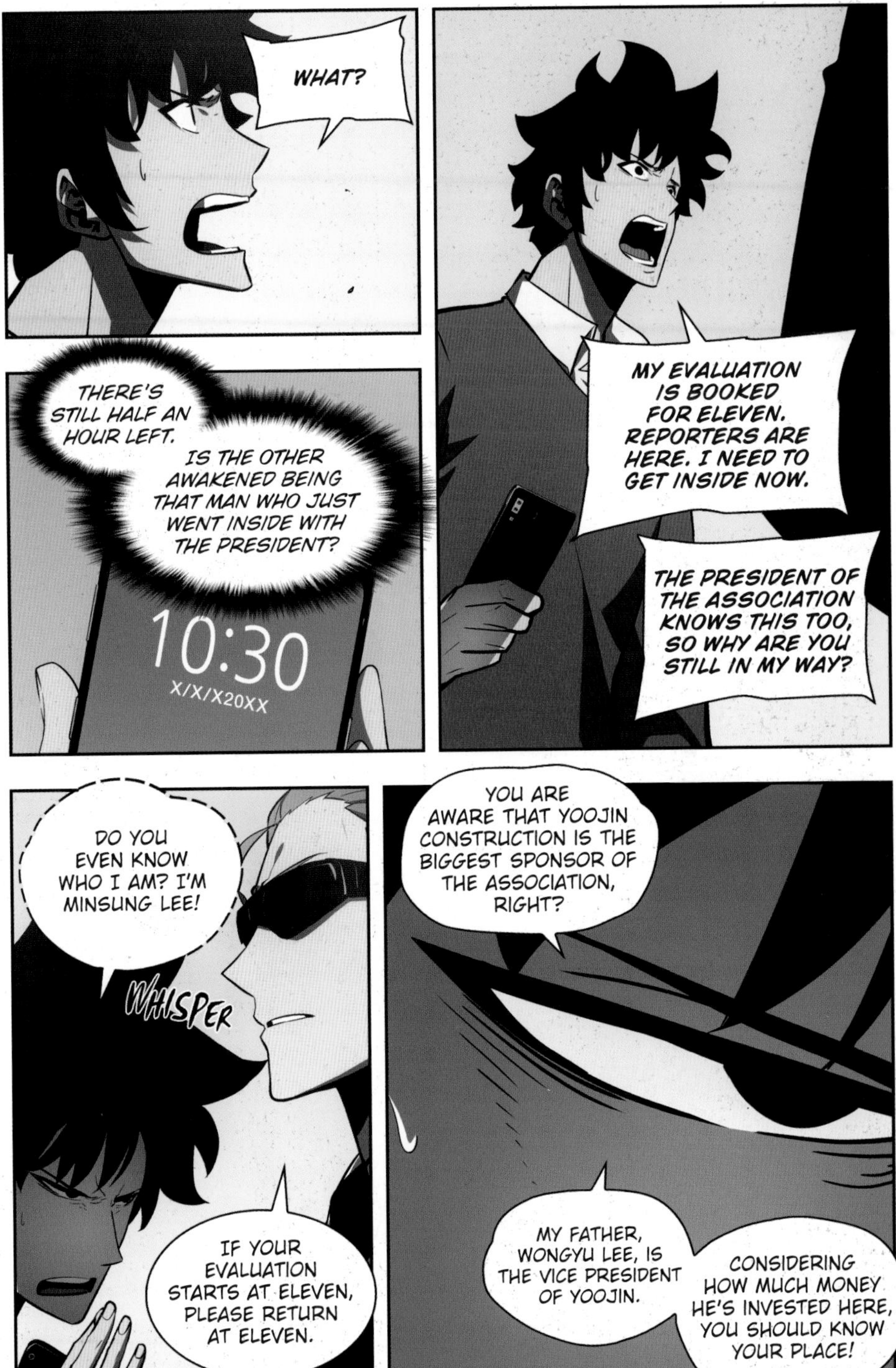
WHAT?
MY EVALUATION IS BOOKED FOR ELEVEN. REPORTERS ARE HERE. I NEED TO GET INSIDE NOW.
THE PRESIDENT OF THE ASSOCIATION KNOWS THIS TOO, SO WHY ARE YOU STILL IN MY WAY?
THERE'S STILL HALF AN HOUR LEFT.
IS THE OTHER AWAKENED BEING THAT MAN WHO JUST WENT INSIDE WITH THE PRESIDENT?
10:30
X/X/X20XX
DO YOU EVEN KNOW WHO I AM? I'M MINSUNG LEE!
WHISPER
IF YOUR EVALUATION STARTS AT ELEVEN, PLEASE RETURN AT ELEVEN.
YOU ARE AWARE THAT YOOJIN CONSTRUCTION IS THE BIGGEST SPONSOR OF THE ASSOCIATION, RIGHT?
MY FATHER, WONGYU LEE, IS THE VICE PRESIDENT OF YOOJIN.
CONSIDERING HOW MUCH MONEY HE'S INVESTED HERE, YOU SHOULD KNOW YOUR PLACE!

DO YOU SEE THOSE PEOPLE?

HOW CAN YOU TREAT ME LIKE THIS WITH SO MANY REPORTERS WATCHING?

ARE YOU PREPARED FOR THE CONSEQUENCES?

CLAMOR

CLAMOR

CLAMOR

YES, I AM.

WHAT?

WH-WHO DO YOU THINK YOU ARE? WHAT'S SO SPECIAL ABOUT THAT OTHER DUDE?

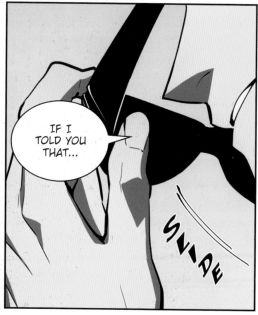

IF I TOLD YOU THAT...

SNIDE

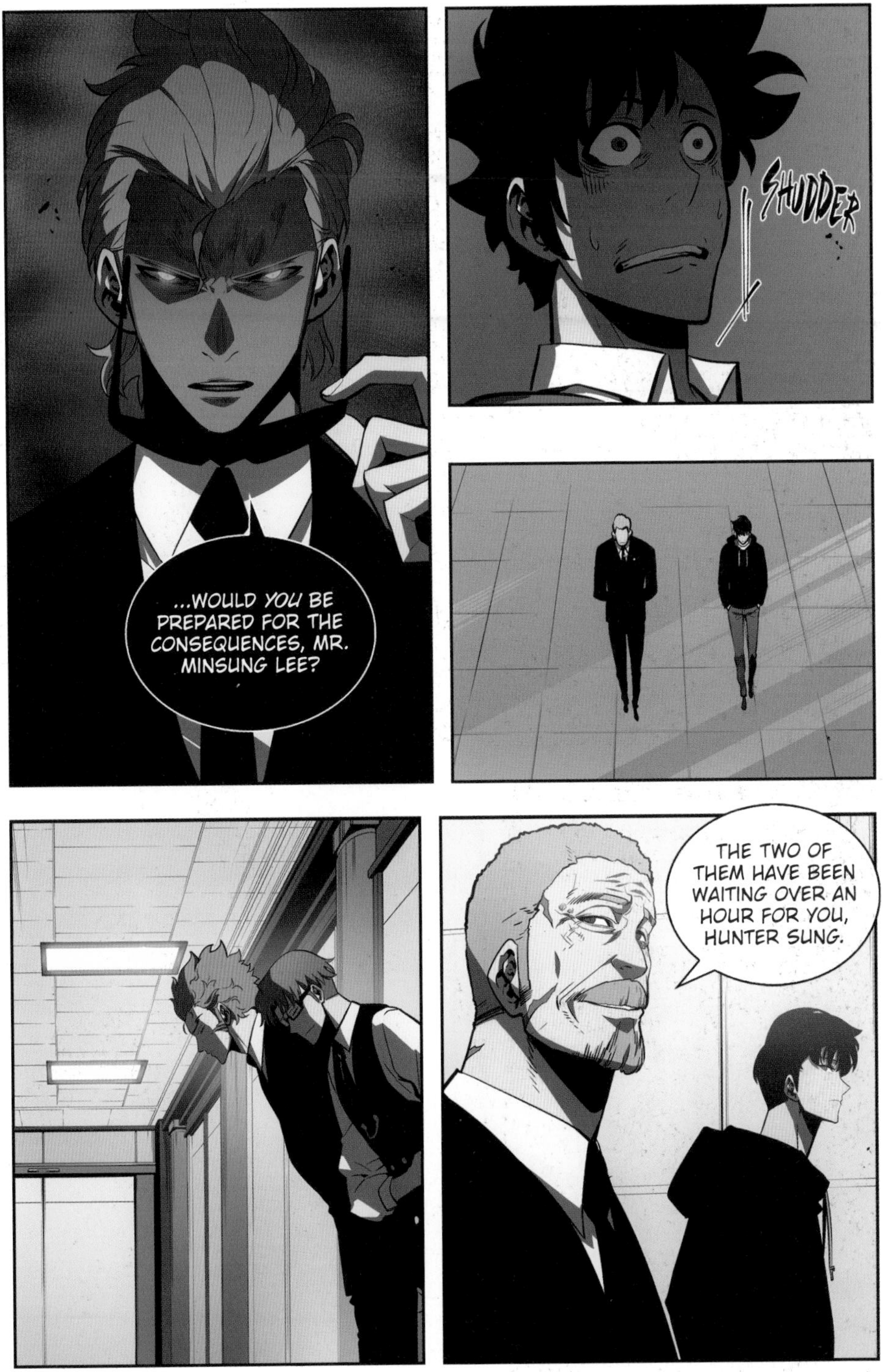
...WOULD YOU BE PREPARED FOR THE CONSEQUENCES, MR. MINSUNG LEE?
SHUDDER
THE TWO OF THEM HAVE BEEN WAITING OVER AN HOUR FOR YOU, HUNTER SUNG.

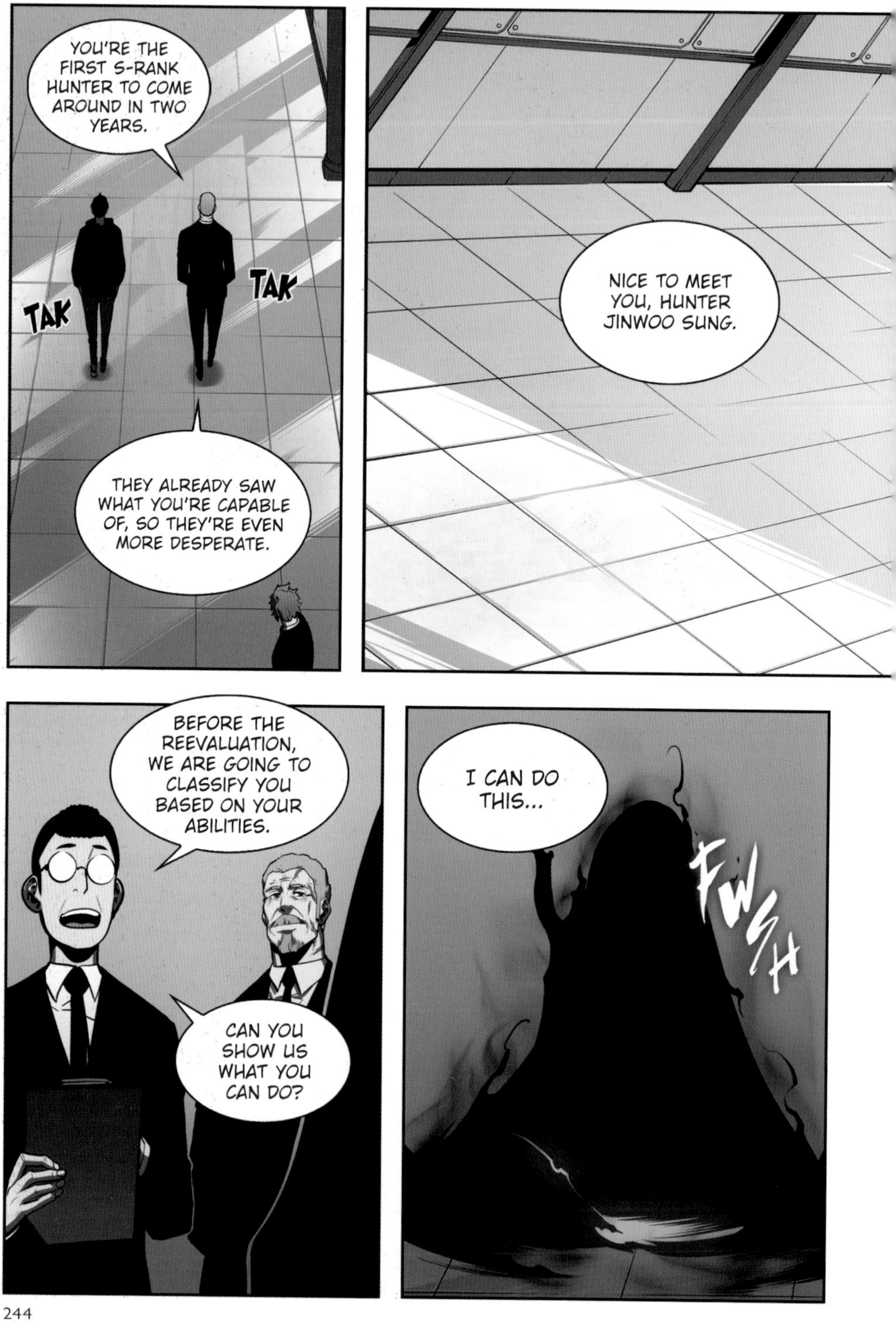
YOU'RE THE FIRST S-RANK HUNTER TO COME AROUND IN TWO YEARS.
TAK
TAK
THEY ALREADY SAW WHAT YOU'RE CAPABLE OF, SO THEY'RE EVEN MORE DESPERATE.
NICE TO MEET YOU, HUNTER JINWOO SUNG.
BEFORE THE REEVALUATION, WE ARE GOING TO CLASSIFY YOU BASED ON YOUR ABILITIES.
CAN YOU SHOW US WHAT YOU CAN DO?
I CAN DO THIS...
FWSH

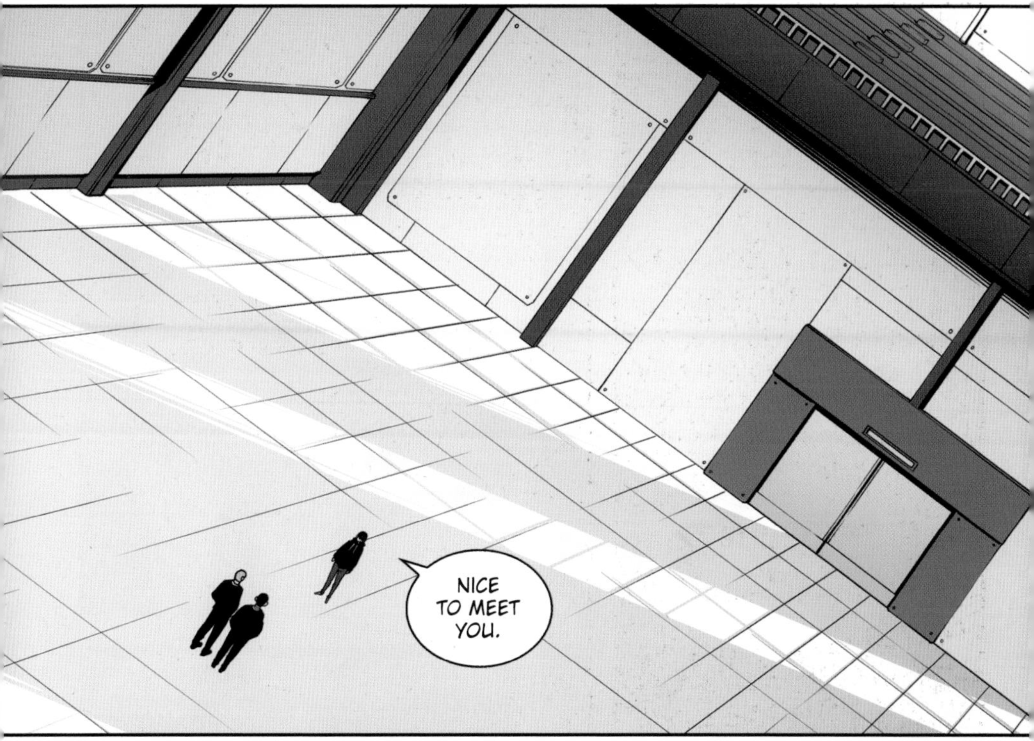
NICE TO MEET YOU.

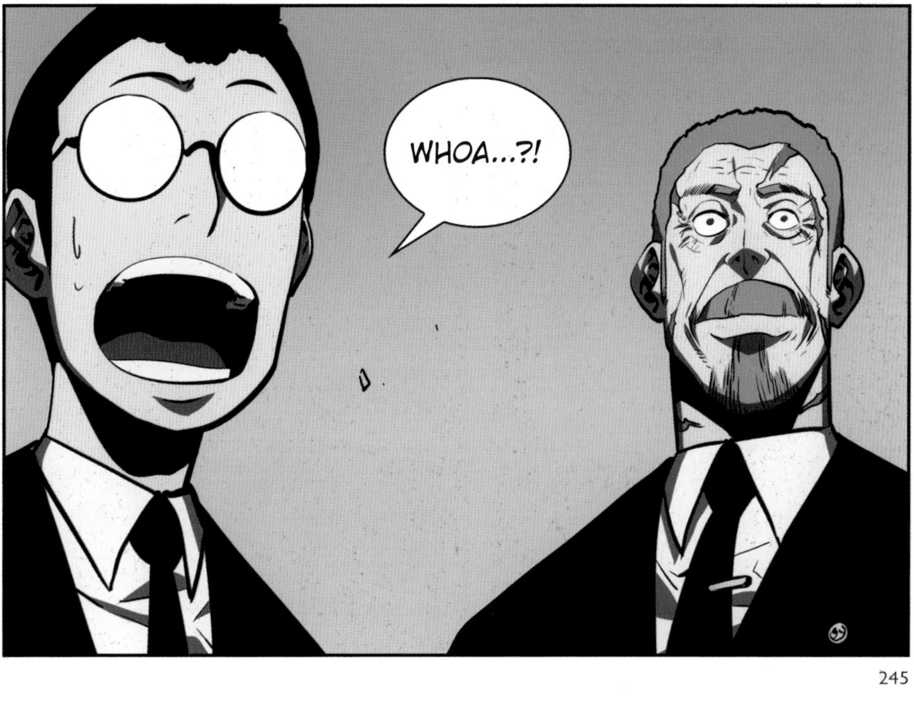
WHOA...?!

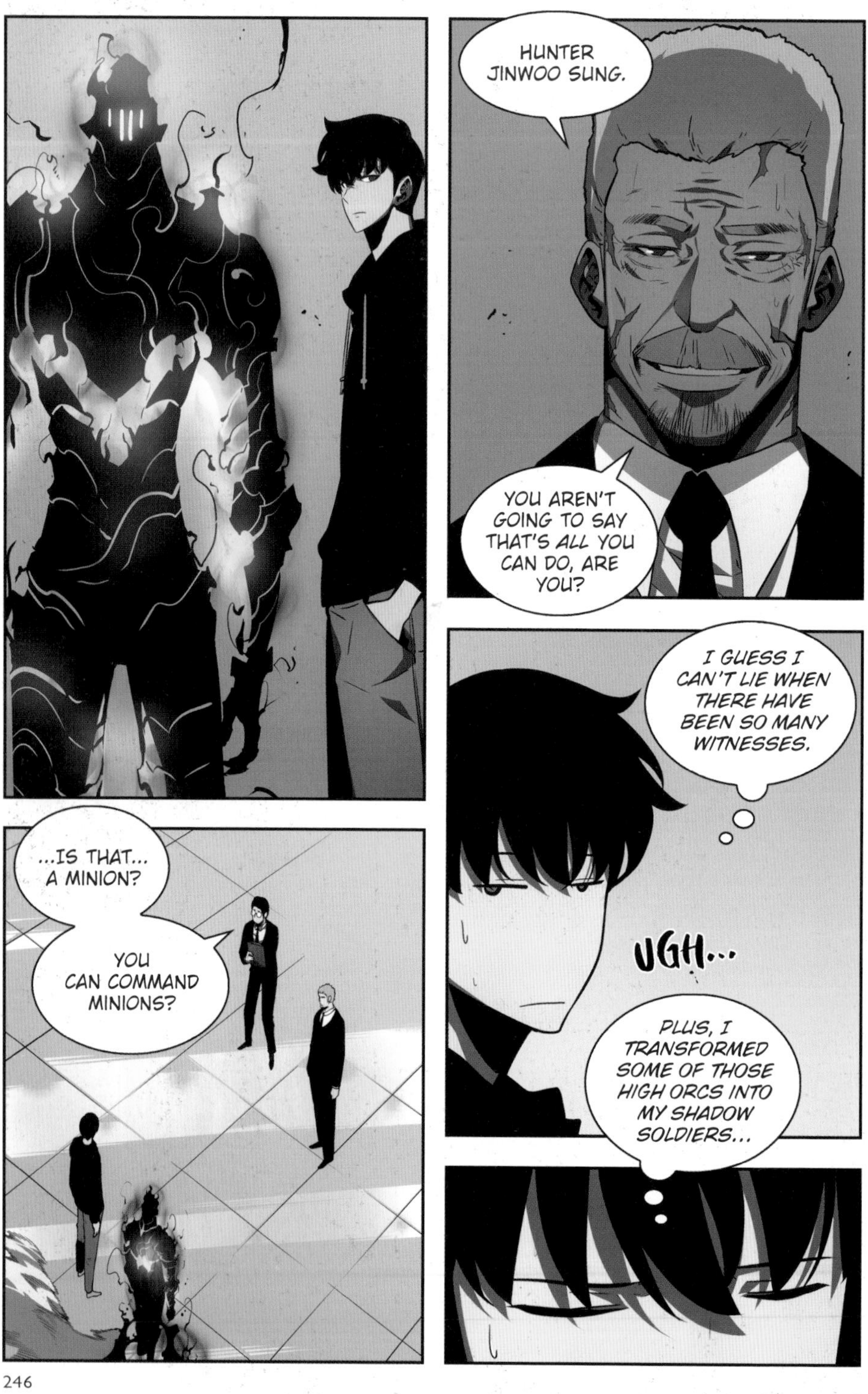
...IS THAT... A MINION?
YOU CAN COMMAND MINIONS?
HUNTER JINWOO SUNG.
YOU AREN'T GOING TO SAY THAT'S *ALL* YOU CAN DO, ARE YOU?
I GUESS I CAN'T LIE WHEN THERE HAVE BEEN SO MANY WITNESSES.
UGH...
PLUS, I TRANSFORMED SOME OF THOSE HIGH ORCS INTO MY SHADOW SOLDIERS...

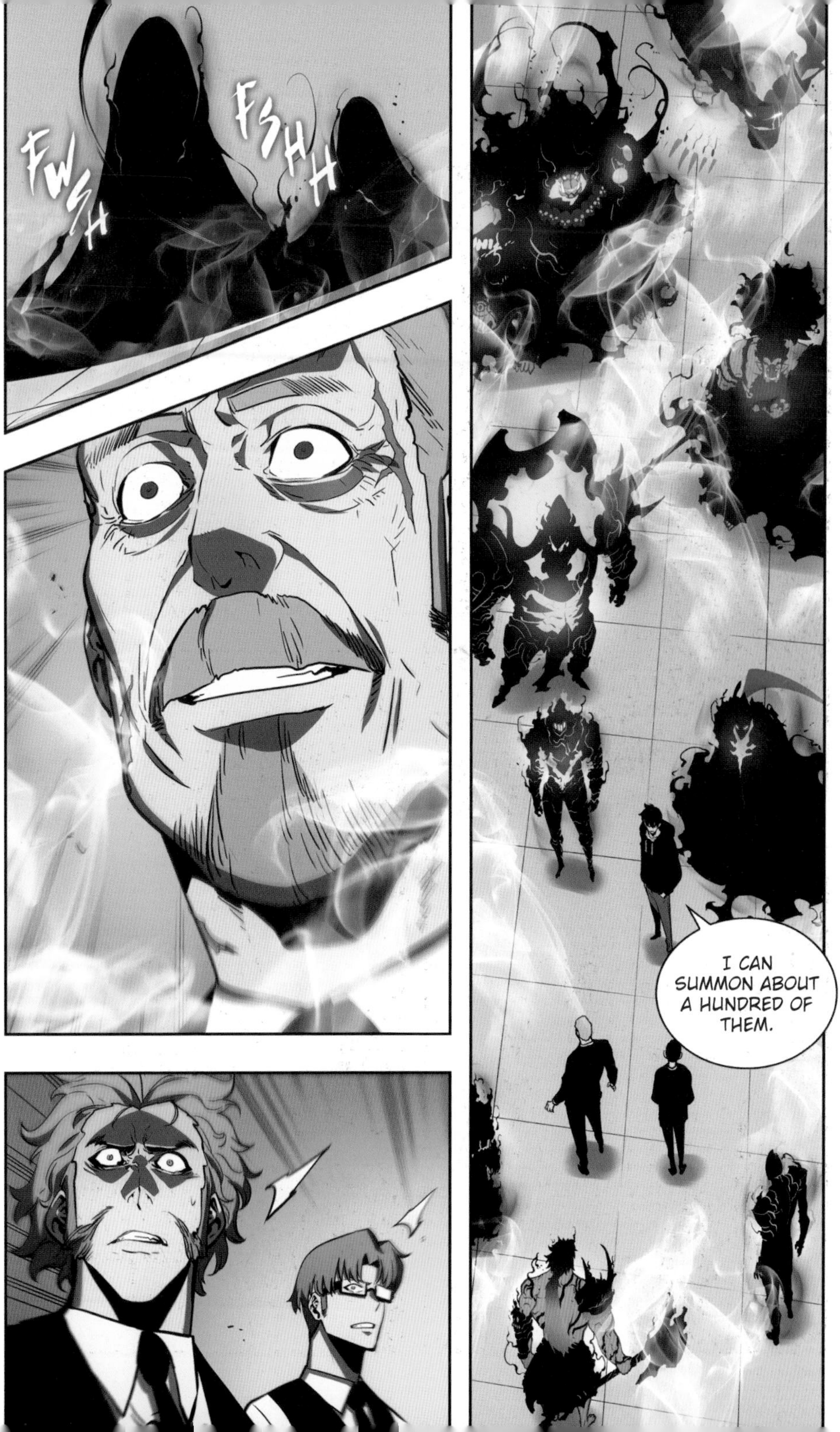
FWSH
FSHH
I CAN SUMMON ABOUT A HUNDRED OF THEM.

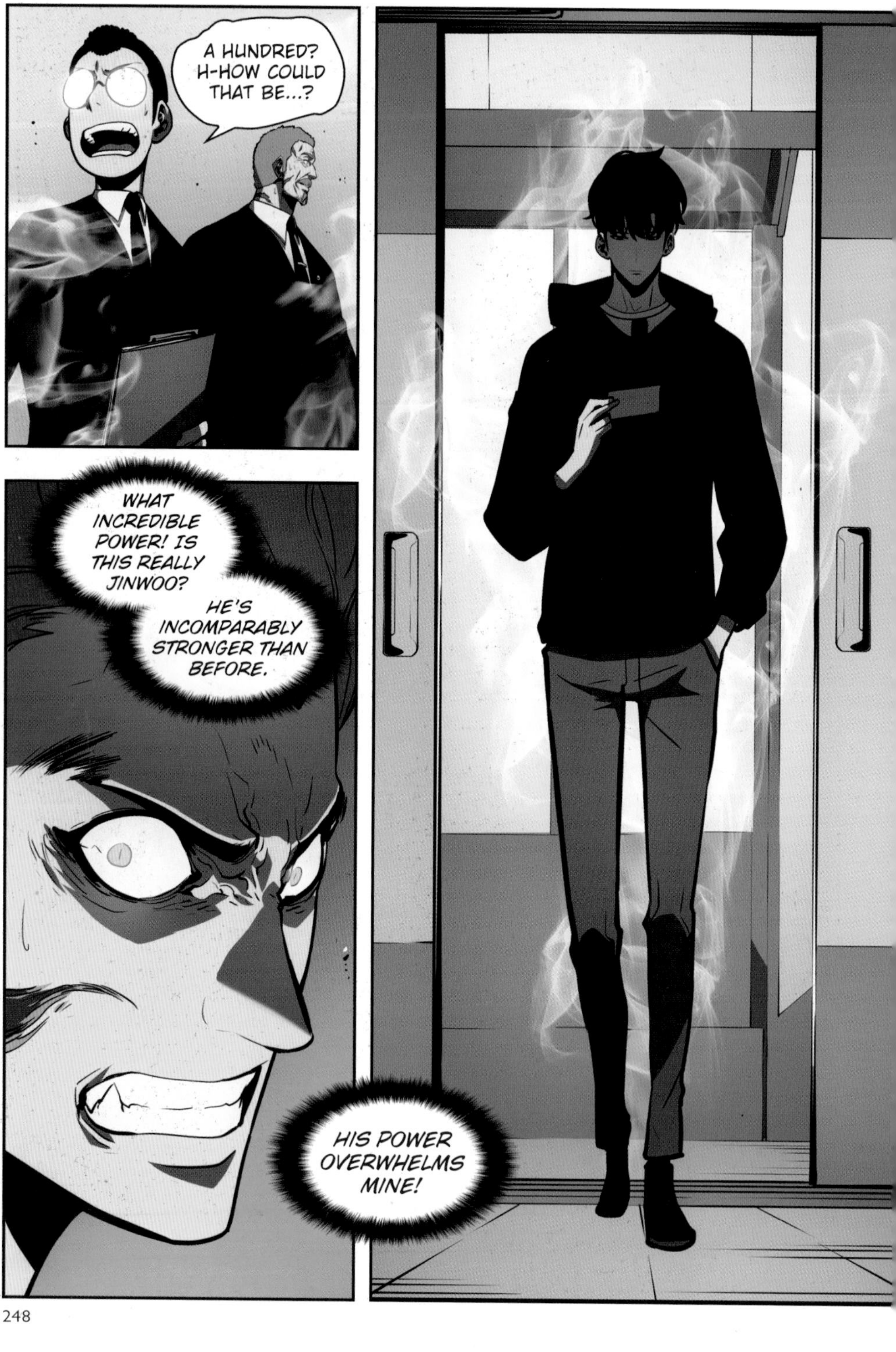
A HUNDRED? H-HOW COULD THAT BE...?
WHAT INCREDIBLE POWER! IS THIS REALLY JINWOO?
HE'S INCOMPARABLY STRONGER THAN BEFORE.
HIS POWER OVERWHELMS MINE!

HUNTER JINWOO SUNG.

er's Association of K
Hunter's License

Jinwoo Su

S-rank

JINWOO, A MOMENT OF YOUR TIME?

I'M SORRY. I'VE GOT SOME ERRANDS TO RUN.

SNEAK

OH, NOT THERE!

IF I WERE YOU, I WOULDN'T GO OUT THAT WAY.

BECAUSE YOU HAVE AN OFFER I CAN'T REFUSE?

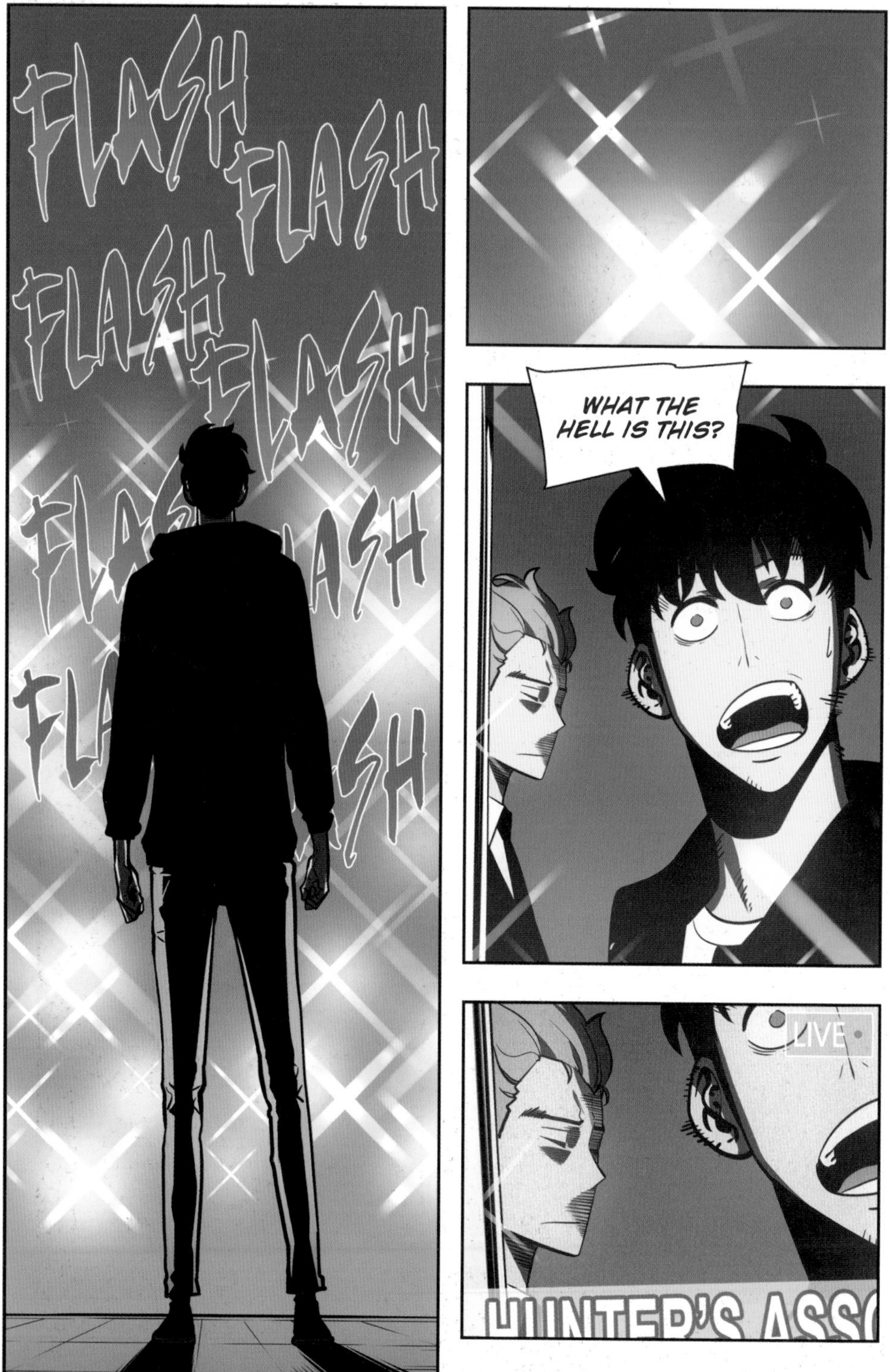
FLASH
FLASH
FLASH
FLASH
FLASH
FLASH
WHAT THE HELL IS THIS?
LIVE
HUNTER'S ASSO

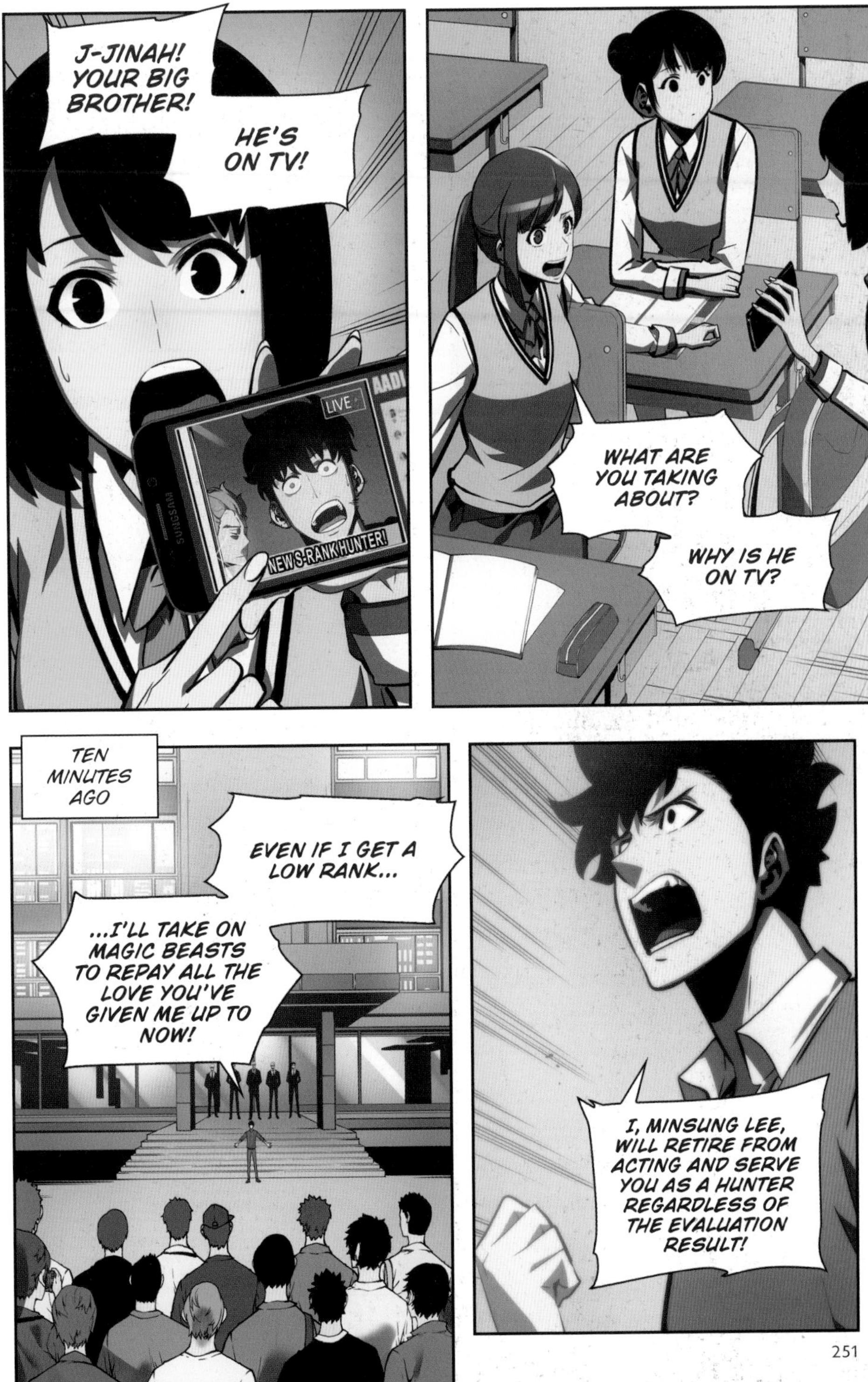
J-JINAH! YOUR BIG BROTHER!
HE'S ON TV!
LIVE
NEW S-RANK HUNTER!
WHAT ARE YOU TAKING ABOUT?
WHY IS HE ON TV?
TEN MINUTES AGO
EVEN IF I GET A LOW RANK...
...I'LL TAKE ON MAGIC BEASTS TO REPAY ALL THE LOVE YOU'VE GIVEN ME UP TO NOW!
I, MINSUNG LEE, WILL RETIRE FROM ACTING AND SERVE YOU AS A HUNTER REGARDLESS OF THE EVALUATION RESULT!

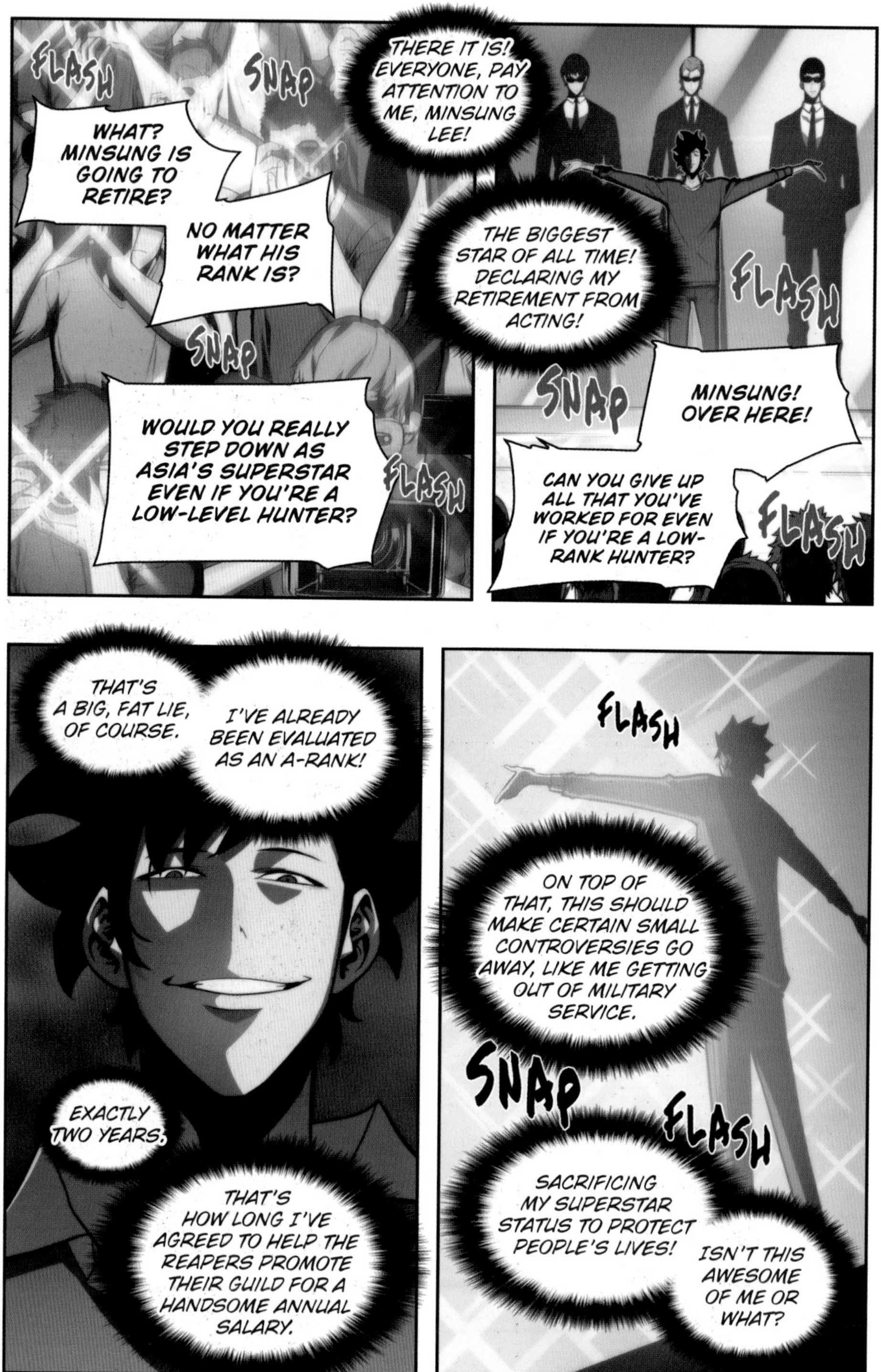
FLASH
SNAP
THERE IT IS! EVERYONE, PAY ATTENTION TO ME, MINSUNG LEE!
WHAT? MINSUNG IS GOING TO RETIRE?
NO MATTER WHAT HIS RANK IS?
THE BIGGEST STAR OF ALL TIME! DECLARING MY RETIREMENT FROM ACTING!
FLASH
SNAP
WOULD YOU REALLY STEP DOWN AS ASIA'S SUPERSTAR EVEN IF YOU'RE A LOW-LEVEL HUNTER?
FLASH
SNAP
MINSUNG! OVER HERE!
CAN YOU GIVE UP ALL THAT YOU'VE WORKED FOR EVEN IF YOU'RE A LOW-RANK HUNTER?
FLASH
THAT'S A BIG, FAT LIE, OF COURSE.
I'VE ALREADY BEEN EVALUATED AS AN A-RANK!
EXACTLY TWO YEARS.
THAT'S HOW LONG I'VE AGREED TO HELP THE REAPERS PROMOTE THEIR GUILD FOR A HANDSOME ANNUAL SALARY.
FLASH
ON TOP OF THAT, THIS SHOULD MAKE CERTAIN SMALL CONTROVERSIES GO AWAY, LIKE ME GETTING OUT OF MILITARY SERVICE.
SNAP
FLASH
SACRIFICING MY SUPERSTAR STATUS TO PROTECT PEOPLE'S LIVES!
ISN'T THIS AWESOME OF ME OR WHAT?

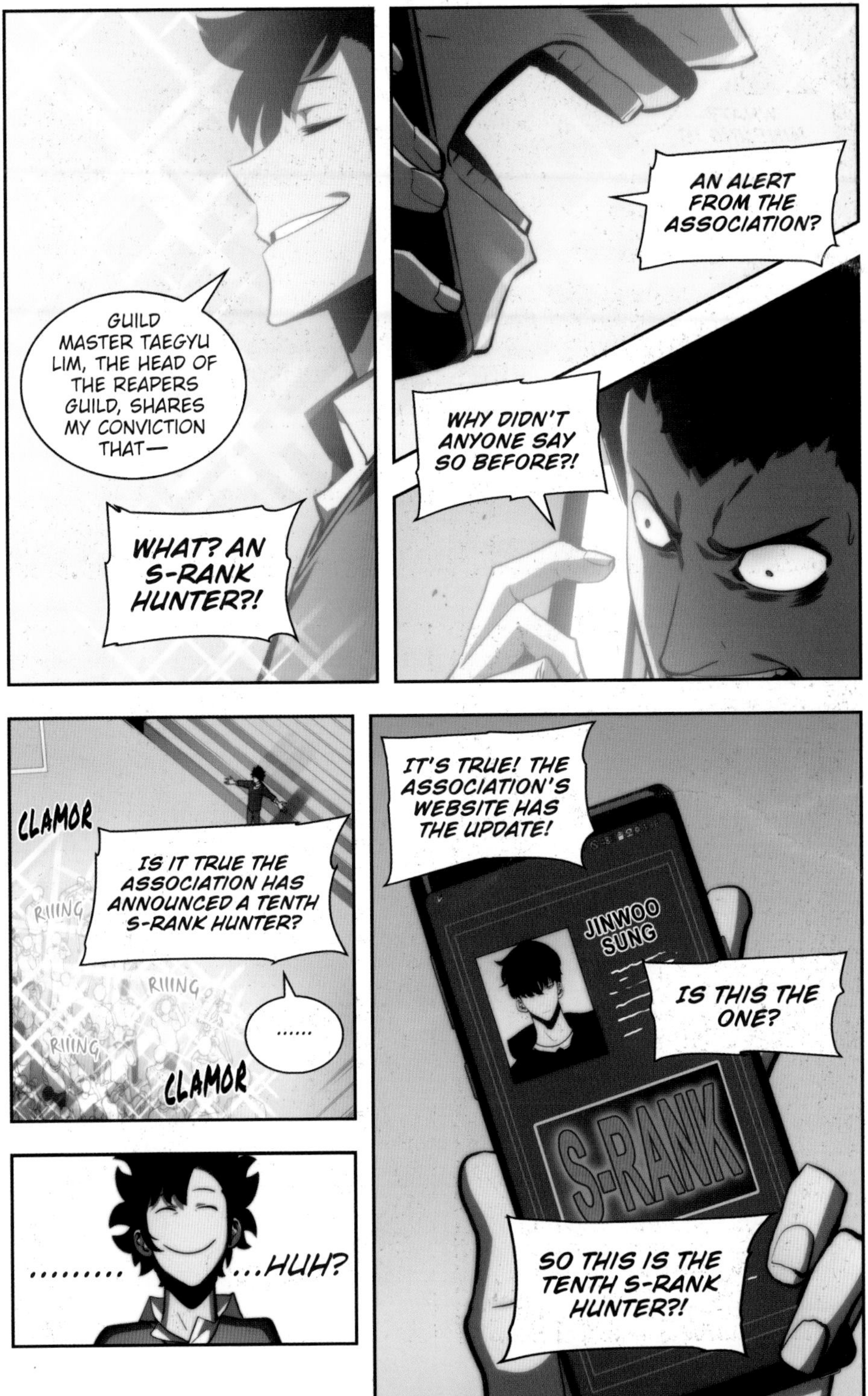
GUILD MASTER TAEGYU LIM, THE HEAD OF THE REAPERS GUILD, SHARES MY CONVICTION THAT—
WHAT? AN S-RANK HUNTER?!
AN ALERT FROM THE ASSOCIATION?
WHY DIDN'T ANYONE SAY SO BEFORE?!
CLAMOR
IS IT TRUE THE ASSOCIATION HAS ANNOUNCED A TENTH S-RANK HUNTER?
RIIING
RIIING
RIIING
......
CLAMOR
....
...HUH?
IT'S TRUE! THE ASSOCIATION'S WEBSITE HAS THE UPDATE!
JINWOO SUNG
IS THIS THE ONE?
S-RANK
SO THIS IS THE TENTH S-RANK HUNTER?!

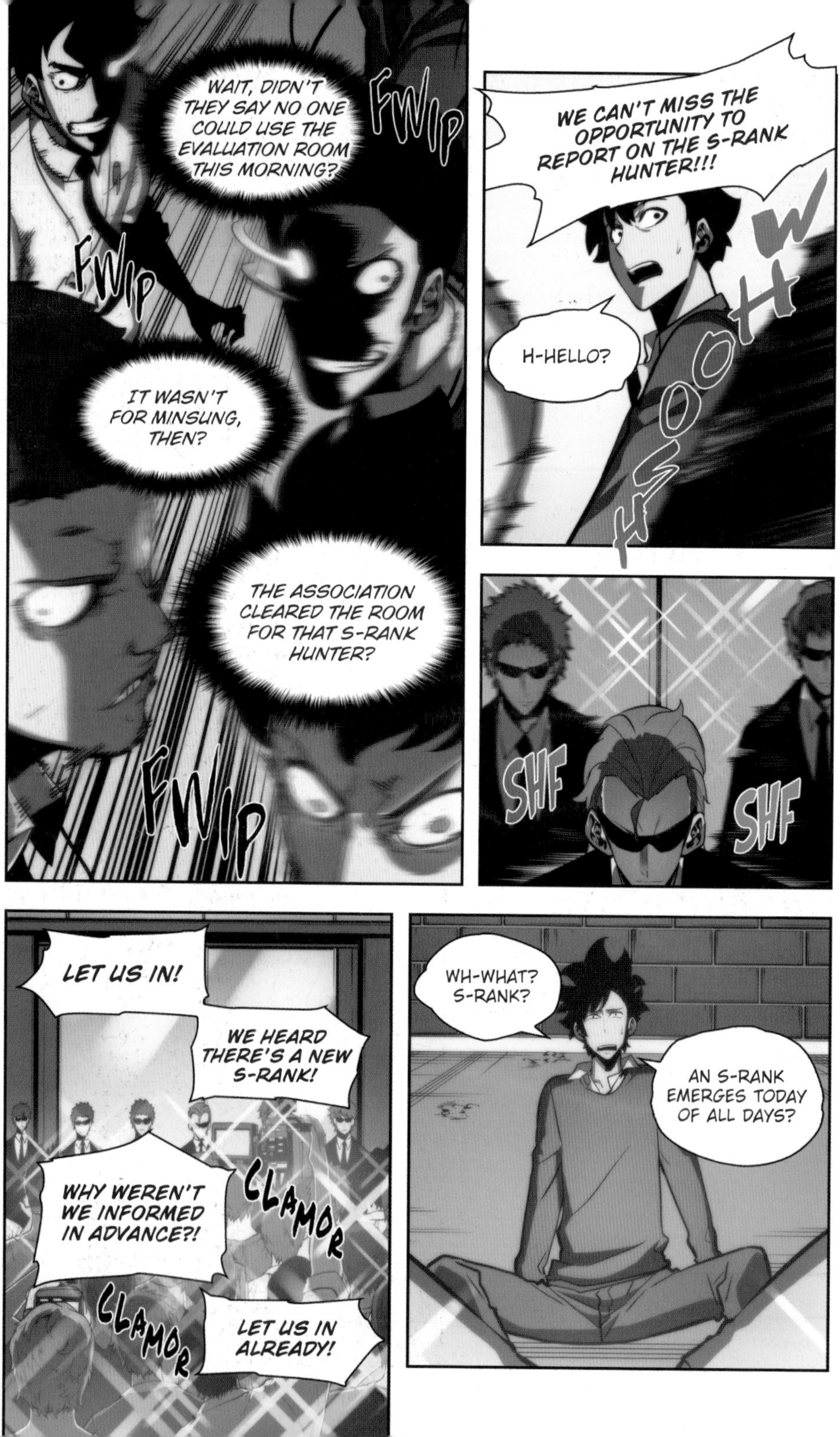
WAIT, DIDN'T THEY SAY NO ONE COULD USE THE EVALUATION ROOM THIS MORNING?
FWIP
FWIP
IT WASN'T FOR MINSUNG, THEN?
THE ASSOCIATION CLEARED THE ROOM FOR THAT S-RANK HUNTER?
FWIP
WE CAN'T MISS THE OPPORTUNITY TO REPORT ON THE S-RANK HUNTER!!!
H-HELLO?
WHOOSH
SHF
SHF
LET US IN!
WE HEARD THERE'S A NEW S-RANK!
WHY WEREN'T WE INFORMED IN ADVANCE?!
CLAMOR
CLAMOR
LET US IN ALREADY!
WH-WHAT? S-RANK?
AN S-RANK EMERGES TODAY OF ALL DAYS?

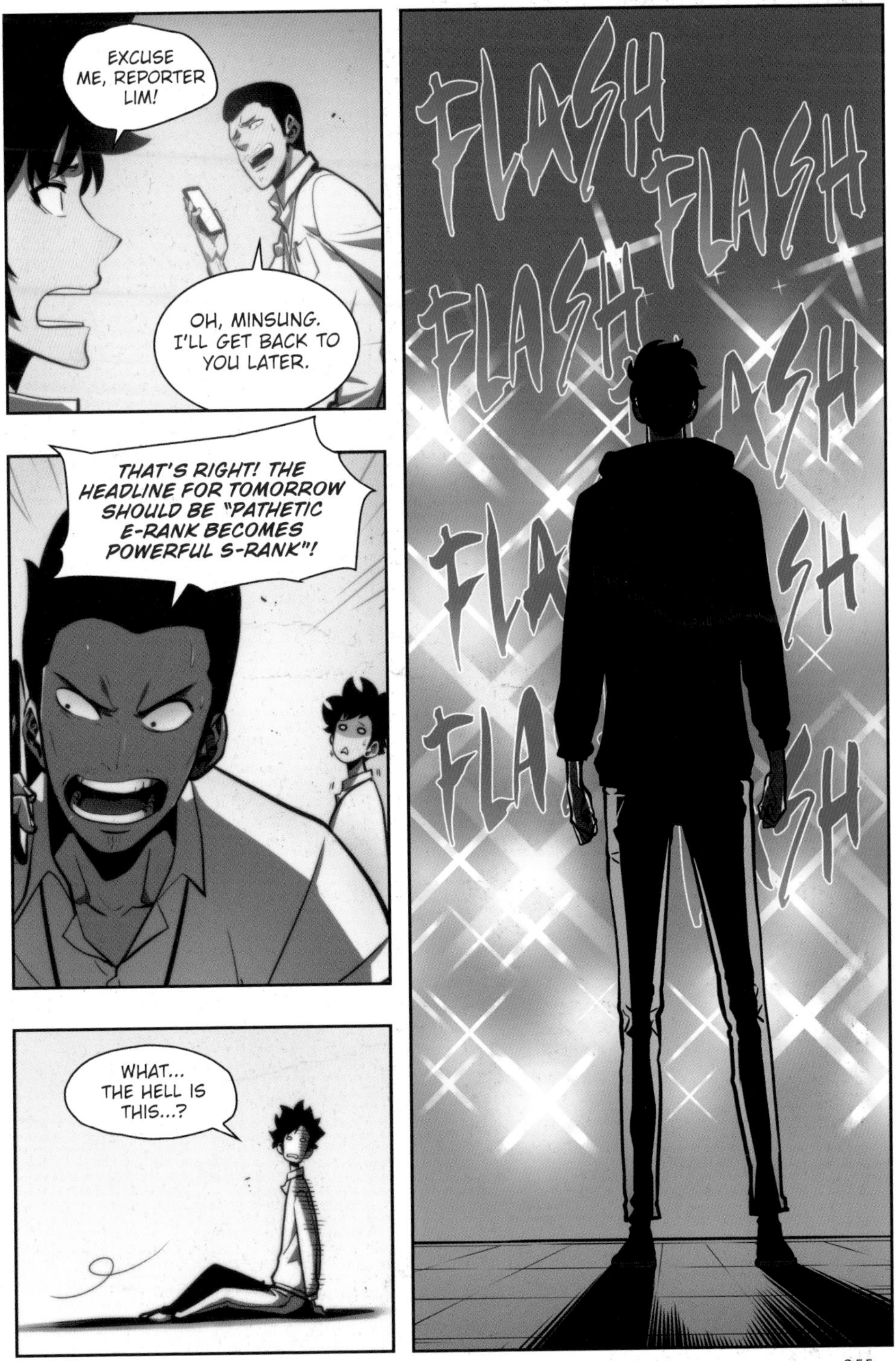
EXCUSE ME, REPORTER LIM!
OH, MINSUNG. I'LL GET BACK TO YOU LATER.
THAT'S RIGHT! THE HEADLINE FOR TOMORROW SHOULD BE "PATHETIC E-RANK BECOMES POWERFUL S-RANK"!
WHAT... THE HELL IS THIS...?
FLASH
FLASH
FLASH

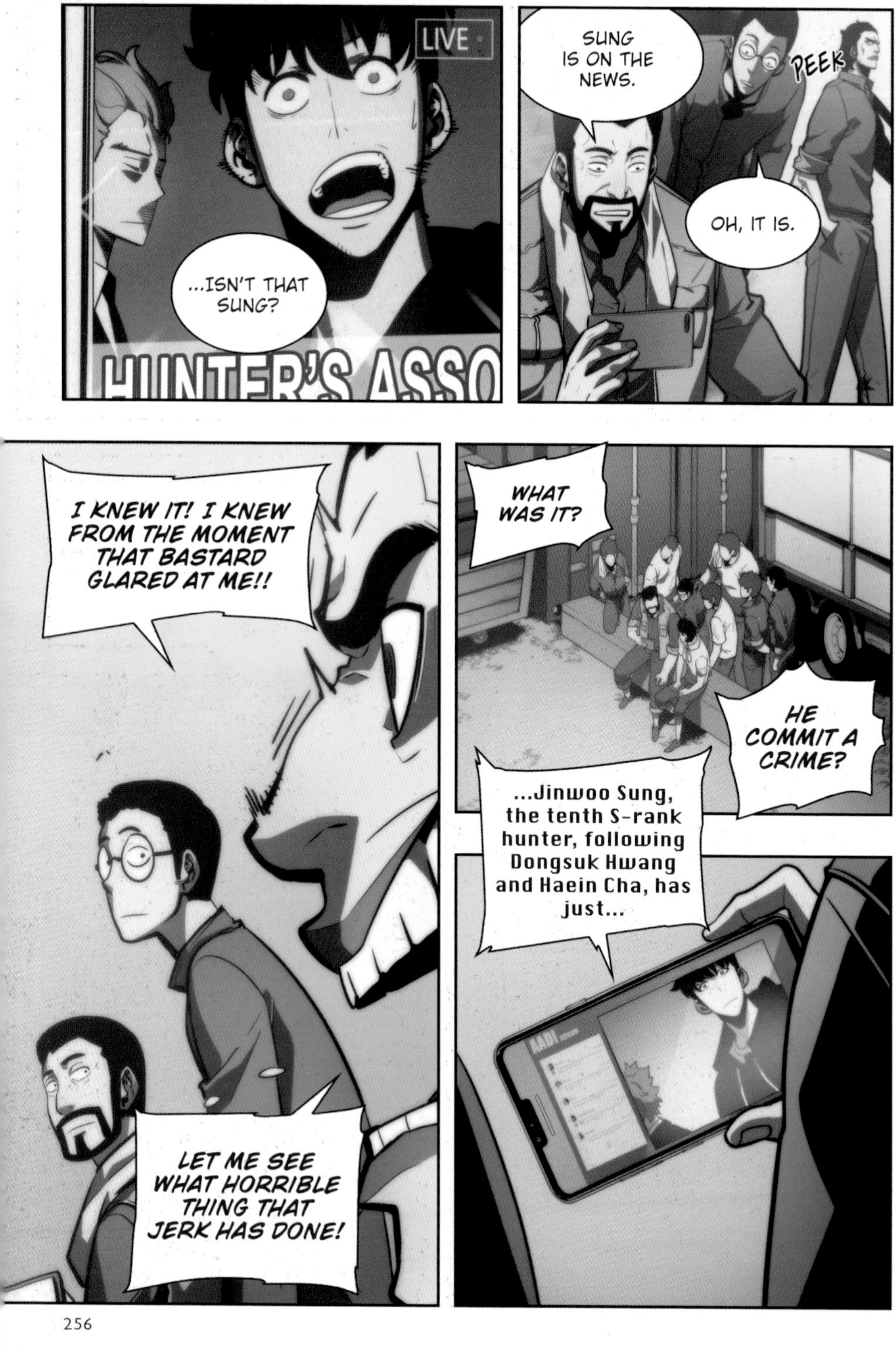
LIVE
HUNTER'S ASSO
...ISN'T THAT SUNG?
SUNG IS ON THE NEWS.
PEEK
OH, IT IS.
I KNEW IT! I KNEW FROM THE MOMENT THAT BASTARD GLARED AT ME!!
LET ME SEE WHAT HORRIBLE THING THAT JERK HAS DONE!
WHAT WAS IT?
HE COMMIT A CRIME?
...Jinwoo Sung, the tenth S-rank hunter, following Dongsuk Hwang and Haein Cha, has just...

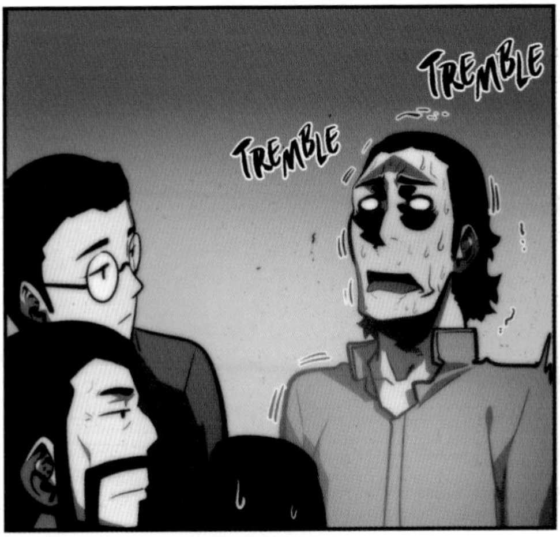
TREMBLE
TREMBLE

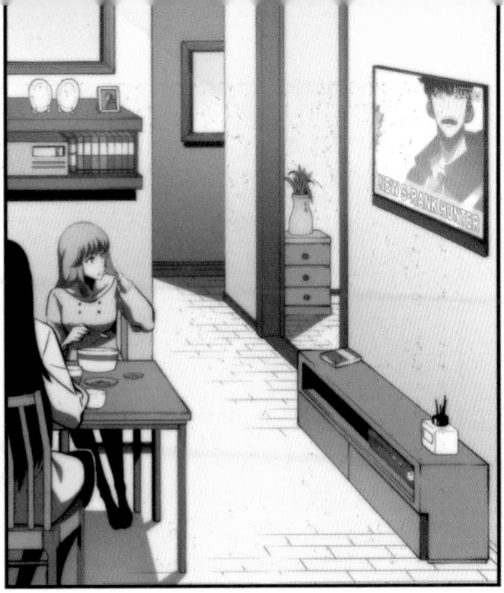
NEW S-RANK HUNTER

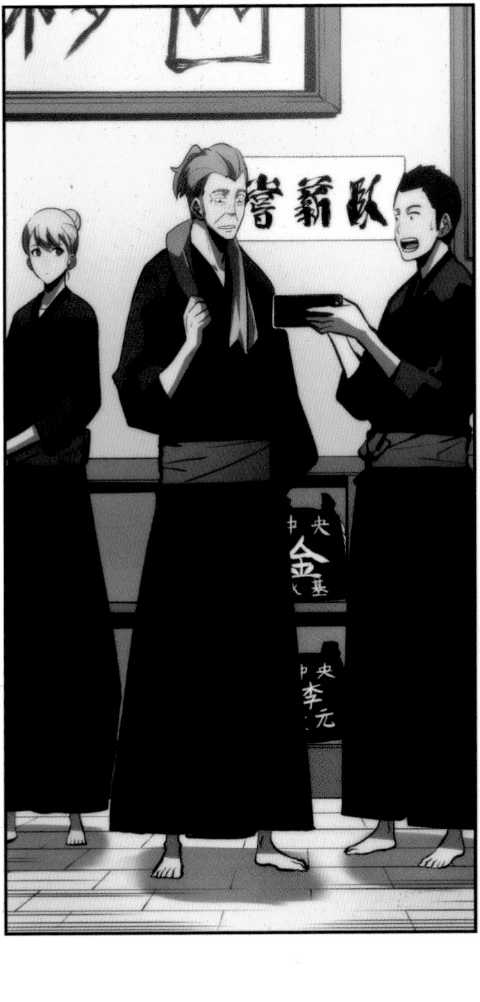

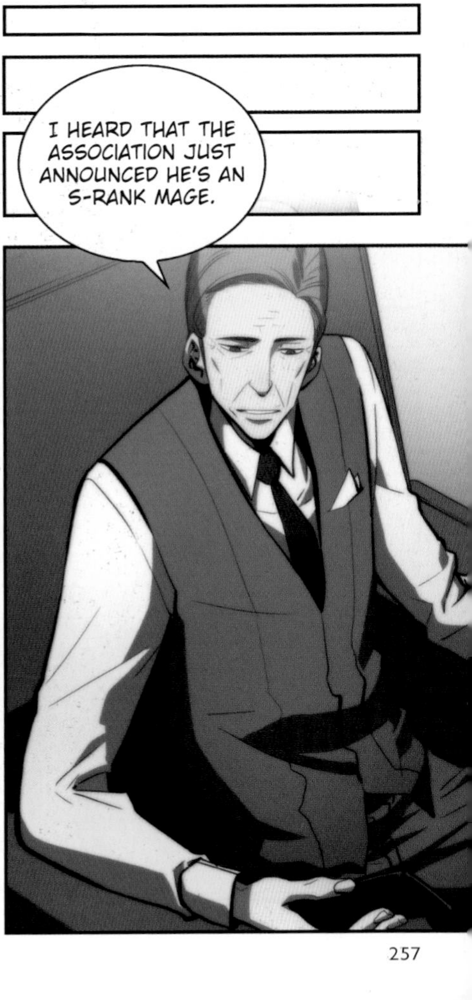
I HEARD THAT THE ASSOCIATION JUST ANNOUNCED HE'S AN S-RANK MAGE.

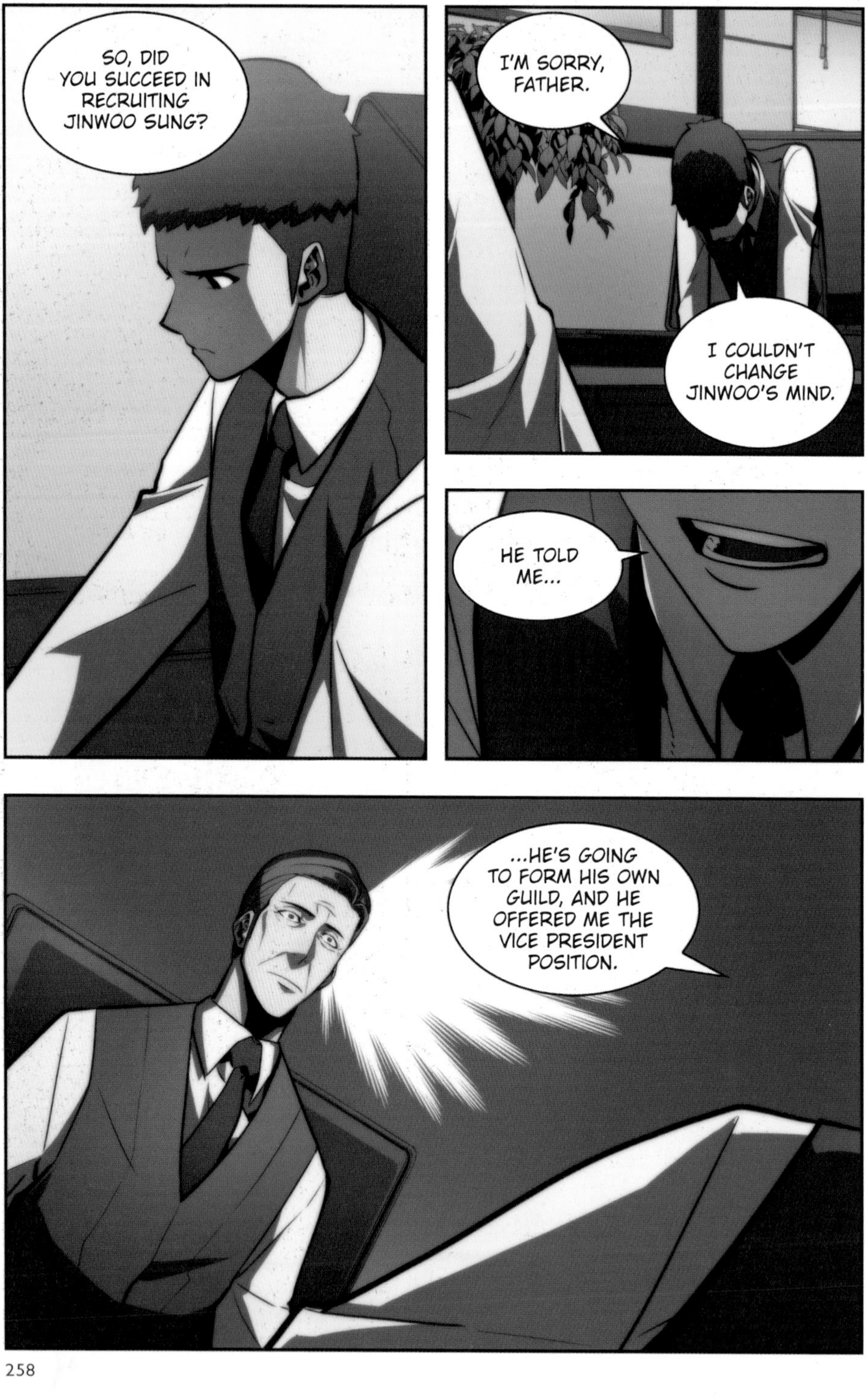
SO, DID YOU SUCCEED IN RECRUITING JINWOO SUNG?
I'M SORRY, FATHER.
I COULDN'T CHANGE JINWOO'S MIND.
HE TOLD ME...
...HE'S GOING TO FORM HIS OWN GUILD, AND HE OFFERED ME THE VICE PRESIDENT POSITION.

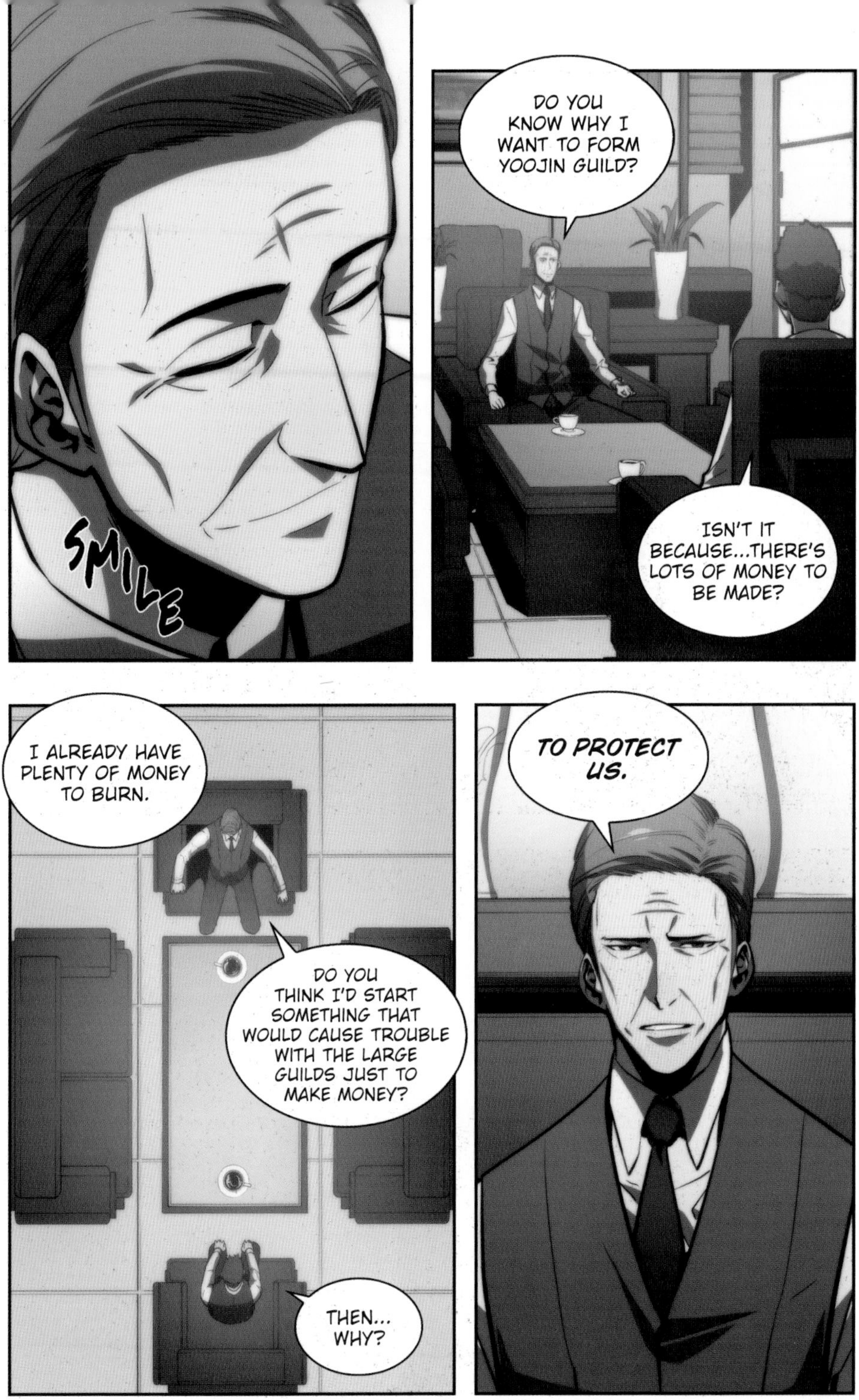
SMILE
DO YOU KNOW WHY I WANT TO FORM YOOJIN GUILD?
ISN'T IT BECAUSE...THERE'S LOTS OF MONEY TO BE MADE?
I ALREADY HAVE PLENTY OF MONEY TO BURN.
DO YOU THINK I'D START SOMETHING THAT WOULD CAUSE TROUBLE WITH THE LARGE GUILDS JUST TO MAKE MONEY?
THEN... WHY?
TO PROTECT US.

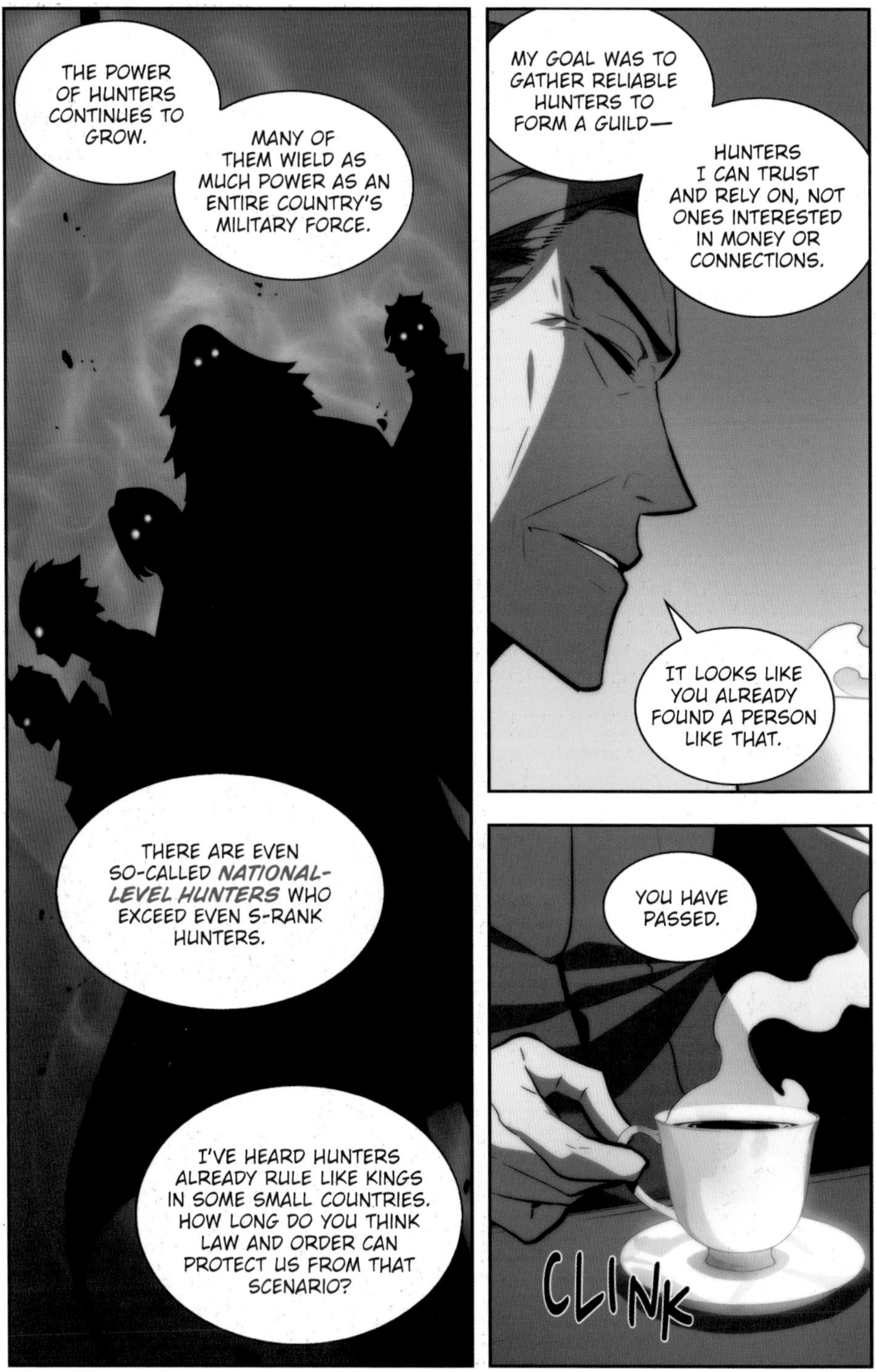
THE POWER OF HUNTERS CONTINUES TO GROW.
MANY OF THEM WIELD AS MUCH POWER AS AN ENTIRE COUNTRY'S MILITARY FORCE.
THERE ARE EVEN SO-CALLED *NATIONAL-LEVEL HUNTERS* WHO EXCEED EVEN S-RANK HUNTERS.
I'VE HEARD HUNTERS ALREADY RULE LIKE KINGS IN SOME SMALL COUNTRIES. HOW LONG DO YOU THINK LAW AND ORDER CAN PROTECT US FROM THAT SCENARIO?
MY GOAL WAS TO GATHER RELIABLE HUNTERS TO FORM A GUILD—
HUNTERS I CAN TRUST AND RELY ON, NOT ONES INTERESTED IN MONEY OR CONNECTIONS.
IT LOOKS LIKE YOU ALREADY FOUND A PERSON LIKE THAT.
YOU HAVE PASSED.
CLINK

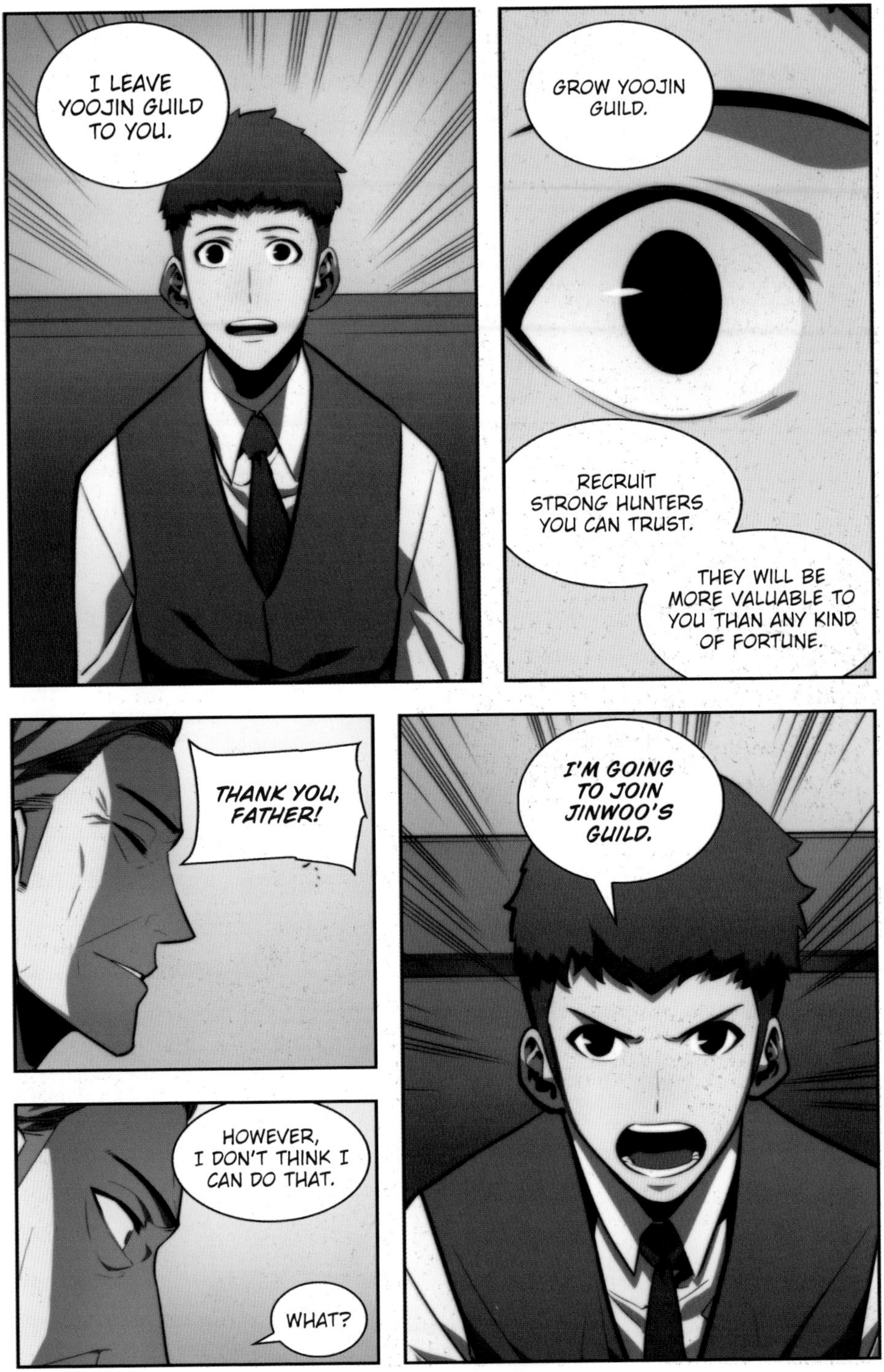
I LEAVE YOOJIN GUILD TO YOU.
GROW YOOJIN GUILD.
RECRUIT STRONG HUNTERS YOU CAN TRUST.
THEY WILL BE MORE VALUABLE TO YOU THAN ANY KIND OF FORTUNE.
THANK YOU, FATHER!
HOWEVER, I DON'T THINK I CAN DO THAT.
WHAT?
I'M GOING TO JOIN JINWOO'S GUILD.

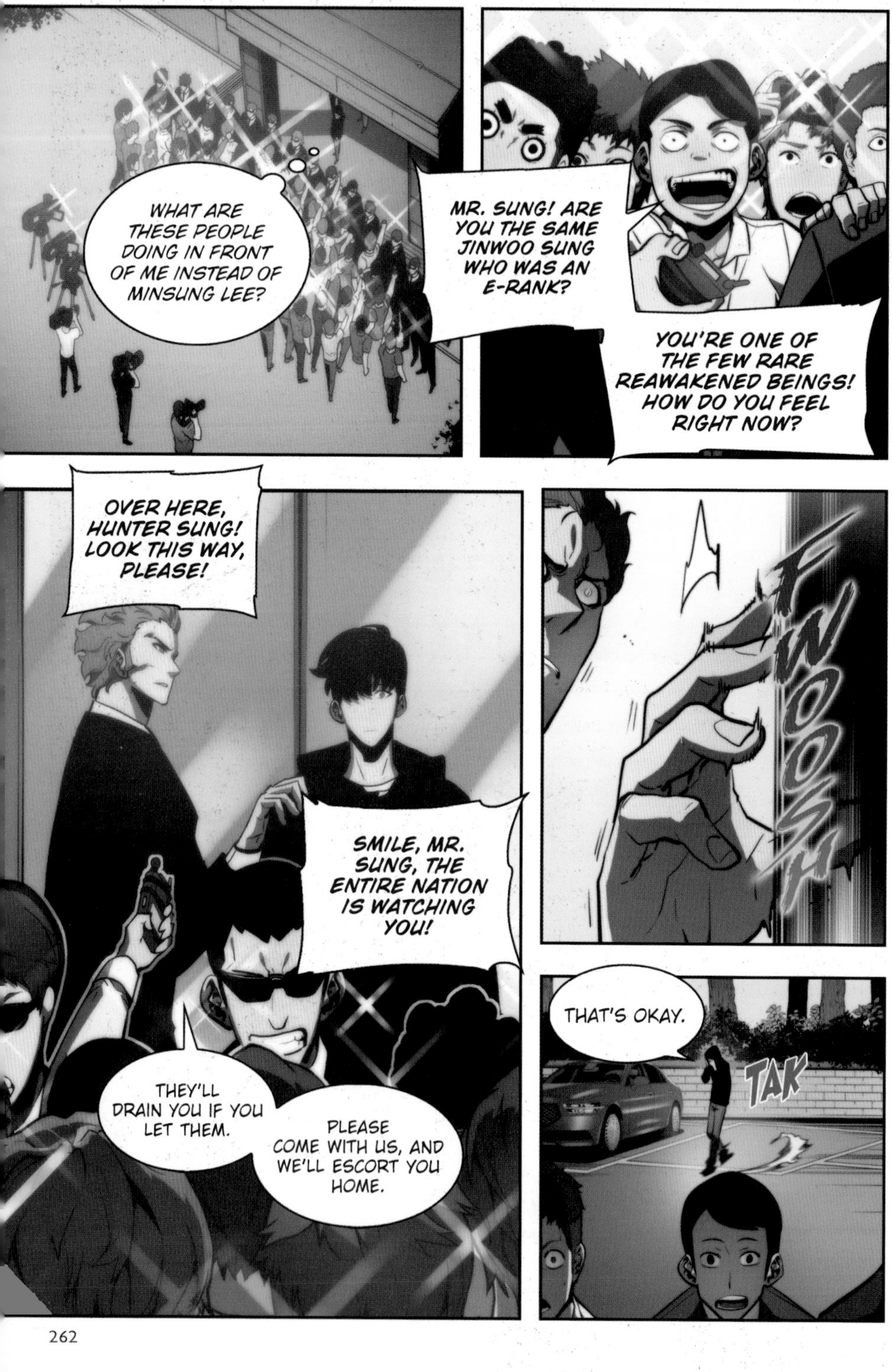
WHAT ARE THESE PEOPLE DOING IN FRONT OF ME INSTEAD OF MINSUNG LEE?
MR. SUNG! ARE YOU THE SAME JINWOO SUNG WHO WAS AN E-RANK?
YOU'RE ONE OF THE FEW RARE REAWAKENED BEINGS! HOW DO YOU FEEL RIGHT NOW?
OVER HERE, HUNTER SUNG! LOOK THIS WAY, PLEASE!
SMILE, MR. SUNG, THE ENTIRE NATION IS WATCHING YOU!
THEY'LL DRAIN YOU IF YOU LET THEM.
PLEASE COME WITH US, AND WE'LL ESCORT YOU HOME.
WHOOSH
THAT'S OKAY.
TAK

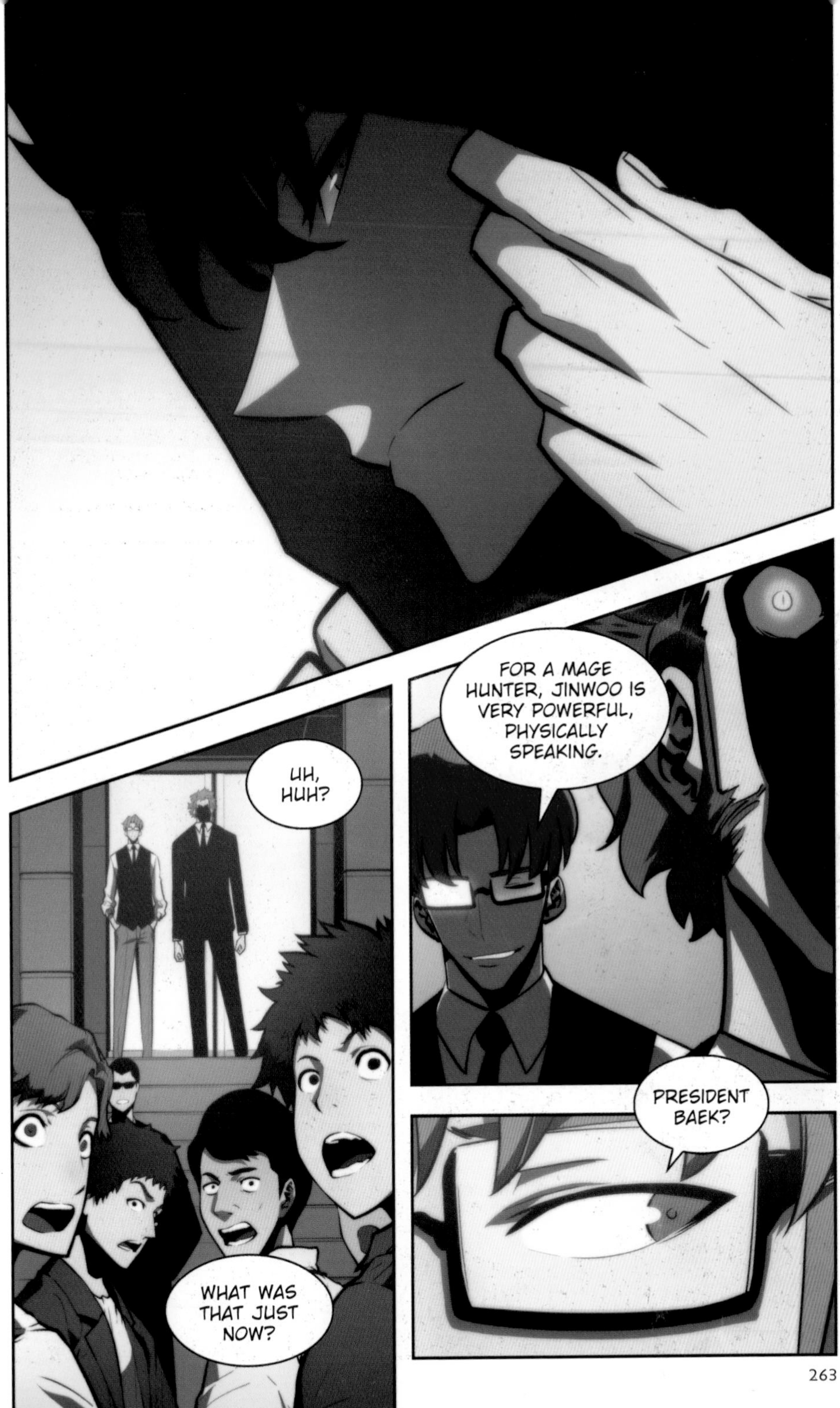
UH, HUH?
WHAT WAS THAT JUST NOW?
FOR A MAGE HUNTER, JINWOO IS VERY POWERFUL, PHYSICALLY SPEAKING.
PRESIDENT BAEK?

HE'S SO QUICK!

HE WAS TOO FAST EVEN FOR MY EYES.

WHAT INCREDIBLE POWER! IS THIS REALLY JINWOO?

THE PHYSICAL POWER HE JUST DEMONSTRATED!

AND THE MAGIC POWER THAT CAME FROM THE EVALUATION ROOM!

HE'S INCOMPARABLY STRONGER THAN BEFORE.

I SAVED THE REMAINING THREE.

AS A SIDE- GUILL HAVE A ASK A REQUEST.

HUNTER SUNG IS STRONGER THAN BEFORE!

BE THANKING ME, FIRST OF ALL?

CURRENTLY, JINWOO SUNG IS LIKELY EVEN MORE POWERFUL THAN US.

I ALREADY KNEW HE WAS STRONG...

...BUT THAT'S NOT THE ISSUE.

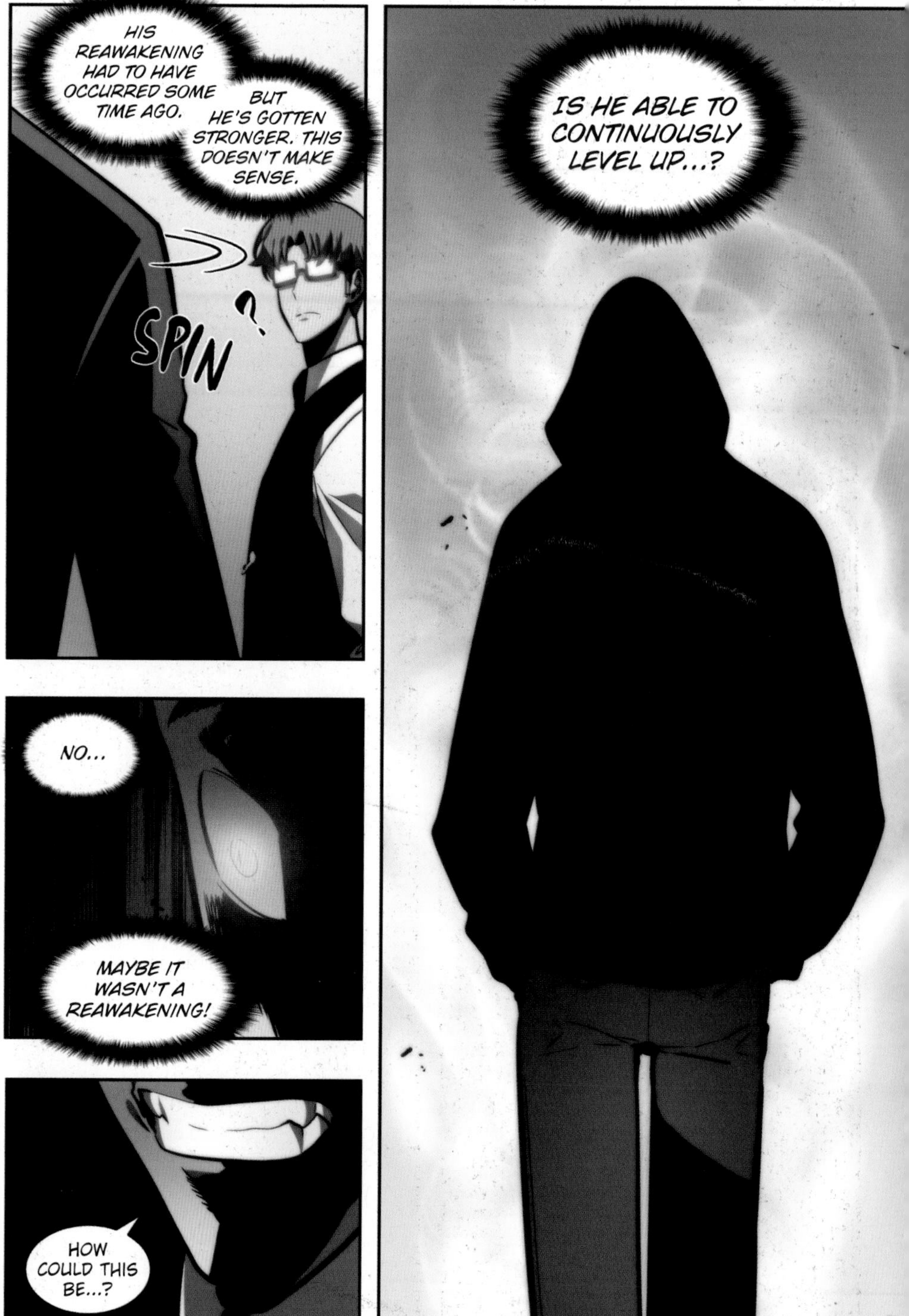
HIS REAWAKENING HAD TO HAVE OCCURRED SOME TIME AGO.
BUT HE'S GOTTEN STRONGER. THIS DOESN'T MAKE SENSE.
SPIN
?
NO...
MAYBE IT WASN'T A REAWAKENING!
HOW COULD THIS BE...?
IS HE ABLE TO CONTINUOUSLY LEVEL UP...?

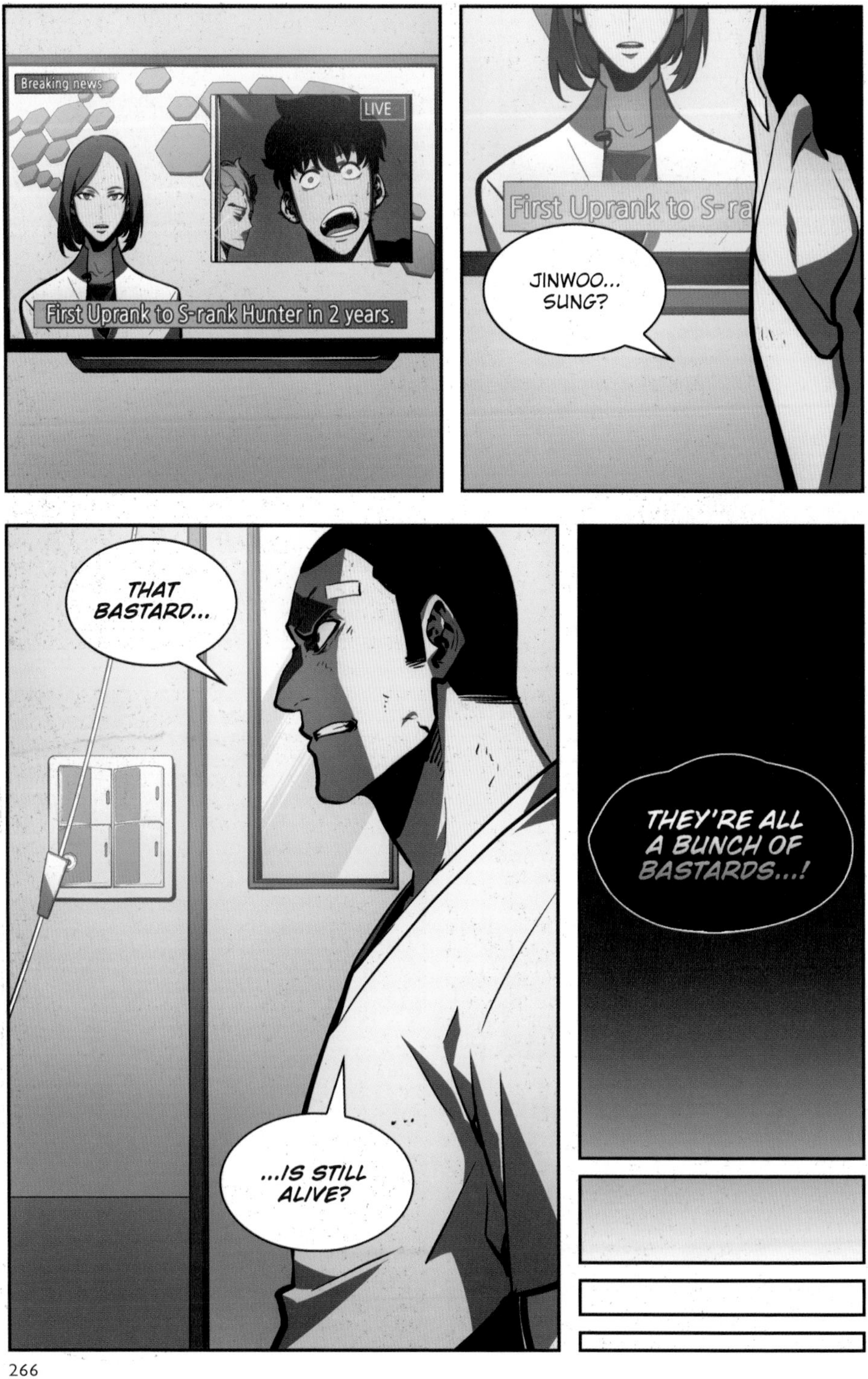

Breaking news
LIVE
First Uprank to S-rank Hunter in 2 years.
First Uprank to S-ra
JINWOO... SUNG?
THAT BASTARD...
...IS STILL ALIVE?
THEY'RE ALL A BUNCH OF BASTARDS...!

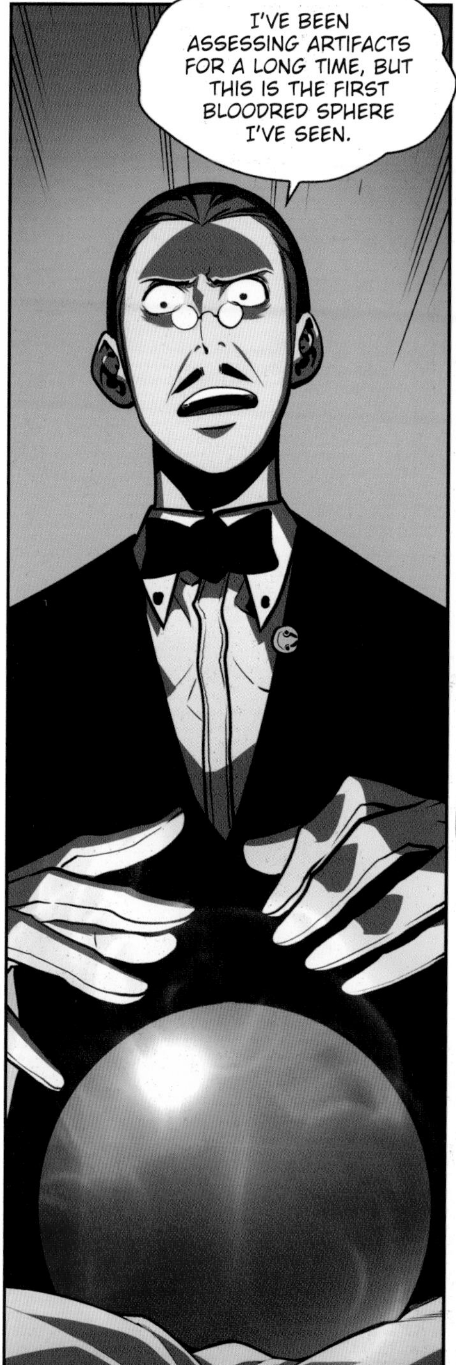
I'VE BEEN ASSESSING ARTIFACTS FOR A LONG TIME, BUT THIS IS THE FIRST BLOODRED SPHERE I'VE SEEN.
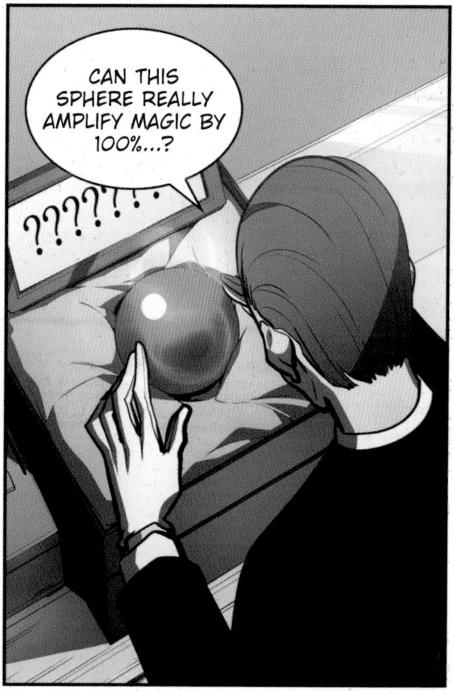
CAN THIS SPHERE REALLY AMPLIFY MAGIC BY 100%...?
????!!!
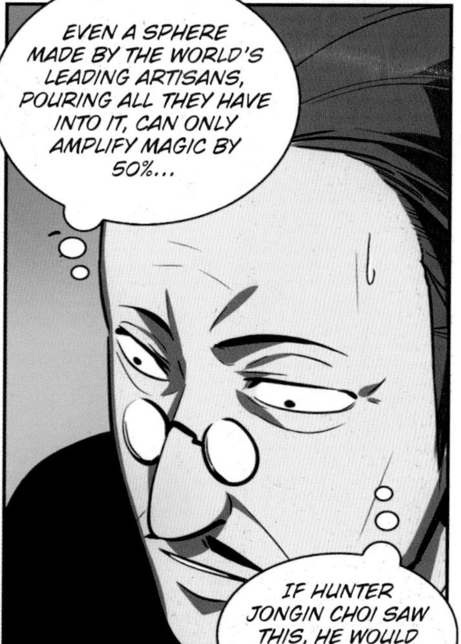
EVEN A SPHERE MADE BY THE WORLD'S LEADING ARTISANS, POURING ALL THEY HAVE INTO IT, CAN ONLY AMPLIFY MAGIC BY 50%...
IF HUNTER JONGIN CHOI SAW THIS, HE WOULD BRING A SUITCASE FULL OF MONEY.

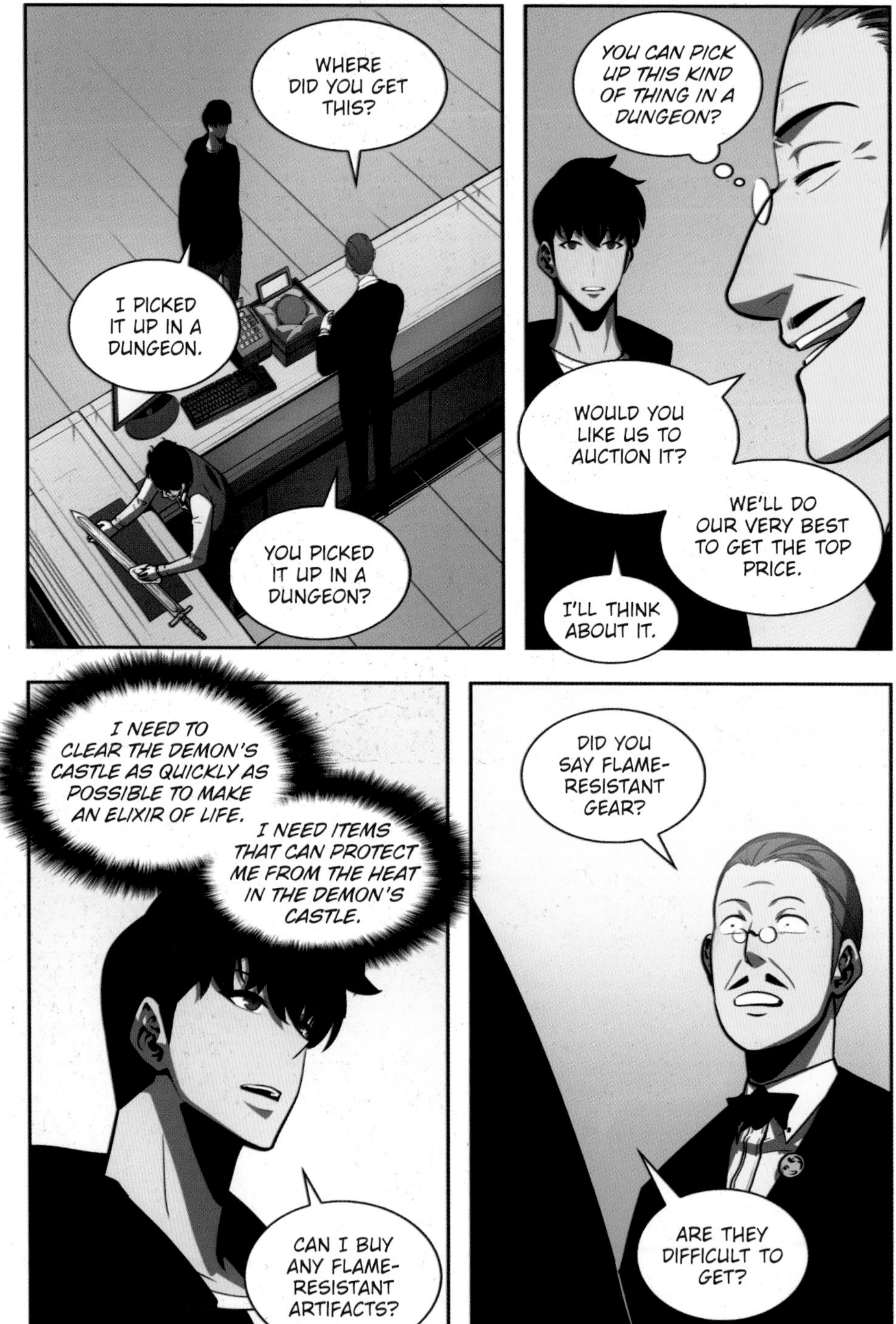
WHERE DID YOU GET THIS?
I PICKED IT UP IN A DUNGEON.
YOU PICKED IT UP IN A DUNGEON?
YOU CAN PICK UP THIS KIND OF THING IN A DUNGEON?
WOULD YOU LIKE US TO AUCTION IT?
WE'LL DO OUR VERY BEST TO GET THE TOP PRICE.
I'LL THINK ABOUT IT.
I NEED TO CLEAR THE DEMON'S CASTLE AS QUICKLY AS POSSIBLE TO MAKE AN ELIXIR OF LIFE.
I NEED ITEMS THAT CAN PROTECT ME FROM THE HEAT IN THE DEMON'S CASTLE.
CAN I BUY ANY FLAME-RESISTANT ARTIFACTS?
DID YOU SAY FLAME-RESISTANT GEAR?
ARE THEY DIFFICULT TO GET?

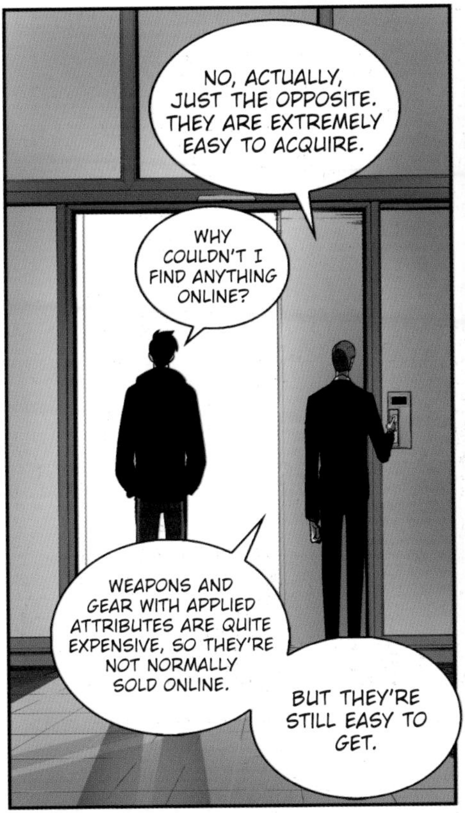
NO, ACTUALLY, JUST THE OPPOSITE. THEY ARE EXTREMELY EASY TO ACQUIRE.
WHY COULDN'T I FIND ANYTHING ONLINE?
WEAPONS AND GEAR WITH APPLIED ATTRIBUTES ARE QUITE EXPENSIVE, SO THEY'RE NOT NORMALLY SOLD ONLINE.
BUT THEY'RE STILL EASY TO GET.

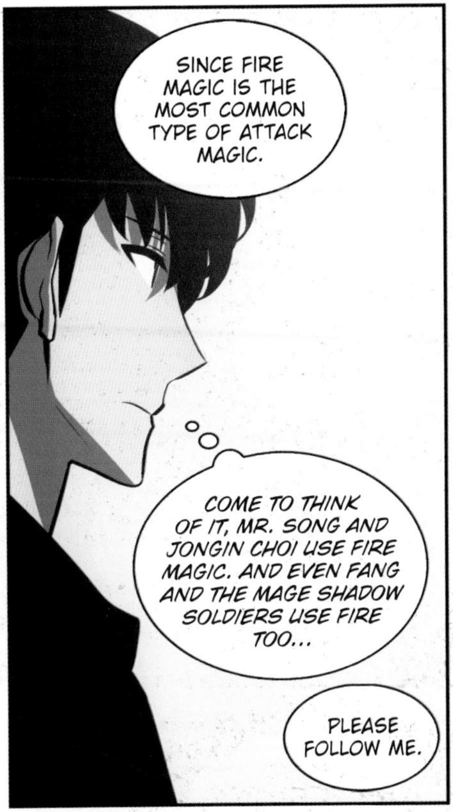
SINCE FIRE MAGIC IS THE MOST COMMON TYPE OF ATTACK MAGIC.
COME TO THINK OF IT, MR. SONG AND JONGIN CHOI USE FIRE MAGIC. AND EVEN FANG AND THE MAGE SHADOW SOLDIERS USE FIRE TOO...
PLEASE FOLLOW ME.

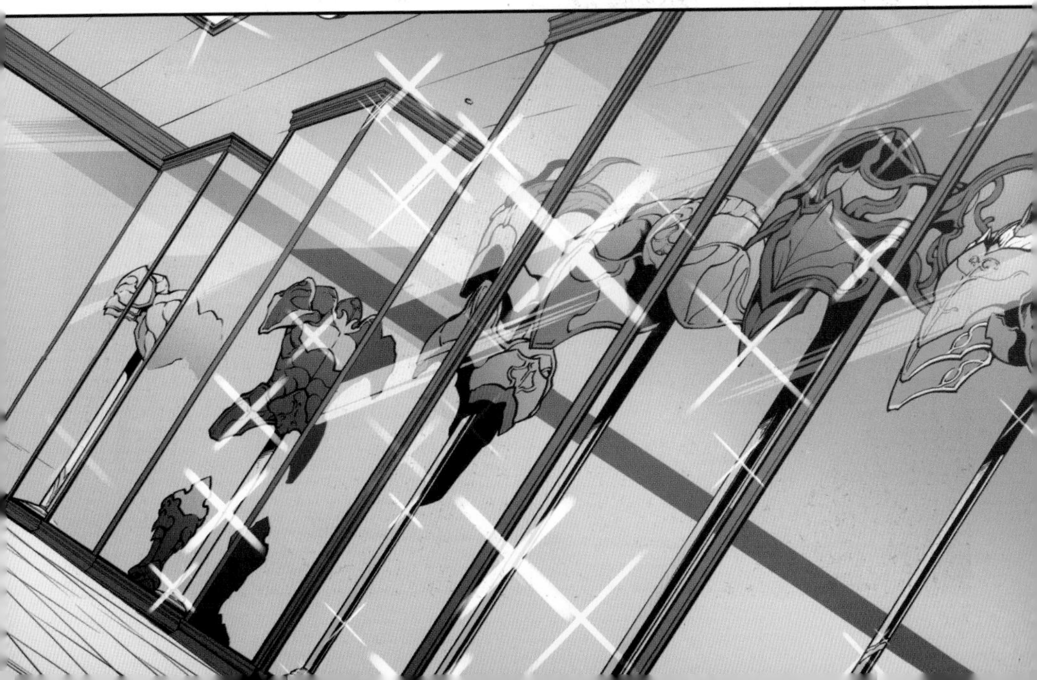

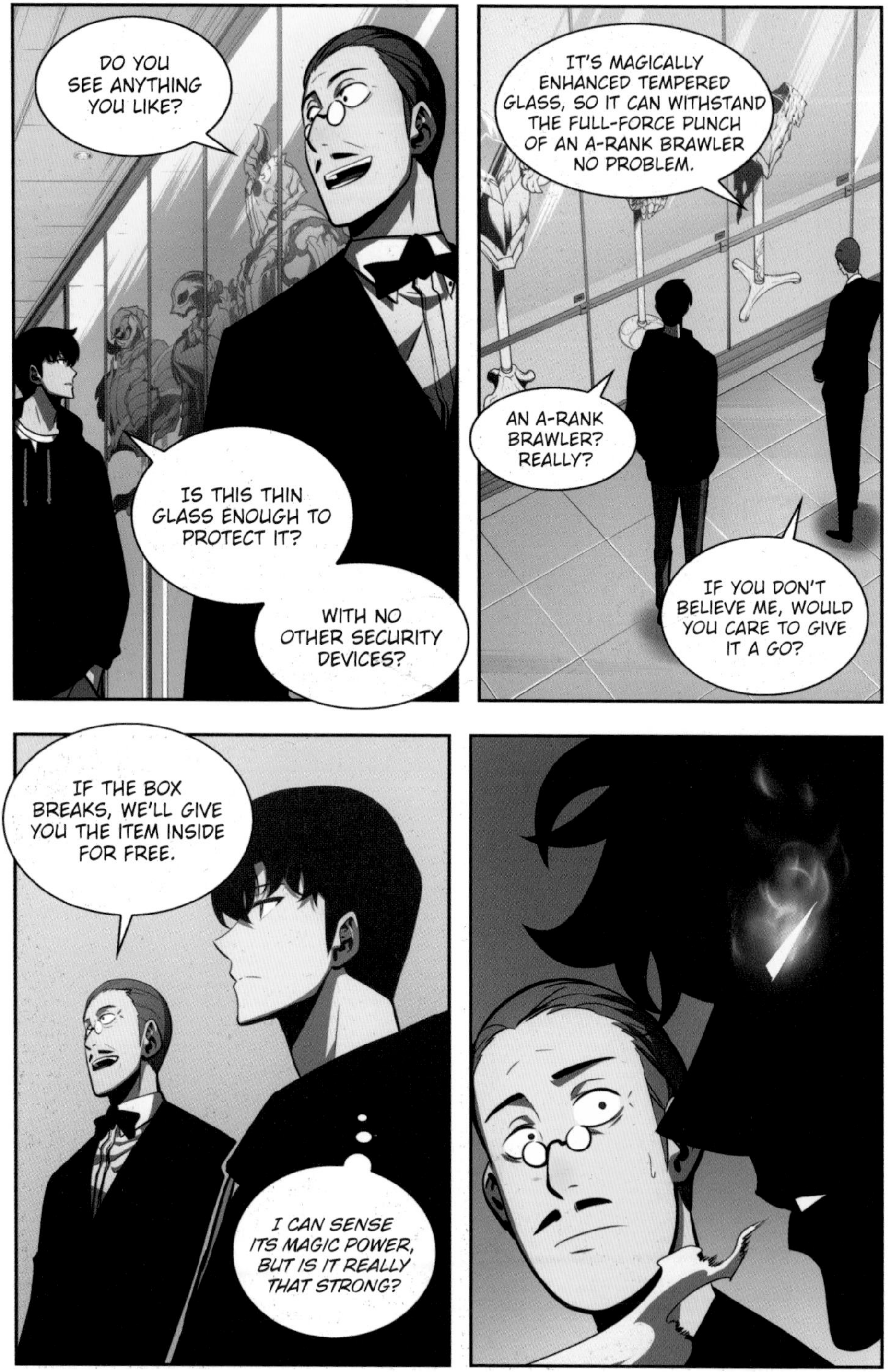
DO YOU SEE ANYTHING YOU LIKE?
IS THIS THIN GLASS ENOUGH TO PROTECT IT?
WITH NO OTHER SECURITY DEVICES?
IT'S MAGICALLY ENHANCED TEMPERED GLASS, SO IT CAN WITHSTAND THE FULL-FORCE PUNCH OF AN A-RANK BRAWLER NO PROBLEM.
AN A-RANK BRAWLER? REALLY?
IF YOU DON'T BELIEVE ME, WOULD YOU CARE TO GIVE IT A GO?
IF THE BOX BREAKS, WE'LL GIVE YOU THE ITEM INSIDE FOR FREE.
I CAN SENSE ITS MAGIC POWER, BUT IS IT REALLY THAT STRONG?

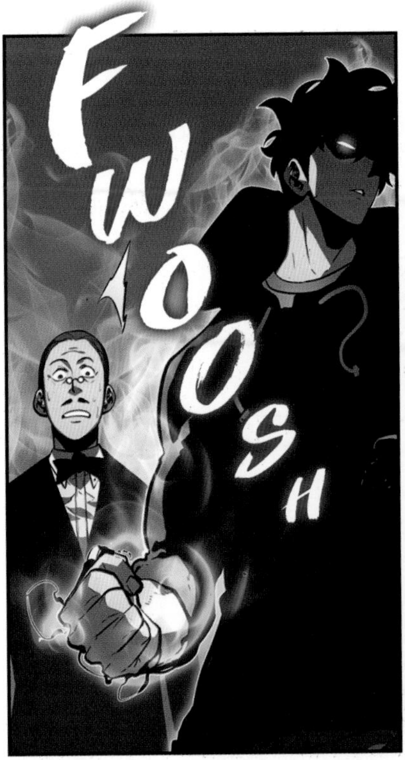
FWOOSH

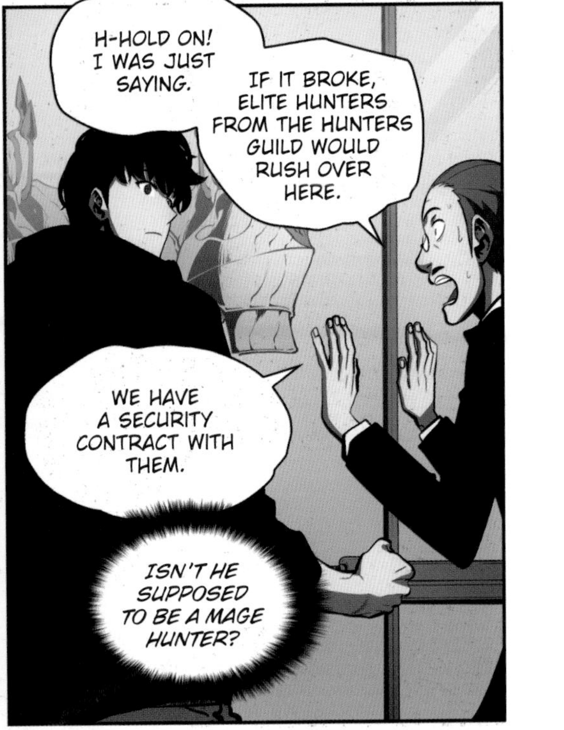
H-HOLD ON! I WAS JUST SAYING.
IF IT BROKE, ELITE HUNTERS FROM THE HUNTERS GUILD WOULD RUSH OVER HERE.
WE HAVE A SECURITY CONTRACT WITH THEM.
ISN'T HE SUPPOSED TO BE A MAGE HUNTER?

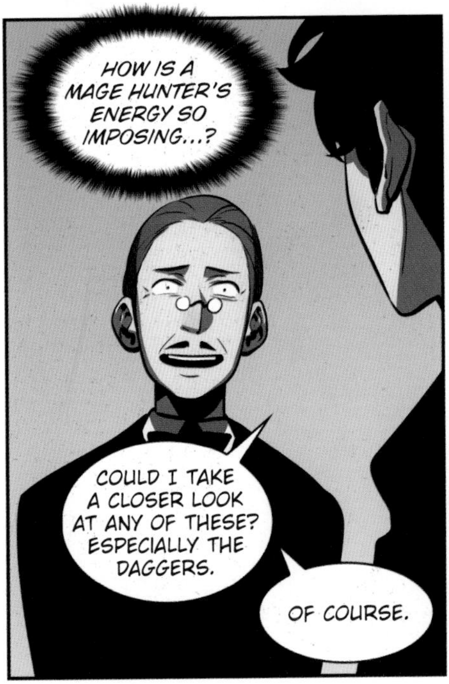
HOW IS A MAGE HUNTER'S ENERGY SO IMPOSING...?
COULD I TAKE A CLOSER LOOK AT ANY OF THESE? ESPECIALLY THE DAGGERS.
OF COURSE.

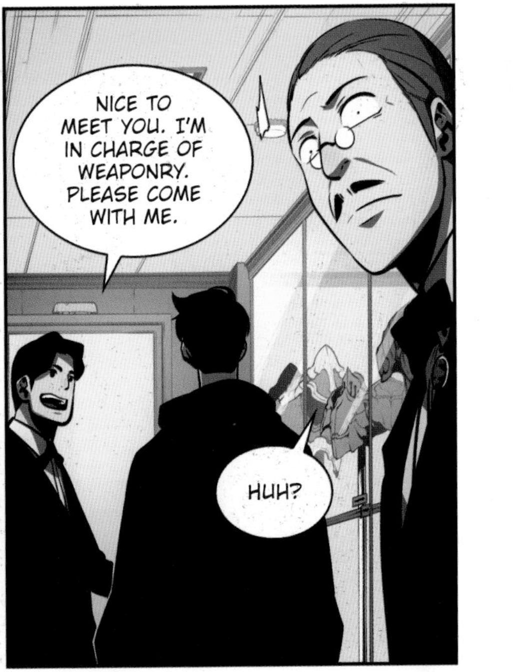
NICE TO MEET YOU. I'M IN CHARGE OF WEAPONRY. PLEASE COME WITH ME.
HUH?

WHEN DID THIS HAPPEN?

HE DIDN'T EVEN TOUCH IT. IT COULDN'T HAVE...

SWEAT

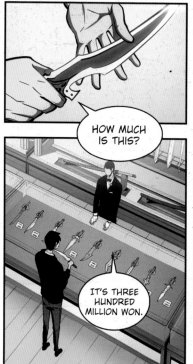

HOW MUCH IS THIS?

IT'S THREE HUNDRED MILLION WON.

IT'S NOT AS GOOD AS KNIGHT KILLER, WITH A B-LEVEL ACQUISITION DIFFICULTY, BUT IT'S MORE EXPENSIVE?

ALTHOUGH, IT'S PROBABLY A SIMILAR LEVEL TO KASAKA'S VENOM FANG.

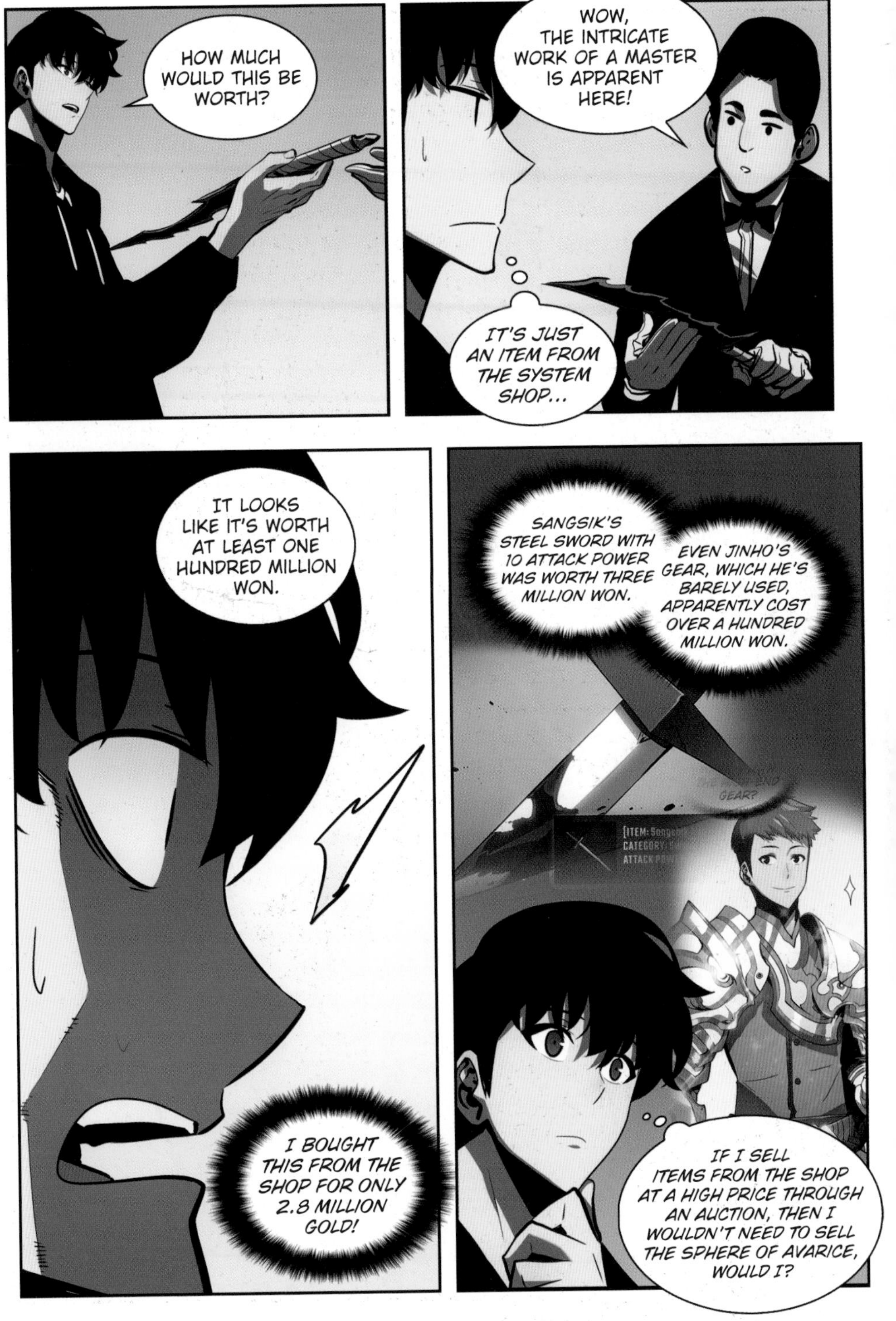

HOW MUCH WOULD THIS BE WORTH?
WOW, THE INTRICATE WORK OF A MASTER IS APPARENT HERE!
IT'S JUST AN ITEM FROM THE SYSTEM SHOP...
IT LOOKS LIKE IT'S WORTH AT LEAST ONE HUNDRED MILLION WON.
I BOUGHT THIS FROM THE SHOP FOR ONLY 2.8 MILLION GOLD!
SANGSIK'S STEEL SWORD WITH 10 ATTACK POWER WAS WORTH THREE MILLION WON.
EVEN JINHO'S GEAR, WHICH HE'S BARELY USED, APPARENTLY COST OVER A HUNDRED MILLION WON.
IF I SELL ITEMS FROM THE SHOP AT A HIGH PRICE THROUGH AN AUCTION, THEN I WOULDN'T NEED TO SELL THE SPHERE OF AVARICE, WOULD I?

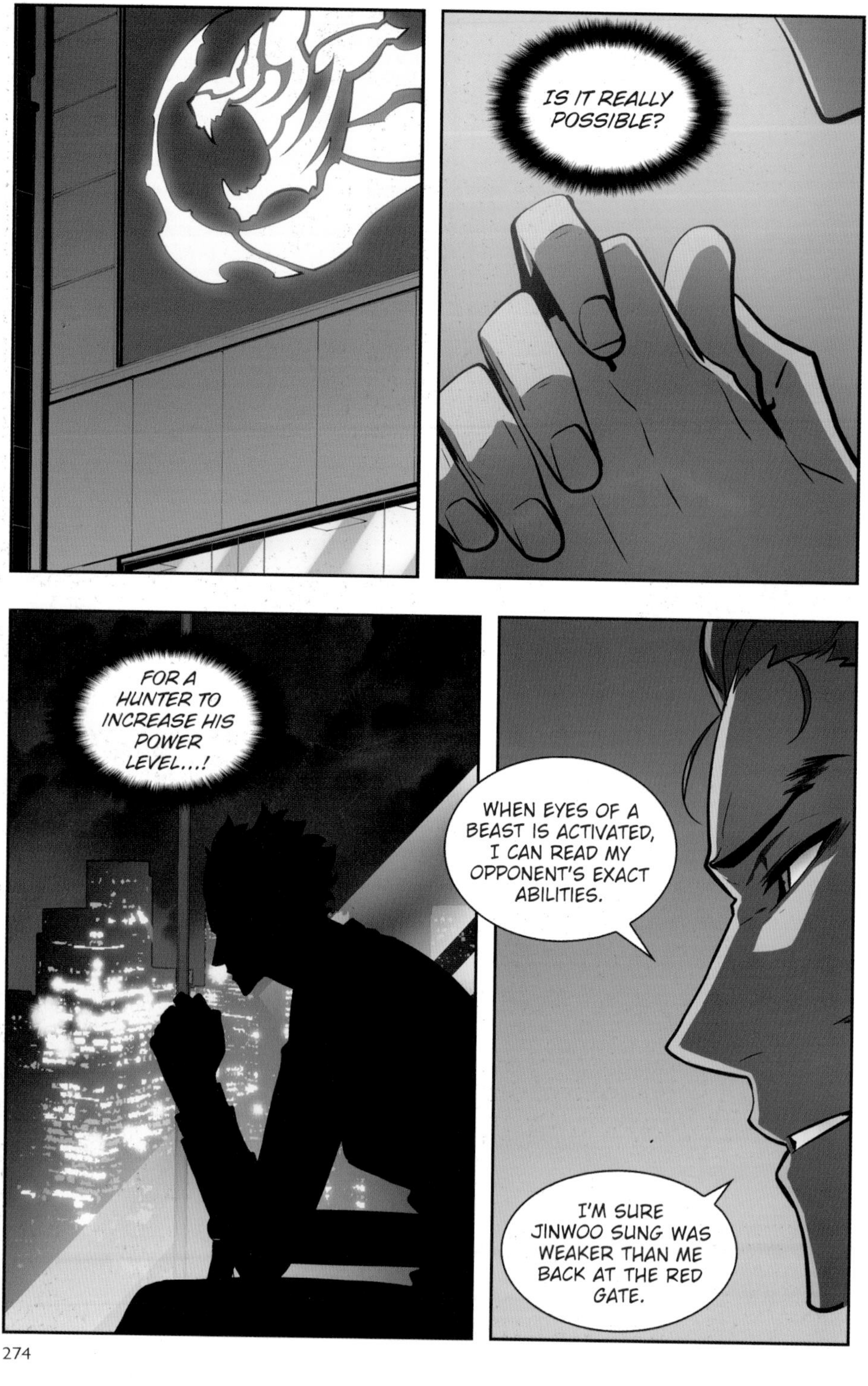
IS IT REALLY POSSIBLE?
FOR A HUNTER TO INCREASE HIS POWER LEVEL...!
WHEN EYES OF A BEAST IS ACTIVATED, I CAN READ MY OPPONENT'S EXACT ABILITIES.
I'M SURE JINWOO SUNG WAS WEAKER THAN ME BACK AT THE RED GATE.

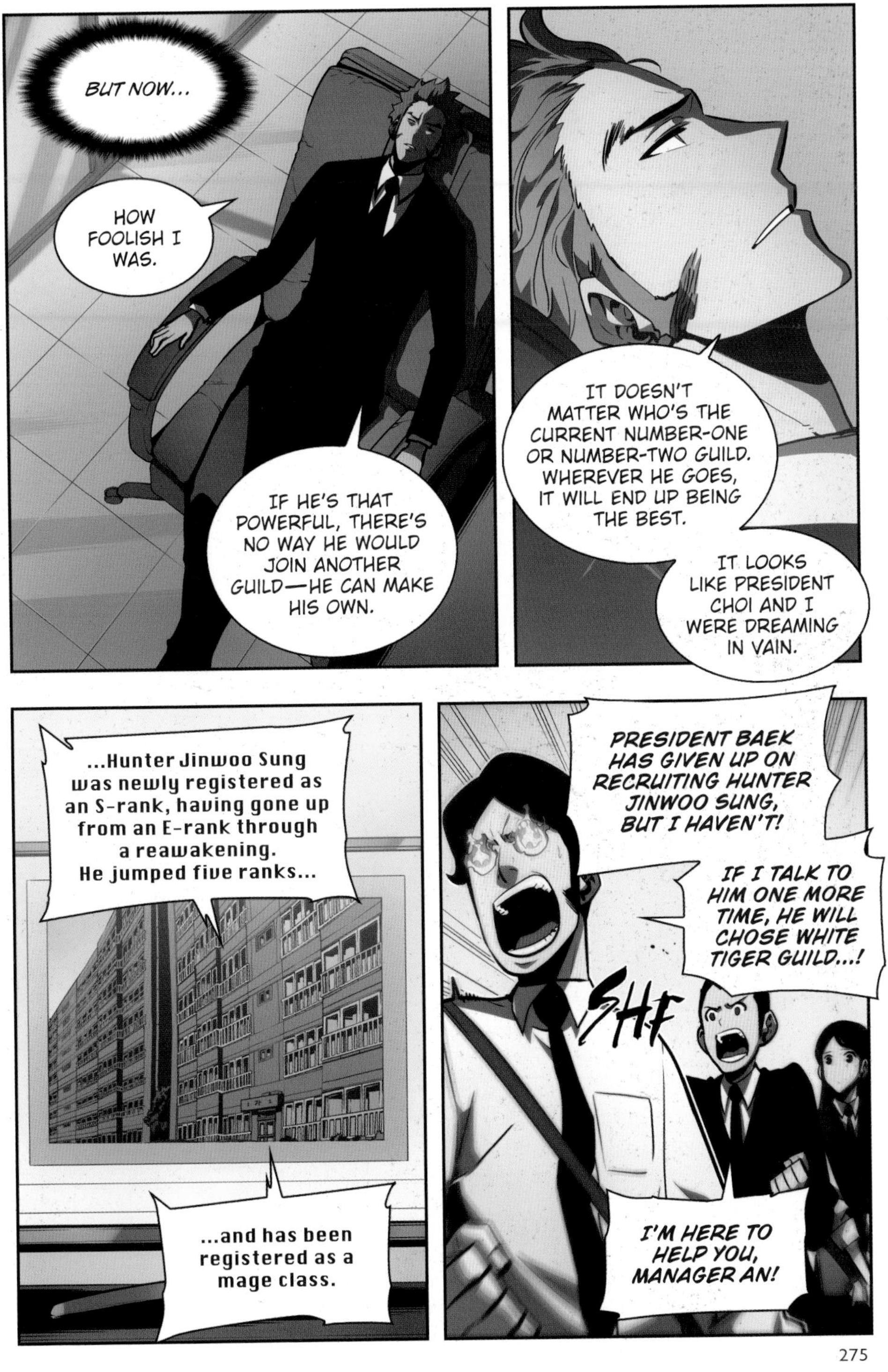
BUT NOW...
HOW FOOLISH I WAS.
IF HE'S THAT POWERFUL, THERE'S NO WAY HE WOULD JOIN ANOTHER GUILD—HE CAN MAKE HIS OWN.
IT DOESN'T MATTER WHO'S THE CURRENT NUMBER-ONE OR NUMBER-TWO GUILD. WHEREVER HE GOES, IT WILL END UP BEING THE BEST.
IT LOOKS LIKE PRESIDENT CHOI AND I WERE DREAMING IN VAIN.
...Hunter Jinwoo Sung was newly registered as an S-rank, having gone up from an E-rank through a reawakening. He jumped five ranks...
...and has been registered as a mage class.
PRESIDENT BAEK HAS GIVEN UP ON RECRUITING HUNTER JINWOO SUNG, BUT I HAVEN'T!
IF I TALK TO HIM ONE MORE TIME, HE WILL CHOSE WHITE TIGER GUILD...!
SHF
I'M HERE TO HELP YOU, MANAGER AN!

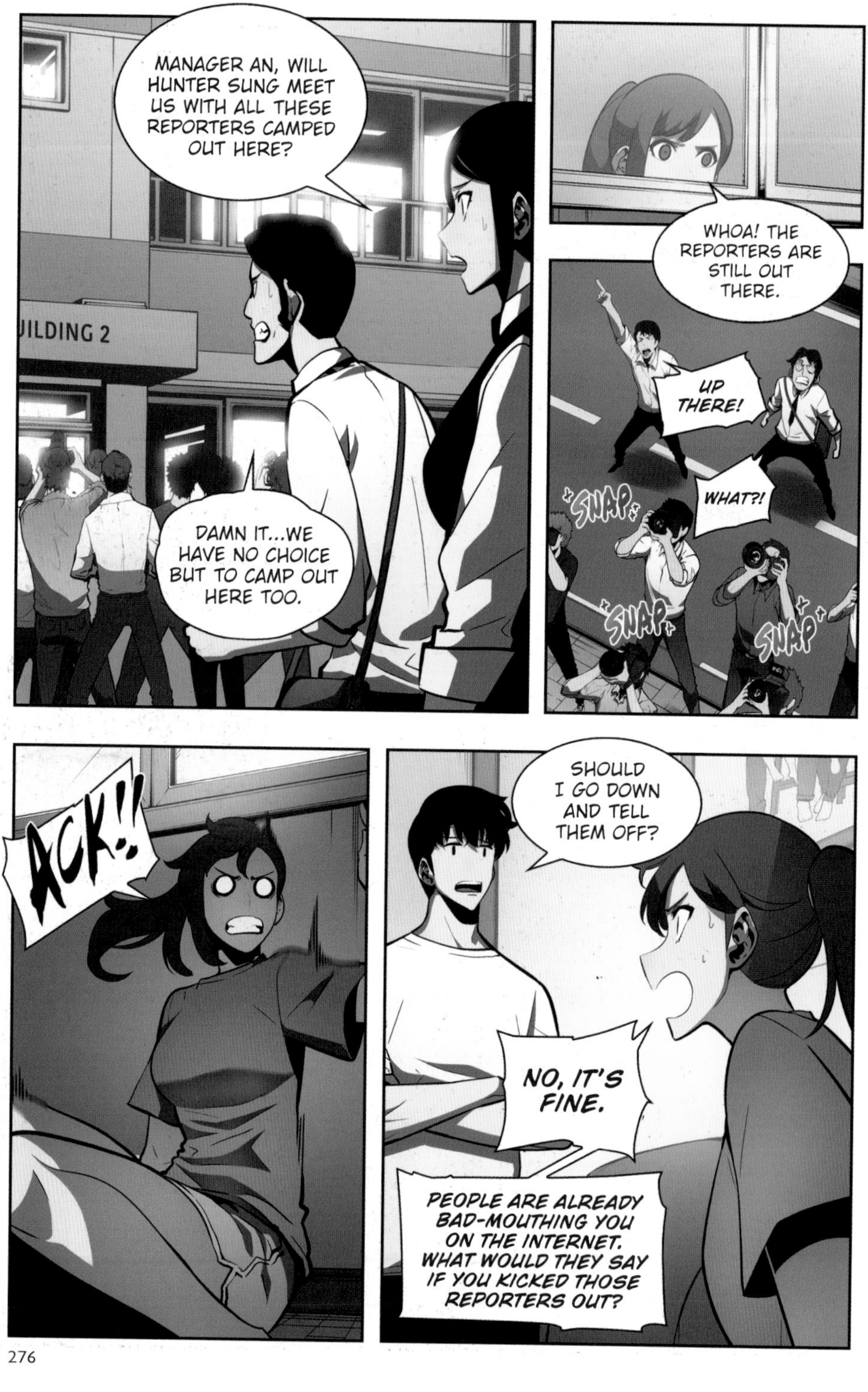
MANAGER AN, WILL HUNTER SUNG MEET US WITH ALL THESE REPORTERS CAMPED OUT HERE?
UILDING 2
DAMN IT...WE HAVE NO CHOICE BUT TO CAMP OUT HERE TOO.
WHOA! THE REPORTERS ARE STILL OUT THERE.
UP THERE!
WHAT?!
SNAP
SNAP
SNAP
ACK!!
SHOULD I GO DOWN AND TELL THEM OFF?
NO, IT'S FINE.
PEOPLE ARE ALREADY BAD-MOUTHING YOU ON THE INTERNET. WHAT WOULD THEY SAY IF YOU KICKED THOSE REPORTERS OUT?

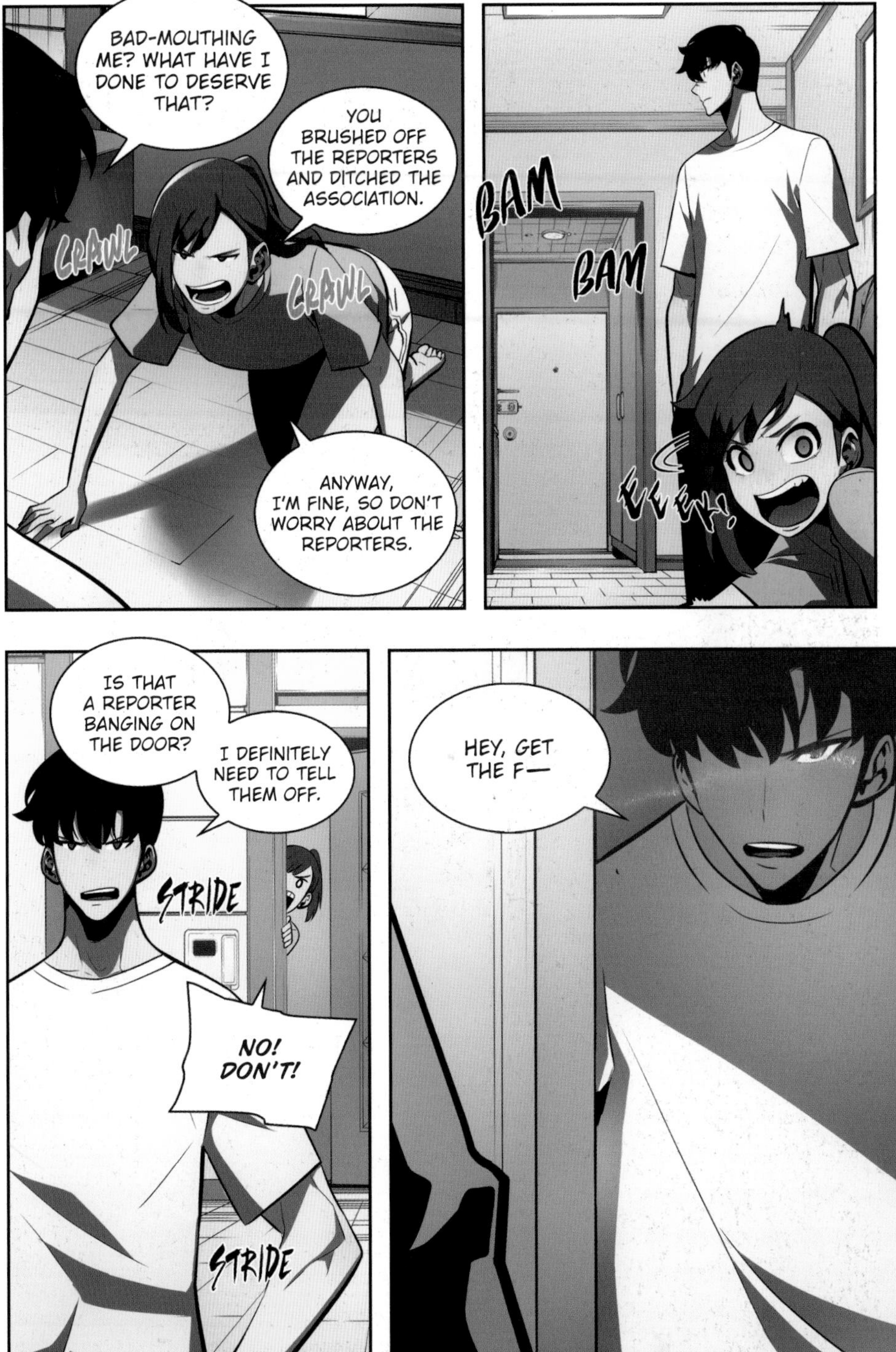
BAD-MOUTHING ME? WHAT HAVE I DONE TO DESERVE THAT?
YOU BRUSHED OFF THE REPORTERS AND DITCHED THE ASSOCIATION.
CRAWL
CRAWL
ANYWAY, I'M FINE, SO DON'T WORRY ABOUT THE REPORTERS.
BAM
BAM
EEEK!
IS THAT A REPORTER BANGING ON THE DOOR?
I DEFINITELY NEED TO TELL THEM OFF.
STRIDE
NO! DON'T!
STRIDE
HEY, GET THE F—

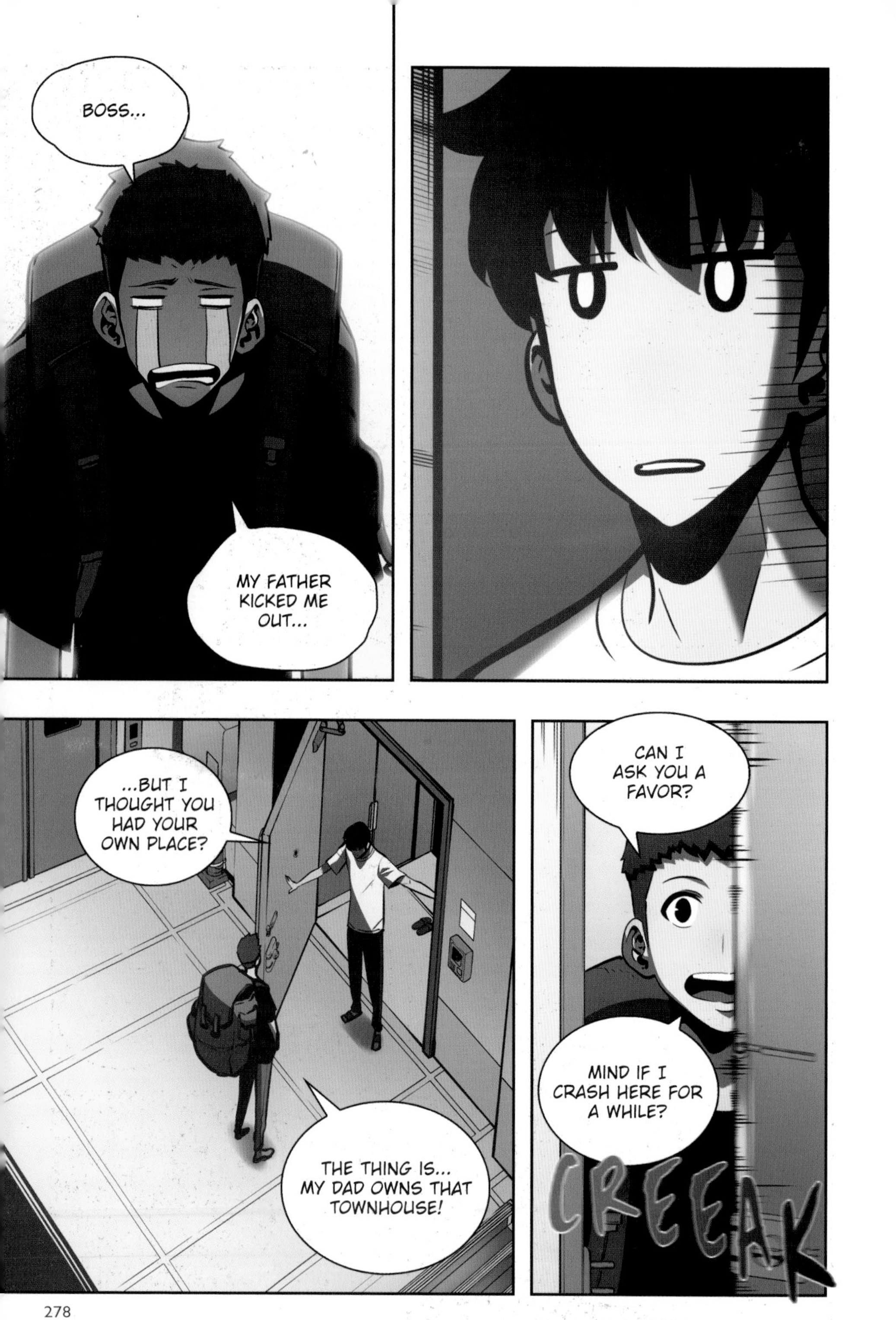
BOSS...
MY FATHER KICKED ME OUT...
...BUT I THOUGHT YOU HAD YOUR OWN PLACE?
THE THING IS... MY DAD OWNS THAT TOWNHOUSE!
CAN I ASK YOU A FAVOR?
MIND IF I CRASH HERE FOR A WHILE?
CREEAK

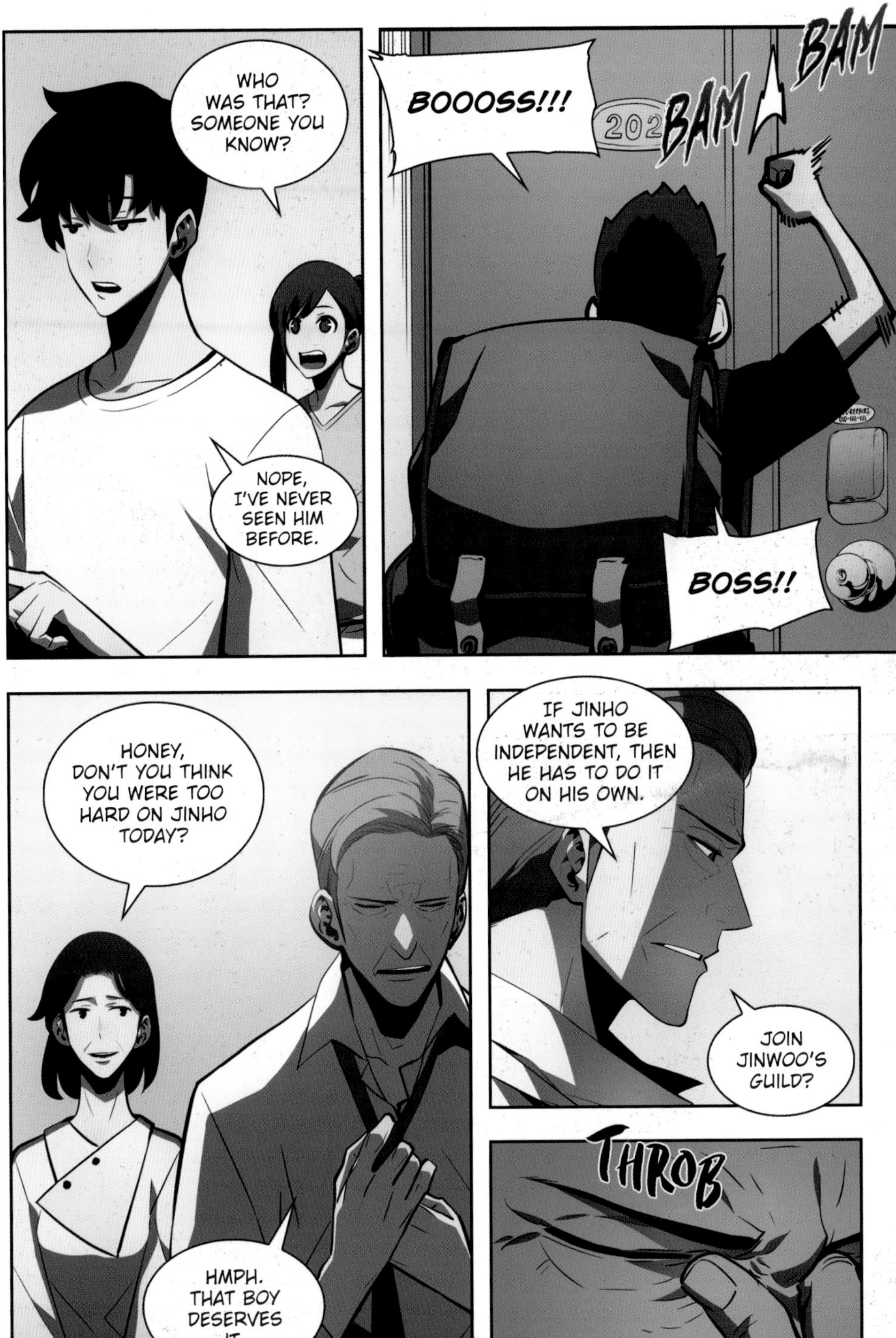
WHO WAS THAT? SOMEONE YOU KNOW?
NOPE, I'VE NEVER SEEN HIM BEFORE.
BOOOSS!!!
202
BAM
BAM
BOSS!!
HONEY, DON'T YOU THINK YOU WERE TOO HARD ON JINHO TODAY?
HMPH. THAT BOY DESERVES IT.
IF JINHO WANTS TO BE INDEPENDENT, THEN HE HAS TO DO IT ON HIS OWN.
JOIN JINWOO'S GUILD?
THROB

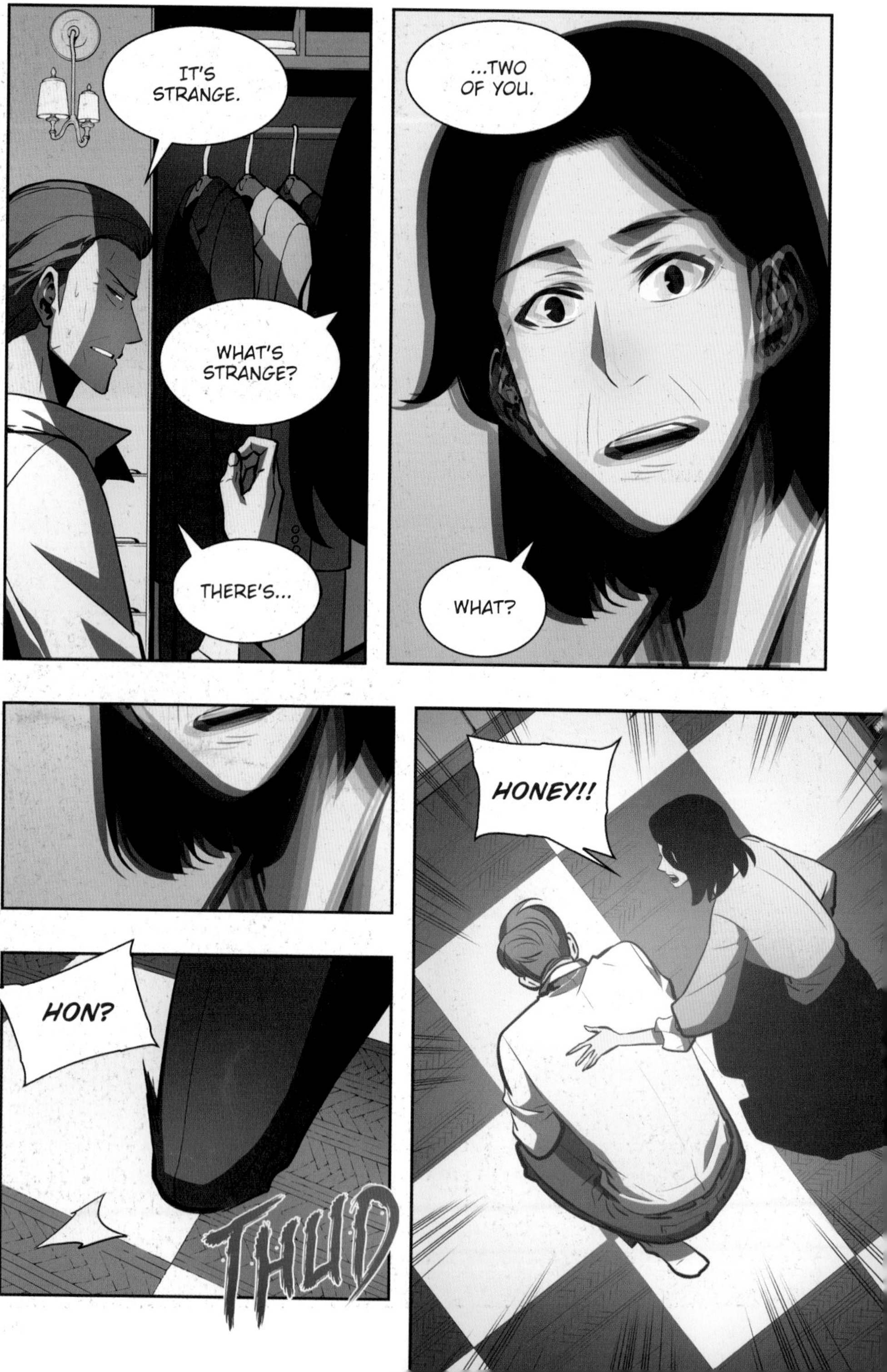
IT'S STRANGE.
WHAT'S STRANGE?
THERE'S...
...TWO OF YOU.
WHAT?
HON?
THUD
HONEY!!

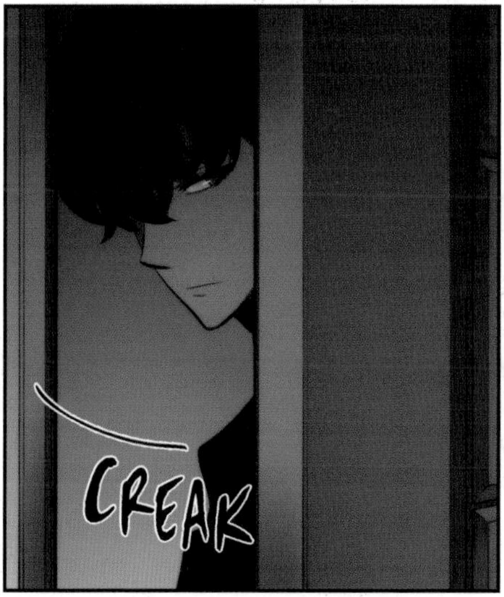
CREAK

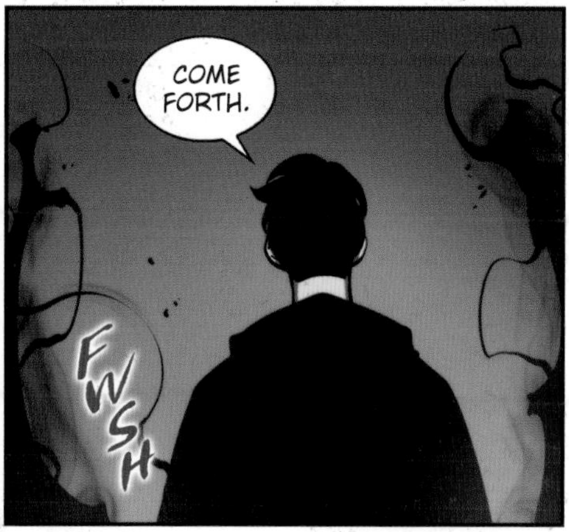
COME FORTH.
FWSH

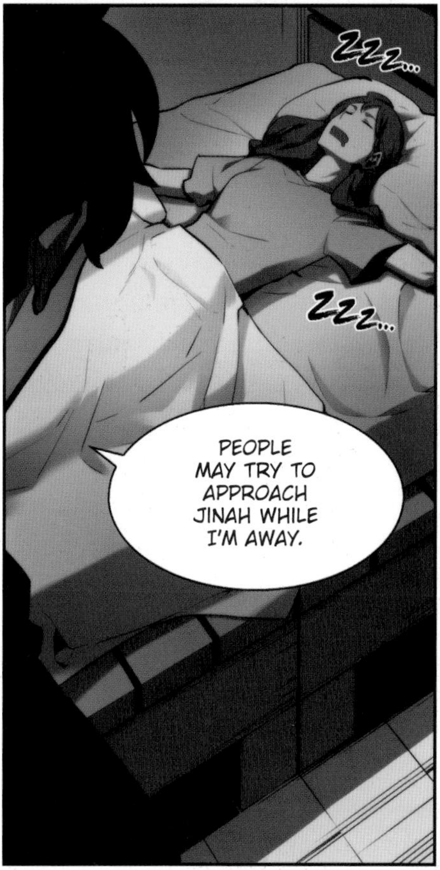
ZZZ...
ZZZ...
PEOPLE MAY TRY TO APPROACH JINAH WHILE I'M AWAY.

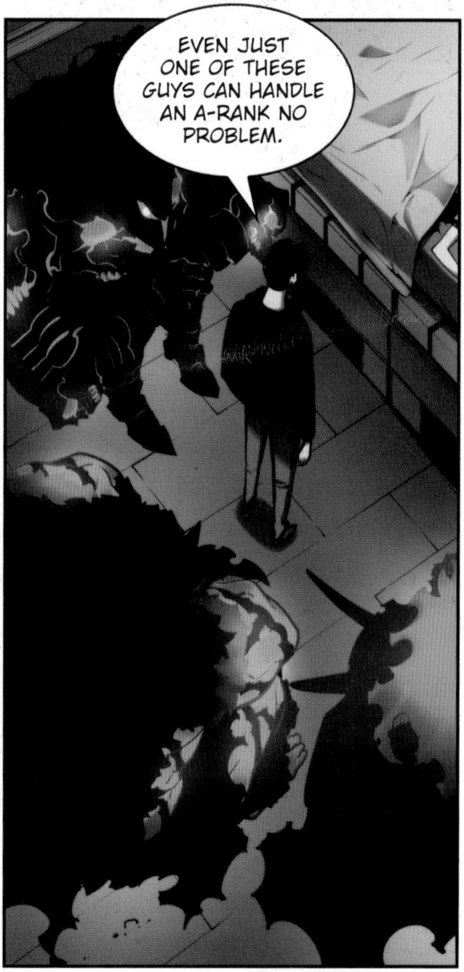
EVEN JUST ONE OF THESE GUYS CAN HANDLE AN A-RANK NO PROBLEM.

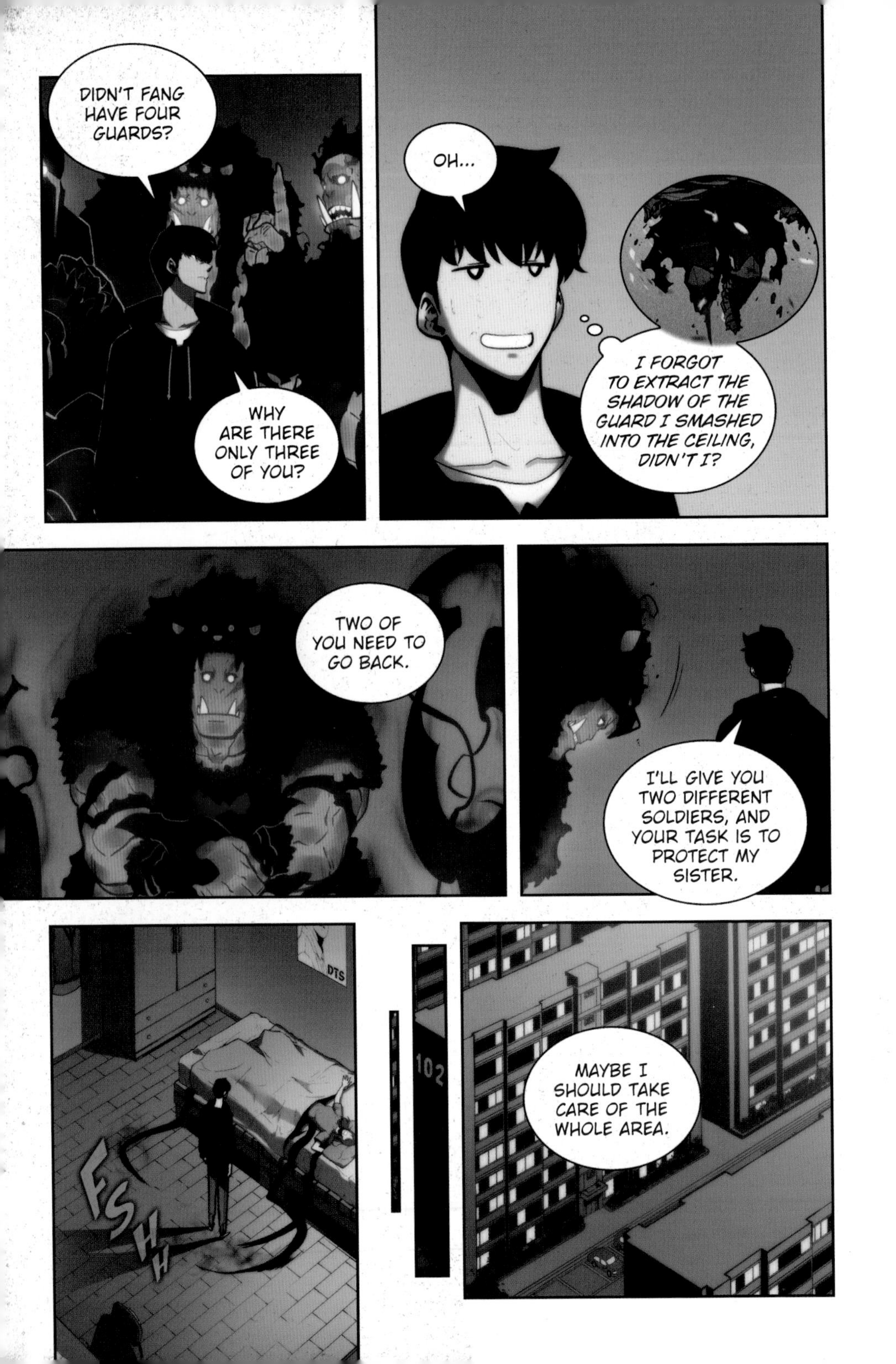
DIDN'T FANG HAVE FOUR GUARDS?
WHY ARE THERE ONLY THREE OF YOU?
OH...
I FORGOT TO EXTRACT THE SHADOW OF THE GUARD I SMASHED INTO THE CEILING, DIDN'T I?
TWO OF YOU NEED TO GO BACK.
I'LL GIVE YOU TWO DIFFERENT SOLDIERS, AND YOUR TASK IS TO PROTECT MY SISTER.
DTS
FSHH
102
MAYBE I SHOULD TAKE CARE OF THE WHOLE AREA.

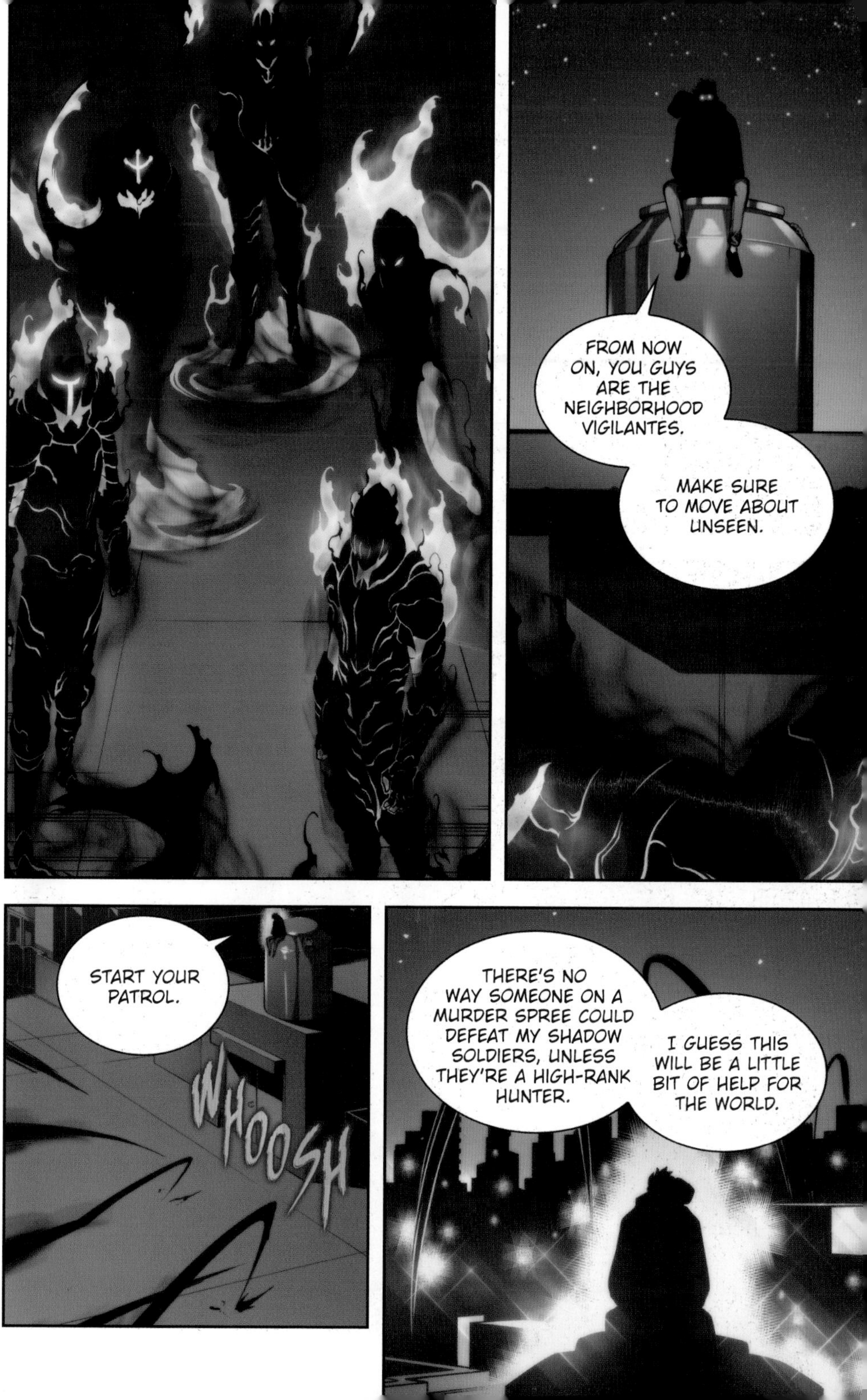
FROM NOW ON, YOU GUYS ARE THE NEIGHBORHOOD VIGILANTES.
MAKE SURE TO MOVE ABOUT UNSEEN.
START YOUR PATROL.
WHOOSH
THERE'S NO WAY SOMEONE ON A MURDER SPREE COULD DEFEAT MY SHADOW SOLDIERS, UNLESS THEY'RE A HIGH-RANK HUNTER.
I GUESS THIS WILL BE A LITTLE BIT OF HELP FOR THE WORLD.

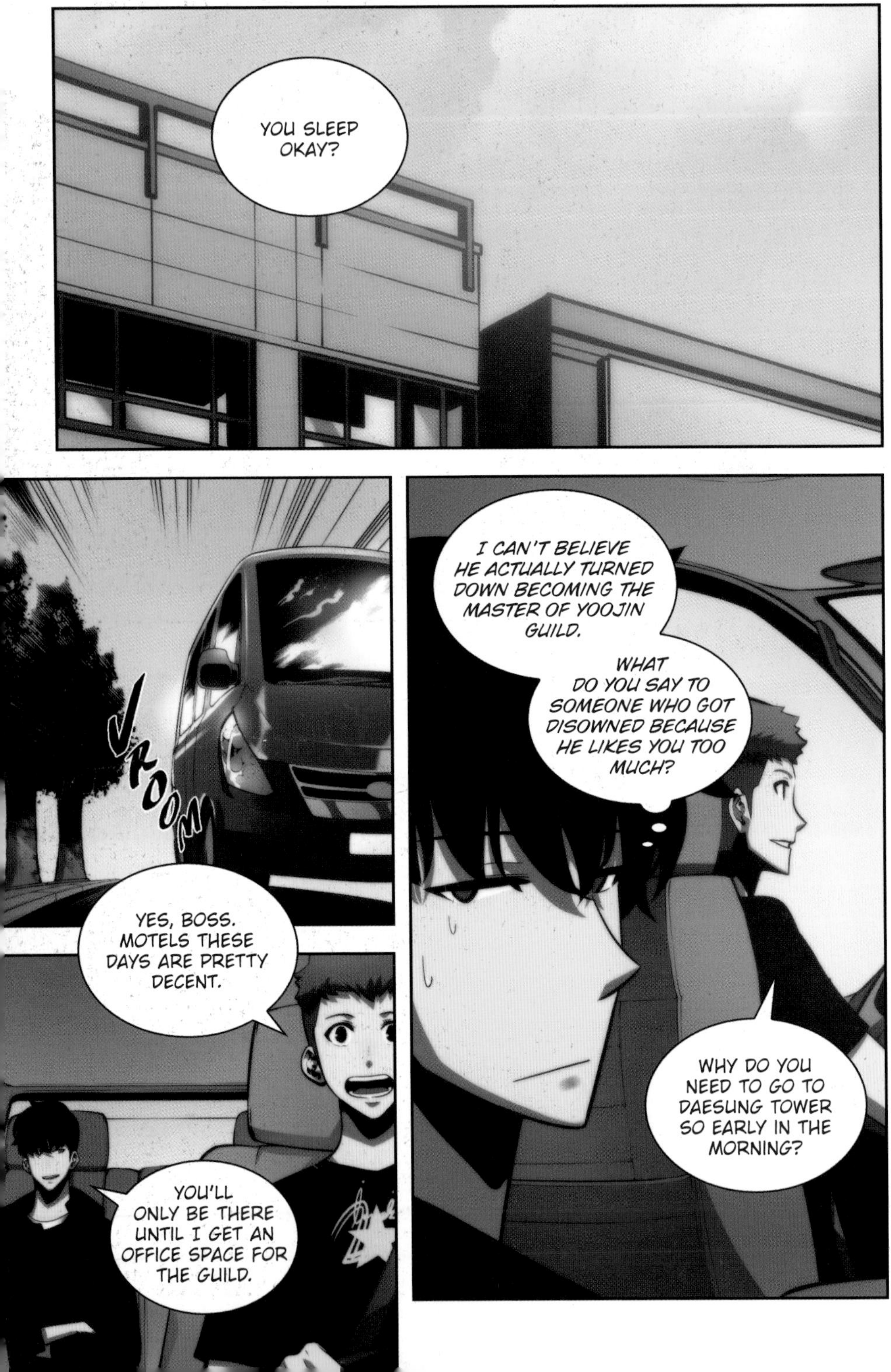
YOU SLEEP OKAY?
VROOM
YES, BOSS. MOTELS THESE DAYS ARE PRETTY DECENT.
YOU'LL ONLY BE THERE UNTIL I GET AN OFFICE SPACE FOR THE GUILD.
I CAN'T BELIEVE HE ACTUALLY TURNED DOWN BECOMING THE MASTER OF YOOJIN GUILD.
WHAT DO YOU SAY TO SOMEONE WHO GOT DISOWNED BECAUSE HE LIKES YOU TOO MUCH?
WHY DO YOU NEED TO GO TO DAESUNG TOWER SO EARLY IN THE MORNING?

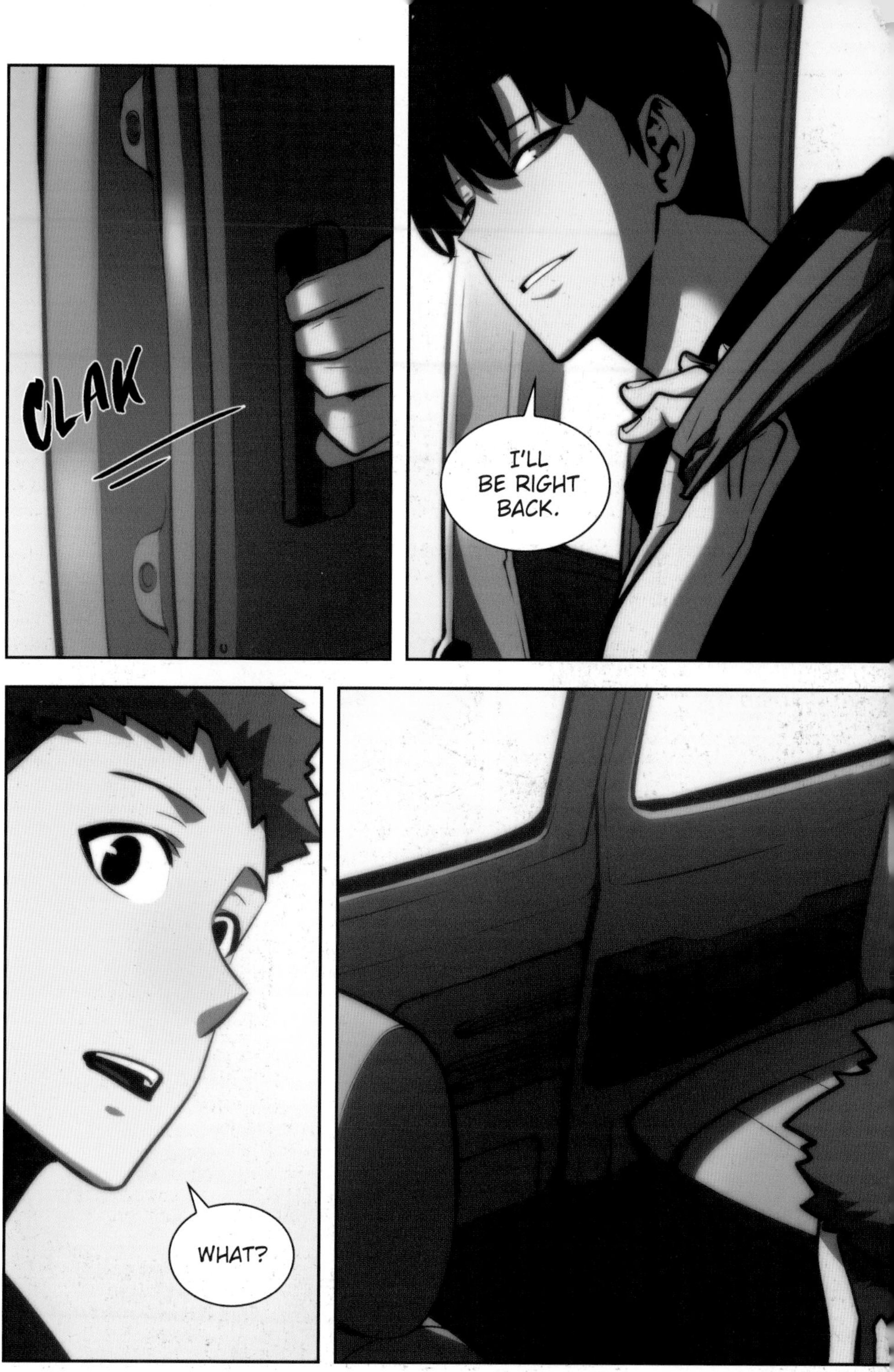
CLAK
I'LL BE RIGHT BACK.
WHAT?

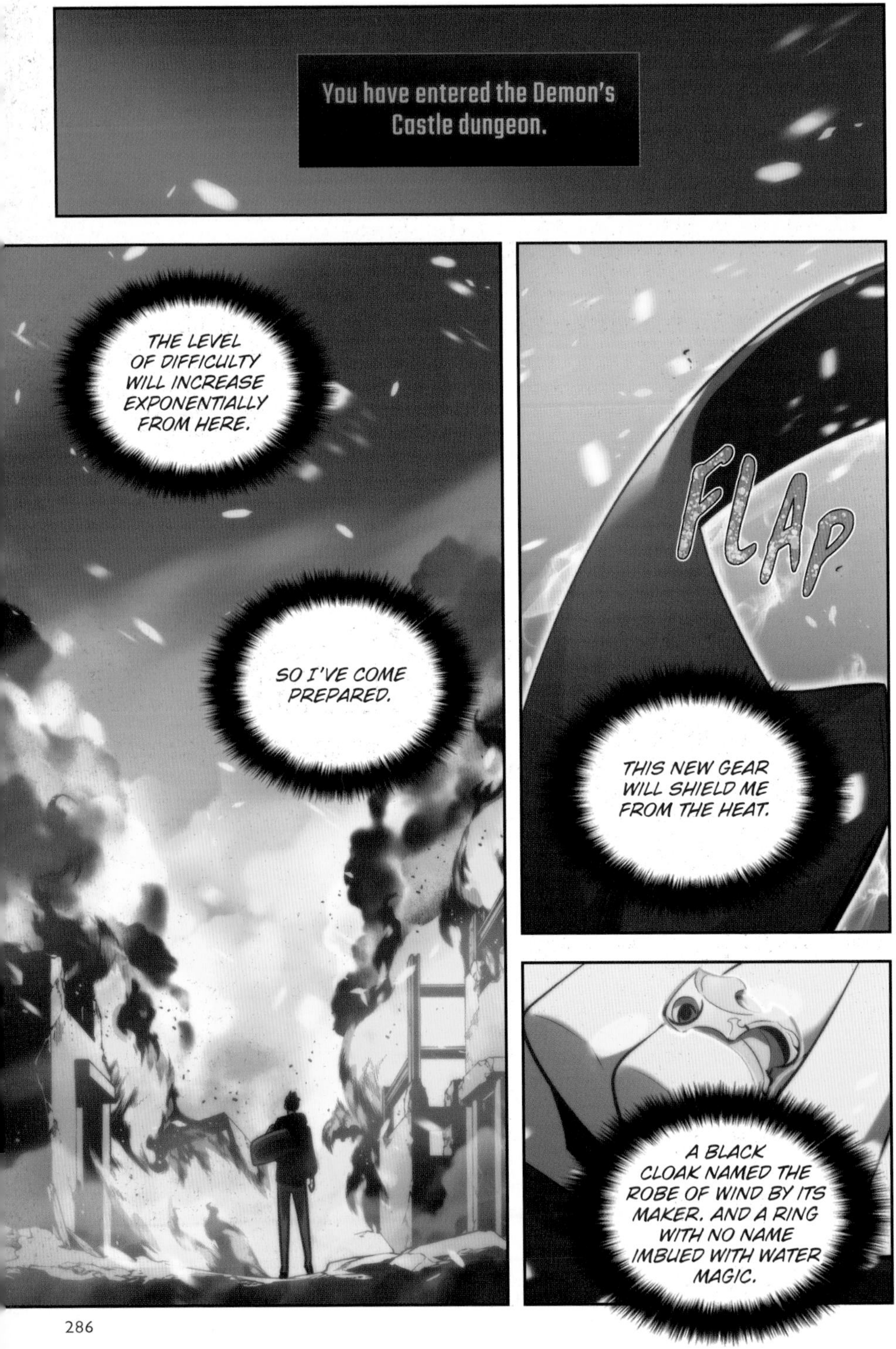
You have entered the Demon's Castle dungeon.
THE LEVEL OF DIFFICULTY WILL INCREASE EXPONENTIALLY FROM HERE.
SO I'VE COME PREPARED.
FLAP
THIS NEW GEAR WILL SHIELD ME FROM THE HEAT.
A BLACK CLOAK NAMED THE ROBE OF WIND BY ITS MAKER. AND A RING WITH NO NAME IMBUED WITH WATER MAGIC.

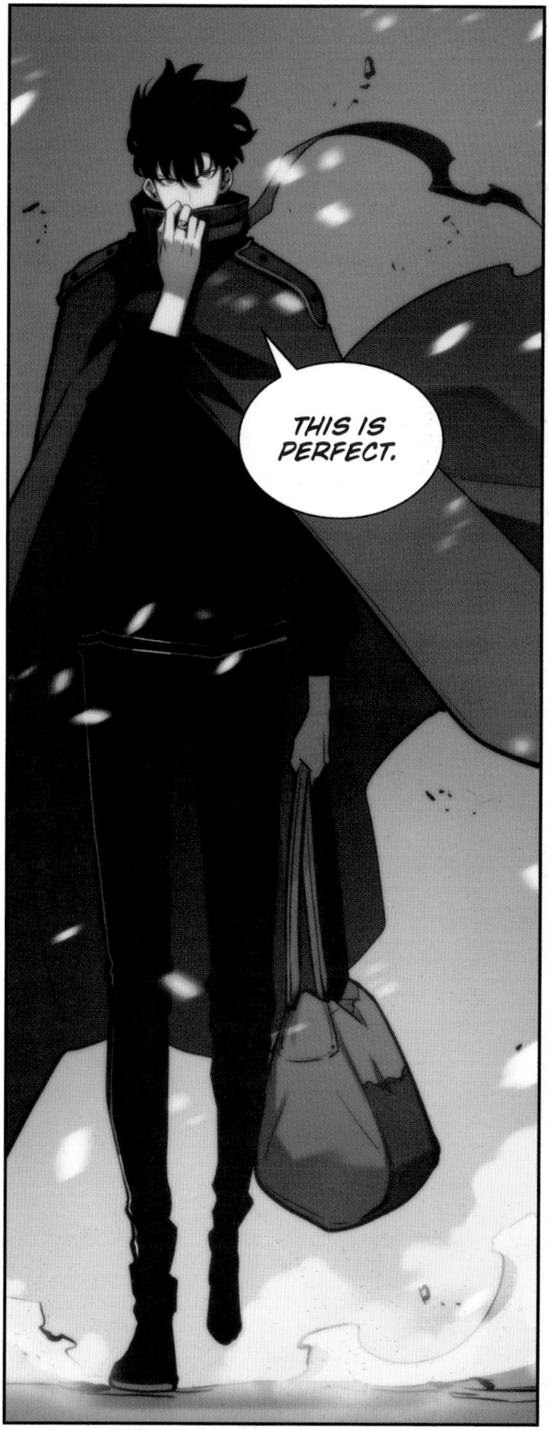
THIS IS PERFECT.

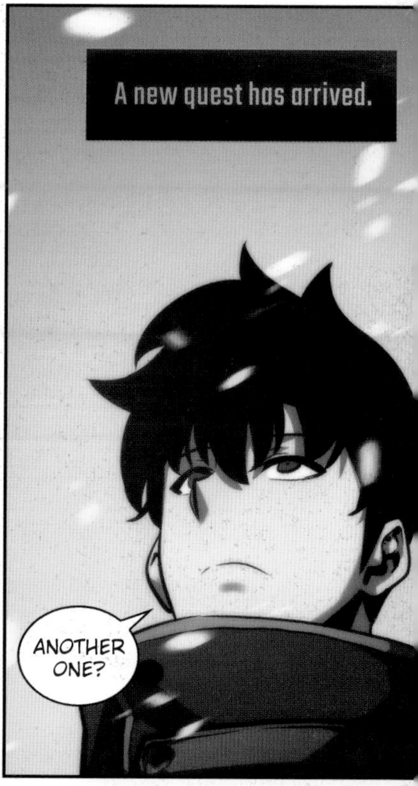
A new quest has arrived.
ANOTHER ONE?

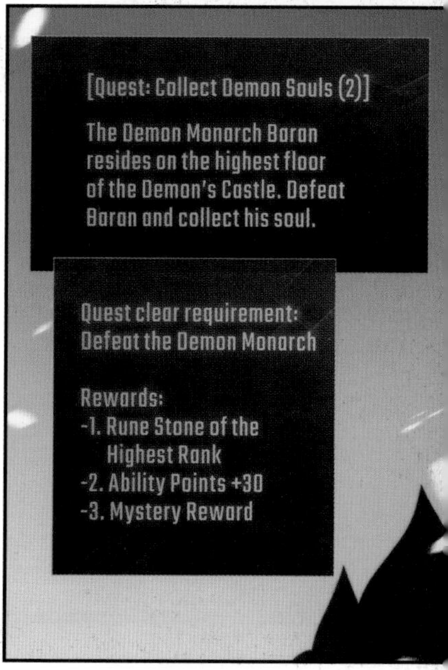
[Quest: Collect Demon Souls (2)]
The Demon Monarch Baran resides on the highest floor of the Demon's Castle. Defeat Baran and collect his soul.
Quest clear requirement: Defeat the Demon Monarch
Rewards:
-1. Rune Stone of the Highest Rank
-2. Ability Points +30
-3. Mystery Reward

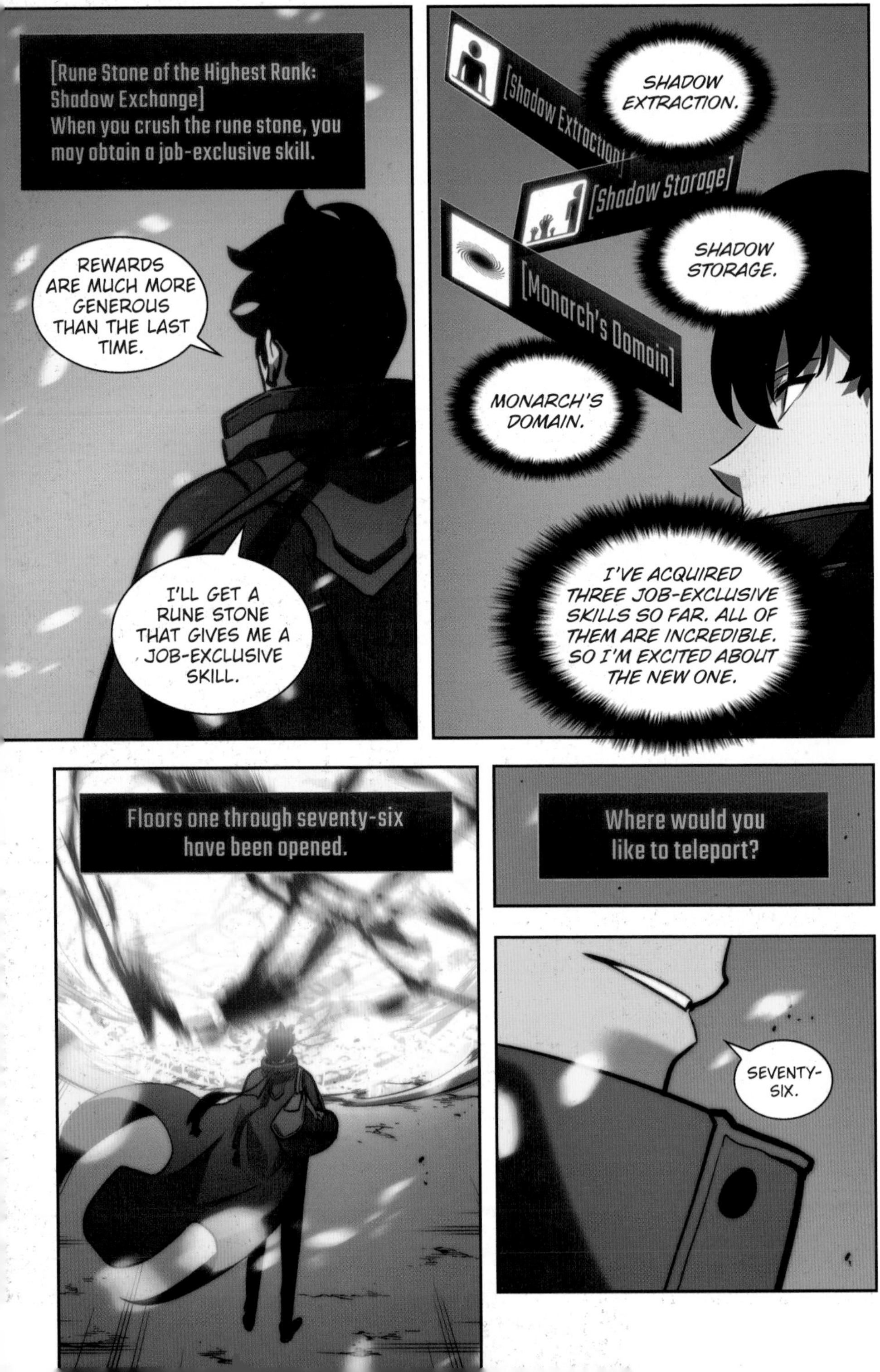
[Rune Stone of the Highest Rank: Shadow Exchange]
When you crush the rune stone, you may obtain a job-exclusive skill.
REWARDS ARE MUCH MORE GENEROUS THAN THE LAST TIME.
I'LL GET A RUNE STONE THAT GIVES ME A JOB-EXCLUSIVE SKILL.
[Shadow Extraction]
SHADOW EXTRACTION.
[Shadow Storage]
SHADOW STORAGE.
[Monarch's Domain]
MONARCH'S DOMAIN.
I'VE ACQUIRED THREE JOB-EXCLUSIVE SKILLS SO FAR. ALL OF THEM ARE INCREDIBLE. SO I'M EXCITED ABOUT THE NEW ONE.
Floors one through seventy-six have been opened.
Where would you like to teleport?
SEVENTY-SIX.

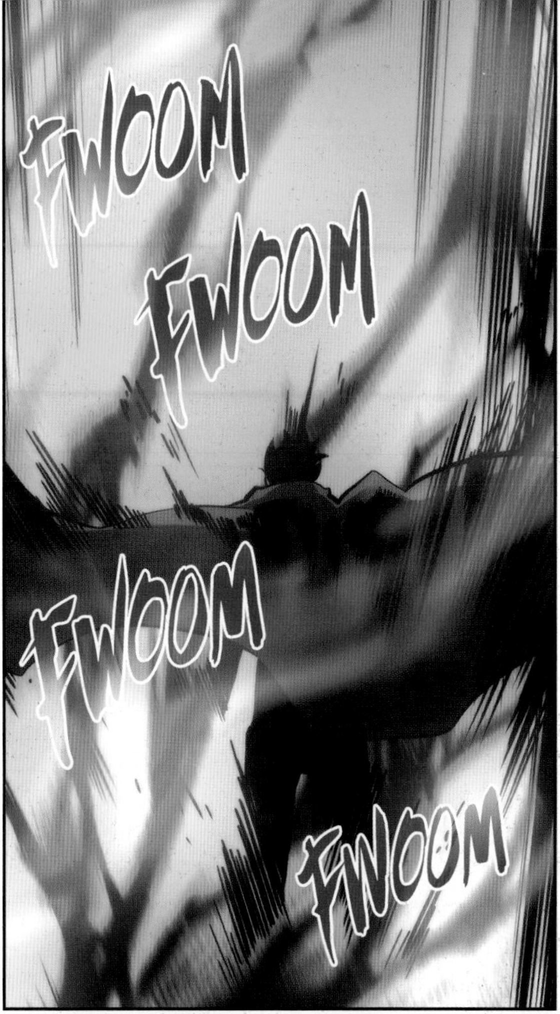
FWOOM
FWOOM
FWOOM
FWOOM
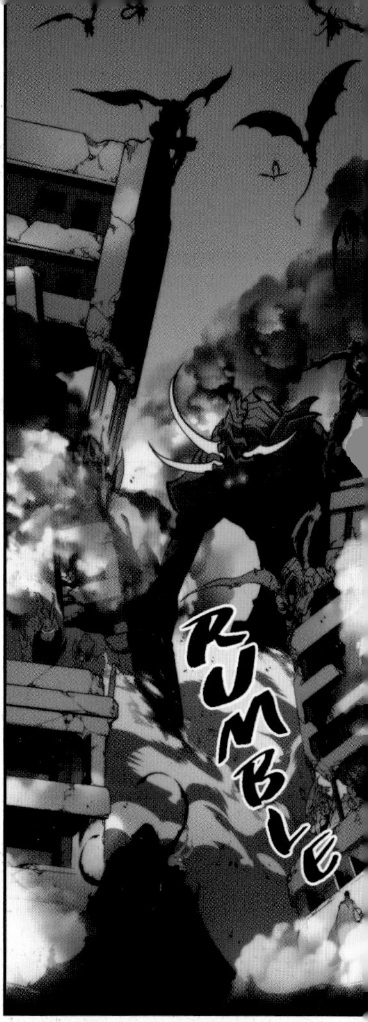
RUMBLE
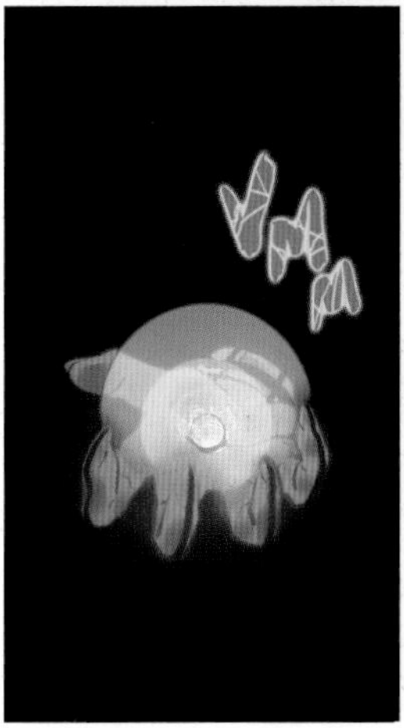
VMM
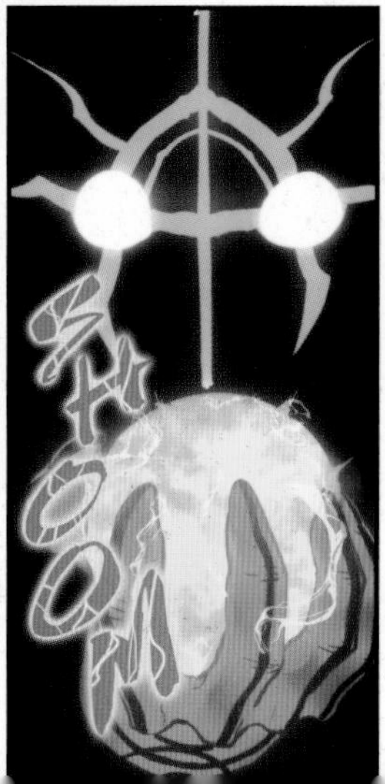
SHOOM
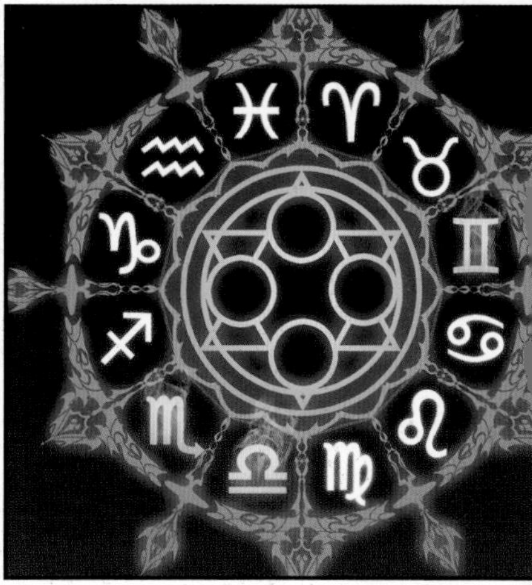

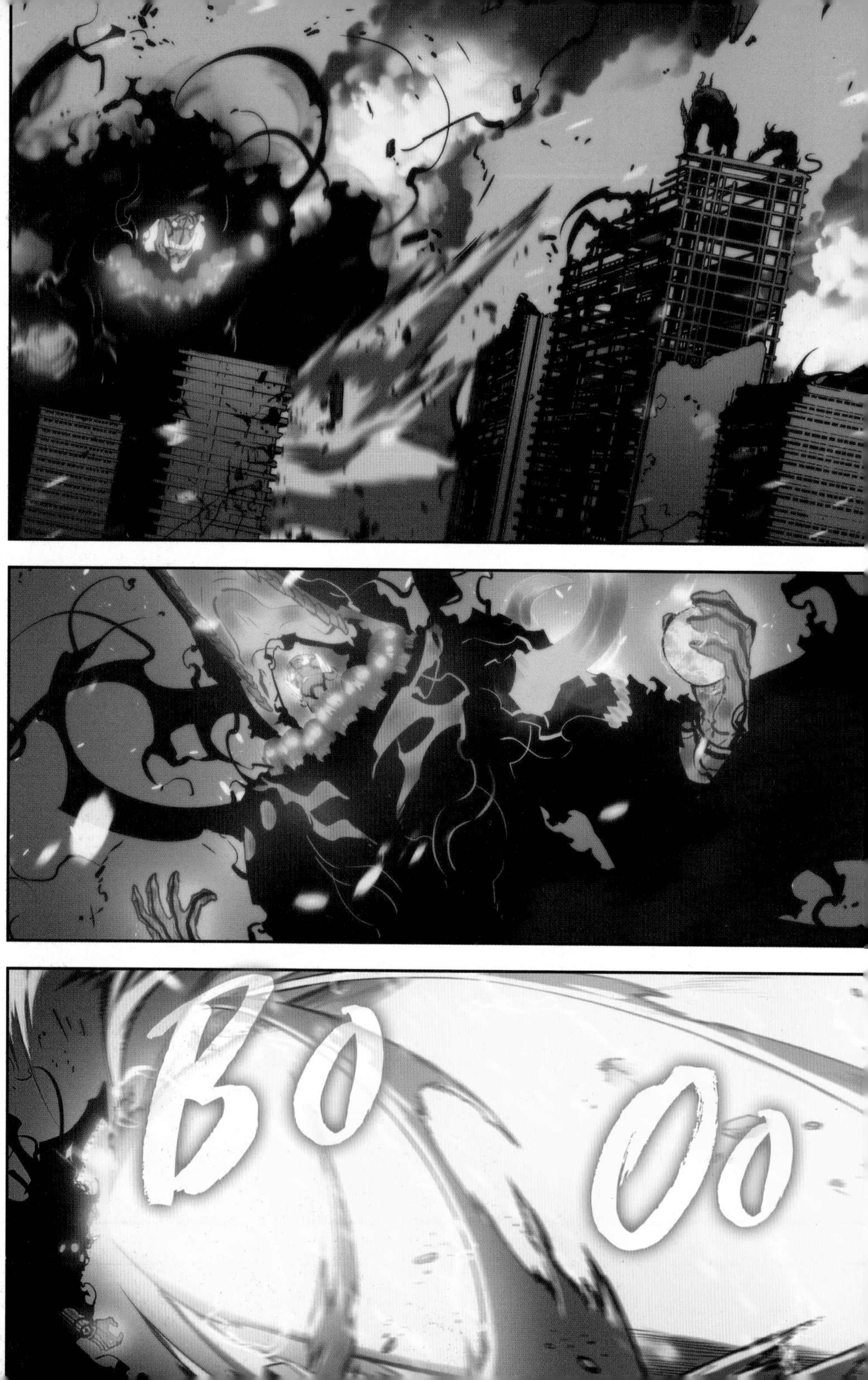
BOOOO

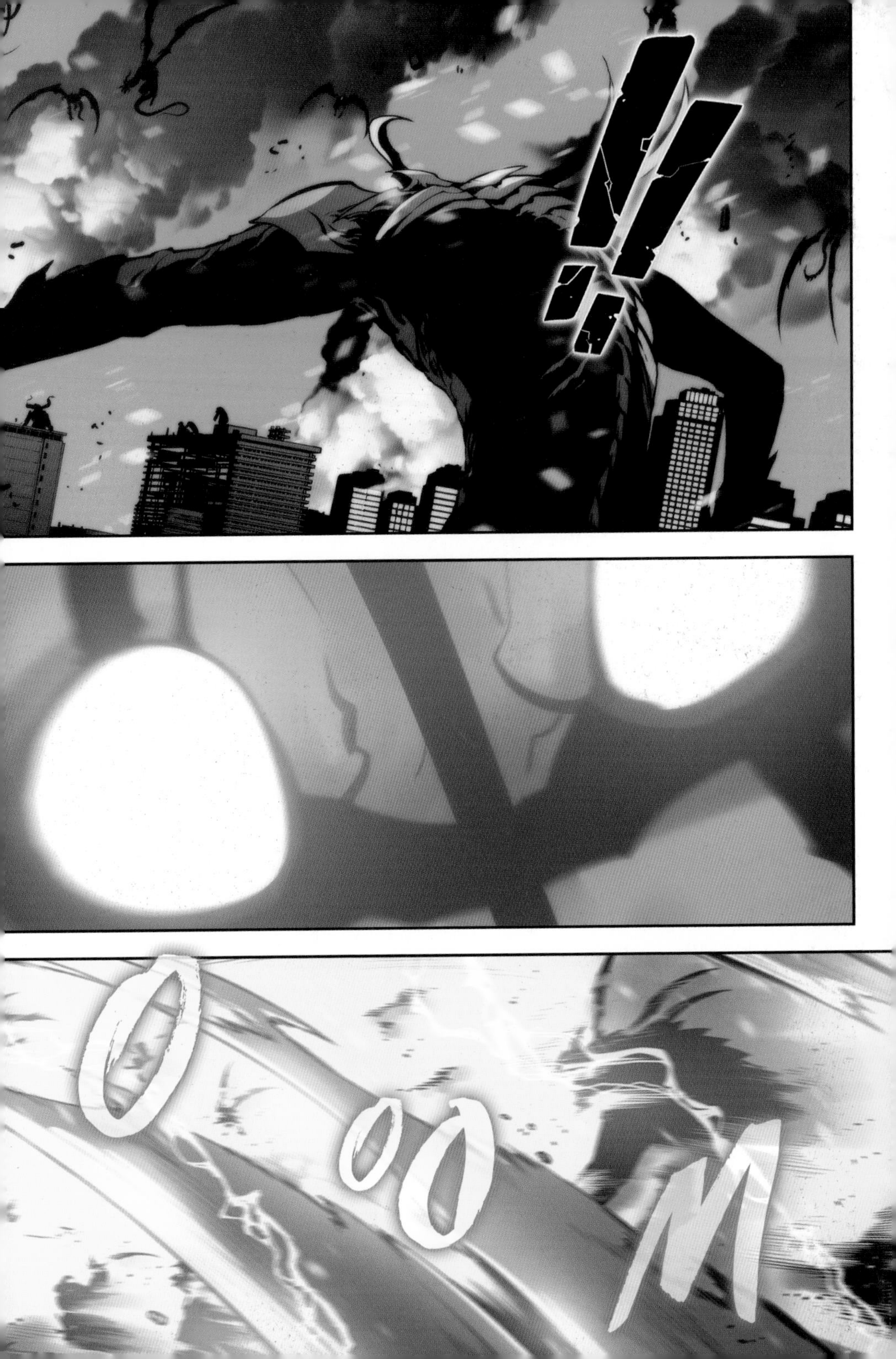
!!
OooM

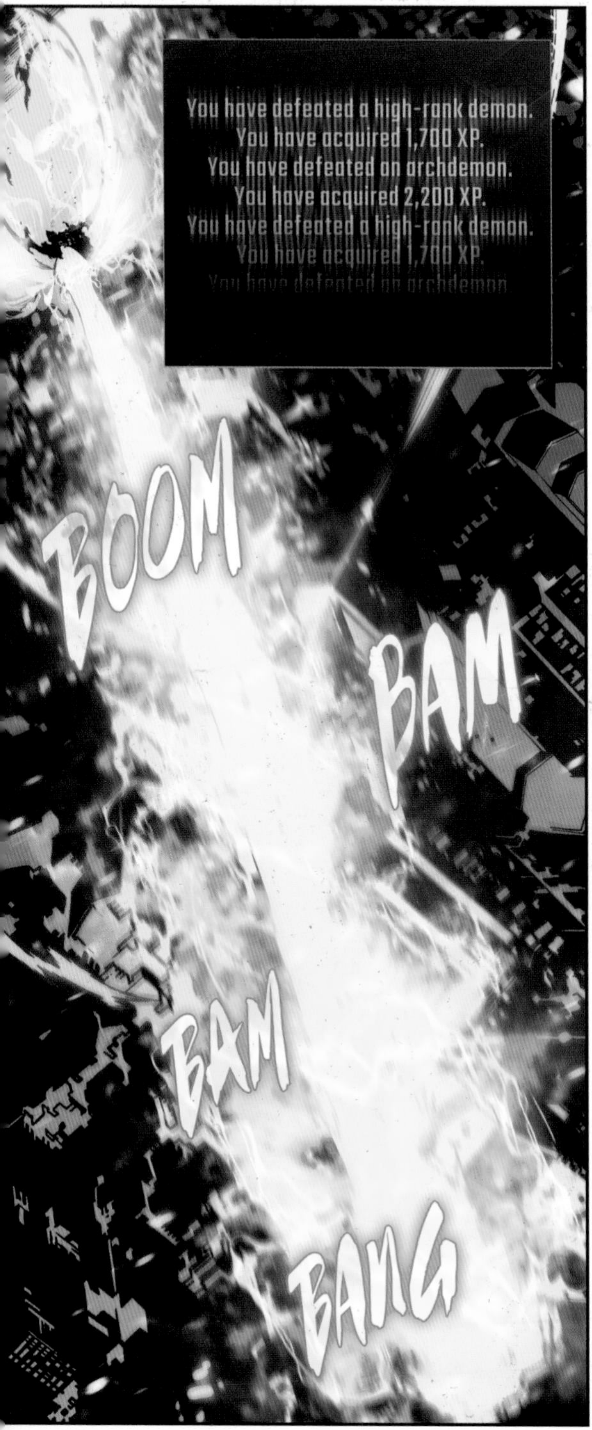
You have defeated a high-rank demon.
You have acquired 1,700 XP.
You have defeated an archdemon.
You have acquired 2,200 XP.
You have defeated a high-rank demon.
You have acquired 1,700 XP.
You have defeated an archdemon
BOOM
BAM
BAM
BANG

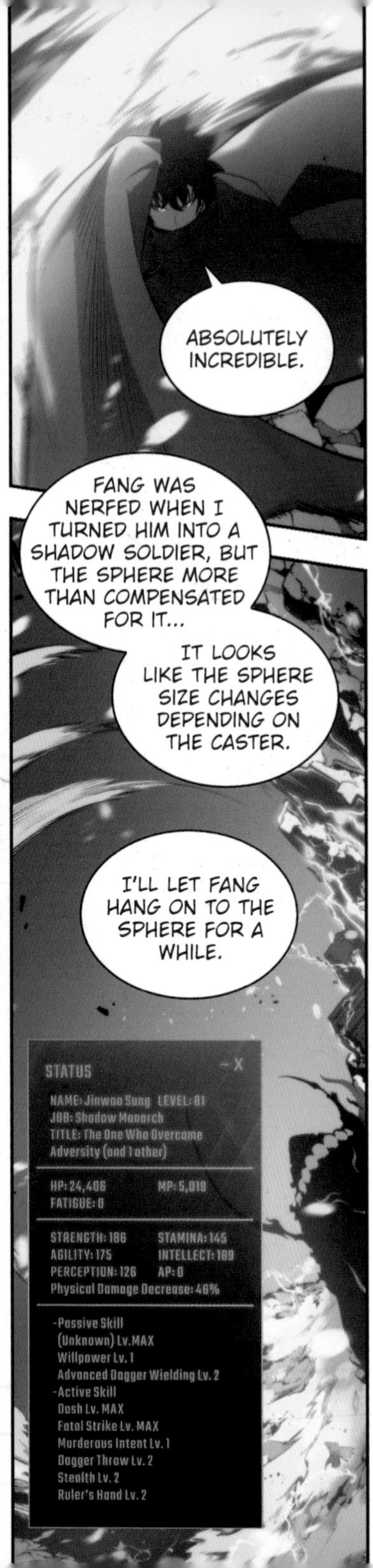
ABSOLUTELY INCREDIBLE.
FANG WAS NERFED WHEN I TURNED HIM INTO A SHADOW SOLDIER, BUT THE SPHERE MORE THAN COMPENSATED FOR IT...
IT LOOKS LIKE THE SPHERE SIZE CHANGES DEPENDING ON THE CASTER.
I'LL LET FANG HANG ON TO THE SPHERE FOR A WHILE.
STATUS
NAME: Jinwoo Sung LEVEL: 81
JOB: Shadow Monarch
TITLE: The One Who Overcame Adversity (and 1 other)
HP: 24,406 MP: 5,019
FATIGUE: 0
STRENGTH: 186 STAMINA: 145
AGILITY: 175 INTELLECT: 189
PERCEPTION: 126 AP: 0
Physical Damage Decrease: 46%
-Passive Skill
(Unknown) Lv.MAX
Willpower Lv. 1
Advanced Dagger Wielding Lv. 2
-Active Skill
Dash Lv. MAX
Fatal Strike Lv. MAX
Murderous Intent Lv. 1
Dagger Throw Lv. 2
Stealth Lv. 2
Ruler's Hand Lv. 2

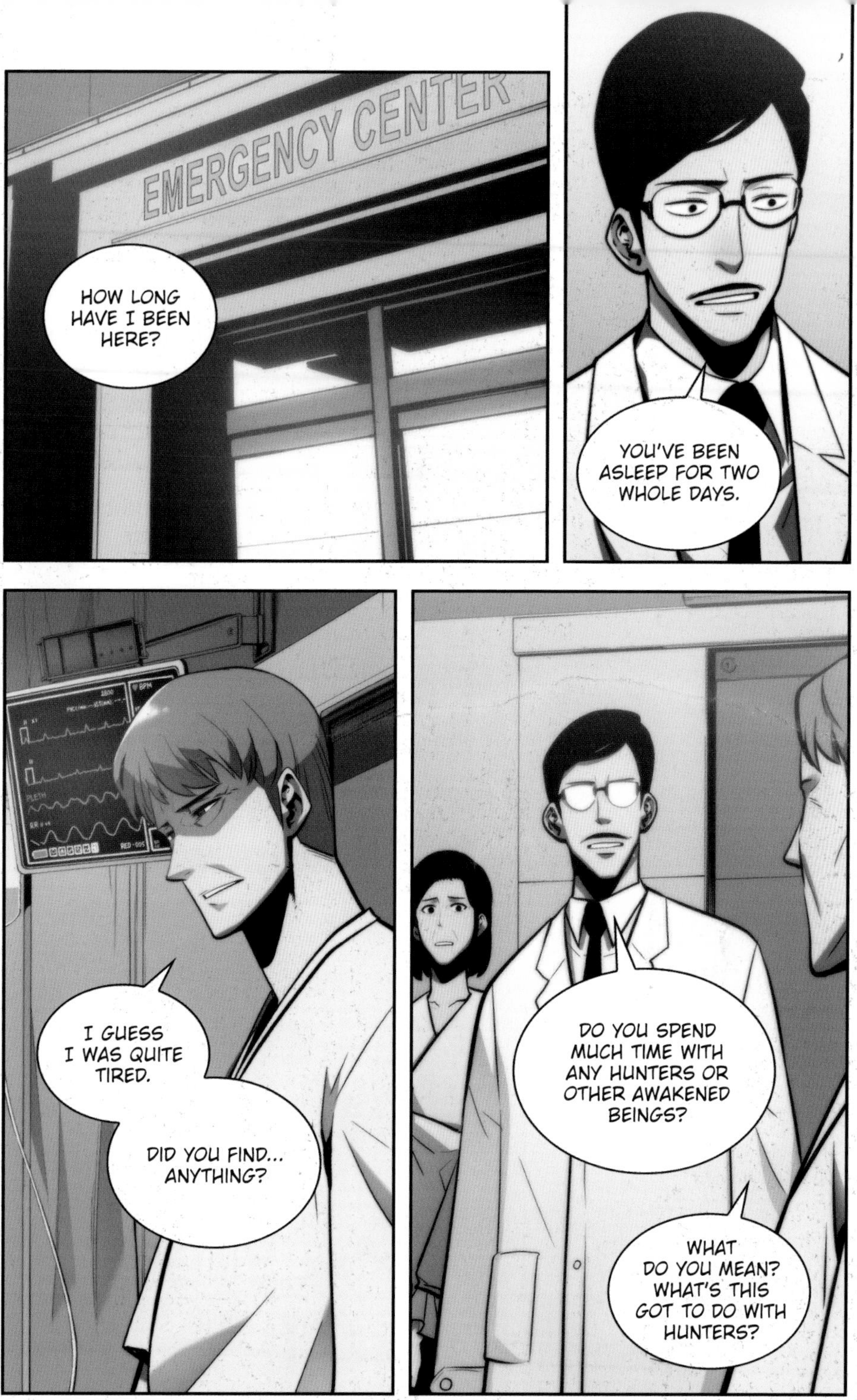
EMERGENCY CENTER
HOW LONG HAVE I BEEN HERE?
YOU'VE BEEN ASLEEP FOR TWO WHOLE DAYS.
I GUESS I WAS QUITE TIRED.
DID YOU FIND... ANYTHING?
DO YOU SPEND MUCH TIME WITH ANY HUNTERS OR OTHER AWAKENED BEINGS?
WHAT DO YOU MEAN? WHAT'S THIS GOT TO DO WITH HUNTERS?

HAVE YOU HEARD ABOUT THE **ETERNAL SLEEP DISEASE**?

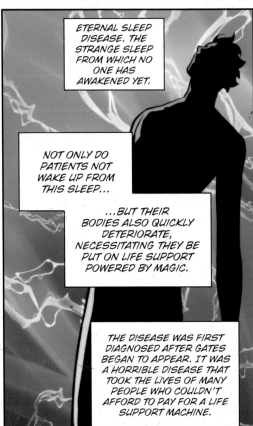

ETERNAL SLEEP DISEASE. THE STRANGE SLEEP FROM WHICH NO ONE HAS AWAKENED YET.

NOT ONLY DO PATIENTS NOT WAKE UP FROM THIS SLEEP...

...BUT THEIR BODIES ALSO QUICKLY DETERIORATE, NECESSITATING THEY BE PUT ON LIFE SUPPORT POWERED BY MAGIC.

THE DISEASE WAS FIRST DIAGNOSED AFTER GATES BEGAN TO APPEAR. IT WAS A HORRIBLE DISEASE THAT TOOK THE LIVES OF MANY PEOPLE WHO COULDN'T AFFORD TO PAY FOR A LIFE SUPPORT MACHINE.

INITIALLY, SUFFERERS ARE SIMPLY DROWSY, BUT EVENTUALLY THEY ARE UNABLE TO WAKE.

SO WHAT DO HUNTERS HAVE TO DO WITH IT?

THERE'S WIDELY BELIEVED TO BE A CONNECTION BETWEEN ETERNAL SLEEP DISEASE AND MANA.

SOME PEOPLE ARE BORN WITH A LOWER TOLERANCE TO MANA.

THOSE TYPES OF INDIVIDUALS ARE FOUND TO BE MORE SUSCEPTIBLE TO ETERNAL SLEEP DISEASE, PARTICULARLY ANYONE WITH PROLONGED EXPOSURE.

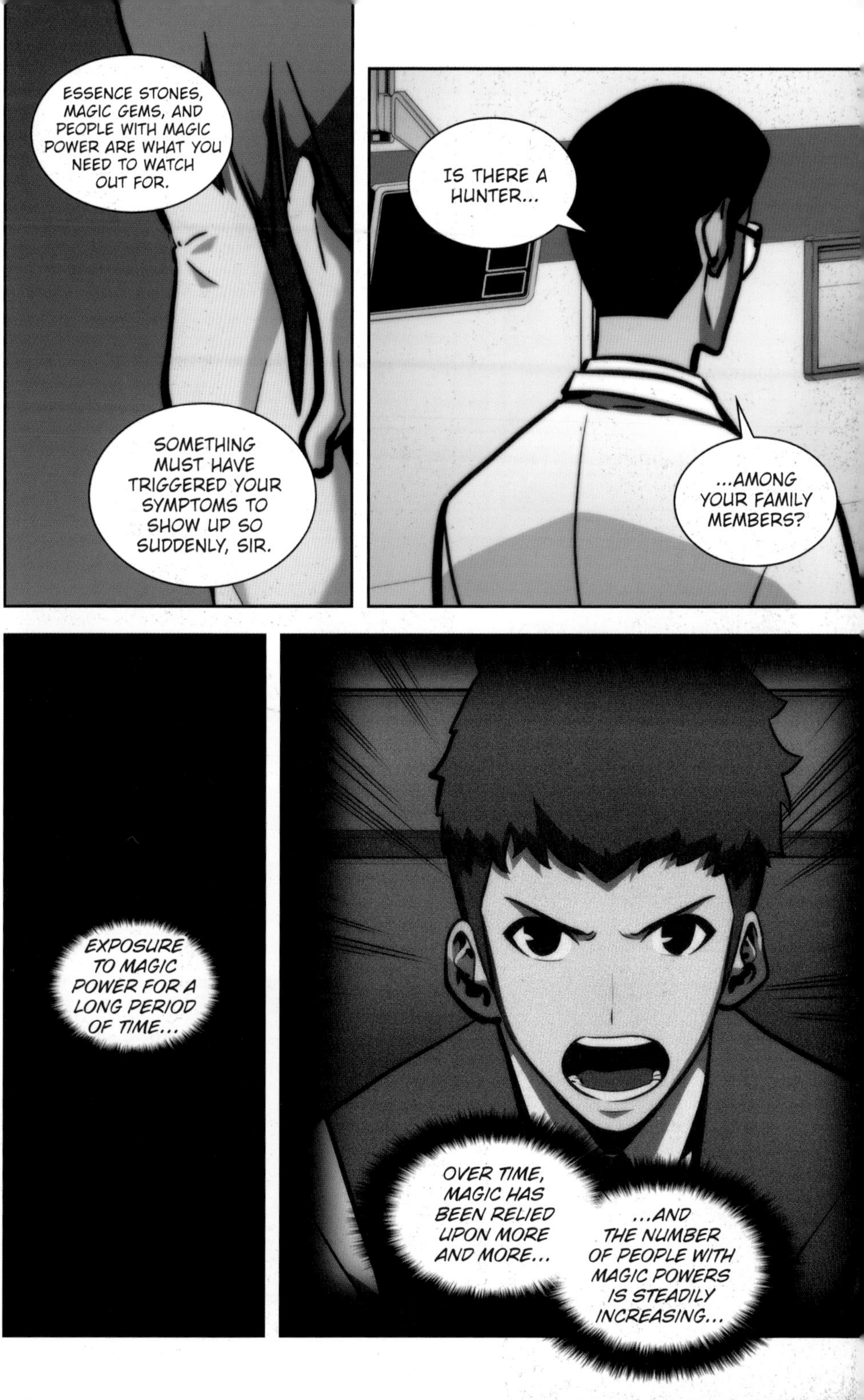
ESSENCE STONES, MAGIC GEMS, AND PEOPLE WITH MAGIC POWER ARE WHAT YOU NEED TO WATCH OUT FOR.
SOMETHING MUST HAVE TRIGGERED YOUR SYMPTOMS TO SHOW UP SO SUDDENLY, SIR.
IS THERE A HUNTER...
...AMONG YOUR FAMILY MEMBERS?
EXPOSURE TO MAGIC POWER FOR A LONG PERIOD OF TIME...
OVER TIME, MAGIC HAS BEEN RELIED UPON MORE AND MORE...
...AND THE NUMBER OF PEOPLE WITH MAGIC POWERS IS STEADILY INCREASING...

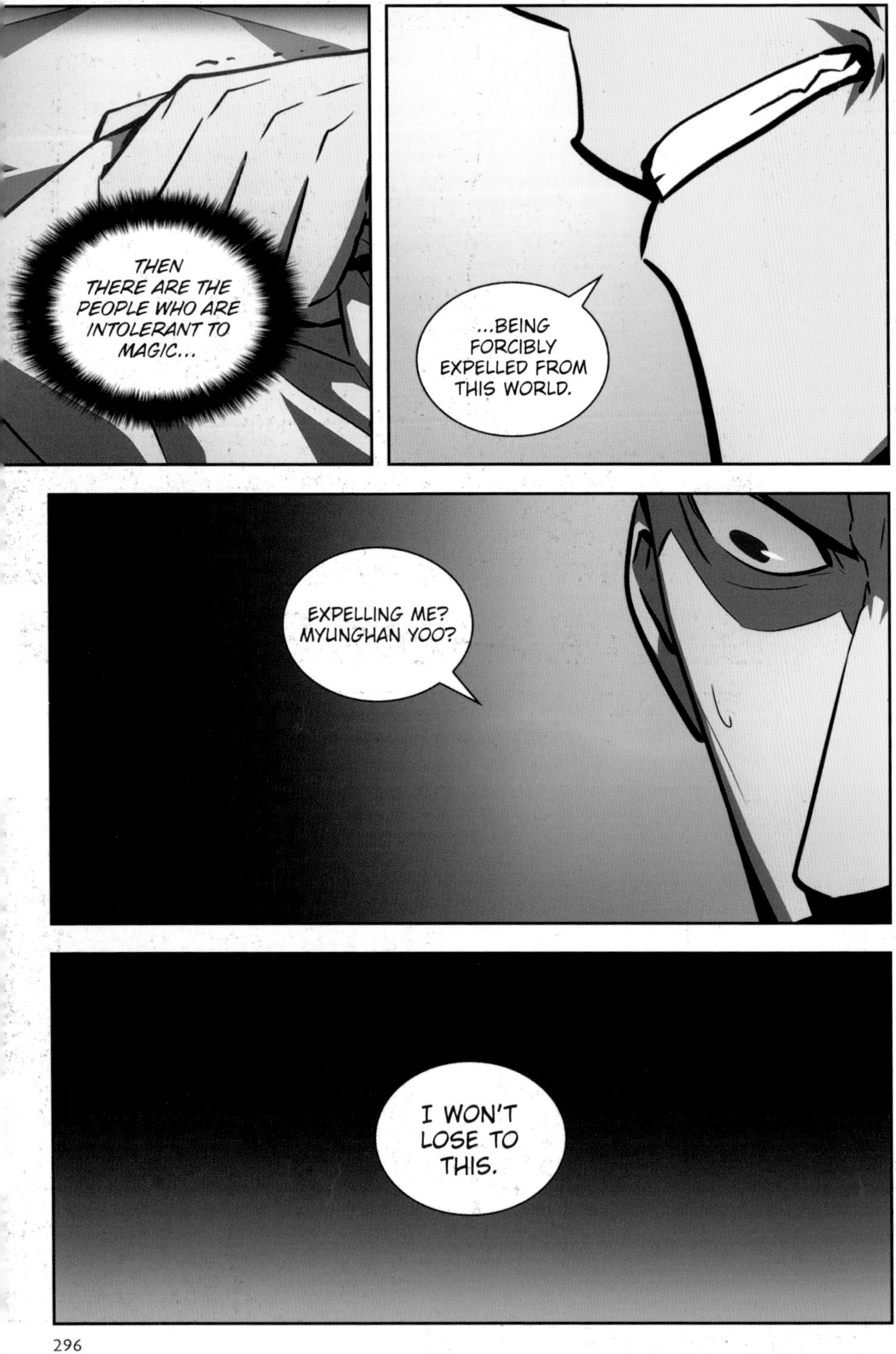
THEN THERE ARE THE PEOPLE WHO ARE INTOLERANT TO MAGIC...
...BEING FORCIBLY EXPELLED FROM THIS WORLD.
EXPELLING ME? MYUNGHAN YOO?
I WON'T LOSE TO THIS.

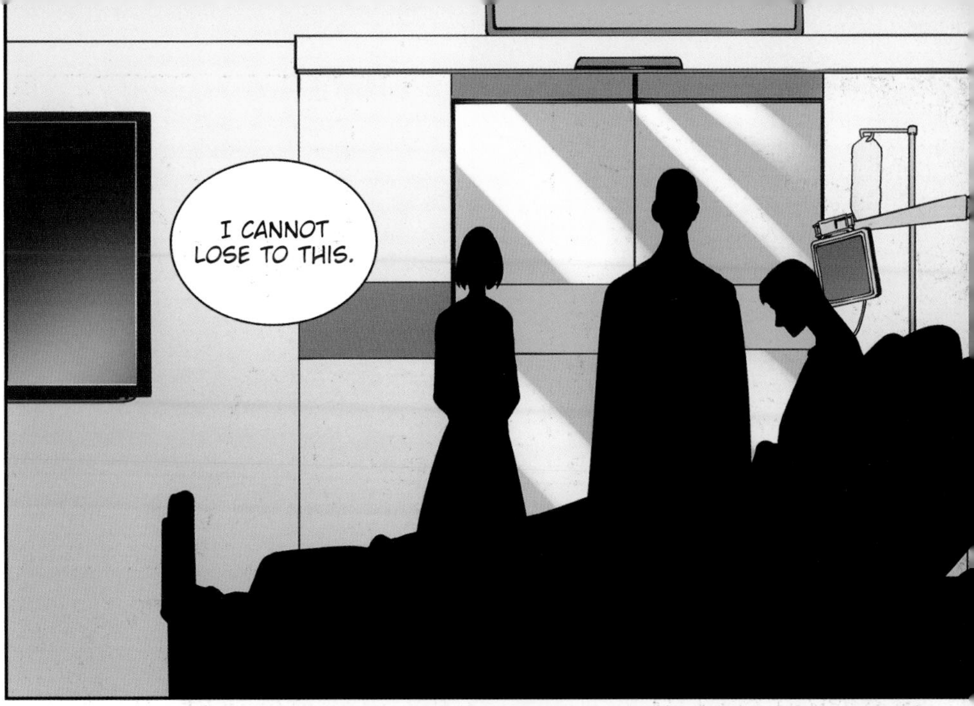
I CANNOT LOSE TO THIS.

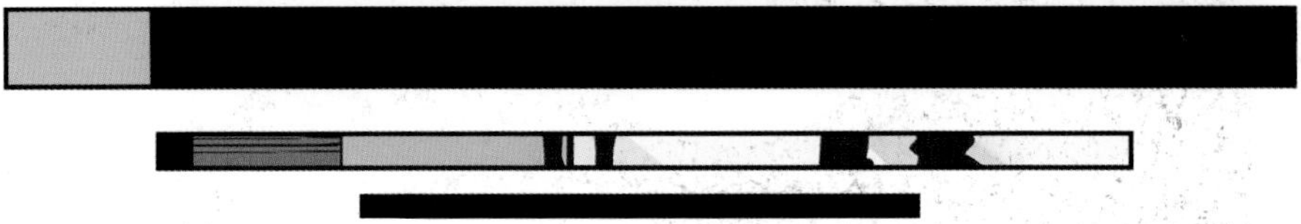

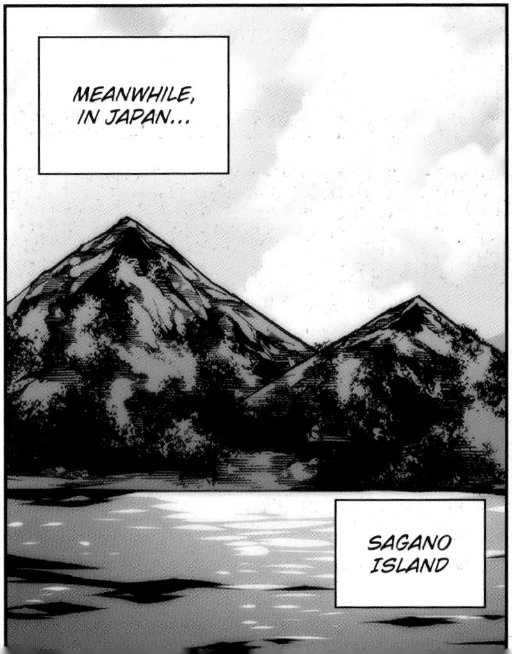
MEANWHILE, IN JAPAN...
SAGANO ISLAND

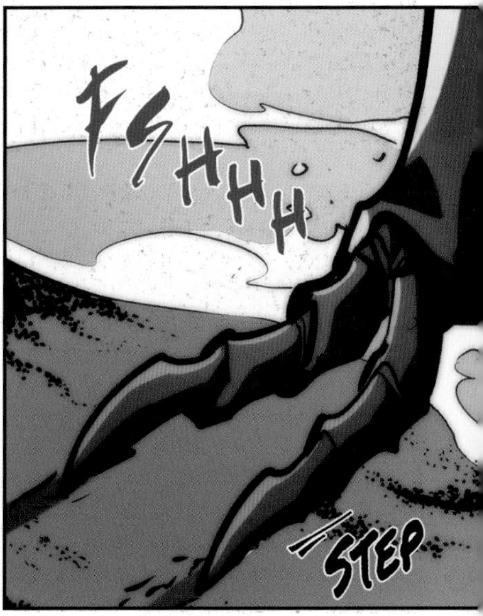
FSHHH
STEP

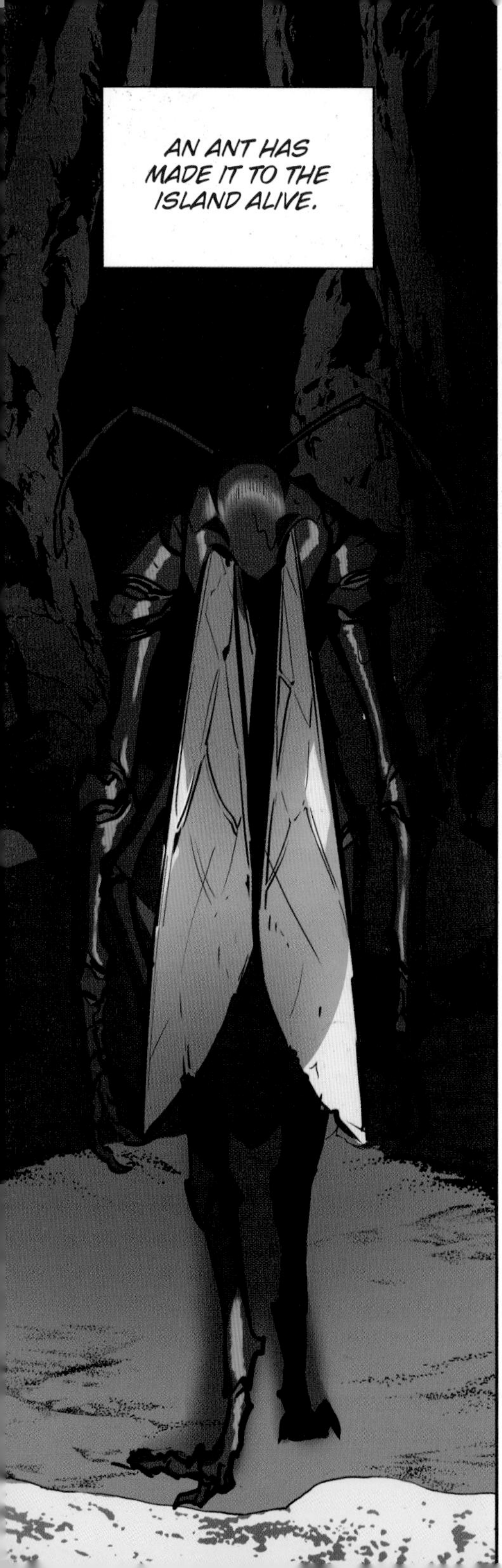
AN ANT HAS MADE IT TO THE ISLAND ALIVE.

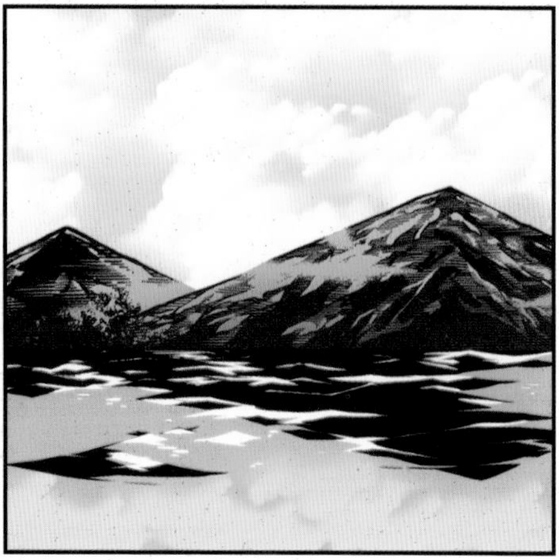

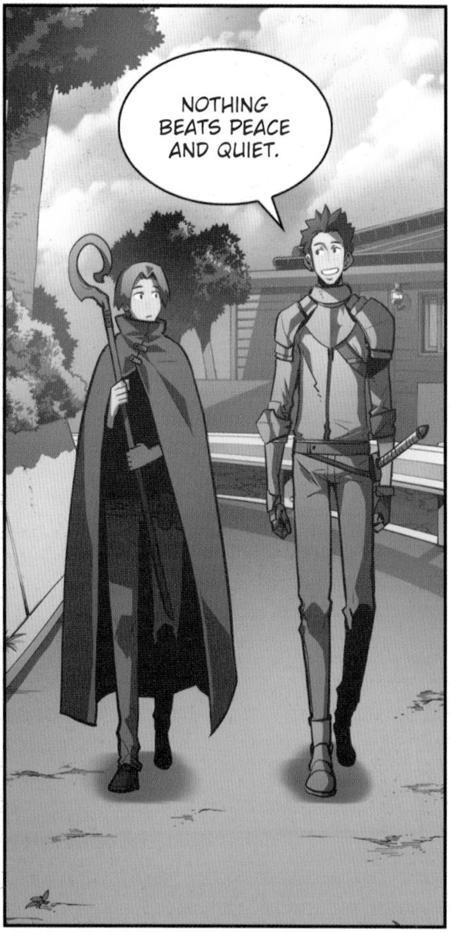
NOTHING BEATS PEACE AND QUIET.

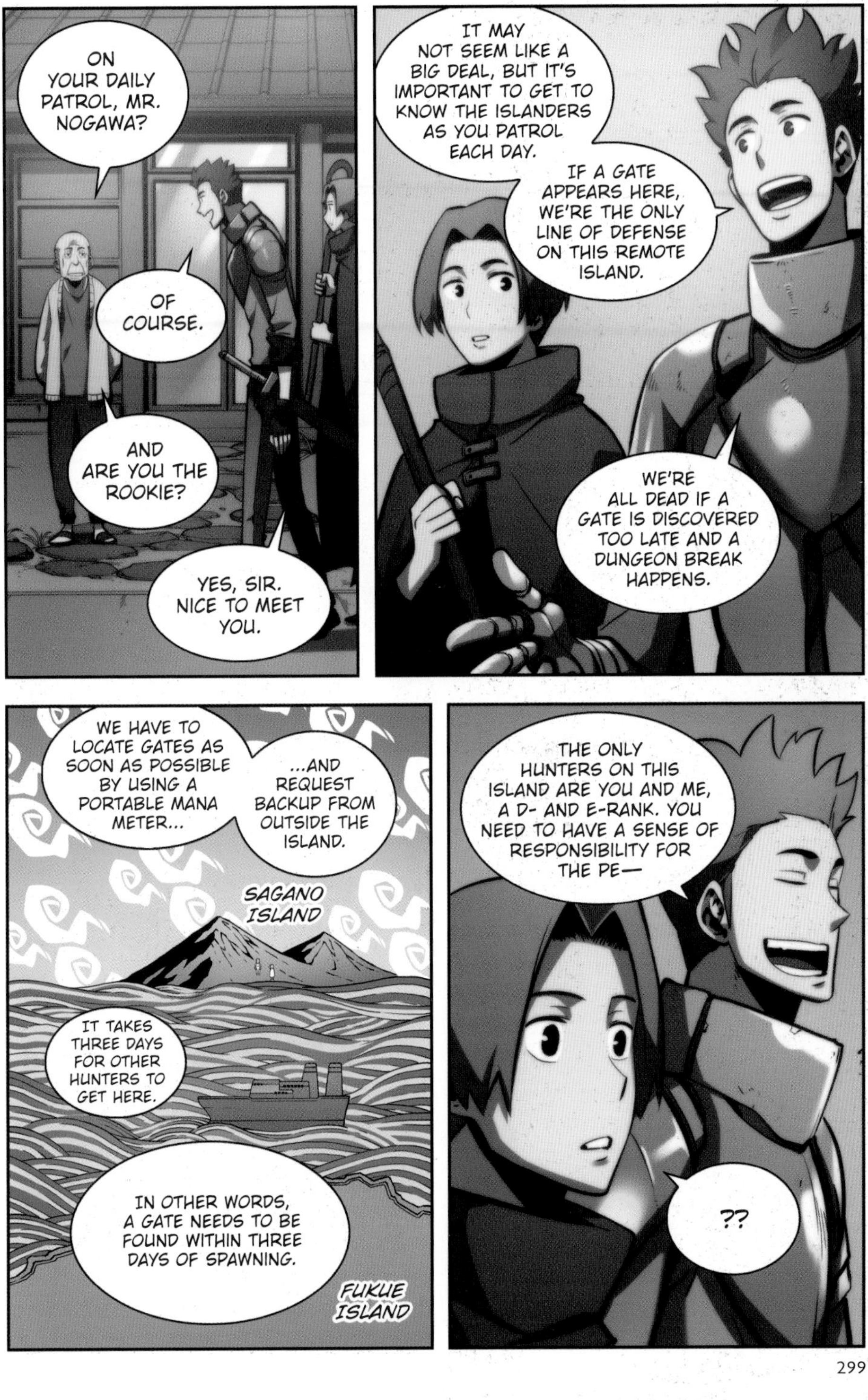
ON YOUR DAILY PATROL, MR. NOGAWA?
OF COURSE.
AND ARE YOU THE ROOKIE?
YES, SIR. NICE TO MEET YOU.
IT MAY NOT SEEM LIKE A BIG DEAL, BUT IT'S IMPORTANT TO GET TO KNOW THE ISLANDERS AS YOU PATROL EACH DAY.
IF A GATE APPEARS HERE, WE'RE THE ONLY LINE OF DEFENSE ON THIS REMOTE ISLAND.
WE'RE ALL DEAD IF A GATE IS DISCOVERED TOO LATE AND A DUNGEON BREAK HAPPENS.
WE HAVE TO LOCATE GATES AS SOON AS POSSIBLE BY USING A PORTABLE MANA METER...
...AND REQUEST BACKUP FROM OUTSIDE THE ISLAND.
SAGANO ISLAND
IT TAKES THREE DAYS FOR OTHER HUNTERS TO GET HERE.
IN OTHER WORDS, A GATE NEEDS TO BE FOUND WITHIN THREE DAYS OF SPAWNING.
FUKUE ISLAND
THE ONLY HUNTERS ON THIS ISLAND ARE YOU AND ME, A D- AND E-RANK. YOU NEED TO HAVE A SENSE OF RESPONSIBILITY FOR THE PE—
??

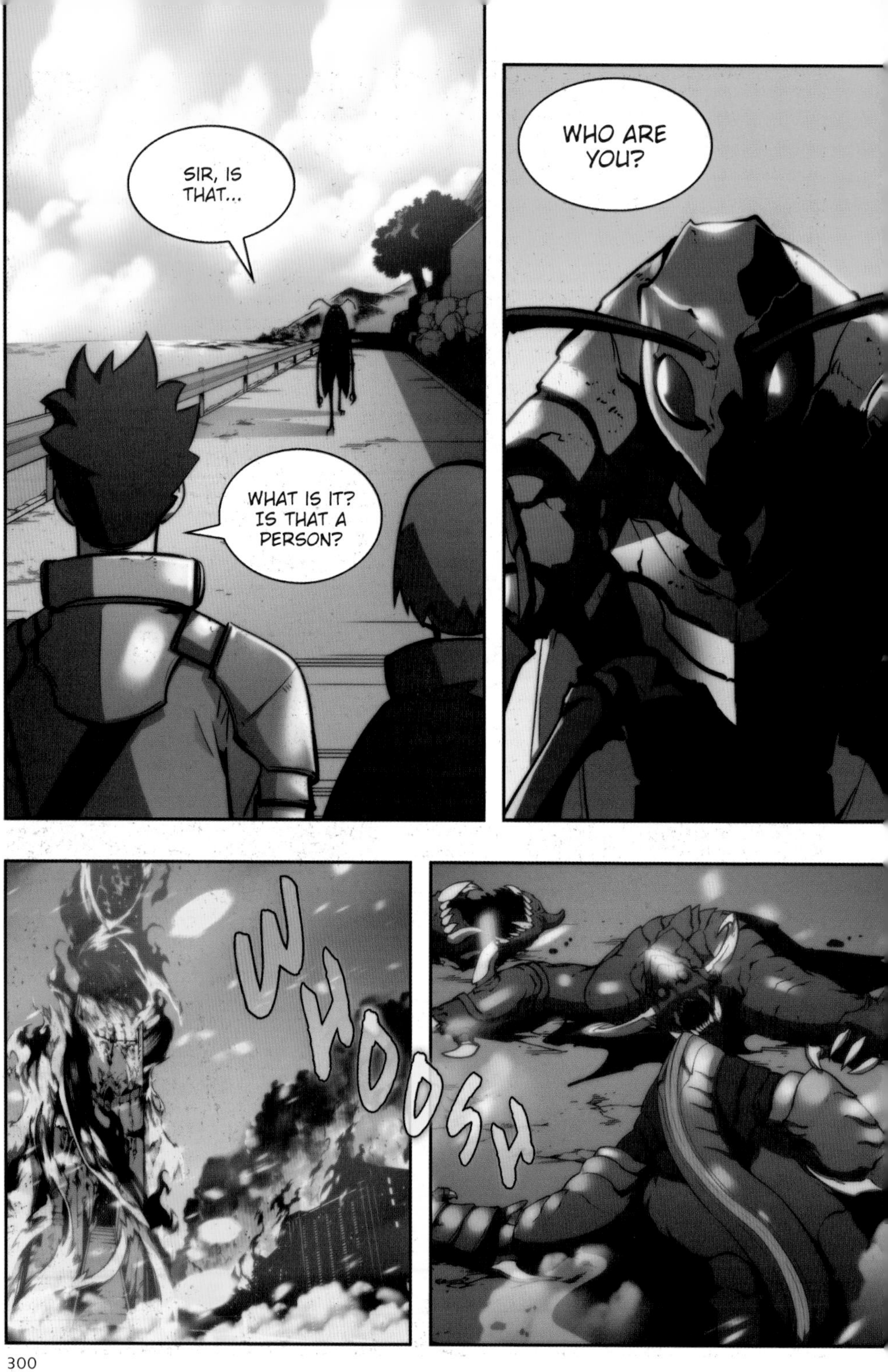
SIR, IS THAT...
WHAT IS IT? IS THAT A PERSON?
WHO ARE YOU?
WHOOSH

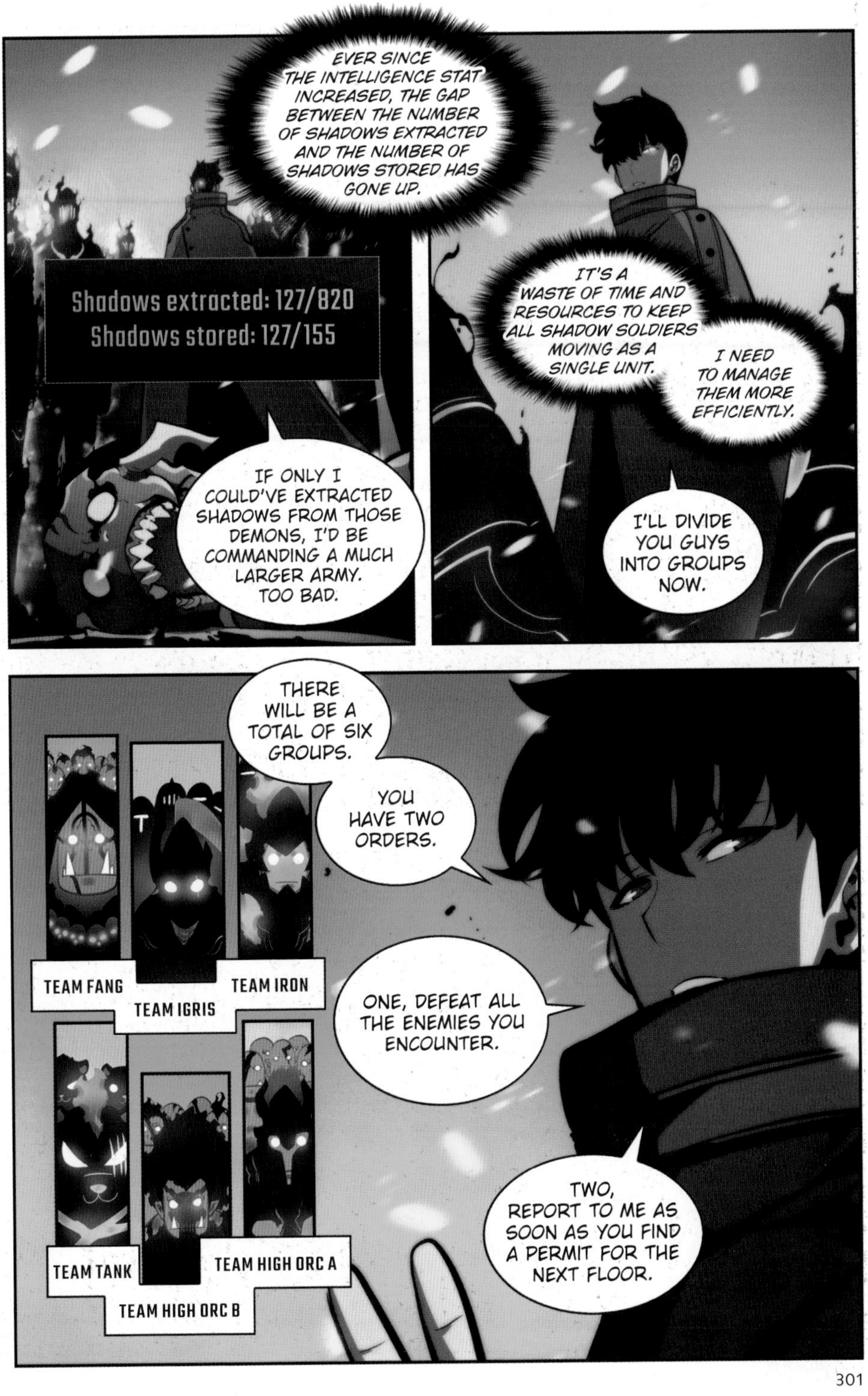
EVER SINCE THE INTELLIGENCE STAT INCREASED, THE GAP BETWEEN THE NUMBER OF SHADOWS EXTRACTED AND THE NUMBER OF SHADOWS STORED HAS GONE UP.
Shadows extracted: 127/820
Shadows stored: 127/155
IF ONLY I COULD'VE EXTRACTED SHADOWS FROM THOSE DEMONS, I'D BE COMMANDING A MUCH LARGER ARMY. TOO BAD.
IT'S A WASTE OF TIME AND RESOURCES TO KEEP ALL SHADOW SOLDIERS MOVING AS A SINGLE UNIT.
I NEED TO MANAGE THEM MORE EFFICIENTLY.
I'LL DIVIDE YOU GUYS INTO GROUPS NOW.
TEAM FANG
TEAM IGRIS
TEAM IRON
TEAM TANK
TEAM HIGH ORC B
TEAM HIGH ORC A
THERE WILL BE A TOTAL OF SIX GROUPS.
YOU HAVE TWO ORDERS.
ONE, DEFEAT ALL THE ENEMIES YOU ENCOUNTER.
TWO, REPORT TO ME AS SOON AS YOU FIND A PERMIT FOR THE NEXT FLOOR.

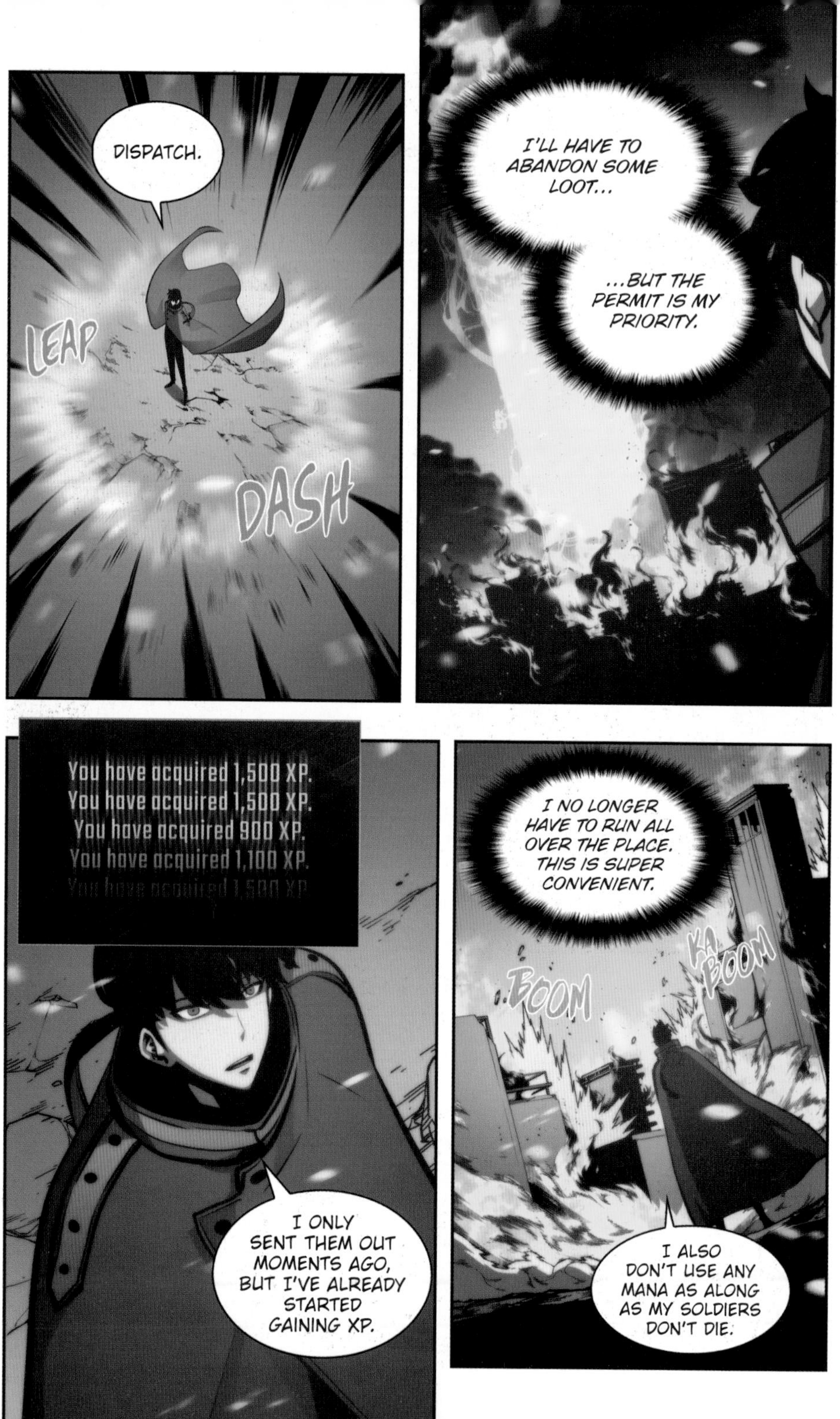
DISPATCH.
LEAP
DASH
I'LL HAVE TO ABANDON SOME LOOT...
...BUT THE PERMIT IS MY PRIORITY.
You have acquired 1,500 XP.
You have acquired 1,500 XP.
You have acquired 900 XP.
You have acquired 1,100 XP.
You have acquired 1,500 XP.
I ONLY SENT THEM OUT MOMENTS AGO, BUT I'VE ALREADY STARTED GAINING XP.
I NO LONGER HAVE TO RUN ALL OVER THE PLACE. THIS IS SUPER CONVENIENT.
BOOM
KA BOOM
I ALSO DON'T USE ANY MANA AS ALONG AS MY SOLDIERS DON'T DIE.

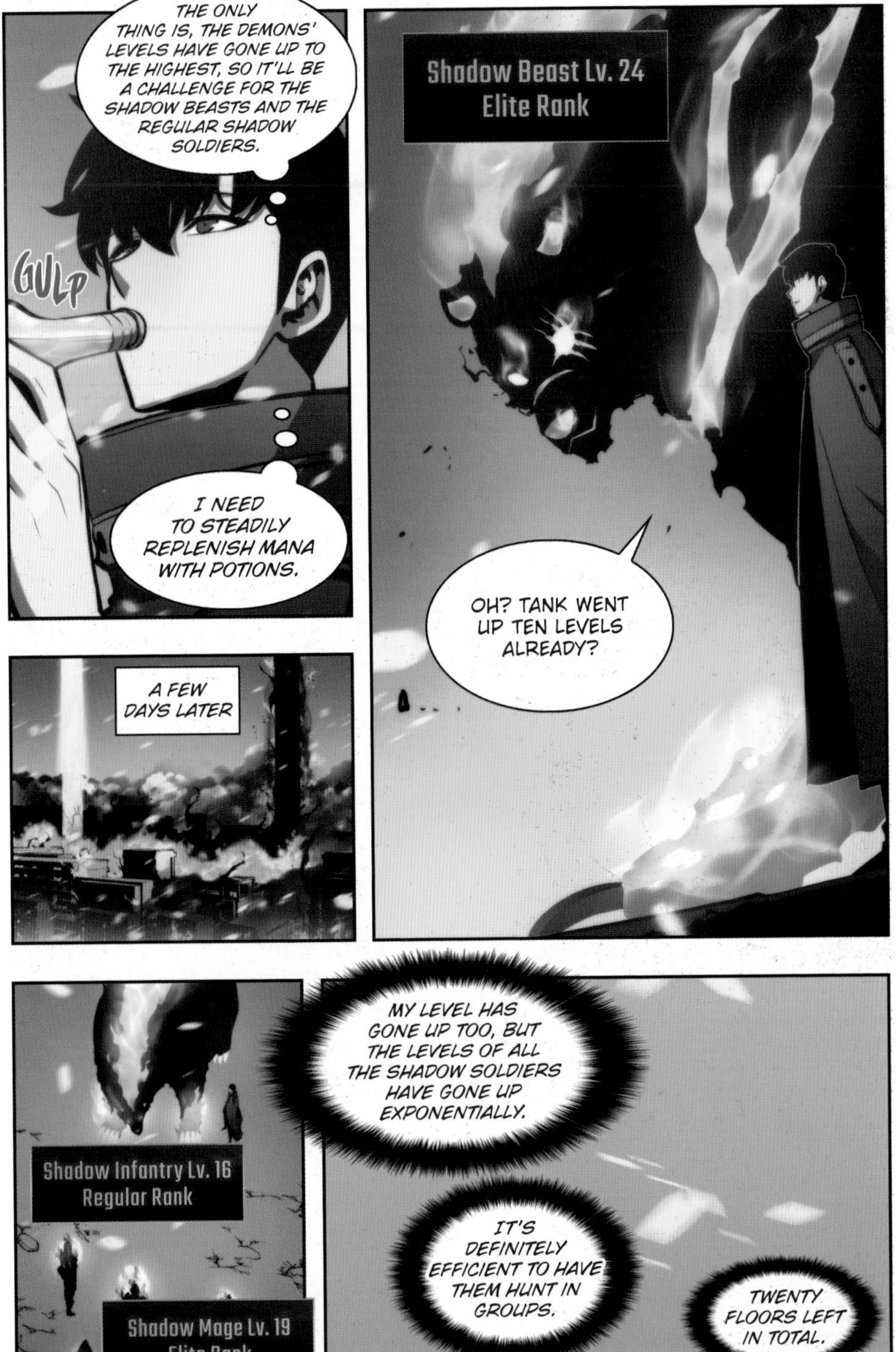
THE ONLY THING IS, THE DEMONS' LEVELS HAVE GONE UP TO THE HIGHEST, SO IT'LL BE A CHALLENGE FOR THE SHADOW BEASTS AND THE REGULAR SHADOW SOLDIERS.
GULP
I NEED TO STEADILY REPLENISH MANA WITH POTIONS.
A FEW DAYS LATER
Shadow Beast Lv. 24
Elite Rank
OH? TANK WENT UP TEN LEVELS ALREADY?
Shadow Infantry Lv. 16
Regular Rank
Shadow Mage Lv. 19
Elite Rank
MY LEVEL HAS GONE UP TOO, BUT THE LEVELS OF ALL THE SHADOW SOLDIERS HAVE GONE UP EXPONENTIALLY.
IT'S DEFINITELY EFFICIENT TO HAVE THEM HUNT IN GROUPS.
TWENTY FLOORS LEFT IN TOTAL.

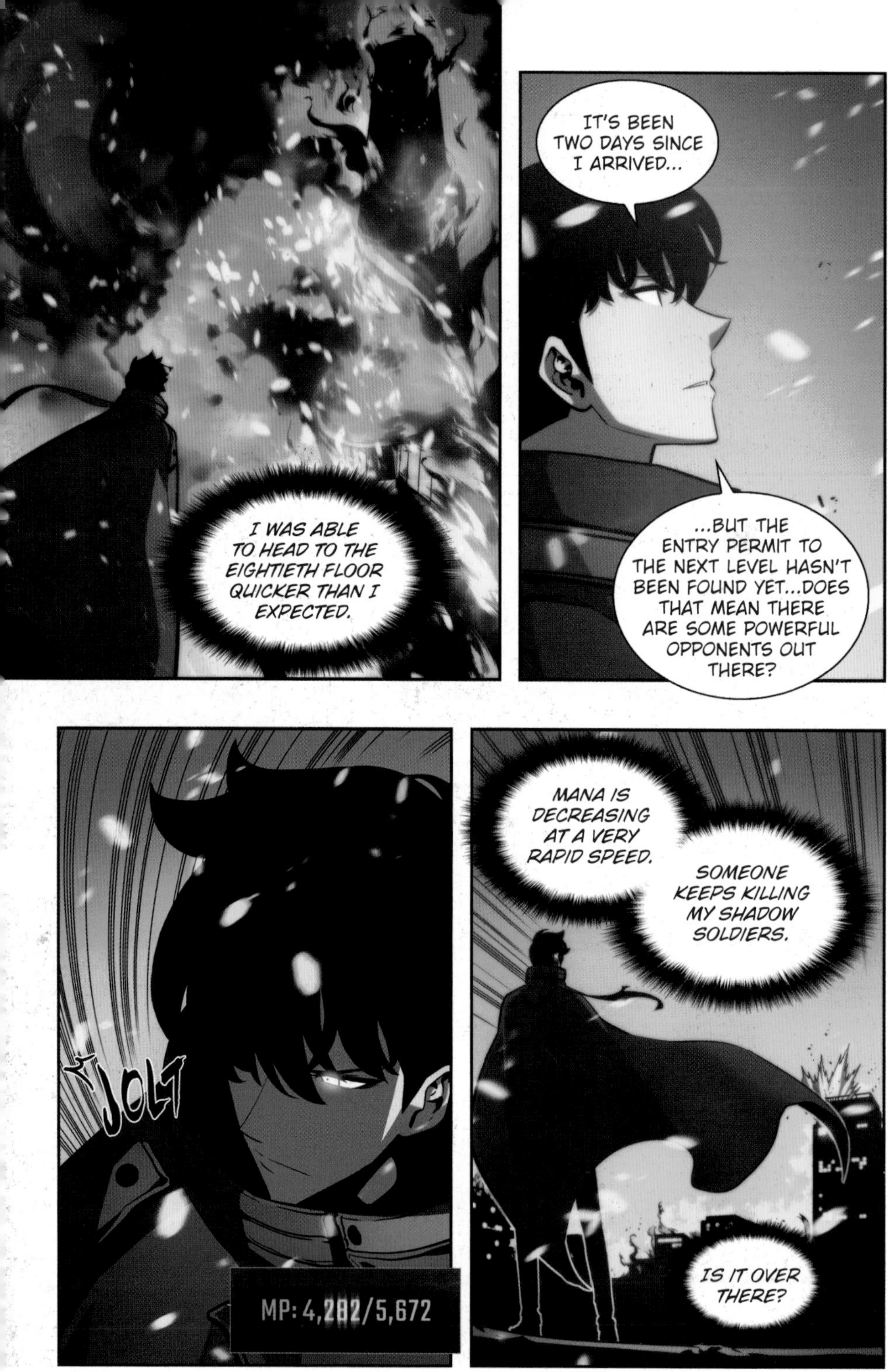
I WAS ABLE TO HEAD TO THE EIGHTIETH FLOOR QUICKER THAN I EXPECTED.
IT'S BEEN TWO DAYS SINCE I ARRIVED...
...BUT THE ENTRY PERMIT TO THE NEXT LEVEL HASN'T BEEN FOUND YET...DOES THAT MEAN THERE ARE SOME POWERFUL OPPONENTS OUT THERE?
JOLT
MP: 4,282/5,672
MANA IS DECREASING AT A VERY RAPID SPEED.
SOMEONE KEEPS KILLING MY SHADOW SOLDIERS.
IS IT OVER THERE?

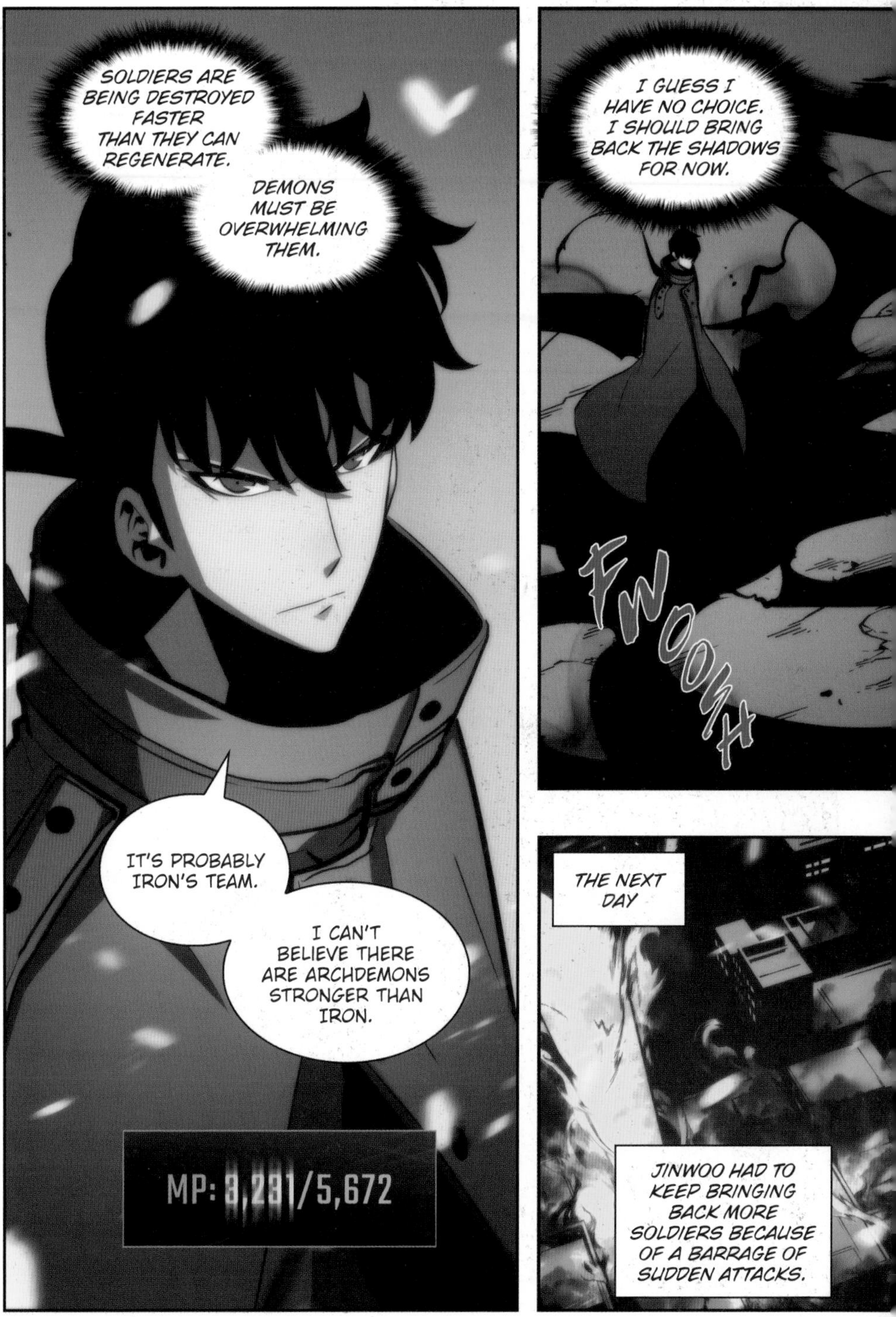
SOLDIERS ARE BEING DESTROYED FASTER THAN THEY CAN REGENERATE.
DEMONS MUST BE OVERWHELMING THEM.
IT'S PROBABLY IRON'S TEAM.
I CAN'T BELIEVE THERE ARE ARCHDEMONS STRONGER THAN IRON.
MP: 3,281/5,672
I GUESS I HAVE NO CHOICE. I SHOULD BRING BACK THE SHADOWS FOR NOW.
FWOOSH
THE NEXT DAY
JINWOO HAD TO KEEP BRINGING BACK MORE SOLDIERS BECAUSE OF A BARRAGE OF SUDDEN ATTACKS.

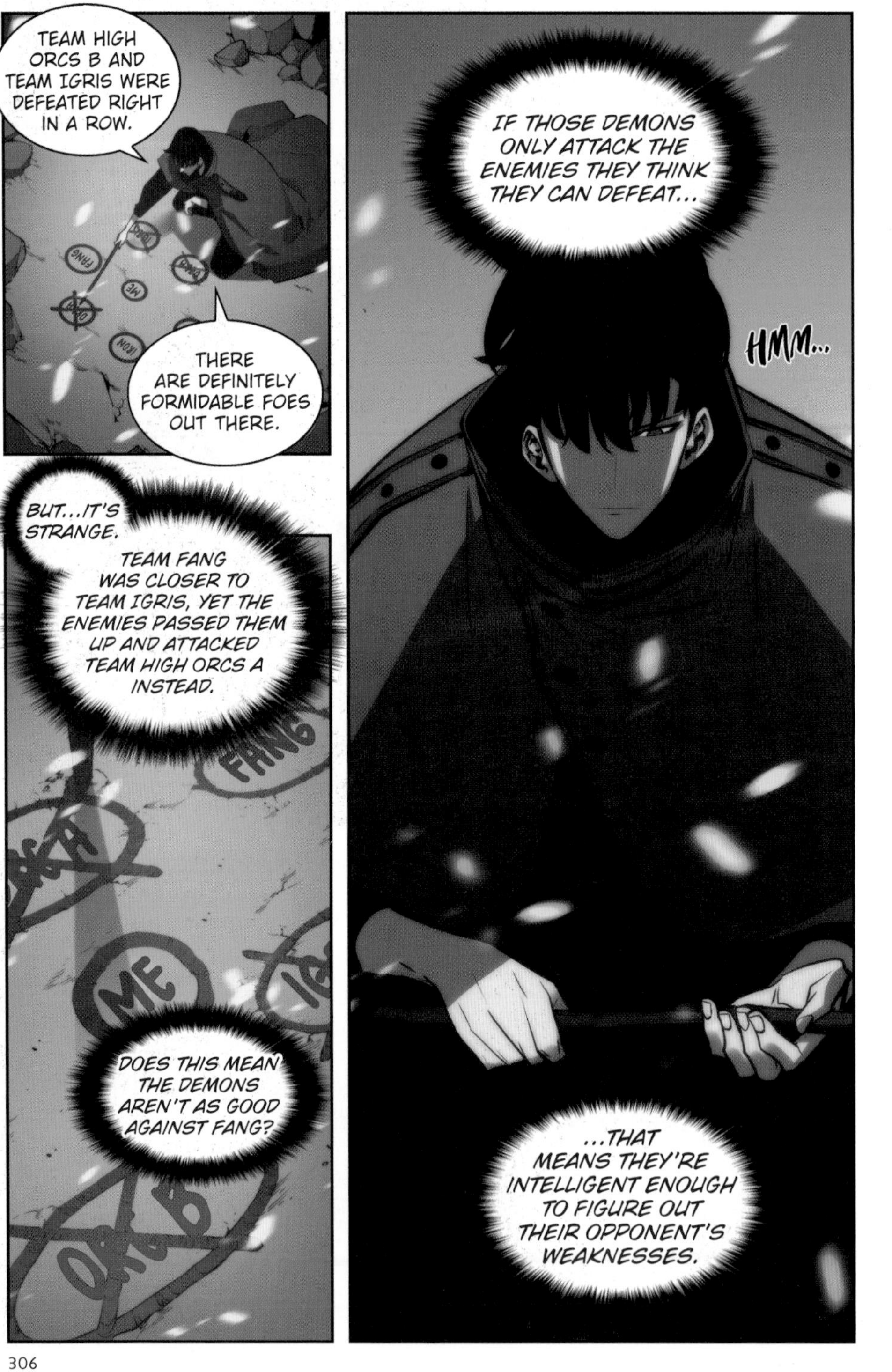
TEAM HIGH ORCS B AND TEAM IGRIS WERE DEFEATED RIGHT IN A ROW.
THERE ARE DEFINITELY FORMIDABLE FOES OUT THERE.
BUT...IT'S STRANGE.
TEAM FANG WAS CLOSER TO TEAM IGRIS, YET THE ENEMIES PASSED THEM UP AND ATTACKED TEAM HIGH ORCS A INSTEAD.
DOES THIS MEAN THE DEMONS AREN'T AS GOOD AGAINST FANG?
IF THOSE DEMONS ONLY ATTACK THE ENEMIES THEY THINK THEY CAN DEFEAT...
HMM...
...THAT MEANS THEY'RE INTELLIGENT ENOUGH TO FIGURE OUT THEIR OPPONENT'S WEAKNESSES.

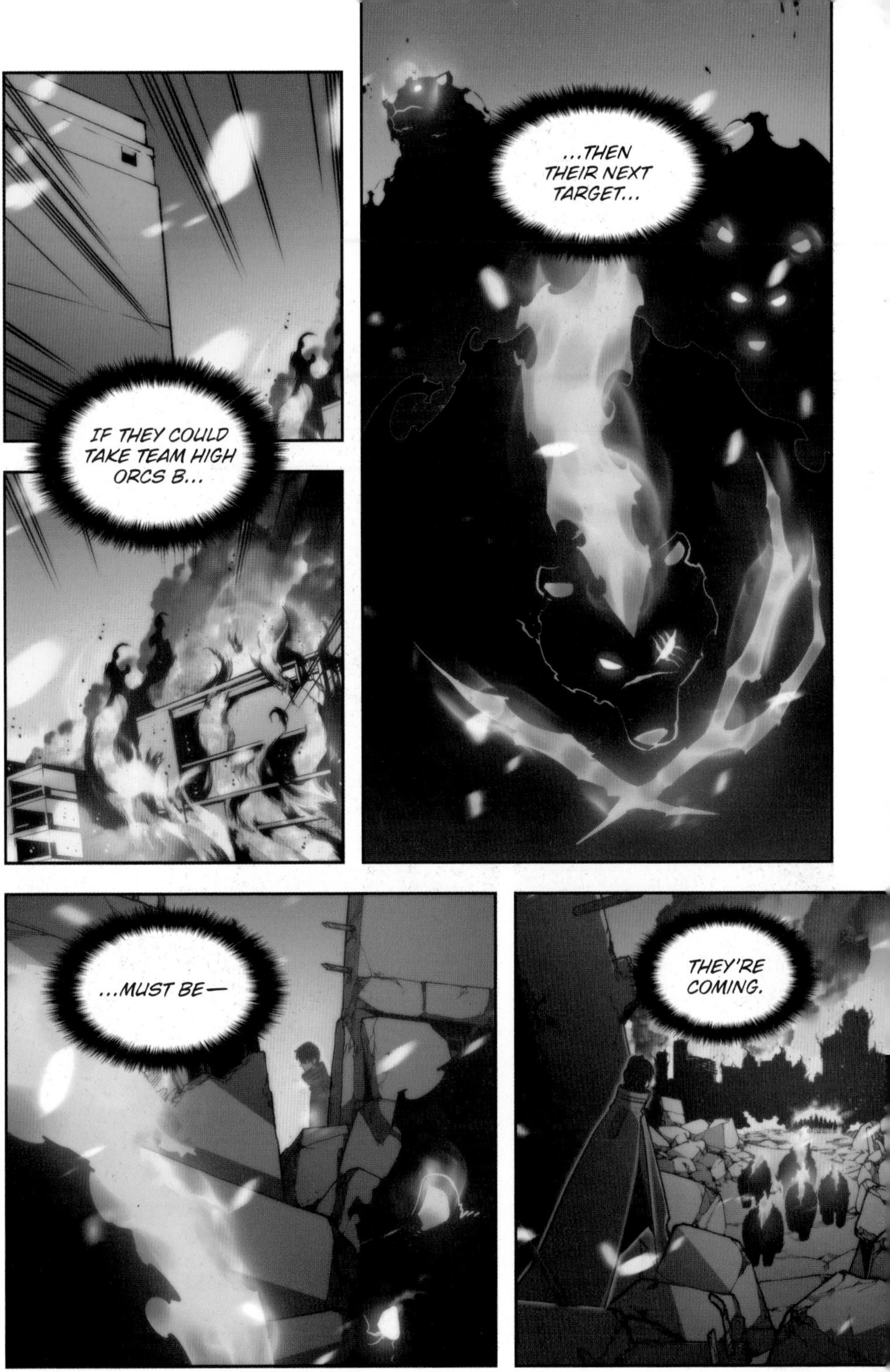
IF THEY COULD TAKE TEAM HIGH ORCS B...
...THEN THEIR NEXT TARGET...
...MUST BE—
THEY'RE COMING.

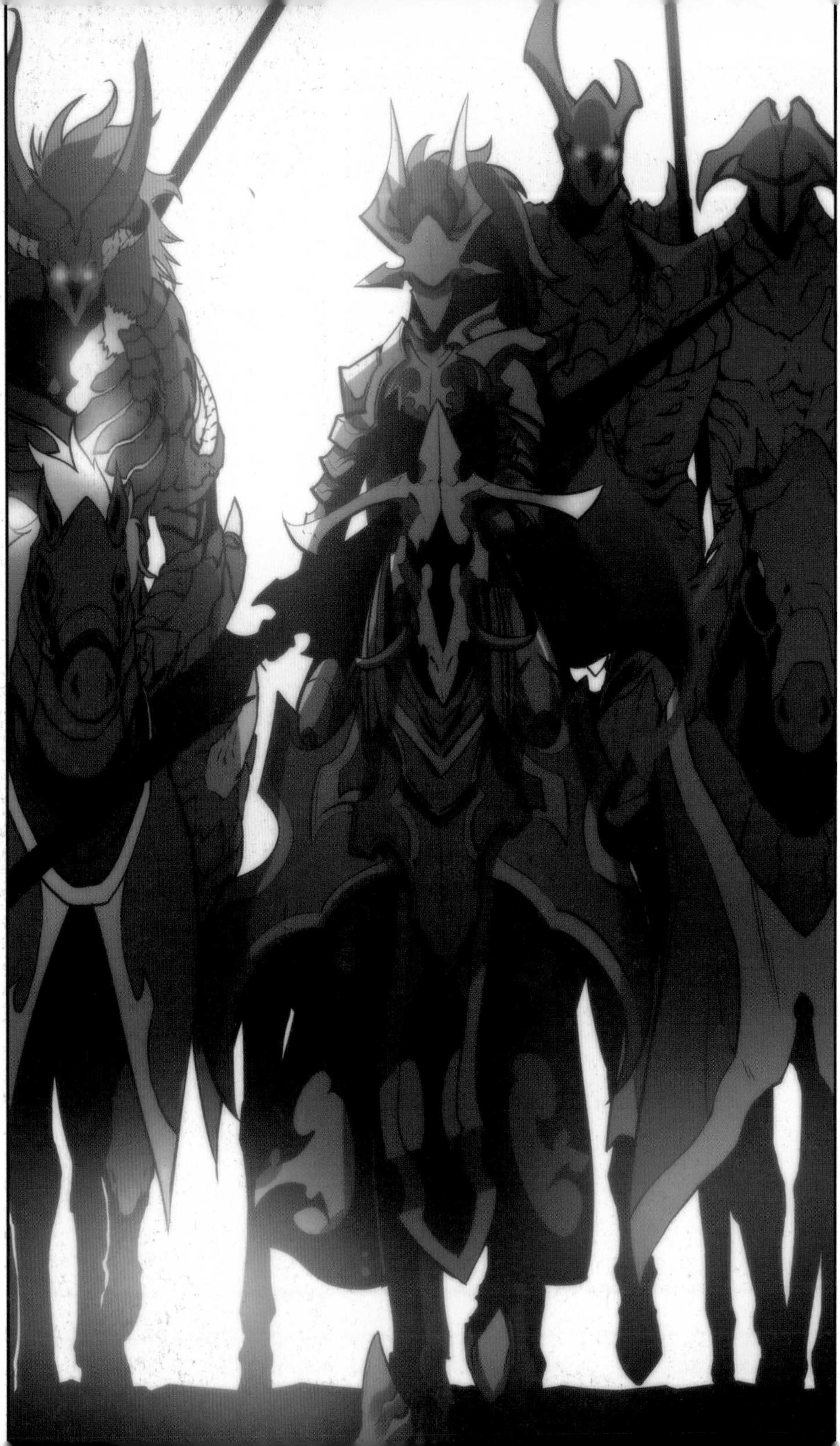

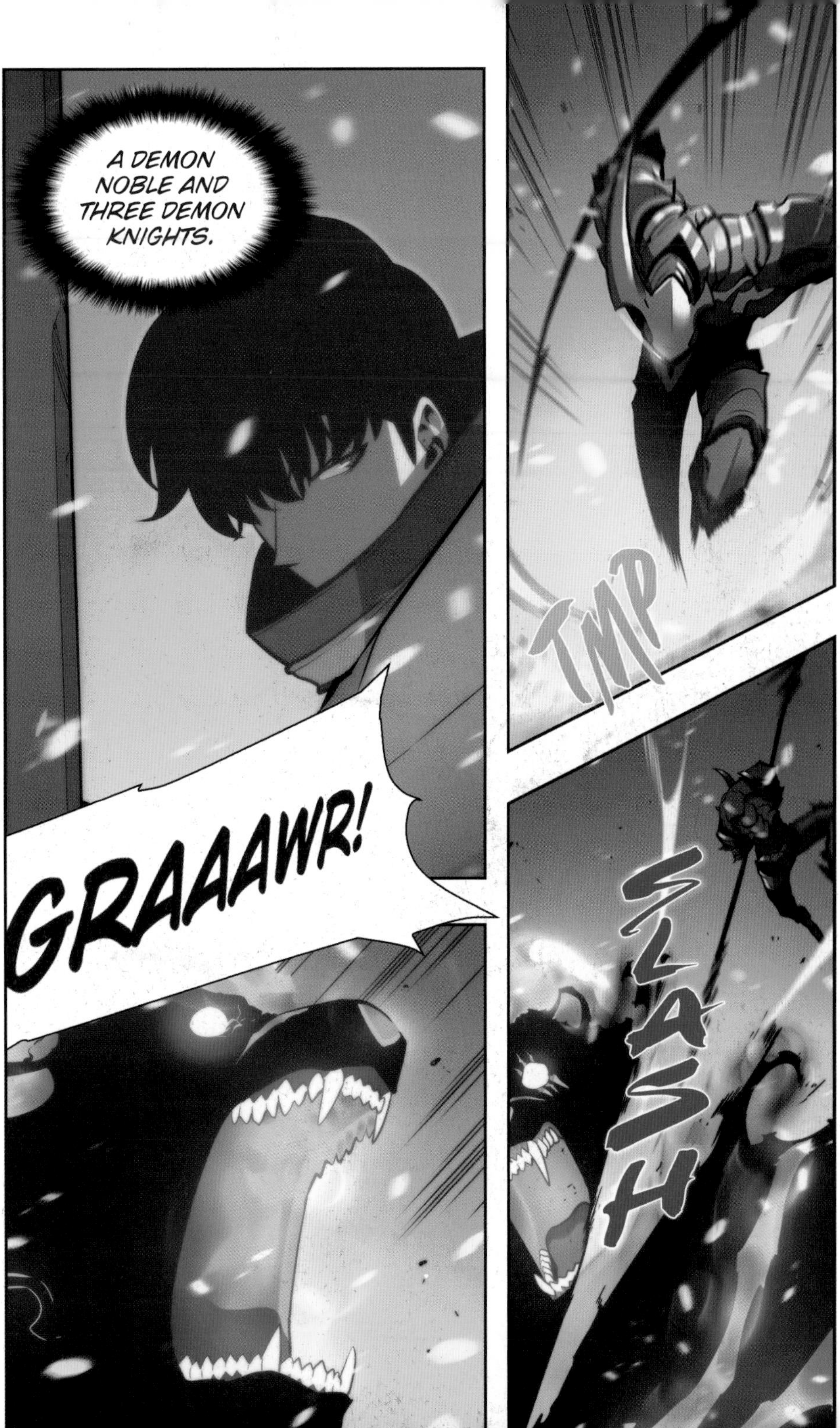
A DEMON NOBLE AND THREE DEMON KNIGHTS.
GRAAAWR!
TMP
SLASH

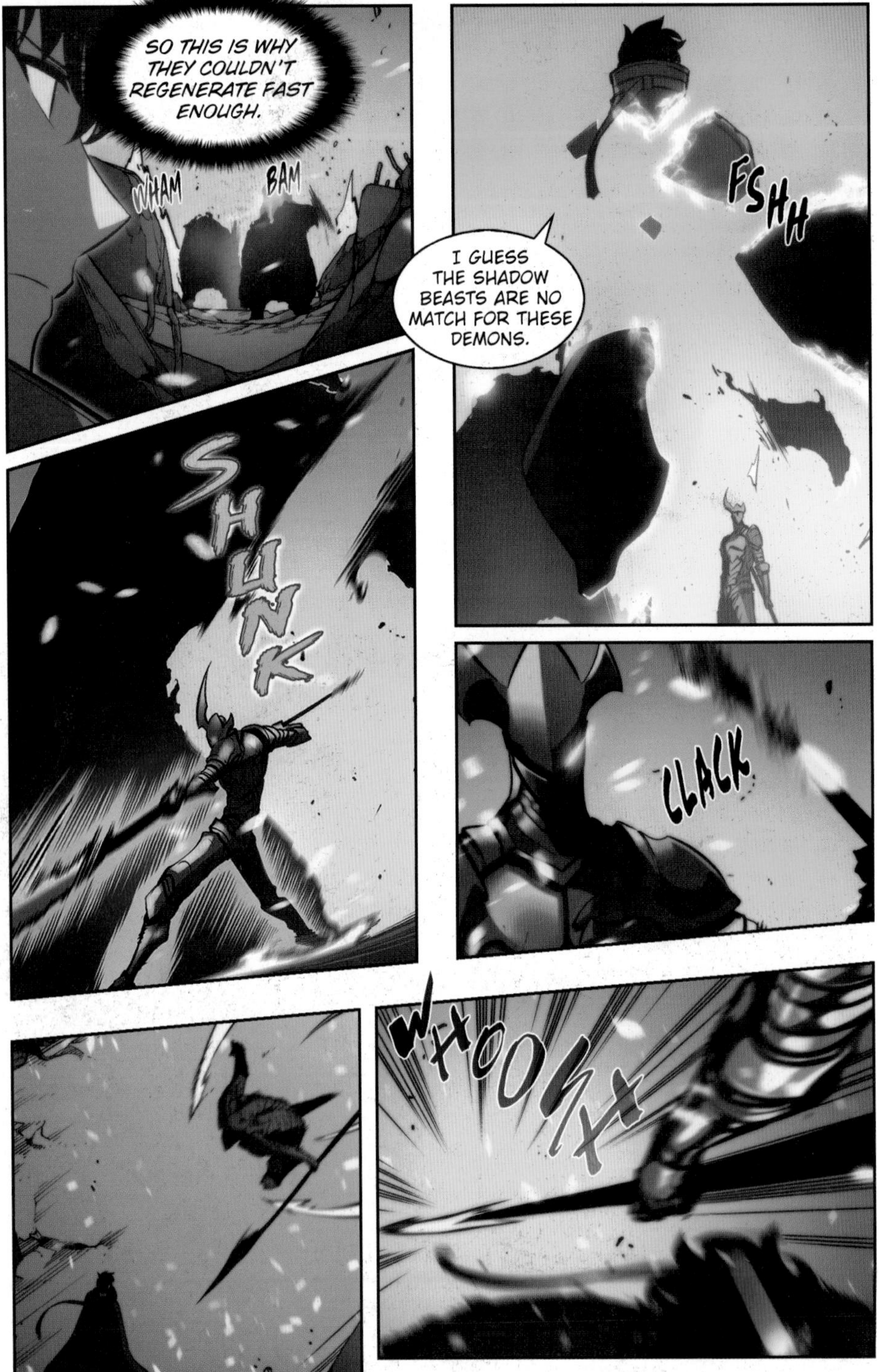
SO THIS IS WHY THEY COULDN'T REGENERATE FAST ENOUGH.
WHAM
BAM
FSHH
I GUESS THE SHADOW BEASTS ARE NO MATCH FOR THESE DEMONS.
SHUNK
CLACK
WHOOSH

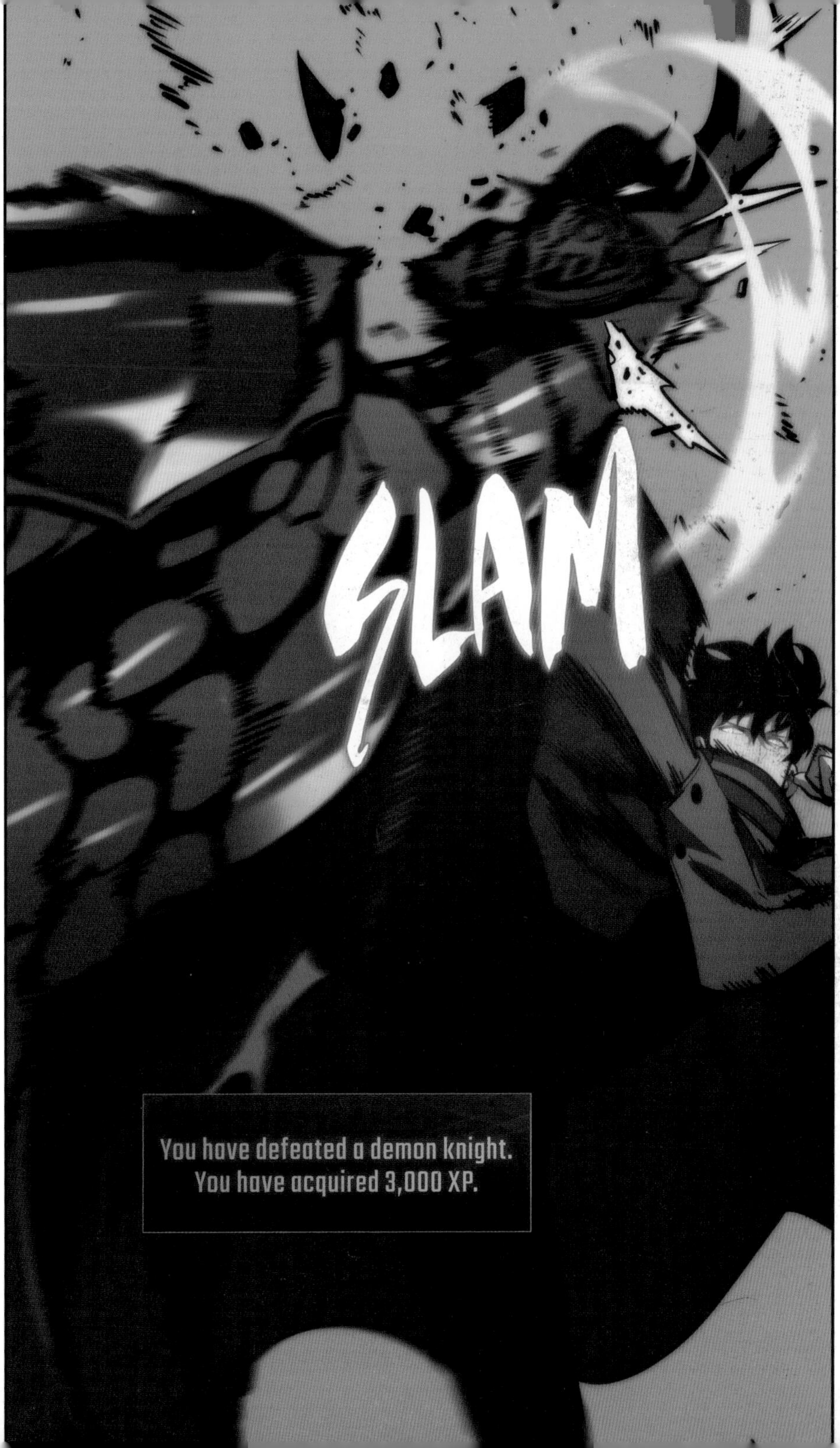
SLAM
You have defeated a demon knight.
You have acquired 3,000 XP.

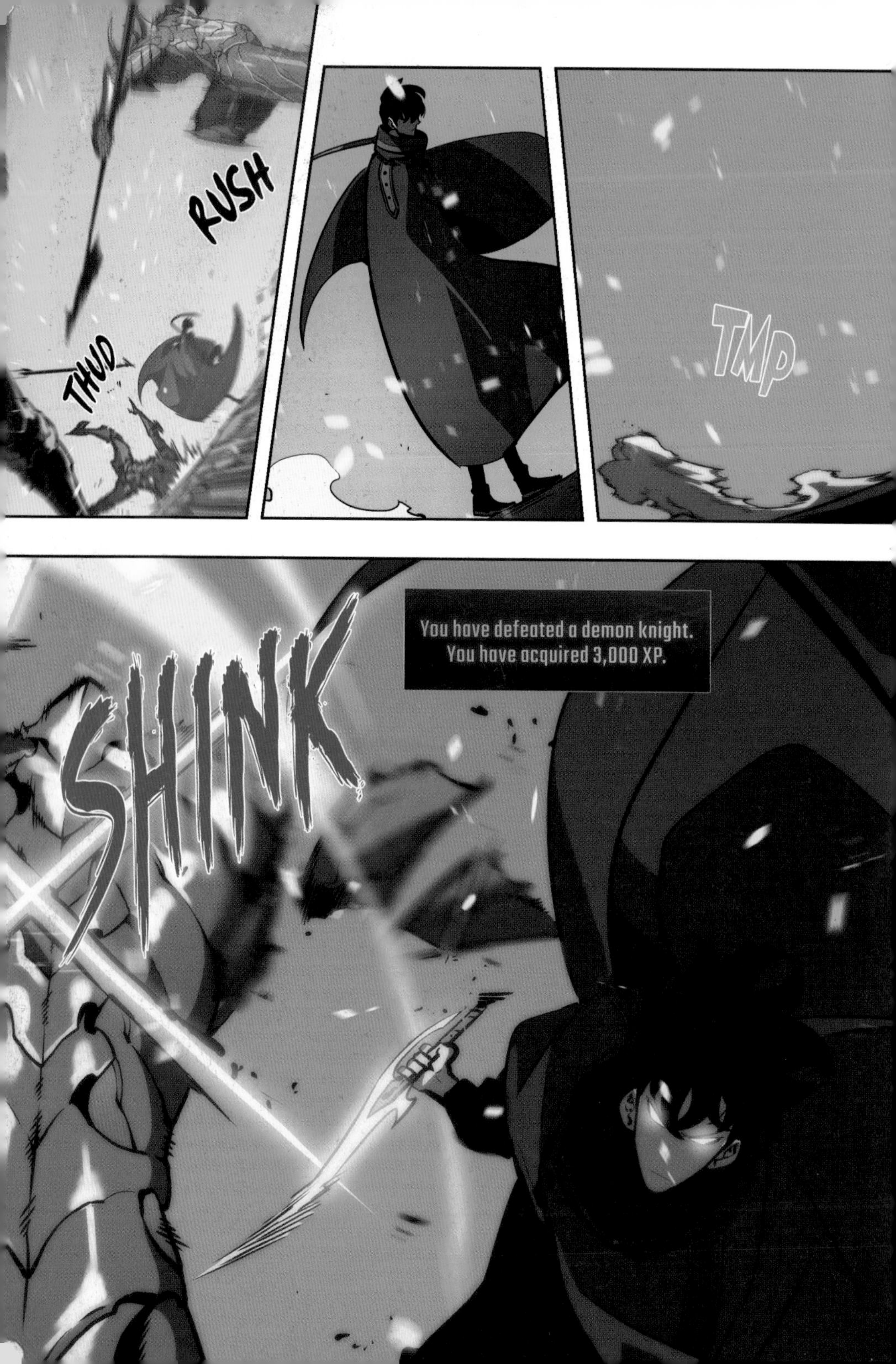
RUSH
THUD
TMP
SHINK
You have defeated a demon knight.
You have acquired 3,000 XP.

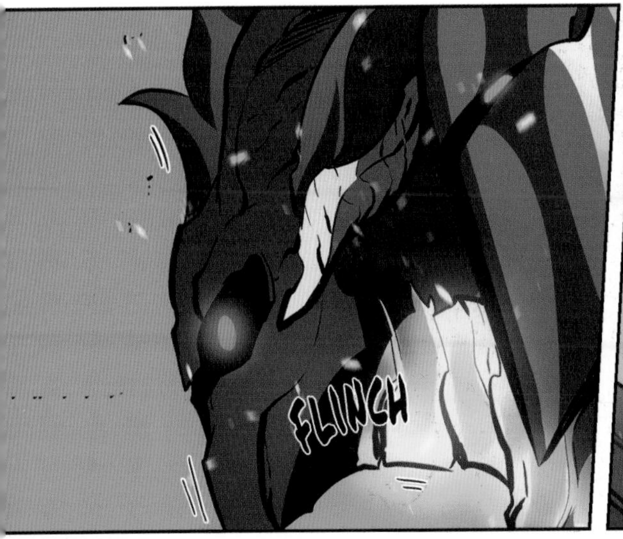
FLINCH
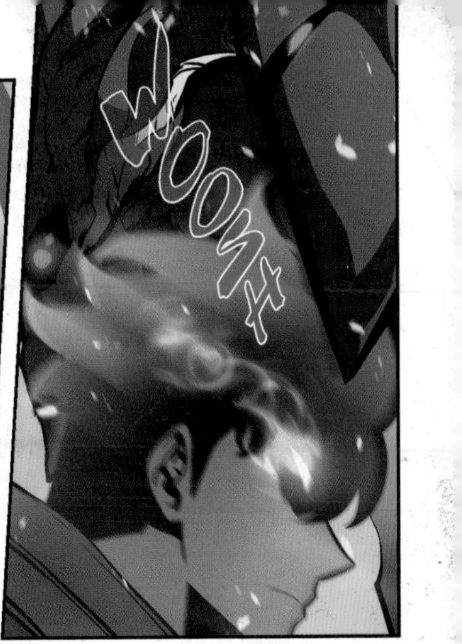
WOOSH
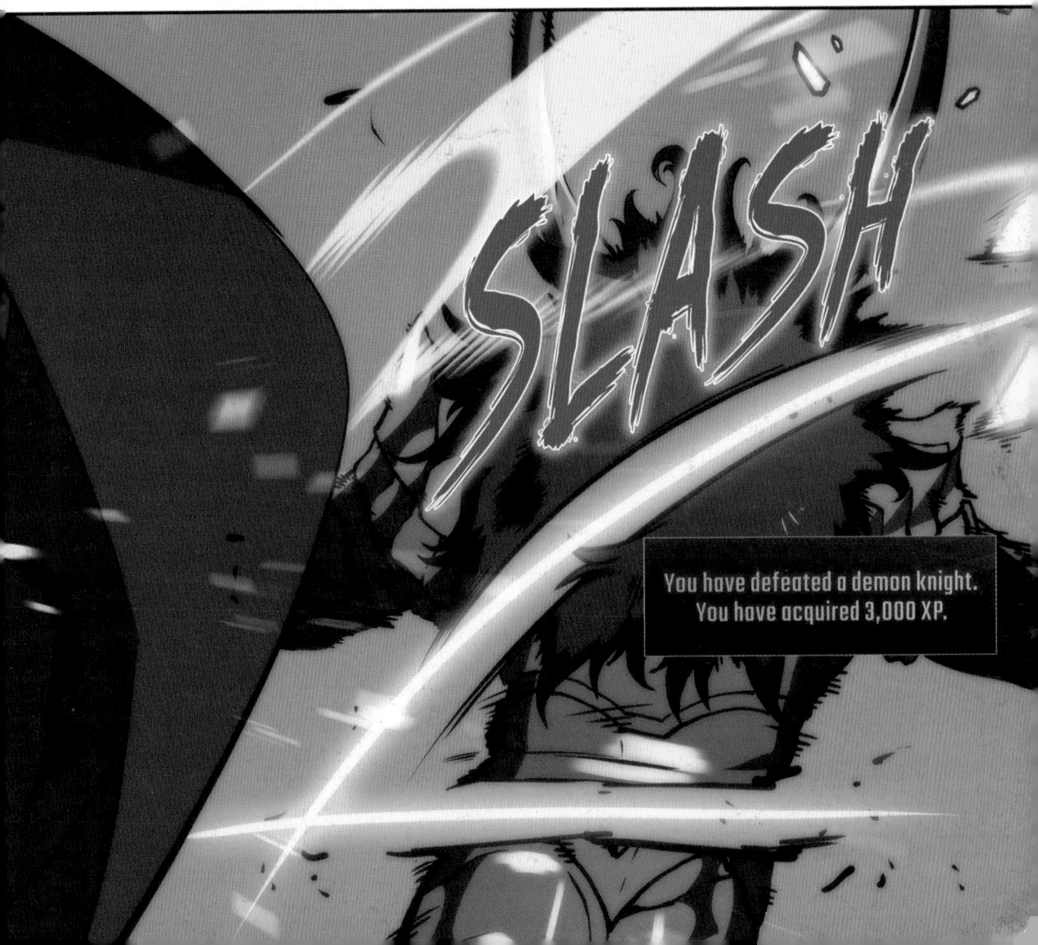
SLASH
You have defeated a demon knight.
You have acquired 3,000 XP.

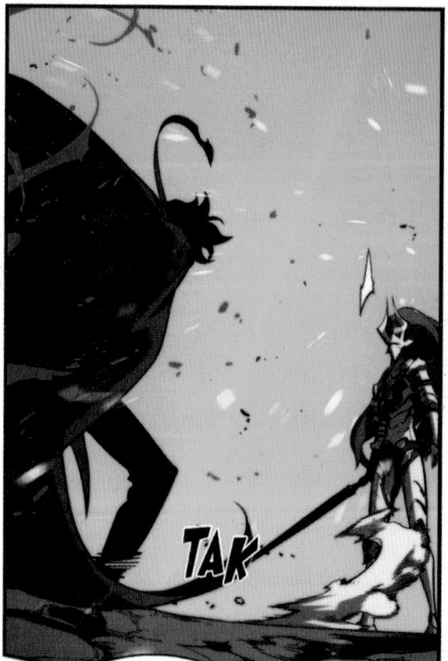
TAK

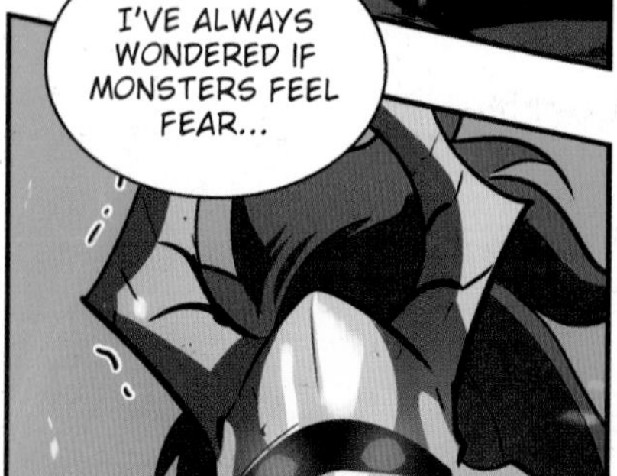
I'VE ALWAYS WONDERED IF MONSTERS FEEL FEAR...

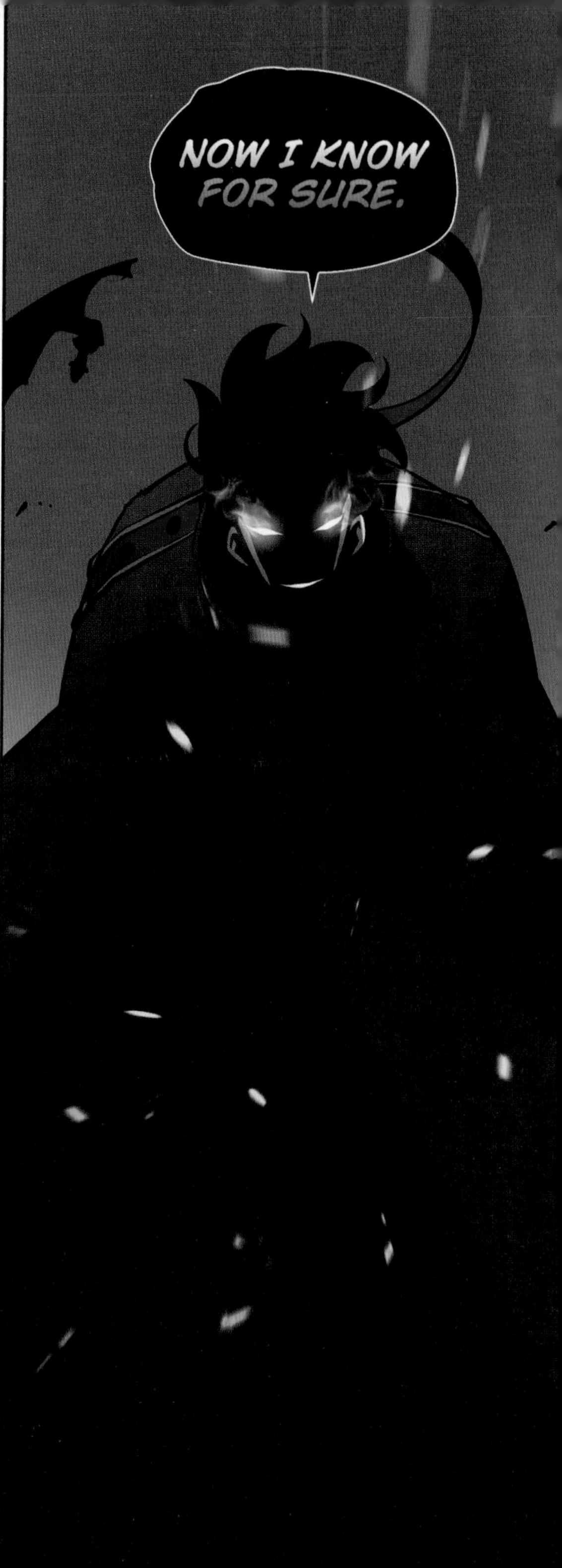
NOW I KNOW FOR SURE.

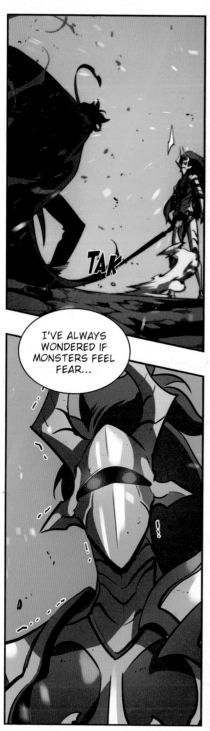